The biology of Canadian weeds

Contributions 1-32

La biologie des mauvaises herbes du Canada

Communications 1 à 32

Gerald A. Mulligan, editor and compiler
Biosystematics Research Institute
Ottawa, Ontario

Publiées sous la direction
de Gerald A. Mulligan
Institut de recherches biosystématiques
Ottawa (Ont.)

Publication 1693

Publication 1693

Reprinted from
Canadian Journal of Plant Science

Extrait du
Canadian Journal of Plant Science

PUBLICATION 1693, available from
Information Services, Agriculture Canada, Ottawa K1A 0C7

©Minister of Supply and Services Canada 1979
Cat. No. A53−1693/1979   ISBN: 0-662-10668-7
Printed 1979   5M−12:79

PUBLICATION 1693
Services d'information, Agriculture Canada, Ottawa K1A 0C7

© Ministre des Approvisionnements et Services Canada 1979
N⁰ de cat. A53−1693/1979   ISBN: 0-662-10668-7
Impression 1979   5M−12:79

Contents

Introduction

An article entitled *A new series — The Biology of Canadian Weeds* appeared in the *Canadian Journal of Plant Science* 52:651-654 in July 1972 and a detailed format for the series was given. The series resulted from a recommendation by the Canada Weed Committee, now known as the Expert Committee on Weeds. I have had the pleasure of editing this series since its inception for the *Canadian Journal of Plant Science* and for the Expert Committee on Weeds. I especially wish to thank Dr. P. B. Cavers and Dr. J. R. Hay for their encouragement and assistance with the creation and editing of this series.

Thirty-two contributions containing accounts of 41 species of weeds were published to the end of 1978. Interest in the series has grown steadily and many workers have endeavored to obtain reprints of all contributions published. Unfortunately, reprints of some of the earlier papers are no longer available. The Expert Committee on Weeds therefore asked me to compile the first 32 contributions in book form.

Individual papers have been reproduced by photo-offset. The page numbers that appeared in the *Canadian Journal of Plant Science* have been replaced by the page numbers of this book. A reference to the source appears in the lower left-hand corner of the first page of each contribution.

I thank the authors and the *Canadian Journal of Plant Science* for permission to reproduce the 32 contributions and Agriculture Canada for publishing this book.

G. A. Mulligan
8 May 1979

Introduction

Le premier article intitulé *A new series — The Biology of Canadian Weeds* a paru dans le numéro de juillet 1972 du *Canadian Journal of Plant Science* 52:651-654. À cette occasion, on y spécifiait la présentation adoptée pour cette nouvelle série d'articles. Cette série est née d'une recommandation du Comité canadien sur les mauvaises herbes, l'actuel Comité d'experts en malherbologie, et j'ai eu le vif plaisir au nom de ce Comité d'experts d'en diriger la publication dès les débuts dans le *Canadian Journal of Plant Science*. Je veux adresser ici mes remerciements particuliers à MM. P.B. Cavers et J.R. Hay pour l'encouragement et l'appui qu'ils ont apportés à la création et à la publication de la série.

À la fin de 1978, on pouvait compter un total de 32 communications portant sur 41 espèces de plantes nuisibles. L'intérêt suscité par la série n'a fait que croître et de nombreux chercheurs ont sollicité des tirés à part de toutes les communications. Malheureusement certains des premiers articles ne sont plus disponibles, c'est pourquoi le Comité d'experts en malherbologie m'a chargé de réunir en un volume les 32 premières monographies.

Les articles ont été reproduits par procédé offset. La pagination du *Canadian Journal of Plant Science* a été changée dans le livre. La source de chaque article est inscrite en renvoi dans le coin inférieur gauche de la première page.

En terminant, je tiens à remercier les auteurs et le *Canadian Journal of Plant Science* qui ont autorisé la reproduction des articles, ainsi qu'Agriculture Canada qui a rendu possible la publication du volume.

G.A. Mulligan
Le 8 mai 1979

THE BIOLOGY OF CANADIAN WEEDS.
1. *Kalmia angustifolia* L.

IVAN V. HALL,[1] LLOYD P. JACKSON,[2] and C. FRED EVERETT[3]

Agriculture Canada: [1]*Research Station, Kentville, Nova Scotia;* [2]*Experimental Farm, Nappan, Nova Scotia; and* [3]*Research Station, Fredericton, New Brunswick. Received 5 Apr. 1973, accepted 1 June 1973.*

HALL, IVAN V., JACKSON, LLOYD P. AND EVERETT, C. FRED. 1973. The biology of Canadian weeds. 1. *Kalmia angustifolia* L. Can. J. Plant Sci. **53**: 865–873.

This contribution on *Kalmia angustifolia* L., sheep-laurel (Ericaceae), is part of a series that presents biological information on plants that are weedy in Canada. *Kalmia angustifolia* is a weed of lowbush blueberry fields and pastures in eastern Canada. It occurs in Newfoundland, Prince Edward Island, Nova Scotia, New Brunswick, Quebec, and Ontario.

Cette contribution à l'étude de *Kalmia angustifolia* L., kalmia à feuilles étroites (Ericaceae), fait partie d'une série qui a pour but de fournir une documentation sur les mauvaises herbes au Canada. *Kalmia angustifolia* est une mauvaise herbe répandue dans les champs le bleuets nains et dans les pâturages de l'est du Canada. On la trouve à Terre-Neuve, à l'Île-du-Prince-Edouard, en Nouvelle-Écosse, au Nouveau-Brunswick, au Québec et en Ontario.

1. Name

Kalmia angustifolia L. — **sheep-laurel** (Canada Weed Committee 1969), lambkill; **kalmia à feuilles étroites**, bois-chaud, crevard de moutons, herbe à commis, herbe forte, kalmia, kalmia à feuilles étoilées, laurier, pétrole, poison de brebis, sacacoumi, tue-moutons (Ferron and Cayouette 1971). Ericaceae, heath family, Éricacées.

2. Description and Account of Variation

A low, erect, woody shrub up to 1 m in height, growing laterally by underground rhizomes and reproducing by seeds; shoots arising from dormant buds on the rhizomes; leaves persistent, in whorls of 3, green but turning reddish-brown in late fall, petioled, simple, entire, waxy on upper surface, bloom on under surface with margin slightly recurved; flowers in lateral corymbs; calyx of 5 sepals; corolla, normally pink, of 5 fused petals; stamens 10, fused to corolla; fruit a 5-parted capsule (Fig. 1A) 4 mm in diam, containing many seeds; seeds small, less than 1 mm long.

Chromosome numbers have not been reported from Canadian populations, but Jaynes (1969) reports $n = 12$ for *K. angustifolia* collected from North Carolina.

Probably the species most resembling *K. angustifolia* is the closely related *K. polifolia* Wang. The young branches of *K. angustifolia* are circular in cross section, whereas those of *K. polifolia* are 2-edged. The flower clusters of *K. angustifolia* are lateral, whereas the flowers of *K. polifolia* are terminal. The calyx of *K. polifolia* has a distinct ring at the base and the lobes overlap, whereas in *K. angustifolia* the calyx lobes do not overlap and a distinct ring is absent.

Fernald (1950) reports that populations differ in flower color, and the white-flowered form he has designated *forma candida* Fern. Jaynes (1968a), who has studied populations from both the United States and Canada, found considerable differences among them with respect to geographic distribution, growth habit, and seed viability.

A seedling is shown in Fig. 1B and both a fruiting and a vegetative shoot are shown in Fig. 1C.

3. Economic Importance

(a) *Detrimental* — *Kalmia angustifolia* is a serious weed of lowbush blueberry fields and pastures of Eastern Canada. In lowbush blueberry fields this species is favored by burning (Hall and Aalders 1968) and if not controlled, will eventually take over as

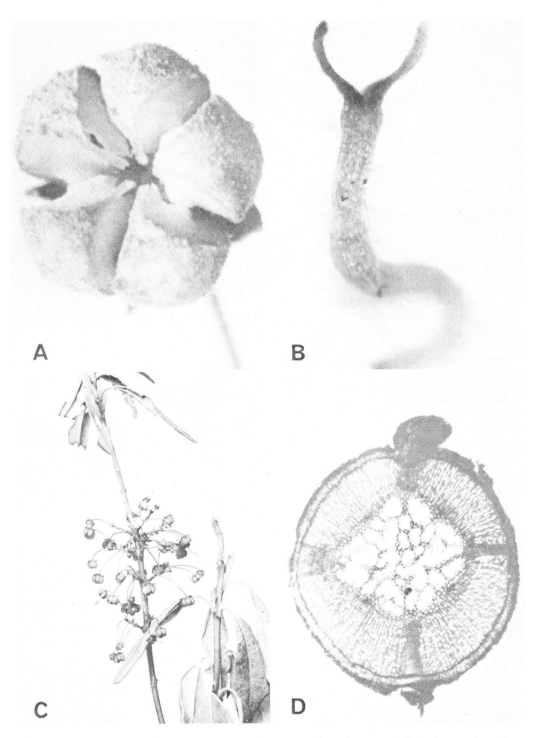

Fig. 1. Capsule 12×; (B) seedling 51×; (C) mature plant 0.4×; and (D) cross section of rhizome of *K. angustifolia* 30×.

the dominant species. When this happens, the field is no longer profitable to operate unless weed control measures are taken. For this reason approximately 10% of all acreage (8,100 ha) of lowbush blueberries in the Maritime Provinces is treated every other year for this weed. A cost of $15.00–$17.00 per hectare is usual for chemical control of sheep-laurel (J. D. Sibley, personal communication). Work by Gagnon (1971) indicates that the problem of controlling this weed is as great in the Province of Quebec.

Poisoning from eating leaves of *K. angustifolia* (Muenscher 1952) occurs in cattle, goats, horses, and particularly sheep. Since the leaves are tough, animals only eat them when other vegetation is lacking, for instance, in winter or early spring. Sheep are usually affected because the type of vegetation associated with this weed is used as pasturage for this animal (Muenscher 1949). Symptoms of poisoning include salivation, watery eyes, running nose, vomiting with convulsions, and paralysis of limbs. The conditions of poisoning are related to availability of food, generally occurring in late fall, winter, or early spring when the persist-

ent leaves of this plant are the only vegetation above a light snowcover (Kingsbury 1964). Clarke and Clarke (1967) state that andromedotoxin is the important toxicological constituent.

(*b*) *Beneficial* — *Kalmia angustifolia* is an attractive native shrub whose pink flowers are quite showy. It provides an important nesting site for the willow ptarmigan, *Lagopus lagopus* L., in Newfoundland (Huxter 1964), but the leaves are seldom eaten by this bird (Peters 1958). This species produces relatively little nectar, but bees do visit the flowers to collect pollen (E. Karmo, personal communication).

4. Geographical Distribution

In Canada, this species occurs in Newfoundland, Prince Edward Island, New Brunswick, Nova Scotia, Quebec, and Ontario (Fig. 2). In the United States, it is commonly found in New England and at the higher elevations as far south as Georgia and west to Michigan.

5. Habitat

(*a*) *Climatic requirements* — In habitat, *K. angustifolia* must be able to withstand a wide

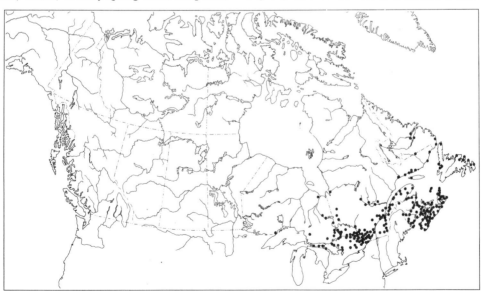

Fig. 2. Canadian distribution of *Kalmia angustifolia* from specimens in the herbaria of Department of Agriculture Herbarium, Ottawa, Ontario; National Herbarium, National Museum of Canada, Ottawa, Ontario; and Acadia University, Wolfville, Nova Scotia.

variety of climatic conditions. In Nova Scotia, which is far from its northern limit, it occurs in areas where minimum temperatures of −40 C (−40 F) have been recorded (Petipas and Hornstein 1963). *Kalmia angustifolia* is common in the lowbush blueberry fields around Lac St. Jean and during the years 1968–71 the mean minima for the month of February at Normandin were −24.5, −17.6, −26.1, and −13.0 C (Department of Transport 1968–71). Fernald (1950) states that its western limit of distribution is Manitoba. Its absence further west may be due to several factors, but probably lack of moisture and a higher soil *p*H are most important. It has considerable resistance to salt spray, for it is found on headlands along the eastern coasts of both Nova Scotia and Newfoundland.

(*b*) *Substratum* — The substratum is believed to play a major role in the distribution of *K. angustifolia*, which occurs typically on podzols. These have developed under a cold to temperate climate on acid parent materials under coniferous, mixed forest, and heath vegetation.

(*c*) *Communities in which the species occur* — This species, along with sweet fern (*Comptonia peregrina* (L.) Coult.) and common lowbush blueberry (*Vaccinium angustifolium* Ait.), are the dominants in the ground cover of the open Jack pine forests to the north of Lac St. Jean (Lavoie 1968). It occurs as a weed in abandoned hayfields, pastures, and blueberry fields of Eastern Canada. Data on percentage of foliage cover and frequency in two fields that had not been cultivated for at least 15 yr are presented in Table 1. At each location there were four replicates and each replicate had 25 contiguous subplots. In estimating foliage cover, each subplot was given a value of 10 and estimates were made down to 0.25. Hall (1959), in studies in Charlotte County, New Brunswick, showed that lowbush blueberry fields that were developed from woodland had a higher frequency of occurrence of *K. angustifolia* than those that were developed from abandoned hay fields.

6. History

Kalmia angustifolia is a native species that was undoubtedly prevalent in forest stands with an open canopy (e.g., Jack pine forest), peat bogs, and exposed headlands prior to the coming of the first European settlers to North America.

7. Growth and Development

(*a*) *Morphology* — A diversified root system in many ericaceous species gives them a distinct advantage on light sandy or gravelly soils. Along the rhizomes are found many adventitious roots that absorb water and nutrients from the upper levels of the soil profile. This species grows laterally by rhizome growth. Older plants have a well-developed tap root that may extend to a depth of at least 1 m where the supply of water and nutrients is sufficient to carry on growth for the entire plant in times of drought (Hall and Mack 1959). The pith of the rhizome in *K. angustifolia* is quite distinctive with aërenchyma cells scattered throughout (Fig. 1D).

(*b*) *Perennation* — Woody shrub that reproduces by seed and new shoot growth arising from dormant buds on rhizomes. Bell and Burchill (1955) found that *K. angustifolia* was relatively slow in development of reproductive tissues in comparison with other ericaceous species native to Nova Scotia. *Kalmia angustifolia* passed the winter with no differentiation of the female gametophyte or pollen.

(*c*) *Physiological data* — Small (1972) has shown that the percent N in leaves of *K. angustifolia* was 1.22, for P 0.072, and for K 0.49. He also found that the bog species, *K. angustifolia*, reabsorbs a greater proportion of the N, P, and K from its leaves preceding leaf fall than do nonbog deciduous species. In the same study it was shown that photosynthetic rates of bog evergreen species were lower than deciduous species expressed on a dry weight basis.

(*d*) *Phenology* — New growth of the shoots commences in Nova Scotia about the last week of May or first week of June. Roland and Smith (1969) state that flowering occurs from 20 June to early July. Capsules were well formed by mid-September and seeds were being released by the first of October.

(*e*) *Mycorrhiza* — Harley (1969) has reviewed in detail the investigations on my-

Table 1. Percentage of foliage cover and frequency of occurrence of species on a 5 × 5 m² plot at two locations in Nova Scotia

	% foliage cover 25 ratings with a value of 10 to each subplot		Frequency of occurrence, 25 subplots	
	Greenwood Road, Yar. Co.†	Onslow, Col. Co.‡	Yar. Co.†	Col. Co.‡
Bare ground	64.3±8.5§	117.1±20.5	20.8±1.3	19.8±0.8
Polytrichum commune Hedw.	3.9±2.2	1.1± 0.7	4.0±0.8	2.2±0.5
Pohlia nutans (Hedw.) Lindb.	1.9±0.7	–	1.8±0.8	–
Lycopodium obscurum L.	0.6±0.4	0.1± 0.0	1.0±0.7	0.2±0.2
Pteridium aquilinum var. *latiusculum* (Desv.) Underw.	–	1.1± 0.7	–	1.0±0.4
Festuca capillata Lam.	1.9±1.9	–	0.2±0.2	–
Poa pratensis L.	–	22.8± 7.8	–	9.5±2.2
Danthonia spicata (L.) Beauv.	43.9±3.3	–	15.5±1.0	–
Agrostis tenuis Sibth	1.8±1.0	3.8± 1.8	0.5±0.3	1.2±0.6
Phleum pratense L.	34.7±3.9	19.1±14.0	15.0±2.0	9.0±5.2
Anthoxanthum odoratum L.	21.0±3.3	–	11.0±1.6	–
Carex scoparia Schkuhr.	–	2.2± 1.9	–	1.0±0.7
Carex sp.	–	1.2± 0.6	–	1.2±0.5
Luzula multiflora (Retz.) Lejeune	1.5±0.6	–	5.2±0.8	–
Maianthemum canadense Desf.	0.1±0.1	–	0.8±0.8	–
Comptonia peregrina (L.) Coult.	1.5±1.5	–	0.5±0.5	–
Rumex acetosella L.	0.4±0.2	0.8± 0.8	4.8±1.5	0.2±0.2
Arenaria lateriflora L.	–	1.1± 0.8	–	1.2±0.7
Fragaria virginiana Duchesne	1.5±0.8	–	2.0±0.6	–
Rubus hispidus L.	7.4±1.0	0.4±0.4	7.2±0.8	0.2±0.2
Rosa carolina L.	–	26.4±10.9	–	12.8±3.1
Trifolium pratense L.	–	2.8± 2.4	–	2.8±2.4
Trifolium hybridum L.	0.1±0.1	–	0.5±0.5	–
Cornus canadensis L.	–	0.2±0.2	–	0.2±0.2
Kalmia angustifolia L.	15.6±4.8	3.1± 0.4	11.0±1.5	4.8±1.0
Gaultheria procumbens L.	4.1±2.0	0.1± 0.1	4.5±1.9	0.2±0.2
Vaccinium myrtilloides Michx.	–	11.2± 4.0	–	6.2±1.5
Vaccinium angustifolium forma *angustifolium* Aalders and Hall	31.2±5.9	18.0± 4.8	17.5±2.2	10.0±1.5
Vaccinium angustifolium forma *nigrum* Aalders and Hall	–	2.4± 2.4	–	1.0±1.0
Lycopus uniflorus Michx.	–	0.3± 0.2	–	0.5±0.3
Plantago major L.	0.5±0.5	–	0.5±0.5	–
Viburnum cassinoides L.	–	1.9± 1.5	–	1.0±0.4
Solidago rugosa Mill.	0.8±0.5	8.6± 1.9	1.2±0.2	4.5±0.6
Solidago graminifolia (L.) Salisb.	–	4.6± 3.8	–	2.0±1.1
Aster sp.	1.0±1.0	–	0.5±0.5	–
Anaphalis margaritacea (L.) C. B. Clarke	4.0±2.4	–	1.5±0.9	–
Achillea millefolium L.	3.1±2.0	–	5.8±3.3	–
Chrysanthemum leucanthemum L.	2.7±2.0	–	3.5±2.0	–
Taraxacum officinale Weber	0.1±0.1	–	0.0	–
Prenanthes trifoliolata (Cass.) Fern.	0.2±0.2	–	0.5±0.5	–

†Records taken at Greenwood Road on 22 May 1958.
‡Records taken at Onslow on 3 June 1958.
§Mean and standard error of four replicates.

11

corrhizas in the Ericaceae. Several workers have been able to grow seeds of various species of this family under aseptic conditions.

8. Reproduction

(a) *Floral biology* — Flowers are insect pollinated by bumble bees, *Bombus terricola* Kirby and *B. ternarius* Say, and solitary bees, *Andrena lata* Vier, *A. carlini* Ckll., and *Dialictus cressonii* (Robt.). The anther sacs are held in small pockets on the limb of the corolla. According to Marie-Victorin (1935), shortly after anthesis the pollen sac dries, enlarges, and the filament springs into an upright position releasing the pollen. Jaynes (1968b) states that most clones tested were found to be self-compatible, but seedlings resulting from selfing were far less vigorous than those that resulted from crossing. We have observed no cases of vivipary in the plants we have examined.

(b) *Seed production and dispersal* — The mean number of seeds per capsule was 181.9 ± 46.2 (SE) (20). (The value in parentheses given here and elsewhere in this paper is the number of observations on which the mean and SE are based.) Counts on shoots collected near Kentville, N.S., showed that the mean number of capsules in each corymb was 4.3 ± 2.5 (80), and the number of corymbs per stem was 9.1 ± 4.4 (20), giving a theoretical total seed production per stem of 7,118.0.

(c) *Viability of seeds and germination* — We were unable, even after 2 mo, to germinate seeds collected on 18 October 1972 and placed immediately in soil inside. Temperature and light conditions were the same as described below for tests on filter paper. Seeds sown on soil had approximately 2 mm of a mixture of sand, peat, and garden soil spread over them. On filter paper, seed germination was 44% after 5 wk. Seeds sown on moist filter paper in culture dishes were placed in a growth chamber that was programmed to give 16 h light and 8 h dark per 24 h with 80% relative humidity. The temperature during the light period was 21 C and during the dark period was 18 C. Light intensity was approximately 2.58×10^4 lm/m². Jaynes (1968b) reports an average 50% seed germination for sheep-laurel.

(d) *Vegetative reproduction* — The rate, time of year, and age of plant when rhizome growth occurs need to be determined.

9. Hybrids

In the wild, *K. angustifolia* does not show any evidence of crossing with the other Canadian species, *K. polifolia* Wang. In experiments at the Connecticut Agricultural Experiment Station, New Haven, Conn., Jaynes (1968a, 1971) has attempted to cross all six species of *Kalmia* native to the United States, but only a few crosses produced any seed. The seedlings that did develop were mostly albinos or lacking in vigor. He concluded that genetic barriers and sterility of F_1 hybrids prevented the potential for gene exchange amongst ornamentals of different species.

10. Population Dynamics

In most fields of the Maritime Provinces of Canada abandoned from forage production, seedlings of *K. angustifolia* arise after the fertility and *p*H of the soil have been much reduced by the natural leaching of the soil. Once the plant is established, lateral growth of the rhizomes is quite variable due to root competition and soil conditions. A single plant of *K. angustifolia* may cover a considerable area. In an abandoned hayfield, which has been without cultivation for 25 yr, the seedling plant is usually less than 1 m wide and it is possible to excavate the entire clone. In a well-established lowbush blueberry field, due to intertwining of rhizomes and roots of *K. angustifolia* and associated *Vaccinium* species, it is almost impossible to excavate clones that appear to cover a diameter of 3 m or more. The problem of determining the limits of plants in weed forest cover consisting chiefly of wire birch (*Betula populifolia* Michx.), trembling aspen (*Populus tremuloides* Michx.), large-toothed aspen (*Populus grandidentata* Michx.), and red maple (*Acer rubrum* L.), is even greater. In the latter case, many parts of the clone must be physiologically separated from others due to decay or breaking of rhizomes. The age of a clone can only be determined by cutting sections from the proximal end of the tap root and counting the growth rings (Hall 1957). The woody tissues of such ericaceous species are difficult to section and it is difficult to count the rings and to know if one ring is formed each year.

11. Response to Herbicides and Other Chemicals

Application of herbicides at sublethal rates to foliage in mixed stands reduced the relative amount of *K. angustifolia* at Fredericton, N.B., and Nappan, N.S. Materials were applied in summer or fall, followed by burning of all foliage before initiation of new growth the following spring. Herbicides reported include amitrole (3-amino-S-triazole), dicamba (3-6-dichloro-*O*-anisic acid), picloram (4-amino-3,5,6-trichloropicolinic acid), 2,4,5-T and 2,4-D ester formulations. Old growth of *K. angustifolia*, 10–15 yr from the last burn, was found to be as susceptible to fall-applied herbicide as was young growth 2 yr from the last burn. Satisfactory reduction of *K. angustifolia* growth was obtained when the herbicide was applied in late fall, and vegetation burned before growth began the next spring (Table 2, 1971).

Foliar sprays of phenoxy herbicide (2,4-D ester formulation) were applied at sublethal rates and in several dilutions to *K. angustifolia* stands in Charlotte Co. and Gloucester Co., N.B. The volume of diluent, from 56.1 to 449.0 liters of water per hectare, used

with the herbicide applied in the fall did not affect the degree of control of *K. angustifolia* (Table 3). Following fall-applied herbicide treatments, the stand of *K. angustifolia* was found to increase or recover steadily during the remaining period of the investigation (Tables 2 and 3).

Entry of ^{14}C-labelled 2,4-D into excised young leaves of *K. angustifolia* varied inversely with the amount of the surfactant Tween 20 (polyoxyethylene sorbitan monolaurate), whereas in older leaves a larger amount of 2,4-D was taken up in the presence of larger amounts of Tween 20 (Webster 1962).

Trevett (1961) reported that 1.4 kg acid equivalent of 2,4-D or 2,4,5-T, and 6.8 kg metallic arsenic, as sodium arsenite, have each effectively reduced populations of sheep-laurel. The killing effect of herbicides decreased with the lateness of the season (60% in September, 32% in November).

12. Response to Other Human Manipulations

When the above-ground parts are removed by burn-pruning, new shoots arise from dormant buds on the rhizomes. Pruning assists lateral growth of the plant by destroying apical dominance of the shoot growing from the end of a rhizome, and this allows two or

Table 2. Reduction of the stand of *K. angustifolia* in lowbush blueberries by selected herbicides and the effects on yield

Herbicide	Rate	Effects on stand[†] of *K. angustifolia*				Yield of blueberries	
		1968	1969	1970	1971	1969	1971[‡]
	kg ai/ha					hl/ha	hl/ha
Dicamba	1.1	6	3	4	3	43	12
Dicamba	2.2	7	6	4	5	42	13
Dicamba	3.3	8	5	5	5	47	13
2,4-D ester + dicamba	1.7+1.7	9	6	6	5	49	16
2,4-D ester + dicamba	2.2+0.6	6	5	4	3	32	6
2,4-D ester + dicamba	2.2+1.1	8	6	6	5	42	12
2,4-D	3.3	6	4	5	3	37	6
2,4-D + dicamba	3.3+0.6	7	6	5	4	44	9
2,4-D + dicamba	3.3+1.1	8	6	8	7	47	11
Check, no herbicide		2	1	3	2	25	10
Check, no herbicide		1	1	2	1	29	7
Check, no herbicide		1	1	2	2	20	4

†Rating based on scale 0 to 10 where 0 = no effects and 10 = stand reduced 100%. Average of four replications. Herbicides applied in 224 liters of water per hectare with 2.07 bars pressure on 5 October 1967. The plots were burnt April 1968 and April 1970.
‡Late spring frost reduced set of berries.

Table 3. Effects of volume of diluent used with a phenoxy herbicide on the stand of *K. angustifolia*

Vol. of diluent	Herbicide	Rate	Rating† of effects on stand of *K. angustifolia*		
			1963	1964	1965
Water, liters/ha		*kg/ha*			
56	2,4-D ester	3.4	5.5	3.5	4.5
112	,,	3.4	7.0	4.0	4.0
56+56†	,,	1.7+1.7	6.0	3.0	4.0
224	,,	3.4	6.5	3.0	3.5
448	,,	3.4	6.0	3.5	3.5
56	2,4,5-T ester	3.4	6.0	3.0	3.5
112	,,	3.4	6.0	3.5	3.5
56+56	,,	1.7+1.7	5.0	3.0	3.0
224	,,	3.4	5.5	3.0	3.0
448	,,	3.4	4.5	2.0	3.0
0	No herbicide		2.0	1.5	2.5
0	,,		1.0	2.0	2.0
0	,,		2.5	1.5	2.0
0	,,		2.0	2.5	2.5

†Rating based on scale 0 to 10 where 0 = no effects and 10 = stand reduced 100%. Average of three replications at two locations in New Brunswick. Herbicides applied at 2.07 bars on 20 October 1962 in Charlotte Co. and 25 October 1962 in Gloucester Co.
‡56 liters sprayed in opposite direction.

more lateral buds to grow as rhizomes in the soil. Ploughing, without cultivation, merely cuts the rhizomes into portions that are capable of growing by themselves, providing sufficient adventitious roots are present to supply water and nutrients (Hall 1963).

In an ecological study carried out in southwestern New Brunswick, the opening of the forest canopy had a marked effect on the vegetative growth and the development of a reproductive phase of six species under full sunlight (Hall 1955). Although *K. angustifolia* was not one of the species listed, its performance was later found to be similar to *Vaccinium myrtilloides* Michx.

Chandler and Mason (1946) have observed that burning, early in October, for 3 yr in succession killed most *K. angustifolia* plants in blueberry fields.

13. Responses to Parasites

Many species of insects inhabit the plants found in a lowbush blueberry field, but *K. angustifolia* is probably the least attractive (G. W. Wood, personal communication). Since sheep-laurel retains its leaves in the fall, it may be more susceptible at this time because leaves of other species have ab-

scissed. He further stated that fields are swept until early October for insects and a few late instar cutworms and a scattering of sawfly larvae are found. These could be responsible for the type of damage seen on the leaves of Fig. 1C, but their low numbers suggest that they are not much of a threat to *K. angustifolia.*

The stems and leaves are relatively free of fungal infections. A list of organisms, occurring mostly on the leaves, is given by Conners (1967). These fungi are: *Gibbera kalmiae* (Pk.) Barr, *Gibberidea kalmiae* (Pk.) Barr, *Lophodermium exaridum* (Cke. & Pk.) Sacc., *Mycosphaerella colorata* (Pk.) Earle, *Phyllachora kalmiae* (Pk.) Petr., and *Synchytrium vaccinii* Thomas.

ACKNOWLEDGMENTS
The authors acknowledge the technical assistance of A. Brydon, D. R. Blenkhorn, and J. Dunphy of the Research Stations, Kentville and Nappan, Nova Scotia, and Fredericton, New Brunswick. We also thank G. A. Mulligan of the Plant Research Institute, Agriculture Canada, Ottawa, Ontario, for helpful suggestions in the preparation of this manuscript. A. Lightfoot of the Kentville Research Station prepared the photographs.

LITERATURE CITED

BELL, H. P. and BURCHILL, J. 1955. Winter resting stages of certain Ericaceae. Can. J. Bot. **33**: 547–561.

CANADA WEED COMMITTEE. 1969. Common and botanical names of weeds in Canada. Can. Dep. Agr. Publ. 1397: 67 pp.

CHANDLER, F. B. and MASON, I. C. 1946. Blueberry weeds in Maine and their control. Maine Agr. Sta. Bull. **443**: 24 p.

CLARKE, E. G. C. and CLARKE, M. L. 1967. Garner's veterinary toxicology. 3rd ed. Baillière Tindall & Cassell, London. 477 pp.

CONNERS, I. L. 1967. An annotated index of plant diseases in Canada and fungi recorded on plants in Alaska, Canada and Greenland. Can. Dep. Agr. Res. Br. Publ. 1251: 381 pp.

DEPARTMENT OF TRANSPORT, METEOROLOGICAL BRANCH. 1968–71. Monthly record meteorological observations in Canada. 315 Bloor Street West, Toronto 181, Ontario.

FERNALD, M. L. 1950. Gray's manual of botany. 8th ed. American Book Co., New York, N.Y. 1632 pp.

FERRON, M. and CAYOUETTE, R. 1971. Noms de mauvaises herbes du Québec. Min. Agr. Colonisation, Québec, P.Q. 113 p.

GAGNON, L. P. 1971. Répression des mauvaises herbes. *Dans* La recherche sur le bleuet. Université Laval, Québec. 184 pp.

HALL, I. V. 1955. Floristic changes following the cutting and burning of a woodlot for blueberry production. Can. J. Agr. Sci. **35**: 143–152.

HALL, I. V. 1957. The tap root in lowbush blueberry. Can. J. Bot. **35**: 933–934.

HALL, I. V. 1959. Plant populations in blueberry stands developed from abandoned hayfields and woodlots. Ecology **40**: 742–743.

HALL, I. V. 1963. Note on the effect of a single intensive cultivation on the composition of an old blueberry stand. Can. J. Plant Sci. **43**: 417–419.

HALL, I. V. and AALDERS, L. E. 1968. The botanical composition of two barrens in Nova Scotia. Natur. Can. **95**: 393–396.

HALL, I. V. and MACK, G. J. A. 1959. Weeds. *In* Blueberry substation Tower Hill, New Brunswick progress report 1954–1959. Can. Dep. Agr., Ottawa, Ontario. pp. 16–19.

HARLEY, J. L. 1969. The biology of mycorrhiza. Leonard Hill, London. 334 pp.

HUXTER, D. S. 1964. Summer habitat of willow ptarmigan in southeastern Newfoundland. M.Sc. Thesis. Acadia University, Wolfville, Nova Scotia.

JAYNES, R. A. 1968*a*. Interspecific crosses in *Kalmia*. Amer. J. Bot. **55**: 1120–1125.

JAYNES, R. A. 1968*b*. Self incompatibility and inbreeding depression in three laurel (*Kalmia*) species. Proc. Amer. Soc. Hort. Sci. **93**: 618–622.

JAYNES, R. A. 1969. Chromosome counts of *Kalmia* species and revaluation of *K. polifolia* var. *microphylla*. Rhodora **71**: 280–284.

JAYNES, R. A. 1971. The *Kalmias* and their hybrids. Quart. Bull. Amer. Rhododendron Soc. **25**: 160–164.

KINGSBURY, J. M. 1964. Poisonous plants of the United States and Canada. Prentice-Hall Inc., Englewood Cliffs, New Jersey. 626 pp.

LAVOIE, V. 1968. La phytosociologie et l'aménagement des bleuetières. Natur. Can. **95**: 397–412.

MARIE-VICTORIN, F. 1935. Flore Laurentienne. Les Frères des Écoles Chrétiennes, 949 rue Côté, Montréal, Québec. 917 pp.

MUENSCHER, W. C. 1949. Poisonous plants of the United States. The Macmillan Company, New York, N.Y. 266 pp.

MUENSCHER, W. C. 1952. Weeds. The Macmillan Company, New York, N.Y. 579 pp.

PETERS, S. S. 1958. Food habitats of the Newfoundland willow ptarmigan. J. Wildlife Manage. **22**: 384–394.

PETITPAS, J. E. R. and HORNSTEIN, R. A. 1963. Plant hardiness zone map Nova Scotia and Prince Edward Island. Dep. Transp. Meteorol. Branch Circ. 3892.

ROLAND, A. E. and SMITH, E. C. 1969. The flora of Nova Scotia. Part II. The dicotyledons. Proc. Nova Scotian Inst. Sci. **26**: 563.

SMALL, E. 1972. Photosynthetic rates in relation to nitrogen recycling as an adaptation to nutrient deficiency in peat bog plants. Can. J. Bot. **50**: 2227–2233.

TREVETT, M. F. 1961. Controlling lambkill in lowbush blueberries. Maine Agr. Exp. Sta. Bull. **600**: 22 pp.

WEBSTER, D. H. 1962. Entry of 2,4-dichlorophenoxyacetic acid into lambkill leaves at varied 2,4-D/tween 20 ratios. Weeds **10**: 250–251.

THE BIOLOGY OF CANADIAN WEEDS. 2. *SPIRAEA LATIFOLIA*

I. V. HALL,[1] R. A. MURRAY,[2] and L. P. JACKSON[3]

[1]*Research Station, Agriculture Canada, Kentville, Nova Scotia, [2]Nova Scotia Department of Agriculture and Marketing, Truro, N.S., and [3]Experimental Farm, Nappan, N.S. Cont.ibution no. 1495, Research Station, Agriculture Canada, Kentville, N.S., received 7 June, 1973, accepted 1 Oct. 1973.*

HALL, I. V., MURRAY, R. A. AND JACKSON, L. P. 1974. The biology of Canadian weeds. 2. *Spiraea latifolia*. Can. J. Plant Sci. **54**: 141–147.

Spiraea latifolia (Ait.) Borkh., broad-leaved meadowsweet (Rosaceae), is a weed of pastures, lowbush blueberry (*Vaccinium angustifolium* Ait. and *V. myrtilloides* Mich.) fields and cranberry (*V. macrocarpon* Ait.) bogs of Eastern Canada, especially where soil moisture content is high during the growing season. Where *S. latifolia* occurs, other vegetation is lacking or depressed. Much time is lost in harvesting lowbush blueberries due to jamming of the *S. latifolia* stems among the tines of the rake or in cranberries due to mechanical damage to the harvesters. In Canada, *S. latifolia* occurs in Newfoundland, Prince Edward Island, Nova Scotia, New Brunswick, Quebec, Ontario, and Manitoba.

La spirée à larges feuilles, *Spiraea latifolia* (Ait.) Borkh. (Rosacée) est une mauvaise herbe des pâturages, des champs de bleuets nains (*Vaccinium angustifolium* Ait. et *V. myrtilloides* Michx.) et des tourbières à canneberges (*V. macrocarpon* Ait.) de l'Est du Canada, particulièrement là où la teneur en eau du sol est élevée durant la saison de croissance. Là où pousse *S. latifolia*, les autres plantes sont absentes ou rabougries. On perd beaucoup de temps dans la cueillette des bleuets nains à cause de l'accumulation de tiges de *S. latifolia* entre les dents du peigne, ou dans celle des canneberges à cause des avaries mécaniques aux récolteurs. Au Canada, on trouve *S. latifolia* à Terre-Neuve, dans l'Île-du-Prince-Édouard, en Nouvelle-Écosse, au Nouveau-Brunswick, au Québec, en Ontario, et au Manitoba.

1. Name

Spiraea latifolia (Ait.) Borkh. — **broad-leaved meadowsweet** (Canada Weed Committee 1969); **spirée à larges feuilles,** aleillant, bois d'Inde, herbe à cheval, reine des prés, spirée sauvage, thé du Canada (Ferron et Cayouette 1970). Rosaceae, rose family, Rosacées.

2. Description and Account of Variation

A vigorous, woody shrub up to 1.5 m in height; bark exfoliating; leaves alternate, simple, margin doubly serrate, entire towards the base, oblanceolate, apex obtuse, base acute; flowers in an elongate panicle, calyx of 5 sepals deeply cut, petals 5, stamens many, pistils usually 5 developing into persisting follicles; seeds about 2 mm long, 3 angled and yellow-brown in color (Fig. 1). Sax (1936) has reported the somatic chromosome number of this species as 36 from material collected in eastern United

Can. J. Plant Sci. **54**: 141-147 (Jan. 1974)

States. More recently Löve and Löve (1966) report that the chromosome number of *S. latifolia* from Mount Washington, New Hampshire was $2n = 36$.

Spiraea latifolia, because of its green leaves, glabrous on both sides, is easily distinguished from *S. tomentosa* L., which has white woolly leaves. The separation of *S. latifolia* from *S. alba* Du Roi is more difficult. Fernald (1950) separated them on the basis of pubescence of the panicle. *Spiraea latifolia* is glabrous, whereas *S. alba* is puberulent or tomentulose.

Mature seeds collected 28 November 1972 from Nappan, Little Forks, and Athol in Cumberland County, Nova Scotia, averaged 87, 92, and 81% germination, respectively, the differences between locations being significant at the 5% level.

At 18 C seedlings attained in 6 wk the four-leaf stage in which the first set of true leaves with serrations was distinguishable from the nonserrated, cotyledon leaves.

Fig. 1. A mature flowering shoot of broad-leaved meadowsweet, *Spiraea latifolia.* 0.75×.

3. Economic Importance

(*a*) *Detrimental* — Areas of pastures in Eastern Canada densely populated with mature plants of *S. latifolia* are of little or no value for grazing. In cultivated crops of lowbush blueberry and cranberry, *S. latifolia* competes for land space, thus reducing potential yield. This weed makes harvesting difficult and incomplete causing additional crop losses. Lowbush blueberry raking crews will by-pass entire areas heavily infested with *S. latifolia.* In areas with a few, weak shoots of this weed, the stems will pass between the teeth of the hand rake crushing the berries already in the rake. In cranberry bogs where the fruit is mechanically harvested, *S. latifolia* may damage the rotating teeth of the harvester causing much time delay for repairs.

A survey carried out on 8,100 ha of lowbush blueberries in Nova Scotia indicated that 3% were severely infested with *S. lati-*

folia, 6% moderately infested, and 12% had a few scattered plants. Of the 24.3 ha of cranberries found in Nova Scotia, 15% of the acreage is severely infested with this weed. A greater financial loss occurs in lowbush blueberries due to the much larger size of this industry. Lowbush blueberry production in 1972 for Nova Scotia was 4,540,000 kg with a gross return of $2,400,000 to the growers. Cranberry production in 1972 for Nova Scotia was 71,732 kg for a gross return to the grower of $28,000. This information on production for 1972 is being prepared by one of us (R.A.M.) for inclusion in the *Quarterly Bulletin of Agricultural Statistics* to be published by Statistics Canada in 1974.

(*b*) *Beneficial* — At the time of flowering this native species has an attractive bloom that is sought out by bumblebees (*Bombus terricola* Kirby and *B. ternarius* Say) and solitary bees (*Andrena lata* Vier., *A. carlinii*

17

Ckll., and *Dialictus cressonii* (Robt.)) for nectar (personal observation).

(*c*) *Legislation* — *Spiraea latifolia* is not listed in any Canadian, federal, or provincial weed or seeds act.

4. Geographical Distribution

In Canada, *S. latifolia* occurs in Newfoundland, Prince Edward Island, Nova Scotia, New Brunswick, Quebec, Ontario, and Manitoba (Fig. 2). In the United States, it occurs west to Michigan and south to North Carolina (Fernald 1950).

5. Habitat

(*a*) *Climatic requirements* — Very few distribution dots of *S. latifolia* on Fig. 2 are in areas of Canada where less than 1,500 degree-days (5.6 C base) occur (Dep. of Energy, Mines and Resources 1971). The northern-most distribution points of Fig. 2 fall within the area having 60 or more frost-free days. The median depth of snow in part of its distribution area is 76.2 cm in February. The average precipitation from April to September in the range of *S. latifolia* is 30.5–50.8 cm. It also exists in an area where the average daily minimum temperature for January is −25 to −30 C and the average daily maximum temperature for the same month is −10 to −15 C.

(*b*) *Substratum* — *Spiraea latifolia* is common on clay soils. The one condition it tolerates exceedingly well is flooding. It is abundant in poorly drained areas such as swamps and ditches. However, it may also occur on very sandy soils when adequate moisture is available throughout the growing season. Cranberry stands in the Annapolis Valley of Nova Scotia have been planted on this type of soil (Townsend and Hall 1971).

(*c*) *Communities in which the species occurs* — Muenscher (1952) stated: "In New York, and to a certain extent in many of the northeastern states, brambles, thorn apples, *Rosa Eglanteria*, spireas and sweetfern are the commonest shrubby weeds invading pastures." *Spiraea latifolia* is one of the worst weeds found in lowbush blueberry fields of Eastern Canada, especially New Brunswick (Jackson and Hall 1972). In 1952 it occurred in 26 out of 100 plots in an old hayfield at Tower Hill, Charlotte Co., New Brunswick (Hall 1953). The associated plants and the abundance of shoots per 20

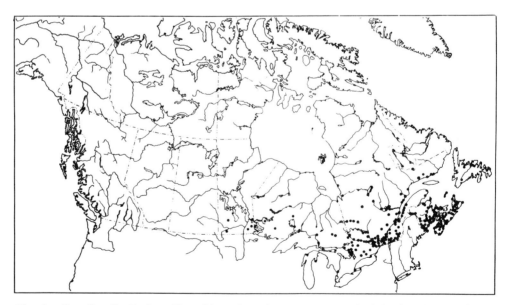

Fig. 2. Canadian distribution of broad-leaved meadowsweet, *Spiraea latifolia,* based on specimens from the herbaria of Department of Agriculture Herbarium, Ottawa, Ontario; National Museum of Canada, Ottawa, Ontario; and Acadia University, Wolfville, Nova Scotia.

cm² quadrat taken from the same field are given in Table 1. *Spiraea latifolia* may survive for a few years in the shade of forest trees, but for maximum growth, flowering, and fruiting it needs full sunlight.

6. History

Fernald (1950) said that *S. latifolia* is a shrub that is native to northeastern North America and that extends from Newfoundland to Michigan and south to North Carolina. Roland and Smith (1969) stated that it is very common throughout Nova Scotia particularly, "in wet land, ditches, swamps, meadows and low pastures, especially in wet mucky soils, where it replaces the heath plants."

Its increase in cranberry bogs is related to the fact that it is resistant to dichlobenil and once it becomes established, the conditions are evidently quite favorable for its growth both above and below ground level.

7. Growth and Development

(*a*) *Morphology* — *Spiraea latifolia* produces an abundant supply of seeds that are carried by either wind or water. It is able to survive burning or cutting because new shoots arise from dormant buds on the rhizomes. A cross-section of the rhizome is shown in Fig. 3. *Spiraea latifolia* also has an extensive root system resembling to a certain degree the tap root in certain ericaceous species (Hall and Mack 1959).

(*b*) *Perennation* — *Spiraea latifolia* is a chamaephyte that is easily recognized in the winter by the persistent, terminal panicles supported by reddish brown stems.

(*c*) *Physiological data* — None are available.

(*d*) *Phenology* — New sprout growth of *S. latifolia* in lowbush blueberry fields of Nova Scotia begins about the last week of May and continues until early July. It flowers in the Maritime Provinces during the last 2 wk of July and throughout August. The range of flowering date is somewhat longer in Quebec and Ontario due to a wider area of distribution with greater diversity of habitats. Mrs. L. Gad, Curatorial Assistant of the University of Toronto, writes the following with regard to the matter in Ontario: "Using specimens with more than ten flowers open per raceme, our earliest collection in flower is around July 6th and our latest in good condition around September 15th.

Table 1. Number of shoots per 20-cm² quadrat in an abandoned hayfield at Tower Hill, Charlotte County, New Brunswick, June 1952; field had not been plowed for at least 20 yr

Species	No. shoots/20 cm² (based on avg of 50 quadrats)	Species	No. shoots/20 cm² (based on avg of 50 quadrats)
Poa pratensis L.	2.5	*Vaccinium angustifolium* forma	
Danthonia spicata (L.) Beauv.	4.0	*angustifolium* Aalders and Hall	8.5
Agrostis tenuis Sibth	19.5	*Vaccinium angustifolium* forma	
Phleum pratense L.	1.4	*nigrum* Aalders and Hall	4.9
Carex spp.	3.0	*Lycopus americanus* Muhl.	1.3
Luzula multiflora (Retz.) Lejeune	6.5	*Solidago rugosa* Mill	2.1
Rumex acetosella L.	1.0	*Solidago canadensis* L.	6.4
Ranunculus acris L.	1.5	*Solidago graminifolia* (L.) Salisb.	6.8
Spiraea latifolia (Ait.) Borkh.	2.7	*Aster lateriflorus* (L.) Britt.	1.8
Pyrus melanocarpa (Michx.) Willd.	4.0	*Aster umbellatus* Mill.	1.2
Fragaria virginiana Duchesne	2.4	*Achillea millefolium* L.	2.4
Potentilla simplex Michx.	3.1	*Chrysanthemum leucanthemum* L.	3.2
Trifolium pratense L.	2.1	*Leontodon autumnalis* L.	1.8
Viola cucullata Ait.	1.0	*Hieracium pilosella* L.	17.5
Gaultheria procumbens L.	13.2	*Hieracium aurantiacum* L.	4.9
Vaccinium myrtilloides Michx.	3.7	*Hieracium florentinum* All.	4.0

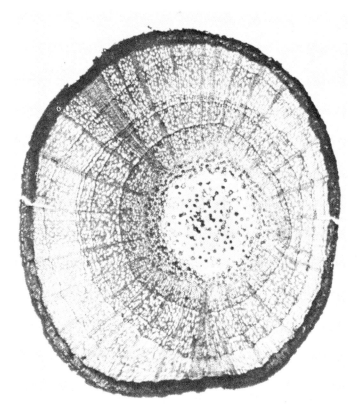

Fig. 3. Cross-section of rhizome of broad-leaved meadowsweet, *Spiraea latifolia.* 30×.

July 1–10th	11–20th	21–31st	
5	8	15	collections
August 1–10th	11–20th	21–31st	
13	9	13 (fruiting 1)	collections
Sept. 1–10th	11–20th	21–30th	
3 (4 fruit)	2	—	collections."

Seed can easily be shaken from the follicles in early winter. Young seedlings have been observed on a moist roadbank in early summer at Tower Hill, Charlotte Co., New Brunswick.

(*e*) *Mycorrhiza* — Information on presence or absence is lacking.

8. Reproduction

(*a*) *Floral biology* — Flowers are pollinated by bumblebees and related types of insects as stated in section 3(*b*). During the late winter of 1973 a series of pollinations on six clones of *S. latifolia* was carried out in the greenhouse at Kentville. Although a minor amount of variation was evident, cross pollinations among plants of different genotypes resulted in 68% development of follicles. Selfing, on the other hand, either with pollen from flowers of the same plant or with pollen from the same flower gave 30% set. Follicles developing from cross pollinations were much larger and more uniform than those resulting from selfing.

(*b*) *Seed production and dispersal* — Based on an average of 10 values, each fruit had 3 seeds, each panicle 9 follicles, and each shoot 40 panicles, giving a potential of 1,080 seeds per shoot. An actual check of 10 samples gave 355.2 ± SE 46.7 follicles per shoot.

(*c*) *Viability of seeds and germination* — Seeds sown in moist soil at a depth of 2–3 mm germinated readily (87%) at a green-

20

house temperature of 21 C day and 16 C night.

(d) *Vegetative reproduction* — *Spiraea latifolia* grows laterally beneath the soil by rhizomes that have many dormant buds. When these buds are released from correlative inhibition (Phillips 1969), they are capable of developing into new shoots.

9. Hybrids

No hybrids involving this species are known.

10. Population Dynamics

Three years after planting, a cranberry stand in the Annapolis Valley was heavily populated with seedlings of *S. latifolia*. The seed probably came from the surrounding area as the cranberry stand was established on a mineral soil and prior to setting the vines, the upper half meter of soil surface containing roots and rhizomes of all species was completely removed with a bulldozer.

The year following seedling establishment, plants of *S. latifolia* can be pulled readily. Although this is a costly labor operation, it is the best recommendation at this time. After seedlings develop thick rhizomes, which are well anchored by adventitious roots, the shoots tend ot break off at the ground level when pulled. New shoots or rhizome branches grow from the crown area that develops. In Wisconsin, on well-cared-for stands, growers cut out the crowns with a machete (*personal communication*).

11. Response to Herbicides and Other Chemicals

Chemical weed control is difficult as this weed is quite resistant to 2,4-D and related compounds, whereas shoots of cranberries and blueberries are quite susceptible. As mentioned previously, *S. latifolia* is also resistant to dichlobenil. The Cranberry Experiment Station, East Wareham, Massachusetts, lists the control measure in their Cranberry Weed Control Schedule for many weeds in cranberry bogs, but they have not listed *S. latifolia* for at least the last 5 yr (Demoranville 1972). This is due to the fact that no control is available (*personal communication*).

12. Response to Other Human Manipulations

Muenscher (1952) suggested that improved drainage will assist control in pastures and that large clumps can be pulled out with a chain. Areas covered with dense growth should be cut and cultivated before reseeding.

13. Responses to Parasites

According to Conners (1967), three fungi, *Cylindrosporium ariaefolium* Ell. & Ev., *Cylindrosporium fairmanianum* Sacc., and *Podosphaera clandestine* (Wallr. ex Fr.) Lév., have been reported as growing on *S. latifolia* in Nova Scotia and several other fungi are reported as occurring on *Spiraea* spp. that could possibly be *S. latifolia*. Insects that attack *Spiraea* spp. are the Spiraea aphid, *Aphis spiraecola*, Spiraea leaf roller, *Olethreutes hemidesma*, and the Spiraea scale, *Eriococcus borealis* (Anonymous 1956).

ACKNOWLEDGMENTS

It is a pleasure to thank A. T. Lightfoot and A. C. Brydon for technical assistance.

ANONYMOUS. 1956. Plant pest handbook. Conn. Agric. Exp. Sta. New Haven Bull. **600**: 194 pp.

CANADA WEED COMMITTEE. 1969. Common and botanical names of weeds in Canada. Can. Dep. Agric. Publ. 1397: 67 pp.

CONNERS, I. L. 1967. An annotated index of plant disease in Canada and fungi recorded on plants in Alaska, Canada, and Greenland. Can. Dep. Agric. Res. Br. Publ. 1251: 381 pp.

DEMORANVILLE, I. E. 1972. 1972 Cranberry weed control. Cranberry Exp. Sta., East Wareham, Massachusetts.

DEPARTMENT OF ENERGY, MINES AND RESOURCES. 1971. The national atlas of Canada. Folios A & B. Queen's Printer, Ottawa, Ontario.

FERNALD, M. L. 1950. Gray's manual of botany. 8th ed. American Book Co., New York, N.Y. 1632 pp.

FERRON, M. and CAYOUETTE, R. 1970. Nom des mauvaises herbes du Québec. Minist. Agric. et Colonisation du Québec. Publ. 288: 113 pp.

HALL, I. V. 1953. Successional studies primarily concerned with three species of *Vaccinium*. Ph.D. Thesis. Cornell University, Ithaca, New York.

HALL, I. V. and MACK, G. J. A. 1959. Weeds. *In* Blueberry substation Tower Hill, New Brunswick progress report 1954–1959. Can. Dep. Agric., Ottawa, Ontario. pp. 16–19.

JACKSON, L. P. and HALL, I. V. 1972. Weeds. *In* Lowbush blueberry production. Agric. Can. Publ. 1477: 17–21 pp.

LÖVE, A. and LÖVE, D. 1966. Cytotaxonomy of the alpine vascular plants of Mount Washington. Univ. Colo. Stud. Ser. Biol. 24: 1–74.

MUENSCHER, W. C. 1952. Weeds. MacMillan Co., New York, N.Y. 579 pp.

PHILLIPS, D. J. 1969. Apical dominance. Pages 163–202 *in* M. B. Wilkins, ed. Physiology of plant growth and development. McGraw-Hill Book Co. London.

ROLAND, A. E. and SMITH, E. C. 1969. The flora of Nova Scotia. Part II. The dicotyledons. Proc. Nova Scotian Inst. Sci. 26: 277–743.

SAX, K. 1936. Polyploidy and geographic distribution in Spiraea. J. Arnold Arbor. Harv. Univ. 17: 352–356.

TOWNSEND, L. R. and HALL, I. V. 1971. Nutrient levels in leaf and soil samples from three cranberry bogs in the Annapolis Valley of Nova Scotia. Cranberries 36(3): 11–12.

THE BIOLOGY OF CANADIAN WEEDS. 3. *CARDARIA DRABA*, *C. CHALEPENSIS*, AND *C. PUBESCENS*

GERALD A. MULLIGAN and JUDY N. FINDLAY

Biosystematics Research Institute, Agriculture Canada, Ottawa, Ontario K1A 0C6. Contribution no. 981, Plant Research Institute, received 1 Aug. 1973, accepted 1 Oct. 1973.

MULLIGAN, GERALD A. AND FINDLAY, JUDY N. 1974. The biology of Canadian weeds. 3. *Cardaria draba, C. chalepensis,* and *C. pubescens.* Can. J. Plant Sci. **54**: 149–160.

This summary of biological information on heart-podded hoary cress (*Cardaria draba* (L.) Desv.), lens-podded hoary cress (*C. chalepensis* (L.) Handel-Mazzetti), and globe-podded hoary cress (*C. pubescens* (C. A. Meyer) Jarmolenko) is the third in a series of contributions on plants that are weedy in Canada. The hoary cresses are weedy in open habitats, particularly in the Prairie Provinces and the interior of British Columbia.

Ce résumé de la documentation biologique sur le cranson dravier (*Cardaria draba* (L.) Desv.), le cranson lenticulaire (*C. chalepensis* (L.) Handel-Mazzetti), et le cranson velu (*C. pubescens* (C. A. Meyer) Jarmolenko) est le troisième d'une série d'articles sur les mauvaises herbes du Canada. On trouve les cransons dans des habitats découverts, particulièrement dans les provinces des Prairies et en Colombie-Britannique intérieure.

1. Names

I. *Cardaria draba* (L.) Desv. — **heart-podded hoary cress** (Canada Weed Committee 1969); **cranson dravier** (Frankton 1958).

II. *Cardaria chalepensis* (L.) Handel-Mazzetti (= *C. draba* (L.) Desv. var. *repens* (Schrenk) Rollins) — **lens-podded hoary cress** (Canada Weed Committee 1969); **cranson rampant** (Frankton 1958).

III. *Cardaria pubescens* (C. A. Meyer) Jarmolenko (= *Hymenophysa pubescens* C. A. Meyer) — **globe-podded hoary cress** (Canada Weed Committee 1969); **cranson velu** (Frankton 1958).

Cruciferae, mustard family, Crucifères.

2. Description and Account of Variation

Until Bellue (1933) reported the presence of three distinct species of *Cardaria* in North America, it was thought that there was only one species, *C. draba*, on this continent. Consequently, it is frequently impossible to determine which *Cardaria* species were being written about by North American authors prior to 1933. In fact, some weed taxonomists still do not distinguish between the three hoary cresses. This is un-

fortunate as Jenkins and Jackman (1938) showed very early that the three species differ in their resistance to herbicides. They reported that at Genesee, Idaho, *C. pubescens* required 909 g per 25.3 m² (2 lb per square rod) of carbon bisulfide for control but *C. draba* required 2,273 g (5 lb) and *C. chalepensis* 1,364 g (3 lb).

The pods (silicles) of *C. draba* are, as the common name suggests, heart-shaped (Fig. 1). Lens-podded hoary cress, *C. chalepensis*, has pods that are nearly round or kidney-shaped in outline (Fig. 2). The pods of this species are compressed perpendicular to the partition. Globe-podded hoary cress, *C. pubescens*, is as the name suggests, completely globular to ellipsoid (Fig. 3). Globe-podded hoary cress has short simple hairs on the sepals and pods whereas the other two hoary cresses have glabrous sepals and pods.

I. *Cardaria draba* — Perennial with a spreading root system from which many aerial shoots are produced; stem stoutish, 30–60 cm, erect to occasionally nearly procumbent, glabrous to nearly so above, slightly to densely pubescent below; basal leaves with scattered to dense pubescence, irregularly toothed to entire, narrowed to a petiole;

middle and upper leaves sparsely pubescent to glabrous, obovate, elliptic-oblong or lanceolate, irregularly toothed to nearly entire, clasping the stem with cordate-sagittate bases, to 9 cm long and 4 cm broad; fruiting inflorescence usually of elongated racemes;

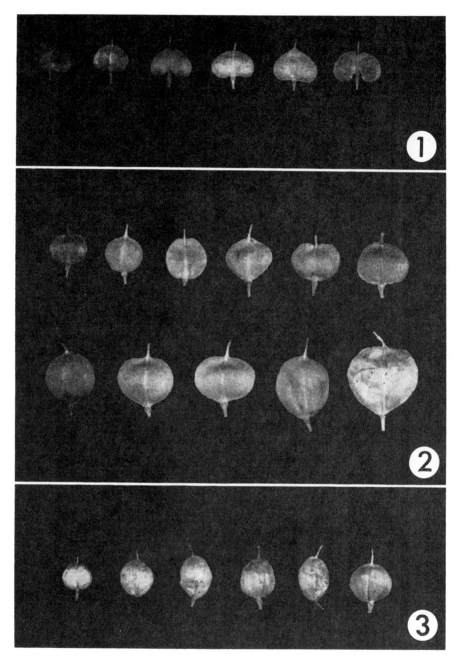

Fig. 1–3. Silicles of three species of *Cardaria*, ×2: 1, *C. draba*; 2, *C. chalepensis*; 3, *C. pubescens*.

petals white, 3–4 mm long; sepals glabrous, white-margined, 1.5–2.0 mm long; pedicels slender, to 1.5 cm long; silicles cordate, glabrous, inflated, usually constricted at septum, broader than long, 3.0–5.0 mm broad, 2.5–3.5 mm long, indehiscent with one ovary in each locule; mature silicles usually with two seeds; style 0.8–1.6 mm long; seeds oval, slightly compressed, red-brown, 1.5 × 2.0 mm; cotyledons incumbent (Mulligan and Frankton 1962).

Plants of *C. draba* from Alberta and Botanic Gardens in Belgium, England, Germany, and the USSR had $2n = 64$ chromosomes (Mulligan and Frankton 1962). Manton (1932) obtained the same chromosome number on plants from Austria and Denmark.

II. *Cardaria chalepensis* — Perennial with a spreading root system from which many aerial shoots are produced; stem stoutish, 20–40 cm, semierect to erect, glabrous or nearly so above, scattered to densely pubescent below; basal leaves with sparse to dense pubescence, irregularly toothed to entire, narrowed to a petiole; middle and upper leaves sparsely pubescent or glabrous, obovate, elliptic-oblong or lanceolate, irregularly toothed to entire, clasping the stem with cordate-sagittate bases, to 8 cm long and 3 cm broad, sometimes much smaller; fruiting inflorescence variable, elongate with spreading racemes to shortened with racemes forming a corymb; petals white, 3–4 mm long; sepals glabrous, very rarely with few simple hairs, white-margined, 2.0–2.5 mm long; pedicels slender, to 1.5 cm long; silicles glabrous, inflated, transversely oval to slightly reniform, nearly reniform to broadly obovate in outline, 2.5–6.0 (8.0) mm long, 4.0–6.0 (7.0) mm broad, indehiscent with usually two, rarely one, ovary in each locule; mature silicles with 1–4 seeds, sometimes seedless; style 1–2 mm long; seeds oval, slightly compressed, red-brown, 1.5 × 2.0 mm; cotyledons incumbent (Mulligan and Frankton 1962).

Plants of *C. chalepensis* from Saskatchewan, Alberta, and British Columbia, and also from a Botanic Garden in the USSR had $2n = 80$ chromosomes (Mulligan and Frankton 1962).

III. *Cardaria pubescens* — Perennial, with a spreading root system from which many aerial shoots are produced; stem rather stoutish, spreading to nearly erect, 10–40 cm, sparsely to densely pubescent; leaves with sparse to dense pubescence, irregularly dentate; basal leaves narrowed to the petiole; middle and upper leaves linear-oblong to oblong-lanceolate with acute sagittate leaf bases, to 8 cm long and 2 cm broad, usually much smaller; fruiting inflorescence of many elongated racemes to racemes much shortened forming a compacted corymb; petals white, 2.0–3.0 (3.5) mm long; sepals pubescent, white-margined, 1.5–2.0 mm long, pedicels slender, pubescent, to 1.0 cm long; silicles sparsely to densely pubescent, strongly inflated, obovoid to subglobose, 3.0–4.5 mm long, 2.5–4.5 mm broad, indehiscent with 1, rarely 2, ovaries in each locule; mature silicles frequently seedless or with 1 or 2, rarely 3 or 4, seeds; style 1.0–1.5 mm long, seeds oval, slightly compressed, red-brown, 1.0–1.5 × 1.5–2.0 mm; cotyledons incumbent (Mulligan and Frankton 1962).

Plants of *C. pubescens* from Saskatchewan, Alberta, and British Columbia, and also from Colorado in the United States, had $2n = 16$ chromosomes (Mulligan and Frankton 1962).

The hoary cresses (*Cardaria* spp.) differ from all other mustards in that they have white flowers, leaf surfaces covered with short simple hairs, upper leaves clasping stem by earlike lobes, and that they spread by underground rootstocks.

There is a marked difference in the susceptibility of different clones of *C. chalepensis* to various herbicides (see section 11).

The illustration of the three hoary cresses shown in Fig. 4 is taken from Frankton and Mulligan (1971).

3. Economic Importance

(a) *Detrimental* — I. *Cardaria draba* — Heart-podded hoary cress is the least weedy of the three hoary cresses in Canada. It is most troublesome in the Prairie Provinces, particularly in southern Manitoba and southern Alberta, and is probably the weediest hoary cress found in the United States. In Australia it causes considerable economic loss (Anonymous 1936) and according to

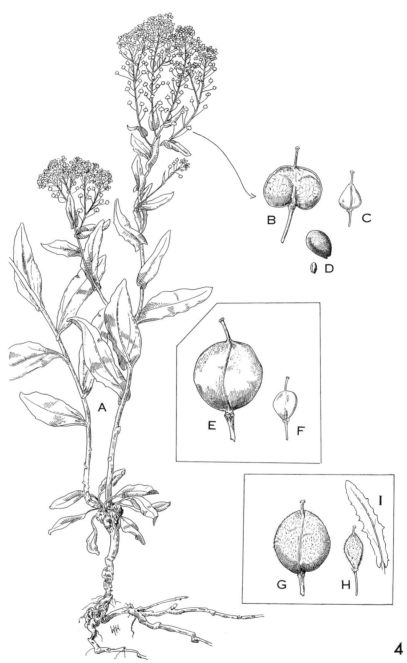

Fig. 4. *Cardaria draba*: (A) plant; (B) mature silicle; (C) immature silicle; (D) seed, *C. chale-pensis*; (E) mature silicle; (F) immature silicle, *C. pubescens*; (G) mature silicle; (H) immature silicle; (I) leaf.

Pemberton and Prunster (1940) has seriously reduced the value of high-priced wheat lands. It has been described as the most serious foreign weed menace in England (Blackman et al. 1949). II. *Cardaria chalepensis* — This species is the most serious of the three hoary cresses as a weed in Canada, particularly in irrigated areas of Saskatchewan, Alberta, and British Columbia. *Cardaria chalepensis* is more widespread and troublesome than either of the other two species in California (Bellue 1933). Keller et al. (1934) states that it is a weed in bogara sowings (sowings in nonirrigated soils) in Kazakhstan and the central Asiatic republics. III. *Cardaria pubescens* — Globe-podded hoary cress occurs in the same areas as does the previous species and frequently grows mixed with it in fields of Canada and United States. It is generally not as aggressive as *C. chalepensis*. A similar situation occurs in the USSR. According to Keller et al. (1934) *C. pubescens* occurs together with *C. chalepensis* as a weed in bogara fields of Kazakhstan and the central Asiatic republics. It also is found in irrigated fields and market gardens in these areas.

(*b*) *Beneficial* — The showy flowers of hoary cresses are frequently visited by insects, probably utilizing the pollen and nectar for food. According to Keller et al. (1934) seeds of *C. draba* may be utilized as a substitute for pepper.

(*c*) *Legislation* — All three species are listed under the Seeds Act and Regulations administered by Agriculture Canada (1967) in the category "Prohibited Noxious Weed Seeds — Class 1." The hoary cresses are listed as noxious weeds in the *Noxious Weeds Acts* of Manitoba, Saskatchewan, Alberta, and British Columbia. Imported seed is prohibited entry into the United States if it contains seeds of any of the hoary cresses (Rollins 1967).

4. Geographical Distribution

I. *Cardaria draba* — Native to the Balkan Peninsula, Georgian SSR, Armenian SSR, Azerbaydzhan SSR, Turkmenia SSR, Kazakhstan SSR, Irkutskaya Oblast, Turkey, Israel, Syria, Iraq, and Iran. It was widely introduced and is naturalized throughout Europe and all other continents. *Cardaria draba* is a widespread weed in Canada and the United States (Mulligan and Frankton 1962). It has been collected in every province of Canada except Prince Edward Island, New Brunswick, and Newfoundland (Fig. 5). It is rare except in the three Prairie Provinces and British Columbia. Of the three hoary cresses found in Canada, it is the least abundant.

II. *Cardaria chalepensis* — Native to Kazakhstan SSR, Uzbekistan SSR, and Turkmenia SSR, and doubtfully native in Pakistan, northern India, Afghanistan, Iran, Iraq, Syria, and Israel. Naturalized in North America, a rare introduction in England and Argentina, and perhaps present but unrecognized elsewhere (Mulligan and Frankton 1962). *Cardaria chalepensis* is a common field weed in central and western Canada and the United States but is nearly absent from eastern North America (Fig. 6).

III. *Cardaria pubescens* — Native to Kazakhstan SSR, Uzbekistan SSR, Turkmenia SSR, northern Iran, and Afghanistan. Naturalized in Argentina and North America. It is an aggressive weed in central and Western Canada and the United States but is rare in eastern North America (Fig. 7).

5. Habitat

(*a*) *Climatic requirements* — *Cardaria* spp. —No specific information is available for *C. draba*. However, most of the general climatic information available for the other two species probably also applies to *C. draba*. At one location in Saskatchewan an infestation of *C. chalepensis* and *C. pubescens* increased from 1953 to 1956 when annual rainfall was 20% above average for the district (38 cm or 15 inches), but decreased from 1956 to 1959 when rainfall was 15% below average (Selleck 1961). Selleck (1961) concluded that *C. chalepensis* and *C. pubescens* are a significant hazard to crop production under moist conditions and on irrigated land but are unlikely to become a major problem under drier conditions.

(*b*) *Substratum* — *Cardaria* spp. — In Alberta, all three hoary cresses occur under a variety of soil conditions where moisture is

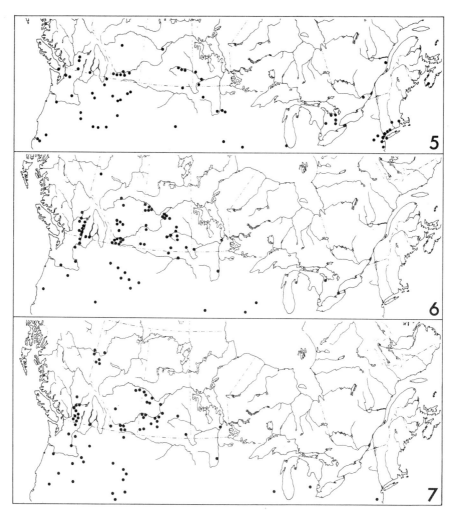

Fig. 5–7. Distribution of three species of *Cardaria* in Canada and the United States from herbarium specimens: 5, *C. draba*; 6, *C. chalepensis*; 7, *C. pubescens*.

at least in moderate supply (Corns and Frankton 1952). *Cardaria* species are often abundant on alkali soils of Alberta, with *Cardaria pubescens* tending to show a preference for this condition (Corns and Frankton 1952). The fact that such soils are often wet late in the spring and proper cultural practice is delayed probably favors the persistence of hoary cresses in this type of habitat.

(*c*) *Communities in which the species occur — Cardaria spp.* — All the hoary cresses grow under similar open unshaded condi-

tions. In Canada, *C. draba* occurs in grainfields, hayfields, and roadsides (Frankton and Mulligan 1971). In Saskatchewan, *C. chalepensis* and *C. pubescens* are found in brome (*Bromus* spp.) and alfalfa (*Medicago* spp.) fields and in other areas of disturbance, e.g., gardens, feed lots, watercourses, and along irrigation ditches (Selleck 1965).

6. History

I. *Cardaria draba* — This species was first collected in the United States at Long Island, New York, in 1862 and in Canada at Barrie, Ontario, in 1878. Many other collections were made in Canada and the United States before 1900. *Cardaria draba* was probably first introduced into North America by early settlers from Europe but may have been introduced later not only from Europe but elsewhere (Mulligan and Frankton 1962).

II. *Cardaria chalepensis* — It was first collected in the United States at Chino, California, in 1918 and in Canada at Grande Prairie, Alberta, in 1926 (Mulligan and Frankton 1962). Groh (1940a, b) indicates that *C. chalepensis* and *C. pubescens* were introduced into Canada and the United States in alfalfa seed that was imported from Turkestan. N. G. Lewis of the Plant Products Division, Agriculture Canada, Calgary, Alberta, wrote the following in a letter to H. Groh dated 5 January 1940: "With respect to the history of the infestations, (*C. chalepensis* and *C. pubescens*) I understand that Mr. R. E. English, Provincial Weed Supervisor, Department of Agriculture, Edmonton, considers all old stands trace to the first distribution of alfalfa by the C.P.R. about 1911-12, and that this is true of the Russian knapweed (*Centaurea repens* L.) as well." Mulligan and Frankton (1962) found additional evidence supporting the view that Turkestan alfalfa was the medium of introduction of these two hoary cresses. Several herbaria (in Ottawa, Los Angeles, and Minnesota) contain duplicates of a collection with the following label data: *Hymenophysa pubescens*, grown from seed in Turkestan alfalfa, Fargo, North Dakota, O. A. Stevens, June 26, 1912. All these duplicates consisted of a fruiting specimen of *C. pubescens* and a vegetative specimen of another *Cardaria*, almost certainly *C. chalepensis*. According to Brown (1914), Turkestan alfalfa was first introduced into the United States in 1898 but was not imported in any great amount until after 1910. There is no evidence that *C. draba* was introduced to North America from Turkestan.

III. *Cardaria pubescens* — It was first collected in the United States at Ypsilanti, Michigan, in 1919 and like *C. chalepensis* was first collected in Canada at Grande Prairie, Alberta, in 1926 (Mulligan and

Frankton 1972). *Cardaria pubescens* was also introduced in North America in alfalfa seed from Turkestan (see *C. chalepensis*).

7. Growth and Development

(*a*) *Morphology* — *Cardaria* spp. — The root systems of all three hoary cresses consist of vertical and lateral roots from which new rosettes and flowering shoots arise. Vigorous vegetative reproduction by means of rootstocks is of prime importance in their survival and spread. Deep vertical penetration of roots makes it difficult to control the hoary cresses easily by cultivation. The vertical roots of *C. chalepensis* disintegrate from the top down when decay starts following repeated cultivations (Rosenfels and Headley 1944). According to Selleck (1965), in Saskatchewan *C. draba* roots frequently penetrate 74–81 cm (29–32 inches) into the soil and occasionally as much as 1.6 m (5 ft). At Leader, Saskatchewan, *C. pubescens* roots were traced vertically to a depth of 5.6 m (18.5 ft), at which level the rootlets became too delicate to follow.

(*b*) *Perennation* — *Cardaria* spp. — The three hoary cresses survive and spread primarily by extremely persistent roots. These roots, with abundant food reserves, overwinter in Canada and produce new shoots in the spring.

(*c*) *Physiological data* — *Cardaria* spp. — There is a seasonal trend of carbohydrate accumulation in roots of *C. chalepensis*, both under cultivated and noncultivated conditions (Barr 1942). In Colorado, Barr (1942) found that samples of *C. chalepensis* roots collected at 2-wk intervals from 25 April to 29 October from noncultivated plots showed a maximum accumulation of carbohydrates about 1 August. "The lowest carbohydrate content was found early in the season when sampling was started. The total sugar content was higher in the roots from the second foot of soil than in those from the first 30 cm (1 ft) level until about the middle of September. The root reserves were present chiefly in the form of starch. The starch content of undisturbed plants reached a maximum of over 21 percent fresh weight but the total sugar content never exceeded 7.44 percent and reducing sugars remained uniformly low, reaching a maximum of 1.41 percent."

(*d*) *Phenology* — *Cardaria* spp. — Cotyledons of *C. draba* appear above ground 5–6 wk after planting and expand to maximum size in about 3 wk (Scurfield 1962). During this period the first leaves emerge and form a loose rosette. Lateral roots develop from the radicle after about 2–3 wk. Lateral stem shoots appear after about 13–14 wk, often arising from the upper regions of the hypocotyl and from the cotyledonary axils of older plants. In Saskatchewan, plants of *C. pubescens* grown from seed planted in October 1957 did not produce an inflorescence until 1959 (Selleck 1965). Shoots from underground parts emerged on 1 May 1959 and produced basal rosettes. Selleck (1965) found that on 18 May 1959, plants of *C. pubescens* were 5.1–12.7 cm (2–5 inches) tall and bore 5–7 leaves. On 3 June plants 12.7–17.8 cm (5–7 inches) tall had 12 leaves and were initiating buds. Some flowers were open on 7 July, but by 14 July flowers were replaced by capsules, some almost fully developed. On 20 July, seeds were fully developed, but immature. Mature plants of *C. pubescens* produced an average of 300 pods, ranging from 30 to 560 per plant. High seed producers developed a much-branched inflorescence, and leaves were usually shed at the time of seed maturity. In Alberta, *C. pubescens* flowers 10–14 days later than either *C. draba* or *C. chalepensis* (Sterling 1951). *Cardaria pubescens* also blooms later than the other two species in Nevada (Rosenfels and Headley 1944). *Cardaria draba* and *C. pubescens* were in flower whereas *C. pubescens* was still in the early bud to flowering stage under comparable conditions in the Lethbridge, Sterling and Calgary areas (Sterling 1951). In California, *C. chalepensis* comes into blossom later than *C. draba* and remains in flower for a longer period. *Cardaria chalepensis* shows a greater ability than *C. draba* both to recover from injury and to persist to seed maturity. *Cardaria pubescens* starts blooming in California at the same time as *C. chalepensis* but *C. pubescens* remains in bloom well into winter.

(*e*) *Mycorrhiza* — None known.

8. Reproduction

(*a*) *Floral biology* — *Cardaria* spp. — Horovitz and Cohen (1972) found that the flowers of *C. draba* do not reflect ultraviolet light. Mulligan and Frankton (1962) state that all three species of hoary cress are self-incompatible and are outcrossed by insects. This is probably the reason why some of the pods of *C. chalepensis* and *C. pubescens* are often seedless. The flowers of *C. draba* are readily accessible to short-tongued insects (Knuth 1908). Knuth (1908) records the following insects visiting the flowers of *C. draba* in Europe: Coleoptera — *Meligethes lepidii* Mill. and *Nacerdes viridipes* Schmidt; Hymenoptera — *Halictus interruptus* Pz., *H. malachurus* K., and *H. minutus* K.

(*b*) *Seed production and dispersal* — *Cardaria* spp. — One plant of *C. draba* produces 1,200–4,800 seeds, of which 1,000 weigh 1.8 g and the number per kilogram is 555,000 (Keller et al. 1934). *Cardaria draba* and *C. chalepensis* yielded large quantities of seed in Alberta in 1950, whereas *C. pubescens* was a poor third (Corns and Frankton 1952). *Cardaria draba* and *C. chalepensis* produced as many as 850 mature fruits per flowering stem.

(*c*) *Viability of seeds and germination* — *Cardaria* spp. — Seed of *C. draba* 1 yr old germinated 84%, 2-yr-old seed germinated 31%, and 3-yr-old seed did not germinate at all (Bellue 1946). Bellue (1946) found that seed of *C. chalepensis* germinated 86% when 1 yr old but only decreased to 52% germination after 3 yr. Seed of *C. pubescens* germinated 9% after 3 yr but the seed was probably immature as it only had 15% germination when collected.

(*d*) *Vegetative reproduction* — *Cardaria* spp. — According to Scurfield (1962) the root system of *C. draba* "consists of a vertical tap-root which develops one or more lateral (first-order) roots. These also eventually turn down to become secondary vertical roots which often reach greater depths than the parent root. Laterals of the second order are developed on first order laterals usually just below the point where the latter bend to become vertical. This method of development is repeated until laterals of the third, fourth and higher orders are formed. Shoot development is from buds which can form on any part of the permanent root system, but tend to occur most often at or just above the point where lateral roots bend down to become vertical. Such buds give rise directly to new rosettes if borne at or near the soil surface. Buds borne at deeper levels may grow out as rhizomes." The root systems of *C. chalepensis* and *C. pubescens* are similar.

The hoary cresses belong to a group of rhizomatous weeds (*Cardaria* spp.; *Cirsium arvense* (L.) Scop., Canada thistle; *Convolvulus arvensis* L., field bindweed; *Centaurea repens* L., Russian knapweed; *Linaria vulgaris* Mill., toadflax) that have vertical roots penetrating several meters into the soil and lateral reproductive roots (Kott 1966). Fragmented roots show poor regeneration in relatively dry soil (Kott 1966). Only *Cirsium arvense* propagates extensively from seed (Kott 1966). The other type of rhizomatous weed, for example *Sonchus arvensis*, is relatively shallow rooting and root fragments regenerate at any time of the year and are resistant to drought and frost.

9. Hybrids

The first generation hybrid, *C. draba* ($2n = 64$) $\times$ *C. chalepensis* ($2n = 80$), was found growing in Alberta at Magrath and at Lethbridge and this hybrid had the expected intermediate chromosome number of $2n = 72$ (Mulligan and Frankton 1962). Seed from one of the F_1 hybrids yielded progeny with $2n = 66, 67, 68, 69$, and ca. 70–72 chromosomes but there is no evidence that anything but first generation hybrids survive in nature. There are no known natural hybrids between *C. pubescens* ($2n = 16$) and either *C. draba* or *C. chalepensis*.

10. Population Dynamics

I. *Cardaria draba* — According to Kirk et al. (1943), at an age of 25 days, single plants developed several shoots, tap roots to a depth of 25 cm (10 inches) and five or six horizontal roots with numerous vegetative buds. After 100 days, these plants developed 48 shoots over an area 61 cm (2 ft) in diameter. More than 80 buds were present on six horizontal and vertical roots. A

single plant of *C. draba* established in the absence of competition has been reported to spread over an area 3.7 m (12 ft) in diameter during the 1st year of development (Selleck 1965). In Saskatchewan, radial increases ranged from 61 to 76 cm (2–2.5 ft) annually (Kirk et al. 1943). Kirk et al. (1943) found that a single plant of *C. draba*, growing without competition, produced 455 shoots in 1 yr.

II. *Cardaria chalepensis* — In Saskatchewan, Selleck (1965) reported that the spread of *C. chalepensis* often exceeded 61 cm (2 ft) per year under favorable conditions. However, at Leader, Saskatchewan, a site dominated by shrubs, *C. chalepensis* receded from 1953 to 1959 from an original infestation of 65 m^2 to only two shoots in 1959. He found that at Glen Kerr, Saskatchewan, both *C. chalepensis* and *C. pubescens* were vigorous, increasing from 12.7% of a transect line in 1956 to 30% in 1957. In this area competition was mostly western wheatgrass, *Agropyron smithii* Rydb., and the site was irrigated twice annually. *Cardaria chalepensis* produced inflorescences at Leader in 1952 and 1953 but failed to produce mature seed. In 1954, plants on the perimeter of the infestation appeared spindly and weak, and desiccated inflorescences were common, particularly in competition with *Rosa* and *Bromus*. During an advanced stage of desiccation, only short leafless stems remained. This occurred with both lens- and globe-podded hoary cresses during 1954–59 but was less marked with the globe-podded species. Shrubs were the most effective competitors for *C. chalepensis* and *C. pubescens* under dry conditions. Presumably the extensive root systems of *Rosa* and *Symphoricarpos* permitted fuller utilization of subsoil moisture (Selleck 1965).

III. *Cardaria pubescens* — According to Selleck (1965), patches of *C. pubescens* increased an average of 76 cm (2.5 ft) in radius at Glen Kerr, Saskatchewan, from 1953 to 1956 and an additional 30 cm (1 ft) from 1956 to 1959. The same species increased 1.7 m (5.7 ft) in radius at Leader, Saskatchewan, from 1953 to 1956, an increase in area of 91%. From 1956 to 1959, however, the perimeter receded 48 cm (1.6

ft). Perimeter extension or recession of hoary cress frequently coincided with the presence or absence of competing species. At both Leader and Glen Kerr, Saskatchewan, *C. pubescens* spread most frequently in denuded areas or where western wheatgrass was the major competitor. Extensions were less frequent, and some recessions occurred, in competition with smooth bromegrass (*Bromus inermis* Leyss.) and Russian knapweed. Recessions occurred at Leader where the shrubs *Rosa* or western snowberry (*Symphoricarpos occidentalis* Hook.) were prevalent. The stand of hoary cress plots at Glen Kerr was initially sparser in mowed than in unmowed plots. A vigorous stand of alfalfa developed in mowed plots after sowing in 1956 and was accompanied by a decrease in density of hoary cress plants, the survivors being stunted and spindly. However, an increase in density of hoary cress and bromegrass occurred in 1959 following winterkilling of alfalfa during the winter of 1958–59. The percentage of shoots of hoary cress that flowered decreased during the study where irrigation was not practiced. At Glen Kerr in mowed and unmowed plots under irrigation, the average percent of flowering shoots of *C. pubescens* increased from 1.4 and 21%, respectively, from 1952 to 1956, to 22 and 42% from 1958 to 1959. In an area not always reached by irrigation water the mean percent of flowering shoots averaged 68 and 42% from 1952 to 1956 in native grass and bromegrass, respectively, and decreased to 12 and 39%, respectively, from 1957 to 1959. Densities of the vigorous perennial competing forbs (Russian knapweed, *Aster* spp. and *Artemisia frigida* Willd. (pasture sage)) remained relatively constant in unmowed plots, but ultimately decreased in mowed plots.

11. Response to Herbicides and Other Chemicals

Cardaria spp. — The reaction of various clones of *C. draba*, *C. chalepensis*, and *C. pubescens* from Alberta to several rates of 2,4-D, 2,3,6-TBA, a mixture of 2,3,6-TBA and MCPA, and amitrole was tested by Sexsmith (1964). His results are given in Table 1. *Cardaria draba* and *C. pubescens* were more susceptible to 2,4-D at rates of 454–907 g/0.4 ha (1–2 lb/acre) than was *C. chalepensis*. There were also marked differences in the susceptibility of various clones of *C. chalepensis* to 2,4-D, 2,3,6-TBA, and the mixture of 2,3,6-TBA and MCPA at some rates.

12. Response to Other Human Manipulations

I. *Cardaria draba* — Cultivation is the major factor in the spread of this species in Australia and according to Pemberton and Prunster (1940) it is not uncommon in that country to see as many as 100 oval-shaped infestations in a fallowed field. Severed portions of the root system readily bud to produce new plants. According to the 1972 report of the Western Section of the Canada Weed Committee it takes 3 consecutive yr of intensive tillage to kill the root system of any of the three hoary cresses. Irrigation facilitates the spread and establishment of the plant by transporting root material from neglected ditch banks (Scurfield 1962). Scurfield (1962) states that flooding will kill *C. draba* if continued sufficiently long on impervious soils but that this species survives "thatching" treatments with straw or tar paper and repeated cutting of the tops. Workers in North Dakota report that seeds of *C. draba* are killed after being buried in moist compacted manure for 1 mo (Anonymous 1970).

II. *Cardaria chalepensis* — Established stands were eradicated on sandy loam soil in Alberta after 6 yr of alternate summer fallow and cropping, and also competition from a mixture of alfalfa and bromegrass (Selleck 1965). Patches of the weed apparently survived only in moist depressions.

III. *Cardaria pubescens* — Alfalfa was more effective competition for both globe- and lens-podded hoary cresses than perennial grasses where moisture was abundant (Selleck 1965). A stand of *C. pubescens* was eradicated in a season and a half by hoeing at intervals of 4 wk (Rosenfels and Headley 1944).

13. Response to Parasites

(*a*) *Insects and other nondomestic animals* — *Cardaria* spp. — Insecta (all on *C. draba*

Table 1. Stand reduction† of different clones of *C. draba*, *C. chalepensis*, and *C. pubescens* resulting from treatment with various herbicides (adapted from Sexsmith 1964)

		% stand reduction									
		2,4-D‡				2,3,6-TBA‡		2,3,6-TBA-MCPA‡ (1:2)		Amitrole‡	
Clones	Hoary cress species	454 g	907 g	2268 g§	9072 g§	2268 g	9072 g§	1134 g	4536 g	907 g§	1814 g
1	*C. chalepensis*	0	85	98	99+	0	40	35	99	99+	96
2		0	30	75	97	0	3	0	99+	96	95
3		30	50	85	95	0	35	30	98	95	95
4		10	40	80	99+	0	8	0	75	99	99+
5		20	80	97	99+	0	3	40	99	99+	98
6		8	85	92	99+	3	15	13	97	99	100
7		3	30	75	99+	0	8	3	80	99+	99+
8		3	93	99+	99+	0	45	60	85	99	99
9		3	65	98	99+	0	3	0	93	99+	99
16		75	93	95	85	0	70	30	88	97	88
18		0	10	98	98	0	75	60	98	96	88
19		10	25	99	99+	0	60	70	97	99+	99
13	*C. draba*	85	95	99+	99+	0	98	88	100	99+	99+
14		75	93	99+	99	0	93	70	80	97	95
15		30	90	98	96	0	70	30	88	97	88
10	*C. pubescens*	95	93	99	100	0	40	40	100	100	99+
11		99	99	98	99+	0	99+	99	100	99	75

†Stand reduction estimated 1 yr after treatments applied in June 1959 to cresses in the early to full-bloom stages.
‡Rates shown are for 0.4 ha.
§Stand reductions as listed may be slightly high for these treatments due to wind drift of soil treated with sodium chlorate during the winter months of 1959–60.

in Poland, Studzinski 1971) — Homoptera: *Brevicoryne brassicae* L. and *Myzodes persicae* Sulz.; Lepidoptera: *Pieris brassicae* L. (larvae on plants) and *Pieris napi* L. (larvae on plants); Coleoptera: *Ceutorrhynchus turbatus* Schul. (larvae in silicles) and *Phyllotreta nemorum* L. (larvae in leaves); Diptera: *Phytomyza horticola* Gour. (larvae in leaves) and *Scaptomyza flaveola* Meig. (larvae in leaves).

(*b*) *Microorganisms and viruses* — *Cardaria* spp. — Fungus — Hyphomycetes: *Cercospora bizzozeriana* Sacc. & Berl on *C. draba* in Manitoba (Bisby et al. 1938).

(*c*) *Higher plant parasites* — *Cardaria* spp. —None recorded.

AGRICULTURE CANADA. 1967. Seeds Act and Regulations. Queen's Printer, Ottawa, Canada. 50 pp.

ANONYMOUS. 1936. Weed destruction. The use of chemical exterminators with a note on hoary cress. Agr. Gaz. 47: 190–192.
ANONYMOUS. 1970. Fresh manure can be a major source of weeds in cropland. Crops Soils Mag. 22: 26.
BARR, C. J. 1942. Reserve foods in the roots of whiteweed. J. Agr. Res. 64: 725.
BELLUE, M. K. 1933. New weeds confused with hoary cress. Monthly Bull. Dep. Agric., State of California, 22: 288–293.
BELLUE, M. K. 1946. Weed seed handbook. Series VI. Calif. Dep. Agr. Bull. 22: 288.
BISBY, G. R., BULLAR, A. H. R., DEARNESS, J., FRASER, J. P. and RUSSELL, R. C. 1938. The fungi of Manitoba and Saskatchewan. Natl. Res. Counc., Ottawa, Canada. 189 pp.
BLACKMAN, G. E., BLACKMAN, M. A., and HOLLY, K. 1949. The control of hoary pepperwort. J. Minist. Agr. 56: 6–11.
BROWN, E. 1914. Commercial Turkestan alfalfa seed. U.S. Dep. Agr. Bull. No. 138: 7 pp.

CANADA WEED COMMITTEE. 1969. Common and botanical names of weeds in Canada. Can. Dep. Agr. Publ. 1397: 67 pp.

CANADA WEED COMMITTEE. 1972. Research report Canada Weed Committee, Western Section. 388 pp.

CORNS, W. G. and FRANKTON, C. 1952. Hoary cresses in Canada with particular reference to their distribution and control in Alberta. Sci. Agr. 32: 484–495.

FRANKTON, C. 1958. Les mauvaises herbes du Canada. Minist. Agr. Can. Publ. 948: 198 pp.

FRANKTON, C. and MULLIGAN, G. A. 1971. Weeds of Canada. Can. Dep. Agr. Publ. 948: 217 pp.

GROH, H. 1940a. Hoary cresses in Canada. Sci. Agr. 20: 750–756.

GROH, H. 1940b. Turkestan alfalfa as a medium of weed introduction. Sci. Agr. 21: 36–43.

HOROVITZ, A. and COHEN, Y. 1972. Ultraviolet reflectance characteristics in flowers of Crucifers. Amer. J. Bot. 59: 706–713.

JENKINS, L. and JACKMAN, E. R. 1938. White Top. Oregon State Coll. Ext. Bull. No. 522: 3 pp.

KELLER, B. A., LUBIMENKO, V. N., MALZEV, A. I., FEPTSCHENKO, B. A., SCHISCHKIN, B. C., ROSHEVITZ, R. J. and KAMENSKY, K. V. (eds.) 1934. Cardaria Desv. In The weeds of USSR. Bot. Inst. USSR Acad. Sci. 3: 27–29.

KIRK, L. E., PAVLYCHENKO, T. K. and KOSSAR, W. 1943. Report of investigations at the Research Laboratory of Plant Ecology. Univ. of Saskatchewan, Regina, Saskatchewan. p. 7.

KNUTH, P. 1908. Handbook of flower pollination, based upon Hermann Muller's work. The fertilization of flowers by insects. Vol. II. Oxford Clarendon Press, London. (Transl. from German by J. A. Ainsworth Davis.) 703 pp.

KOTT, S. A. 1966. Control of rhizomatous weeds. Zemledelie. 28: 56–61.

MANTON, I. 1932. Introduction to the general cytology of the Cruciferae. Ann. Bot. 46: 509–566.

MULLIGAN, G. A. and FRANKTON, C. 1962. Taxonomy of the genus Cardaria with particular reference to the species introduced into North America. Can. J. Bot. 40: 1411–1425.

PEMBERTON, E. J. and PRUNSTER, R. W. 1940. A survey of the problem of hoary cress (Lepidium draba L.) as a weed in Victoria. J. Counc. Sci. Indust. Res. 13: 107–114.

ROLLINS, S. F. 1967. Seed legislation in the United States of America. Proc. Int. Seed Testing Assoc. 32: 437–444.

ROSENFELS, R. S. and HEADLEY, F. B. 1944. Whitetop eradication. Univ. Nev. Agr. Exp. Sta. Bull. 170: 18 pp.

SCURFIELD, G. 1962. Biological flora of the British Isles. No. 84. Cardaria draba (L.) Desv. (Lepidium draba L.). J. Ecol. 50: 489–499.

SELLECK, G. W. 1961. An ecological study of Cardaria spp. in Saskatchewan. Proc. 11th West. Can. Weed Control Conf. Saskatoon, Sask. 1961.

SELLECK, G. W. 1965. An ecological study of lens- and globe-podded hoary cresses in Saskatchewan. Weeds 13: 1–5.

SEXSMITH, J. J. 1964. Morphological and herbicide susceptibility differences among strains of hoary cress. Weeds 12: 19–22.

STERLING, G. R. 1951. The control of hoary cresses in Alberta. Direction Field Crops Branch, Alta. Dep. of Agric. 3 pp.

STUDZINSKI, A. 1971. Survey and study of insects associated with cruciferous plants in Poland and surrounding countries. Annual report of researches conducted under grants authorized by public law 480 for the U.S. Dep. Agric. Inst. Plant Protection Rep. period: November 1, 1969 to December 31, 1970.

THE BIOLOGY OF CANADIAN WEEDS. 4. *PLANTAGO MAJOR* AND *P. RUGELII*

WAYNE R. HAWTHORN[1]

Department of Plant Sciences, University of Western Ontario, London, Ontario N6A 3K7.

Received 17 Oct. 1973, accepted 20 Dec. 1973.

HAWTHORN, WAYNE R. 1974. The biology of Canadian weeds. 4. *Plantago major* and *P. rugelii*. Can. J. Plant Sci. **54**: 383–396.

This summary of biological information of *Plantago major* L. (broad-leaved plantain) and *P. rugelii* Decne. (Rugel's plantain) is part of a series on the biology of Canadian weeds. *P. major* is a weed of disturbed habitats throughout Canada whereas *P. rugelii* is restricted to similar habitats in eastern Canada.

Le présent résumé d'information biologique sur *Plantago major* L. (plantain majeur) et *P. rugelii* Decne. (plantain de Rugel) fait partie d'une série d'articles sur la biologie des mauvaises herbes du Canada. *P. major* est une mauvaise herbe des habitats perturbés dans tout le Canada, tandis que *P. rugelii* occupe des habitats semblables dans l'est du Canada seulement.

1. Names

I. *Plantago major* L. — **broad-leaved plantain** (Canada Weed Committee 1969); **plantain majeur** (Ferron & Cayouette 1971).

II. *Plantago rugelii* Decne. — **Rugel's plantain** (Canada Weed Committee 1969); **plantain de Rugel** (Marie-Victorin 1964).
Plantaginaceae, plantain family, Plantaginacées.

2. Description and Account of Variation

(*a*) Both species can be described as annual, biennial, or perennial herbs (Tessene 1968; Mulligan and Findlay 1970; Bassett 1973) each with a fibrous, adventitious root system arising from a stout caudex that bears a rosette of spirally arranged leaves. The following descriptions have been taken from Tessene (1968) and Bassett (1973).

I. *Plantago major* — Leaves glabrous or hirsute, ovate to cordate shape, entire or slightly toothed margins; 50 cm long, the lamina 2–20 cm long, 1–12 cm wide, and have 3–7 main veins; scapes 1–30 per plant, up to 50 cm long; linear-cylindric spikes up to 25 cm long and 6 mm wide; flowers ca. 16 per cm of spike; bracts obtuse-acute, 0.5–1.0 mm long, about one-third the length of 1.5–2.0- mm long sepals; flowers small and inconspicuous; capsule rhombic-ovate, 4–5 mm long, and dehiscent near the middle; seeds 5–22 per capsule, black to dark brown, 0.5–1.5 mm long with a deeply sculptured testa, variable in shape; hilum and micropyle are adjacent to each other. Chromosome counts of $n = 6$ (Mulligan and Cody 1968) and $2n = 12$ (Mulligan 1959; Bassett and Crompton 1968; Kapoor 1972) from Canadian material are the same as numbers from plants found in Britain (Sagar and Harper 1964), Germany (Rahn 1957), and the United States (Tessene 1968).

II. *Plantago rugelii* — Leaves glabrous or inconspicuously hairy, 6–50 cm long, and broadly elliptic to ovate or cordate-ovate; lamina 2–22 cm long, about two-thirds as wide, entire or irregularly toothed margin bearing 5–9 small pectinate teeth, and 5–9 main veins; scapes 1 to 8 per plant, up to 50 cm long; spikes up to 30 cm long and 6 mm wide, with ca. 10 flowers per cm; bracts attenuate, about 2 mm long, one-half as long as sharply keeled, acute sepals; capsule ellipsoid, oblong, 4–8 mm long and dehiscent below the middle; seeds 4–9 per capsule, black to dark brown; seeds slightly sculptured, 1.5–2.0 mm long; hilum and micropyle separated. Chromosome count, $2n = 24$ (Bassett and Crompton 1968) matches those obtained in Sweden (Rahn 1957) and the United States (Tessene 1968).

---

[1]Present address: Department of Biology, University of Waterloo, Waterloo, Ontario N2L 3G1.

Can. J. Plant Sci. 54: 383-396 (Apr. 1974)

(*b*) These two species are very similar morphologically but they can be separated on the basis of the leaf, bract, sepal, and capsule characters mentioned above. The base of the petiole in *P. rugelii* is usually dark red or purple but this character may be absent in *P. rugelii* and present in *P. major*. *P. rugelii* may have pale green leaves whereas those of *P. major* are darker. In eastern Canada either species can be easily confused with the other when found growing under depauperate conditions.

Both *P. major* and *P. rugelii* can be distinguished from other morphologically similar plantains. *P. virginica* L. has been found in only one location of southwestern Ontario, is usually annual, small, and produces two seeds per capsule. Vegetative plants of *P. media* L. have elliptic, thick leaves tapering gradually to the petiole. The spikes are densely packed near the tip of the long scapes. Each capsule contains two to four brown–black seeds. The entire plant is covered with woolly hairs. In dense grassland both plantains reported here can appear similar to *P. lanceolata* L. However, this species produces lanceolate to lance-oblong leaves tapering to a short petiole. The spikes are similar to those of *P. media* but each capsule contains one or two seeds and the sepals are fused. Both *P. media* and *P. lanceolata* reproduce vegetatively more extensively than *P. major* and *P. rugelii*. Unlike the two latter species, the seeds of *P. virginica*, *P. media*, and *P. lanceolata* are concave.

(*c*) Infraspecific variation is extensive in *P. major* and this has resulted in a number of lengthy subdivisions into subspecies, varieties, and forms (Pilger 1937; Hitchcock et al. 1959; Gleason 1968). For example, the var. *scopulorum* Fries & Broberg has leathery, villous leaves with broad and short petioles. Plants of this variety collected on beaches in Wisconsin reverted to the "typical" form in the greenhouse (Tessene 1968). In contrast, *P. major* from two different habitats in the Netherlands when grown in the same greenhouse showed differences in gross morphological characters (lengths of petiole and lamina, and the width of the lamina) that persisted for two generations (Groot and Boschhuizen 1970). Bassett

(1973) recognized only two forms in Canada, f. *bracteata* (Moench) Hegi and f. *ramosa* Beckh. Until taxonomic clarification of this taxon is accomplished, the species should be treated as *Plantago major sensu lat.* (Tessene 1968).

Only two varieties of *P. rugelii* have been named but they are simply ecological variants (Tessene 1968).

(*d*) Figure 1 shows the main diagnostic features of seed, seedling, and mature plant of each species.

3. Economic Importance

(*a*) *Detrimental* — Both species are nuisances that mar, according to some, the appearance of lawns, gardens, roadsides, and waste places. They are also found in damp shorelines, open woods, and pastures. In local situations each species can reduce the early growth of crops such as corn and oats, although no dollar value on the crop losses is available. In New Jersey, *P. rugelii* and, to a lesser extent, *P. major* may be reservoirs for strains of tobacco-virus mosaic (*Marmor tabaci* H.) that causes internal browning of tomato (*Lycopersicon esculentum* Mill.) fruits (Holmes 1950). About 35% of the tomato plants in one field in New Jersey were affected.

P. major may be a host of aster yellows disease that is transmitted by the six-spotted leaf hopper, *Macrosteles fascifrons* Stal. (Pirone 1970; Freitag and Smith 1969).

In Italy, petunia asteroid mosaic virus has been isolated from roots of *P. major* (Lovisolo et al. 1965) and in the Netherlands, *P. major* is a host for *Verticillium alboatrum* Reinke & Berth. and *V. lecanii*, which cause serious wilting in lucerne (*Medicago sativa* L.) (Kort and Van Rheenen 1959).

In Ontario *P. major* is used as a transient host by the pear psylla, *Psylla pyricola* Foer., when the weed is the prominent field plot cover crop (Wilde 1970).

Neither species is known to be toxic to farm animals or man. Pollen from both species shed in large amounts may cause hay fever.

(*b*) *Beneficial* — Since both weeds are invading species they quickly colonize disturbed areas and restrict soil erosion. *P. major* var. *rosea*, with purple leaves, is oc-

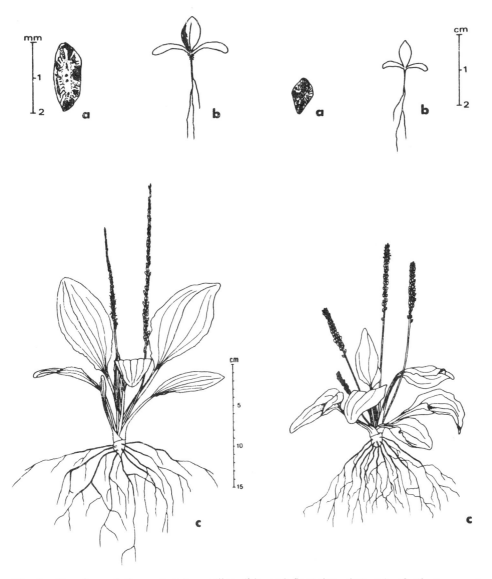

Fig. 1. Drawings of the seed (a), seedling (b), and flowering plant (c) of *Plantago major* (right side) and *P. rugelii* (left side). The scale for the seeds is in mm and in cm for the seedlings and flowering plants. Adapted from Tessene (1968).

casionally grown for ornamental purposes in England (M. F. Tessene, *personal communication*). Both species are eaten by domestic animals (see Section 7c).

(c) *Legislation* — Provincial Weed Control regulations for both species exist explicitly for Manitoba only (where *P. rugelii* is not present!) but provisions allow for their declaration as weeds in the other provinces except Ontario and Newfoundland. Since *P. major* can colonize agricultural land throughout Canada, it is grouped as an 'other' weed seed under provisions of the Canada Seeds Act (see Montgomery and Switzer 1967).

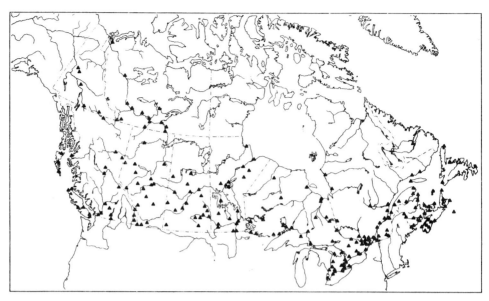

Fig. 2. The distribution of *Plantago major* in Canada.

4. Geographical Distribution

In Canada, the distribution of *P. major* is more extensive than that of *P. rugelii*, which is confined to the southeastern section (Fig. 2 and 3). These maps are based only on herbarium specimens seen from the Plant Research Institute, Ottawa (DAO); the National Museum of Canada, Ottawa; the University of Guelph, Guelph; the University of Waterloo, Waterloo; and the University of Western Ontario, London. *P. major* is recorded to 1,460 m in Banff National Park

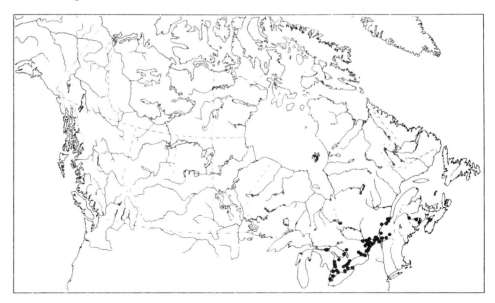

Fig. 3. The distribution of *Plantago rugelii* in Canada.

(DAO). The ascent of *P. rugelii* is considerably less with reports to only 300 m; more commonly it is found near sea level.

5. Habitat

(a) *Climatic requirements* — *P. major* has spread from Europe throughout North America. Its northern limit appears to be influenced by cold temperatures and is 200–500 km south of the tree line. It is rarely found in shaded sites or in sites that are continually wet during the growing season.

P. rugelii is native to eastern North America with its northern limit southeastern Canada from Nova Scotia to Ontario, southward to Georgia, west to Texas and North Dakota (Bassett and Crompton 1968). In Wisconsin, Tessene (1968) suggested that there was a weedy, adventive form of disturbed areas and a native, robust form associated with rich bottom-lands frequently in shaded areas. *P. rugelii* in Quebec appears to be confined to regions where the annual radiant energy exceeds 23.5 kg cal (Rousseau 1968). The westerly limits of *P. rugelii* coincide generally with those of several plant species such as *Eupatorium rugosum* Houtt., *Solanum nigrum* L., *Glechoma hederacea* L., *Polygonum pensylvanicum* L., and *Nymphaea odorata* Ait. (Anonymous 1971).

(b) *Substratum* — Both species occupy a wide range of soils such as loam, clay and sand but not sphagnum peat (Sagar and Harper 1964; Tessene 1968; I. J. Bassett, *personal communication*).

(c) *Communities in which the species occur* — A close association was found in the fertile neutral pastures of the Netherlands between *Plantago major*, *Poa annua* L., *Trifolium pratense* L., and *Lolium perenne* L. (De Vries 1953). *Plantago major* is a constituent of dry mesic prairie and *P. rugelii* a member of the southern wet mixed forest, with its nitrogen-rich soil (Curtis 1959, *in* Tessene 1968). Each species grows both in the open and in the shade, although *P. rugelii* can persist longer in the shade of other plants. The distribution of *P. major* and *P. rugelii* in different pastures, near London, Ontario is recorded in Table 1.

6. History

P. major had been observed in New England in 1672 and Montreal in 1821 (Rousseau 1968) and recorded on the west coast in 1899 (DAO).

P. major in North America may consist of both native populations and those naturalized from Eurasia. Since it was found in isolated habitats that were not thought to have been disturbed earlier by white man, it may have been indigenous north of 50° latitude (Rousseau 1968) and around the Gulf of St. Lawrence (Rousseau 1966). However, Bassett and Crompton (1968) studied pollen of several present-day North American *Plantago* taxa and they felt that *Plantago* pollen in postglacial deposits in the eastern half of the continent would probably come from several taxa, including *P. rugelii*; they did not include *P. major*.

Introduction and rapid spread of *P. major* was probably due to its occurrence as an impurity in crop seed. Also, the seeds can adhere to soil particles which would be attached to various modes of transportation. Since *P. major* was one of the first weeds carried by the white man, the Indians called it "white man's foot" (Rousseau 1966).

Earlier botanists may have confused *P. rugelii* with *P. major* so that the first taxonomic record for *P. rugelii* was not made until the mid-19th century. Rousseau (1968) believed that it had been present in Montreal since 1821. Reports of its occurrence in the Canadian prairies are doubtful (Budd and Best 1964). *P. rugelii* probably was a rare plant of the native flora but its distribution and abundance in eastern Canada have increased since the time of European settlement.

7. Growth and Development

(a) *Morphology* — The short stem, or caudex, in each species is the food storage organ from which adventitious roots and the rosette arise each year. Since the caudex is usually just below the ground surface, the plant is not easily destroyed by compaction or treading. The mature root system of *P. major* may exceed 80 cm in depth and 80 cm in diameter (Kutschera 1960), which enables the species to survive drought conditions. The root system of *P. rugelii* is just as extensive.

Table 1. Community lists for different pastures near London, Ontario

Species	Community		
	12-yr-old pasture	Ploughed pasture, sown	Ploughed pasture, fallow
Acer sp.		r	
Achillea millefolium L.	r†		
Agrostis stolonifera L.		r	va
Ambrosia artemisiifolia L.		o	va
Aster sp.	f	o	f
Brachythecium rutabulum (L.) B.+S.	f		
Bromus inermis Leyss.	f		va
Cyperaceae			r
Cerastium vulgatum L.	a		r
Chrysanthemum leucanthemum L.	a	va	va
Cirsium arvense (L.) Scop.			r
Convolvulus arvensis L.		o	
Crataegus sp.	r		
Dactylis glomerata L.	va		va
Daucus carota L.	va	r	va
Equisetum arvense L.		r	
Erigeron annuus (L.) Pers.	a	f	va
Erigeron philadelphicus L.		o	o
Festuca pratense L.			f
Festuca rubra L.	f		o
Fragaria vesca L.	r		
Geum sp.	r		
Lotus corniculatus L.		d	
Medicago lupulina L.	va	f	va
Medicago sativa L.	o		r
Oxalis stricta L.	r	o	r
Phleum pratense L.	va	va	va
Picea glauca (Moench.) Voss	f		
Plantago lanceolata L.	va		a
Plantago major L.	r	r‡	o
Plantago rugelii Decne.	va	r	va
Poa compressa L.	f	o	va
Poa pratensis L.	va	f	f
Potentilla sp.			r
Prunella vulgaris L.	f	f	va
Ranunculus acris L.	a		o
Rumex crispus L.		r	
Solidago sp.	o	r	
Sonchus asper (L.) Hill	f		f
Taraxacum officinale Weber	va	va	va
Trifolium pratense L.	va	o	va
Trifolium repens L.	r	f	r
Ulmus americana L.			r
Veronica serpyllifolia L.	a		a

†The ratings are based on the following percentage frequencies: (r), rare, 0–20%; (o) occasional, 21–40%; (f) frequent, 41–60%; (a) abundant, 61–80%; (va) very abundant, 81–100%; and (d) dominant, 100% and covering more than ¾ of the area.
‡In 1969 P. major was very abundant. It was quickly eliminated.

(b) *Perennation* — Both species are hemi-cryptophytes. They are capable of vegetative reproduction but it is of local importance and relatively rare (Hawthorn 1973).

(c) *Physiological data* — Plants which compete with forage crop species may not be serious weeds if their nutrient content and palatability are high. The composition of *P. rugelii* compared with accompanying crop plants was analyzed by Vengris et al. (1953). They noted that *P. rugelii*, among other weeds, was able to accumulate about as much Ca (2.55%, air-dry basis) and Mg (0.46%) as *Trifolium pratense* L. and as much K (2.10%) as *Phleum pratense* L. It is not known whether a similar situation exists for *P. major*.

(d) *Phenology* — Root and shoot growth of each species in southern areas of Canada occurs from mid-April to late October (Hawthorn 1973). This information agrees with that of Sagar and Harper (1964) who observed that for *P. major* new growth above ground ceased by August in undisturbed communities in Britain.

Flowering can continue from mid-June to October, with a peak in July for both species (Tessene 1968; McWilliams and Ludwig 1972; W. R. Hawthorn, *personal observation*). Both species are long-day plants. Plants of both species were grown in the laboratory with supplementary fluorescent and incandescent lighting under one of the photoperiods 8, 13, 14, and 16 h. The temperature fluctuated by approximately 5 C about a mean of 22 C. Both species failed to flower unless the photoperiod was greater than 13 h. With a 14-h photoperiod *P. rugelii* did not initiate flowering as rapidly (170 days from the start of germination) as *P. major* (65 days). Stearns (1955) showed that plants of *P. rugelii* grown at 27 C flowered within 49 days whereas those grown at cooler temperatures of 21 C and 16 C flowered later, after 56 and 116 days, respectively.

Fruits of both species mature 2–3 wk after anthesis (Tessene 1968) and seeds of *P. major*, from the first formed capsules, are dispersed earlier in the autumn than those of *P. rugelii*. Some seeds of both species are not shed until the following spring or summer.

Seeds germinate intermittently throughout the growing season.

(e) *Mycorrhiza* — No mycorrhizal system in either species has been found, although mycorrhizae have been suspected in the Plantaginaceae (Tessene 1968).

8. Reproduction

(a) *Floral biology* — Both species have chasmogamous flowers (Bassett and Crompton 1968) which are wind-pollinated and are also self-compatible (Mulligan and Findlay 1970; Bassett 1973). Each flower of *P. major* is protogynous but since the scentless flowers on the spike open in acropetal successsion, only the first-opened flowers are certain to be cross-pollinated (Sagar and Harper 1964). The same situation applies to *P. rugelii*. Apparently reproduction is amphimictic. Vivipary has not been recorded in either species.

Sexual reduction of the normally hermaphroditic flowers of *P. major* was not observed by Tessene (1968) nor by the present writer. However, Knuth (1909) reported gynomonoecism and gynodioecism, with about 10% of the flowers female. Ross (1970) stated also that 100 plants from a natural population in Nova Scotia consisted of seven male steriles, 74 hermaphrodites, and 19 gynomonoecious plants. Male sterile plants of *P. rugelii* have not been reported but Ross (M. D. Ross, *personal communication*) suspects that they may be present in small numbers.

Pollen studies show that each anther of *P. major* can produce almost three times as many pollen grains as one of *P. rugelii* (600 vs. 240) and that these spheroidal and reticulate grains of *P. major* are smaller (average diameter 22.5 μ) than the similarly shaped grains of *P. rugelii* (25.0 μ) (Bassett and Crompton 1968).

(b) *Seed production and dispersal* — Variable numbers of seeds per capsule are produced in each species but more seeds of smaller size are found in capsules of *P. major* (Tables 2 and 3).

In pasture, *P. rugelii* produced longer spikes with more flowers (capsules) per cm. However, *P. major* in most other habitats had a greater number of capsules per cm (see Section 2a). Also, per unit area, the

Table 2. Data on reproduction for *Plantago major* and *P. rugelii* in pasture fields at London, Ontario

Attribute		*P. major*	*P. rugelii*
(a)	Length of spike (cm)	2.7±0.2†	16.4±0.7
(b)	Total no. capsules/spike	20.4±1.6	176.0±21.5
(c)	No. viable capsules/spike	20.4±1.6	126.7±20.9
(d)	No. capsules/cm of spike length	7.6	10.7
(e)	Seeds/capsule	12.7±0.3	3.0±0.1
(f)	Seeds/viable capsule	12.7±0.3	4.2±0.1
(g)	No. seeds/spike	257.4±30.8	414.4±44.8
(h)	No. spikes/ flowering plant	2.2	1.6
(i)	Seeds/plant	565	662
(j)	Flowering plants/m²	95	26
(k)	Seeds/m²	53675	17212

†Standard error.

Table 3. The mean wt per seed averaged on a per capsule basis for spikes of *P. major* and *P. rugelii* in London, Ontario

	P. major		*P. rugelii*	
Spike code†	Mean wt/seed capsule ($g \times 10^{-4} \pm SE$)		Spike code†	Mean wt/seed per capsule ($g \times 10^{-4} \pm SE$)
2–4	.55±.04	*	2–1	3.53±.07
1–2	.60±.05		5–1	4.05±.12
1–4	.62±.05		1–2	4.60±.16
3–1	.65±.05		1–3	4.64±.30
1–3	.78±.04		4–1	5.04±.13
1–1	.79±.06		3–1	5.39±.11
2–3	.79±.11		1–1	5.82±.21
4–2	.99±.04			
3–2	1.03±.09			
4–1	1.04±.07			
2–1	1.04±.05			
4–3	1.05±.09			
5–2	1.24±.03			
3–3	1.32±.09			
4–6	1.35±.08			
3–4	1.43±.14			
5–1	1.57±.05			
2–2	2.27±.59			
4–5	2.87±.25			

*Means in each column joined by a single vertical line are not significantly different at the 5% level according to the SNK test (Sokal and Rohlf 1969).
†The spike code consists of the plant number followed by the number arbitrarily assigned to each spike on that plant.

total seed production of *P. major* exceeded that of *P. rugelii*.

In water, the adhesive mucilage on the seed coat of *P. major* swells to increase the original seed size by about 40% (Young and Evans 1973). Responses by seeds of *P. rugelii* appear to be similar. This ability of each species to imbibe water increases the stickiness of the seeds to soil particles, feathers, and fur and enhances the potential for dispersal.

The circumscissile dehiscence in *P. rugelii* is similar to that of *P. major*, which is due to contraction of the fruit wall as the capsule ripens and turns brown (Rethke 1946).

(c) Viability of seeds and germination — Seeds of both species exhibit intermittent germination from late April to late September. Not all relatively fresh seeds of both species collected in the autumn were innately dormant (*sensu* Harper 1957) but there is evidence that most seeds formed in midsummer are dormant (Steinbauer and Grigsby 1957). In Canada, fresh seeds of both species start germinating early in May, following their formation, with peak flushes in late May. Germination then occurs intermittently throughout the entire growing season. In the spring most seeds of *P. major* germinated more quickly than those of *P. rugelii*. This brief difference of 2 days in the rapidity of germination under controlled conditions might enable seedlings of *P. major* to appear first in an area and become established earlier than the initially larger seedlings of *P. rugelii*.

The longevity of seeds of both species is at least 21 yr (Toole and Brown 1946); seeds of *P. major* gave 10% germination after burial for 40 years (Crocker 1938).

Seed viability, as determined by either the tetrazolium test (Machlis and Torrey 1956) or as germination in 0.01 M gibberellic acid, varied among plants, but generally 80% of the seeds were viable. Seeds of *P. rugelii* obtained from plants previously treated with 2,4-D and 2,4,5-T mixture at the start of flowering had significantly lower viability (50%) than seeds from untreated plants or those treated with fertilizer. No plants of *P. major* survived the herbicide treatment to produce seed.

Based on spring trials in the greenhouse, seeds that overwintered 15 cm above the ground with chaff were less viable and more dormant than seeds that overwintered on, or 15 cm below, the surface in the presence or absence of chaff. Thus the reservoir of seeds in the soil may be a more important source of recruits to the standing population than seeds retained on the plant. This difference was not detected during the subsequent field germination trials; rather, the fluctuating environment imposed an intermittent germination pattern on the seeds, regardless of previous treatment. Also, germination polymorphism might account for the germination pattern in *P. major* (Palmblad 1969).

Light was necessary for germination although a small proportion of seeds of both species germinated in total darkness. Either chilling or higher temperature regimes, or both, increased germination (Deschênes and Moineau 1972; Hawthorn 1973).

(d) Vegetative reproduction — Although reproduction is primarily by seed, about 20% of the sampled populations of both species in laneway and recently disturbed sites had reproduced vegetatively by producing ramets from buds on the persistent crown (Table 4). No plants in pasture produced ramets. The ramet remains attached to the parent plant for 2–3 yr at which time the bond breaks and the ramet initiates root development.

Ramets are immediately capable of seed production. Seed production by the entire plant is greater than if the plant had produced spikes from one caudex.

9. Hybrids

No hybrids for either species have been reported and attempts to cross *P. major* and *P. rugelii* with each other and with several other *Plantago* species have failed (Rahn 1957; Sagar and Harper 1964; Tessene 1969; Bassett 1973).

10. Population Dynamics

The population dynamics of each species in hay-pasture communities (see Table 1) was studied, using permanent quadrats 40 × 40 cm square, during three successive years in London, Ontario, at sites where either both species or only one were present. All individuals of *P. major* and *P. rugelii* were mapped at 3-wk intervals from May to October. In different treatments, mature seeds of each species were added to, or removed from, the plots. There were four replicates for each treatment. Seedling mortality per year for both species was greater than 90%, a value comparable to figures for seedling mortality of perennial herbaceous species (Rabotnov 1969). Regardless of the time of appearance, seedlings of both species suffered greater mortality during their first 6 to 9 wk of life.

Table 4. Ramet production and densities of *Plantago major* and *P. rugelii* in three sites in London, Ontario

| | Species and sites | | | | |
| | P. major | | | P. rugelii | |
Attribute	Laneway	Laneway	Recently disturbed field	Laneway	Recently disturbed field
Sample size	99	98	97	40	70
No. (%) ramet individuals	11 (11.1)	24 (24.5)	7 (7.2)	8 (20.0)	11 (15.7)
Avg no. ramets/ ramet individual	2.6±0.4†	3.1±0.4	2.4±0.7	4.0±1.1	1.8±1.1
Density of the same species in 40×40-cm square centred on the sampled individual	*nonramet* 1.8±0.2 *ramet* 5.0±0.6	2.7±0.2 4.4±0.8	0.9±0.1 1.9±0.8	0.7±0.6 3.6±0.9	0.6±0.1 1.6±0.5

†Standard error.

43

For both species, survivorship of the mature plants present at the start of the study and of most cohorts, first observed as seedlings, could be adequately described by Deevey's Type II or the negative exponential model — a straight line relationship (Deevey 1947).

A seasonal fluctuation was superimposed on the exponential death rate. Mortality was greater during the period of most vigorous growth in the spring and in late summer after growth of the community had generally ceased; it was less during the relatively dry summer period and the cold winter.

From these data it was possible to calculate values of half-life, the time taken for elimination of one-half of the original population (Harper 1967). Mature populations of *P. major* had a short half-life, ca. 16.2 wk in a newly sown pasture and ca. 42 wk in a ploughed but unseeded pasture. The species was being rapidly eliminated. For seedlings, the values were ca. 18 wk and 27 wk, respectively, in the above areas. In contrast, mature populations of *P. rugelii* had a half-life of ca. 4.1 yr in old pasture and ca. 1.1 yr in recently disturbed pasture areas. Seedlings, derived mostly from introduced seeds, had values ca. 32 wk and ca. 37 wk, respectively, in the above areas. The mature plants were at least 8 mo old at the start of the study but this age was not included in the determination of half-life. *P. major* is indeed a short-lived species compared with *P. rugelii*.

The number of viable seeds of *P. major* in the soil declined exponentially and was halved each year (Roberts 1962). Therefore, a weed-free environment would be obtained most rapidly where the soil was not disturbed, so that most of the viable seed population could be ignored (Roberts and Dawkins 1967). *P. major* appears to have greater seed longevity in the soil than does the longer-lived perennial, *P. rugelii*. Toole and Brown (1946) observed that *P. major* had 1% germination after 30 yr burial and *P. rugelii* failed to germinate.

In a pasture, plants of *P. major* flowered earlier in life, produced more seeds, but had a shorter life span than did those of *P. rugelii*. By investigating the proportionality of organs to the total dry weight of plant,

we may find reasons for the success or failure of the species in competition in natural communities (Harper 1967; Whitehead 1969; Harper and Ogden 1970).

In detailed grass–plantain competition experiments (Hawthorn 1973), it was shown that plants of *P. major* made better actual growth, flowered earlier, and suffered greater subsequent mortality than did plants of *P. rugelii*. In an earlier study based on plants grown in pure stands, Palmblad (1968) had also shown that *P. major* behaved "like a weedy annual" and produced "seeds at all costs." In the present study the longer-lived plants of *P. rugelii* usually remained vegetative and devoted proportionally more resources to root growth.

Ramet production in both species was reduced by increased competitive stress; this reduction was greater with plants of *P. rugelii*.

P. rugelii is probably better adapted for a continued existence in grassland. Plants of *P. rugelii* showed a more diverse flowering pattern during three growing seasons. Some plants were polycarpic, some monocarpic, others flowered once and then remained vegetative, and still others remained vegetative in all 3 yr. The existing population is being maintained and flowering can take place in some future year.

Although *P. major* may be scattered where the ground is trampled (Bates 1935), both species usually form small or large aggregations (Hawthorn 1973) because, as noted for *P. major*, offspring tend to remain associated together in the neighbourhood of their parent (Skellam 1952).

11. Response to Herbicides and Other Chemicals

Plantains in general are susceptible to 2,4-D; 2,4,5-T; MCPA; fenoprop and to greater applications of 2,4-DB; MCPB; and dicamba (Switzer 1969).

Forty-day-old plants of *P. rugelii* were resistant to 'Brush and Poison Ivy' herbicide but they were just as susceptible as *P. major* to a similar application given 76-day-old plants (Table 5). Except for a nitrogen treatment (34-0-0) applied to 40-day-old plants, which affected *P. rugelii* more than *P. major*, defoliation or fertilizer treatments did not in-

Table 5. Percentage survival of plants of *Plantago major* and *P. rugelii* 1 mo. after the application of different treatments

Treatment	Applied 16 June, to 35 40-day-old plants/species		Applied 22 July, to 25 76-day-old plants/species	
	P. major	P. rugelii	P. major	P. rugelii
Control	100	94	96	91
Herbicide				
(2,4-D & 2,4,5-T) Niagara				
Brand Brush and Poison Ivy†	23	71	4	0
Esso Flint†	3	3	13	8
Fertilizer (NPK)‡				
10–6–4	97	100	100	100
34–0–0	80	54	87	100
0–20–0	94	100	96	100
0–0–50	100	100	96	100
Defoliation				
Leaves	97	100	91	92
Leaves and spikes	94	100	100	83

†Not an endorsement. Applied at manufacturer's recommended rate.
‡Application rates in 15-cm radius around plant: NPK, 9.7 kg/100 m²; N, 9.7 kg/100 m²; P, 2.4 kg/10 m²; K, 0.5 kg/10 m².

crease mortality of either species. This nitrogen treatment did not result in noticeable mortality when the plants were 76 days old. Since the fertilizers were not watered-in thoroughly immediately after application, this response to the nitrogen treatment may be a result of the application technique.

12. Response to Other Human Manipulations

Both species in pasture benefit from occasional mowing, as the tall vegetation of competing species is temporarily eliminated. Fertilizing chemicals usually benefit growth and survival (see Section 11). Both species grew better in hay pasture where grazing and trampling were prevalent. Removal of the cattle plus increased growth of the community rapidly eliminated *P. major*.

13. Responses to Parasites

An index of plant diseases (mostly fungi and viruses) on each species is available for Canada (Conners 1967) and the United States (Anonymous 1960). Sagar and Harper (1964) presented an extensive list of animal feeders and parasites on *P. major*, but the extent to which they regulate the population size of the host is unknown.

Table 6 lists parasites on *P. major* and *P. rugelii* in Canada.

ACKNOWLEDGMENTS

Much of this paper is based on research carried out for the Ph.D. degree at the University of Western Ontario. This work was made possible by grants from the National Research Council of Canada and Agriculture Canada to Dr. P. B. Cavers, who has given valued advice. Thanks are due to Mrs. Doris Rowley and Miss Ellen Edwards for assistance in the field work. Helpful comments were provided by Mr. I. J. Bassett and Mr. W. J. Cody, Plant Research Institute, Ottawa. Thanks are due to Dr. P. Harris, Regina Research Station, for a partial list of insects.

ANONYMOUS. 1960. Index of plant diseases in the United States. Agric. Handbook no. 65. U.S. Dep. Agric. 531 pp.
ANONYMOUS. 1971. Common weeds of the United States. U.S. Dep. Agric. Dover Publications, Inc., New York, N.Y. 463 pp.
BASSETT, I. J. and CROMPTON, C. W. 1968. Pollen morphology and chromosome numbers of the family Plantaginaceae in North America. Can. J. Bot. **46**: 349–361.
BASSETT, I. J. 1973. The plantains of Canada. Monograph no. 7. Agriculture Canada, Ottawa, Ontario. 47 pp.

Table 6. Parasites on *P. major* and *P. rugellii* in Canada

Species	*P. major*	*P. rugelii*
NEMATODA		
Meloidogyne sp.	Root-knot nematode in greenhouse; B.C. (Conners 1967)	–
INSECTA		
Homoptera		
Cicadellidae		
Macrosteles fascifrons	Leaf hopper; Ont. (Hawthorn)	Leaf hopper; Ont. (Hawthorn)
Coleoptera		
Chrysomelidae		
Dibolia borealis Chev.	Flea beetle; Ont. (Hawthorn), south of Washington, D.C. (Needham et al. 1928)	–
Scarabaeidae		
Phyllophaga sp.	White grub; Ont. (Hawthorn)	–
Diptera		
Agromyzidae		
Liromyza sorosis (Williston)	Leaf miner in *Plantago;* Ont. (Frick 1959; Spencer 1969)	–
Liriomyza trifolii (Burgess)	Leaf miner in *Plantago*; Ont. (Frost 1924; Spencer 1969)	–
Phytomyza plantaginis R.-D.	Leaf miner; Ont. (Spencer 1969)	–
Phytomyza syngenesiae (Hardy)	Leaf miner; Alta, B.C.? (Frost 1924)	–
ARACHNIDA		
Acarina		
Tetranychus telarius (L.)	2-spotted leaf mite in greenhouse; Ont. (Hawthorn)	In greenhouse; Ont. (Hawthorn)
FUNGI		
Phycomycetes		
Peronospora alta Fckl.	B.C., Man., Ont., N.S. (Conners 1967)	–
Ascomycetes		
Erysiphe cichoracearum DC. ex. Mérat	N.B.,N.S., P.E.I., B.C., Man., Ont., Que. (Conners 1967)	Que. (Conners 1967)
Mycosphaerella tassiana Var. *arthopyrenioides* (Auersw.) Barr	Que. (Conners 1967)	–
Basidiomycetes		
Ceratobasidium anceps (Bres. & Syd.) Jackson	Ont. (Conners 1967)	–
Fungi Imperfecti		
Phyllesticta plantaginicola Tehon & Daniels	Man. (Conners 1967)	–
Phyllosticta plantaginis Sacc.	Man. (Conners 1967)	–
Septoria plantaginea Pass. var. *plantaginis-majoris* Sacc.	Man. (Conners 1967)	–
VIRUS		
Aster yellows virus	Ont., N.B. (Conners 1967)	–

BATES, G. H. 1935. The vegetation of footpaths, sidewalks, cart-tracks and gateways. J. Ecol. 23(2): 420–427.

BUDD, A. C. and BEST, K. F. 1964. Wild plants of the Canadian Prairies. Publ. 983. Can. Dep. Agric. 519 pp.

CANADA WEED COMMITTEE. 1969. Common and botanical names of weeds in Canada. Publ. 1397. Can. Dep. Agric., Ottawa, Ontario. 67 pp.

CONNERS, I. L. 1967. An annotated index of plant diseases in Canada and fungi recorded on plants in Alaska, Canada and Greenland. Publ. 1251. Can. Dep. Agric., Ottawa, Ontario. 381 pp.

CROCKER, W. 1938. Life span of seeds. Bot. Rev. 4: 235–274.

DEEVEY, E. S. Jr. 1947. Life tables for natural populations of animals. Q. Rev. Biol. 22: 283–314.

DESCHÊNES, J. M. et MOINEAU, D. 1972. Conditions de germination de quatre mauvaises herbes du Québec. Naturaliste Can. 99: 103–114.

DE VRIES, D. 1953. Objective combinations of species. Acta Bot. Neerl. 1: 497–499.

FERRON, M. et CAYOUETTE, R. 1971. Noms des mauvaises herbes du Québec. 2ᵉ ed. Ministère Agriculture et Colonisation, Québec, Québec. 113 pp.

FREITAG, J. H. and SMITH, S. H. 1969. Effects of tetracyclines on symptom expression and leafhopper transmission of aster yellows. Phytopathology 59(12): 1820–1823.

FRICK, K. E. 1959. Synopsis of the species of agromyzid leaf-miners described from North America (Diptera). Proc. U.S. Nat. Mus. 108: 347–465.

FROST, S. W. 1924. A study of the leaf-mining Diptera of North America. Cornell Univ. Agric. Exp. Sta. Mem. 78. 228 pp.

GLEASON, H. A. 1968. The new Britton and Brown illustrated flora of the northeastern United States and adjacent Canada. Vol. 3. Hafner Publishing Co., Inc., New York, N.Y. 595 pp.

GROOT, J. and BOSCHHUIZEN, R. 1970. A preliminary investigation into the genecology of Plantago major L. J. Exp. Bot. 21: 835–841.

HARPER, J. L. 1957. The ecological significance of dormancy and its importance in weed control. Proc. 6th Congr. Crop Protection, Hamburg. 1: 415–420.

HARPER, J. L. 1967. A Darwinian approach to plant ecology. J. Ecol. 55(2): 247–270.

HARPER, J. L. and OGDEN, J. 1970. The reproductive strategy of higher plants. I. The concept of strategy with special reference to Senecio vulgaris L. J. Ecol. 58(3): 681–698.

HAWTHORN, W. R. 1973. Population dynamics of two weedy perennials, Plantago major L. and P. rugelii Decne. Ph.D. thesis, University of Western Ontario, London, Ont. 317 pp.

HITCHCOCK, C. L., CRONQUIST, A., OWNBEY, M. and THOMPSON, J. W. 1959. Vascular plants of the Pacific Northwest, Part 4. University of Washington Press, Seattle, Wash. 510 pp.

HOLMES, F. O. 1950. Internal-browning diseases of tomato caused by strains of tobacco-mosaic virus from Plantago. Phytopathology 40: 487–492.

KAPOOR, B. M. 1972. IOPB chromosome number reports XXXV. Taxon 21(1): 161–166.

KNUTH, P. 1909. Handbook of flower pollination. Vol. 3. Clarendon Press, Oxford, England. 644 pp.

KORT, J. and VAN RHEENEN, H. A. 1959. Some observations on the occurrence of lucerne wilt disease in Zeeland in 1957. Tijdschr. Plantenziekten 65(4): 147–157. (from Rev. Appl. Mycol. 39: 324).

KUTSCHERA, L. 1960. Wurtzelatlas Mitteleuropaischer Ackerunkrauter und Kulturplantzen. DLG-Verlags., Frankfurt Am Main, Deutschland. 574 pp.

LOVISOLO, O., BODE, O. and VÖLK, J. 1965. Preliminary studies on the soil transmission of petunia asteroid mosaic virus (= 'Petunia' strain of tomato bushy stunt virus). Phytopathology 53(4): 323–342.

MACHLIS, L. and TORREY, J. G. 1956. Plants in action: a laboratory manual of plant physiology. W. H. Freeman and Co., San. Francisco, California. 282 pp.

MARIE-VICTORIN, FRÈRE. 1964. Flore laurentienne, 2ᵉ ed. Entièrement revue et mise à jour par E. Rouleau, Montréal. Les presses de l'Université de Montréal, Montréal, Québec. 924 pp.

McWILLIAMS, E. L. and LUDWIG, L. K. 1972. Floral phenology at the Matthaei Botanical Gardens: 1969-1971. Mich. Bot. 11: 83–114.

MONTGOMERY, F. H. and SWITZER, C. M. 1967. Ontario weeds. Publ. 505. Ont. Dep. Agric. Food. Toronto, Ont. 141 pp.

MULLIGAN, G. A. 1959. Chromosome numbers of Canadian weeds. II. Can. J. Bot. 37: 81–92.

MULLIGAN, G. A. and CODY, W. J. 1968. IOPB chromosome number reports XVII. Taxon 17(3): 285–288.

MULLIGAN, G. A. and FINDLAY, J. N. 1970. Reproductive systems and colonization in Canadian weeds. Can. J. Bot. 48(5): 859–860.

NEEDHAM, J. G., FROST, S. W. and TOTHILL, B. H. 1928. Leaf-mining insects. Williams and Wikins Co. Baltimore, Maryland. 351 pp.

PALMBLAD, I. G. 1968. Competition in experimental populations of weeds with emphasis on the regulation of population size. Ecology 49(1): 26-34.

PALMBLAD, I. G. 1969. Populational variation in germination of weedy species. Ecology 50(4): 746-748.

PILGER, R. 1937. Plantaginaceae. *In* Engler and Diels, eds. Das Pflanzenreich. Vol. IV, 269 (Heft 102). W. Englemann, Leipzig, Deutschland. 441 pp.

PIRONE, P. P. 1970. Diseases and pests of ornamental plants. 4th ed. Ronald Press Co., New York, N.Y. 546 pp.

RABOTNOV, T. A. 1969. On coenopopulations of perennial herbaceous plants in natural coenoses. Vegetatio 19: 87-95.

RAHN, K. 1957. Chromosome numbers in *Plantago*. Bot. Tidsskr. 31: 300-307.

RETHKE, R. V. 1946. The anatomy of circumscissile dehiscence. Amer. J. Bot. 33: 677-683.

ROBERTS, H. A. 1962. Studies on the weeds of vegetable crops. II. Effects of six years of cropping on the weed seeds in the soil. J. Ecol. 50(3): 803-813.

ROBERTS, H. A. and DAWKINS, P. A. 1967. Effect of cultivation on the numbers of viable weed seeds in soil. Weed Res. 7(4): 290-301.

ROSS, M. D. 1970. Breeding systems in *Plantago*. Heredity 25: 129-133.

ROUSSEAU, C. 1968. Histoire, habitat et distribution de 200 plantes introduites au Québec. Naturaliste Can. 95(1): 49-171.

ROUSSEAU, J. 1966. Movements of plants under the influence of man. *In* R. L. Taylor and R. A. Ludwig, eds. The evolution of Canada's flora. University of Toronto Press, Toronto, Ontario. 137 pp.

SAGAR, G. R. and HARPER, J. L. 1964. Biological flora of the British Isles. 95. *Plantago*

major L., *P. media* L., and *P. lanceolata* L. J. Ecol. 52: 189-221.

SKELLAM, J. G. 1952. Studies in statistical ecology. I. Spatial pattern. Biometrika 39: 346-362.

SOKAL, R. R. and ROHLF, F. J. 1969. Biometry: the principles and practice of statistics in biological research. W. H. Freeman and Co., San Francisco, California. 776 pp.

SPENCER, K. A. 1969. The Agromyzidae of Canada and Alaska. No. 64. Mem. Entomol. Soc. Can. 311 pp.

STEARNS, F. 1955. The influence of light and temperature on germination and flowering of five species of *Plantago*. Proc. 12th N. Cent. Weed Control Conf., Omaha, Nebraska.

STEINBAUER, G. P. and GRIGSBY, B. 1957. Dormancy and germination characteristics of the seeds of four species of *Plantago*. Proc. Assoc. Off. Seed Anal. N. Amer. 47: 157-146.

SWITZER, C. M., Chairman. 1969. Guide to chemical weed control, 1969. Publ. 75. Ont. Dep. Agric. Food, Toronto, Ontario. 87 pp.

TESSENE, M. F. 1968. Preliminary reports on the flora of Wisconsin No. 59. Plantaginaceae-Plantain Family. Trans. Wisc. Acad. Sci. Arts Lett. 56: 281-313.

TESSENE, M. F. 1969. Systematic and ecological studies on *Plantago cordata*. Mich. Bot. 8: 72-104.

TOOLE, E. H. and BROWN, E. 1946. Final results of the Duvel buried seed experiment. J. Agric. Res. 72: 201-210.

VENGRIS, J., DRAKE, M., COLBY, W. G. and BART, J. 1953. Chemical composition of weeds and accompanying crop plants. Agron. J. 45: 213-218.

WHITEHEAD, F. H. 1969. Rationale of physiological ecology. Intecol. Bull. 1: 34-42.

WILDE, W. H. A. 1970. Common plantain as a host of pear psylla (Homoptera: Psyllidae). Can. Entomol. 102(3): 384.

YOUNG, J. A. and EVANS, R. A. 1973. Mucilaginous seed coats. Weed Sci. 21(1): 52-54.

THE BIOLOGY OF CANADIAN WEEDS

5. *Daucus carota*

HUGH M. DALE

Department of Botany and Genetics, College of Biological Science, University of Guelph, Guelph, Ontario N1G 2W1. Received 24 Sept. 1973, accepted 3 May 1974.

DALE, HUGH M. 1974. The biology of Canadian weeds. 5. *Daucus carota*. Can. J. Plant Sci. **54**: 673–685.

This summary of biological data is for wild carrot, *Daucus carota* L. ssp. *carota*, as a weed in Canada, particularly in central Ontario. Brief reference is made to wild carrot in Europe and to the related cultivated carrot which have many pests in common. Weedy populations of this biennial occur in areas formerly occupied by deciduous forests in eastern Canada, and by the coastal Douglas fir forest in British Columbia. It belongs to association of plants of roadsides, old pastures and open spaces which are disturbed periodically.

Ce résumé d'information biologique porte sur la carotte sauvage (*Daucus carota* L.; spp *carota*), mauvaise herbe au Canada, plus spécialement dans le centre d'Ontario. Nous nous sommes référés brièvement à la carotte sauvage d'Europe et à la carotte cultivée (*Daucus carota* ssp *sativa*) — qui, en plusieurs cas, sont atteints des mêmes ennemis naturels. Des populations de la carotte sauvage — plante bisannuelle — se présentent dans les régions autrefois couvertes de forêts. Il s'associé aux plantes qui se retrouvent au bord des routes, dans les vieux pâturages, et dans les terrains découverts qui sont défrichés de temps à autre.

1. Name

Daucus carota L. ssp. *carota* — **wild carrot** (Canada Weed Committee 1969), Queen Anne's-lace, bird's-nest, devil's-plague; **carotte sauvage**, carotte commune, dauce carotte (Ferron and Cayouette 1964). Umbelliferae, parsley family, Ombellifères.

2. Description and Account of Variation

(*a*) *Biennial, annual or short lived perennial* — Reproduces by single-seeded half-fruits (mericarps) 3 to 4 mm long, 2 mm wide, broadest at middle, with rows of bristles on curved surface; taproot slender, less than 5 cm in diameter, whitish and becoming woody; basal leaves 5 to 40 cm long, three-pinnate, frequently divided into segments; flowering stalk 0.1 to 1.2 m, solid, frequently colored red or purple where it arises from the basal rosette, ridged, hairless to rough-bristly with alternate leaves, each attached by a sheathing base; leaves frequently finely divided with pinnatifid segments, lobes 5 mm wide. Axillary leafy, flowering stalks are produced in succession until the plant dies,

Can. J. Plant Sci. 54: 673-685 (Oct. 1974)

in our zone frequently still bearing immature umbels. Flower umbels are compound, terminal and normally consist of over 1,000 white flowers developing from a convex into a flat circle at fertilization, becoming concave during fruit maturation, producing the bird's nest effect which flattens during seed dispersal; pedicels unequal in length, 3 to 10 mm, outer flowers in umbels surrounded by a whorl of green, finely-divided bracts. A flowering plant may produce up to 100 umbels during flowering season mid-July to September. The characteristic odor of carrot is apparent when tissue from any part of the plant is crushed. Chromosome number $2n = 18$ for Canadian material (Mulligan 1961) and European (Darlington and Wylie 1955).

(*b*) *Similar plants* — *Carum carvi* L., caraway, is also a member of the Umbelliferae. It is more open in habit than wild carrot and flowers earlier, from the end of May, with seeds maturing in July (Clark and Fletcher 1906; Frankton 1955; Roland 1949; Rousseau 1968). The umbel is compound as in *Daucus*, but in *Carum* the umbellets are small and separate from each other; bracts which may appear below the umbel are inconspicuous and narrow; the seeds are ribbed but without bristles and when crushed they give the characteristic odor of caraway; the flower stalks and leaves are glabrous; the root is brownish with crescent-shaped ridges below the crown. Caraway is found by roadsides and field edges (Clark and Fletcher 1909).

(c) *Variations within the subspecies* — Collections made in the 18th and 19th centuries in North America were so variable in their appearance that several entities were described (Gronovius 1739, 1762; Walter 1788; Rafinesque 1836); however, Mathias and Constance (1944-45) recognized only two species, which included 16 entities of the previous authors. Heywood (1968) recognized 12 subspecies of *D. carota* in Europe.

One population can yield plants of such variation that representatives are present for each class separated by four parameters of root morphology and size, six for leaves and four for flowers and flower stalks. This was apparent in a collection of 100 plants taken at random from a pasture 4 mi NE of Arthur, Ontario. For example, leaves and flower stalks were rated on a scale of 0 to 3 for hairs and bristles; the results showed that half the plants were hairless or slightly hairy, but the other half were rated 2 or 3. Such variation within a single population is not confined to one area of Canada. Similar variation was found when 100 herbarium sheets of diverse origin (deposited in DAO, CAN, TRT, and OAC) were rated for the same parameters (Dale unpublished). Nor is this variability exclusive to Canadian populations, since it has been recorded for wild carrot plants in the U.S.S.R. (Rubashevskaia 1931).

(d) *Figures 1-4* — Photographs of wild carrot. Figure 3 is a young rosette with cotyledons present and three expanded leaves. Figure 4 illustrates a mature rosette in the pre-flowering stage; the leaves are no longer parallel to the ground surface but have assumed a more upright position. Figures 1 and 2 are of plants from a pasture – Fig. 1 is an ungrazed mature plant, while Fig. 2 is of a plant with all flowering stalks removed by grazing.

3. Economic Importance

(a) *Detrimental* — Wild carrot occurs in waste places, road allowances, meadows and underutilized or depleted pastures (Bates 1937, 1955; Clark and Fletcher 1909; Ellenberg 1950, 1952; Frankton 1955; Frankton and Mulligan 1970; Georgia 1914; Klapp 1956; Renney unpublished; Sylwester 1960). As it is not a weed of cultivated fields on prime agricultural land, it is difficult to assess the loss produced by its interference and resultant reduced production of animals or plants. The milk of dairy cattle can be tainted when large amounts of herbage of *D. carota* are eaten along with that of other plants, but it has never been reported that cattle will graze upon it from choice (Muenscher 1961).

Several disease organisms and insect pests, such as aster yellows and carrot rust fly, have been found harboring on wild carrot (see section 13); but a five-year study found that wild carrot in natural stands and in field plots was remarkably free from disease or parasites (Dale 1967b).

Wild carrot may affect the commercial production of carrot either by transmitting pests or harboring diseases common to both cultivated and wild carrot (see section 13) or by causing the production of poor seed of commercial varieties when hybridization occurs (Frankton 1955). In Canada, carrot seed is grown commercially only in British Columbia (1,200 kg/yr, 5-yr average) (Canada Department of Agriculture 1973). Adamson (unpublished) has stated in discussion that it is not feasible to grow commercial carrot for seed on Vancouver Island due to the populations of wild carrot that occur there. Therefore, production is restricted to central British Columbia, away from areas infested with large populations of wild carrot.

(b) *Beneficial* — Digestibility and nutritive value of the herbage of wild carrot are similar to those of legumes (Ellenberg 1952; Harrison and Dale 1966; Klapp 1956) and therefore this plant should be regarded with greater tolerance when found in pastures among plants of low nutritive value (Klapp 1956; Tribe et al. 1952). Clark and Fletcher (1909) reported that sheep will feed on it.

Fig. 1. Wild carrot mature flowering plant, typical pasture condition. Fig. 2. Plant from heavily grazed pasture, all flowering stalks removed. Fig. 3. Rosette, taken from above, with cotyledons and three expanded leaves. Fig. 4. Rosette with large leaves in upright position assumed in the immediate pre-flowering condition.

51

Cattle and horses will also graze on wild carrot.

The adult of a parasite (*Orgilus obscurator* Nees) of the European pine shoot moth (*Rhyacionia buoliana* Schiff.) feeds on the flower of wild carrot. The size of the population of the parasite is influenced by the length of time the adult survives in its egg-laying stage and this depends on the availability of suitable food such as wild carrot flowers. Foresters concerned with the establishment of red pine (*Pinus resinosa* Ait.), a native species of considerable importance, may question the status of wild carrot as a noxious weed (Syme 1966, 1973).

The flowers of wild carrot have considerable aesthetic appeal as indicated by its popular name, Queen-Anne's-lace. In Jamaica, a variety with particularly large petals on the outer flowers of the umbel is grown as an ornamental (Adams 1971).

(*c*) *Legislation* — Wild carrot or *Daucus carota* is 1 of 12 plants in the secondary noxious class of the Canada Seed Act of 1961. It is listed in the Weed Control Acts of Manitoba, Nova Scotia, Ontario and Quebec.

4. Geographical Distribution

Figure 5 gives the geographical distribution of collection sites of plants of *D. carota* in Canadian herbaria. Data are from the National Herbarium and maps by the Plant Research Institute, Agriculture Canada, Ottawa, and are acknowledged, as well as information in various floras (Erskine 1960; Rousseau 1968; Scoggan 1957; Roland 1949; Baldwin 1958). Wild carrot, in populations large enough to qualify as weedy, is found in eastern Canada, in the area formerly occupied by deciduous forests; in western Canada, in the coastal Douglas Fir Zone.

Daucus carota ssp. *carota* is found throughout the eastern states and along the south and west coasts of the United States, in Mexico, Central America and the West Indies (Mathias and Constance 1944-45). It occurs throughout the British Isles and is especially abundant near the sea. It also occurs from Norway and central Sweden south to North Africa and the Canary Islands, and eastward through Siberia to northern and eastern India (Clapham et al. 1952).

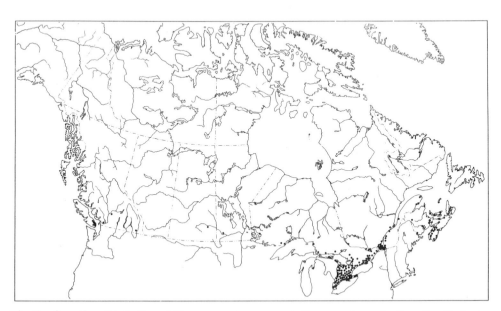

Fig. 5. Canadian distribution of *Daucus carota* ssp. *carota* from specimens in Canadian Herbaria and maps by the Plant Research Institute, Agriculture Canada, Ottawa, Ontario.

5. Habitat

(a) *Climatic* — *D. carota* is not found in central Canada where the climate is Continental. It occurs in areas of > 2,500 F° days of heat (Rousseau 1968), > 120 consecutive days frost free, and annual precipitation from 80 to 100 cm (Canada Department of Mines and Technical Surveys 1957). Wild carrot in Canada, as in Britain, is limited by altitude; it grows between sea level and 450 m (Gimingham 1964; Hepburn 1952; Salisbury 1961).

Photoperiod does not limit the range of *D. carota*. It is adventive throughout the warmer parts of the world, occurring in Central America and Mexico (Mathias and Constance 1944-45) where the day length is relatively constant; and, at the other extreme, it occurs north of 65°N in Sweden (Hultén 1950) where day length is 24 h in June each year, and in Asia on the Kamchatka Peninsula in the Bering Sea at approximately 60°N (Clapham et al. 1952). It grows in full sunlight (Clark and Fletcher 1909; Dale et al. 1965; Ellenberg 1952; Frankton 1955; Sylwester 1960). When shaded its vigor drops, and, with severe shading, its reproductive method may change to short-lived perennial (Harrison 1965).

(b) *Substratum* — In eastern Canada wild carrot is associated with calcareous soil (Dale et al. 1965) but not confined to it (Frankton 1955). In Britain also, wild carrot is associated with calcareous or chalk soil (Anderson 1927; Salisbury 1961), but it appears indifferent to this factor in Europe (Ellenberg 1952, 1963; Klapp 1956) where it is associated with well drained sites: as Linnaeus (1753) stated, "Habitat in Europae campis exaridis" or dried-out fields or meadows. A good supply of water, however, is beneficial where the soil is aerated and not waterlogged (Dale et al. 1965; Ellenberg 1952; Klapp 1956).

In Ontario, soil of fine-particle size was associated with fast growth and early maturing of wild carrot plants (Harrison 1965). Also, wild carrot established on a drained millpond only on areas where the soil was of fine-particle size and high nutrient status (Dale 1964). Harrison and Dale (1966) found that severe frost-heaving during the early spring prevented the maintenance of a population and its subsequent reproduction on poorly drained muck or clay soil. In Britain, the preference shown by wild carrot for soil particle size varies with other environmental factors from sand near the sea coast (Gimingham 1964) to fine chalk on the Downs (Anderson 1927). In Europe, wild carrot showed a preference for medium to high levels of nitrogen (Ellenberg 1950, 1963; Klapp 1956; Williams 1968), but was indifferent to phosphorus levels on well fertilized sites in hay meadows in Germany (Kühner 1951, quoted *in* Williams 1968).

(c) *Communities in which Daucus carota occurs* — In Quebec, Dansereau and Gille (1949) listed the following with *D. carota* in pastures which were ploughed from time to time: *Phleum pratense* L., *Trifolium hybridum* L., *Plantago major* L., *Ambrosia artemisiifolia* L., *Trifolium repens* L., *Agrostis stolonifera* L., *Taraxacum officinale* (L.) Weber, *Stellaria graminea* L., *Trifolium pratense* L., *Poa pratense* L., *Polygonum* sp., *Cirsium arvense* (L.) Scop., *Chrysanthemum leucanthemum* L., *Agropyron repens* L. and *Prunella vulgaris* L.

In Ontario, Thomson (1965) found the additional associated species: *Fragaria virginiana* Duchesne, *Geum aleppicum* Jacq., *Vicia cracca* L., *Hypericum perforatum* L., *Solidago nemoralis* Ait., *Solidago canadensis* L., *Cichorium intybus* L., and *Sonchus arvensis* L., and Dale (1966) found *D. carota* concurring most frequently on sites with the following species: *P. vulgaris, Potentilla recta* L., *S. nemoralis* Ait., *Achillea millefolium* L.

In Germany, Williams (1968) found *D. carota* in the *Arrhenatheretum* association in well fertilized meadows with high nitrogen levels. Other species of this association common in Canada are *Chrysanthemum leucanthemum, Taraxacum officinale, Dactylis glomerata* L., *Tragopogon pratense* L., *Achillea millefolium* L., *Medicago lupulina* L. and *Leontodon hispidus* L. Ellenberg (1963) found *D. carota* associated with *C. leucanthemum, D. glomerata, Centaurea jacea* L., *Poa pratensis, A. millefolium,* and *Agrimonia eupatoria* L.

Klapp (1956) reported that in grasslands in Germany, *D. carota* occurred in 21% of 4,000 areas surveyed and contributed 0.19% to the cover. It was more frequent in meadows than in pastures (36 vs. 16%) and contributed greater cover (0.42 vs. 0.07%).

6. History

No Canadian collection of wild carrot from the province of Quebec and housed in Canadian herbaria is more than 100 yr old, or more than 90 yr old from Ontario (Macoun 1883-1890); and most collections are less than 28 yr old. The plant has a longer documented history in the United States (Gronovius 1739, 1762; Walter 1788; Rafinesque 1836). It was considered a serious weed in Connecticut in 1881 (Committee of Connecticut Botanical Society 1910) and was listed as a farm weed in Canada 25 yr later (Clark and Fletcher 1906). Many aspects of its natural history and suggestions for its control were outlined by Clark and Fletcher (1909).

The origin of Canadian wild carrot is stated to be Eurasia (Frankton 1955). It has been treated as an introduced species in Ontario (Montgomery 1957) and Quebec (Rousseau 1968), but the method of introduction and whether the route was via the United States is a matter of conjecture. Mathias and Constance (1944-45) claimed a solely Eurasian origin for it in North America. The history of the west coast of Canada populations, and whether they were introduced from Russia, or from elsewhere, may prove difficult to document (Renney unpublished).

As this is a species that grows in full sunlight (section 5a) and in areas formerly occupied by deciduous forest (section 4), its distribution and abundance in Canada have increased as land has been cleared of trees. Many changes in its distribution can be associated with changes in land use and patterns of availability of seed. Unfortunately, collectors of plants frequently pass over common weeds to over-sample some rarer or more interesting species. The collection of a plant is positive evidence of its presence, but its non-collection is a less valuable criterion upon which to assume absence.

7. Growth and Development

(*a*) *Morphology* — Wild carrot propagates solely by seeds (half-fruits) which have a flat surface and an outer curved one, covered with five hairy ribs and four rows of large spines. These spines and the aromatic flavor may protect the seeds from birds.

(*b*) *Perennation* — Wild carrot passes the winter either as a seed or as a tap root surmounted by a rosette of leaves. No plant that has flowered has been observed to survive and grow in the subsequent year (Harrison and Dale 1966).

(*c*) *Physiological data* — *Daucus carota* has been used for many physiological studies, the most spectacular being the development of whole plants from cultured cells of the cultivated carrot (Steward 1958, 1963, 1970). It would be difficult to extract from these studies what unique or special characteristics of carrot is relevant to the career of wild carrot as a weed in Canada.

(*d*) *Phenology* — The author is not aware of studies of time of maximum root growth, shoot growth or initiation of growth in the spring. Flushes of germination occur following rain, chiefly in the spring, but also in the summer and fall (Dale and Harrison 1966). In Europe, germination is in the autumn (Ellenberg 1950, 1963). In annual plants, flowering may occur 6 wk after spring germination (*see* section 2c). There is not a critical root weight which plants must reach before flowering. However, when grown in field plots, the plants that flowered first were those with larger root weight, length and diameter (Harrison 1965). In Ontario, full flowering has been observed as early as 29 June, but the peak is usually in the last 2 wk of July. Flowering continues all summer until the first heavy frost, which may be as late as October in sheltered sites (Harrison 1965).

(*e*) *Mycorrhiza* — There is no report of mycorrhiza occurring on this plant.

8. Reproduction

(*a*) *Floral biology* — Wild carrot plants are generally cross-fertilized. As in other species of Umbelliferae, the number of different pollinating agents is large, often between two and three hundred. These comprise *Dipterans*, such as flies, mosquitoes and gnats; and *Hymenoptera*, unspecialized bees, wasps and ants (Bell 1971). Wild carrot plants are visited by a wide spectrum of insects (Flemion and Hendrickson 1949) and the pollen is incorporated into bumble bees' nests, particularly in the larval meconia (Edwards-Anderka 1967; Wyatt 1970).

Daucus carota is protandrous, with the gynoecium only weakly developed when pollen is shed. Although generally cross-fertilized, it is self-fertile. When insect pollination fails, fertilization by adjacent flowers is facilitated by the long filament on the anthers (Bell 1971). The first-formed umbels have fewer staminate flowers — 16% in terminal umbels vs. 40% in laterals and 60% in sublaterals (Braak and Kho 1958). European wild carrot is similar (Rubashevskaia 1931). Wild carrot crosses with cultivated carrot to produce fertile hybrids (*see* sections 3a and 9).

(*b*) *Seed production and dispersal* — The terminal umbel is formed first; others develop successively. The seeds of the terminal umbel ripen first, are the heaviest (0.84 vs. 0.61 mg), have the highest percentage germination (21 vs. 5%) and have two or three times as many seeds as the second- or third-order umbels (Harrison 1965). However, in commercial carrot seed production, it was found that over 50% of the total seed yield was produced consistently by the second-order umbels (Hawthorn et al. 1962).

When fertilization takes place, the flower head is still concave or flat, but as the fruits increase in size and are still green, the rays are curved inward forming a nest-shaped structure (bird's nest phase). As the fruits mature and become dry, the rays flex outwards, causing the umbel to open and the ripe fruit to scatter. The rays are hygroscopic, opening the umbel when dry and closing it when the weather is damp. The fruits on the outer edge of the umbel ripen first and are released first. The percentage germination is independent of the region of the umbel from which the seed is taken (Harrison 1965).

The 1,000 to 40,000 seeds per plant are normally released from the dry, open umbel between mid-summer and mid-winter and may be dispersed for short distances by the wind. Some late-developing umbels retain 30% of their seeds until mid-January when the wind may blow the seeds a long way over the crusty surface of the snow. However, the wind is not the only method of dispersing the seeds; they may be carried on animals' fur, attached by their hooked spines (Hehn 1885), and may pass undamaged through the digestive tract of a horse (Salisbury 1961).

(*c*) *Viability of seeds and germination* — Freshly ripened seed when tested in the laboratory gave less than 1% germination in early October, but, 6 mo later, the same seed lot gave 20% germination (Dale and Harrison 1966). Germination ability and speed of germination varies greatly between seed lots and within one lot of seeds (Arnott 1956; Barton 1953; Borthwick 1931; Dale 1970; Dale and Harrison 1966; Flemion and Hendrickson 1949; Harrison 1965). Delayed germination was attributed to immature embryos (Borthwick 1931; Flemion et al. 1949), but it has been shown recently that the embryo is partially enclosed by the endosperm and this mechanical constriction delays germination until removal by breaking or by digestion (Dale and Harrison 1966). Extracts from leaves and roots inhibited germination, reducing it from 64% in a control using distilled water to 20% using extracts (Smith 1966). Dormancy has also been induced by environment in up to 60% of viable seeds when fully imbibed seeds were subjected to conditions in which only a single environmental factor inhibited their germination. This induced dormancy was broken by drying and storing seed for several months (Dale unpublished).

Seeds of wild carrot are not uniform in their response to light. Maguire and Overland (1959) reported 72% germination in light, and 84% in darkness. Gardner (1921) and Mitchell (1926) found that a larger number of seeds germinated in light. Dale and Harrison (1966) showed an interaction of light and temperature in different combinations. Below 20 C, higher percentage germination took place in darkness, whereas above this temperature a 16-h photoperiod produced higher germination. Rogers and Stearns (1958) found that when seeds were freshly collected, more germinated in the light, but with 2-yr-old seeds, more germinated in darkness. Germination in the dark is increased with increased oxygen concentration (Gardner 1921). It can be concluded that light is essential for the germination of only a small proportion of any one collection of wild carrot seeds.

The number of seeds germinating can be influenced by their environment during storage (Barton 1953) and by the length of time stored under constant conditions (e.g. dry, and at 4 C) (Dale 1970). Seeds may remain viable but dormant in the soil for several years (Sylwester 1960) and then appear as seedlings when an old pasture is ploughed (Dansereau and Gille 1949) or when a meadow is disturbed for fertilization (Williams 1968).

(*d*) *Vegetative reproduction* — There is no evidence for vegetative reproduction either in the field or in the laboratory, although wild carrot root tissue has been used successfully for tissue culture (Halperin et al. 1964; Halperin and Weatherall 1964; Levine 1947).

9. Hybrids

Hybrids occur between the two subspecies of *Daucus carota*, wild carrot and cultivated carrot, when they are in the same area. Economic loss may occur if wild carrot crosses with the cultivated carrot, causing hybrid seed to be set (section 3a).

10. Population Dynamics

Under favorable conditions and low density, wild carrot populations have a large proportion of annuals (Frankton quoted *in* Harrison 1965). Seeds planted in rows had 50% annuals (Dale 1967b). Table 1 presents data on annual and biennial flowering of plants seeded, at rate stated, in May 1967. Some germination and seedling growth occurred between the analysis of annuals in 1967 and that of biennials in 1968. Harrison (1965) observed that when conditions are unfavorable, flowering may be delayed until the 3rd or 4th yr after germination. The slowing down of the life cycle tends to reduce the rate of population growth, whereas the annual production of seeds encourages rapid expansion of the population by compounding the production of seed (Rempel and Dale 1969). Many plants die during the winter, 25% of the population on clay loam and 50% on sandy loam on sites examined (Harrison 1965) (see section 5b). In comparing the success of wild carrot in fallow vegetation of different ages, Holt (1968) has shown that germination of seeds, establishment of seedlings and subsequent reproductive behavior were more successful in younger fallowed fields.

Rempel (1970) examined population dynamics within and between populations that had been planted and found that: (1) there was little interaction between plants when they were seedlings or young vegetative plants; (2) among older plants, when densities were high, intraspecific interference caused plants to become less vigorous and thus to flower later and set fewer seeds; (3)

Table 1. Comparison of flowering plants, annuals in September 1967 and biennials in September 1968. Means of 10 replicates (from Rempel 1970)

| | Seeding density (no./m^2) | | | | | |
| | 1,000 | | 5,000 | | 9,000 | |
	Ann.	Bienn.	Ann.	Bienn.	Ann.	Bienn.
No reproductive/m^2	29.0	143.3	44.6	348.3	40.6	534.9
% reproductive	10.3	85.6	5.3	78.3	3.8	70.3
Dry weight/plant	0.9	13.4	0.4	6.1	0.2	3.5
Cpd. umbels/plant	2.9	13.1	2.4	10.6	2.6	9.3
Cpd. umbels/m^2	100	1836	120	3755	102	5429

in sparse *D. carota* populations and in mixtures with one other species of the following: *Rumex crispus* L., *Verbascum thapsus* L., *Medicago lupulina* L., *Asclepias syriaca* L. and *Potentilla recta* L., the wild carrot established in larger numbers, grew larger and matured faster than in more dense carrot populations. The companion species was thought to reduce the intraspecific competition between wild carrot plants; and (4) the presence of *D. carota* affected the test species of *P. recta*, *M. lupulina* and *A. syriaca* by reducing the population size and causing reduced growth, but did not affect *R. crispus* or *V. thapsus*.

11. Response to Herbicides and Other Chemicals

Young wild carrot plants are susceptible to 2,4-D and 2,4,5-T, especially when plants are 4–6 inches high (Sylwester 1960). A strain resistant to 2,4-D at normally applied levels, but not to 2,4,5-T, was reported (Switzer 1957; Whitehead and Switzer 1963). The most serious problem in effective control is that the populations are of heterogeneous age (Dale 1967b; Harrison 1965).

12. Response to Other Human Manipulations

Populations of wild carrot are maintained by occasional disturbance. In Quebec, Dansereau and Gille (1949) found that wild carrot occurred only on pastures which were ploughed from time to time and planted in grain–pastures "dans une rotation." It was present in one-fifth of the quadrats in this type of pasture. The species was absent when ploughing was an annual event.

Williams (1968) found wild carrot occurring on fertilized meadows in Germany and, although this plant is considered an indicator of dry sites (see section 5b), it established on wet meadows as a result of manipulation. The sites were disturbed when fertilizer was applied. The association of plants which includes wild carrot in meadows recurs throughout Europe and is known as the *Arrhenatheretum* (Kornas 1968; see 5c). Medwecka-Kornas and Kornas (1964) noted the replacement of wild carrot by lady's mantle, *Alchemilla crinita* and *A. micans* and by higher populations of short grasses

in this association when there was no disturbance of a meadow. This change produced an increased plant cover and reduced light intensity at the seedling level.

The flowering stalk is grazed in pastures. The central stalk is grazed first, followed by the branches when the grazing is heavy. Older plants become woody and older flower stalks are less palatable than younger ones. Figure 2 shows a mature plant from a heavily grazed pasture with all flower stalks removed, in contrast with an ungrazed plant in Fig. 1.

The degree of weediness of any species depends on its interference with other plants and the size of populations is a measure (Dale 1967a). In wild carrot, successful seedling establishment determines population size. Prevention of seed production is paramount in the control of wild carrot as a weed (Sylwester 1960). Simulated grazing by pruning or mowing is a means of control. Harrison (1965) found the flowering stage of the plant to be the most vulnerable to clipping. The more frequent the clipping, the smaller the plant and the lower the reproductive capacity. A single mowing late in summer was also a most effective control (Harrison and Dale 1966).

13. Response to Parasites

Plant bug species (*Lygus* spp.) contribute to embryoless seeds in cultivated and wild carrot (Arnott 1956; Flemion and Hendrickson 1949; Kho and Braak 1956). Seeds produced late in the growing season have their embryos destroyed at almost every stage of development by the abundant nymphal stage of the plant bug (*Lygus*). These nymphs cause no apparent harm to the developing endosperm or seed coat (Flemion et al. 1949).

Roots of wild and cultivated carrots are eaten by the larval (maggot) stage of the carrot rust fly, *Psila rosae* (F.), which burrows in the roots (Work and Carew 1955; Ontario Ministry of Agriculture and Food 1973). Roots are also attacked by larvae and adults of the lesion nematode, *Protylenchus* (Agrios 1969), and the root knot nematode, *Meloidogyne* species, particularly in the Montreal district (Conners 1967).

57

Aster yellows commonly accounts for 10 to 25% losses in cultivated carrot crops, while occasionally losses are reported as high as 80–90%. The disease is reported almost annually in the Maritime Provinces and is sporadically severe in New Brunswick, Nova Scotia and Prince Edward Island (Conners 1967). The mycoplasm is transmitted by leaf hoppers (*Macrosteles fascifrons* (Stal)) and other species that feed for several hours on the diseased plant. Reservoirs of aster yellows mycoplasm are in weedy plants: thistles, wild chicory, wild carrot, dandelion, field daisy, black-eyed Susan and common plantain (Agrios 1969). Conners (1967), for Canada, included as reservoirs the following perennial weeds: *Chrysanthemum leucanthemum, Erigeron canadensis, Leontodon taraxacum* and *Plantago major*. Large inocula may also build up in fields of diseased vegetable crops. Walker (1952) lists the following as susceptible: lettuce (*Lactuca sativa* L.), endive (*Ciclorium endiva* L.), tomato (*Lycopeisicon escolentum* Mill.), potato (*Solanum tuberosum* L.), parsley (*Petroselinum crispum* Nym.), onion (*Allium* sp.), salsify (*Trogopoxon porrifolius* L.) and celery (*Apium graveolens* L.). (The genus and species names used for the eight crop plants are the author's, not Walker's.) The suggested controls are the eradication of all the perennial and biennial weed hosts (Agrios 1969) or leaf hopper control (Ontario Ministry of Agriculture and Food 1973).

Conners (1967) has listed 15 disease organisms associated with carrot plants in Canada in addition to 36 fungi isolated from seeds. The index of plant diseases on carrot plants in the United States lists 36 disease organisms in addition to virus, mycoplasm and unknowns (United States Department of Agriculture 1960).

Two leaf blights restricted to the genus *Daucus* are *Cercospora carotae* (Pass.) Solh. and *Alternaria dauci* (Kühn) Groves and Skolko. The latter has caused losses in British Columbia, Quebec and Nova Scotia. Wild carrot in Nova Scotia is suspected of harboring *Cercospora*, allowing it to overwinter on rosettes (Conners 1967). Humid weather greatly encourages the spread of these blight diseases.

Xanthomanas carotae (Kendr.) Dawson, the bacterial blight of carrot, may occur in 4.3% of carrot seed. The pathogen actively and directly penetrates the seeds and spreads to the plant as it develops (Ark and Gardner 1944). It may also be spread by soil or insects. This blight occurs in seed crops in the British Columbia interior (Conners 1967).

The control of weedy populations of wild carrot by these parasites is not feasible, particularly in areas where the closely related subspecies, cultivated carrot, is grown for food.

ACKNOWLEDGMENTS

The author appreciates the large volume of data collected and analyzed by various students and assistants. He has benefitted greatly by their discussions and enthusiasm for the problems of wild carrot. Financial assistance is acknowledged from the Ontario Agricultural College, Agricultural Institute of Ontario and the National Research Council of Canada. Assistance in preparing the manuscript has been given generously by colleagues and the editorial committee for this series. C. B. Kelly kindly read section 13. R. M. Adamson and A. J. Renney have assisted by discussing wild carrot in British Columbia.

ADAMS, C. D. 1971. The blue mahoe and other bush. McGraw-Hill, Singapore. 159 pp.
AGRIOS, G. N. 1969. Plant pathology. Academic Press Inc., New York, N.Y. 629 pp.
ANDERSON, V. L. 1927. Studies on the vegetation of English chalk. J. Ecol. **15**: 72–129.
ARK, P. A. and GARDNER, M. W. 1944. Carrot bacterial blight as it affects the roots. Phytopathology **34**: 415–420.
ARNOTT, D. A. 1956. Some factors reducing carrot seed yields in British Columbia. Proc. Entomol. Soc. B.C. **52**: 27–30.
BALDWIN, W. K. W. 1958. Plants of the clay belt of northern Ontario and Quebec. Can. Dep. North. Aff. and Nat. Resour., Nat. Mus. Can., Bull. 156, Ottawa, Ontario. 324 pp.
BARTON, L. V. 1953. Seed storage and viability. Contrib. Boyce Thompson Inst. Plant Res. **17**: 87–103.
BATES, G. H. 1937. The vegetation of wayside and hedgerow. J. Ecol. **25**: 469–481.
BATES, G. H. 1955. Weed control. Jarrold Ltd., Norwich, England. 235 pp.
BELL, C. R. 1971. Breeding systems and floral biology of the Umbelliferae or evidence for specialization in unspecialized flowers. *In* V. H. Heywood, ed. Biology and chemistry of the Umbelliferae. Bot. J. Linn. Soc., Vol. 64, Suppl. I. Academic Press Inc., New York, N.Y. 438 pp.

BORTHWICK, H. A. 1931. Carrot seed germination. Proc. Amer. Soc. Hortic. Sci. **28**: 310–314.

BRAAK, J. P. and KHO, Y. O. 1958. Some observations on flowering biology of carrot, *Daucus carota*. Euphytica **7**: 131–139.

CANADA DEPARTMENT OF AGRICULTURE. 1973. Final seed crop report 1972 crop. Plant Prod. Div., Prod. Marketing Branch, Ottawa, Ontario. Tables 1–15.

CANADA DEPARTMENT OF MINES AND TECHNICAL SURVEYS. 1957. Atlas of Canada. Queen's Printer, Ottawa, Ontario. 110 pp.

CANADA WEED COMMITTEE. 1969. Common and botanical names of weeds in Canada. Can. Dep. Agric. Publ. 1397, Ottawa, Ontario.

CLAPHAM, A. R. TUTIN, T. G. and WARBURG, E. F. 1952. Flora of the British Isles. Cambridge University Press, Cambridge, England, 1591 pp.

CLARK, G. H. and FLETCHER, J. 1906. Farm weeds of Canada. Dep. Agric., Ottawa.

CLARK, G. H. and FLETCHER, J. 1909. Farm weeds of Canada. Dep. Agric., Ottawa.

COMMITTEE OF CONNECTICUT BOTANICAL SOCIETY. 1910. Conn. Geol. Nat. Hist. Surv. Bull. 14. 569 pp.

CONNERS, I. L. 1967. An annoted index of plant diseases in Canada and fungi recorded on plants in Alaska, Canada and Greenland. Res. Branch, Can. Dep. Agric. Publ. 1251. Queen's Printer, Ottawa, Ontario. 381 pp.

DALE, H. M. 1964. Influence of soil on weed vegetation on a drained river millpond. Can. J. Bot. **42**: 823–830.

DALE, H. M. 1966. Weed complexes on abandoned pastures as indicators of site characteristics. Can. J. Bot. **44**: 11–17.

DALE, H. M. 1967a. The biology of the weed habit. Symposium paper. Can. Bot. Assoc., University of Ottawa, Ottawa, Ontario.

DALE, H. M. 1967b. Factors influencing early flowering in wild carrot. Minutes Nat. Weed Comm. Can., East. Sect., Que. 21–24.

DALE, H. M. 1970. Germination patterns in *Daucus carota* ssp. *carota*. Variations in the 1967 collections. Can. J. Bot. **48**: 413–418.

DALE, H. M. and HARRISON, P. J. 1966. Wild carrot seeds, germination and dormancy. Weeds **14**: 201–204.

DALE, H. M., HARRISON, P. J. and THOMSON, G. W. 1965. Weeds as indicators of physical site characteristics in abandoned pastures. Can. J. Bot. **43**: 1319–1327.

DANSEREAU, P. and GILLE, A. 1949. Ecologie des principaux types de pâsturages des environs de Granby. Bull. Serv. Biogeo., Univ. de Montréal, 4. 59 pp.

DARLINGTON, C. D. and WYLIE, A. P. 1955. Chromosome atlas of flowering plants. Allen and Unwin, London, England. 519 pp.

EDWARDS-ANDERKA, C. J. 1967. Ecology of the genus *Bombus* Latr. (Hymenoptera, Apidae) in southern Ontario with emphasis on pollen analysis. M.Sc. Thesis, Univ. of Guelph, Guelph, Ontario. 87+ 20 pp.

ELLENBERG, H. 1950. Landwirtschaftliche pflanzensoziologie. Band I. Unkrautgemeinscheftenals Zeiger für Klima und Boden. E. Ulmer, Stuttgart. 138 pp.

ELLENBERG, H. 1952. Landwirtschaftliche pflanzensoziologie. Band II. Wiesen und Weiden und ihre standörliche Bewertung. E. Ulmer, Stuttgart. 143 pp.

ELLENBERG, H. 1963. Vegetation mitteleuropas mit den Alpen. E. Ulmer, Stuttgart. 943 pp.

ERSKINE, D. 1960. Flora of Prince Edward Island. Can. Dep. Agric., Queen's Printer, Ottawa, Ontario. 270 + 1 pp.

FERRON, M. and CAYOUETTE, R. 1964. Noms des mauvaises herbes du Québec, Division de la Recherche, Ministère de l'Agriculture et de la Colonisation du Québec. Publ. No. 288. 68 pp.

FLEMION, F. and HENDRICKSON, E. T. 1949. Further studies on the occurrence of embryoless seeds, and immature embryos in Umbelliferae. Proc. Boyce Thompson Inst. **15**: 291–297.

FLEMION, F., POOL, H. and OLSEN, J. 1949. Relationship of *Lygus* bugs to embryoless seeds in dill. Proc. Boyce Thompson Inst. **15**: 299–310.

FRANKTON, C. 1955. Weeds of Canada. Queen's Printer, Ottawa, Ontario. 196 pp.

FRANKTON, C. and MULLIGAN, G. A. 1970. Weeds of Canada. Queen's Printer, Ottawa, Ontario. 217 pp.

GARDNER, W. A. 1921. The effect of light on light sensitive seeds. Bot. Gaz. **71**: 249–288.

GEORGIA, A. E. 1914. A manual of weeds. Macmillan Co., New York, N.Y. 593 pp.

GIMINGHAM, C. H. 1964. Maritime and sub maritime communities. *In* Burnett, J. The vegetation of Scotland. Oliver and Boyd Ltd., Edinburgh, Scotland. 613 pp.

GRONOVIUS, J. F. 1739-1743. Flora virginica, exhibens plantas quas Johannes Clayton in Virginia observavit atque collegit. Vol. 1 and 2. C. Haak, Lugduni Batavorum (Leyden). 206 pp.

GRONOVIUS, J. F. 1762. Flora virginica. Lugduni Batavorum. Photolithographed 1946. Arnold Arboretum, Cambridge, Mass. 176 pp.

HALPERIN, W., ABENDROTH, E. A. and WETHERELL, D. F. 1964. Studies in nutrition and morphogenesis of wild carrot callus. Amer. J. Bot. **51**: 669.

HALPERIN, W. and WETHERELL, D. F. 1964. Adventitive embryony in tissue cultures of wild carrot, *Daucus carota*. Amer. J. Bot. **51**: 274-283.

HARRISON, P. J. 1965. The effect of grazing and clipping on wild carrot (*Daucus carota* L.) performance, grown on different soil textures. M.Sc. Thesis, Univ. of Guelph, Guelph, Ontario. 74 + 40 pp.

HARRISON, P. J. and DALE, H. M. 1966. The effects of grazing and clipping on the control of wild carrot. Weeds **14**: 285-288.

HAWTHORN, L. R., BOHART, G. E. and TOOLE, E. H. 1956. Carrot seed yield and germination as affected by different levels of insect pollination. Proc. Amer. Soc. Hortic. Sci. **67**: 384-389.

HAWTHORN, L. R., TOOLE, E. H. and TOOLE, V. K. 1962. Yield and viability of carrot seeds as affected by position of umbel and time of harvest. Proc. Amer. Soc. Hortic. Sci. **80**: 401-406.

HEHN, V. 1885. Wanderings of plants and animals. Swan Sonnenschein & Co., London, England. 399 pp.

HEPBURN, I. 1952. Flowers of the coast. Collins, N. N. ser. London, England. 236 pp.

HEYWOOD, V. H. 1968. *Umbelliferae*. Pages 373-375 *in* T. G. Tutin, V. H. Heywood, N. A. Burges, D. M. Moore, D. H. Valentine, S. M. Walters, and D. A. Webb, eds. Flora Europaea. 3 vols. Cambridge University Press, Cambridge, England.

HOLT, B. R. 1968. Experimental study of establishment and subsequent reproduction of *Daucus carota* L. in fallow vegetation of two ages. Bull. Ecol. Soc. Amer. **49**: 156.

HÜLTÉN, E. 1950. Atlas of the distribution of vascular plants in North West Europe. Kartografiska Institutat, Stockholm. 512 pp.

KHO, Y. O. and BRAAK, J. P. 1956. Reduction in yield and viability of carrot seed in relation to the occurrence of plant bug *Lygus campestris*. Euphytica **5**: 146-156.

KLAPP, E. L. 1956. Wiesen und Weiden. P. Parey, Berlin. 519 pp.

KORNAS, J. 1968. Plant communities of the Gorce Mountains (Polish Western Carpathians). II Synanthropic communities. Fragm. Florist. Geobot. (Krakow) **14**: 83-124.

LEVINE, M. 1947. Differentiation of carrot root tissue grown in vitro. Bull. Torrey Bot. Club **74**: 321-328.

LINNAEUS, C. 1753. Species Plantarum. Fasc. 1957. The Ray Society, London, England. 1200 pp.

MACOUN, J. M. 1883-1890. Catalogue of Canadian plants. Dawson Brothers, Montreal, Quebec. 5 parts.

MAGUIRE, J. D. and OVERLAND, A. 1959. Laboratory germination of seeds of weedy and native plants. Wash. Agric. Exp. Sta. Circ. 349. 15 pp.

MATHIAS, M. E. and CONSTANCE, L. 1944-1945. *Umbelliferae* in North Amer. Flora **28B**: 43-297. New York Botanical Gardens, New York, N.Y.

MEDWECKA-KORNAS, A. and KORNAS, J. 1964. Vegetation map of the Ojcow National Park. Ochrona Przyrody, Krakow **29**: 1-87.

MITCHELL, E. 1926. Germination of seeds of plants native to Dutchess County, N.Y. Bot. Gaz. **81**: 108-112.

MONTGOMERY, F. H. 1957. The introduced plants of Ontario growing outside of cultivation (Part II). Trans. R. Can. Inst. **32**: 3-34.

MUENSCHER, W. C. 1961. Poisonous plants of the United States. Macmillan Co., New York, N.Y. 277 pp.

MULLIGAN, G. A. 1961. Chromosome numbers of Canadian weeds III. Can. J. Bot. **39**: 1051-1066.

ONTARIO MINISTRY OF AGRICULTURE AND FOOD. 1973. Vegetable production and recommendations. Publ. 363. 71 pp.

RAFINESQUE, C. S. 1836. New flora and botany of North America. Part IV. Neobotanon. Philadelphia. Fasc. Arnold Aboretum, Cambridge, Mass. 1946. 112 pp.

REMPEL, E. 1970. Interference studies on *Daucus carota* (wild carrot). M.Sc. Thesis. Univ. of Guelph, Guelph, Ontario. 102 pp.

REMPEL, E. and DALE, H. M. 1969. Interference studies on *Daucus carota*. Ontario Technical Sessions in Biology. Carleton University, Ottawa, Ontario.

ROGERS, B. J. and STEARNS, F. W. 1958. Preliminary studies on the germination of weed seeds. Proc. Northeast. Weed Contr. Conf. **12**: 7-10.

ROLAND, A. E. 1949. The flora of Nova Scotia. Proc. N.S. Inst. Sci. **21**: 552 pp.

ROUSSEAU, C. 1968. Histoire, habitat et distribution de 220 plantes introduites au Québec. Nat. Can. (Que.) **95**: 49-171.

RUBASHEVSKAIA, M. K. 1931. Observations on wild carrot in cultivation and under natural conditions. Bull. Appl. Bot. Gen. and Plant Breed., Leningrad (English summary) **26**: 194-252.

SALISBURY, E. 1961. Weeds and aliens. Collins, N.N. ser., London, England. 384 pp.

SCOGGAN, H. J. 1957. Flora of Manitoba. Can. Dep. North. Aff. Nat. Resour. Nat. Mus. Can. Bull. 140, Ottawa, Ontario. vi + 619 pp.

SMITH, C. G. 1966. Some effects of extracts of *Daucus carota* on germination and growth. *In* Occasional papers of the C. C. Adams Center for Ecological Studies, Western Michigan University, Kalamazoo, Michigan. **14**: 9–18.

STEWARD, F. C. 1958. Growth and organized development of cultured cells. III. Interpretation of growth from free cells to carrot plant. Amer. J. Bot. **45**: 709–713.

STEWARD, F. C. 1963. The control of growth in plant cells. Sci. Amer. **209**: 104–117.

STEWARD, F. C. 1970. Totipotency, variation and clonal development of cultured cells. Endeavour **29**: 117–124.

SWITZER, C. M. 1957. The existence of 2,4-D resistant strains of wild carrot. Proc. Northeast. Weed Contr. Conf. **11**: 315–318.

SYLWESTER, E. P. 1960. Beware of the wild carrot. Hoard's Dairyman **105**: 330–331.

SYME, P. D. 1966. The effects of wild carrot on a common parasite of the European Pine shoot moth. Dep. For. Bimon. Res. Notes **22**: IV, 3.

SYME, P. D. 1973. Effectiveness of insect pest parasites increased by enhancement of plantation environments. Forest. Res. Newsl. 3,2. Great Lakes Forest Research Station, Environment Canada. (unnumbered).

THOMSON, G. W. 1965. Plant communities on different soils in abandoned pastures in West Luther township. M.Sc. Thesis, Univ. of Guelph, Guelph, Ontario. 53 pp.

TRIBE, D. E., GORDON, J. G. and GIMINGHAM, C. H. 1952. The nutritive value of weeds and coarse herbage (browse) for young cattle grazing a temporary pasture. Emp. J. Exp. Agric. **20**: 240–248.

UNITED STATES DEPARTMENT OF AGRICULTURE. 1960. Index of plant diseases in U.S. Crop Res. Div. Agric. Handb. no. 165. 531 pp.

WALKER, J. C. 1952. Diseases of vegetable crops. McGraw-Hill, New York, N.Y. 529 pp.

WALTER, T. 1788. Flora Caroliniana. London.

WHITEHEAD, C. W. and SWITZER, C. M. 1963. The differential response of strains of wild carrot to 2,4-D and related herbicides. Can. J. Plant Sci. **43**: 255–262.

WILLIAMS, J. T. 1968. The nitrogen relations and other ecological investigations on wet fertilized meadows. Veröffentlichungen des Geobotaneschen Institutes der ETH, Stiftung Rübel, Zürich **41**: 71–190.

WORK, P. and CAREW, J. 1955. Vegetable production and marketing. John Wiley and Sons, New York, N.Y. 537 pp.

WYATT, B. K. 1970. Ecology of bumble bees, *Bombus* Latr. in southern Ontario with reference to nest development and pollen sources. M.Sc. Thesis, Univ. of Guelph, Guelph, Ontario. 178 pp.

THE BIOLOGY OF CANADIAN WEEDS.
6. *CENTAUREA DIFFUSA* AND *C. MACULOSA*

A. K. WATSON[1] and A. J. RENNEY

Department of Plant Science, University of British Columbia, Vancouver 8, B.C.
Received 13 May 1974, accepted 14 June 1974.

WATSON, A. K. AND RENNEY, A. J. 1974. The biology of Canadian weeds. *Centaurea diffusa* and *C. maculosa*. Can. J. Plant Sci. **54**: 687–701.

A summary of biological information on *Centaurea diffusa* Lam. (diffuse knapweed) and *C. maculosa* Lam. (spotted knapweed) is presented. The knapweeds are common on semiarid rangeland, highway and railroad right-of-ways and waste places in southern British Columbia. Spotted knapweed is also common in eastern Canada.

Les auteurs présentent un résumé de l'information biologique sur *Centaurea diffusa* Lam. (centaurée diffuse) et *C. maculosa* Lam. (centaurée tachetée). Les centaurées sont fréquentes dans les grands pâturages semi-arides, le long des grandes routes et des chemins de fer et dans les terres incultes du sud de la Colombie-Britannique. La centaurée tachetée est répondue aussi dans l'est du Canada.

1. Names

Centaurea diffusa Lam. — diffuse knapweed (Canada Weed Committee 1969); centaurée diffuse (Frankton 1958).

Centaurea maculosa Lam. — spotted knapweed (Canada Weed Committee 1969); centaurée maculée, centaurée tachetée (Ferron et Cayouette 1964).

Compositae, composite family, Composées.

2. Description and Account of Variation
(some data from Moore 1972)

Diffuse knapweed (Fig. 1 and 3A) is a biennial or triennial, pubescent, with an elongated tap root; stems erect, 50–80 cm tall, heavily branched; leaves alternate, basal leaves in a whorl, much divided, up to 20 cm long and 5 cm wide, lower stem leaves much divided, uppermost leaves bractlike and entire; flower heads radiate, 3 mm diam, 14–16 mm high, numerous and solitary, bracts pale yellowish-green, upper part narrowed into a stiff spine; flowers generally white, occasionally pink to purple; achenes 2–3 mm long, light brown to black; pappus generally absent or mere fringe less than 1 mm long.

Spotted knapweed (Fig. 2 and 3B) is a biennial or short-lived perennial, reproducing by seeds; stems erect or ascending, branched, pubescent, 30–100 cm high; leaves alternate, much divided, upper leaves linear; flower heads eradiate, 6 mm diam, 16–20 mm high, mainly terminal, numerous, corymbs or corymbose panicles, bracts with a black-fringed tip 1–2 mm long; flowers tubular, purple, rarely white; achenes brownish, 3 mm long; pappus of simple bristles, 1–2 mm long, persistent.

The chromosome complement of diffuse knapweed is diploid with $2n = 18$ and spotted knapweed is tetraploid with $2n = 36$ (Moore and Frankton 1954).

3. Economic Importance

(*a*) *Detrimental* — Diffuse and spotted knapweeds are not generally utilized as forage and their dense and spiny overstory reduces the availability of more desirable forage species. The spines of diffuse knapweed may cause mechanical injury to the mouth and digestive tracts of grazing animals. Because of its growth habits, diffuse knapweed limits the use of many recreational areas.

The rosettes are not grazed, but the flower shoots are utilized in overgrazed areas. The rosettes of diffuse and spotted knapweeds have some nutritive value, but mature plants

[1]Present address (A.K.W.): Agriculture Canada, Regina Research Station, Regina, Saskatchewan S4P 3A2.

Can. J. Plant Sci. 54: 687-701 (Oct. 1974)

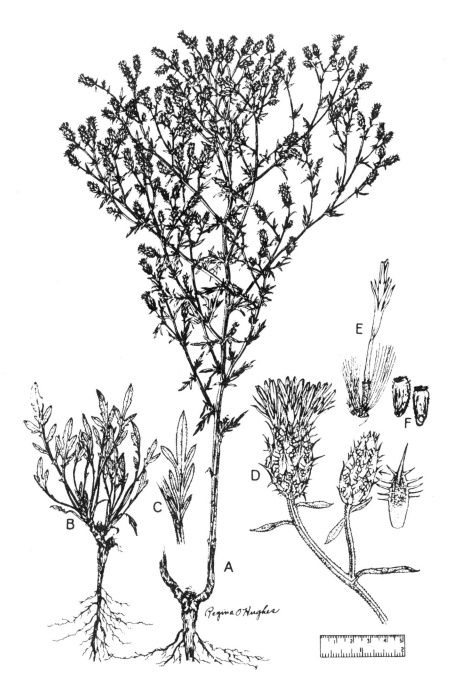

Fig. 1. *Centaurea diffusa* Lam. Diffuse knapweed. A, Habit (× 0.5); B, rosette (× 0.5); C, cauline leaf (× 2.5); D, flower head (× 5); E, flower (× 5); F, achenes (× 5). Source: Reed, C. F. and Hughes, R. O. (1970).

63

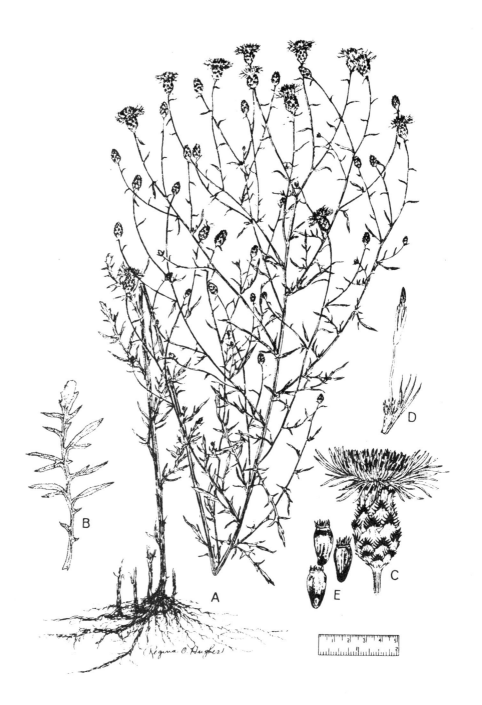

Fig. 2. *Centaurea maculosa* Lam. Spotted knapweed. A, Habit (× 0.5); B, leaf (× 1); C, flower head (× 2); D, disk flower (× 3.5); E, achenes (× 4). Source: Reed, C. F. and Hughes, R. O. (1970).

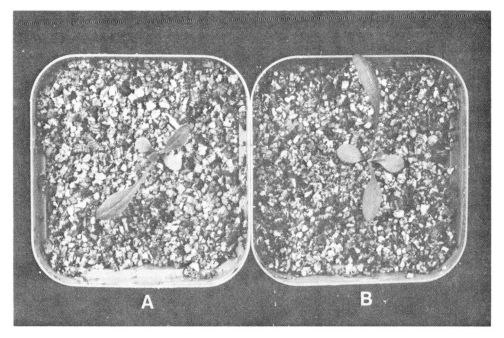

Fig. 3. Knapweed seedlings, A, *Centaurea diffusa*; B, *C. maculosa.*

have very high fibre content with little nutritive value (Fletcher 1961; Popova 1964).

Line transects were established in diffuse knapweed infestations to determine the effect of knapweed on forage yield. Random m² quadrats were harvested and the dry matter yields (kg/ha) of infested and non- infested rangeland were compared (Table 1). The decrease in forage yield at site 2 was significantly ($P < 0.05$) correlated with increased production of knapweed. The site was not stocked with cattle. The other two sites were located on stocked rangeland. Occasionally, large forage and knapweed

Table 1. Dry matter yield (kg/ha) of forage and *Centaurea diffusa* from infested rangeland in B.C.†

Site 1		Site 2		Site 3	
Knapweed	Forage	Knapweed	Forage	Knapweed	Forage
(kg/ha)		(kg/ha)		(kg/ha)	
0	1450	0	880	0	970
0	1440	0	590	0	940
0	1150	0	440	0	630
0	300	0	350	40	320
140	710	10	400	130	170
150	530	60	980	250	540
220	820	150	400	340	260
370	310	290	530	750	840
390	1100	810	20	820	750
660	210	820	70	850	220

†Data calculated from random m² quadrats along line transects.

yields were recorded, indicating that forage may not be available to the cattle under the knapweed overstory.

"Bluebunch wheatgrass–rough fescue" range in "good" condition produces, on the average, 896.8 kg/ha (800 lb/acre) of forage and would have a stocking rate of 0.61 ha (1.5 acre) per animal unit month (McLean and Marchand 1968). Knapweed-infested range may produce only 112 kg/ha (100 lb/acre) of forage resulting in a stocking rate of 4.86 ha (12.0 acre) per animal unit month.

The knapweeds produce allelopathic effects on other plant species. Fletcher and Renney (1963) isolated an inhibitory substance in diffuse and spotted knapweeds with the leaves containing the highest proportions of the inhibitor. The inhibitor was partially characterized as an indole derivative, a possible auxin precursor. There have been no reports of poisoning from diffuse or spotted knapweed.

(b) *Beneficial* — Diffuse and spotted knapweeds are valuable pioneer species. The rapid establishment of plant cover in the form of rosettes on barren soil prevents soil erosion and leads to an accumulation of organic matter. The knapweeds provide substantial pollen and nectar for domestic bees in the interior of British Columbia. However, nectar samples collected from working bees have a bitter taste which lowers the quality of the honey. Spotted knapweed with its bright purple flowers has an aesthetic value, particularly along roadsides. However, this is lost after flowering. Consumption of knapweed seeds by birds or rodents has not been observed, but numerous neat piles of spotted knapweed chaff were observed, indicating rodent utilization of the seed. Diffuse knapweed has been used for amara ("bitters") (Racz et al. 1963) and an antibacterial substance has been isolated

from spotted knapweed (Cavallito and Bailey 1949; Monya et al. 1968). Spotted and diffuse knapweeds are listed as noxious weeds in the Noxious Weeds Act of British Columbia and Manitoba. Ontario lists *Centaurea* species as noxious weeds in its Weed Control Act.

4. Geographical Distribution

Diffuse knapweed is native to Eurasia and spotted knapweed is native to Europe (Frankton and Mulligan 1970). Frankton and Mulligan (1970) indicated that the Canadian distribution of diffuse knapweed was limited to southern B.C. However, Boivin (1972) reported diffuse knapweed at Grassy Lake, Alberta. Spotted knapweed is abundant in B.C., and is common in Ontario, Quebec, and the Maritimes (Moore 1969, 1972; Frankton and Mulligan 1970). Spotted knapweed has also been observed at Carway and Pincher Creek in southern Alberta (V. C. Brink, personal communication). The Canadian distributions of diffuse and spotted knapweeds are illustrated in Fig. 4 and 5. Diffuse and spotted knapweeds are widely distributed in the U.S.A. where significant increases have been observed in recent years (Reed and Hughes 1970). Diffuse knapweed is common in Roumania, Yugoslavia, northern Italy, eastern shore of the Mediterranean, Turkey, Greece, Bulgaria, Asia Minor, Syria, and the U.S.S.R., especially in the Ukraine and the Crimea (Popova 1960). Spotted knapweed is common throughout Europe and western Asia (Englert 1971).

5. Habitat

(a) *Climatic requirements* — The knapweeds are well adapted to the climatic range of the arable southern interior of B.C. (Table 2). Diffuse knapweed is common in the semiarid areas of the Okanagan–Kamloops area of B.C., whereas spotted knapweed is prevalent in the mesic regions of the

Table 2. Climatic ranges of knapweed infested areas in the southern interior of B.C.

Species	Annual mean temp. (C)	Annual ppt. (cm)	April–Aug. ppt. (cm)
C. diffusa	7.2–9.4	24.1–41.7	10.4–18.3
C. maculosa	6.1–7.8	25.1–64.8	14.7–24.9

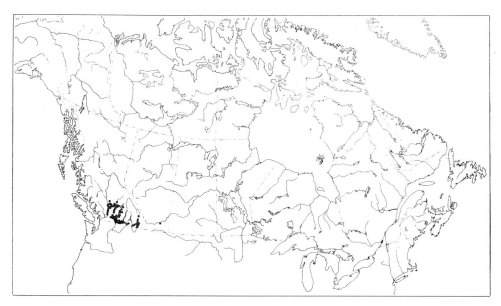

Fig. 4. Canadian distribution of *Centaurea diffusa* (from B.C. survey by A.K.W. and Boivin, 1972).

province. The climatic range of spotted knapweed would possibly explain its wide Canadian distribution. Spotted knapweed has a more northern limit than diffuse knapweed in B.C. The northern boundary of diffuse knapweed in the Crimea is approximately 53°N Lat. (Popova 1960). In B.C. the present northern distribution of diffuse knapweed is 51°N Lat.

Diffuse knapweed has been observed at

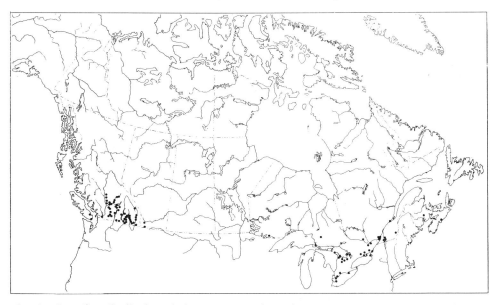

Fig. 5. Canadian distribution of *Centaurea maculosa* (from B.C. survey by A.K.W., herbarium records and Rousseau, 1968).

Table 3. Range of chemical and physical properties of soils infested with *Centaurea diffusa* and *C. maculosa* in B.C.

Measurements	*C. diffusa*	*C. maculosa*
Plant density (plants/m^2)	26–545	138–463
pH (H$_2$O)	5.9–8.4	6.4–7.4
pH (0.01 M CaCl$_2$)	5.3–7.8	5.8–6.4
Conductivity (umhos/cm^2)	93.8–244.3	115.8–128.0
Sulfur (%)	.008–.065	.014–.047
Carbon (%)	0.51–4.04	1.34–3.64
Organic matter (%)	0.87–6.87	2.27–6.19
Nitrogen (%)	0.035–.319	.102–.329
C/N	10.5–15.0	11.5–16.5
Phosphorus (ppm)	1.45–5.43	2.20–3.03
Total exchange capacity (meq/100g)	8.56–32.07	15.34–28.32
Texture (hand method)	Silty clay loam to medium sand	Loam to gravelly loamy sand

altitudes ranging from 150 m to over 900 m, with spotted knapweed ranging from 30 m to over 1,200 m.

(*b*) *Substratum* — Diffuse and spotted knapweeds readily colonize different soils with a wide range of chemical and physical properties (Table 3). The densities of diffuse and spotted knapweeds varied considerably from location to location and were significantly ($P < 0.05$) correlated only with the degree of soil disturbance, which was rated subjectively. The greater the disturbance, the higher the plant density of these knapweeds. These results support the report of Atkinson and Brink (1953) that any soil in the dry interior of B.C. with a disturbed A horizon is subject to knapweed infestation.

(*c*) *Communities in which the species occur* — These knapweed species are not common on cultivated land nor on irrigated pasture. The knapweeds prefer open habitats and are not commonly found in shaded areas. These pioneer species quickly invade disturbed sites and are common along road and railroad right-of-ways, in waste places and on overgrazed rangeland. The density of knapweeds varies from single plants to over 500 plants/m^2 for diffuse and over 400 plants/m^2 for spotted knapweed. The density of the knapweed is dependent upon the age of the infestation and the degree of disturbance of the habitat. The plants associated with knapweed communities are those commonly characteristic of dryland range and pioneer sites in B.C. (Table 4).

6. History

The earliest western collection of diffuse knapweed was made in an alfalfa (*Medicago sativa* L.) field at Bingen, Klickitat County, Washington in 1907 by Suksdorf (Howell 1959). The first B.C. record was at Oyama, in 1936 by Tisdale, followed by subsequent collections (1939-40) by Eastham at Penticton and Grand Forks (Groh 1944). Renney (1959) suggested that diffuse knapweed infestations occurred prior to 1930, as the weed was observed at Lytton and Pritchard at this time. Diffuse knapweed has spread rapidly and has infested 25,952 ha (64,079 acres) of dryland ranges and roadsides in southern interior of B.C.

Spotted knapweed was first collected in Canada at Victoria, B.C. by Macoun in 1893 (Groh 1944). Renney (1959) indicated that extensive infestations of spotted knapweed occurred in B.C. at Canford, west of Merritt, the west arm of Kootenay Lake and in the Slocan Valley. Presently, spotted knapweed infests 3,410 ha (8,420 acres) in B.C.

7. Growth and Development

(*a*) *Morphology* — In addition to their prolific seed production (up to 40,000/m^2), morphological characteristics that contribute to the aggressiveness of these weeds and their absence of control by grazing animals are rosette growth habit, unpalatable and fibrous foliage, and spiny heads. The resistance of knapweed to chemical control may

Table 1. Plant species commonly associated with *Centaurea diffusa* and *C. maculosa* in the southern interior of B.C.

Achillea lanulosa Nutt.	Western yarrow
Agropyron spicatum (Pursh) Rydb.	Bluebunch wheatgrass
Antennaria umbrinella Rydb.	Pussytoes
Astragalus miser Dougl. var. *serotinus* (Gray) Barneby	Timber milk-vetch
Artemisia frigida Willd.	Pasture sage
Balsamorhiza sagittata (Pursh) Nutt.	Balsamroot
Bromus tectorum L.	Downy brome
Chrysothamnus nauseosus (Pall.) Britt.	Stinking rabbitbush
Festuca idahoensis Elmer.	Idaho fescus
Festuca scabrella Torr.	Rough fescue
Koeleria cristata (L.) Pers.	Junegrass
Lappula echinata Gilib.	Bluebur
Lupinus sericeus Pursh	Silky lupine
Poa pratensis L.	Kentucky bluegrass
Poa secunda Presl.	Sandburg's bluegrass
Potentilla recta L.	Sulphur cinquefoil
Rumex acetosella L.	Sheel sorrel
Stipa comata Trin. and Rupr.	Needle-and-thread
Taraxacum officinale Weber	Dandelion
Tragopogon pratensis L.	Meadow goat's-beard
Verbascum thapsus L.	Common mullein

result from pubescence sufficient to limit either retention or penetration of herbicidal sprays (Ormrod and Renney 1968).

(*b*) *Perennation* — The knapweeds overwinter as rosettes or as seeds. Occasionally, severe winter conditions cause rosette mortality. However, the knapweed population is not adversely affected due to the large number of seeds germinating in the spring. Spotted knapweed regrows from the root crowns for a number of years. Diffuse knapweed has been observed to regrow only one season after initial seed production, but this regrowth is not common.

(*c*) *Physiological data* — None are available.

(*d*) *Phenology* — Seeds of diffuse and spotted knapweeds germinate in the fall or early spring when environmental conditions are suitable. Moisture appears to be the most limiting factor in the dry interior of B.C. Seedlings develop into rosettes and maximal root growth occurs in this stage. Plants that have overwintered in a rosette bolt in early May. Diffuse knapweed rosettes produce one stem, rarely two, but spotted knapweed rosettes produce 1–6 stems, and perennial plants commonly produce 15 or more stems. Numerous flower buds are formed in early June. Flowering occurs in July and August, with spotted knapweed flowering about 2 wk earlier than diffuse knapweed. Mature seeds are formed by mid-August. Shedding of seed occurs immediately with spotted knapweed and is delayed with diffuse knapweed. If moisture is adequate the seeds will germinate and develop into rosettes by fall.

(*e*) *Mycorrhiza* — None observed.

8. Reproduction

(*a*) *Floral biology* — The knapweeds are entomophilous, although both diffuse and spotted knapweeds are self-compatible (R. T. Taylor, personal communication). Seed is produced allogamously and there is no evidence of vivipary in diffuse or spotted knapweed populations.

(*b*) *Seed production and dispersal* — The production of diffuse and spotted knapweed seed is illustrated in Table 5. Assuming 80% survival of all seeds, the annual reproductive capacities of diffuse and spotted knapweed plants are 740 and 349, respectively. The average weight per seed of 500 diffuse and

Table 5.   Average seed production of *Centaurea diffusa* and *C. maculosa* in B.C.

Species and location	Flower heads per plant		Seeds per head		Seeds per plant	Annual reproductive capacity
	X̄	SE	X̄	SE		
C. diffusa — rangeland[†]	74.23 ±	8.24	12.46 ±	2.06	925	740
C. maculosa — rangeland	16.35 ±	4.44	26.64 ±	2.88	436	349
C. diffusa — irrigated[‡]	1403.66 ±	303.11	13.00 ±	1.72	18,248	14,598
C. maculosa — irrigated	706.66 ±	64.81	35.75 ±	4.00	25,263	20,210

[†]Data collected from a number of natural rangeland infestations near Kamloops, B.C.
[‡]Data collected from plants grown in irrigated plots at Kamloops, B.C.

500 spotted knapweed seeds was 1.099 mg and 1.778 mg, respectively.

Seed dispersal of diffuse knapweed is mainly by wind as the mature plants break off at ground level and become "tumbleweeds" or become attached to vehicles. The achenes are individually dispensed through the small distal opening in the flower heads. Dispersal close to the parent plant is facilitated by horizontally placed involucres, which open as dehydration occurs, dropping their achenes readily (Atkinson and Brink 1953). The majority of diffuse knapweed heads remain closed in the fall.

Spotted knapweed does not break off at ground level, and populations extend largely through peripheral enlargement of existing stands. Seed dispersal is achieved by a flicking action which spreads seeds up to a meter from the parent plant. Dehydration and subsequent opening of the bracts of spotted knapweed heads, 2-3 wk after maturity, enables the loosely held achenes to be expelled from the head if movement of the stem occurs. Released achenes may become attached to passing animals and be transported some distance from the parent plant.

(c) *Viability of seeds and germination* — The effect of light, temperature and depth of sowing on germination of these two weed species was studied. A linear temperature gradient bar was constructed with temperatures along the bar ranging from 7 to 34 C (± 0.5 C). The effect of light was studied in growth chambers with a constant tempera-

ture of 25 C. Studies to determine the effect of sowing depth on percent germination and subsequent seedling emergence were conducted under greenhouse conditions. Seeds were sown at depths of 0, 0.5, 1, 3 and 5 cm in 12.5 cm pots filled with greenhouse soil. Soils were brought to field capacity daily.

Diffuse and spotted knapweed seeds germinated readily over a broad range of environmental conditions. Diffuse knapweed seed that has been retained in the flower head overwinter under field conditions exhibited 88% germination. Seeds removed from knapweed heads at maturity exhibited 40% germination for diffuse and 20% for spotted knapweed. Twenty-five-day-old seed stored under dry conditions exhibited 68 and 80% germination, respectively. The above germination tests were conducted on moist filter paper at 20 C.

Continuous light significantly ($P < 0.05$) reduced the germination of both species after 2, 4 and 6 days (Table 6). There were no significant differences between the germination of the two species in the light-plus-dark and dark treatments after 4 and 6 days. However, after 2 days, germination of spotted knapweed in the dark was significantly ($P < 0.05$) greater than diffuse knapweed in the dark and significantly greater than both species in the light-plus-dark treatment.

Germination of both species occurred over the temperature range of 7–34 C (Fig. 6). Germination of over 80% occurred in the range of 13–28 C for diffuse and 10–

Table 6. The effect of light on germination of *Centaurea diffusa* and *C. maculosa* at 25 C

Species	Treatment	Duration (days)		
		Two	Four	Six
C. diffusa	Light (24 h)	58† c‡	67 b	72 b
	Dark (24 h)	69 b	83 a	87 a
	Light (12 h) + dark (12 h)	69 b	83 a	87 a
C. maculosa	Light (24 h)	58 c	67 b	72 b
	Dark (24 h)	82 a	83 a	87 a
	Light (12 h) + dark (12 h)	69 b	83 a	87 a

†Adjusted means.
‡Means in the same column sharing the same letter do not differ significantly at the 5% level according to simple multiple regression.

28 C for spotted knapweed. Germination of both species was delayed at the lower temperatures with spotted knapweed showing higher cumulative percent germination at 7 and 10 C than diffuse knapweed. Diffuse knapweed exhibited higher germination at the warmest temperature at the end of the experiment. Optimum temperatures were calculated from the fitted curves drawn from the regression analysis (Table 7). These results suggest that spotted knapweed will germinate at slightly lower temperatures than diffuse knapweed which is consistent with its more northern distribution in B.C.

Twenty-four days after sowing, spotted knapweed exhibited a significantly ($P <$ 0.05) larger cumulative percent emergence than diffuse knapweed at all sowing depths (Fig. 7). The optimum emergence of both species was at the soil surface but spotted knapweed was capable of emergence from 5 cm. Diffuse knapweed did not emerge from depths below 3 cm which confirmed Popova's (1960) findings.

Seedling mortality was recorded in the emergence study. Under greenhouse conditions, 7.6 and 4.0% of the diffuse and spotted knapweeds died. Seedling mortality in the field was observed to be over 55% in some instances, but generally was approximately 12% in quadrats where phenological data were obtained.

(*d*) *Vegetative reproduction* — Vegetative reproduction does not naturally occur in diffuse knapweed populations. However, spotted knapweed does reproduce vegetatively. A number of lateral shoots arise just beneath the soil surface and grow horizon-

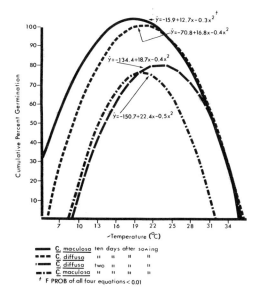

Fig. 6. Effect of temperature on germination of *Centaurea diffusa* and *C. maculosa* (curves fitted from regression analysis).

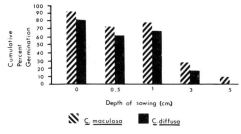

Fig. 7. Seedling emergence of *Centaurea diffusa* and *C. maculosa* when seed was sown at different soil depths.

71

Table 7. Optimum germination temperatures for *Centaurea diffusa* and *C. maculosa*

Time after sowing (days)	Optimum temperature (C)	
	C. Diffusa	C. maculosa
1	25.5†	22.9
2	23.0	21.6
3	21.8	20.8
4	21.0	20.3
5	20.6	19.6
6	20.6	19.4
7	20.5	19.4
8	20.5	19.0
9	20.5	19.0
10	20.5	19.0

†Calculated from regression analysis – see Figure 6.

tally for approximately 3 cm before forming a rosette. These rosettes mature the following season, but do not become detached from the parent root stock. The triennial habit of diffuse knapweed results from regrowth of the parent rootstock and not from the development of lateral shoots. The knapweeds are particularly well adapted to reproduction by seeds. The reproductive strategy was not observed to be different in the various habitats of the two species.

9. Hybrids

Hybridization between diffuse and spotted knapweed was suspected because of the variation which appeared in populations of diffuse knapweed (Renney 1959). However, cytological studies by Moore and Frankton (1954) did not reveal any plants with a triploid chromosome number which would be expected if hybridization between diffuse knapweed ($2n = 18$) and spotted knapweed ($2n = 36$) had occurred. R. T. Taylor (personal communication) has confirmed these results and suggests that the degree of variation within the diffuse knapweed populations is possibly due to more than one introduction of the species into the area. He also suggests that the variable genotypes expressed by flower color in diffuse knapweed populations may be due to loose multiple gene control.

10. Population Dynamics

In recent years diffuse and spotted knapweeds have spread rapidly and have colonized large acreages of semiarid rangeland in the southern interior of B.C. Disturbance of any area by overgrazing or by road construction has resulted in rapid establishment of knapweed populations. Plots on the perimeter of knapweed infestations on overgrazed rangeland became completely covered with knapweed after one season. Knapweed populations in well managed rangelands do not increase rapidly.

Diffuse knapweed generally forms large dense infestations, but solitary plants and small patches are common in recently invaded areas. Spotted knapweed has a more patchy distribution, but large stands are not uncommon in areas where the weed has become well established. The mean length of life of diffuse knapweed plants is 2 yr and 3–5 yr for spotted knapweed plants. Ample seed is produced by both species each year. Numerous seedlings can be observed in the fall, with a characteristic flush of seedlings in the spring. If dry conditions prevail after seedling emergence, many seedlings perish.

The aggressive knapweeds are strong competitors and exhibit allelopathic effects on associated species establishing essentially single-species stands (Fletcher and Renney 1963).

11. Response to Herbicides and Other Chemicals

Popova (1960) reported that 2,4-D at 1 kg/ha completely eliminated diffuse knapweed and associated forbs. Furrer and Fertig (1965) reported complete control of spotted knapweed with 2,4-D at 1.5 kg/ha and with dicamba at 1 kg/ha. Control of the knapweeds with 2,4-D was found to be temporary and did not prevent heavy seedling establishment in the fall in trials conducted in B.C. (Renney and Hughes 1969). Renney and Hughes reported that picloram (4-amino-3,6-trichloropicolinic acid) exhibited selective control of diffuse and spotted knapweeds for 3 to 4 yr on semiarid rangeland sites in the interior of B.C. Picloram is presently recommended at the rate of 0.42-0.56 kg/ha (6-8 oz/acre) for the control of diffuse and spotted knapweed in B.C. (British Columbia Department of Agriculture 1971). The long residual life and high cost of this herbicide has limited its use.

12. Response to Other Human Manipulations

(a) *Cultivation* — Popova (1960) found that shallow plowing (7 cm) did not control diffuse knapweed, but deep plowing (18 cm) eliminated knapweed with subsequent vigorous grass growth. Atkinson and Brink (1953) found regeneration from plowed-under crowns of diffuse knapweed was not common, but incompletely covered crowns regenerated readily.

(b) *Fertilizer* — The application of fertilizer on areas heavily infested with knapweed enhanced the weed growth (Popova 1960).

(c) *Mowing* — Populations of diffuse knapweed in the Crimea increased after mowing (Popova 1960). The rosettes of the knapweeds escape mowing, but the bolting and fruiting stems can be mown. Meter-square plots were mown with a hand scythe once at the bud stage, once at flowering or once at bud stage and again at flowering. A significant ($P < 0.05$) reduction in the number of plants that produced seed occurred in all treatments and the percent germination was significantly ($P < 0.05$) reduced by mowing in the flowering stage and by mowing twice (Table 8). Secondary flowering, with capitula forming below the cutting height, was observed in diffuse knapweed populations.

(d) *Burning* — Burning has been shown to be an effective control measure of diffuse knapweed with vigorous grass regrowth (Popova 1960). However, burning is not ac-

ceptable for most rangelands in B.C. because of associated forest areas.

(e) *Integrated control* — Hubbard (1970) has established plots to determine the effects of several variables on the control of diffuse knapweed. His results indicate that forage production can be substantially increased through proper management practices in dryland situations. Where native grasses have been drastically reduced, reseeding to crested wheatgrass (*Agropyron cristatum* (L.) Gaertn.) increased forage yields. The major limiting factor in the use of cultural control methods for rangeland is the difficulty with rough terrain since much of the area infested with knapweeds is not suitable for common farm implements.

13. Response to Parasites

(a) *Insects and other non-domestic organisms* —

I. *Centaurea diffusa*

INSECTA (Majority of data from M. G. Maw, unpublished)

DIPTERA.

Trypetidae: *Urophora affinis* Frfld., (biology from Zwölfer 1970) larvae form galls within the receptacle of flower heads reducing seed production, host range restricted to diffuse and spotted knapweed, released as a biological control agent near Kamloops, B.C. in 1970; populations increasing, but not sufficient to cause stand reduction.

HEMIPTERA.

The following insects were swept from diffuse knapweed at Pritchard, B.C. (the biology from Britton 1923 and Kelton 1955).

Lygacidae: *Nysins thymi* (Wolff), general feeder.

Table 8. The effects of mowing on *Centaurea diffusa* and *C. maculosa*

Treatment	No. seed producers at end of Aug.	Germination of seed formed by end of Aug. (%)
1 mowing (bud stage)	7.8† a*	48.0 b
1 mowing (flower stage)	0.3 a	17.9 a
2 mowings (bud and flower stage)	1.2 a	19.9 a
Control	34.3	91.1 b

*Means in the same column sharing the same letter do not differ significantly at the 5% level according to Duncan's New Multiple Range Test.
†There was no difference between species, therefore, data is combined.

Miridae: *Campylomma verbasci* (Meyer), reproduces on *Verbascum thapsus* L. and occasionally on *Malus sylvestris* Mill., often associated with aphids; *Lygus shulli* (Kngt.), breeds on *Solidago* spp., *Cirsium arvense* and occasionally on alfalfa.

HOMOPTERA.

Cicadelidae: (biology from Beirne 1956) The following were swept from diffuse knapweed at Pritchard, B.C.: *Aceratagallia sanguinolenta* Prov., alfalfa, *Trifolium* spp., *Aster* spp. and other herbaceous plants are hosts, common throughout Canada where alfalfa grows; *Auridius flavidus* Beir., grass hosts; *Colladonus geminatus* (Van D.), widely distributed, common in southern British Columbia, vector of a number of virus diseases of *Prunus* spp., *Empoasca filamenta* Del., variety of host plants, common in semiarid regions; *Macrostele fascifrons* (Stal.), common, found on grasses and herbaceous species throughout Canada, virus vector.

Pseudococcinae: (biology from Essig 1958). *Phenacoccus* sp. nr. *solani* Ferris, root feeder, infests roots of numerous plants, common, on diffuse and spotted knapweeds in southern interior of B.C.

LEPIDOPTERA.

Nymphalidae: (biology from Essig 1958). *Vanessa cardui* (Linn.), larvae cause periodic defoliation of a number of Compositae and other hosts, widely distributed.

II. *Centaurea maculosa*

INSECTA (Majority of data from M. G. Maw, unpublished)

DIPTERA.

Trypetidae: *Urophora affinis* Frfld. (see above).

COLEOPTERA.

Chrysomelidae: (biology from Blake 1955). *Graphops curtipennis* Mels. known hosts are *Hypericum perforatum* and *Asyrum hypericoidus*, may be chance capture on *Centaurea maculosa*. *Monoxia* sp.

HEMIPTERA.

The following insects were swept from spotted knapweed at Chase, B.C. (biology from Britton 1923):

Lygacidae: *Geocoris bullatus* (Say), common about roots of grasses and weeds; *Nysins thymi* (Wolff), general plant feeder; *Ortholomus scolopan* (Say).

Scutelloridae: *Homaemus bijugis* (Uhler), feeds on many species of herbaceous plants.

HOMOPTERA.

Cicadellidae: (biology from Beirne 1956). The following were swept from spotted knapweed at Chase, B.C.: *Aceratagallia sanguinolenta* Prov.; *Chlorotettix unicolor* (Fitch), occurs in grasslands, widely distributed in Canada; *Empoasca filamenta* DeL.; *Gyponana hasta* Del., vector of California aster yellows, common in southern B.C.; *Macrosteles fascifrons* (Stal.); *Sorhoanus debilis* (Uhl.), local in grasslands of southern B.C.; *Xerophloea viridis* (Fab.), grass hosts, grassland regions of the western provinces.

Pseudococcinae: *Phenacoccus* sp. nr. *solani* Ferris (see above).

LEPIDOPTERA.

Gelechiidae: *Metzneria paucipunctella* Zel. (biology from Englert 1971), larvae feed within flower heads, host range restricted to spotted knapweed, released in 1973, but not recovered at two sites in B.C.

(*b*) *Microorganisms and viruses* —

I. *C. diffusa*

FUNGI

ASCOMYCETES.

Sclerotinia sclerotiorum (Lib.) deBary (DAOM 137933), ubiquous wilt pathogen, damage to numerous crops, observed locally at Vernon, B.C.

DEUTEROMYCETES.

Microsphaeropsis centaureae Morgan-Jones, leaf necrosis, may be pathogenic to some crops, parasitizes the sclerotia of *S. sclerotiorum*.

II. *C. maculosa*

None observed, but *M. centaureae* will cause leaf necrosis under laboratory conditions.

A number of *Puccinia* (Basidomycetes) have been reported on diffuse and spotted knapweeds in Europe and Asia (Guyot

1967; Savile 1970, 1973). These *Puccinia* species may prove to be valuable biological control agents of diffuse and spotted knapweeds in Canada.

ACKNOWLEDGMENTS

The authors are grateful for the co-operation and assistance of Dr. P. Harris, Dr. J. E. Miltimore, M. G. Maw, and B.C. Dep. Agric. personnel at Kamloops, Vernon and Cranbrook, B.C. The assistance of Dr. G. W. Eaton with statistical analysis is gratefully appreciated. Technical assistance of A. Harris, I. Derics and J. Gibson is appreciated. Financial support from the Bostock Grant and National Research Council of Canada (bursary to A.K.W.) is acknowledged.

ATKINSON, T. G. and BRINK, V. C. 1953. Progress report on the biology and control of diffuse knapweed (*Centaurea diffusa* Lam.) in British Columbia. Dep. Agronomy, Univ. of British Columbia, Vancouver, B.C.

BRITISH COLUMBIA DEPARTMENT OF AGRICULTURE. 1971. Chemical Weed Control Guide 1972-73. B.C. Dep. Agric. Publ., by Authority of the Minister of Agriculture, Victoria, B.C. 86 pp.

BEIRNE, B. P. 1956. Leafhoppers (Homoptera: Cicadellidae) of Canada and Alaska. Can. Entomol. Vol. 88, Supplement No. 2. 180 pp.

BLAKE, D. H. 1955. A study of LeConte's species of the chrysomelid genus *Graphops* with descriptions of some new species. Bull. Mus. Comp. Zool. 113: 263–301.

BOIVIN, B. 1972. Flora of the Prairie Provinces. Phytologia 22–23, Part III. 224 pp.

BRITTON, W. E. 1923. The Hemiptera or sucking insects of Connecticut. Guide to the insects of Connecticut. Part IV. State Geological and Natural History Survey. Paper No. 47. Bulletin No. 34. Hartford, Connecticut. 807 pp. 20 plates.

CANADA WEED COMMITTEE. 1969. Common and botanical names of weeds in Canada. Can. Dep. Agric. Publ. 1397. 67 pp.

CAVALLITO, C. J. and BAILEY, J. H. 1949. An antibacterial principle from *Centaurea maculosa*. J. Bacteriol. 57: 207–212.

ENGLERT, W. 1971. *Metzneria paucipunctella* Zel. (Gelechiidae:Lepidoptera): a potential insect for the biological control of *Centaurea stoebe* L. in Canada. Prog. Rep. Commonw. Inst. Biol. Control 28: 1–12.

ESSIG, E. O. 1958. Insects and mites of western North America. Macmillan Company, New York, N.Y. 1050 pp.

FERRON, M. et CAYOUETTE, R. 1964. Noms des mauvaises herbes du Québec. Minist. Agric. et Colonization du Québec. Publ. 288. 113 pp.

FLETCHER, R. A. 1961. A growth inhibitor found in *Centaurea* spp. M.Sc. Thesis, Dep. Plant Science, University of British Columbia, Vancouver, B.C.

FLETCHER, R. A. and RENNEY, A. J. 1963. A growth inhibitor found in *Centaurea* spp. Can. J. Plant Sci. 43: 475–481.

FRANKTON, C. 1958. Les mauvaises herbes du Canada. Minist. Agric. Can. Publ. 948. 198 pp.

FRANKTON, C. and MULLIGAN, G. A. 1970. Weeds of Canada. Can. Dep. Agric. Publ. 948. 217 pp.

FURRER, A. H. and FERTIG, S. N. 1965. Progress report on herbicide treatments for the control of spotted knapweed (*Centaurea maculosa*). Proc. 19th Northeast. Weed Contr. Conf. pp. 324–326.

GROH, H. 1944. Canadian weed survey. 2nd Ann. Rep. Can. Dep. Agric. 74 pp.

GUYOT, A. L. 1967. Les rouilles des Centaurées. Uredineana 6: 59–61.

HOWELL, J. T. 1959. Distributional data on weedy thistles in western North America. Leafl. West. Bot. 9: 17–29.

HUBBARD, W. A. 1970. Knapweed control. Canadex 641. Can. Dep. Agric.

KELTON, L. A. 1955. Species of *Lygus*, *Liocoris* and their allies in the prairie provinces of Canada (Hemiptera:Miridae). Can. Entomol. 87: 531–556.

McLEAN, A. and MARCHAND, L. 1968. Grassland ranges in the southern interior of British Columbia. Can. Dep. Agric. Publ. 1319. 28 pp.

MONYA, M., SABAU, M. and RACZ, G. 1968. Die antibiotische Wirkung von Auszügen aus *Centaurea-Arten* [English summary]. Planta Med. 16: 58–62.

MOORE, R. J. 1969. How weedy thistles came to Canada. Greenhouse–Garden–Glass. 8: 1–2.

MOORE, R. J. 1972. Distribution of native and introduced knapweeds (*Centaurea*) in Canada and the United States. Rhodora 74: 331–346.

MOORE, R. J. and FRANKTON, C. 1954. Cytotaxonomy of three species of *Centaurea* adventive in Canada. Can. J. Bot. 32: 182–186.

ORMROD, D. J. and RENNEY, A. J. 1968. A survey of weed leaf stomata and trichomes. Can. J. Plant Sci. 48: 197–209.

POPOVA, A. YA. 1960. *Centaurea diffusa* Lam., a steppe-pasture weed in the Crimea [English transl.]. Bot. Zh. (Moscow) 45: 1207–1213.

POPOVA, A. YA. 1964. Composition of nutritional substances of *Centaurea diffusa* Lam. in Crimea [English transl.]. Bot. Zh. (Moscow) **49**: 863–865.

RACZ, A., AUGUSTIN, G., and RACZ-KO-TILLA, E. 1963. Valorificarea speciilor indigene de centaura ca plante medicinale cu continut in princippii amare [English transl.]. Lucrarile Grandini Bot. Bucuresti 1961/1962 (1): 521–524.

REED, C. F. and HUGHES, R. O. 1970. Selected weeds of the United States. U.S. Dep. Agric., Handb. **366**. 463 pp.

RENNEY, A. J. 1959. *Centaurea* spp. infestation in British Columbia. Proc. Joint Meet. North Cent. Weed Control Conf. **16** and West. Can. Weed Control Conf. **10**: 18–19.

RENNEY, A. J. and HUGHES, E. C. 1969. Control of knapweed, *Centaurea* species in British Columbia with Tordon herbicides. Down to Earth **24**: 6–8.

ROUSSEAU, C. 1968. Histoire, habitat et distribution de 220 plantes introduit au Québec. Nat. Can. (Qué.) **95**: 49–169.

SAVILE, D. B. O. 1970. Some Eurasian *Puccinia* species attacking Cardueae. Can. J. Bot. **48**: 1553–1566.

SAVILE, D. B. O. 1973. A variety of *Puccinia centaureae* on *Centaurea diffusa*. Can. J. Bot. **51**: 1077–1078.

ZWÖLFER, H. 1970. Investigations on the host-specificity of *Urophora affinis* Frfld. (Diptera, Trypetidae). Prog. Rep. Commonw. Inst. Biol. Control no. **25**. 28 pp.

THE BIOLOGY OF CANADIAN WEEDS
7. *Myrica pensylvanica* Loisel.

IVAN V. HALL[1]

Agriculture Canada: [1]Research Station, Kentville, Nova Scotia B4N 1J5.
Received 15 July 1974, accepted 30 Aug. 1974.

HALL, IVAN V. 1975. The biology of Canadian weeds. 7. *Myrica pensylvanica* Loisel. Can. J. Plant Sci. **55**: 163–169.

Myrica pensylvanica Loisel., bayberry (Myricaceae) is a native shrub occurring mainly along or near the seacoast of the Maritime Provinces. *M. pensylvanica* grows on light sandy soils that are highly acidic, and is the major weed problem of lowbush blueberry (*Vaccinium angustifolium* Ait. and *V. myrtilloides* Michx.) fields developed on the Culloden soil series in Prince Edward Island. Lateral growth of *M. pensylvanica* is by rhizome, and following burning, new shoots grow from dormant buds of the stem or rhizome. Due to the waxy nature of the upper surface of the leaves, *M. pensylvanica* is quite resistant to salt spray and the herbicides 2,4-D and 2,4,5-T in oil applied to cut branches will control this weed.

Le cirier de Pennsylvanie *Myrica pensylvanica* Loisel, (Myricacées) est un arbuste indigène que l'on rencontre surtout sur le littoral des provinces Maritimes. Il pousse sur des sols sableux légers fortement acides; c'est l'adventice la plus nuisible des bleuetières (*Vaccinium angustifolium* Ait. et *V. myrtilloides* Michx.) établies sur les séries de sols Culloden de l'Île-du-Prince-Édouard. La croissance latérale de *M. pensylvanica* se fait par rhizome, et, après brûlage, les bourgeons dormants de la tige ou du rhizome produisent de nouvelles pousses. La nature cireuse de la surface supérieure des feuilles de *M. pensylvanica* lui permet de résister assez bien aux embruns marins. On peut le détruire par des émulsions d'herbicide 2,4-D et 2,4,5-T dans l'huile appliquées à la surface de coupe des branches.

1. Name

Myrica pensylvanica Loisel. — **bayberry** (Canada Weed Committee 1969), **candleberry**; **arbre à cire.** Myricaceae, wax-myrtle family, Myricacées.

2. Description and Account of Variation

A woody shrub up to 2.5 m in height, reproducing from the seed of a nutlet and growing laterally by rhizomes; plants dioecious, the male and female catkins (aments) are on different individuals (Fig. 2B); bark of previous year's growth brown with glands and hairs, bark of older wood sooty gray; leaves aromatic when crushed, nearly entire, oblanceolate, obtuse at the apex, acute at the base; male catkins up to 1.2 cm in length, borne directly on previous year's wood; female catkins borne similarly and up to 1.0 cm in length; fruit a gray nutlet (2.5–3 mm in diam) covered with wax.

Stokes (1937) reported that the haploid number of chromosomes in three species of *Myrica* including *M. caroliniensis* = *M. pensylvanica* was eight. His plants came from Valdosta, Georgia. Vegetative buds of *M. pensylvanica* from near Kentville, Nova Scotia had $2n = 16$.

The species most closely resembling *M. pensylvanica* is the congeneric species *M. gale* L. In *M. gale* the catkins are borne at the end of the previous year's growth, whereas in *M. pensylvanica* they occur along the entire length of the previous year's growth. The nutlets of *M. pensylvanica* are covered with wax and are without bracts, whereas the fruit of *M. gale* has two bracts and has no appreciable wax coating.

At the two-leaf stage, the most distinctive feature of the seedling is the bright red color of the stem below the cotyledons. The cotyledons are nearly oval in shape, being 5 cm in length in the direction of the petiole and 4 cm at right angles to this axis. The first true leaves are bronze in color and are serrate near the apex.

3. Economic Importance

(a) Detrimental — *Myrica pensylvanica* is the major weed problem in stands of lowbush blueberries (*Vaccinium angustifolium* Ait. and *V. myrtilloides* Michx.) on the Culloden soil series of eastern Prince Edward Island. These soils account for about 14% of the area of that province (Whiteside 1965). In the summer of 1973, it cost $180.00 per hectare to remove *M. pensylvanica* from a stand of lowbush blueberries with a herbicide treatment of 2,4,5-T in oil (K. Yeo, personal communication).

Although prolonged exposure to quantities of pollen of this species may cause some irritation to the eyes and nose, *M. pensylvanica* is not a major cause of hay fever. Bassett and Crompton (1969) found only very small amounts of pollen from *Myrica* spp. in their survey of air-borne pollen of Eastern Canada. The general period of collection for pollen grains of this type was from 9 to 20 May. Probably this pollen was produced on plants growing farther west, as examination of herbarium specimens showed the period of pollen production from local plants to be 13 to 29 June.

(b) Beneficial — The wax from the fruit of *M. pensylvanica* was melted and used by the early settlers of Prince Edward Island in the making of candles (Erskine 1960). The fruit of a closely related species, *M. cerifera* L., was widely collected for the same purpose in southeastern United States (U.S. Dep. Agric. Forest Service 1948). The dormant branches of female plants with the attractive gray fruit are used to decorate window boxes in winter.

(c) Legislation — *Myrica pensylvanica* is not listed in any Canadian, federal or provincial, weed or seeds act.

4. Geographical Distribution

Myrica pensylvanica has a rather unique distribution in Canada (Fig. 1). It is only found in Ontario next to the sandy beach at Turkey Point, Charlotteville Township, Norfolk Co. (Soper and Heimburger 1961). In the Province of Quebec, it occurs only in the Magdalen Islands (Marie-Victorin 1964). *M. pensylvanica* has been found on the Burin Peninsula of Newfoundland (Rouleau 1956). In the Maritime Provinces its main occurrence is along the seacoast.

5. Habitat

(a) Climatic requirements — *Myrica pensylvanica* occurs in an area of Canada having 2,500 to 3,500 degree-days above 5.6 C (Can. Dep. of Energy, Mines and Resources 1970). The average length of the frost-free period in this region ranges from 100 to 140 days. Since *M. pensylvanica* grows very close to the sea, the average date of the end of the growing season is 5 to 25 November. The start of the growing season occurs between 15 April and 5 May. The average daily minimum temperature for February in the range of *M. pensylvanica* varies from -15 to -5 C, while the average daily maximum temperature varies from -5 to 5 C. The average daily minimum temperature for July in the area where *M. pensylvanica* occurs varies from 10 to 15 C, while the average daily maximum temperature varies from 20 to 30 C. The habitat of *M. pensylvanica* receives from 25.4 to 50.8 cm of precipitation from April to September.

(b) Substratum — *Myrica pensylvanica* becomes the most serious weed problem in the blueberry fields of the Culloden soil series of eastern Prince Edward Island. These fine sandy loams are naturally very strongly acid and have developed on water-worked sandy till (Whiteside 1965).

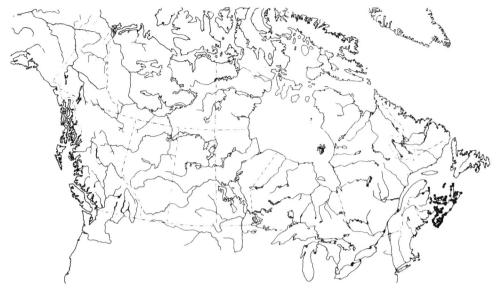

Fig. 1. Canadian distribution of *Myrica pensylvanica* from specimens in the herbaria of Department of Agriculture Herbarium, Ottawa, Ontario; National Herbarium, National Museum of Canada, Ottawa, Ontario; and Acadia University, Wolfville, Nova Scotia.

(c) Communities in which the species occurs — Erskine (1960) reports that if pastures are neglected on Prince Edward Island they soon revert to a stand of white spruce, *Picea glauca* (Moench) Voss. *M. pensylvanica* is one of the first woody shrubs to invade the area, but within 15 yr white spruce has shaded it out. *M. pensylvanica* is also the first woody species to colonize sand dunes. Fernald (1950) states that it occurs, in general, on dry or wet sterile soil near the coast or on the Coastal Plain. The abundance and frequency of *M. pensylvanica* in a lowbush blueberry field of Kings County, Prince Edward Island are given in Table 1.

In the literature, no information was found on the proportion of male to female plants in natural stands. Counts of male and female plants from three fields showed a slightly higher number of male than female plants. Field no. 1 near Sheffield Mills, Kings Co., Nova Scotia had 52 female and 61 male plants. Field no. 2 near Kentville, Nova Scotia had 38 female and 52 male

plants. Field no. 3 at Mount Vernon, Kings Co., Prince Edward Island had 138 female and 139 male plants. Counts were taken on the two fields in Nova Scotia on 5 June 1974 and for the one in Prince Edward Island on 20 June 1974.

Table 1. Frequency of occurrence of *Myrica pensylvanica* and associated species, 100 points on a 100-m line transect at Mount Vernon, Kings Co., Prince Edward Island (Data collected 14 May 1974)

Bare ground	1
Polytrichum commune Hedw.	1
Agropyron repens (L.) Beauv.	1
Danthonia spicata (L.) Beauv.	1
Agrostis tenuis Sibth.	2
Salix bebbiana Sarg.	3
Myrica pensylvanica Loisel.	46†
Betula populifolia Marsh.	3
Alnus rugosa (Du Roi) Spring	7
Rosa micrantha Sm.	1
Vaccinium myrtilloides Michx.	4
Vaccinium angustifolium Ait.	30

†At each location where *Myrica pensylvanica* occurred the number of stems of this species per 20 cm² was counted and the mean was 4.6±0.2 SE (46).

6. History

Myrica pensylvanica is a native species that has formed a part of the flora of coastal communities for quite some time. It probably moved into the Atlantic Provinces from eastern United States following the retreat of the last glacial ice.

7. Growth and Development

(a) Morphology — The upper surface of the leaves is quite waxy, a factor that prevents the salt of the ocean spray from penetrating into the leaves. The young rhizome of *M. pensylvanica* is more succulent than that of many ericaceous shrubs due to the presence of a wide layer of cortex (Fig. 2C). A considerable layer of cortex is also found in ₊ne young root (Fig. 2D). Laycock (1967) found in upland communities of New Jersey that some roots of *M. pensylvanica* extend as deep as 75 cm. He also found that the rhizomes grow mainly in the organic matter

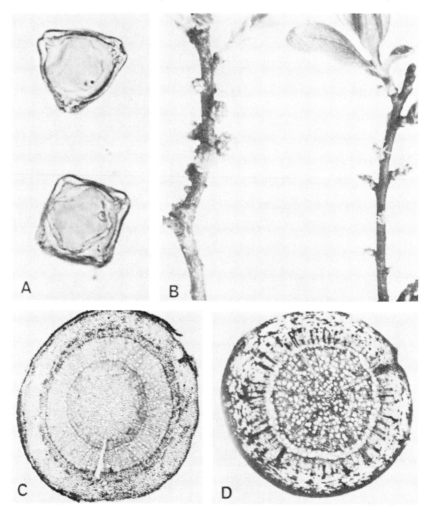

Fig. 2. A. Pollen (75×): the normal triporate type (above); the tetraporate type (below). B. Branches of male (left) and female (right) plants with their respective catkins (0.75×). C. Cross section of rhizome (32×). D. Cross section of root of *M. pensylvanica* (18×).

layer. Excavations of plants in Nova Scotia and Prince Edward Island have also shown that the rhizomes are in the top 5 cm of soil.

(b) Perennation — *Myrica pensylvanica* is a chamaephyte that passes the winter in a dormant state. In winter, female plants are conspicuous with their persistent gray fruit attached to the short receptacle. If the fruits have been removed, the ends of the receptacles are nearly as sharp as thorns. The male plants can easily be mistaken for sterile female plants.

(c) Physiological data — None is available.

(d) Phenology — In the Maritime Provinces vegetative growth of *M. pensylvanica* begins about 24 May. The resumption of growth in this species is decidedly later than in many other species growing in the same habitat. For instance, *Vaccinium angustifolium* Ait. and *Comptonia peregrina* (L.) Coult. are nearly at anthesis on this date. Male catkins start to shed pollen about mid-June and continue to do so until the end of the month. Pistils of the female inflorescences are sufficiently advanced during this same period to receive the pollen. Fruits are about one-third final size by the 3rd wk of July and a month later are full size. Wax develops on the nutlets during late August or the first week of September.

(e) Mycorrhiza — Mycorrhiza have not been reported for *M. pensylvanica* (Harley 1969) but root nodule bacteria are present. Fred et al. (1932) state, "The nodules on the roots of *Myrica* are unique in having at their tips elongated, slender, root-like processes which are in reality extensions of the control cylinder of the modified root." These same authors consider that the bacterium present in the nodules is a species of *Rhizobacterium* and that the relationship is pathogenic rather than symbiotic.

8. Reproduction

(a) Floral biology — Pollination in *M. pensylvanica* is by wind. The catkins of the male plants produce clouds of pollen when agitated by wind or other sources. A brief description of the pollen is as follows: grains triporate, rarely tetraporate; grains circular to triangular in polar view, 25–35 μ (microns), avg 29 μ in diam; pores equally distributed around the equator of the grain, 2.5–3.5 μ in diam; circular; annulus (including pore) up to 10 μ in diam, scabrate sculpturing; tectate structure; complete wall 2 μ thick (Fig. 2A).

(b) Seed production and dispersal — There is one seed per fruit. The mean number of nutlets per inflorescence was 2.82±0.17 (SE), as based on 60 observations. The number of nutlets per plant is related to the age and size of the plant. Two plants, 1 m in diam, averaged 2,446 nutlets with a weight of 64.9 g. The weight of the wood producing this weight of fruit was 446.5 g. Seeds are dispersed by birds and rodents. According to Martin et al. (1951), 25–50% of the diet of tree swallows along the Atlantic coast consists of bayberries. These are practically the only fruits in their diet.

(c) Viability of seeds and germination — In contrast to *Kalmia angustifolia* L. (Hall et al. 1973) and *Spiraea latifolia* (Ait.) Borkh. (Hall et al. 1974) seeds of *M. pensylvanica* obtained from freshly harvested fruits were difficult to germinate. A sample of 50 seeds collected from the wild, placed in the glasshouse at approximately 20 C on 28 November 1973, and held under those conditions until 26 March 1974, failed to germinate. In addition, no differences were noted among seeds planted on the surface of the soil, planted under 1 cm of soil, or planted in synthetic media. Another sample of 360 seeds was held in cold storage at 0 C from 22 January to 24 April 1974. Then the seeds were allowed to grow in soil at 20 C in the glasshouse and germinated 20% by 2 June 1974. In 1974, a different plant of *M. pensylvanica* was dug each week to note the date when rhizome growth began. The plant dug on 5 June had a piece of new rhizome 5 cm in length.

9. Hybrids

Although the two species of *Myrica, M. gale* and *M. pensylvanica* flowered at approximately the same time, no evidence of hydridization between them has been reported.

10. Population Dynamics

On Prince Edward Island, seedlings of *M. pensylvanica* quickly establish in neglected pastures of the Culloden soil series Erskine (1960). Browntop, *Agrostis tenuis* Sibth. gives way to hawkweeds, *Hieracium* spp.; goldenrods, *Solidago* spp.; and asters, *Aster* spp., and these in turn are followed by *Vaccinium angustifolium* Ait. and *M. pensylvanica*. In 10–15 years, *M. pensylvanica* is shaded out of the upland soils by white spruce, *Picea glauca* (Moench) Voss or wire birch, *Betula populifolia* Marsh. *M. pensylvanica* provides strong competition for blueberries because of its greater height, heavy foliage and compact clonal habit.

11. Response to Herbicides and Other Chemicals

The Guide to Chemical Weed Control (Ontario Herbicide Committee 1971) approved by the Atlantic Provinces Herbicide Committee does not include *M. pensylvanica* in the list showing susceptibility to 2,4-D; 2,4,5-T MCPA; 2,4-DB; Fenoprop; Mecoprop; and Dicamba. Trevett (1952) considered bayberry (*M. pensylvanica*) to be very resistant to 2,4-D and recommended in Maine a 4,000 parts per million water solution of 2,4,5-T acid from amine formulations for control by spraying of foliage. For stub treatments he recommended applying kerosene or fuel oil that contained 8 lb (3,624 g) of total acids from a mixture of 2,4-D and 2,4,5-T ester formulations per 100 gal (454.61) of oil. Jackson and Hall (1972) recommend that large bushes of *M. pensylvanica* be cut first and that the herbicide be applied to the basal stumps. This reduces the amount of area to be treated and lessens the danger of killing lowbush blueberries in the understory.

12. Response to Other Human Manipulations

Burning does not destroy the entire plant, but merely consumes the above-ground stems. Following burning, new shoot growth arises from dormant buds on stem bases or rhizomes below ground. The underground stems of *M. pensylvanica* are fewer per unit area and are considerably larger than those of most ericaceous shrubs. For these reasons the rhizomes can be grubbed out with a pick or pulled with a chain.

13. Responses to Parasites

According to Pirone et al. (1960), the major insect pest of *M. pensylvanica* is the red-humped caterpillar, *Schizura concinna* (J. E. Smith). This insect feeds on a variety of trees and shrubs. It is known better from its feeding on apple (*Pyrus malus* L.) leaves rather than *M. pensylvanica* in Nova Scotia (C. J. S. Fox, personal communication).

Both *Apioporthe phomaspora* (Ck. & Ell.) Wehm. and *Diaporthe eres* Nit. have been reported as fungal pests of *M. pensylvanica* from Nova Scotia (Connors 1967). Pirone et al. (1960) report also that two leaf spotting fungi *Mycosphaerella myricae* Miles and *Phyllosticta myricae* Cke., as well as the rust fungus *Gymnosporangium ellisii* (Berk.) Farl., occur on this species.

ACKNOWLEDGMENTS

The author acknowledges the technical assistance of A. Brydon, G. Brown and A. Lightfoot of the Kentville Research Station. The description of the pollen and the photograph of the pollen grains were kindly donated by I. J. Bassett and C. W. Crompton of the Biosystematics Research Institute, Canada Department of Agriculture, Ottawa. L. E. Aalders of the Kentville Station prepared the slide for the chromosome count reported herein.

BASSETT, I. J. and CROMPTON, C. W. 1969. Air-borne pollen surveys in Eastern Canada. Can. J. Plant Sci. **49**: 247–253.

CANADA WEED COMMITTEE. 1969. Common and botanical names of weeds in Canada. Can. Dep. Agric. Publ. 1397. 67 pp.

CANADA DEPARTMENT OF ENERGY, MINES and RESOURCES. 1970. The national atlas of Canada. Folio A. Map Distribution Office, 615 Booth St., Ottawa, Ont. K1A 0E9.

CONNORS, I. L. 1967. An annotated index of plant diseases in Canada and fungi recorded on plants in Alaska, Canada and Greenland. Can. Dep. Agric. Res. Br. Publ. 1251. 381 pp.

ERSKINE, D. S. 1960. The plants of Prince Edward Island. Can. Dep. Agric. Res. Br. Publ. 1088. 270 pp.

FERNALD, M. L. 1950. Gray's manual of botany. 8th ed. American Book Co., New York, N.Y. 1632 pp.

FRED, E. B., BALDWIN, I. L. and McCOY, E. 1932. Root nodule bacteria and leguminous plants. Univ. Wisc. Studies in Sci. 5: 343 pp.

HALL, I. V., JACKSON, L. P. and EVERETT, C. F. 1973. The biology of Canadian weeds. 1. *Kalmia angustifolia* L. Can. J. Plant Sci. 53: 865–873.

HALL, I. V., MURRAY, R. A. and JACKSON, L. P. 1974. The biology of Canadian weeds. 2. *Spiraea latifolia*. Can. J. Plant Sci. 54: 141–147.

HARLEY, J. L. 1969. The biology of mycorrhiza. Leonard Hill, London, England. 344 pp.

JACKSON, L. P. and HALL, I. V. 1972. Weeds. Pages 17–21 in Lowbush blueberry production. Agric. Can. Publ. 1477.

LAYCOCK, W. A. 1967. Distribution of roots and rhizomes in different soil types in the pine barrens of New Jersey. U.S. Dep. Interior, Geolog. Survey Prof. Pap. 563-C. p. 9.

MARIE-VICTORIN, FRÈRE. 1964. Flore Laurentienne. Deuxième Edition. Les Presses de L'Université de Montréal. Montréal 3, Qué. 925 pp.

MARTIN, A. C., ZIM, H. S. and NELSON, A. L. 1951. American wildlife and plants. McGraw-Hill Book Company, Inc., New York, N.Y. 500 pp.

ONTARIO HERBICIDE COMMITTEE. 1971. Guide to chemical weed control. Ont. Dep. of Agric. Publ. 75. 78 pp.

PIRONE, P. P., DODGE, B. O. and RICKETT, H. W. 1960. Diseases and pests of ornamental plants. The Ronald Press Company, New York, N.Y. 494 pp.

ROULEAU, E. 1956. III. A check-list of the vascular plants of the Province of Newfoundland. Contrib. de l'Institut Botanique de l'Université de Montréal – No. 69. p. 58.

SOPER, J. H. and HEIMBURGER, M. L. 1961. 100 shrubs of Ontario. Ont. Dep. of Commerce and Develop., Toronto, Ont. 100 pp.

STOKES, J. 1937. Cytological studies in the Myricaceae. Bot. Gaz. 99: 387–399.

TREVETT, M. F. 1952. Control of woody weeds in lowbush blueberry fields. Maine Agric. Exp. Sta. Bull. 499. 23 pp.

U.S. DEP. AGRIC. FOREST SERVICE. 1948. Woody-plant seed manual, 244 pp. Misc. Publ. 654. U.S. Gov. Printing Office, Washington, D.C.

WHITESIDE, G. B. 1965. Soil survey of Prince Edward Island. Canada Dep. Agric. and P.E.I. Dep. Agric. 70 pp.

THE BIOLOGY OF CANADIAN WEEDS.
8. *Sinapis arvensis* L.

G. A. MULLIGAN and L. G. BAILEY

Biosystematics Research Institute, Research Branch, Agriculture Canada, Ottawa, Ontario K1A 0C6. Received 20 Aug. 1974, accepted 19 Sept. 1974.

MULLIGAN, G. A. AND BAILEY, L. G. 1975. The biology of Canadian weeds. 8. *Sinapis arvensis* L. Can. J. Plant Sci. **55**: 171–183.

This contribution on *Sinapis arvensis* L., wild mustard (Cruciferae), is part of a series which presents biological information on plants that are weedy in Canada. Wild mustard is a serious weed of cultivated land, particularly in cereal crops. It occurs in all provinces of Canada and in the Mackenzie District, Northwest Territories.

Le présent travail sur la moutarde des champs *Sinapis arvensis* L. (Crucifères) fait partie d'une série sur la biologie de plants trouvées à l'état adventice au Canada. La moutarde est une mauvaise herbe nuisible dans les cultures, et particulièrement dans les céréales. On la trouve dans toutes les provinces du Canada et dans le district de Mackenzie (Territoires du Nord-ouest).

1. Name

Sinapis arvensis L. (*Brassica kaber* (DC.) Wheeler var. *pinnatifida* (Stokes) Wheeler) — **wild mustard** (Canada Weed Committee 1969), charlock; **moutarde des champs**, jotte, moutarde, moutarde commune, moutarde d'été, moutarde sauvage, petit bouquet jaune, ravonée jaune, sauve, sanve, sendre, sené, sénevé, sénevé des champs, snôve (Ferron et Cayouette 1971). Cruciferae, mustard family, Crucifères.

2. Description and Account of Variation

Annual; stems 30–100 cm high, usually with stiff downward-pointing hairs, at least at the base; stem simple or branched, branches often purple at their junction with the main stem; leaves alternate, somewhat hairy, particularly on the veins of the lower surface; lowest leaves stalked, deeply divided and consisting of a large terminal segment and a few smaller lateral lobes; upper leaves stalkless, usually undivided but coarsely toothed; flowers more than 1.3 cm across; petals bright yellow; pods normally spreading from the stem on thick

stalks that are less than 0.6 cm long; pods glabrous or sometimes with bristly hairs, usually prominently ribbed lengthwise, from 2.5 cm to 3.8 cm long without the beak; beak angular, about as wide as the pod, 0.6–1.3 cm long, often containing a single seed at the base; seeds round, about 1.5 mm across, black, appearing netted at high magnification (Frankton and Mulligan 1970).

Wild mustard plants growing in fields of Ontario and Saskatchewan had $n = 9$ chromosomes (G. A. Mulligan, unpublished). Meiosis was completely regular. The same chromosome number has been reported for plants from the United States, Europe and Asia (Bolkhovskikh et al. 1969).

Wild mustard is confused with a number of other annual yellow-flowered mustards: *Sinapis alba* L. (white mustard), *Brassica nigra* (L.) Koch (black mustard), *Brassica juncea* (L.) Czern. (Indian mustard), *Brassica campestris* L. (bird rape, cultivated turnip and cultivated turnip rape), *Brassica napus* L. (cultivated Swede rape), and *Raphanus raphanistrum* L. (wild radish). Wild mustard differs from all of these mustards by having a seed in the beak of the pod in addition to those within the valves. Both wild mustard and white mustard have stiff downward-directed hairs on the stems. However, the beak of white mustard is flattened and seedless, whereas the beak of wild mustard is not flattened and contains a single seed. Illustrations of wild radish, wild mustard, Indian mustard, bird rape, black mustard and white mustard are shown in Frankton and Mulligan (1970) (the hairs on the illustration of wild mustard should have been drawn pointing downwards rather than upward). Mature plants with pods can be identified with the following key.

A. Pods strongly constricted, breaking off at the constrictions . . . .
. . . .*Raphanus raphanistrum.*
A. Pods not strongly constricted, splitting lengthwise.
   B. Pods each with three to five conspicuous parellel veins, beak one-seeded or strongly flattened; stem with short stiff downward-directed hairs.
   C. Pods and at least base of beak with white bristly hairs; beak flattened, curved, equalling to exceeding length of valves, beak seedless . . . . .*Sinapis alba.*
   C. Pods glabrous or with bristly hairs; beak glabrous, long-conical, straight, slightly winged, one-seeded, beak considerably shorter than length of valves . .
   . . . . *Sinapis arvensis.*
   B. Pods each with a conspicuous midrib and much weaker lateral veins and so more or less one-veined; beak neither one-seeded nor strongly flattened; stem lacking short stiff downward-directed hairs.
   D. Upper stem leaves stalked or narrowed into a stalk-like base, not clasping.
      E. Leaves green; pods appressed to stem, 1.0–2.0 cm, with mature pods more or less quadrangular; beak 1.5–3.0 mm; fruiting pedicels 1.5–3.0 mm, appressed to stem . . . .
      . . . . *Brassica nigra.*
      E. Leaves glaucous; pods ascending, 3.0–5.0 cm, with mature pods slightly flattened perpendicular to partition, beak 5.0–10.0 mm long; fruiting pedicels 8.0–14.0 mm long spreading . . . . .
      . . . . *Brassica juncea.*
   D. Upper stem leaves one-half to completely clasping stem, broadened at base; petals 6.0–13.0 mm long; beak longer than 6.0 mm, gradually tapering.
      F. Petals 6.0–10.0 (rarely 11.5) mm; beak usually 1.0–1.7 cm long, beak (rarely 1/4) 1/3 – 1/2 length of valves . .
      . . . . *Brassica campestris.*
      F. Petals 10.0–13.0 mm; beak usually 0.8–1.0 cm, beak (rarely 1/4) 1/5–1/6 (rarely 1/7) length of valves . . . .
      . . . . *Brassica napus.*

According to Quartley and Wellington (1962), the mature seeds of wild mustard can be distinguished from those of cultivated *Brassica* by their relatively small size (1.5–2.0 mm in diam), completely round shape, and black, slightly greasy testa with a faint reticulation. A stereoscan photomicrograph of the seed surface of *S. arvensis* showing its characteristic reticulation is shown in Fig. 1. Quartley and Wellington (1962) also consider the diffusion of a red substance from the testa of wild mustard, when seeds are placed in a few drops of a cold concentrated solution of chloral hydrate, a good test for identifying mature seeds of wild mustards. However, these two authors developed a test that confirms the identity of wild mustard seeds at any stage of maturity. The testa of the doubtful seed is removed and placed in a small pyrex glass tube with 1 ml of 2 N (8%) sodium hydroxide solution. The tube is then heated in a boiling water bath for 20 min. If the doubtful seed is of wild mustard, the solution shows a bright green–yellow fluorescence when examined in ultraviolet light. The testa of *Sinapis alba* and *Brassica* species turn other colors with this test.

Wild mustard is morphologically and cytologically quite uniform throughout its Canadian range. Pods can be glabrous or hairy, but hairy pods are rare. Occasional

Fig. 1 and 2. *S. arvensis*. 1. Seed coat (×500). 2. Seedling.

populations of wild mustard occur that have slender, strongly torulose pods.

A photograph of a seedling of wild mustard is shown in Fig. 2 and of more mature parts of the plant in Fig. 3, 4 and 5. The cotyledons shown in Fig. 2 and 3 are also characteristic of a number of other related mustards. According to Musil (1950), the cotyledons of wild mustard are 0.8–1.4 cm across, the first foliage leaves are spatulate

Fig. 3 to 5. *S. arvensis*. 3. Lower portion of plant. 4. Upper portion of plant. 5. Pods.

with a long first internode and uniformly shallow dentate margins, and the stem and petioles of seedlings are bristly hairy.

3. Economic Importance

(a) Detrimental — *Sinapis arvensis* is a serious weed of cultivated land. It is responsible for reductions in crop yields, for dockage losses, and for costly chemical and cultural control measures. Wild mustard markedly reduces the yield of wheat (*Triticum aestivum* L.) (Pavlychenko and Harrington 1935; Burrows and Olson 1955a; Anderson 1956), flax (*Linum usitatissimum* L.) (Burrows and Olson 1955b), soybeans (*Glycine max* Meir.) (Berglund and Nalewaja 1969), oats (*Avena sativa* L.) (Anderson 1956; Rademacher 1964), barley (*Hordeum vulgare* L.) (Anderson 1956), potato (*Solanum tuberosum* L.) (Appel 1965), corn (*Zea mays* L.) (Vorob'ev 1968), and kale (*Brassica oleracea* L.) (Welbank 1963). At Regina, Saskatchewan the average yield reduction due to dense infestations of wild mustard in wheat, oats and barley was found, over a 9-yr period, to be 53, 63 and 69%, respectively (Anderson 1956).

Wild mustard is regarded as palatable in young stages, but seeds may cause serious illness in livestock if ingested in large quantities. Wild mustard seed poisoning has the symptoms of severe gastroenteritis. These symptoms are: "severe pain, salivation, diarrhea and irritation of the mouth and upper digestive tract. Symptoms may appear soon after ingestion of a toxic amount and may terminate in death" (Kingsbury 1964). Long (1924) identified the toxic ingredients of the seeds as *Allyl-isothiocyanate* (C_3H_5NCS), the alkaloid *Sinapine* ($C_{10}H_{33}NO_5$) and the alkaloidal glucoside *Sinalbin*.

Wild mustard is a source of infection by insect, nematode, fungus, virus and bacterial pests that cause damage to various cultivated crops, particularly Cruciferae (*see* Section 13).

(b) Beneficial — Wild mustard is much visited by pollinating insects (Mulligan and Kevan 1973) and is probably a prime source of pollen and nectar when it is in flower. It has been used for oilseed and as a source of protein, particularly weed screenings from crop seed (Wood et al. 1958). However, the product is generally of low quality and must be treated cautiously to avoid poisoning. In Europe, wild mustard has been used as a leafy vegetable, and oil from the seeds has been used for making soap, for cooking, and as a lubricant (Vaughan and Hemingway 1959).

(c) Legislation — *Sinapis arvensis* is classified as a noxious weed in the Provincial Weeds Acts of Nova Scotia, Quebec, Manitoba, Saskatchewan and Alberta (Anonymous, 1964, 1965, 1968, 1970, 1973). It has recently been deleted from the Noxious Weeds Acts of Ontario and British Columbia because of effective control measures available. Newfoundland, Prince Edward Island, New Brunswick and the Territories do not have active legislation controlling noxious weeds. The Federal Seeds Act and Regulations, administered by Agriculture Canada (1967) and enforced in all Provinces and Territories, lists mustard seed as "primary noxious." This limits the number of wild mustard seeds permitted in commercial seed to a specified minimum that varies from crop to crop.

4. Geographical Distribution

Wild mustard occurs in all provinces of Canada and in the Mackenzie District, Northwest Territories (Fig. 6). It reaches its greatest abundance in cultivated fields of the Prairie Provinces and occasionally forms almost solid stands in fields elsewhere in Canada. It is indigenous throughout most of the temperate regions of the world: Europe (except northern Scandinavia), Iceland, the Faeröes, Siberia, Asia Minor, southwest Asia to the Himalayas, North Africa (excluding the Sahara), Madeira, and the Canary Isles (Fogg 1950). It has recently been acciden-

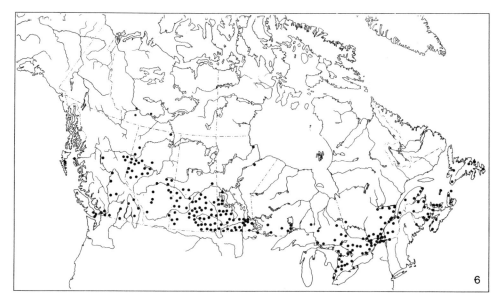

Fig. 6. Distribution of *S. arvensis* in Canada from herbarium specimens and Groh (1947).

tally introduced into North and South America, South Africa, Australia and New Zealand.

Sinapis arvensis was the most common weed found by Friesen and Shebeski (1960) in 142 Manitoba grain fields surveyed during the years 1956, 1957 and 1958 and it was the dicotyledonous weed recorded most in four surveys carried out in cereal fields of Britain during 1962 and 1967 (Fryer and Chancellor 1970). There has been some reduction in the relative abundance of *S. arvensis* in recent years due to its susceptibility to herbicides. This has resulted in an increase in the abundance of species more resistant to the common herbicides (*see* Section 11).

5. Habitat

(a) Climatic requirements — Wild mustard is an annual species that is readily killed by frost. It grows mainly in habitats with a high light intensity. In England, Idris and Milthorpe (1966) found that photosynthesis in *S. arvensis* was 30–40% less when grown in barley than in a pure stand. Barley is able to suppress *S. arvensis* mainly through competition for light. However, in years with normal rainfall, competition between cereal crops and wild mustard is for both light and nitrogen (Blackman and Templeman 1938).

(b) Substratum — In the Prairie Provinces, wild mustard is most common and competitive on the heavy clay soils of the Dark Brown soil zone (Ripley 1949; Friesen and MacKay 1949).

(c) Communities in which the species occurs — It occurs in a wide variety of habitats in Canada: spring cereal fields, fallow fields, roadsides, waste places, potato fields, rape fields, clover fields, corn fields, gardens, riverbanks, etc. It is most common in cultivated fields and frequently forms almost solid stands in fields of spring-sown cereals. Wild mustard often appears unexpectedly on recently disturbed soil and is associated with a wide variety of primary colonizers.

6. History

Sinapis arvensis was common in fields of Albany, New York as early as 1748 (Kalm in Benson 1966). In 1829 it was recorded for Nova Scotia, and by about 1840 it had reached only the western and northern parts of the state of New York and Lower Canada (Groh 1947). It was reported from Fort Garry, Manitoba in 1860, and Dufferin, Manitoba in 1875 (Scoggan 1957). Wild mustard has since spread throughout all settled areas of Canada.

7. Growth and Development

(a) Morphology — Pods of wild mustard ripen in the first year from seed and, in cereals, mature pods usually remain intact until the crop is harvested. During harvesting operations, seed is either gathered with the crop seed or falls in the vicinity of parent plants. Large quantities of seed are not only left in the original field, but are also introduced into other fields as impurities in crop and forage seed.

(b) Perennation — Wild mustard is annual with one generation per year under Canadian conditions. There is no vegetative reproduction.

(c) Phsyiological data — Greenhouse studies indicate that after spraying, 3,6-dichloro-o-anisic acid (dicamba) accumulates in meristematic tissues of wild mustard, but in barley and wheat it is distributed throughout the plant (Chang and Vanden Born 1971). The ability to "detoxify" dicamba in the three species studied correlates well with the degree of resistance of each species to dicamba. The ability of the species to absorb and translocate dicamba shows an inverse relationship to resistance.

Wild mustard and a number of cereals have many more stomata per plant than do nine common weeds (Pavlychenko and Harrington 1934). Wild mustard had 79,800 stomata per plant, Marquis wheat had 40,300, Hannchen barley had 64,300, Banner oats had 43,300 and Prolific spring rye had 63,700. Pavlychenko and Harrington (1934) suggest that the high number of stomata on young seedlings facilitates physiological activities, and best fitted *S.*

arvensis and cereals to compete with other weeds at early stages of growth.

(d) Phenology — Five days after emergence, wild mustard had a root system 87 cm in length, and 21 days after emergence the length was 12,055 cm (Pavlychenko and Harrington 1934). This root system, at 21 days, was larger than were the roots of 11 cereals and eight other weeds after a similar period. The root system of wild mustard was approximately one-half as long (3,576 cm) under competition with Hannchen barley as when competing with Marquis wheat (6,815 cm).

Seeds of *S. arvensis* collected in the wild on 12 August 1954 were seeded in field plots at Ottawa on 17 August of the same year. Although some of the seed germinated in 1954 and plants grew to 18 cm in height, none of the plants overwintered. Additional seed germinated on 18 April of the following year and intermittently for the remainder of that spring and early summer. Plants flowered first on 30 May 1955 and the first seed matured on 14 July 1955. Although this early seed was immediately planted in other plots and some of it germinated very quickly, none of the resulting plants matured before they were killed by the first severe frosts of 1955.

(e) Mycorrhiza — None known.

8. Reproduction

(a) Floral biology — Plants of wild mustard are self-incompatible and, although this weed was introduced into North America, cross-pollination is performed by a wide variety of native insects (Mulligan 1972). According to Mulligan and Kevan (1973), individual plants of wild mustard present a large flower target for pollinating insects, and flowers have a high reflectance in the yellow and ultraviolet wavelengths that are noticeable to insects. The large solid yellow infestations of wild mustard that are so evident to man must be obvious to insects, even at a long distance. Pollinating insects see not only the color yellow, but the high ultraviolet reflectance that is invisible to

man. Insects are also attracted to the odoriferous flowers, and the large ultraviolet-free spot in the center of the corolla serves as a guide to the sexual parts. Mulligan and Kevan (1973) reported the following insects visiting the flowers of *S. arvensis* at Ottawa:

HYMENOPTERA (10 species) — *Agapostemon radiatus* (Say), *Andrena forbesii* Robt., *Bombus terricola* Kby., *Calliopsis andreniformis* Sm., *Ceratina calcarata* Robt., *Dialictus cressonii* (Robt.), *Evylaeus foxii* (Robt.), *Halictrus rubicundus* (Chr.) *Lasioglossum athabascence* (Sandh.) and *Lasioglossum leucozonium* (Schr.).

DIPTERA (7 species) — *Eristalis arbustorum* (L.), *Eristalis tenax* (L.), *Helophilus laetus* Lw., *Helophilus latifons* Lw., *Helophilus stipatus* Walk., *Lucilia illustris* (Mg.) and *Sphaerophoria* sp.

Fogg (1950) lists a large number of insects visiting the flowers of wild mustard in Britain and on the Continent.

(b) Seed production and dispersal — Plants grown in cultivated fields of Canada have from 10 to 18 seeds per pod and from 2,000 to 3,500 seeds per plant. Plants growing without competition are larger and have much more seed. The seed is contained in pods that usually split when a crop is harvested. Some of the seed may remain as an impurity in the crop seed and the remainder falls on the ground in the immediate vicinity of the parent plants.

(c) Viability of seeds and germination — Some seed of wild mustard is capable of germination as soon as it is mature. In Saskatchewan, when moisture was abundant, seed of wild mustard germinated in 4 days and had a total germination of 21% after 14 days. When moisture was scarce it took 11 days for first germination, and after 20 days 20% of the seed germinated (Pavlychenko and Harrington 1934).

In experiments at Ottawa, first germination of seeds occurred 2–3 days after being placed in an inside germinator and 5–7 days after being sown in field plots. However, some of the seed sown in field plots remained dormant for a considerable period of time.

Germination of wild mustard seed is sporadic. Many years may elapse before all seeds in a sample will germinate. Seed may remain viable in the soil for as long as 60 yr (Evans 1962), particularly when they are buried at considerable depths in the soil (Long 1910; Hopp 1957). When buried, germination capacity (about 85%) did not change for 10 yr, whereas seeds from the same sample were only 24% viable after 10 yr in dry storage (Dorph-Petersen 1910). Germination of wild mustard seed did not decrease after being buried in a pasture for 5 yr (Thurston 1966). There is evidence that dormancy and longevity of buried seed of wild mustard are the result of low amounts of oxygen beneath the soil surface.

Edwards (1968a,b,c; 1969) suggests that dormancy in wild mustard is maintained by a specific growth-inhibiting substance that is produced at low oxygen concentrations in the embryo. This substance diffuses to the meristems, preventing root elongation. A layer of mucilages and phenols, present in the seed coat, retards diffusion of oxygen into the embryo and permits the formation of this growth-inhibiting substance.

There are conflicting reports on the eti of light on the germination of seeds. Kolk in Fogg (1950) states that seeds germinate best in weak light or darkness, whereas Povilaitis (1956) reports that light was beneficial in increasing germination. Mullverstedt (1963) found that *S. arvensis* was indifferent to light during germination but that soil aeration, due to cultivation, significantly increased the emergence of seedlings when compared with unaerated controls.

(d) Vegetative reproduction — There is no vegetative reproduction.

9. Hybrids

No interspecific hybrids involving *S. arvensis* are known to occur in nature.

10. Population Dynamics

Wild mustard is an annual plant that produces only one complete generation each year. It requires from 2½ to 3 mo to produce mature plants from seed and it never overwinters under Canadian conditions. It is most common in spring-planted annual crops, particularly cereals, and is virtually absent from land that has not been recently disturbed. When pastures, hayfields, roadsides, etc. are cultivated, plants of wild mustard often appear in abundance because of the germination of dormant seed (*see* Section 8c).

Wild mustard germinates on bare soil early in the spring, and in the early stages of growth the developing seedlings outgrow the seedlings of other plants (Pavlychenko and Harrington 1935). This rapid early growth depresses crop yield (Rademacher 1966).

The competitive success of wild mustard depends greatly on the plants with which it is competing and the abundance of its competitors. *Sinapis arvensis* and cow cockle (*Saponaria vaccaria* L.) were seeded at various densities in spring wheat at Regina, Saskatchewan (Alex 1970). Both species emerged at about the same time, just after the wheat. Growth in height of the two weeds was similar during the first 3–4 wk, but thereafter wild mustard increased in height faster and averaged 10 cm taller than cow cockle after 7 wk. About half as much cow cockle seed was produced in plots containing 128 wild mustard plants per square meter as in similar plots where *S. arvensis* was absent. Cow cockle, however, had little or nor effect on the yield of wild mustard. Wild mustard caused greater reductions in yield of wheat than did cow cockle at similar densities. In mixed infestations of cow cockle and wild mustard in wheat, the presence of one weed species tended to obscure the effect of the other on yield of wheat, and the combined effect of both was only a little worse than the effect of each individually. In Manitoba, the presence of wild mustard affected the growth, tillering and yield of spring wheat (Burrows and Olson 1955a). As the density of mustard increased, there was a reduction in seed bolls per plant, weight of straw and yield of seed in flax (Burrows and Olson 1955b). According to Koch (1967), the greatest competitive effect of wild mustard on oats occurred up to the middle of shooting, when there was a depression in plant weight of 25–32%. Oats could not overcome the initial damage even when weeds were removed at the beginning of tillering. The effects of *S. arvensis* were much less when there was a high nutrient level in the soil than when the nutrient level was low.

11. Response to Herbicides and Other Chemicals

Sinapis arvensis is successfully controlled by a wide range of selective herbicides. In fact, it has been suggested that the effective control of wild mustard in the grain fields of western Canada was responsible for the rapid and widespread acceptance of selective weed control by farmers of the Canadian prairie. Wild mustard is killed by one application of 0.45 liter/0.4 ha (16 oz/acre) or less of 2,4-D, MCPA or mecoprop; by 0.56 liter/0.4 ha (20 oz/acre) or less of 2,4-DB or MCPB; by 0.13 liter/0.4 ha (6 oz/acre) or less of dicamba (Saidak and Bandeen 1973). *Sinapis arvensis* is susceptible to benazolin (4-chloro-2-oxo-3 benzothiazoline acetic acid) at 0.56- and 0.84-kg/ha rates of application (Salam and Downey 1973). Benazolin may be effective for the control of wild mustard in some cruciferous crops, particularly white mustard (*Sinapis alba* L.) and *Crambe* species.

Wild mustard continues to be a common weed in Canadian cereal crops in spite of the fact that plants are easily killed by a wide range of herbicides. This is due to various factors in the reproduction and growth of wild mustard, not due to the development of herbicide-resistant strains. However, there is some evidence that the effectiveness of control of wild mustard by herbicides has resulted in an increase in the abundance of weed species that are resistant to the most widely used selective herbicides.

In Britain, species that are susceptible to herbicides commonly used in cereal crops, particularly *Sinapis arvensis, Papaver rhoeas* L. (common poppy) and *Ranunculus arvensis* L. (corn buttercup) have greatly diminished in abundance whereas many of the herbicide-tolerant weeds have increased in numbers (Fryer and Chancellor 1970). According to Alex (1970), the widespread use of 2,4-D in grain fields of the Canadian Prairie Provinces has reduced densities of *Sinapis arvensis* and increased the numbers of the more resistant weed cow cockle (*Saponaria vaccaria* L.). Other weeds of the Prairie Provinces that are fairly resistant to 2,4-D and are apparently favored by the removal of wild mustard and other susceptible weeds are wild buckwheat (*Polygonum convolvulus* L.), Tartary buckwheat (*Fagopyrum tataricum* (L.) Gaertn.), hemp-nettle (*Galeopsis tetrahit* L.), corn spurry (*Spergula arvensis* L.), green foxtail (*Setaria viridis* (L.) Beauv.), and wild oats (*Avena fatua* L.) (Hay 1968). Nalewaja and Arnold (1970), at an International Conference on Weed Control, stated that the development, introduction and use of 2,4-D in the mid-1940's produced a considerable change in weed populations. They reported that competition from weeds such as wild mustard, stinkweed (*Thlaspi arvense* L.), and Russian thistle (*Salsola pestifer* A. Nels.) was reduced by 2,4-D, but allowed other more resistant weed populations to increase.

12. Response to Other Human Manipulations

Since wild mustard is an annual weed that does not reproduce from vegetative parts, plants of this weed can easily be killed by cultivating the soil after seed has germinated. However, cultivation of infested land is often impossible due to the fact that mustard seed usually germinates about the same time as annual crops. Wild mustard in annual crops is most easily controlled with herbicides. Increasing the seeding rate of wheat increased grain yield in Manitoba plots infested with wild mustard (Burrows and Olson 1955a). In six experiments in Wales, with *S. arvensis* the dominant weed species, application of nitrogen fertilizer increased yields of marrowstem kale (*Brassica oleracea* L.) in the absence of weed control measures (Hammerton 1964). The benefits were 60% greater if treatment was combined with weeding from the four-leaf stage onward, and 120% greater when weeding began at crop emergence.

13. Responses to Parasites

(a) Insects and other non-domestic animals —

INSECTA

HOMOPTERA: *Myrus persicae* (Sulz.) and *Brevicoryne brassicae* (L.) — British Isles (Fogg 1950) and Canada (Biosystematics Research Institute Entomologists, Ottawa, unpublished).

THYSANOPTERA: *Melanothrips fuscus* (Sulz.), *M. gracilicornis* (Maltb,), *Aelothrips fasciatus* (L.), *Taeniothrips vulgatissimus* (Hal.) and *Thrips angusticeps* (Uzel.) — Canada (Biosystematics Research Institute Entomologists, unpublished) and all except *Aelothrips fasciatus* in British Isles (Fogg 1950).

LEPIDOPTERA: *Pieris napae* (L.) and *Plutella maculipennis* (Curt.) — Canada (Biosystematics Research Institute Entomologists, unpublished), *Pieris brassicae* (L.), *Euchloë cardamines* (L.) and *Evergestis extimalis* (Scop.) — British Isles (Fogg 1950).

COLEOPTERA: *Agroites obscurus* (L.), *Meligethes aeneus* (Fab.) and *Ceuthorrhynchus assimilis* (Payk.) — Canada (Biosystematics Research Institute Entomologists, unpublished) and British Isles (Fogg 1950), *Phyllotreta atra* (Fab.), *Phyllotreta nigripes* (Fab.), *Phyllotreta undulata* Kuts. and *Ceuthorrhynchus pleurostigma* (Marsh.) — British Isles (Fogg 1950).

93

HYMENOPTERA: *Elinora flaveola* (Gmel.) — British Isles (Fogg 1950).

DIPTERA: *Hylemya floralis* (Fallén), *H. brassicae* (Bouché), *Liromyza brassicae* (Riley), *Phytomyra rufipes* (Mergon) — Canada (Biosystematics Research Institute Entomologists, unpublished), *Contarinia nasturtii* (Kieff.), *Dasyneura brassicae* (Winn.) and *Clortophila floralis* (Fall.) — British Isles (Fogg 1950).

NEMATODA

Heterodera schachtii Schmidt, the sugar beet nematode was found on the host plant *Sinapis arvensis* near Sarnia, Ontario (Baker 1941). In England, wild mustard is a host for the nematode *Longidorus elongatus* (de Man) and the viruses that this nematode transmits, tomato black ring virus and raspberry ringspot.

(b) Microorganisms and viruses —

FUNGI

In Canada, *Peronospora brassicae* Gaüman, *Albugo candidus* (Pers.) O. Ktze, *Albugo cruciferarum* S. F. Gray and *Plasmodiophora brassicae* Wor. have been found on *Sinapis arvensis* (CDA, Mycology Herbarium). Wild mustard is an important alternative host for clubroot of crucifers, *Plasmodiophora brassicae* (Peterson 1961; Maklakova 1959).

VIRUSES

Sinapis arvensis harbors the turnip mosaic virus (Lu 1971).

BACTERIA

Wild mustard is a host plant for *Bacterium campestre* (Pammel) E. F. Smith a disease attacking the vascular system of many vegetables (Elliot 1930).

ACKNOWLEDGMENT

We thank Judy N. Findlay for her assistance in abstracting information on *Sinapis arvensis*.

AGRICULTURE CANADA. 1967. Seeds Act and Regulations. Queen's Printer, Ottawa, Canada. 50 pp.

ALEX, J. F. 1970. Competition of *Saponaria vaccaria* and *Sinapis arvensis* in wheat. Can. J. Plant Sci. **50**: 379–388.

ANDERSON, E. G. 1956. What weeds cost us in Canada. Botany and Plant Pathology Lab., Sci. Serv., Ottawa, Canada. pp. 1–15.

ANONYMOUS. 1964. Réglement concernant les mauvaises herbes. Ministère de l'Agriculture, Québec, Qué. pp. 639–641.

ANONYMOUS. 1965. An act respecting noxious weeds. Queen's Printer, Regina, Sask. pp. 3937–3953.

ANONYMOUS. 1968. Regulations to the Weed Control Act, pp. 1–6.. Queen's Printer, Halifax, N.S. pp. 1–6.

ANONYMOUS. 1970. The Noxious Weeds Act. Queen's Printer, Winnipeg, Man. pp. 1–20.

ANONYMOUS. 1973. The Weed Control Act. Queen's Printer, Edmonton, Alta. 3 pp.

APPEL, G. O. 1965. Effects of weed infestation on potato stands. Kartoffelbau **16**: 134–135.

BAKER, A. D. 1941. New host records for the sugar beet nematode, *Heterodera schachtii* Schmidt, in Canada. Can. Entomol. **73**: 196.

BENSON, A. B., ed. 1966. Peter Kalm's travels in North America. I. Dover Publ. Inc. New York, N.Y. 797 pp.

BERGLUND, D. R. and NALEWAJA, J. D. 1969. Wild mustard competition in soybeans. Proc. 24th N. Central Weed Control Conf., Sioux Falls, N.D. p. 83.

BLACKMAN, G. E. and TEMPLEMAN, W. G. 1938. The nature of the competition between cereal crops and annual weeds. J. Agric. Sci. **28**: 247–271.

BOLKHOVSKIKH, Z.,GRIF, V., MATVEJEVA, T. and ZAKARYEVA, O. 1969. Chromosome numbers of flowering plants. Academy of Science of the U.S.S.R., V. L. Kamarov Bot. Inst., Lenningrad. 926 pp.

BURROWS, V. D. and OLSON, P. J. 1955a. Reaction of small grains to various densities of wild mustard and the results obtained after their removal with 2,4-D or by hand. I. Experiments with wheat. Can. J. Agric. Sci. **35**: 68–75.

BURROWS, V. D. and OLSON, P. J. 1955b. Reaction of small grains to various densities of wild mustard and the results obtained after their removal with 2,4-D or by hand. II. Experiments with flax. Can. J. Agric. Sci. **35**: 193–201.

CANADA WEED COMMITTEE. 1969. Common and botanical names of weeds in Canada. Can. Dep. Agric. Publ. 1397. 67 pp.

CHANG, F. Y. and VANDEN BORN, W. H. 1971. Dicamba uptake, translocation metabolism and selectivity. Weed Sci. **19**: 113–117.

DORPH-PETERSEN, K. 1910. Kurze Mitteilungen über Keimuntersuchungen mit Samen verschiedener wildwachsenden Pflanzen. I. ber. Ver. angew. Bot. Stud. **8**: 239–247.

EDWARDS, M. M. 1968a. Dormancy in seeds of charlock. I. Developmental anatomy of the seed. J. Exp. Bot. **19**: 575–582.

EDWARDS, M. M. 1968b. Dormancy in seeds of charlock. II. The influence of the seed coat. J. Exp. Bot. **19**: 583–600.

EDWARDS, M. M. 1968c. Dormancy in seeds of charlock. III. Occurrence and mode of action of an inhibitor associated with dormancy. J. Exp. Bot. **19**: 601–610.

EDWARDS, M. M. 1969. Dormancy in seeds of charlock. IV. Interrelationships of growth, oxygen supply and concentration of inhibitor. J. Exp. Bot. **20**: 876–894.

ELLIOTT, C. 1930. Manual of bacterial plant pathogens. Williams and Williams Co., Baltimore, Md. 349 pp.

EVANS, S. A. Weed destruction; a farmers' and students' guide. Blackwell Scientific Publ., Oxford, England. 172 pp.

FERRON, M. et CAYOUETTE, R. 1971. Noms des mauvaises herbes du Québec. Min. Agric. et Colonisation du Québec. Publ. 288. 113 pp.

FOGG, G. E. 1950. Biological flora of the British Isles. J. Ecol: **38**: 415–429.

FRANKTON, C. and MULLIGAN, G. A. 1970. Weeds of Canada. Can. Dep. Agric. Publ. 948, 217 pp.

FRIESEN, G. and SHEBESKI, L. H. 1960. Economic losses caused by weed competition in Manitoba grain fields. I. Weed species their relative abundance and their effect on crop yields. Can. J. Plant Sci. **40**: 457–467.

FRIESEN, H. A. and MACKAY, J. W. 1949. Weeds of grain fields. Agric. Inst. Rev. **4**: 91–94.

FRYER, J. D. and CHANCELLOR, R. J. 1970. Herbicides and our changing weeds. The flora of a changing Britian. Bot. Soc. Brit. Isles. Rep. 11. pp. 105–118.

GROH, H. 1947. Canada weed survey. Fourth annual report (1945). Can. Dep. Agric., Ottawa. pp. 1–56.

HAMMERTON, J. L. 1964. Aspects of weed competition in kale. Proc. 7th Brit. Weed Control Conf. Aberystwyth, Wales. pp. 389–395.

HAY, J. R. 1968. The changing weed problem on the prairies. Agric. Inst. Rev. Can. Dep. Agric., Mar.-Apr. pp. 17–19.

HOPP, H. 1957. A study of the longevity of weed seeds, using new methods. Thesis, Landw. Hochsch. Hohenhein. 72 pp.

IDRIS, H. and MILTHORPE, F. L. 1966. Light and nutrient supplies in the competition between barley and charlock. Oecologia Pl. **1**: 143–164.

KINGSBURY, J. M. 1964. Poisonous plants of the U.S. and Canada. Prentice-Hall Inc., Englewood Cliffs, N.J. 626 pp.

KOCH, W. 1967. Competition between crop plants and weeds. 2. Effect of annual weeds on cereals. Weed Res. **7**: 22–28.

LONG, H. C. 1910. Common weeds of the farm and garden. Smith, Elder and Co., London, England. 451 pp.

LONG, H. C. 1924. Plants poisonous to livestock. 2nd ed. Cambridge University Press, London, England. 119 pp.

LU, J. 1971. Study of transmission agents of turnip mosaic virus. Phytoprotection **52**: 35–44.

MAKLAKOVA, G. E. 1959. *Plasmodiophora brassicae* var. on Cruciferous weeds. Bot. Zh. U.S.S.R. **44**: 1649–1653.

MULLIGAN, G. A. 1972. Autogamy, allogamy and pollination in some Canadian weeds. Can. J. Bot. **50**: 1767–1771.

MULLIGAN, G. A. and KEVAN, P. G. 1973. Colour, brightness and other floral characteristics attracting insects to blossoms of some Canadian weeds. Can. J. Bot. **51**: 1939–1952.

MULLVERSTEDT, R. 1963. Investigations on the causes of increased emergence of weeds following mechanical weed control measures (post-emergence). Weed Res. **3**: 298–303.

MUSIL, A. F. 1950. Identification of Brassicas by seedling growth or later vegetative stages. U.S.D.A. circular 857. 26 pp.

NALEWAJA, J. D. and ARNOLD, W. E. 1970. Weed control methods, losses and costs due to weeds and benefits of weed control in wheat and other small grains. 1st F.A.O. Int. Conf. Weed Control. Davis, Calif. 668 pp.

PAVLYCHENKO, T. K. and HARRINGTON, J. B. 1934. Competitive efficiency of weeds and cereal crops. Can. J. Res. **10**: 77–94.

PAVLYCHENKO, T. K. and HARRINGTON, J. B. 1935. Root development of weeds and crops in competition under dry farming. Sci. Agric. **16**: 151–160.

PETERSON, H. I. 1961. Examples of the importance of the weed flora for plant pests and diseases. Horticultura **15**: 120–122.

POVILAITIS, B. 1956. Dormancy studies with seeds of various weed species. Proc. Intern. Seed Test. Assoc. **21**: 88–111.

QUARTLEY, C. E. and WELLINGTON, P. S. 1962. Biochemical tests for seed indentification. J. Nat. Inst. Agric. Bot. **9**: 179–185.

RADEMACHER, B. 1964. Beginning of competition between cereals and weeds. Z. Pftkrankh. Pflpath. Pflschutz. (Sonderh. 1): 88–93.

RADEMACHER, B. 1966. The current status and achievements of agro-chemical and agro-biological research. B. Weed control in cereals viewed as a problem in soil fertility. Landw. Forsch. (Sonderh. 20): 21–38.

RIPLEY, P. O. 1949. Regional weed problems. Agric. Inst. Rev. **4**: 79–86.

SAIDAK, W. J. and BANDEEN, J. D. 1973. Report of research appraisal and research planning committees for eastern Canada. Can. Weed Comm., Eastern Section, Québec, Qué. p. 97.

SALAM, M. A. and DOWNEY, R. K. 1973. Selectivity of benzolin in Cruciferae. Can. J. Plant Sci. **53**: 891–896.

SCOGGAN, H. J. 1957. Flora of Manitoba. Nat. Museum Can., Ottawa, Bull. 140. 619 pp.

THURSTON, J. M. 1966. Survival of seeds of wild oats (*Avena fatua* and *Avena ludoviciana*) and charlock (*Sinapis arvensis*) in soil under logs. Weed Res. **6**: 67–80.

VAUGHAN, J. G. and HEMINGWAY, J. S. 1959. The utilization of mustards. Econ. Bot. **13**: 196–204.

VOROB'EV, N. E. 1968. Competition between maize and weeds. Vestn. sel-khoz. Nauki. Mask. **13**: 30–35.

WELBANK, P. J. 1963. A comparison of competitive effects of some common weed species. Ann. Appl. Biol. **51**: 107–125.

WOOD, A. J., ROBERSTON, M. C. and KITTS, W. D. 1958. Studies on the nutritive value of refuse screenings. I. The essential amino acid content of certain weed seeds. Can. J. Animal Sci. **38**: 97–102.

THE BIOLOGY OF CANADIAN WEEDS

9. *Thlaspi arvense* L.

K. F. BEST and G. I. MCINTYRE

Regina Research Station, Box 440, Regina, Saskatchewan.
Received 10 May 1974, accepted 23 Sept. 1974.

BEST, K. F. AND MCINTYRE, G. I. 1975. The biology of Canadian weeds. 9. *Thlaspi arvense* L. Can. J. Plant Sci. **55**: 279–292.

An account is given of various aspects of the biology of *Thlaspi arvense* L. This species, commonly known as stinkweed or field pennycress, is found in almost all parts of Canada, but is particularly prevalent as a weed in the cultivated fields of the Prairie Provinces. The paper is one of a series on the biology of Canadian weeds and is concerned primarily with those characteristics of the species which appear to present the main obstacles to its effective control.

Les auteurs passent en revue la description biologique de *Thlaspi arvense* L., espèce communément appelée tabouret des champs, qui pousse dans presque toutes les régions du Canada, mais qui s'est surtout implantée comme mauvaise herbe dans les cultures des provinces des Prairies. L'article s'inscrit dans le cadre d'une étude sur la biologie des mauvaises herbes du Canada, et s'intéresse en premier lieu aux caractéristique de l'espèce qui semblent le plus en entraver la lutte.

1. Name

Thlaspi arvense L. — **stinkweed** (Canada Weed Committee 1969). Other common English names are: bastard cress, fanweed, field pennycress, frenchweed, mithridate mustard, pennycress, and wild garlic (Best 1965). The French common name is **tabouret des champs** (Ferron and Cayouette 1971). Cruciferae (Mustard Family) Crucifères.

2. Description and Account of Variation

A smooth annual or overwintering herb with an unpleasant odor. The seedling develops as a compact vegetative rosette (Fig. 1A,B). When well illuminated, stem elongation normally occurs only with the onset of flowering. Stem erect to 80 cm in height, simple or branched above. Leaves glabrous, alternate, undivided, with margins entire or sparingly toothed. Basal leaves stalked but soon wither. Stem leaves eared at base and clasping stem. Flowers in racemes, white, perfect, regular with four sepals, four petals and six stamens, two of

which are shorter than the other four (Fig. 1C). Silicles borne on slender upward curving stalks; bright green, becoming yellowish or greenish orange; circular, compressed at right angles to the septum; 8–12 mm wide with a very short style which persists in the narrow notch of the broadly winged fruit (Frankton and Mulligan 1970; Gleason 1958) (Fig. 1D). There are from five to eight seeds in each of the two locules. Seeds compressed, ovoid, reddish brown to black, each side with several concentric ridges resembling a fingerprint, 1.2–2.3 mm long, 1.0–1.5 mm wide.

T. arvense is diploid (Mulligan 1960) with a chromosome count of $2n = 14$ (Mulligan 1957).

Stem height and branching behavior show a high degree of environmental plasticity. When growing in dry, shallow or infertile soil, the stem remains unbranched and may reach only 1.0 cm in height; in a deeper, more fertile soil and in relative absence of competition, many flowering lateral branches are produced from buds at basal nodes, and stems may reach a height

Can. J. Plant Sci. 55: 279-292 (Jan. 1975)

of 80 cm (Best and McIntyre 1972; Fig. 1). Plants collected in the vicinity of Swift Current and Regina, Sask., and grown under controlled conditions, revealed the occurrence of early- and late-flowering strains differing markedly in the time required for flowering to occur (Best and McIntyre 1972). Although genetically distinct, the two strains have the same number of chromosomes (personal communication, G. A. Mulligan, Biosystematics Research Institute, Agriculture Canada, Ottawa). During the summer they are distinguishable by differences in leaf shape. The leaves of the late-flowering plants have longer petioles and deeper serrations than those of the early-flowering strain (Fig. 2).

Stinkweed bears some resemblance to field pepper-grass (*Lepidium campestre* (L.) R. Br.) which also has clasping leaves, white flowers and seed pods of a similar shape. The leaves of pepper-grass, however, are densely villous, the flowers are much smaller than those of stinkweed, and the pods contain only two seeds.

3. Economic Importance

(a) Detrimental — *T. arvense* is generally recognized as a serious agricultural weed, particularly in the Prairie Provinces, where it competes with crops for a limited moisture supply, causing significant reductions in yield. E. Molberg (Research Station, Agriculture Canada, Regina, Sask., personal communications of unpublished data) found that a 16% infestation of stinkweed (percentage of total vegetation on an air-dried basis) reduced wheat yields by an average of 36% over a 5-yr period. Where a 61% infestation occurred, the yields were reduced by 51% over hand-weeded checks.

T. arvense produces seed that is rich in oil glucocides. Under certain conditions, these are acted upon by enzymes and liberate mustard oil or similar substances. According to Kingsbury (1964), allyl *iso*-thiocyanate present in the seeds of this plant (Kjaer et al. 1953) is undoubtedly responsible for the gastric distress in livestock reported to result from ingestion of grain containing stinkweed seed (Thompson et al. 1922). The mustard oils are very strong irritants. Livestock feeding on considerable quantities of ground seeds may develop chronic enteritis, haemorrhagic diarrhoea, colic, abortion, nephritis and haematuria, apathy and paralysis of heart and respiration (Steyn 1934). Feeds containing ground stinkweed seed should not be moistened with cold water before feeding or the enzymes will liberate mustard oil before the feed enters the stomach. Boiling water poured over the feed tends to inactivate the enzymes responsible for the liberation of the mustard oils (Muenscher 1940).

King (1966) noted that while flavors such as onion (*Allium* L.) will appear in milk 4 or 5 min after feeding, and will require 5-6 h of grazing for the flavor to disappear, the flavor and odor of stinkweed does not disappear until 7-8 h after the weed is eaten.

(b) Beneficial — Coupland (1950) concluded that *T. arvense* is one of the four primary colonizers in the annual stage of succession on abandoned land in the mixed prairie. Stabilization of these areas is achieved within 15–40 yr. Wood et al. (1958), investigating the nutritive value of refuse screenings, found that ground raw seed of *T. arvense* had a crude protein of 16.0%. Analysis indicated that the amino acid content of the seeds tends to follow the general pattern found in rapeseed (*Brassica napus* L.). It would appear that the seeds offer a satisfactory source of protein for ruminants and for monogastric animals, provided feeds for the latter are supplemented with suitable sources of sulphur-containing amino acids. Lips and Grace (1949) discussed the edible properties of stinkweed oil and shortening.

(c) Legislative — *T. arvense* is listed under the Seeds Act and Regulations administered by Agriculture Canada (1967) where it is included in a category of "Secondary Noxious Weeds." It is also classified as a noxious weed in the Noxious Weeds Act of Saskatchewan.

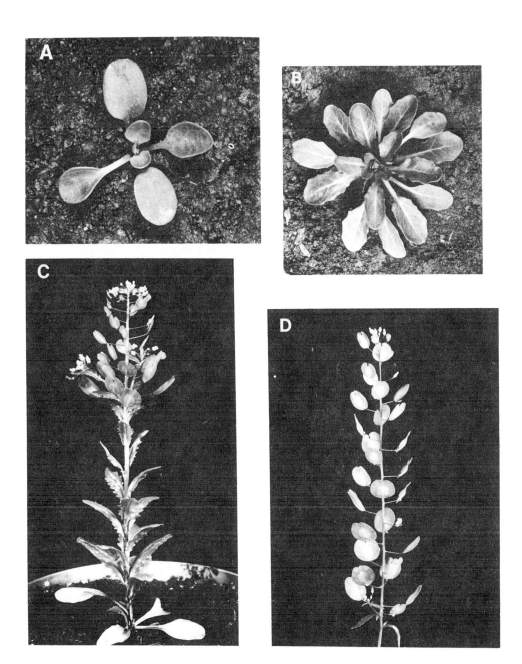

Fig. 1. Stages in the growth and development of *Thlaspi arvense* L. (A). A young seedling showing the cotyledons and the first four true leaves (×2.5). (B) A vegetative rosette which had overwintered at this stage and was photographed in the field at the Regina Research Station on 25 April. Note the healthy condition of the leaves and the apparent absence of frost injury (×1). (C) The flowering stage (×0.5). (D) Infloresence with mature seed pods (silicles) (×0.5).

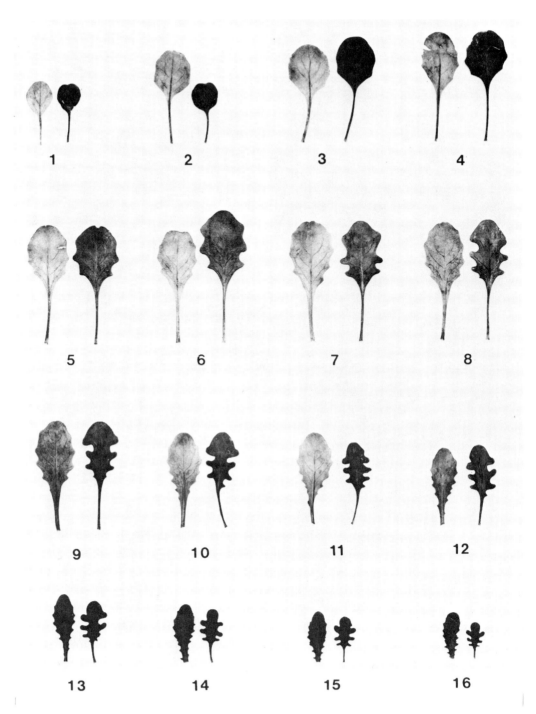

Fig. 2. Leaves from early- and late-flowering strains of *Thlaspi arvense* illustrating differences in leaf shape. The nodes are numbered acropetally from the base of the stem. The cotyledons are not included, node 1 being the node of the first true leaf. Of the two leaves shown at each node, the one on the left is from the early-flowering strain and the one on the right from the late-flowering strain (×0.48).

4. Geographical Distribution

It occurs in all provinces of Canada and in the North West Territories, being particularly abundant in the Prairie Provinces (Fig. 3), especially on the heavier soils (Frankton and Mulligan 1970; Alex 1966). According to Mulligan (1965), it is to be found in all agricultural areas of the country. It also occurs throughout the United States (Reed 1970), and according to Clapham et al. (1962), it occurs in most areas of the British Isles, except in the outer Hebrides and the Shetland Islands, and is also found in Europe to 79°N, N. Africa, W. Asia, Siberia, and Japan.

Polunin (1959) found stinkweed growing on wasteland and in other disturbed areas in West Greenland where it appeared to have become established in a few locations following introduction, and cites reports from as far north as Spitsbergen. He also listed the species at several locations in Alaska.

5. Habitat

(a) Climatic requirements — The remarkably widespread distribution of *T. arvense* is evidence that it has become adapted to a wide range of environmental conditions, and, at least in the North American continent, its spread does not appear to have been significantly restricted by climatic factors. Stinkweed grows successfully in both dry and wet habitats, from exposed knolls to moist valleys, from sea-level to an altitude of 2,739 m in Colorado as reported by Jones (herbarium specimen 31403 in Department of Agriculture, Ottawa, DAO).

(b) Substratum — According to Smith (1917), stinkweed generally takes possession of the best soil on the farm, while Granstrom (1962) claims that distribution of this species is unaffected by soil type.

(c) Communities in which the species occurs — Stinkweed may grow as isolated

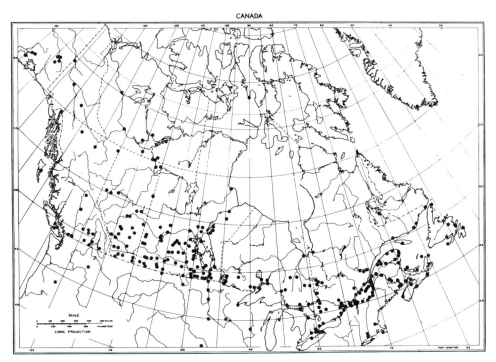

Fig. 3. The distribution in Canada and northern United States of *Thlaspi arvense* L. based on specimens from various Canadian herbaria.

plants, in small patches or in pure stands. A pioneer of disturbed soil, it readily invades cultivated land. It is often plentiful in areas where winter wheat (*Triticum aestivum* L.) is grown (Smith 1917). Hamel and Dansereau (1949) indicated that stinkweed was characteristic of two habitats in Quebec — in cereal fields and on young prairies. It is considered to be one of the principal plants of the annual weed stage of succession on abandoned sandy land in the Brown soil zone of the mixed prairie. Associated species are *Sisymbrium altissimum* L., *Salsola pestifer* A. Nels., and *Lepidium densiflorum* Schrad. (Coupland 1950, 1952). Stinkweed is reported present in cereals and in oil seed, forage and vegetable crops in western Canada. Species with which it is frequently associated in these crops include *Agropyron repens* (L.) Beauv., *Amaranthus retroflexus* L., *Avena fatua* L., *Capsella bursa-pastoris* (L.) Medic., *Chenopodium album* L., *Cirsium arvense* (L.) Scop., *Crepis tectorum* L., *Echinochloa crusgalli* (L.) Beauv., *Equisetum arvense* L., *Fagopyrum tataricum* (L.) Gaertn., *Galium spurium* L., *Galeopsis tetrahit* L., *Kochia scoparia* (L.) Schrad., *Lappula echinata* Gilib., *Malva pusilla* Sm., *Polygonum convolvulus* L., *Polygonum persicaria* L., *Portulaca oleracea* L., *Salsola pestifer* A. Nels., *Saponaria vaccaria* L., *Setaria viridis* (L.) Beauv., *Sonchus arvensis* L., *Stellaria media* (L.) Vill., *Tragopogon dubius* Scop., and *Taraxacum officinale* Weber (Canada Weed Committee 1973).

6. History

Darlington et al. (1940) cites stinkweed as an introduced weed, a native of Europe and Asia, but becoming widely distributed throughout the northern United States and in areas of cultivation in Canada. It was collected at Fort Garry, Manitoba by Schultz in 1860 (herbarium specimen 230340 in National Museum, Ottawa, CAN) and at Anticosti, Quebec, in 1865 (Groh 1943). Fletcher (herbarium specimen 31234 in DAO) collected stinkweed at Ottawa in 1878 and Macoun collected the species in 1879 at White Horse Plains, Manitoba (herbarium specimen 59929 in CAN). Wood (1955) quoting from a paper entitled "History of weeds in western Canada" by A. C. Budd, noted that stinkweed was introduced onto the prairies as early as 1882 in bales of trading and food stuffs by factors and traders. Macoun, in 1883, described stinkweed as being abundant in many parts of Quebec; scarce in Ontario; but a real pest in Manitoba and around Hudson Bay Company posts in the North West Territories (Groh 1943). He recorded stinkweed in 1885 at James Bay, Ontario (herbarium specimen 59927 in CAN) and at Morley, Alberta (herbarium specimen 59925 in CAN), while Fowler (herbarium specimen 31399 in DAO) found stinkweed near Emerson, Manitoba in 1918. Muenscher (1935) observed that the high incidence of stinkweed on the Canadian prairies appeared to correspond with its similar abundance in the Northwestern States. Groh (1943) noted in the Canadian Weed Survey of 1943 that a considerable proportion of the westernmost records were in the Peace River district where stinkweed was already a major weed on land devoted intensively to grain production. He noted that Nuttall had classified stinkweed as a common weed around Detroit in his publication of 1818 more likely dating back to the founding of the colony of the Detroit River by Cadillac in 1701. By 1937, stinkweed was distributed throughout the United States from Maine to Florida and westward to California and Washington (Dayton et al. 1937). Chael (1953) recorded the species in New South Wales for the first time in 1935.

7. Growth and Development

(a) Morphology — The low, rosette habit of the vegetative phase protects overwintering plants from low temperatures and drying winds, enabling them to gain maximum advantage from the insulating effect of snow cover. Klebesadel (1969)

reported that in Alaska, winter snow cover was a significant factor in promoting the survival of overwintering rosettes. The racemose inflorescence and the capacity of the plant to produce numerous additional inflorescences from lateral branches, in response to favorable growing conditions, largely accounts for the prolific seed production characteristic of the species.

(b) Perennation — Gates (1940) classified *Thlaspi arvense* as therophyte, the species overwintering either as a seed or as a vegetative rosette. It appears well adapted to the winter annual habit, and vegetative rosettes from fall-germinating seeds may overwinter without the loss of a single leaf (Batho 1939) (Fig. 1B). Individuals that flower in late fall freeze when winter sets in, but in spring resume growth and mature seed with no sign of injury (Clark and Fletcher 1909).

(c) Physiological data — Experiments at Regina with the early-flowering strain of stinkweed, grown under controlled conditions (Best and McIntyre 1972), showed that while flowering occurred under both long (16-h) and short (8-h) days, its occurrence was significantly accelerated by the longer photoperiod (Table 1). On this evidence *T. arvense*, with respect to flowering response, may be categorized as a quantitative, long-day species. The effect of day length interacted with the N supply, the promotion of flowering by long days being considerably increased by growing the plants at a reduced N level. The morphogenetic nature of the photoperiod response was indicated by data on leaf number which was increased to a similar extent both by reducing the day length and by increasing the N supply. Shading, which reduced the light intensity from 34,000 to 3,800 lx, caused effects on days-to-flower and leaf number similar to those produced by reducing the day length. This suggests that the day-length response may be mediated by an effect on the carbohydrate supply.

It was shown in the same investigation that leaf number was increased, and the onset of flowering significantly delayed, by increasing the nitrogen supply. In addition to its effect on flowering, N also caused a striking increase in lateral branching, presumably by reducing apical dominance. Although the effect on seed yield was not determined, it may be assumed that the large number of flowering laterals produced at high N levels greatly increased the capacity for seed production.

A comparative study of the effects of temperature on the flowering of early- and late-flowering strains under controlled conditions (McIntyre and Best, unpublished data) showed that increasing the temperature (from 10 to 25 C) significantly accelerated flowering and reduced leaf number of

Table 1.   Effects of day length, light intensity and nitrogen supply on flowering in *Thlaspi arvense*

Treatments[†]	Days to flower[‡]		Number of leaves[*]	
	Low nitrogen	High nitrogen	Low nitrogen	High nitrogen
A High light 16-h day	44.3±0.58	49.6±0.54	18.4±0.41	34.2±0.88
B High light 8-h day	80.6±1.47	72.4±1.25	34.1±0.94	45.7±1.38
C Low light 16-h day	93.1±1.83	89.3±1.86	30.8±1.27	34.2±0.62

[†]The light intensity was 34,000 lx in treatments A and B and 3,800 lx in treatment C.
[‡]Mean values (±SE) based on 18 plants in treatments A and B and on 17 plants in treatment C. The long and short day treatments at high light intensity (i.e. treatments A and B) were analyzed statistically as a 2×2 factorial by analysis of variance. All main effects are significant at the 1% level. There is a significant interaction ($P < 0.01$) of day length and nitrogen supply on days to flower, but no significant interaction of their effects on leaf number.

Table 2. Effects of day temperature on the flowering of early- and late-flowering strains of *Thlaspi arvense*

Day‡ Temp (C)	Days to flower†		Number of leaves†	
	Early-flowering strain	Late-flowering strain	Early-flowering strain	Late-flowering strain
10±1	79.6±1.06	108±1.31	38.3±0.40	56.9±1.20
25±1	56.2±0.60	128±2.40	32.3±0.51	87.9±1.23

†Data are mean values (±SE) based on 20 plants per treatment. All effects of temperature and strain are significant at the 1% level, as determined by analysis of variance.
‡The night temperature was 3±1 C in both treatments and the day length was 12 h.

plants of the early-flowering type, but delayed flowering and increased leaf number in the late-flowering strain (Table 2).

A preliminary investigation of the response of plants of the late-flowering strain to vernalizing treatments (Best and McIntyre, unpublished data) showed that exposure of vegetative plants, at the six-to-seven true-leaf stage, to a temperature of 2±1 C significantly accelerated flowering. The response increased with the duration of the low temperature treatment over the experimental range of 2-6 wk.

Anderson and Best (1965) found that stinkweed was rather inefficient in water usage in comparison to weed-free barley (*Hordeum vulgare* L.), Russian thistle *Salsola pestifer* A. Nels.), and green foxtail (*Setaria viridis* (L.) Beauv.), requiring 405 kg of water to produce 0.453 kg of dry matter.

Clark and Fletcher (1909) noted that no mucilage developed when stinkweed seeds were soaked in water.

(d) Phenology — Chepil (1946) observed that 50% of *T. arvense* seedlings emerged by 30 April at Swift Current and that the average date of mature seed production was 7 July. While seeds germinate in greatest numbers early in the spring, from mid-April to mid-May, there is a second flush of emergence in the fall. Some germination may also occur sporadically throughout the summer, particularly when the soil has been cultivated or otherwise disturbed and where rain has provided an adequate moisture supply (Best and McIntyre, unpublished data). Seedlings of the spring emerging

population normally flower within 30–50 days and produce mature seed by the early part of July. Much of the seed is shed during the following weeks, but the extent to which it germinates and contributes to the population of seedlings emerging in the fall does not appear to have been recorded. Although it has been shown (McIntyre and Best, unpublished data) that freshly harvested seed has the capacity for immediate germination if provided with light, adequate water and a fluctuating temperature (Table 3), it cannot be assumed that such seeds germinate as readily under more natural field conditions, and the question requires further investigation. Seedlings emerging in the fall may overwinter as vegetative rosettes or at various stages of floral development, depending on their date of germination, and flower early in the following growing season.

Table 3. Effects of light and temperature on germination of seeds from early- and late-flowering strains of *Thlaspi arvense*

Temp† (C)	% germination‡			
	Early-flowering strain		Late-flowering strain	
	Light	Dark	Light	Dark
A 10	2.0	2.5	0.5	0.5
B 25	44.5	0.0	0.0	0.0
C 10–25	99.0	9.5	96.5	0.0

†In treatments A and B the temperature was kept constant, in C it alternated on a 12-h cycle. Light (2,300 lx) was supplied for 12 h daily (during the 25° cycle in treatment C).
‡All values are the means of two petri dish cultures each containing 100 seeds. Germination was recorded after 14 days.

104

Observations recorded at Regina, from an area of stinkweed known to include plants of both early- and late-flowering strains, showed that all seedlings emerging in the spring behaved like plants of the early-flowering type. However, when plants were grown under controlled conditions (20 ± 1 C, 16-h photoperiod), from seeds collected from the same spring-emerging population, both the early- and late-flowering types were found to be present in approximately equal proportions. These observations suggest that exposure of the seed and/or seedling to the low temperature of winter and/or early spring may prevent the expression of the late-flowering genotype, resulting in a uniformly early-flowering population. This conclusion is supported by the results of the seedling vernalization experiment reported above (Section 7c). Much further work is required, however, before the influence of low temperatures on germination and flowering in this species can be fully described.

(e) Mycorrhiza — No information available.

8. Reproduction

(a) Floral Biology — Experiments at Regina (Best and McIntyre, unpublished data), in agreement with Mulligan (1972), showed that plants whose flowers were covered to prevent cross-pollination invariably gave a high yield of viable seed, indicating that the species is self-compatible and readily autogamous. A similar conclusion was reached by Knuth (1908) who noted that of the six stamens present in the flower, the anthers of the four longest ones reached the same level as, or slightly higher than, the stigma and as their pollen-covered surfaces turned inwards at maturity, their proximity to the stigma made automatic self-pollination inevitable. Knuth also remarked that the two shorter stamens serve for cross-pollination by insects. Mulligan (1972), however, reported that *T. arvense* was rarely visited by insects and although it seems probable that some cross-pollination by insects does occur,

evidence as to its frequency and importance for the species appears to be lacking. Mulligan and Kevan (1973) listed the following insects as occasional visitors on *T. arvense* at Ottawa:
LEPIDOPTERA (1 species) — *Pieris rapae* L.;
HYMENOPTERA (7 species) — *Andrena* sp., *Andrena forbesii* Robt.; *Andrena* near *fragilis* Sm., *Andrena wilkella* Kby., *Dialictus lineatulus* (Cwfd.), *Evylaeus foxii* (Robt.), *Halictus confusus* Sm.;
DIPTERA (6 species) — *Eristalis anthophorinus* (Fall.) *Eristalis arbustorum* (L.), *Eristalis dimidiatus* Wied., *Helophilus fasciatus* Walk., *Helophilus lunualatus* Mg., *Metasyrphus* sp.

(b) Seed production and dispersal — Stinkweed is a prolific seeder; a single plant may produce from 1,600 to 15,000 seeds that shatter readily (Best, unpublished data). There are generally 5–8 seeds in each of the two locules of the silicle (Polunin 1959). Stevens (1954) gives an average of 7,040 seeds per plant with an average weight of 0.8 mg and also estimates that there are 1,235 seeds/g. Batho (1939) estimated that a field heavily infested with stinkweed may yield as much as 1,345 kg/ha of pure stinkweed seed, exactly the weight of 20 bu of wheat. Howitt (1911) estimated production at 20,000 seeds per plant. Seed-drill surveys (Saskatchewan Department of Agriculture 1929) indicated that there was an average of four seeds of stinkweed per kilogram of wheat; or if seeding were calculated at 80 kg/ha, there were 374 weed seeds sown on each hectare.

Soil samples from a cultivated field at Swift Current, Sask., taken to a depth of 15 cm, were subjected to germination conditions in the greenhouse and had 327 emerging seedlings per 1/4 m². Similar samples, air-dried for 5 mo, had 69 seedlings emerge per 1/4 m² (Best 1959).

Klebesadel (1969) claimed that the older the seedling at the onset of winter, the greater was the number of seed pods produced the following year.

Seeds mature and many scatter before and during harvest. In comparison with Thatcher wheat, with a rating of 100, stinkweed has a rating of 35 in its resistance to shattering (Chepil 1946). Howitt (1911) noted that dispersal is chiefly by wind while Helgelson (1958) found that 90% of stinkweed seeds would float for 24 h on still water.

(c) Viability of seeds and germination — In a study of environmental effects on germination (McIntyre and Best, unpublished data), freshly harvested seed from plants of the early- and late-flowering strains were placed on moist filter paper in petri dishes and assigned to the several combinations of light and temperature shown in Table 3. Results recorded after 14 days showed that maximum germination of both early- and late-flowering genotypes was obtained with a 10–25 C temperature alternation where seeds were also exposed to light. In darkness, germination at this temperature regime was restricted to seeds from early-flowering plants and was much reduced. Relatively few seeds germinated at a constant temperature of 10 C whereas at 25 C, germination was restricted to illuminated seeds from plants of the early-flowering strain. The greater effectiveness of a fluctuating temperature in promoting germination in this species was also noted by previous investigators (Cross 1931; Everson 1949; Steinbauer et al. 1955.)

Literature relating to the germination of *T. arvense* was reviewed by Kolk (1962) and Anderson (1968). Evidence of the stimulating effect of light on germination was also provided by Courtney (1966) who showed that when seed samples were collected from the field in darkness, germination of seeds retained in the dark was less than 5% of those subsequently exposed to light. Courtney concluded that the promotion of germination that results from cultivation can be largely or entirely attributed to the consequent illumination of the seeds. Several workers have found that removal of the seed coat greatly promotes germination

of this species (Best and McIntyre, unpublished data; Crocker 1906; Schulte and Balback 1941; Pelton 1956), even under conditions otherwise unfavorable to germination. That this response to dehulling is due to removal of a permeability barrier rather than to elimination of a seedcoat inhibitor is substantiated by the fact that scarification of the seed, either with sandpaper (Schulte and Balback 1941) or sulphuric acid (Pelton 1956) is also effective in promoting germination.

A number of workers have noted that the viability of stinkweed seed is considerably greater in the soil than in dry storage under laboratory conditions. For example, Kjaer (1940) reported that dry-stored seed lost its viability completely within 2 yr, whereas seeds from the same sample were still alive after 10 yr burial in the soil. Dorph-Peterson (1924) obtained 87% germination from seed that had remained for 9 yr in the soil, while Crocker (1938) and Smith (1917) reported that even after 20 yr burial some seeds were still capable of germination. This persistant viability of stinkweed seeds in the soil, their capacity to germinate when brought to the surface by cultivation, and the very large reservoir of dormant seeds present in the soil of a heavily infested area (Batho 1939) are all factors that must contribute significantly to the persistance of this troublesome weed.

Gibberellic acid is very effective in promoting germination of stinkweed seeds of various ages. Corns (1960) found that 4-day-old seed at 21 C in darkness failed to germinate, but germinated 91% when treated with 500 ppm gibberellic acid. Three-week-old and 2-mo-old seed (dry-stored at 3 C), germinated 99–100% on filter paper moistened with water after being pre-soaked in a 1,000 ppm solution of gibberellic acid for 24 h. Six-month-old seed (dry-stored at room temperature) germinated 96% on filter paper moistened with a 500 ppm solution.

The dormancy of stinkweed seed has been investigated by several workers.

Chepil (1946) recorded the dormancy of stinkweed seeds in cultivated land and noted that few if any seeds survive for more than 6 yr in the soil under cultivation. Courtney (1966) observed that the germination of freshly harvested seed was primarily restricted by the seed coat, and that the seeds appear to develop a secondary dormancy during late spring and summer. Bibbey (1948) noted that stinkweed seeds displayed marked environmental dormancy and were very sensitive to low oxygen or high carbon dioxide concentrations. He further observed that although samples of seed might vary widely in the occurrence of after-ripening in the fall, marked changes take place during winter, and by spring most of the seeds have lost their primary dormancy and are able to germinate. Seeds may lie dormant in the soil for several years and are generally readily germinable, but in a condition of environmental dormancy.

Courtney (1966) noted that changes in the dormancy status took place in stinkweed seed independent of depth of burial. The response to soil disturbance is governed by the environmental conditions prevailing at the time, the germination requirements of the species, and the dormancy status of the seed.

9. Hybrids

No evidence of hybridization has been reported.

10. Population Dynamics

The number of stinkweed seeds in the soil increases materially in both the first and second grain crop after fallow, with the greatest increase occurring in the first crop after fallow (Budd et al. 1954). Batho (1939) refers to a crop of Garnet wheat, sown in 1931 at 67.3 kg/ha without fertilizer, which yielded 740 kg/ha of wheat and 1,038 kg/ha of stinkweed seed. In plots under less severe conditions of weed infestation, stinkweed produced over 10,500 seeds per square meter when crops were sown light and without fertilizer.

Kirk et al. (1941) found that stinkweed was a poor competitor with such forage crops as *Agropyron cristatum* (L.) Gaertn., *A. trachycaulum* (Link.) Malte and *Bromus inermis* Leyss. during the first season of establishment. Harrington et al. (1936) noted that in the second season of growth of *Agropyron cristatum*, the grass stand was thick and uniform with only the occasional weak plant of stinkweed. In the fall, an excellent stand of grass was observed with no stinkweed present. Harrington et al. (1937) found that in the third season of growth, *Agropyron cristatum* had produced an excellent stand with only an occasional empty space, and the stinkweed had apparently been eliminated. *Bromus inermis* was also an excellent competitor, giving good stands with a number of bare spaces that were free of stinkweed. *Agropyron trachycaulum* was rather a poor competitor, giving a rather sparse stand, with half of the surface bare and a few stinkweed plants present. Kirk et al. (1941) noted that in competition with *Agropyron cristatum*, the density of stinkweed was reduced from 2,051/m² 24 days after emergence to none after 82 days. *Agropyron cristatum* in competition with stinkweed was effectively retarded in development during the first 2½ mo after emergence, but produced a perfect stand after the weed was removed.

11. Response to Herbicides and Other Chemicals

Stinkweed is very susceptible to amine and ester formulations of 2,4-D and MCPA, and to many of the commercial mixtures containing them: for example, bromoxynil-MCPA-dicamba; 2,4-D-mecoprop; linuron-MCPA; dichlorprop-2,4-D. Stinkweed is less susceptible to dicamba or bromoxynil alone than when mixed with 2,4-D or MCPA (Canada Weed Committee 1972).

12. Response to Other Human Manipulations

Best (1959) found that by delaying the seeding of wheat at Swift Current, the

107

stinkweed population of fallow and stubble seeded fields was reduced by over 90%.

13. Response to Parasites

Vinducka (1967) reported that stinkweed served as a host for the sugar beet eel worm (*Heterodera schachtii* Schmidt), but that the nematode preferred the sugar beet (*Beta vulgaris* L.), winter rape (*Brassica napus* L. var. *arvensis* (Lam.) Thellung), kale (*Brassica oleraceae* L. var. *acephala* DC.) and kohlrabi (*Brassica caulorapa* Pasq.). The fungus *Plenodomus (Phoma) lingam* (Tode ex Fr.) Desm., which causes a troublesome disease of other cruciferous species, was found on stinkweed in central Saskatchewan by Petrie (1965). At least two cultural types occurred, each appearing to have its own primary host. A third type, recently discovered, was found on rape. All three types overwinter on dead plant material with the "Thlaspi" type, which has stinkweed as its primary host, also being commonly borne by infected seed.

No information is available on higher plant-parasites.

ACKNOWLEDGMENTS

We wish to thank William Fleming for his assistance with the illustrations and Dr. J. R. Hay for his critical appraisal of the manuscript.

AGRICULTURE CANADA. 1967. Seeds Act and Regulations. Queen's Printer, Ottawa, Ontario. 50 pp.

ALEX, J. F. 1966. Survey of weeds of cultivated land in the prairie provinces. Exp. Farm, Res. Br., Agric. Can., Regina, Saskatchewan. p. 68.

ANDERSON, C. H. and BEST, K. F. 1965. Water use efficiency of barley and weeds grown in the greenhouse. Soil Horiz. **6**: 15–16.

ANDERSON, R. N. 1968. Germination and establishment of weeds for experimental purposes. W. F. Humphrey Press, Inc., Geneva, N.Y. 236 pp.

BATHO, G. 1939. Stinkweed and common mustard. Man. Dep. Agric. Immigr. Circ. 129. 8 pp.

BEST, K. F. 1959. Effect of dates of seeding on stinkweed population. Res. Rep. Nat. Weed Comm. (West. Sect.) p. 67.

BEST, K. F. 1965. Common names of weeds of Canada. Exp. Farm Publ. S. C. 110. Can. Dep. Agric., Swift Current, Sask.

BEST, K. F. and McINTYRE, G. I. 1972. Studies on the flowering of *Thlaspi arvense* L. I. The influence of some environmental and genetic factors. Bot. Gaz. **133**: 454–459.

BIBBY, R. O. 1948. Physiological studies of weed seed germination. Plant Physiol. **23**: 467–484.

BUDD, A. C., CHEPIL, W. S. and DOUGHTY, J. L. 1954. Germination of weed seeds. III. The influence of crops and fallow on the weed seed population of the soil. Can. J. Agric. Sci. **34**: 18–27.

CANADA WEED COMMITTEE. 1969. Common and botanical names of weeds in Canada. Can. Dep. Agric. Publ. 1397. 67 pp.

CANADA WEED COMMITTEE (WEST. SECT.) 1972. Rep. Res. Appraisal Comm. and Res. Planning Comm.

CANADA WEED COMMITTEE (WEST. SECT.) 1973. Res. Rep. 438 pp.

CHAEL, E. 1935. Penny cress (*Thlaspi arvense*) serious pest reported for the first time. Agric. Gaz. N. S. W. **46**: 185–186.

CHEPIL, W. S. 1946. Germination of weed seeds. 1. Longevity, periodicity of germination and vitality of seeds in cultivated soil. Sci. Agric. **26**: 307–346.

CLAPHAM, A. R., TUTIN, T. G. and WARBURG, E. F. 1962. Flora of the British Isles. Cambridge Univ. Press, Cambridge, England. 1269 pp.

CLARK, G. H. and FLETCHER, J. 1909. Stinkweed (*Thlaspi arvense* L.) Farm weeds of Canada. Can. Dep. Agric. pp. 80–82.

CORNS, W. G. 1960. Combined effects of gibberellin and 2,4-D on dormant seeds of stinkweed (*Thlaspi arvense* L.). Can. J. Bot. **38**: 871–874.

COUPLAND, R. T. 1950. Ecology of mixed prairie in Canada. Ecol. Monogr. **20**: 271–315.

COUPLAND, R. T. 1952. Grassland communities of the Western Canadian prairies — climax and subclimax. Proc. 6th Int. Grassl. Congr. pp. 625–631.

COURTNEY, A. D. 1966. Germination ecology. Nat. Veg. Res. Sta., Wellesbourne, England. Annu. Rep. pp. 80–81.

CROCKER, W. 1906. Role of seed coats in delayed germination. Bot. Gaz. **42**: 265–291.

CROCKER, W. 1938. Life span of seeds. Bot. Rev. **4**: 235–274.

CROSS, H. 1931. Laboratory germination of weed seeds. Proc. Assoc. Off. Seed Anal. **24**: 125–128.

DARLINGTON, H. T., BESSEY, E. A. and MEGEE, C. R. 1940. Some important Michigan weeds. Mich. Agric. Exp. Sta. Bull. 304 pp.

DAYTON, W. A., LOMMASSON, T. and PARK, B. C. 1937. Range plant handbook. U.S. Dep. Agric. p. W187.

DORPH-PETERSON, K. 1924. Examinations of the occurrence and vitality of various weed species under different conditions, made at the Danish State Testing Station during the years 1896-1923. Rep. 4th Int. Seed Test. Congr. pp. 124–138.

EVERSON, L. 1949. Preliminary studies to establish laboratory methods for germination of weed seeds. Proc. Assoc. Off. Seed Anal. **39**: 84–89.

FERRON, M. and CAYOUETTE, R. 1971. Noms des mauvaises herbes du Quebec, Min. Agric. Colon. Que. Publ. 288. p. 65.

FRANKTON, C. and MULLIGAN, G. A. 1970. Weeds of Canada. Can. Dep. Agric. Publ. 948, p. 76.

GATES, F. C. 1940. Weeds in Kansas. Kansas Board Agric. Rep. **60**: 149.

GLEASON, H. A. 1958. Illustrated flora of the northeastern United States and adjacent Canada. Lancaster Press. Lanc: Penn. Vol. 2. p. 216.

GRANSTROM, B. 1962. Studies on weeds in spring sown crops. Medd. Statens. Jordbrforsok, Uppsala. 188 pp.

GROH, H. 1943. *Thlaspi arvense* L. Canadian Weed Survey, Annu. Rep. 2nd. p. 21.

HAMEL, A. and DANSEREAU, P. 1949. L'aspect ecologique du probleme des mauvaises herbes. Bull. Serv. Biogeogr. **5**: 1–41.

HARRINGTON, J. B., PAVLYCHENKO, T. K., KOSSAR, W. and KNOWLES, P. 1936. Report of investigations carried on during 1935 at the Weed Research Nursery, University of Saskatchewan, Saskatoon, Sask. p. 2.

HARRINGTON, J. B., PAVLYCHENKO, T. K., KOSSAR, W. and ANDERSON, O. M. 1937. Report of investigations carried on during 1936 at the Weed Research Nursery, University of Saskatchewan, Saskatoon, Sask. p. 40.

HELGELSON, E. A. 1958. A weed problem in irrigation. N. D. Agric. Exp. Sta. Bull. **20**: 24–25.

HOWITT, J. E. 1911. Weeds of Ontario. Ont. Dep. Agric. Bull. 188.

KING, L. J. 1966. Weeds of the world. Plant Sci. Monogr. Intersci. Publ. Inc. N.Y.

KINGSBURY, J. M. 1964. Poisonous plants of the United States and Canada. Prentice-Hall, Inc. Englewood Cliffs, N. J. 626 pp.

KIRK, L. W., PAVLYCHENKO, T. K., KOSSAR, W. and ANDERSON, D. M. 1941. Report of investigations carried on in 1939 at the Research Laboratory of Plant Ecology, University of Saskatchewan, Saskatoon, Sask. p. 75.

KJAER, A. J., CONTI, J. and LARSEN, I. 1953. *iso* Thiocyanates IV. A systematic investigation of the occurrence and chemical nature of volatile *iso*Thiocyanates in seeds of various plants. Acta Chem. Scandinavica **7**: 1276.

KJAER, A. 1940. Germination of buried and dry stored seeds. Proc. Int. Seed Test. Assoc. **12**: 167–190.

KLEBESADEL, L. J. 1969. Life cycles of field pennycress in the subarctic as influenced by time of seed germination. Weed Sci. **17**: 563–566.

KNUTH, P. 1908. Handbook of flower pollination. Vol. II. Ranunculaceae to Stylidiae. Clarendon Press, Oxford, England, p. 74.

KOLK, H. 1962. Viability and dormancy of dry stored weed seeds. Växtodling (Uppsala) **18**: 192 pp.

LIPS, H. J. and GRACE, N. H. 1949. Canadian erucic oils. IV. Edible properties in fanweed (pennycress) oil and shortening. Can. J. Res. Sect. Food Technol. **27**: 311–317.

MUENSCHER, W. C. 1935. Weeds of New York, Cornell Univ. Agric. Exp. Sta. Bull. 635 p. 12.

MUENSCHER, W. C. 1940. Poisonous plants of the United States. The Macmillan Co., New York, N.Y. pp. 14, 105, 108.

MULLIGAN, G. A. 1957. Chromosome numbers of Canadian weeds. Can. J. Bot. **35**: 779–789.

MULLIGAN, G. A. 1960. Polyploidy in Canadian weeds. Can. J. Genet. Cytol. **2**: 150–161.

MULLIGAN, G. A. 1965. Recent colonization by herbaceous plants in Canada. Pages 127–146 *in* The genetics of colonizing species. Academic Press Inc. New York, N.Y.

MULLIGAN, G. A. 1972. Autogamy, allogamy, and pollination in some Canadain weeds. Can. J. Bot. **50**: 1767–1771.

MULLIGAN, G. A. and KEVAN, P. G. 1973. Color, brightness, and other floral characteristics attracting insects to the blossoms of some Canadian weeds. Can. J. Bot. **51**: 1939–1957.

PELTON, J. 1956. A study of seed dormancy in eighteen species of high altitude Colorado plants. Butler Univ. Bot. Studies, Indianapolis, Ind. **13**: 74–84.

PETRIE, G. A. 1965. A potentially severe disease of rape widespread on cruciferous weeds in Saskatchewan. Can. Dep. Agric. Res. Br. Highlights. 88 pp.

POLUNIN, N. 1959. Circumpolar arctic flora. Oxford Univ. Press, London, Eng.

REED, C. F. 1970. Selected weeds of the United States. U.S. Dep Agric. Handb. 366, p. 214.

SASKATCHEWAN DEPARTMENT OF AGRICULTURE. 1929. Rep. Weed Conf. 27 p. 13.

SCHULTE, R. B. and BALBACK, P. 1941. Germination of seeds of *Agropyron* spp. (probably quackgrass) and *Thlaspi arvense*, pennycress. Proc. Assoc. Off. Seed Anal. **33**: 44–45.

SMITH, J. D. 1917. Weeds of Alberta. Alta. Dep. Agric. Bull. 2.

STEINBAUER, G. P., GRIGSBY, B., CORREA, L. and FRANK, P. 1955. A study of methods for obtaining laboratory germination of certain weed seeds. Proc. Assoc. Off. Seed Anal. **45**: 48–52.

STEVENS, O. A. 1954. Weed seed facts. N. D. Agric. Coll. Circ. p. A218.

STEYN, D. G. 1934. The toxicology of plants in South Africa. Central News Agency Ltd. Johannesburg, S. Africa. 631 pp.

THOMSON, R. B. and SIFTON, H. B. 1922. A guide to the poisonous plants and weed seeds of Canada and northern United States. Univ. Toronto Press, Toronto, Ont. 169 pp.

VINDUCKA, L. 1967. Weeds and the sugar beet eel-worm *Heterodera schachtii* Schmidt. Ochr. Rost. **3**: 219–224.

WOOD, A. J., ROBERTSON, M. C. and KITTS, W. D. 1958. Studies on the nutritive value of refuse screenings. I. The essential amino acid content of certain weed seeds. Can. J. Anim. Sci. **38**: 97–102.

WOOD, H. E. 1955. Fifty years of weed control in Western Canada. Proc. Can. Weed Contr. Conf. 8th, Regina, Sask. pp. 1–6.

THE BIOLOGY OF CANADIAN WEEDS
10. *Iva axillaris* Pursh

K. F. BEST

Research Station, Agriculture Canada, Regina, Saskatchewan S4P 3A2.
Received 20 Aug. 1974, accepted 3 Oct. 1974.

BEST, K. F. 1975. The biology of Canadian weeds. 10. *Iva axillaris* Pursh. Can. J. Plant Sci. **55**: 293–301.

Iva axillaris Pursh, povertyweed, is a native, colony-forming herbaceous perennial, generally associated with poorly drained alkaline regions on clay and clay loam soils and is one of the most persistent weeds of agriculture in western North America. This is one of a series of papers dealing with the biology of Canadian weeds and is concerned primarily with those characteristics of the species which appear to present the main obstacles to its effective control.

L'herbe de pauvreté, *Iva axillaris* Pursh, est une plante vivace herbacée et indigène, formant colonies, que l'on observe généralement sur argile et sur loam argileux alcalins et mal drainés; c'est une des mauvaises herbes d'importance agricole les plus persistantes dans l'ouest de l'Amérique du Nord. Ce résumé fait partie d'une série d'articles sur la biologie des mauvaises herbes du Canada et porte surtout sur les caractéristiques de l'espèce qui en rendent la lutte particulièrement difficile.

1. Name

Iva axillaris Pursh — **povertyweed** (Canada Weed Committee 1969). Other common names include small-flowered marsh elder (Best 1965), death-weed or devil's-weed (Muenscher 1955) and bozzleweed or salt sage (Rydberg 1932); **herbe de pauvreté** (Frankton 1958). Compositae, composite family, Composées.

2. Description and Account of Variation

Povertyweed is a native colony-forming perennial with creeping roots and an unpleasant odor. It is herbaceous, or slightly woody near the base; often bushy-branched, and grows from 10 to 60 cm high (Fig. 1). The leaves are opposite on the lower part of the stem but alternate on the upper portion of the stem, upper leaves smaller than the lower ones. The leaves are thick, pale green, linear to elliptic or ovate, all leaves glabrous to rough-hairy, sessile or sub-sessile, 1- to 3-nerved and generally 0.5–3.0 cm long, 0.1–1.0 cm wide. Flower heads are solitary in the axils of the upper leaves, nodding on short peduncles; the phyllaries of the involucral cup have four to six lobes, united or separate, heads with

staminate and pistillate florets, the central florests staminate, generally 5–15; the corolla funnel-shaped, 2–3 mm long with five stamens and a reduced, sterile ovary; the marginal florets are pistillate, usually 2–11, with cylindrical corollas. The achenes are grayish-brown to brownish-black, resinous and generally 2–3 mm long and 1.5–2.0 mm wide. Pollen grains from diploid plants were 19.3–26.3 μ in diameter and guard cells were 24.5–35.0 μ long, while the triploid had pollen grains 27.5–32.5 μ in diameter and guard cells 38.5–42.0 μ long (Bassett et al. 1962). The diploid plant has a chromosome count of $2n=36$; the triploid material has a count of $2n=54$ (Mulligan 1961).

No gross morphological differences have been found between plants with different chromosome numbers (Bassett et al. 1962). In western Canada, another subspecies of povertyweed, *Iva axillaris* Pursh ssp. *robustior* (Hook.) Bassett, can be separated from ssp. *axillaris* by the following key of Bassett et al. (1962).

Leaves mostly linear to linear-lanceolate, rarely elliptic, upper surface glabrous or nearly so, margins and lower surface with many, mostly pustulate,

Fig. 1. *Iva axillaris* Pursh ssp. *axillaris*.

simple hairs; phyllaries of involucral cup generally separated nearly to base; plant with sessile resinous glands that remain colorless after drying ....
.... 1. **ssp. axillaris.**
Leaves mostly elliptic or ovate to obovate, rarely linear, upper and lower surfaces with many simple hairs, pustulate hairs absent or few; phyllaries of involucral cup generally united nearly to top; plant with sessile resinous glands that turn brown after drying ....
.... 2. **ssp. robustior.**
Povertyweed is not likely to be mistaken for other plants. Perennial ragweed (*Ambrosia coronopifolia* T. & G.) also has creeping rootstocks and is about the same height as povertyweed, but perennial ragweed has lobed leaves and the flower heads contain only one kind of flower (Frankton and Mulligan 1970).

3. Economic Importance

(a) Detrimental — Povertyweed (ssp. *axillaris*) is usually found on slightly to heavily alkaline areas on the Canadian Prairies. In cultivated fields it produces dense patches that significantly reduce crop yields (Canada Dep. Agric. 1938). Almost no crop is produced in heavily infested areas (Fig. 3). Surveys conducted in the Prairie Provinces between 1929 and 1932 by the National Research Council of Canada classed povertyweed as one of the most serious weed problems of the prairies (Manson 1932). Areas of pasture in western Canada densely populated with *Iva axillaris* ssp. *axillaris* are of little or no value for grazing. Plants of *I. axillaris* ssp. *axillaris* and ssp. *robustior* shed large amounts of pollen and, although considered as unimportant in California (Rowe 1928), the pollen has long been regarded as causative agent for hay fever (Pammel 1911; Wodehouse 1935). Scheppegrell (1917) claimed it to be next to sagebrush (*Artemisia tridentata* Nutt.) in this regard. Povertyweed is able to absorb selenium compounds from the soils of Cretaceous or Eocene shales in sufficient quantities to make it poisonous to animals (Muenscher 1940).

(b) Beneficial — None known.

(c) Legislation — Povertyweed is listed under the Seeds Act and Regulations administered by Agriculture Canada (1967) in the category "other weeds" and is classed as noxious by the Government of Saskatchewan (1966) and by the Government of Manitoba (1971).

4. Geographical Distribution

Povertyweed is native to western Canada (Fig. 2). It is listed as a new weed in southern Australia (Johnson 1933), but the plant is not known to occur on other continents (Godel 1934). Ssp. *axillaris* is common on the Canadian Prairies, being found east of the Continental Divide to Manitoba, in the Peace River area of Alberta and southward through the Dakotas to Colorado (Bassett et al. 1962). Manson (1932) noted that in Alberta the weed appeared to be confined to the Drumheller area, while Alex (1966) recorded light infestations in 23 municipalities, medium infestations in 12 municipalities and heavy infestations in 4 municipalities. Best (unpublished data) found the weed as far west as Lundbreck in the Porcupine Hills. Povertyweed was found to exist in 205 of 897 townships in Saskatchewan in surveys between 1929 and 1932, the two main centers of infestation being on the fine-textured soils of the Regina plains and southwest of Rosetown to the Alberta border. However, the weed was not confined to fine-textured soils, but was found throughout the province from Lloydminster to Arcola and from Lafleche to Melfort (Manson 1932). Coupland et al. (1953), summarizing the Saskatchewan Weed Surveys of 1949–1953, suggested that povertyweed probably occurs throughout the area in native grassland, and appeared to be more abundant in the fine-textured soils. A brief sampling survey of the area between Rosetown and the Saskatchewan Landing, made in 1951, revealed that 28% of the quarter-sections supported troublesome infestations, each averaging 10.5 hectares in extent. Coupland et al. (1953) calculated that 4,434 hectares were infested in 458 quarter-sections in a 9.66-km strip through the three municipalities involved. In the rest of the surveyed area, farmers reported infestations in a total of 5,177 quarter-sections in 25 municipalities. Alex (1966) recorded light infestations in 140 municipalities in

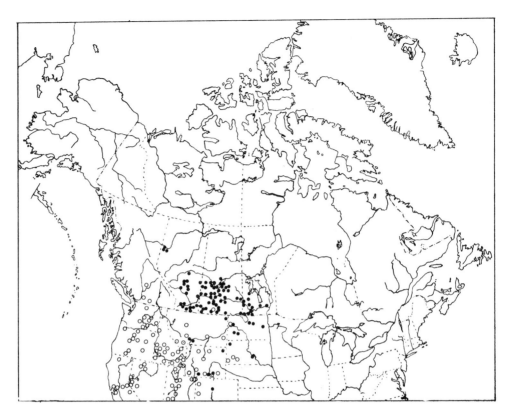

Fig. 2. Distribution of *Iva axillaris* Pursh ssp. *axillaris* and ssp. *robustior* (Hook.) Bassett in Canada and the northern United States (after Bassett et al. 1962). *Legend* — ● *Iva axillaris* ssp. *axillaris*; ○ *Iva axillaris* ssp. *robustior*.

Saskatchewan, medium infestations in 35 municipalities and heavy infestations in 10 municipalities.

Surveys between 1929 and 1932 did not report the presence of *I. axillaris* from Manitoba at that time (Manson 1932); Alex (1966) reported light infestations in 20 municipalities from Manitoba, medium infestations in 7 municipalities, but none classified as heavy infestations. Best (unpublished data) found the weed as far east as Rosser, near Winnipeg.

Ssp. *robustior* occurs mainly west of the Continental Divide, from southern British Columbia to California and New Mexico, and eastward to the Dakotas. This subspecies has been found at one location on the Canadian Prairies, at Wood Mountain in

Saskatchewan (herbarium specimen 10917 in National Museum of Canada, Ottawa, Ont.). The distribution of ssp. *robustior* is much more widespread in the United States than that of ssp. *axillaris* (Bassett et al. 1962).

5. Habitat

(a) Climatic — Povertyweed (ssp. *axillaris*) is adapted to the climatic conditions existing in western North America. A slow-growing species, it seldom exhausts its root reserves and can remain relatively dormant for long periods of time under severe competition or adverse weather conditions (Canada Dep. Agric. 1938).

(b) Substratum — Ssp. *axillaris* is generally found in poorly drained alkaline regions on

114

Fig. 3. Suppression of wheat growth in a heavy infestation of *Iva axillaris* Pursh ssp. *axillaris*.

clay and clay loam soils and frequently in cultivated fields (Bassett et al. 1962). The fact that such soils are often wet late in the spring, and proper cultivation practice is delayed, probably favors the persistence of povertyweed in this type of habitat. Godel (1934) found povertyweed to be prevalent on soils with a high clay content, but it also thrives on other types of soil. Harding (1939) reported that the species showed a preference for low, slightly alkaline areas, but that it was also often found on high, well drained locations. Soil from 79 infestations and from 32 adjacent areas that were free of the weed was sampled to a depth of 7.5 cm. Ssp. *axillaris* was found on soils varying from sandy loam to clay, with pH from 6.59 to 8.77. Sodium content ranged from a low of 2.83 to a high of 6.10. There were no significant differences between the pH and the sodium content from the in-fested and adjacent non-infested soil (Best 1962).

(c) Communities in which the species occurs — Surveys have shown that in low areas the presence of povertyweed is often associated with *Hordeum jubatum* L., *Suaeda depressa* (Pursh) S. Wats. and *Salicornia rubra* Nels. (Best 1960; K. F. Best, unpublished data).

6. History

Iva axillaris ssp. *axillaris* was collected by Bradbury in 1809–1811, probably in the North Central and Western States, which was then part of upper Louisiana. Macoun collected the subspecies in 1896 on open saline prairie 32 km north of Brandon, Manitoba. *Iva axillaris* ssp. *robustior* was collected by Douglas on the Columbia River in 1824–1825 (Bassett et al. 1962).

7. Growth and Development

(a) Morphology — Povertyweed (ssp. *axillaris*) seldom develops as a seedling, due to the scarcity of viable seeds. The root system consists of a large number of deep and profusely branched taproots that contain strong, corky or resinous layers in the bark that are practically impervious to moisture. These thick, generally succulent perennial structures are abundantly supplied with root reserves (Pavlychenko 1943). The extent of root development is indicated (Fig. 4) where a soil monolith 30.5 cm × 15.25 cm × 1.2 m deep was removed from an infested pasture, and washed to remove the soil without disturbing the pattern of root growth. Although the monolith was taken to the 1.2-m depth, roots were still present at a depth of 1.8 m. Laterals were observed at 20 cm and again at a depth of 60 cm.

(b) Perennation — Ssp. *axillaris* survives and spreads primarily by extremely persistent roots. These roots, with abundant food reserves, overwinter in the Canadian Prairies and produce new shoots in the spring. Individual patches are probably genetically one clone and spread by vigorous underground roots.

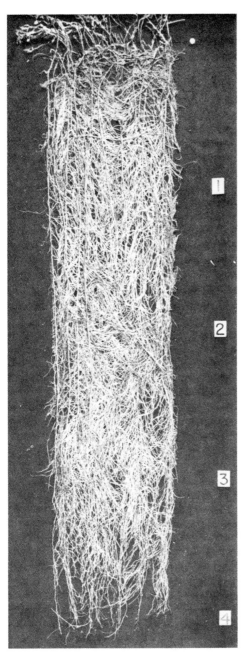

Fig. 4.   Roots of *Iva axillaris* Pursh ssp. *axillaris* from a soil monolith 30.5 cm by 15.3 cm to a depth of 1.2 m.

(c) Physiological data — When povertyweed occurs in dense patches on cropland, there is usually a marked reduction in the stand of the crop in the immediate area of the patch (Fig. 3). Germination of wheat (*Triticum aestivum* L.) in pots of soil was reduced when moistened with extracts from topgrowth of povertyweed. There was also a suppression of shoot and root development of those seeds that did germinate. Growth of wheat and flax (*Linum usitatissimum* L.) in soil from a field infested with povertyweed (ssp. *axillaris*) was suppressed when compared with crops seeded in povertyweed soil from adjacent areas of the same field (Best 1963a). Water extracts of the roots of povertyweed (ssp. *axillaris*) inhibited germination and seedling development of several grass and legume species (Lawrence and Kilcher 1962).

(d) Phenology — Time of maximum root development is not known. Ssp. *axillaris* flowers from June to August, producing relatively few seeds which rarely germinate. Regrowth of the roots begins by mid-March in south-western Saskatchewan (Best 1963a).

(e) Mycorrhiza — None known.

8. Reproduction

(a) Floral biology — Individual plants of povertyweed (ssp. *axillaris*) are evidently self-incompatible, or nearly so. Collections of self-pollinated material produced achenes with underdeveloped embryos. Achenes with developed embryos that germinate readily were produced from crosses between material from different clones established at Ottawa. Vivipary has not been recorded (Bassett et al. 1962).

(b) Seed production and dispersal — Viable seed is seldom produced in nature, as it is often destroyed by insect larvae (Sect. 13a), and no specialized types of dispersal are reported.

(c) Viability of seeds and germination — Periodic testing of povertyweed seed (presumably ssp. *robustior*) at 20–22 C gave no

germination even after 22 mo of dry storage. Scarification was not effective in promoting germination. Achenes stored in screen bags in an irrigation canal showed no germination after being held for 1 mo. Germination of the seed increased to a peak of 43% after 7 mo of fresh-water storage in the canal, but declined to less than 3% after 10 and 11 mo. Germination again increased as water temperature declined. Evidently, a relatively high percentage of povertyweed seeds maintain sufficient viability after 22 mo of fresh-water storage to produce seedlings when placed under suitable conditions for germination (Bruns and Rasmussen 1953).

(d) Vegetative reproduction — Vigorous vegetative reproduction by means of rootstocks is the primary method of survival and spread. The shallow roots, active only in favorable years, are responsible for lateral spread, production of new shoots and storage of food. In 4 yr, a portion of perennial runner had expanded to form a patch 18.6 m in diameter (Pavlychenko 1943). Best (1962, 1963c) found that after 15 mo, isolated transplants of root cuttings produced as many as 52 shoots at distances up to 1.3 m from a parent plant. The deep roots remain relatively inactive in good years, producing only an occasional shoot despite large food reserves. Prolonged drought induces these roots to grow upwards to within 5–10 cm of the surface. They then turn horizontally and produce several shoots and a vertical root to support the new plants. This ecological adaptation enables povertyweed to grow luxuriously in years when all other vegetation perishes or just barely exists (Pavlychenko 1943).

9. Hybrids

Intermediates between the two subspecies have been recorded from locations in Colorado and Wyoming where ssp. *axillaris* and ssp. *robustior* occur together, but none have been found in Canada (Bassett et al. 1962).

10. Population Dynamics

Povertyweed (ssp. *axillaris*) in the Canadian Prairies is occasionally found as solitary plants, but more usually in small or large patches. Chepil (1936) classifies patches with up to 12 shoots per square meter as light infestations, and those with from 13–30 shoots/m^2 as medium infestations. When the density of povertyweed exceeds 30 shoots/m^2, it is regarded as a heavy infestation. In its native state, growing amongst prairie grasses, it is small and inconspicuous, 7.5–12.5 cm in height, and has rather woody roots. The patches are small but persistent and the plants have only a few stems. When this land is cultivated, these patches increase in size; the weed grows taller and becomes more branched, with the roots penetrating the soil to depths of 2.5 m or more. Under favorable moisture conditions, the roots are close to the surface and fairly abundant in number. Under moisture stress or in competition with other plants, such as grain crops, weeds or grass, no roots are found close to the surface; patches spread very little under these conditions (Chepil 1935, 1936; Harding 1939).

11. Response to Herbicides and Other Chemicals

Povertyweed (ssp. *axillaris*) is classed as being resistant to 2,4-D at rates that are recommended for use in cultivated crops. It may be practically eliminated from established stands of grass on rangelands and native pastures with annual applications of 2,4-D esters at 2.24 kg/ha, or 2,4-DB at 1.48 kg/ha over at least a 5-yr period. Small patches may be controlled with fall applications of sodium chlorate at 100–200 g/m^2. Picloram at 0.84 kg/ha on non-cropland and permanent pastures will control povertyweed, although some grass damage may result (Canada Weed Committee 1971).

12. Response to Other Human Manipulations

Povertyweed (ssp. *axillaris*) is most difficult to eradicate by tillage methods. Practically all of the methods tried have failed to eradicate the weed. Even 3 yr of black summer fallow, with continuous cultivation throughout the entire period, have failed to eradicate the weed completely. Povertyweed can be effectively kept in check on the western prairies by an alternating wheat (*Triticum aestivum* L.) and summer-fallow system. Experiments have shown that a fair crop could be produced on weedy land following summer fallow, but the growing of stubble crops on infested land is practically useless. Perennial hay crops such as smooth brome (*Bromus inermis* Leyss.), crested wheatgrass (*Agropyron cristatum* (L.) Gaertn), alfalfa (*Medicago sativa* L.) and sweet clover (*Melilotus officinalis* (L.) Lam.) will suppress the weed to some extent. A uniform 4-yr-old stand of smooth brome was found to have less suppressing effect on povertyweed than did a 4-yr-old stand of alfalfa, possibly due to the shallower root system of the smooth brome (Chepil 1936). Povertyweed is able to withstand much trampling.

13. Response to Parasites

(a) Insects and other nondomestic animals — Ssp. *axillaris* is not usually grazed by livestock or other animals. Large numbers of this weed are untouched in well grazed fields and it appears that animals learn to avoid it. The larvae of a small curculionid beetle (*Smicronyx utilis* Buchanan) have been found in well developed achenes, resulting in complete embryo destruction and sterile heads (Remple and Shevkenek 1941). A beetle, identified as *Zygospila conjuncta conjuncta* (Rog.), has been observed methodically stripping the emerging shoots of povertyweed in many locations in the southern part of the prairies. Though appearing to be native to the area, the beetle lacks a common name and little is known regarding its host plants (Best 1963b). Several plant feeders have also been recorded as active on ssp. *axillaris*. These include a member of the squash bug family, *Rhophalus viridicatus* (Uhler) (hemip-

tera: Coreidae), and a hop flea beetle *Psylliodes punctulata* Melsh. (Coleoptera: Chrysomelidae). Other leaf feeders belonging to the Chrysomelidae found on the subspecies include *Systena blada* (Melsh.) *Monoxia angularis* (Le Conte) and a species of *Calligrapha*. Two predators, a softwinged flower beetle *Collops vittatus* (Say) (Coleoptera: Melridae) and the ladybird beetle *Hippodamia parenthesis* (Say) (Coleoptera: Coccinellidae) have been collected from the typical subspecies (M. Maw, personal communication, Agriculture Canada, Research Station, Regina, Saskatchewan).

(b) Micro-organisms and virusus — Povertyweed (ssp. *axillaris*) is attacked almost every year by rust, but does not appear to be noticeably weakened (Godel 1934). Arthur (1934) and Bisby et al. (1938) reported *Puccinia intermixta* Pk. on povertyweed in Saskatchewan and Manitoba. Bisby et al. (1938) recorded *Albugo tragopogonis* (Pers.) S. F. Gray on povertyweed in Saskatchewan.

(c) Higher plant parasites — No information available.

AGRICULTURE CANADA. 1967. Seeds Act and Regulations. Queen's Printer, Ottawa. Ont. 50 pp.
ALEX, J. F. 1966. Survey of weeds of cultivated land in the Prairie Provinces. Exp. Farm, Regina, Saskatchewan. 68 pp.
ARTHUR, J. C. 1934. Manual of the rusts in the United States and Canada. Purdue Res. Foundation, Lafayette, Ind.
BASSETT, I. J., MULLIGAN, G. A. and FRANKTON, C. 1962. Povertyweed (*Iva axillaris*) in Canada and the United States. Can. J. Bot. **40**: 1242–1249.
BEST, K. F. 1960. Exp. Sta. Ann. Rep., Swift Current, Saskatchewan.
BEST, K. F. 1962. Res. Rep. Weed Comm. (West. Sect.).
BEST, K. F. 1963a. Exp. Sta. Ann. Rep. Swift Current, Sask.
BEST, K. F. 1963b. *Zygospila conjuncta conjuncta*. Soil Horizons **4**: 9–10.
BEST, K. F. 1963c. Povertyweed. Res. for Farmers **8**: 14–15.

BEST, K. F. 1965. Common names of weeds of Canada. S.C. 110, Exp. Farm, Swift Current, Saskatchewan. 27 pp.

BISBY, G. R., BULLER, A. H. R. and DEARNESS, J. 1938. The fungi of Manitoba and Saskatchewan. Nat. Res. Counc. Can., Ottawa, Ont.

BRUNS, V. F. and RASMUSSEN, L. W. 1953. The effect of fresh water storage on the germination of certain weed seeds. Weeds 2: 138–147.

CANADA DEPARTMENT OF AGRICULTURE. 1938. Experiments on the control of povertyweed. Weekly letter, June 9, Dom. Range Exp. Sta., Manyberries, Alta.

CANADA WEED COMMITTEE. 1969. Common and botanical names of weeds in Canada. Can. Dep. Agric. Publ. 1397. 67 pp.

CANADA WEED COMMITTEE. 1971. Rep. Res. Appr. Comm. for western Canada. 72 pp.

CHEPIL, W. S. 1935. Report on the control of povertyweed, experimental plots Eston, Sask. Can. Agric., Exp. Sub-Sta., Regina, Saskatchewan. 10 pp.

CHEPIL, W. S. 1936. Results of experiments on the eradication of povertyweed at Eston, Sask. Dom. Exp. Sta., Swift Current, Sask. 25 pp.

COUPLAND, R. T., SELLECK, G. W., ZILKE, S., and SELLECK, V. 1953. Survey of the abundance and distribution of persistent perennial weeds in Saskatchewan 1952. Dep. of Plant Ecology, Univ. of Saskatchewan, Saskatoon, Sask.

FRANKTON, C. 1958. Les mauvaises herbes du Canada. Minst. Agric. Can. Publ. 948. 198 pp.

FRANKTON, C. and MULLIGAN, G. A. 1970. Weeds of Canada. Can. Dep. Agric. Publ. 948. 217 pp.

GODEL, G. L. 1934. Povertyweed, Sask. Dep. Agric. Bull, 24/26. pp.

GOVERNMENT OF MANITOBA. 1971. The Noxious Weeds Act. Prov. of Man., Queen's Printer, Chap. N 110: 19

GOVERNMENT OF SASKATCHEWAN. 1966. The Noxious Weeds Act. Prov. of Sask. Queen's Printer, Chap. 236: 3937.

HARDING, W. H. 1939. Investigations on the control and eradication of povertyweed and wild morning glory. Proc. 5th Meeting Assoc. Comm. on Weeds. (West Div.) Nat. Res. Counc. 61 pp.

JOHNSON, W. C. 1933. Povertyweed, notes on the occurrence of a new weed at Sevenhills. South. Aust. Dep. Agric. J. 36: 1039.

LAWRENCE, T. and KILCHER, M. R. 1962. The effect of fourteen root extracts upon germination and seedling length of fifteen plant species. Can. J. Plant Sci. 42: 308–313.

MANSON, J. M. 1932. Weed survey of the Prairie Provinces. Nat. Res. Counc., Rep. 26. 34 pp.

MUENSCHER, W. C. 1940. Poisonous plants of the United States. The Macmillan Co., New York, N.Y. 277 pp.

MUENSCHER, W. C. 1955. Weeds (2nd Edition). The Macmillan Co., New York, N.Y. 479 pp.

MULLIGAN, G. A. 1961. Chromosome numbers of Canadian weeds. Can. J. Bot. 39: 1057–1066.

PAMMEL, L. H. 1911. A manual of poisonous plants. The Torch Press, Cedar Rapids, Iowa. 975 pp.

PAVLYCHENKO, T. K. 1943. Mode of vegetative propagation and ecological adaptation of the roots of perennial weeds. Sci. Agric. 23: 410–439.

REMPLE, J. G. and SHEVKENCK, W. 1941. Notes of the morphology, life history and economic importance of *Smicronyx utilis* Buchanan. Can. Entomol. 73: 100–104.

ROWE, A. H. 1928. A study of the atmospheric pollen and botanic flora of the east shore of San Francisco Bay. J. Lab. Clin. Med. 13: 416–439.

RYDBERG, P. A. 1932. Flora of the prairies and plains of central North America. Science Press Printing Co., Lancaster, Pa. 969 pp.

SCHEPPEGRELL, W. 1917. Hayfever, its cause and prevention in the Rocky Mountain and Pacific states. Public Health Rep. 412: 1135–1152.

WODEHOUSE, R. P. 1935. Pollen grains. McGraw-Hill Book Co. Inc., New York, N.Y. 574 pp.

THE BIOLOGY OF CANADIAN WEEDS.
11. *Ambrosia artemisiifolia* L. and *A. psilostachya* DC.

I. J. BASSETT and C. W. CROMPTON

Biosystematics Research Institute, Agriculture Canada, Ottawa, Ontario K1A 0C6.
Received 9 Oct. 1974, accepted 17 Jan. 1975.

BASSETT, I. J. AND CROMPTON, C. W. 1975. The biology of Canadian weeds.
11. *Ambrosia artemisiifolia* L. and *A. psilostachya* DC. Can. J. Plant Sci. **55**:
463–476.

This account of *Ambrosia artemisiifolia* L. (common ragweed) and *A. psilostachya*
DC. (perennial ragweed) summarizes the most recent biological information on
these species as part of a series of contributions on plants that are weedy in Canada.
Common ragweed is weedy in open disturbed habitats, particularly in southern
Ontario and Quebec and portions of the Maritime Provinces. Perennial ragweed is
most abundant in southern Saskatchewan and Manitoba.

Cette contribution à l'étude de la petite herbe à poux (*Ambrosia artemisiifolia* L.) et
de l'herbe à poux vivace (*A. psilostachya* DC.) résume les plus récentes données
biologiques sur ces espèces, et fait partie d'une série d'articles sur les mauvaises
herbes du Canada. On trouve la première dans les habitats ouverts dérangés,
notamment dans le sud de l'Ontario et du Québec, et dans certaines régions des
provinces Maritimes. La seconde est la plus répandue dans le sud de la Saskatchewan et du Manitoba.

1. Names

I. *Ambrosia artemisiifolia* L., Sp. Pl.
2:988. 1753. — **common ragweed**
(Canada Weed Committee 1969); **petite
herbe à poux** (Frankton and Mulligan
1974; Ferron et Cayouette 1970). Payne
(1970) has listed 20 scientific names including species, subspecies, varieties and forms
which he refers to synonymy under *A.
artemisiifolia* L. Of these, *A. elatior* L. and
A. artemisiifolia L. var. *elatior* (L.) De-
scourtils are those most frequently occurring in the weed literature.

II. *Ambrosia psilostachya* DC., Prodr.
5:536. 1836. — **perennial ragweed**
(Canada Weed Committee 1969); **l'herbe à
poux vivace** (Frankton and Mulligan 1974;
Ferron et Cayouette 1970). Payne (1970)
has listed 11 scientific names including
species, subspecies and varieties which he
refers to synonymy under *A. psilostachya*
DC. Of these, only *A. coronopifolia* T. &
G. and *A. psilostachya* DC. var.

Can. J. Plant Sci. 55: 463–476 (Apr. 1975)

coronopifolia (T. & G.) Farwell are frequently used.
Compositae, composite family, Composées.

2. Description and Account of Variation

I. *Ambrosia artemisiifolia* L. is an erect
annual herb 5–70 (–200) cm high with a tap
root. Spreading by seeds. Stems unbranched to bushy branched, glabrous to
rough hairy. Leaves short-stalked, mostly
opposite below, alternate above, thin, pinnatifid to tri-pinnatifid, blades of uppermost
cauline leaves occasionally unlobed.
Flower heads contain either male or female
flowers. Male heads 10–100 (–200) flowered, in spikes terminating the stems and
branchlets, bracts of flower heads united.
Female heads 1-flowered, sessile, inconspicuous in small clusters or single in the
axils of the upper leaves; male and female
flower heads are usually on different parts
of the same plant, plants are rarely entirely
female. Achenes obovate, 2.5 mm broad,
3.5 mm long with a central terminal beak up

to 2 mm long that is usually surrounded by a ring of spines to 1 mm long; outer coat of achene woody; within the outer coat is a whitish, oily, soft seed, that is enclosed by a brown membrane. Pappus lacking. Plants very variable in size, leaf shape, inflorescence form, and degree of hairiness.

Mulligan (1957) has reported chromosome counts of $2n = 36$ for *A. artemisiifolia* from eastern and western Canada. Payne et al. (1964) have reported the haploid number, $n=18$, for this species from Wyoming, U.S.A.

II. *Ambrosia psilostachya* DC. is an erect perennial herb 3–105 cm high with horizontal running root stocks. Spreading by seeds and rhizomes. Stems unbranched or branched, harshly pubescent with stiff, short, minutely glandular hairs. Leaves mostly opposite below, alternate above, thickish, light green to grayish green, subsessile or occasionally on short-winged petioles, pinnately to bi-pinnately lobed (rarely unlobed), margins entire or sparsely serrate. Flower heads contain either male or female flowers and are on different parts of the same plant. Male heads, 10–40 flowered, stalked to subsessile, arranged in spikes terminating the stems and branchlets, the involucre is hirsutulous with usually tuberculate-based hairs; corolla five-lobed. Female heads 1-flowered, sessile, single or clustered in the upper axils. Achene obovate, body 3 (–6) mm long and 3.5 mm broad with a short blunt beak about 0.6 mm long, outer achene coat woody; spines surrounding the beak usually blunt, sometimes lacking. Pappus absent.

Mulligan (1957) has reported a chromosome count of $2n = 72$ for *A. psilostachya* from Espanola, Ontario. Counts of $n=36$ or $2n=72$ or near that number were made on plants from eight different counties in Michigan (Wagner and Beals 1958). Payne et al. (1964) have reported chromosome counts for this taxa of $n=36$, 54, and 72. Miller et al. (1968) found that six populations investigated from central Texas and one from Mexico were diploid ($n=18$), a

condition not previously reported for *A. psilostachya*.

The morphological variability of *A. psilostachya* is probably related, at least in part, to the presence in this species of a polyploid series, although no correlation between particular ploidal levels and particular morphological expressions has yet been demonstrated (Payne 1970).

A. psilostachya (perennial ragweed) is very similar in appearance to *A. artemisiifolia* (common ragweed) except that the former is a perennial with horizontal creeping roots whereas the latter is an annual with a tap root. Perennial ragweed is usually a smaller plant with rougher, thicker, less lobed leaves and with involucral spines blunt or absent.

Bur-ragweed (*A. acanthicarpa* Hook.) is similar to common ragweed, especially in the flowering stage. However, bur-ragweed is usually decumbent and spreading, rarely erect and is strigose-hispid to hirsute with leaves mostly deeply bipinnatifid. Bur-ragweed occurs sporadically on sand dunes of southern Alberta and Saskatchewan.

A mature plant of *A. artemisiifolia* and the lower part of a plant of *A. psilostachya* illustrating underground root-stocks and leaf shape are shown in Fig. 1. Also shown are seedlings of the two taxa. The drawings are modified from Frankton and Mulligan (1970).

3. Economic Importance

(a) *Detrimental* — I. *A. artemisiifolia* (common ragweed) is weedy in grain fields, cultivated fields, open disturbed habitats, and along roadsides, particularly in southern Ontario and Quebec. Alex (1964) listed this annual species along with five other taxa as the most widespread and abundant of the 103 weedy species found in 88 fields of tomatoes (*Lycopersicon esculentum* Mill.) and sweet corn (*Zea mays* L.) surveyed in Prince Edward, Essex, and Kent counties of Ontario. Vengris (1953) estimated that common ragweed was in 69% of the corn fields, 50% of the potato (*Solanum*

Fig. 1. Common ragweed, *Ambrosia artemisiifolia*. A, plant; B, head of male flowers; C, "seed". Perennial ragweed, *A. psilostachya*. D, lower part of plant showing underground rootstocks; E, seedling of *A. artemisiifolia*. F, seedling of *A. psilostachya*.

tuberosum L.), 24% of the onion (*Allium cepa* L.), and 18% of the tobacco (*Nicotiana tabacum* L.) fields in the Connecticut River Valley, U.S.A.

The prevalance of common ragweed in all types of crops is well known, yet precise values of losses are difficult if not impossible to obtain (Dickerson 1968).

Common ragweed is the most abundant of the ragweeds and the most important cause of hay fever in eastern North America (Bassett and Frankton 1971). The plant or its pollen may produce a dermatitis in some people who are not necessarily sufferers from hay fever (Frankton and Mulligan 1970). Ragweed oil dermatitis commonly affects male outdoor workers over 40 years of age (Fromer and Burrage 1953).

II. *A. psilostachya* (perennial ragweed) is weedy in abandoned fields, vacant lots, along roadsides and railway embankments, particularly in the Prairie Provinces.

Perennial ragweed does shed large quantities of air-borne pollen that causes hay fever symptoms (Wodehouse 1971). However, the more localized occurrence of plants and their smaller size lessens the importance of perennial ragweed as a cause of hay fever.

(b) *Beneficial* — Many primitive medical uses have been reported for common ragweed (*A. artemisiifolia*). The fluid extract of the flowering herb has been used to stop local bleeding (Bausor 1937). It is a bitter tonic sometimes used for dyspepsia. Baldwin and Handley (1946) have reported that in Virginia, between 15 November and 31 January (1929–1931), common ragweed was second only to legumes as winter food for the quail. Roedel and Thornton (1942) reported that common ragweed has about the same oil content as soybean (*Glycine max* Merr.), but better drying properties; they suggested utilizing ragweed oil in paints or varnishes.

No beneficial uses are known for *A. psilostachya* although, where abundant, seeds are probably used as a winter food by a number of bird species.

(c) *Legislation* — Common ragweed is classified as a secondary noxious weed under the seeds act and regulations administered by the Plant Products Division, Agriculture Canada (1967).

Common ragweed is included in the noxious weed list published for British Columbia (Anonymous 1960). Only the name "ragweed" is listed in the Saskatchewan Weed Act (Anonymous 1965). Common and perennial ragweeds are listed in the noxious weed act of Manitoba (Anonymous 1970). The revised Weed Control Act and Regulations for Ontario (Anonymous 1973a) includes ragweed, *Ambrosia* spp., in its list. In Quebec (Anonymous 1964), common ragweed is considered noxious when growing on the borders of roads, lanes or streets, along railways, transmission lines and ditches on farms, vacant and occupied lots. In the counties of Bonaventure, Gaspé-Nord, Gaspé-Sud, Matapedia, Rimouski, Matane, Rivière-du-Loup, and Témiscouata, perennial ragweed is considered noxious. In the regulations to the weed control act for Nova Scotia (Anonymous 1968) ragweed is considered secondary noxious.

4. Geographical Distribution

I. *A. artemisiifolia*: In Canada, common ragweed has been reported from all provinces and the Mackenzie District, N.W.T. (Fig. 2). Information gathered from herbarium sheets, floras and recent surveys suggest that it is very rare in the Mackenzie District and in British Columbia; rare in Alberta, except in the areas around Medicine Hat and Empress where it is firmly established in depressions, on banks of ponds, small lakes and occasionally at the edges of cultivated land; rare in Saskatchewan, except in the southern portion around Estevan, where a few small patches occur in disturbed habitats; found in small patches about communities and along roadsides in the southeastern portion of Manitoba; abundant and widespread in southern Ontario and Quebec; occurring frequently

123

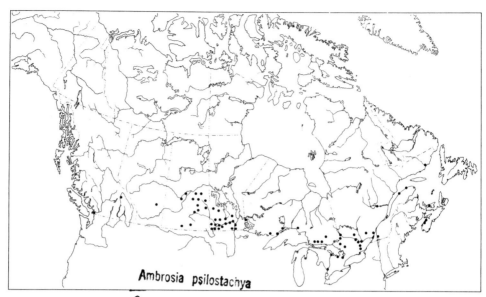

Fig. 3. Distribution of *Ambrosia artemisiifolia* in Canada.

in patches in disturbed habitats around communities and along roadsides in New Brunswick; fairly common along roadsides and disturbed habitats in the Annapolis Valley, and scattered about the larger communities along the south and east coastline of Nova Scotia; found in small patches in disturbed habitats throughout Prince Edward Island; and very rare in Newfoundland. It has been widely introduced in Europe, Asia, and South America.

II. *A. psilotachya*: Perennial ragweed occurs in all provinces except Newfoundland (Fig. 3). It is rare in British Columbia,

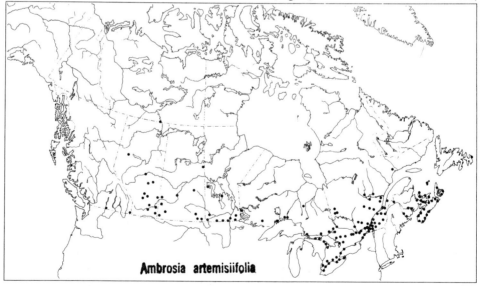

Fig. 2. Distribution of *Ambrosia psilostachya* in Canada.

124

Alberta, Ontario and the rest of eastern Canada. The area of greatest concentration of the perennial ragweed lies in southeastern Saskatchewan and southern Manitoba. Outside North America, the perennial ragweed has been found in many countries of Europe (Lawalrée 1947) and in Australia (Eardley 1944). Allard (1943) states that all ragweeds are most common between latitudes 45° and 30°, both north and south, throughout most of the earth's surface.

5. Habitat

(a) *Climatic requirements* — I. *A. artemisiifolia*: Temperature is the most important factor affecting the germination of common ragweed. Dickerson (1968) attempted to closely define the optimum temperature for germination. Temperatures of 10, 20, 30, and 40 C and all combinations for durations of 8, 16, and 24 h (continuous) were used. Alternating temperatures are required for maximum germination; after 28 days with continuous temperatures of 10, 20, 30, and 40 C, germination was 6.9, 8.6, 8.1 and 0.8%, respectively. Alternating temperatures of 10 C for 16 h and 30 C for 8 h in 24-h cycles (mean 16.7 C) resulted in 75% germination. Alternating temperatures of 20 C for 16 and 30 C for 8 h in a similar cycle with a mean of 23.3 C produced 50.1% germination. The alternating temperatures of 10–30 C relate closely to field conditions during the spring and early summer, in southern Ontario and Quebec, an area where the common ragweed is most abundant in Canada.

Another experiment by Dickerson (1968) determined that soil moisture levels of from 14 to 22% are required for germination of *A. artemisiifolia*.

Erosional disturbances such as rain-wash channels or gulleys, and microdisturbances such as soil heaps from the runways of burrowing animals also play an important role in the presence of common ragweed in some areas (Gebben 1965). Curtis and Partch (1948) noted that *A. artemisiifolia* increased greatly after the burning of grasslands.

Turner (1928) states that common ragweed grows most successfully on soils from *p*H 6.0–7.0; its optimum soil type is silt loam and silt clay loam. Plants growing at an optimum *p*H are vigorous, very abundant, and range in height from 30 to 90 cm. Plants growing in a strongly acid soil are less vigorous, fairly abundant and range in height from 7.5 to 15.0 cm.

II. *A. psilostachya*: No specific information on climatic requirements is available for the perennial ragweed.

(b) *Substratum* — I. *A. artemisiifolia*: Common ragweed is widespread on arable land and in ruderal situations grows in clay, silt and sand mixtures. The stiff, erect stem ranges from a few centimeters in height, on plants in light sandy soils, to over one meter on plants in heavy fertile soils (Gebben 1965).

II. *A. psilostachya*: In Michigan, Wagner and Beals (1958) noted that the species forms large clones by proliferation from underground parts in disturbed habitats such as along roadsides and railways, especially around populated areas. Perennial ragweed will invade grassy fields. In southern Saskatchewan and Manitoba perennial ragweed is often found growing in sandy alkaline regions in open habitats.

(c) *Communities in which the species occur* — I. *A. artemisiifolia*: Common ragweed is abundant in cereal crops, cultivated row crops, in recently disturbed fields, waste places and occasionally along the edges of roadsides. In fields seeded down to clover (*Trifolium* sp.), and alfalfa (*Medicago* sp.), scattered plants may occur in the first year of growth. In permanent pastures, lawns, marshes, and woodlands, common ragweed is very rare or absent.

II. *A. psilostachya*: Perennial ragweed occurs in abandoned fields, open prairie, vacant lots, roadsides, and railway embankments. In Michigan, perennial ragweed thrives in disturbed sites (Wagner and Beales 1958). In southern Saskatchewan and Manitoba it often occurs in poor pasture fields and along the edges of alkaline sloughs (Bassett and Crompton, unpublished).

6. History

I. *A. artemisiifolia*: Common ragweed, native to North America, was recorded as early as 1838 in Michigan, U.S.A., according to Wagner and Beals (1958). One of the earliest collections of *A. artemisiifolia* in eastern Canada was taken in 1860 by B. Billings at Prescott, Ontario (Bassett and Terasmae 1962). An early collection (1879) of the species by Macoun in Saskatchewan, critically studied by Frankton as to date and locale, might be taken to establish that it is native to the Canadian Prairies (Moss 1956). Further evidence that *A. artemisiifolia* is native to the Canadian Prairies is the listing of the plant by Bourgeau in 1860 published by Palliser (1863).

In Ontario, *Ambrosia* fossil pollen is present all through the postglacial time (Bassett and Terasmae 1962). It may be of interest to note that *Ambrosia* pollen has been found in southern Ontario and Quebec in interglacial deposits older than 60,000 yr. Thus *Ambrosia* has a long history in eastern Canada. Its pollen is somewhat more abundant in late-glacial sediments than in younger postglacial ones except subrecent ones. Open unvegetated land in late-glacial time apparently provided suitable habitats for the migration and spread of ragweeds to the north. Another explanation of the higher percentages of *Ambrosia* at that time is the fact that the quantity of tree pollens was relatively low. It is only within the last 200 yr or so that ragweeds have again become abundant. This increase coincides with settlement by the white man, the removal of trees in favor of large agricultural development, and the resultant provision of numerous disturbed habitats.

II. *A. psilostachya*: Although perennial ragweed is certainly native in western North America there is evidence that this species has been in eastern Canada for a considerable time. *A. psilostachya* has been collected at several locations in eastern Canada, in open undisturbed habitats, along with other species now largely confined to western America. Seventeen native western species including perennial ragweed, have been collected at Nomininingue, Quebec. This suggests that shortly after the retreat of the Wisconsin ice, *A. psilostachya* migrated from the southwest into these eastern areas. With changing conditions brought about by the establishment of forest, this species survived only as a relict at a few locations. There is also evidence, from its frequency along railways, that perennial ragweed has been intoduced in recent times from western into eastern Canada (Bassett and Terasmae 1962).

7. Growth and Development

(a) *Morphology* — I. *A. artemisiifolia*: At Ottawa the growth of the common ragweed, observed over several seasons, was not as great through May and June as in July and August. The rate of growth was at its peak between 15 July and 15 August. Mature seed was formed on plants near the end of August and early September (Bassett and Crompton, unpublished).

II. *A. psilostachya*: Along the rhizomes of the perennial ragweed are found many adventitious roots that absorb moisture and nutrients from the upper levels of the soil profile. The new shoots arising from these creeping rootstocks may take more than 1 yr to reach flowering. Generally, only a few seeds develop at maturity on these shoots (Wagner and Beals 1958).

(b) *Perennation* — *A. psilostachya*: Perennial ragweed survives and spreads primarily by spreading rootstocks. In areas of southern Saskatchewan and Manitoba where the winters are extremely cold, the roots are able to survive and continue growing the following spring.

(c) *Physiological data* — I. *A. artemisiifolia*: Prince (1957) conducted several comparative analyses of ragweed and corn in New Jersey and found that ragweed generally absorbed much more boron, cop-

126

per, manganese, strontium, zinc, tin, galium, vanadium, bismuth, nickel, and chromium than corn. Large amounts of potassium, calcium, and magnesium were also generally found in ragweed as compared to corn leaves harvested at the tassel stage. Robinson et al. (1947) found approximately seven times as much zinc in common ragweed as in corn in plants growing in soil with a heavy concentration of that metal. They also noted that common ragweed would grow well on soils that contained enough available zinc to be toxic to other plants. The data from these experiments point out that ragweed will accumulate large quantities of trace elements. Dickerson (1968) states that it is difficult, however, to draw any firm conclusions concerning the occurrence, ecology, and competitive ability of common ragweed from these data.

In shade experiments, common ragweed was found to grow as well as sweet corn or dry beans (*Vicia* spp.), in 30% shade but much poorer in 73% shade. Common ragweed was also found to utilize much more water to produce an equivalent amount of fresh or dry weight than sweet corn or dry beans (Dickerson 1968).

II. *A. psilostachya*: No physiological information is available.

(d) *Phenology* — I. *A. artemisiifolia*: In 1961 at Ottawa, 90% of the total emergence of common ragweed in an experimental plot occurred before 15 June (Bassett and Crompton, unpublished). At Ithaca, N.Y., the same percentage of the total emergence in test plots occurred before 9 June (Dickerson 1968).

In Canada it has been observed that plants from more northerly latitudes flowered earlier and produced less vegetative growth (Bassett and Crompton, unpublished). Payne (1962) states that Wagner found that plants from Nova Scotia, Michigan, and Louisiana required 45, 95, and 125 days, respectively, to reach full anthesis. Dickerson (1968) observed that plants from southern latitudes remained vegetative for longer periods before producing floral structures. Plants from Edmonton, Alta.; Winnipeg, Man.; Halifax, N.S.; and Ottawa, Ont. were grown in test plots at Ottawa. The more northerly plants flowered earlier and produced less vegetative growth than the Ottawa plants. These tests point out that *A. artemisiifolia* in Canada is adapted to different day lengths and that the flowering characteristics of the more northerly plants are inherited by their progeny (Bassett and Crompton, unpublished).

Over an 8-yr period the mean first flowering date at Ottawa for the common ragweed was 7 August (Bassett et al. 1961).

In relation to the photoperiodic response, seedlings emerging in early July at Ithaca, N.Y. produced approximately one-third as much fresh or dry weight as those emerging in mid-May (Dickerson 1968). Seedlings emerging in mid-May produced more than 32,000 seeds, while those that emerged in early July produced only about 3,100 seeds. A significant linear correlation was obtained between fresh weight and the number of seeds per plant.

II. *A. psilostachya*: Wagner and Beals (1958), in carrying out field studies in Michigan, found that the pollen and morphological development of perennial ragweed preceded that of the common ragweed by 2–3 wk. In *A. psilostachya*, 18% of the branches bore staminate spikes which were over 3 cm in length; many of these carried mature flowers.

(e) *Mycorrhiza* — *Opidium brassicae* (Woronin) Dang. in the Chytridiales is found on the roots of *A. artemisiifolia* in Ontario (D. J. S. Barr, personal communication). No other information is available.

8. Reproduction

(a) *Floral biology* — I. *A. artemisiifolia*: Common ragweed is primarily anemophilous (wind-pollinated). If insects ever visit the flowers it is only to eat the pollen (Wodehouse 1971). Greenhouse studies at Ottawa indicate that the plant produces viable seed autogamously and allogamously. There is no evidence that agamospermy or vivipary takes place (Bassett and Crompton, unpublished).

About 95% of plants of common ragweed are monoecious, a few are completely pistillate, and some plants exhibit an intermediate condition, being predominantly staminate or pistillate (Gebben 1965).

II. *A. psilostachya*: Perennial ragweed is primarily anemophilous. Wagner and Beals (1958) obtained 55% seed set on plants growing in Michigan. No greenhouse experiments have been carried out on this plant to determine whether viable seeds are produced autogamously.

(b) *Seed production and dispersal.* — I. *A. artemisiifolia*: Plants produce one seed per flowering head; the number per small plant averages slightly more than 3,000 seeds while large plants produce up to 62,000 seeds (Dickerson and Sweet 1971).

The fruit possesses no obvious dispersal mechanism. Gebben (1965) states that seed dispersal by water, birds, and man are important for the spread of common ragweed. Apparently wind plays a minor role in dispersal as no seeds were found beyond 2 m from experimental plants (Dickerson 1968).

II. *A. psilostachya*: The plant produces one seed per flowering head; Wagner and Beals (1958) counted a total of 118 flowering heads on one plant from which only 66 fruits developed to maturity. Since reproduction takes place largely by vegetative means, seed production in this plant is of secondary importance in its survival and spread.

The hybrid *A. artemisiifolia* × *A. psilostachya* (*A. intergradiens* Wagner) failed to produce a single fully formed fruit (Wagner and Beals 1958).

(c) *Viability of seeds and germination* — I. *A. artemisiifolia*: Durvel's (1905) study of buried seed vitality, initiated in the fall of 1902 at the Arlington Experimental Station near Baltimore, Maryland, involved seed burial at three depths in a heavy clay soil. These depths were: (1) 15–30 cm below the surface, (2) 45–55 cm (below the frost line at that latitude), and (3) 90–105 cm, where conditions of moisture, temperature, and oxygen were assumed to be nearly constant. The seeds were dug up and germination was attempted under laboratory conditions from 1903 to 1941 by Toole and Brown (1946). Their germination tests showed that ragweed seeds can remain viable for 39 yr or more when buried in the soil.

Gebben (1965) found that seedling emergence from seeds planted at the soil surface greatly exceeded seedling emergence from those buried at depths ranging from 2.5 to 15.5 cm in indoor and outdoor experiments. Dickerson (1968) noted that seeds subjected to frost and several months' storage exhibited from 25 to 86% germination. In recent studies Bazzaz (1970) found that when attempts were made to germinate stratified seeds of common ragweed in darkness they developed a secondary dormancy which was largely broken by re-stratification and subsequent exposure to light. In view of this and previous studies on the germination requirements of common ragweed, Bazzaz (1970) suggested that this complex germination behavior has ecological adaptations which allow this species to colonize disturbed areas and to maintain large populations on them.

II. *A. psilostachya*: No specific information is available on the viability of seeds and germination.

(d) *Vegetative reproduction* — I. *A. artimisiifolia*: No vegetative reproduction is known.

II. *A. psilostachya*: Through its spreading rootstocks, an area can be readily colonized by one or a few original plants despite the small seed set. Unlike common ragweed, perennial ragweed will invade grassy fields. The reproductive strategy appears similar in all habitats but the plant prefers sandy or gravelly well drained soils. In the 1st yr from seed the individual plant does not appear to produce additional shoots from its root system. In the 2nd yr new shoots emerge from the creeping rootstocks, thus establishing a clone which can cover about 2 m² (Wagner and Beals 1958).

9. Hybrids

The first interspecific hybrid described was a cross between *A. artemisiifolia* and *A. trifida* L. (Wylie 1915). The F_1 hybrids between these two plants resemble *A. trifida* with their coarsely lobed leaves, and are completely sterile.

A. artemisiifolia × *A. psilostachya (A. intergradiens* Wagner) has been found in several locations in Michigan by Wagner and Beals (1958) but has not yet been discovered in Canada. Wagner and Beals state that this hybrid often forms clonal populations that persist for many years. It is not known whether viable seeds are produced in these patches. Somatic chromosome counts from three localities of this hybrid were $2n = 54$.

Payne (1962) developed a fertile artificial hybrid between *A. artemisiifolia* and *A. acanthicarpa* in the greenhouse at Ann Arbor, Michigan. The leaves of the F_1 hybrid are larger and more finely divided than either of the parents. The seeds resemble those of *A. artemisiifolia* except that they have longer beaks and more spines. The staminate flowers of the hybrid are similar to those of *A. artemisiifolia*.

10. Population Dynamics

I. *A. artemisiifolia:* Gebben (1965) states that common ragweed in Michigan is most abundant in cereal crops, less abundant in cultivated row crops, common in fields in initial stages of abandonment, and sparse in clover and alfalfa hay fields the season following seeding. He also found that in Michigan, 59% of the total seasonal emergence of common ragweed occurred between 20 April and 4 May. Although seedlings were recorded in June they were fewer in number and very few seedlings emerged during the month of July.

Gebben (1965) further states that it appears that as temperature increases to a mean temperature of approximately 14 C, the germination and emergence of viable, vernalized seeds increases rapidly. Seeds germinating during subsequent periods are fewer in number due to the exhaustion of the supply of available, germinable seed at or near the surface, and continued later emergence is due to more deeply buried seeds. This study by Gebben in Michigan would also apply to southern Ontario and Quebec since the latitude, climate, and soil conditions are similar. Geben also states that "following emergence, the vegetative growth of the plant involves geometric increase in the number of nodes and a geometric increase in height of the vegetative plant axis. Elongation of the inflorescence followed a pattern similar to that of the vegetative portion of the plant axis, so that elongation of the axis appeared to continue uninterruptedly from the vegetative portion into the inflorescence."

In southern Illinois, fields are usually abandoned after corn cultivation. Bazzaz (1968) found that in the first season after abandonment, *A. artemisiifolia* was dominant in fields sampled during the 3rd wk of July. In the 2nd yr, common ragweed was also abundant (frequency 97%), but few individuals were more than 15 cm tall. In the 3rd yr, common ragweed had a frequency of 80%; however, the plants were rather small and inconspicuous. In the 4th yr, common ragweed was not listed in the plants dominating the undisturbed fields. From the 4th yr on it maintained a low importance value but was found on eroded areas in fields of all ages.

Survival of ragweed seedlings at Willow Run, Michigan was high (approximately 85%) according to Gebben (1965). Few predators kill growing ragweed plants. Although seedling mortality prior to emergence was not investigated, fungal "damping off" of postemergence seedlings probably is insignificant in field environments (Gebben 1965).

129

II. *A. psilostachya*: Wagner and Beals (1958) noted that the vast majority of plants in typical exposed situations on sterile soil along roadsides and railways have a simple axis with only a single terminal staminate spike or with one or a few laterals in the upper fourth of the plant. They observed that a few more lateral branches may tend to develop from axillary buds as the season progresses, thus extending the potential flowering time. If the main stem of a plant is cut off or otherwise damaged during the first half of the summer, a short, "bushy" specimen will result with numerous branches arising from the base of the stem.

The morphology and maturation of fruits varies to some extent from clone to clone. It is not uncommon to find populations of perennial ragweed in which only a small number of fruits have been produced (Wagner and Beals 1958).

11. Response to Herbicides and Other Chemicals

I. *A. artemisiifolia*: Common ragweed is killed by one application of 2,4-D; 2, 4, 5-T; MCPA; Fenoprop (Silvex) or Mecoprop at concentrations of 180 ml/ha (16 oz/acre) or by 228 ml (20 oz) or less of 2,4-D B or MCPB or with one application of Dicamba at 24 ml/ha (6 oz/acre) (Anonymous 1973b). Spraying is effective during the months of June, July, and August.

II. *A. psilostachya*: Perennial ragweed infesting a pasture near Lincoln, Nebraska was effectively controlled by one application of Picloram (Tordon) at concentrations of 1.8 kg/ha (1 lb/acre) but 2,4-D at 3.6 kg/ha (2 lb/acre) was inconsistent (McCarty and Scifres 1972). Picloram and Dicamba at concentrations of 0.9, 1.8 and 3.6 kg/ha (0.5, 1.0 and 2.0 lbs/acre) and 2,4-D at 3.6 kg/ha (2 lbs/acre) provided effective control for perennial ragweed when applied for 2 successive yr.

No information is available on the chemical control of perennial ragweed in Canada.

12. Response to Other Human Manipulations

I. *A. artemisiifolia*: Common ragweed is able to adapt to mowing, trampling, and grazing. In an experiment carried out at Ottawa, 48 plants grown in a waste lot and averaging 5 cm high at the end of May were cut slightly above the cotyledon leaves. A week later 40 of the 48 plants were growing quite normally. Also, in surveying several grain fields near Ottawa, it was observed that ragweed plants cut in July developed several new stems and flowered about 10 days later than adjacent uncut plants. Several cuttings, therefore, are required in August to prevent flowering and seed development (Bassett and Crompton, unpublished).

Common ragweed responds to, and counteracts the effects of, cultivation and ploughing by the longevity of its seeds (Toole and Brown 1946). It has been shown by Dickerson (1968) that stirring (i.e. ploughing) the soil will decrease but not eradicate the growth of common ragweed. Gebben (1965) implies that agricultural techniques, with modern equipment applied to row crops, kills many weed seedlings including those of common ragweed. Harrington (1960) noted that in Michigan airborne ragweed pollen counts were higher in rural tilled land than in a section of untilled land.

II. *A. psilostachya*: Continuous cutting during the summer months is necessary to prevent flowering and subsequent seed development. This practice must be carried out for several years to eradicate the plant clones through starving the spreading rootstocks.

13. Responses to Parasites

(a) *Insects and nondomestic stock* — *A. artemisiifolia* meets the criteria established by Harris (1971) and is deemed by him to be a plant suitable for biological control.

A comprehensive review of the insects found on *Ambrosia* spp. in North America is given by Harris and Piper (1970). They listed 217 taxa as occurring on *Ambrosia* spp. No evaluation is given, however, of the effects these insects might have in biological control. Recently Goeden et al. (1974) reported arthropods of Californian origin as being found on nine *Ambrosia* spp. These arthropods are: *Tarachidia candefacta* Hübner (Lepidoptera: Noctuidae); *Coleophora* sp. near *annulatella* Braun (Lepidoptera: Coleophoridae); and *Eriophyes boycei* Keifer (Acarina: Eriophyidae). These arthropods were recently exported to the U.S.S.R., from California, for biological control purposes.

(b) *Microorganisms and viruses* — Many parasitic fungi have been found on North American *Ambrosia* spp. Only those fungi considered to have some importance in reducing plant vigor are included in the following list. The names are from Connors (1967) or from the host index at the National Mycological Herbarium, Ottawa (DAOM). *Erysiphe cicharaceum* DC. ex Mérat (Erysiphales); *Albugo tragopogonis* (Pers.) S. F. Gray (Phycomycetes); *Plasmopara halstedii* (Farl.) Berl. & de Toni (Peronosporales); *Entyloma compositorum* Farl. (Ustilaginales); *Entyloma polysporum* (Pk.) Farl. (Ustilaginales).

Parmelee (1969) lists *Puccinia xanthii* Schw. as being the only autoecious rust occurring on *Ambrosia* spp. in Canada. This rust also infects *Xanthium* spp. *A. psilostachya* is reported as an aecial host for another rust, *Uromyces junci* (Desm.) L., which alternates on *Juncus* spp.

Aster yellow virus is reported on *A. artemisiifolia*, resulting in stunted plants with a one-sided infection (Kunkel 1926).

(c) *Higher plant parasites* — Dean (1934) reported that *A. artemisiifolia* serves as a host plant for *Cuscuta gronovii* Willd. in West Virginia, U.S.A.

AGRICULTURE CANADA 1967. Seeds Act and Regulations. Queen's Printer. Ottawa, Canada. 50 pp.

ALLARD, H. A. 1943. The North American ragweeds and their occurrence in other parts of the world. Science **98**: 292–294.

ALEX, J. F. 1964. Weeds of tomato and corn fields in two regions of Ontario. Weed Res. **4**: 308–318.

ANONYMOUS. 1960. Revised statutes of British Columbia, Chapter 267. Queen's Printer, Victoria, B.C.

ANONYMOUS, 1964. Réglement concernant les mauvaises herbes. Ministère de l'Agric. Qué. 639–641.

ANONYMOUS, 1965. An Act respecting noxious weeds. Queen's Printer, Regina, Sask. pp. 3939–3953.

ANONYMOUS. 1968. Regulations to the Weed Control Act. Queen's Printer, Halifax, N.S. pp. 1–6.

ANONYMOUS. 1970. The Noxious Weeds Act. Queen's Printer, Winnipeg, Man. pp. 1–20.

ANONYMOUS. 1973a. Revised Weed Control Act. Ministry of Agric. and Food, Toronto, Ont.

ANONYMOUS. 1973b. Guide to chemical weed control. Publ. 75. Prepared by: Members of the Ontario Herbicide Committee, Minister of Agric. Newfoundland–New Brunswick, Nova Scotia–Prince Edward Island. 87 pp.

BALDWIN, W. P. and HANDLEY, C. O. 1946. Winter food of bobwhite quail in Virginia. J. Wildl. Manage. **10**: 142–149.

BASSETT, I. J., HOLMES, R. M. and MACKAY, K. H. 1961. Phenology of several plant species at Ottawa, Ontario, and an examination of the influence of air temperatures. Can. J. Plant Sci. **41**: 643–652.

BASSETT, I. J. and TERASMAE, J. 1962. Ragweeds, *Ambrosia* species, in Canada and their history in postglacial time. Can. J. Bot. **40**: 141–150.

BASSETT, I. J. and FRANKTON, C. 1971. Canada havens from hay fever. Information Canada, Ottawa, Ont. 28 pp.

BAUSOR, S. C. 1937. A review of some medicinal plants. Part 2. Medicinal plants of our local flora. Torreya **37**: 45–54.

BAZZAZ, F. A. 1968. Succession on abandoned fields in the Shawnee hills, southern Illinois. Ecology **49**: 924–936.

BAZZAZ, F. A. 1970. Secondary dormancy in the seeds of the common ragweed, *Ambrosia artemisiifolia*. Bull. Torrey Bot. Club. **97**: 302–305.

CANADA WEED COMMITTEE. 1969. Common and botanical names of weeds in Canada. Can. Dep. Agric. Publ. 1397. 67 pp.

CONNORS, I. L. 1967. An annotated index of plant diseases in Canada. Can. Dep. Agric. Res. Br. Publ. 1251. 381 pp.

CURTIS, J. T. and PARTCH, M. L. 1948. Effect of fire on the competition between bluegrass and certain prairie plants. Amer. Midl. Nat. **39**: 437–443.

DEAN, H. L. 1934. Host plants of *Cuscuta gronovii*. Rhodora **36**: 372–375.

DICKERSON, C. 1968. Studies on the germination, growth, development and control of common ragweed (*Ambrosia artemisiifolia* L.) Univ. Microfilms Inc. Ann Arbor, Mich. 162 pp.

DICKERSON, C. T. and SWEET, R. D. 1971. Common ragweed ecotypes. Weed Sci. **19**: 64–66.

DURVEL, J. W. T. 1905. The vitality of buried seeds. U.S. Dep. Agric. Plant Ind. Bull. 83. 20 pp.

EARDLEY, C. M. 1944. Control of perennial ragweed (*Ambrosia psilostachya*). J. Dep. Agric. S. Australia **47**: 430–434.

FERRON, M. et CAYOUETTE, R. 1970. Noms des mauvaises herbes du Québec. Publ. 288-71. Minist. de l'Agric. et de la Colonisation du Québec. 113 pp.

FRANKTON, C. and MULLIGAN, G. A. 1974. Les mauvaises herbes du Canada. Minist. Agric. Can. Publ. 948 Révisée. 218 pp.

FRANKTON, C. and MULLIGAN, G. A. 1970. Weeds of Canada. Can. Dep. Agric. Publ. 948. 217 pp.

FROMER, J. L. and BURRAGE, W. S. 1953. Ragweed oil dermatitis. J. Allergy **24**: 425–433.

GEBBEN, A. I. 1965. The ecology of common ragweed (*Ambrosia artemisiifolia* L.) in southeastern Michigan. Univ. Microfilms Inc., Ann Arbor, Mich. 234 pp.

GOEDEN, R. D., KOVALEV, O. V. and RICKER, D. W. 1974. Arthropods exported from California to the U.S.S.R. for ragweed control. Weed Sci. **22**: 156–158.

HARRINGTON, J. B. 1960. Atmospheric pollution by aeroallergens. Progress report No. 4, part 3. Univ. of Michigan Office of Research Administration.

HARRIS, P. 1971. Biological control of weeds in Canada. Current approaches to biological control of weeds. Pages 67-76 *in* Technical communication No. 4. Commw. Inst. Biol. Control.

HARRIS, P. and PIPER, G. L. 1970. Ragweed (*Ambrosia* spp.: Compositae) its North American insects and the possibilities for its biological control. Tech. Bull. No. 13. Commw. Inst. Biol. Control. 117–140.

KUNKEL, L. D. 1926. Studies on aster yellows. Amer. J. Bot. **13**: 647–705.

LAWALRÉE, A. 1947. Les *Ambrosia* adventices en Europe occidentale. Bull. Jard. Bot. Etat Bruxelles **18**: 305–315.

McCARTY, M. K. and SCIFRES, C. J. 1972. Herbicidal control of western ragweed in Nebraska pastures. J. Range Manage. **25**: 290–292.

MILLER, H. E., MABRY, T. J., TURNER, B. L., and PAYNE, W. W. 1968. Infraspecific variation of sequiterpene lactones in *Ambrosia psilostachya* (Compositae). Amer. J. Bot. **55**: 316–324.

MOSS, E. H. 1956. Ragweed in southeastern Alberta. Can. J. Bot. **34**: 763–767.

MULLIGAN, G. A. 1957. Chromosome numbers of Canadian weeds I. Can. J. Bot. **35**: 779–789.

PALLISER, J. 1863. The journals, detailed reports and observations relative to the exploration of British North America, No. 11: 243–263. Botanical report. Eyre and Spottiswoode, London.

PARMELEE, J. A. 1969. The autoecious species of *Puccinia* on Heliantheae (Ambrosiaceae) in North America. Can. J. Bot. **47**: 1391–1402.

PAYNE, W. W. 1962. Biosystematic studies of four widespread weedy species of ragweeds (*Ambrosia*: Compositae) Univ. Microfilms Inc., Ann Arbor, Mich. 319 pp,.

PAYNE, W. W. 1970. Preliminary reports on the flora of Wisconsin No. 62. Compositae family U.I. The genus *Ambrosia* — the ragweeds. Wisconsin Acad. Sci. Arts and Letters **58**: 351–371.

PAYNE, W. W., RAVEN, P. H., and KYHOS, D. W. 1964. Chromosome numbers in Compositae. IV. Ambrosiae. Amer. J. Bot. **51**: 419–424.

PRINCE, A. L. 1957. Influence of soil types on the mineral composition of corn tissue as determined spectrographically. Soil. Sci. **83**: 399–405.

ROBINSON, W. O., LAKIN, H. W. and REICHEN, L. E. 1947. The zinc content of plants on the Friedensville zinc slime ponds in relation to geochemical prospecting. Econ. Geol. **42**: 572–582.

ROEDEL, G. F. and THORNTON, M. H. 1942. The composition and properties of rag-

132

weed seed oil. J. Amer. Oil Chem. Soc. **19**: 153–156.

TOOLE, E. H. and BROWN, E. 1946. Final results of the Durvel buried seed experiment. J. Agric. Res. **72**: 201–210.

TURNER, J. A. 1928. Relation of the distribution of certain Compositae to the hydrogen concentration of the soil. Bull. Torrey Bot. Club **55**: 199–213.

VENGRIS, J. 1953. Weed population as related to certain cultivated crops in the Connecticut River Valley, Massachusetts. Weeds **2**: 125–134.

WAGNER, W. H. and BEALS, T. F. 1958. Perennial ragweeds (*Ambrosia*) in Michigan, with the description of a new, intermediate taxon. Rhodora **60**: 177–204.

WODEHOUSE, R. P. 1971. Hayfever plants. Ed. 2. Hafner Publ. Co., New York, N.Y. 280 pp.

WYLIE, R. B. 1915. A hybrid ragweed. Proc. Iowa Acad. Sci. **22**: 127–128.

THE BIOLOGY OF CANADIAN WEEDS
12. *Dipsacus sylvestris* Huds.

PATRICIA A. WERNER

Department of Botany and Plant Pathology, Michigan State University, E. Lansing, Michigan.
Contribution no. 271, W. K. Kellogg Biological Station, Hickory Corners, Mich. 49060,
received 10 Jan. 1975, accepted 17 Mar. 1975.

WERNER, PATRICIA A. 1975. The biology of Canadian weeds. 12. *Dipsacus sylvestris* Huds. Can. J. Plant Sci. **55**: 783–794.

Dipsacus sylvestris Huds., wild teasel, is an introduced weed of pastures, abandoned fields and roadsides occurring in widely-spaced but very dense patches in southern Ontario, Quebec, northeastern U.S.A., and northwestern U.S.A. Original research and information from other studies are incorporated into a summary of the biology of this fugitive plant species.

Dipsacus sylvestris Huds., cardère des bois, est une mauvaise herbe introduite dans les pâturages, les champs abandonnés et les talus des routes. On le trouve en plaques dispersées, mais denses, dans le sud de l'Ontario, au Québec et dans le nord-est et le nord-ouest des Etats-Unis. L'auteur utilise ses recherches propres et les résultats d'autres études dans un résumé de la biologie de cette espèce fugitive.

1. Name

Dipsacus sylvestris Huds. — **Teasel** (Canadian Weed Committee 1969), wild teasel, card thistle; **cardère des bois**, cabaret des oiseaux, cardère sylvestre, chardon des forêts (Ferron et Cayouette 1970). Dipsacaceae, teasel family, Dipsacacées.

The binomial *D. sylvestris* Huds. has been used for the wild teasel by the majority of authors especially those in North America (e.g., Small 1913; Fernald 1950; Hitchcock et al. 1959; Gleason and Cronquist 1963), and the binomial *D. fullonum* L. reserved for the cultivated teasel. However, in several European and Asian floral treatments, the binomial *D. fullonum* L. is used for the wild teasel and *D. sativus* L. for the cultivated teasel (e.g., Bobrov 1957; Butcher 1961; Clapham et al. 1962). Ferguson and Brizicky (1965) discuss the taxonomic problem in detail and conclude that *D. fullonum* L. is the proper name for the wild teasel; however, in an effort to maintain consistency with current North American treatments, the binomial *D. sylvestris* Huds. is used here.

Can. J. Plant Sci. 55: 783-794 (July 1975)

2. Description and Account of Variation

Commonly classified as biennial, producing a low vegetative rosette up to 60 cm in diameter which overwinters and is followed in a succeeding growing season by a stout flowering stem 0.5–2.5 m in height; thick taproot often exceeding 75 cm in length; leaves lanceolate to oblanceolate, entire or undulate, rigid spines on underside of the midrib, also smaller spines set upon papillate bases on the upper surface of rosette leaves, leaves of the flowering stem are opposite, basally connate, forming a "cup" which may be filled with rainwater (hence the name *Dipsacus* from the Greek word meaning thirst); flowering stem pithy or hollow, opposite branching, each branch terminating in a capitulum (head); heads cylindric, 2.5–10 cm long, subtending involucral bracts linear with spiny midribs, those in the outer cycle curving upward and extending in length beyond the head; receptacular bracts ovate to lanceolate, acuminate into an awn surpassing the flowers; calyx reduced, silky; corolla lilac or dark pink of 4 fused petals, 10–15 mm; stamens 4; ovary inferior, 1-celled, with a single pendulous ovule; fruit an achene, 4–5 mm in length, enclosed in an adhering involucel (epicalyx), strongly 4-angled, slightly hairy, grayish brown in color (Fig. 1). The erect stems and capitula become woody in the autumn and are persistent throughout the winter, sometimes for 2–3 yr. Both the rosette and flowering forms resemble plants of the Compositae family in general appearance.

Chromosome numbers have not been reported from Canadian populations, but Werner (unpublished) reports $n=9$ in anthers from one plant collected in Michigan.

Two other species of *Dipsacus* have been introduced into North America but have relatively minor distributions in Canada. *D. laciniatus* L., slashed teasel, differs from *D. sylvestris* in the irregularly-cut pinnatifid leaves, white flowers, and the shorter involucral bracts which do not surpass head length. *D. fullonum* L., cultivated teasel or fuller's teasel, mainly differs from *D. sylvestris* in the awns of the receptacular bracts each of which are shorter, stiffer, and recurved into a strong "hook"; also, flowers are pinkish-lilac and the involucral bracts are similar to *D. laciniatus*.

Defoliation of large rosettes in the spring or early summer may result in delayed flowering (September–October instead of July) and stunted stems (0.1–0.5 m high). Should a flowering stem be broken during growth, its apex will continue to grow vertically, sometimes resulting in a contorted stem with several right-angled bends.

3. Economic Importance

(*a*) *Detrimental* — *Dipsacus sylvestris* is not a serious agricultural weed since it does not become established where the vegetation is removed each year (Ehrendorfer 1965). In some cases it may be a local nuisance, i.e., by becoming established in fallow fields or roadsides where human passage is hindered by large prickly stems. The plants are highly reduced in size in areas where cattle graze, probably by trampling of the rosettes. Unidentified lepidopteran stem borers have been found, one to a stem, in poorly-growing populations under partial shade; however, it is doubted that teasel serves as a significant refuge for insects harmful to crop plants. *Dipsacus sylvestris* is not known to be allelochemic, allergenic, or poisonous.

(*b*) *Beneficial* — The dried, empty flower heads are used in flower arrangements, outdoor wreaths, and for making toys or holiday decorations. When dry, the plant yields a blue coloring matter (dipsacotine) similar to indigo (Bobrov 1957). The showy flowers are frequently visited by insects which collect both pollen and nectar. Teasel plants are often found along the steep roadside banks of new highways where the potential for severe erosion is high without a covering vegetation. The large seeds serve as food for ants in the natural community. (Until 1950 *D. fullonum*, cultivated teasel, was grown commercially for its head which was used to "tease," or raise the nap on wool cloth. Mullins, 1951, gives an historical account of the use of fuller's teasel.)

4. Geographical Distribution

In Canada, *D. sylvestris* occurs in Ontario, Quebec and British Columbia. Teasel populations are especially common and abundant in southeastern Ontario (Fig. 2). In North America, *D. sylvestris* reaches greatest abundance in a triangle marked by Montreal, west-central lower Michigan, and eastern Virginia. Populations are quite scattered but locally abundant, perhaps indicative of multipe introductions from Eurasia (*see* section 6).

5. Habitat

(*a*) *Climatic requirements* — Ehrendorfer (1965) states that species of the genus *Dipsacus* are found in summer-humid temperate climates. In North America the northern limit of teasel distribution closely follows isopleths where less than 1% of the minimum daily temperatures fall below 0 C in May and below 10 C in July (Rayner

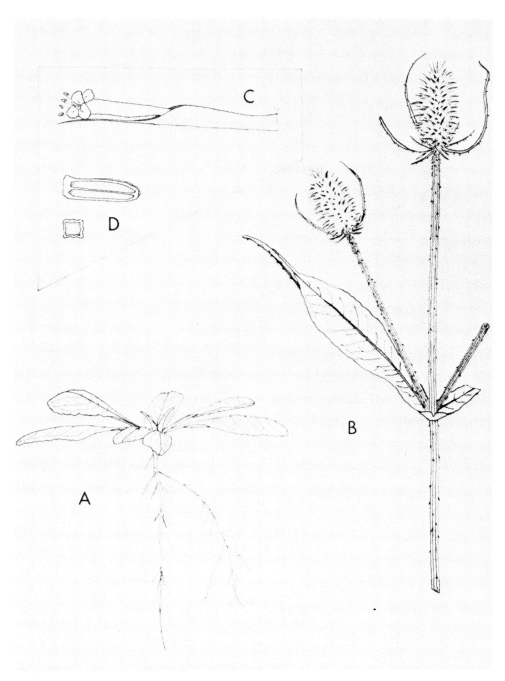

Fig. 1. *Dipsacus sylvestris* Huds. A. Rosette habit. B. Flowering habit, upper portion. C. Individual flower with receptacular bract. D. Achene. An individual leaf in A and B is approximately 30 cm in length; the involucral bract in C is 11 mm in length; the seed in D is 4 mm in length.

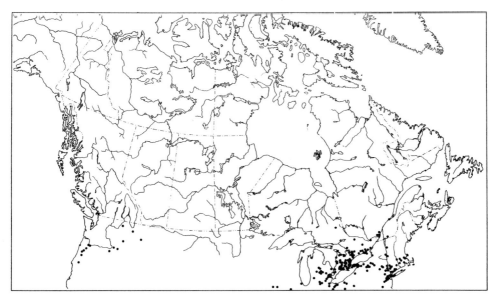

Fig. 2. Distribution of *Dipsacus sylvestris* in Canada and adjacent United States from herbarium specimens (see acknowledgments).

1961). No more specific information is available. In eastern Canada teasel's western and northern limits may be due to several factors, but probably cold climate and lack of adequate moisture are important.

(*b*) *Substratum* — The substrata in the distributional area of teasel are typically Gray–Brown Podsols, having been developed under temperate climates on alkaline parent materials under mixed hardwood forests. Within this group, *D. sylvestris* is found on a variety of soils, from sandy soils when abundant moisture is available, to heavy clay soils in poorly-drained areas such as ditches or low spots. Teasel also tolerates spring flooding very well. The largest teasel plants are found when conditions are such that soil moisture is maintained relatively high throughout the growing season. (*D. laciniatus* is found in a narrower range of, and somewhat wetter, habitats than *D. sylvestris*.)

(*c*) *Communities in which the species occur* — The species of the genus *Dipsacus* are found mainly in the later stages of succes-sion of abandoned crop or hay fields, on roadsides along irrigation ditches and creeks, and in other areas of disturbance; they may also be found in moist forest openings or cuttings. Table 1 presents data on percentage of foliage cover in eight abandoned fields in Kalamazoo Co., Mich. In estimating foliage cover, 26 subplots, each 0.25 m^2, are averaged for each field. Data for teasel growing in open facies in forests are not available. Both the rosette and flowering stages of *D. sylvestris* usually grow in open sunlight with leaf surfaces above dead plant litter or other vegetation.

6. History

Dipsacus is an Old World genus with about 15 species whose center of distribution is eastern Europe and western Russia (Bobrov 1957). In Canada, *D. sylvestris* was first collected in 1877 in Niagara Falls, Ontario. Collections throughout its current range of distribution were made before 1900. Introduction was probably made by early settlers deliberately as an ornamental or coincidentally with decorations or toys made from the heads.

7. Growth and Development

(a) *Morphology* — *Dipsacus sylvestris* plants possess a well-developed taproot that may extend to 75 cm in mesic soils, deeper than the roots of *Agropyron repens* L., its main competitor in many abandoned fields (Werner 1972). Spines on the leaves and stems discourage grazing by larger herbivores. The seeds float in water up to 22 days without any loss in numbers of viable seeds (Werner, unpublished).

(b) *Perrennation* — A biennial that produces new above-ground plant parts from the overwintering meristematic tissue in the crown at, or just below, ground level which has been protected by the bases of the rosette leaves. The blades of the rosette leaves often become brownish-green and portions die during the winter months.

(c) *Physiological data* — None are available.

(d) *Phenology* — Seeds germinate mainly from early April to early June; a few germinate in early September. The rosettes that develop from the seedlings continue to increase in size until late autumn. A plant may remain vegetative for several growing seasons; however, many reach the critical minimum size necessary for producing an erect flowering stem within the second growing season (Werner 1975a). The flowering stem usually begins to grow out of the old rosette base in May and reaches full height by early July. Flowers are continuously produced from July to early September. Within a single head, flowers first mature in a ring midway on the height of the head; then a ring of maturing flowers "moves" upward and another "moves" downward over several weeks' time. Seeds mature within the head and are dispersed from September to late November. The phenology of Ontario populations is about 2 calendar wk ahead of Michigan populations.

(e) *Mycorrhiza* — None known.

8. Reproduction

(a) *Floral biology* — The flowers are protandrous, the stamens ripening earlier than the pistil, their bent filaments becoming straight. The two posterior stamens develop earlier than the two anterior stamens (Szabo 1923). Flowers are visited by bumblebees (*Bombus* spp.) and other smaller bees which collect nectar and become covered with pollen (personal observation). In the summer of 1973, a field experiment was conducted in Michigan to determine whether plants of *D. sylvestris* are out-crossers. In early July, prior to flower development on each of five plants, one head of the pair immediately beneath the single central head was covered with a nylon airflow pollination bag that allowed passage of moisture and air, but not pollen or insects. The bags were fitted so that there was no contact with the flowers themselves; each was secured tightly under the head close to the stem. The opposite head in each pair was designated a control. In August, after flowering was finished, the bagged and control heads were removed to the laboratory where 10 seeds from each head were randomly selected, weighed, and viability determined using tetrazolium. No mold or visible differences between heads was observed.

When cross-pollination was prevented, the mean weight of seeds was 0.6 ± 0.1 (SE) mg, compared to 1.1 ± 0.2 (SE) mg for controls. A t test produced a t-value of -4.27 (df = 4) with a probability of 0.01 that the two groups of seeds are of the same weight. Only 4% of the seeds produced were viable when cross-pollination was prevented, compared to 70% of the controls (Table 2). Interestingly, it is likely that the control head on plant number 1 was missed by pollinators since it produced no viable seeds, compared to an average value of 87.5% for the remaining four controls. The above results indicate that allogamy is the most common means of fertilization, but that a few seeds are produced by some type of selfing.

138

Table 1. Percentage of foliage cover of species in eight fields in Kalamazoo Co., Michigan in August, 1970. All fields were abandoned cropland; fields A–D were 4th-yr fallow and fields J–M, 5th-yr fallow in 1970. Values are mean and standard error of 26 subplots, each 0.5 × 0.5 m

	Field							
	A	B	C	D	J	K	L	M
MONOCOTYLEDONAE								
Annual grasses								
Panicum capillare L.	–	–	–	–	<0.1	–	–	–
Setaria glauca (L.) Beauv.	<0.1	<0.1	–	<0.1	–	–	<0.1	–
Perennial grasses								
Agropyron repens (L.) Beauv.	71.7±4.3	70.0±2.4	61.5±4.7	70.0±3.3	21.4±5.3	92.5±1.4	70.3±5.4	64.5±3.8
Bromus inermis L.	–	–	–	–	–	–	5.8±3.0	–
Dactylis glomerata L.	–	–	–	–	–	–	<0.1	–
Phleum pratense L.	–	–	–	–	–	–	–	0.1±0.1
Poa compressa L.	–	<0.1	–	7.8±2.6	<0.1	–	0.4±0.2	8.7±3.6
DICOTYLEDONAE								
Summer annuals								
Ambrosia artemisiifolia L.	0.3±0.1	0.6±0.2	0.4±0.1	0.7±0.2	–	0.1±0.1	0.3±0.1	<0.1
Cerastium vulgatum L.	–	–	–	<0.1	–	–	–	<0.1
Chenopodium album L.	0.1±0.0	0.2±0.1	<0.1	<0.1	0.1±0.0	–	0.3±0.1	–
Lychnis alba Mill.	0.2±0.2	0.1±0.1	–	<0.1	0.4±0.2	–	0.6±0.2	0.2±0.1
Malva neglecta Wallr.	0.1±0.1	–	–	0.2±0.1	–	–	–	–
Oxalis stricta L.	<0.1	0.2±0.1	0.2±0.1	0.2±0.0	0.9±0.5	<0.1	2.3±0.9	0.2±0.1
Stellaria media (L.) Cyrill	–	–	–	<0.1	–	<0.1	–	<0.1
Winter–spring annuals								
Arabis spp.	–	–	–	–	1.2±0.7	–	0.1±0.1	–
Barbarea vulgaris R. Br.	0.4±0.2	0.1±0.0	0.2±0.1	<0.1	0.3±0.2	–	<0.1	–
Capsella bursa-pastoris (L.) Medic.	–	<0.1	–	1.2±0.6	–	–	–	–
Erigeron annuus (L.) Pers.	0.5±0.2	0.2±0.1	–	2.8±0.9	1.4±0.3	–	0.1±0.0	1.0±0.4
Erigeron strigosus Muhl.	<0.1	<0.1	–	–	–	–	–	–
Medicago lupulina L.	–	<0.1	–	<0.1	<0.1	–	–	0.1±0.0
Polygonum convolvulus L.	–	–	–	0.1±0.1	–	–	–	–
Thlaspi arvense L.	–	–	–	<0.1	–	–	–	–
Veronica peregrina L.	–	–	–	0.2±0.2	–	–	–	–
Veronica arvensis L.	–	–	–	0.2±0.1	–	–	–	<0.1

139

Table 1 (*Continued*)

	Field							
	A	B	C	D	J	K	L	M
Biennials								
Daucus carota L.	<0.1	–	0.4±0.2	0.7±0.4	5.4±1.9	–	8.6±3.4	0.1±0.1
Dipsacus sylvestris Huds.	21.5±5.3	25.7±4.0	7.6±2.0	6.7±1.3	5.5±1.7	2.5±1.2	10.1±3.8	25.8±5.1
Lactuca biennis (Moench.) Fern.	<0.1	<0.1	0.1±0.1	<0.1	0.6±0.4	0.1±0.1	<0.1	0.1±0.0
Lactuca canadensis L.	–	–	–	0.1±0.1	–	–	0.2±0.1	–
Melilotus spp.	<0.1	1.3±0.6	0.1±0.0	0.5±0.3	1.0±0.8	–	0.1±0.0	1.0±0.3
Sonchus oleraceus L.	–	–	–	0.3±0.1	<0.1	–	<0.1	<0.1
Verbascum thapsus L.	–	–	0.4±0.4	–	–	–	0.4±0.2	0.1±0.1
Verbascum blattaria L.	–	–	–	–	–	–	–	0.5±0.5
Woody perennials								
Lonicera spp.	6.7±2.5	–	–	–	2.0±1.0	–	–	–
Parthenocissus quinquefolia (L.) Planch.	–	–	–	–	–	4.8±2.0	1.0±0.6	–
Rhus typhina L.	–	19.2±4.8	54.9±6.5	36.6±6.4	58.1±6.6	0.6±0.4	7.0±3.2	25.2±7.3
Herbaceous perennials								
Achillea millefolium L.	0.2±0.2	–	–	0.1±0.1	–	–	–	–
Asclepias syriaca L.	–	–	–	0.6±0.6	–	–	–	–
Aster pilosus Willd.	0.1±0.1	<0.1	1.0±0.6	3.8±1.4	5.0±2.1	–	<0.1	0.1±0.0
Aster sagittifolia Willd.	–	0.3±0.2	2.1±0.8	0.4±0.2	31.6±4.2	–	0.8±0.4	–
Cirsium arvense (L.) Scop.	0.1±0.0	0.2±0.1	0.1±0.0	0.5±0.3	–	–	–	0.1±0.1
Hieracium spp.	–	–	<0.1	0.1±0.1	–	–	<0.1	–
Hypericum perforatum L.	–	–	23.3±5.3	–	–	–	0.1±0.0	–
Lotus corniculata L.	–	–	–	–	2.7±1.0	–	0.3±0.3	–
Nepeta cataria L.	–	–	–	0.3±0.3	–	–	0.1±0.0	–
Plantago spp.	–	0.5±0.3	–	–	–	–	0.4±0.4	0.2±0.2
Potentilla recta L.	–	–	–	4.0±1.9	<0.1	–	0.1±0.1	–
Rumex acetosella L.	0.8±0.8	–	–	–	–	–	0.2±0.1	–
Rumex crispus L.	0.5±0.2	–	–	–	–	–	–	–
Solidago canadensis L.	–	0.2±0.1	–	0.8±0.4	<0.1	–	0.4±0.1	–
Solidago graminifolia (L.) Salisb.	–	–	–	–	–	–	–	0.7±0.4
Taraxacum officinalis Weber	–	0.1±0.1	0.5±0.5	1.1±0.3	0.1±0.1	–	0.1±0.1	0.2±0.2
Trifolium pratense L.	–	0.1±0.1	–	<0.1	0.3±0.2	–	–	–
Trifolium repens L.	<0.1	<0.1	<0.1	0.9±0.7	<0.1	–	–	<0.1
OTHER								
Dicot litter	0.9±0.3	3.1±0.4	5.0±1.4	7.1±1.7	20.1±2.3	<0.1	3.1±0.6	6.7±2.0
Monocot litter	70.1±4.3	67.1±2.1	79.1±3.6	77.1±3.7	29.5±4.9	92.8±1.3	84.7±3.0	74.2±3.0
Bare ground	1.7±0.4	6.5±1.1	2.4±0.5	2.5±0.5	7.3±1.0	0.6±0.1	1.4±0.5	3.4±0.7

Table 2. Effect of preventing cross-pollination on numbers of viable seeds and weight of seeds produced

Plant no.	Mean weight of all seeds (mg)		Number of viable seeds per 10 seeds	
	X-pollination prevented	Control	X-pollination prevented	Control
1	0.7	0.8	0	0
2	0.5	1.6	0	9
3	0.9	1.6	2	6
4	0.5	2.0	1	10
5	0.3	1.9	0	10
$\bar{X}$ (± SE)	0.6 (±0.1)	1.1 (±0.2)	0.4	7.0

(b) *Seed production and dispersal* — As a member of the family *Dipsacaceae*, teasel produces one seed per fruit (achene). The number of seeds per inflorescence varies directly with the size of the capitulum and may be calculated from the equation $y = 186.5 x - 27.0$ where x = the length of the core of the flowering head and y = the number of involucral bracts, each of which supports one ovule (Fig. 3). These data indicate the average number of potential seeds per inflorescence is 854.6 ± 375.7 (SD). (Values may be multiplied by 0.8 to approximate the number of fertilized, hence viable, seeds.) The number of inflorescences per plant also varies with size of the plant, usually 3–9 in number, but as few as 1 or as many as 35 are not uncommon. A roadside population in Michigan had 3.9 ± 2.4 (SD; $n = 15$) per plant; hence, a single

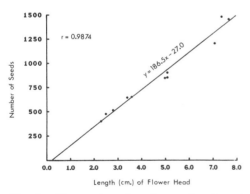

Fig. 3. The number of seeds as a function of the length of the central woody core of a flower head (capitulum) in *Dipsacus sylvestris* (wild teasel).

teasel plant might be expected to produce approximately 854.6 × 3.9 or 3,333, seeds. The seeds do not possess morphological adaptations for dispersal by wind or animals. When mature, they fall passively from the parent plant; 99.9% are deposited a distance less than 1.5 m (Werner 1975b).

For long-distance dispersal, the species probably depends upon the seeds' ability to float in water. Seeds in the laboratory germinate after floating up to 16 days in distilled water, and the spread of teasel through North America has been mainly along waterways. Goldfinches (Ridley 1930) and blackbirds (Pohl and Sylwester 1963) have been reported to feed on the seeds of *Dipsacus* species, although field observations of these birds in the study area by Caswell (personal communication) do not confirm this.

(c) *Viability of seeds and germination* — In natural conditions teasel seedlings are most often found in small open places such as those that occur when frost or mammals disturb the soil or the ''holes'' in the vegetation created when teasel rosette leaves die back during plant flowering. Natural plant litter, especially from quackgrass (*Agropyron repens*), inhibits seed germination (Werner 1975c). Although seeds are dispersed in the autumn, few seedlings are found until the germination pulse the following spring.

In the laboratory or greenhouse, teasel seeds harvested in October germinate in a few days at rates over 90% on soil or on moist Whatman #3 filter paper in petri dishes. No pre-germination requirements of freezing or cold have been found. Seeds fail to germinate in temperatures below 0 C.

In a study by the author on seeds collected in Michigan in October of 1968, '69, '72, '73, and '74, fresh seeds were germinated each year; and in 1973 seeds from 1968 and 1972 were also germinated using the following procedure. Seeds were shaken free of the heads, cleaned of chaff in an Erickson Seed Blower, and then germinated in replicated lots of 100 per petri dish on Whatman #3 filter paper (distilled water, 12 h light), in November. Temperatures were 30 C daytime and 20 C nighttime. (Differences between populations were minimal and values pooled here.) Fresh seed germination was 99.7% ± 0.6 (SD). Time to 50% germination was 4 days for fresh seed, 7 days for 2-yr-old seed, and 13 days for 5-yr-old seed. (Similarly, seeds collected in Wurzburg, W. Germany and germinated under the same conditions yielded 99.3% ± 1.5 in the 1st yr and 98.5% ± 2.1 in the 2nd yr.) Seeds stored under dry conditions for up to 6 yr decrease in viability only about 14%, although older seeds take longer to germinate once they are put in moist conditions.

Seeds introduced into the fields listed in Table 1 germinated in either the 1st or 2nd yr after introduction (Werner 1972). Germination rate was the lowest (28.0% ± 5.7 SD) in field K which had a thick cover of quack grass (*Agropyron repens*) and its litter. Germination rate was highest (86.0% ± 5.7 SD) in field J which had the least quack grass and the highest amount of bare ground of the eight fields. However, most seedlings in field J failed to live more than a year, possibly due to the combined effects of > 50% cover by sumac (*Rhus typhina* L.) and > 30% cover of *Aster sagittifolia* Willd. Seedlings in the other fields grew to produce rosettes and, eventually, flowering plants.

(*d*) *Vegetative reproduction* — No vegetative reproduction has been observed in *Dipsacus sylvestris*. Mechanical damage to the crown of a plant may be followed by regeneration of a single plant only.

9. Hybrids

No hybrids involving this species have been described. Since isolation of species of *Dipsacus* is mainly geographic and ecological (Ehrendorfer 1965), it is probable that extensive hybridization could be expected when species do come in contact. In several floral treatments (e.g. Georgia 1914; Montgomery 1964; Smith 1966) various combinations of the characteristics of the three species of *Dipsacus* found in North America are attributed to one species of wild teasel; however, these are very unlikely descriptions of hybrids. Plants having intermediate characteristics or combinations of characteristics of the three *Dipsacus* species are only very rarely found in herbaria specimens or field populations.

10. Population Dynamics

A typical teasel population might occupy 2,000 m² of a field, or extend for several kilometers along a roadway. Individual plants are usually spaced 0.5–1.5 m apart although they may be so close together that leaves of adjacent rosettes become intertwined. Typically, the center of a population of teasel will comprise a thick intermingling of robust rosettes and large flowering plants to the extent that passage by humans is difficult. In such a situation in a population in Michigan, there were approximately 13.0 (±9.8 SD, $n = 8$) flowering stalks and 7.1 (±5.5) mature rosettes per square meter.

Populations of teasel have been collected from the same field and roadsides for up to 25 yr (records at the Beal-Darlington Herbarium, Michigan State Univ.). Explanations for the longevity of the population on one site are lacking. Mechanisms of competition for individual plants include the wide, horizontally-oriented rosette leaves which produce heavy shading, and the deep taproot which extends to depths beyond roots of many of the grasses found in abandoned fields (Werner 1972). A rosette which has survived the early stages of growth has an increasing probability of continued survival in the competitive field situation, having preempted the site and its resources. The probability that an individual plant will die, remain vegetative, or flower during a particular growing season is related to the size of its vegetative rosette at the end of the growing season of the preceding year. A rosette forms a flowering stalk only after attaining a critical size of approximately 30 cm in diameter (Werner 1975a).

In fields presenting optimal conditions, (e.g., fields A, L, and M, Tables 1 and 3) teasel rosettes may grow rapidly and flower in their 2nd yr. In less suitable areas (e.g., fields B, C, and D, Tables 1 and 3) the rosettes grow more slowly and populations may consist of plants on a 3- or 4-yr reproductive cycle (Werner 1972).

In a study of colonization teasel seeds were introduced in known numbers into the fields listed in Table 1 in the winter of 1968–69. Seedlings were marked with color-coded toothpicks to measure recruitment and survivorship from 1969 to 1972. In fields A, L, and M teasel plants flowered in 1970, but heads were removed prior to

seed dispersal. In 1971, all heads were allowed to remain and in 1972 seedlings marking the second generation were first observed. Hence, in terms of numbers, the populations in each field decreased from an initial seed innoculum between 1969 and 1971; at the same time individual plants were growing in size and assuming an increasing role in the vegetation in terms of area of ground covered by the teasel population. Table 3 illustrates this latter point. It is suspected that teasel numbers fluctuate greatly and the spread of a population is relatively slow compared to other weeds because the generation time of teasel is longer than 1 yr and there is no vegetative reproduction. Interestingly, in all fields where teasel successfully colonized (fields A–D, L, M), the annual number of seeds produced on an aerial basis was approximately the same ($4,500/m^2$) by 1973, regardless of the number of flowering plants or the age of the plants.

11. Response to Herbicides and Other Chemicals

Repeated applications of the herbicides 2,4-D, 2,5,6-T, or Silvex (or a single application > 16 oz/acre) may be used to

Table 3. Survivorship of a cohort of 1,000 teasel seeds introduced in 1968 into each of eight fields in Kalamazoo Co., Michigan and percentage cover of the developing teasel plants

	A	B	C	D	J	K	L	M
					Field			
				Survivorship				
1968	1,000	1,000	1,000	1,000	1,000	1,000	1,000	1,000
1969	278	302	291	478	582	233	583	383
1970	35†	73	29	49	17	9	26†	49†
1971	12†	51†	21†	34	5	2	7†	26†*
1972	2†	18†	0	12†	0	0	0	14†
				Ground cover (%)				
1968	0	0	0	0	0	0	0	0
1969	10.1	7.0	1.1	1.4	4.8	0.6	3.9	13.0
1970	21.5	25.7	7.6	6.7	5.5	2.6	10.1	25.8
1971	29.5	53.5	22.2	28.4	5.0	2.3	11.1	39.1
1972‡								

†A year when some plants of the cohort flowered.
‡Percentage ground cover for 1972 not available.

control teasel (Ontario Herbicide Committee 1968). Control by repeated cuttings prior to flowering also effectively eradicates a·population (Werner, unpublished.)

12. Response to Other Human Manipulations

When the above-ground portion of a teasel rosette is removed by clipping leaves down to crown level, a new shoot may arise from the old rootstock. New leaves are observed 1-5 days after clipping. Rosettes 10 cm in diameter reconstruct new leaves more than 50% of the time.

13. Response to Parasites

No endoparasites of seeds, roots or rosettes have been observed. The erect flowering stem may become infested with unidentified stem-boring lepidopteran larvae (especially in shaded conditions) which sometimes weakens the stem to the extent that head development is hindered (hence seed numbers reduced). Maguire (1959) listed the aquatic biota of the water collected in the bases of teasel leaves but found no pattern of species composition. Leaf damage from slugs and leaf miners is rarely seen.

The stems and leaves are relatively free of fungal infections. A list of organisms found on teasel is listed by the United States Department of Agriculture (1960). These fungi are: *Cercospora elongata* Pk., *Mycosphaerella asterinoides* (Ell. & Ev.) Fairm., *Peronospora dipsaci* Tul., *Phoma oleracea* Sacc. var. *dipsaci* Sacc., *Phyllactinia corylea* Pers. ex Karst., and *Phymatotrichum omnivorum* (Shear) Dug. No higher plant parasites are recorded.

ACKNOWLEDGMENTS

Thanks is expressed to herbarium personnel at the following institutions: Department of Agriculture, Ottawa; University of Western Ontario; University of Guelph; University of Toronto; Acadia University; Michigan State University; Arnold Arboretum, Harvard University; New York Botanical Garden. The assistance of M. H. Moreland, C. D. Caswell, and J. A. Oostveen in the field research is gratefully acknowledged. S. A. Wineriter prepared the drawings, photographs, and figures. The research was supported in part by National Science Foundation grants GB-6941X to J. E. Cantlon and S. N. Stephenson, GI-20 to H. E. Koenig and W. E. Cooper, and GB-40425 to the author.

BOBROV, E. G. 1957. Genus 1411. *Dipsacus* L. Pages 16-20 *in* B. K. Shishkin and E. G. Bobrov, eds. Flora of the USSR, Vol. XXIV. Izdatel'stvo Akademii Nauk SSSR, Moskva-Leningrad. (Transl. from Russian.) Israel Prog. for Sci. Transl., Jerusalem.

BUTCHER, R. W. 1961. A new illustrated British flora, Vol. II. Leonard Hill, London.

CANADIAN WEED COMMITTEE. 1969. Common and botanical names of weeds in Canada. Can. Dep. Agric. Publ. 1397. Ottawa, Ontario. 67 pp.

CLAPHAM, A. R., TUTIN, T. G. and WARBURG, E. F. 1962. Flora of the British Isles. Cambridge Univ. Press, Cambridge, England.

EHRENDORFER, F. 1965. Dispersal mechanisms, genetic systems, and colonizing abilities in some flowering plant families. Pages 331-352 *in* H. G. Baker and G. L. Stebbins, eds. The genetics of colonizing species. Academic Press, New York.

FERGUSON, I. K. and BRIZICKY, G. K. 1965. Nomenclatural notes on *Dipsacus fullonum* and *Dipsacus sativus*. J. Arnold Arb. **46**: 362–365.

FERNALD, M. L. 1950. Gray's manual of botany. 8th ed. American Book Co., New York, N.Y. 1632 pp.

FERRON, M. and CAYOUETTE, R. 1970. Noms des mauvaise herbes du Québec. Min. Agric. Colonisation, Québec, Qué. 113 p.

GEORGIA, A. E. 1914. A manual of weeds. Macmillan Co., New York, N.Y. 593 pp.

GLEASON, H. A. and CRONQUIST, A. 1963. Manual of vascular plants of northeastern United States and adjacent Canada. Van Nostrand Co., Princeton, N.J. 810 pp.

HITCHCOCK, C. L., CRONQUIST, A., OWNBEY, M. and THOMPSON, J. W. 1959. Vascular plants of the Pacific northwest. Univ. Washington Press, Seattle, Wash.

MAGUIRE, B. Jr. 1959. Aquatic biotas of teasel (*Dipsacus sylvestris*) waters. Ecology **40**: 506.

MONTGOMERY, F. H. 1964. Weeds of Canada and the northern United States. F. Warne, New York, N.Y. 226 pp.

MULLINS, D. 1951. Teasel growing, an ancient practice. World Crops 3: 146–7.

ONTARIO HERBICIDE COMMITTEE. 1968. Guide to chemical weed control. Ontario Dep. Agric. and Food, Toronto, Ont. 88 pp.

POHL, R. W. and SYLWESTER, E. P. 1963. *Dipsacus* in Iowa. Proc. Iowa Acad. Sci. **70**: 53–54.

RAYNER, J. N. (ed.) 1961. Surface temperature frequencies for North America and Greenland. Arctic Meteorol. Res. Group Publ. 33., Montreal, Que.

RIDLEY, H. N. 1930. The dispersal of plants throughout the world. L. Reeve and Co., Ashford, Kent.

SMALL, J. K. 1913. Flora of the southeastern United States. Publ. by author. New York, N.Y. 1,130 pp.

SMITH, H. V. 1966. Michigan wild flowers. Cranbrook Inst. Sci., Bloomfield Hills, Mich. 468 pp.

SZABO, Z. 1923. The development of the flower of the Dipsacaceae. Ann. Bot. **37**: 325–334.

U.S. DEPARTMENT OF AGRICULTURE. 1960. Index of plant disease in the United States. Agric. Handb. no. 165. U.S. Gov. Print. Off., Washington, D.C. 531 pp.

WERNER, P. A. 1972. Effect of the invasion of *Dipsacus sylvestris* on plant communities in early old-field succession. Ph.D. thesis, Michigan State University. 140 pp. University Microfilms, Ann Arbor, Mich.

WERNER, P. A. 1975a. Predictions of fate from rosette size in teasel, *Dipsacus fullonum* L. Oecologia (in press).

WERNER, P. A. 1975b. A seed trap for determining patterns of seed deposition in terrestrial plants. Can. J. Bot. **53**: 810–813.

WERNER, P. A. 1975c. The effects of plant litter on germination in teasel. Amer. Midl. Natur. (in press).

145

THE BIOLOGY OF CANADIAN WEEDS.
13. *Cirsium arvense* (L.) Scop.

R. J. MOORE

Biosystematics Research Institute, Research Branch, Agriculture Canada, Ottawa, Ontario.

Received 28 Feb. 1975, accepted 27 May 1975.

MOORE, R. J. 1975. The biology of Canadian weeds. 13. *Cirsium arvense* (L.) Scop. Can. J. Plant Sci. **55**: 1033–1048.

This contribution on *Cirsium arvense* (L.) Scop., Canada thistle (Compositae) is part of a series which presents biological information on plants that are weedy in Canada. Canada thistle is a serious weed of agricultural land of all types and is one of the most serious weeds of temperate regions. Introduced from Europe in the 17th century, it now occurs in all provinces of Canada.

Ce texte sur *Cirsium arvense* (L.) Scop., le chardon des champs (Composé) fait partie d'une série d'articles sur la biologie des plantes trouvées à l'état adventice au Canada. Le chardon des champs est une importante mauvaise herbe des terres cultivées de toutes sortes et l'une des principales mauvaises herbes des régions tempérées. Introduit d'Europe vers le XVIIe siècle, on le rencontre maintenant dans toutes les provinces du Canada.

1. Name

Cirsium arvense (L.) Scop.
Synonyms in recent weed literature: none.
Common names: **Canada thistle** (Canada Weed Committee 1969); **chardon des champs**, chadron, chardon, chardon commun, chardon des prés, chardon du Canada, chardron, chaudron, cirse des champs, minou (Ferron et Cayouette 1971).
Compositae, Composite family, famille de Composées.

2. Description

Perennial herb spreading rapidly by horizontal roots which give rise to aerial shoots. Stems 3–15 dm tall, slender, green, freely branched. Leaves alternate, the base sessile and clasping or shortly decurrent; leaves generally oblong in outline, margin variable from entire to deeply pinnately segmented. Variation in leaf characters (texture, vesture, segmentation, spininess) is the basis for the varieties described hereafter. Plants dioecious, all heads of a plant either male or female. Flower heads numerous, 1–5 per branch, 15–25 mm high and 1/3 to 1/4 as wide; male heads globular, somewhat smaller than the flask-shaped female heads. Involucre 10–20 mm high, outer phyllaries ovate, tough-textured, subulate-tipped (0.5- to 0.75-mm stout spine), surface and margins glabrous or lightly arachnoid and with a narrow glandular mid-line; inner phyllaries progressively longer, the innermost unarmed, apex flat, chartaceous, often purplish and erose. Florets all tubular, rose–purple to pinkish, less commonly white. Florets of female heads 23–26 mm long; tube 20–23 mm, lobes about 2 mm; the pistil well-developed but anthers vestigial or absent; florets of male heads 12–14 mm long, tube 7–8.5 mm, lobes 3–4 mm, pistil absent or present and superficially normal but with a vestigial ovary; anther 4 mm long, pollen 42–44 μ diam, tricolporate, exine spiny. Pappus copious, white, feathery, 20–30 mm long on mature achenes; achenes 2.5–4 mm $\times$ 1 mm, straight or slightly curved, straw or light brown in color. The chromosome number $2n = 34$ has been reported for all the varieties, both in Europe and in Canada. Counts on Canadian plants were reported by Moore (1968).

Can. J. Plant Sci. 55: 1033-1048 (Oct. 1975)

146

Canada thistle is our only thistle, native or introduced, with separate male and female plants. It differs from other species of *Cirsium* also in the combination of smooth (without spiny wings), green, glabrous stems, numerous, small, almost spineless heads and the vigorous creeping roots. Like other species of *Cirsium, C. arvense* has a pappus composed of branched hairs, rather than the unbranched pappus hairs of the closely related genus *Carduus*, whose members also are often called "thistles."

Four varieties are usually recognized, as separated in the following key (Moore and Frankton 1974).
A. Leaves gray-tomentose below . . . .
. . . . var. *vestitum* Wimm. & Grab.
A. Leaves glabrous or only lightly arachnoid below.
   B. Leaves thin, flat, marginal spines few, fine and short.
      C. Leaves all entire or the upper leaves entire and the lower stem leaves shallowly and regularly pinnatifid or undulating . . . . . var. *integrifolium* Wimm. & Grab.
      C. Leaves shallowly to deeply pinnatifid, often asymmetrical . . . . . . var. *arvense*.
   B. Leaves thick, subcoriaceous, surface wavy, marginal spines long and stout . . . .
. . . . var. *horridum* Wimm. & Grab.

The above varieties are interfertile and Detmers (1927) found that seed from a plant of the variety *vestitum* produced seedlings of all the varieties. The variety *horridum* is the commonest phase and is known from the entire range in Canada. Collections of the other varieties are known from the following provinces: var. *arvense* — N.S., Que., Ont., Man.; var. *integrifolium* — Que., Ont., Man., Sask., Alta., B.C.; var. *vestitum* — Que., Ont., Man., Sask. These varieties may be expected to occur anywhere in the range of the species. White-flowered plants of the var. *horridum* (f. *albiflorum* (Rand. & Redf.) R. Hoffm.) have been found in all provinces.

Many physiological variants have been reported. Selected ecotypes show differences in phenology and photoperiodism, vigor and growth habit, stomatal frequency and response to herbicides, seed dormancy and germination. These variations are mentioned hereafter under the respective subjects.

3. Economic Importance

(a) Detrimental — Canada thistle is found in all crops — wheat and other cereals, corn, peas, beans, sugarbeets, potatoes, etc. — and is also common in pastures and ranges, reducing forage yields (Hodgson 1968b). The weed uses light, moisture and nutrients needed by the crop and hence reduces the crop yield.

Hodgson (1968a,b) reported a reduction in yield of spring wheat in Montana as follows: 2 weed shoots per 0.84 m² reduced wheat yield by 15%; 12 shoots, by 35%; 25 shoots, by 60%.

In a 4-year study in Indiana, Schreiber (1967) studied the number of alfalfa plants surviving in plots which had initial densities of 0, 0.5, 1, 2 plants of *Cirsium arvense* per 0.09 m². Measures for weed control used were: no control, mowing after each grazing, herbicide treatment. Over the period, the number of alfalfa plants declined in all plots, but the decline was accelerated by the weed. Mowing was found to be the most effective control and in plots with initial weed frequency of two plants per 0.09 m², mowing increased the forage yield by 13.9 tonnes/ha over the 4 yr. Comparison of plots with initial weed densities of zero and of two plants per 0.09 m² showed that the loss in alfalfa due to the weed was 16.5 tonnes/ha over the 4 yr.

The weed also harbors insects (bean aphid, stalk borer) that attack corn and tomatoes and it is an alternate host for some pathogenic organisms. Grazing animals may be scratched by the weed and develop infections. Small buds of the thistle may be harvested with canning crops, such as peas, and special precautions in the canneries are required to remove the thistle buds (Link and Kommedahl 1958).

(b) Beneficial — Detmers (1927) remarked that Canada thistle is "wonderfully fragrant and very attractive to honey bees. It may therefore be listed as a honey plant." Young thistle shoots are sometimes eaten by grazing animals, at least in Europe (Detmers 1927), and Rogers (1928) reports that roots and shoots have been eaten by man in Russia, and by North American Indians.

(c) Legislation — *Cirsium arvense* is listed as a Canadian noxious weed in the federal Seeds Act 1937. It has long been declared a noxious weed by most of the provinces and is currently listed as such in the Revised Statutes of Quebec 1964, Ontario 1970, Manitoba 1970, Saskatchewan 1965, Alberta 1970 and British Columbia 1960.

4. Geographical Distribution — *Cirsium arvense* is a naturalized weed in all provinces of Canada (Fig. 1, 2) as far north as 58–59°N. It is most common in agricultural areas. In weed surveys made across Canada between 1922 and 1947 (Groh and Frankton 1949), all common weeds were listed in selected survey areas, which were districts in settled agricultural areas. *Cirsium arvense* was found in the following percentages of the survey areas, as summarized by provincial regions (% and total number of areas): B.C. and Peace River, 39.3% (713); Alta. and W. Sask., 40.7% (364); Sask. and W. Man., 73.7% (427); Man. and W. Ont., 81.2% (192); Cent. Ont. and N. Que., 83.1% (947); E. Ont. and Cent. Que., 81.6% (921); Maritimes and Gaspé, 76% (1005). On the whole, the incidence of Canada thistle was lower from the Pacific coast to western Saskatchewan than in the eastern provinces. Details of the density of Canada thistle infestations in the southern portions of the Prairie Provinces are shown on a map compiled from reports of a survey made in 1963–64 (Alex 1966). The survey covered the agricultural areas, approximately 30 million hectares, and the weed incidence in each municipal unit is indicated in terms of the percentage of agricultural land infested and the severity of the infestation. Some occurrence of the weed is indicated in almost every municipal

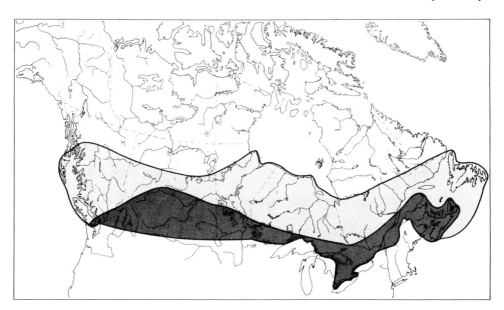

Fig. 1. Distribution of *Cirsium arvense* in Canada — the darker shading indicates the area of greater abundance.

unit and most units have medium or heavy infestations of the two area classes 5–33% or 34–67% of the agricultural land.

It is naturalized also in the United States north of approximately 37°N but does not survive in the southern states. It is more serious as a weed in the northwestern and north central states. Probably originally native to southeastern Europe and the eastern Mediterranean area, *C. arvense* now occurs throughout Europe, North Africa, Asia Minor and across central Asia to Japan. In

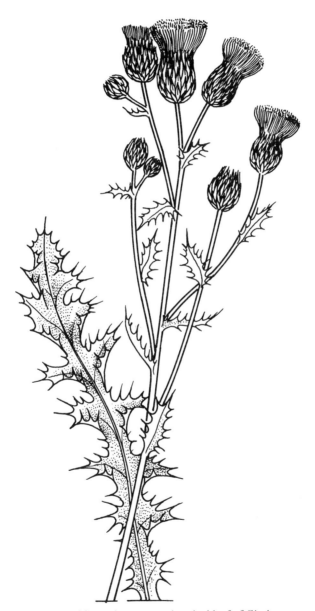

Fig. 2. Drawing of flowering stem and typical leaf of *Cirsium arvense*.

Europe, it extends north to 68°N (Scandinavia). Kolokolinikov (1931) found that in the Vyatka region of Siberia the weed does not flower north of approximately 58°N latitude. The species extends south to approximately 30°N latitude in North Africa and Afghanistan. *Cirsium arvense* has become naturalized also in the southern hemisphere, in South Africa, New Zealand and southeastern Australia.

5. Habitat

(a) Climatic requirements — Canada thistle is found in open mesophytic areas. Writing in Ohio, Detmers (1927) stated that a moderate temperature range, 0 C – 32 C, is best. Rainfall of 400 mm–750 mm per year is favorable (Hodgson 1968a).

The extremes of temperature found in the areas of Canada in which the weed occurs (Fig. 1) may be stated as follows (Anonymous 1959–60): mean January temperatures −22 C to −7 C; mean July temperatures 10 C to 20 C.

The northern limit of the zone of greater density of the weed (Fig. 1) corresponds roughly with the 18 C (0 F) mean January isotherm. Low winter temperatures of −27 C to −35 C are common through much of the range of the weed. Annual precipitation over the Canadian area is diverse, from 300 to 1,000 mm. In the state of Victoria, Australia *C. arvense* is found mainly in areas with annual rainfall of 700–1,000 mm (Amor and Harris 1974). Canada thistle is a long-day plant and this requirement, together with unsuitably high summer temperatures, probably limits the southerly distribution.

(b) Substratum — Detmers (1927) concluded that clay soil is most favorable to growth, as judged by the length of roots developed in clay, gravel and limestone soils. According to Hodgson (1968a) silt loams are well suited to growth; productive, deep, well-aerated soils produce good growth whereas poorly aerated soils or high water tables limit growth. Reed and Hughes (1970) state that Canada thistle grows in a wide variety of soils, even in soils with a salt content up to 2%, and Rogers (1928) states that the weed can grow in any soil except peat. It can survive in very dry areas but does not do well in wet soils, where root development is shallow. Korsmo (1930) observed that in Germany the weed is most lasting on agricultural land that contains chalk.

Canadian collections of *C. arvense* have been made in areas described as clay loam, sandy loam, sandy clay and even sand dunes.

(c) Communities — *Cirsium arvense* has been collected in Canada in almost every plant community touched by man. It is found most frequently along roadsides, railway embankments, lawns, gardens and abandoned fields in which it has been associated with such weeds as *Echium vulgare* L., *Ambrosia artemiisifolia* L., *Oxalis*. As a weed of agricultural land it occurs in pastures (*Agropyron, Agrostis*) and in cereal crops (wheat, oats, barley), hayfields and hoed crops. It is occasionally found in dry habitats — sand dunes and open sandy areas — although it prefers moister locations. It is found also on banks of streams, lakeshores, cleared swamps, even wet ditches and on the edge of muskeg, but does not survive in very wet locations. The weed is frequently seen in grassy opening in woods and on the margins of woods, both deciduous (maple, alder thickets, poplar) and coniferous (cedar–hemlock associations).

Good light intensity is required; in shade the plants become tall and lax and produce few flowers. In a favorable environment (unshaded, moist, aerated clay loam) Bakker (1960) observed 39 shoots per square meter with 41 heads per shoot, whereas in a shaded forest habitat there were only 11 shoots per square meter with 18 heads per shoot.

According to Friesen and Shebeski (1960) 7.7% of 142 grain fields in Manitoba contained 12 or more shoots of thistle per 0.4 ha (acre). Doyon (1968) found the weed in 2 of 37 stations in pastures of *Agrostis tenuis* Sibth. in Montmorency Co., Quebec but absent in pastures of *Festuca rubra* L., *Danthonia spicata* (L.) Beauv. and *Carex nigra* (L.) Reichard.

Hamel and Dansereau (1949) class Canada thistle as a weed of low vigor, not completing its life cycle in deteriorated undergrowth. They found the weed in the following types of culture, listed in order of abundance: (1) cultivated (2) cereal fields (3) young prairie (4) old prairie. The weed was much less abundant in the last culture than in the other three.

6. History

Apparently Canada thistle was introduced to North America very early in the colonial period, probably in the 17th century.

Dewey (1901) states that *Cirsium arvense* was a troublesome weed throughout southern Europe by the beginning of the 16th century and by the mid-18th century was common throughout Europe. He believed that it was first introduced into North America in the French settlements (early 17th century). Hansen (1918) believes that the weed was probably brought in as a contaminant in farm seed in both New France and New England independently and did not come from Canada to New England. The weed was so common that control legislation was enacted in Vermont in 1795 and by New York in 1831. Canada thistle was not reported west of the Allegheny Mountains until after 1835. Canada thistle was common in Montreal in 1821 (Rousseau 1968).

7. Growth and Development

(a) Morphology — The obnoxious character of the weed is due mainly to the highly successful vegetative propagation carried on by the creeping horizontal roots which survive winters and continue to extend, year after year, giving rise to numerous aerial shoots and thus establishing independent plants.

(b) Perennation — The plants survive indefinitely through the root system. The aerial shoots are killed by heavy frost but the roots, containing abundant food reserve, survive winter.

Rogers (1929) in Iowa studied the root system in soil frozen to a depth of 50 cm, from mid-December to mid-March. He found that aerial and subterranean shoots were killed back to the roots when the soil froze. During January new roots and shoots began to develop on the old roots and 4- to 7-cm shoots were present in early February. In early March, the new roots and shoots were larger and after the soil thawed in mid-March, development proceeded rapidly and leaves appeared on the surface of the soil in mid-April.

The root system is described more fully in Section 8 (d).

(c) Physiological data — Studies on day length and flower induction are mentioned hereafter. Numerous other physiological studies compare the response of various ecotypes of the weed to different herbicides and compare growth rates of ecotypes. Factors affecting the action of herbicides are under investigation.

Present researches concern the movement and activity of the herbicide within the plant. Radioactive picloram applied through leaves or roots was found to accumulate in shoot apices. The herbicide was not metabolized to a significant degree even after 40 days. It was concluded that differences in the location of accumulation of herbicides within the plant can account for differences in susceptibility to herbicide damage between the different species tested (Canada thistle, soybeans, barley) (Sharma and Vanden Born 1973). Atrazine labelled with ^{14}C was observed to move with the transpiration stream in the shoot. The herbicide therefore has slight effect on portions of the plant basipetal to the area of application (Burt 1974).

(d) Phenology — Shoots emerge after the soil and air temperatures have warmed. Hodgson (1968a) found that emergence began when the mean weekly temperature

151

reached 5 C and was best when the temperature was at least 8 C. There was some difference in the emergence time of different ecotypes. In Montana, the shoots begin to emerge in early May. They then develop rosettes and rapid vertical growth commences about 3 wk after emergence. The most rapid growth, averaging 3 cm a day, occurred in the last 2 wk of June. Throughout July, the growth rate decreased to almost zero by early August.

Flowering begins in Canada in mid-June or early July and continues into September. Canada thistle is a long-day plant, flowering freely under 18 h illumination but not flowering under 8- to 12-h days (Link and Kommedahl 1958). Hunter and Smith (1972) studied seven ecotypes and found that all flowered under a 16-h photoperiod; only five flowered under 14-h and the flowering of three of these was temperature-dependent.

(e) Mycorrhiza — None have been reported.

8. Reproduction

(a) Floral biology — Canada thistle is dioecious, the male and female flowers being borne on separate plants. Staminate flowers usually contain a vestigial ovary and probably this may be functional under favorable conditions since male flowers occasionally produce a seed. It may be that some ecotypes of the species tend toward some degree of perfect flowers (Hodgson 1964).

Hayden (1934) observed that large amounts of seed were formed when male and female plants were within 33 m but that only 2–3 seeds per head were formed when the sexes were separated by 160–200 m. Hodgson (1968a) observed large amounts of seed when the two sexes were growing within 16.5 m and Amor and Harris (1974) found some seed when the sexes were within distances up to 390 m.

The flowers are insect-pollinated. Detmers (1927) stated that honey bees were the chief agent of pollination. Derscheid and Schultz (1960) observed that honey bees and a black beetle were active in patches of Canada thistle and sow thistle and that there was only a light seed set when the male and female plants of Canada thistle were 184 m apart. They compared the importance of insect pollination with wind pollination in greenhouse experiments during two consecutive winters. When honey bees were allowed to visit the plants, averages of 43.5 and 45.6 mature achenes per head were produced in the 2 yr. When a fan was used to blow across the plants for 9 h daily for 2 wk, only 0.76 and 0.21 achenes per head were formed.

Anthrax flava, members of the families Stratiomyidae and Calliphoridae (Diptera) and of Sphecidae (wasps) are listed as visitors to the flowers of *C. arvense* in Europe by Proctor and Yeo (1973).

(b) Seed production and dispersal — Carpellate heads contain an average of about 100 florets; average 100 (Detmers 1927); about 100 (Hayden 1934); 84 to 132, average 100 (Bakker 1960). Detmers observed that one vigorous shoot may bear 100 heads in a season and Bakker found 32–69 heads per shoot in favorable growing conditions.

The number of seeds produced depends upon the thoroughness of pollination. Hayden (l.c.) found up to 98 seeds per head and Derscheid and Schultz (1960) counted up to 83. The latter determined that viable achenes were formed 8–10 days after flowering. Hay (1937) reports that one plant may produce up to 5,300 seeds, but the average production was 1,530.

Hodgson (1968a) found that seed size varied widely among the ecotypes under study. The largest size was equivalent to 298,000 achenes to the pound; the smallest size, to 677,000. An average weight of 0.096 g per 100 seeds was determined from a 2-yr study of eight ecotypes.

Some authors have questioned the effectiveness of the plumose achene of this species as a method of widespread dispersal. Frequently the achenes remain in the head while the pappus breaks off readily.

Bakker (1960) observed that at a distance of 10 m from female plants, only 9.9% of the floating plumes bore achenes and at a distance of 1 km only 0.2% of floating plumes had an attached seed.

Long distance dispersal by other means is possible. Hope (1927) found that seeds of *C. arvense* were among seeds trapped in irrigation water in Alberta.

(c) Viability of seeds and germination — Numerous studies of seed germination have been reported; only some of these will be summarized here. Some authors have stated that the seed has a dormancy period, but most authors agree that fresh seed will germinate well. Malvez (1931) states that the seed germinates best at high temperatures (25–30 C) and Bakker (1960) also found that germination was best at 30 C or with intermittent temperatures of 10–28 C, and that at lower temperatures (15–20 C) germination is aided by high light intensity. Kolk (1947) also reported that germination is better at 30 C than at 20–22 C and that young seeds germinate well in bright daylight whereas old seeds germinate well in weak daylight.

Amor and Harris (1974) found that of samples of seed from 37 sites in Australia, stored 6 mo at 20 C, 52–97% germinated (average 78%). Germination was tested at 15/30 C with a 12-h photoperiod. Seed stored for 10 or 15 wk was tested at constant and alternating temperatures. At constant 20 C, but not at alternating temperatures, the germination was increased by prechilling. A constant temperature of 30 C resulted in a better germination than a constant temperature of 20 C. Alternating temperatures of 15/30 C produced better germination than 15/40 C. High soil temperatures, therefore, may depress germination.

Hayden (1934) found that freshly gathered seed germinates up to 95% and Hodgson (1964) reported 50–80% germination of fresh seed. He found that the amount of germination varies with the ecotype and that seed of some ecotypes consistently germinates less than others. Seed of 10 ecotypes harvested on five dates in three consecutive summers showed the following ranges of germination: 0–44%, 13–81%, 45–85%, 43–90%, 33–92%.

Germination of 42–66% after dry storage at room temperature is reported by Derscheid and Schultz (1960). Bruns and Rasmussen (1957) found 62% germination after 8 mo dry storage and 25% after 12 mo, but 70% after 6 mo submerged in water. Germination of the submerged seed decreased after longer storage, reaching 0 after 54 mo. Hayden (1934) found that samples of 2-yr-old seed germinated 38–71% (average 50%). Chipil (1946) observed that seeds may remain dormant for up to 3 yr and that they germinate most readily in late May.

Duval initiated a series of experiments to test the viability of various species planted in pots of soil and buried at different depths, over the period 1902 to 1941. It was found for *Cirsium arvense* that the highest germination was obtained from the most deeply buried samples and that some viability was retained for 21 yr. The results are summarized in Table 1, from Toole and Brown (1946).

Lund and Rostrup (1901) found that seed sown at a depth of 4–5 mm germinated, on average, in 8–9 days; at depths of 2.5 cm, in 10–12 days; and at more than 5 cm, in

Table 1. Germination of stored seed (from Toole and Brown 1946)

Storage depth (cm)	Percent germination after (yr)							
	1	3	6	10	16	21	30	39
20	21	35	15	6	3	1	0	–
55	23	29	16	10	1	1	0	0
105	29	39	26	21	3	5	0	0

13–18 days. In the latter case, few seedlings emerged. Kolk (1947) also concluded that the seeds germinate better at a shallow depth (optimum depth for emergence 1 cm) but will emerge from depths up to 6 cm (maximum tested).

The young seedling was well described by Hayden (1934). Elongation of the hypocotyl pushes the two cotyledons, in an upright position, from the earth. Occasionally the hypocotyl arches and pulls the cotyledons from the soil. The oval cotyledons are slighlty puberulent. The first foliage leaves are ovate to round, the margins bearing coarse hairs and becoming spinose. Early leaves become serrate and lobed (Fig. 3–6).

Seedlings become established in recently plowed or disturbed soils. They survive only if competition is limited and the light intensity is high (Hodgson 1968a; Bakker 1960). According to Bakker, seedlings die when the light intensity falls below 20% of full daylight and growth is reduced in light of 60–70% full daylight. In the laboratory it was found that growth was stunted in light of less than 500 lx, but above 4,000 lx, growth was rapid and rhizomes were formed within 8 wk. Detmers (1927) also reported that rhizome formation began early. She found that a 4-mo-old seedling, raised in greenhouse, had a 101-cm rhizome which bore 19 shoot buds.

(d) Vegetative reproduction — The root system assures the persistence and spread of the species by vegetative means.

Seedlings first develop a tap-fibrous root, and within a few months the main root thickens and produces lateral roots which

Fig. 3–6.   Seedlings of *Cirsium arvense* at age of 3-wk (Fig. 3); 4 wk (Fig. 4); 2 mo (Fig. 5 and 6).

spread out horizontally, arching upwards or downwards. After growing 6–12 cm, the horizontal roots bend downwards, growing toward the water table. At the point of bending a new horizontal root usually develops and continues the horizontal spreading. Aerial shoots develop from the original vertical root or from buds on the arching branches of the horizontal system. The shoots that arise from the horizontal roots and form aerial shoots are rhizomes. The vertical roots produce numerous small rootlets for absorption and are the main source of absorption for the plant and also the main storage organ (Rogers 1928; Hayden 1934). Rogers found that individual roots live only about 2 yr, being replaced by new roots which develop from the old.

Horizontal extension of the root system is rapid. Hayden (1934) and Rogers (1928) report extensions of 6 m in one season. Aerial shoots appear as the root system spreads.

Hodgson (1968a) found that 54% (by dry weight) of the root system was within 7.5–22.5 cm of the surface of the soil; 30% was 22.5–37.5 cm below the surface and 16% lay at depths of 37.5–52.5 cm. These data were determined on recently established plants and the author suggests that in an older stand, a greater proportion of the roots might be deeper. Hayden (1934) concluded that the length and form of the root system depended on the soil environment (soil texture, fertility, moisture, vegetative cover) and found that the vertical roots penetrate to the water table. Penetration to depths of 2–3 m is commonly observed; Malzev (1931) reported penetration to a depth of 5.5 m in the cotton-growing regions of Russia, and Rogers (1928) states that vertical roots have been found at a depth of 6.75 m.

Of great importance to the weedy character of the plant is the ability of the root to survive adversity and regenerate from small pieces. Prentiss (1889) found that 5 of 36 root fragments 3–6 mm thick and 8 mm in length could produce shoots and that 100%

of 12.5-mm segments produced shoots. Sagar and Rawson (1964) removed 3 × 6-cm segments of roots and subterranean shoots from the soil in December (in Wales) and found that one or more aerial shoots were developed by these segments, in some cases, within 5 days. Hayden (1934) also found that pieces of either horizontal or vertical roots only 3–6 mm long were able to grow into plants. Upright subterranean shoots can produce roots and buds at any node and both horizontal and vertical roots can form buds and roots at any point. Rogers (1928) states that a root fragment which is more than 6 wk and less than 2 yr old can regenerate an entire plant.

A program of mowing aerial shoots and cultivating the soil has often been used to control the weed, but to be effective, cultivation must be repeated to prevent the roots building up new food reserves. Seely (1952) found that for approximately 30 days after cultivation, the carbohydrate reserve in the root remained more or less constant but thereafter began to increase.

The low point in the carbohydrate reserves in the root system occurs in early June, when flowering begins (Welton et al. 1929). Bakker (1960), working in Holland, found that the amount of water-soluble sugars (as percentage of fresh weight) decreased during spring until June, remained relatively constant during flowering (June–August) and thereafter increased rapidly to a high level in September and October. Hodgson (1968a) also found that in Montana, carbohydrate reserves (percentage dry weight) decreased from early spring to late June and then increased through June to September, when they level off.

9. Hybrids

Approximately nine hybrids between C. arvense and Old World species of Cirsium have been reported in Europe (Hegi 1929) but only one of the latter species (C. palustre) has been introduced into North America and it is rare here. Only one

155

possible hybrid has been reported in North America — *C. arvense* × *C. hookerianum* Nutt., the latter a native species of British Columbia and Alberta. This hybrid, found in British . Columbia, was described by Moore and Frankton (1965, p. 603). It is a very rare occurrence and of no economic significance.

10. Population Dynamics

A single seedling can form a large patch of stems through the vegetative propagation of the root system, as described above. The spread of the clone may continue indefinitely, groups of stems becoming independent as the root system breaks up. Canada thistle therefore occurs usually as a clump of stems. A large area may become infested by a single introduction but no seed will be produced in such a case. Seed production requires the presence of plants of both sexes and, hence, of more than one introduction in an area.

Some of the seeds formed during summer may germinate immediately, form rosettes before winter and flower in the following spring. Other seeds may remain dormant until spring or even later and thus a succession of seedlings will be produced. The abundance of the weed depends on the history of the infestation and the vigor of control measures. Hayden (1934) reported an incidence of 150 shoots per 0.84 m² (sq. yd) in an infestation which had been established for 25 yr.

Competitive plants vary in effectiveness against the thistle. The percentage of thistles increased by 192% in 4 yr in continuous spring wheat cropping, but decreased to 1% in alfalfa mowed for hay (Hodgson 1968a).

Bendall (1975) has recently reported that water and alcohol extracts of roots and foliage of *C. arvense* inhibit the germination of its own seed and that of *Trifolium* and inhibit the growth of seedlings of seven test species. Phytotoxins in the soil of areas of southern Tasmania infested with *C. arvense* may hinder the establishment of cultivated species.

11. Response to Herbicides and Other Chemicals

Since Canada thistle is such a serious weed, a great many studies on control methods have been carried out. Before the introduction of modern herbicides, various chemicals (sodium chloride, sodium arsenite, calcium arsenite, sodium chlorate, carbon bisulfide) were used effectively. Canada thistle was early classed as intermediate in response to the new herbicide 2,4-D (2,4-dichlorophenoxyacetic acid), and repeated treatments were needed to maintain control. It was found that 2,4-D and MCPA (((4-chloro-o-tolyl)oxy) acetic acid) were about equally effective and were better than 2,4,5-T (2,4,5-trichlorophenoxyacetic acid) (Hodgson 1968a).

Soil sterilants, such as Monuron (3-(p-chlorophenyl)-1,1,-dimethylurea) wipe out Canada thistle for a season, but the weed usually recovers from the deep roots and is more successful than any competitors in the treated area. Repeated sterilization is needed to wipe out Canada thistle and this type of chemical is not recommended (Hodgson 1968a).

Selective herbicides which control Canada thistle but do not seriously harm grass are 2,4-D, dicamba (3-6-dichloro-o-anisic acid) and picloram (4-amino-3,5,6-trichloropicolinic acid). Picloram at 2.24 kg or more per ha eliminated Canada thistle. Perennial grasses were unharmed by picloram at 1.12 kg per ha (Hodgson 1968a). Picloram causes little damage to the foliage of Canada thistle, but completely destroys the root system (Hunter and Smith 1972). A differential response of *Cirsium arvense* ecotypes to herbicide treatments has been claimed (Hodgson 1970). This is not related to leaf form or flower color, or to stomatal frequency (Hodgson and Moore 1972). Hunter and Smith (1972) found that the rate at which herbicides killed foliage was faster at 27 C than at lower temperatures.

New herbicides are continually being tested and it is impossible here to summarize these numerous experiments. Herbicide treatments to control *Cirsium ar vense* recommended by the Saskatchewan Department of Agriculture (Leavitt 1973) represent current practice. These are summarized in Table 2.

12. Response to Other Human Manipulation

Shallow cultivation of the soil breaks up the root system but does not eliminate an infestation unless repeated regularly. Seely (1952) found that cultivations repeated over a period of 122 days eradicated the weed in mild infestations in Idaho. He recommended that cultivation be repeated at 21-day intervals. Repeated mowing will weaken surviving stems and prevent seeding. Mowing is often effective in controlling the weed in pastures and in areas where the infestation is not severe. Grazing similarly reduces the weed population. Competitive crops, especially alfalfa and forage grasses, have been used to control an infestation. Alfalfa, with mowing twice each year, reduced the count of Canada thistle to 14% of the original figure after 1 yr and to 0 after 4 yr. (Hodgson 1968a).

Combinations of cultivation, mowing and competitive crops used with herbicides are more effective than herbicides alone. Various combinations have been tested.

Nitrogen fertilizer used with 2,4-D on wheat produced a much higher grain yield and also controlled the weed. The combined fertilizer and herbicide resulted in a yield of 43.2 hl per ha, compared with 29.6 hl after either fertilizer or herbicide alone and 19.8 for the untreated check field (Hodgson 1968a).

13. Responses to Parasites

(a) Insects and other nondomestic animals—
ANIMALS.
The American gold finch (*Spinus tristis* (L.)) eats Canada thistle seed (Detmers 1927). Root knot nematode (*Meloidogyne* sp.) has been reported in Canada (Conners 1967) and in U.S.A. (U.S. Department of Agriculture (USDA) 1960).
INSECTS.
Larvae of the painted lady butterfly (*Cynthia cardui* (L.)) defoliate the thistle; larvae of Canada thistle midge (*Dasyneura gibsoni* Felt) damage the seed; and larvae of *Orellia ruficauda* (F.) (as *Trypeta florescentiae* L.) infest the heads (Detmers 1927). None of these native North American insects cause sufficient damage to control the thistle.

Zwolfer (1965) lists 86 species of insects found on *C. arvense* in some areas of Europe (France, Switzerland, Austria, southern Great Britain and southern Germany, Dalmatia). Approximately half of the insect species were found within plant organs; the remainder were external, on stems, roots and leaves. Almost all of the insects were believed to feed only on plants

Table 2.   Herbicide control of *Cirsium arvense* (after Leavitt 1973)

Crop	Herbicide and rate per hectare (acre)	Stage of crop at application
Wheat Barley	2,4-D or MCPA, 560–840 g (8-12 oz)	4-leaf to flag leaf stage and when maximum number of thistle shoots emerged. Use MCPA only on oats.
Oats	Dicamba, 140 g (2 oz) Dicamba, 140 g (2 oz) plus 2,4-D or MCPA at 420 g (6 oz) Bromoxynil + MCPA (1:1) 560 g (8 oz)	 2- to 4-leaf stage 2-leaf stage to early flag leaf, in 112.3 liters water per ha (10 gal per acre)
Flax	MCPA at 700–840 g (10–12 oz)	5 cm high to bud formation
Peas	MCPB at 1.4 kg (20 oz)	Vine length 10–20 cm
Non-crop land	Picloram at 0.56–1.12 kg (8–16 oz) Dicamba at 2.24 kg (32 oz)	Apply in fall or spring

157

of the tribe Cynareae and, in many cases, only on *C. arvense*. Approximately 50 additional species were recorded as occasional visitors. Maw (personal communication, 1974) has compiled an extensive list of insects found associated with *Cirsium arvense* in Canada. Eighty-four species are believed to damage the plant. Many of these insects were found within plant organs and others were taken from the plant surface. An additional 44 species are listed as plant visitors or predators on insects which inhabit the weed.

Species which damage *Cirsium arvense* are:

ORTHOPTERA: *Tetrix sublata* (L.), *Melanoplus angustipennis* (Dodge), *M. differentialis* (Thom.), *M. mexicanus mexicanus* (Sauss.), *M. sanguinipes* (F.), *Conocephalus* spp.

THYSANOPTERA: *Frankliniella tritici* (Fitch).

HEMIPTERA: *Plagiognathus obscurus* Uhler, *Campylomma verbasci* (Meyer), *Poecilocapsus lineatus* (Fab.), *Adelphocoris rapidus* (Say), *Lygus columbiensis* (Kngt.) *L. lineolaris* (Beauv.), *L. shulli* (Kngt.), *L. varius* (Kngt.), *Liocoris borealis* Kelton, *L. unctuosus* Kelton, *Lygaeus kalmii* Stal., *Corimelaena pulicaria* (Germar), *Euschistus variolarius* (Beauv.), *Cosmopepla bimaculata* (Thomas).

HOMOPTERA: *Campylenchia latipes* (Say), *Entylia carinata* (Forst.), *Stictocephala basalis* (Walk.), *S. bubalus* (Fab.), *S. diceros* (Say), *Hebecephalus occidentalis* Beam. & Tuth., *Euscelidus schenkii* (Kirsch.), *Rosenus obligus* (DeL. & Dav.), *Aceratagallia sanguinolenta* (Prov.), *Erythroneura aspera* Beam. & Griff., *Empoasca filamenta* DeL., *Macrosteles salina* (Reut.), *Gyponana hasta* DeL., *Helochara communis* Fitch, *Agallia quadripunctata* (Prov.), *Philaenus spumarius* (L.), *Capitophorus braggii* (Gillette), *C. carduinis* (Walk.) *C. elaeagni* (del Guericio), *Dactynotus cirsii* L., *Myzus persicae* (Sulzer).

COLEOPTERA: *Disonycha pennsylvanica* (Illiger), *Longitarsus melanurus* Melsh., *Hydrothassa vittata* (Oliv.), *Cassida rubiginosa* (Mull.), *Pyrrhalta* sp., *Altica carduorum* Guer., *Psylliodes* spp., *Acanthascelides fracterculus* Horn, *Lixus concavus* Say, *Cosmobaris americana* Csy, *Otiorhynchus ovatus* (L.), *Baris subsimilis* Csy., *Hypera postica* (Gyll.), *Sciaphilus muricatus* (F.), *Cleonus piger* Scop., *Ceutorhynchus litura* (Fab.), *Miccotrogus picirostris* (Fab.), *M. griseus* (Schaeffer), *Anthonomus* sp., *Metriona bivittata* (Say), *Crioceris duodecimpunctata* (L.), *Tanysphyrus lemnae* (Fab.), *Gymnetron antirrhini* Payk.

LEPIDOPTERA: *Choristoneura rosaceana* (Harr.), *Aphelia pallorana* (Rob), *Macrobotys pertextalis* (Lederer), *Platyptilia carduidacyla* Riley, *Feltia subgothica* (Haw.), *Agrotis vancouverensis* Grt., *Peridroma saucia* Hbn., *Papaipema nitela* (Guen.), *P. cataphracta* (Grt.), *Amphipyra tragopoginis* (L.), *Autogragha californica* (Speyer), *Caenurgina crassiuscula* (Haw.), *Phyciodes mylitta* (Edw.), *Cynthia cardui* (L.).

DIPTERA: *Pegomyia carduorum* Huckett, *Dasineura gibsoni* Felt, *Euaresta bella* (Loew), *Orellia occidentalis* (Snow), *O. ruficauda* (Fab.).

The following three insects from continental Europe have been studied for biological control of *Cirsium arvense* in Canada.

Altica carduorum Guer. (flea beetle) was found by Harris (1964) to eat the leaves of only certain *Cirsium* species and to refuse the foliage of closely related genera. This insect was released in Ontario, Nova Scotia, Alberta and British Columbia during 1963–68 but does not seem to have become established well (Peschken 1971). It survived only in Alberta. Colonies survived at other locations when protected by cages and it appears that predation of the immature stages wiped out unprotected colonies (Peschken et al. 1970). The beetle was released again in Ontario in 1970 (Williamson 1971). It has been released in some states (U.S.A.) and in Great Britain as well.

Adults of *Ceutorhynchus litura* (F.) (Coleoptera) eat young thistle shoots but do not cause serious damage. Eggs are laid in the main vein of leaves in the rosette stage and larvae mine from the veins into the stem and root collar. The weevil was released near Belleville, Ontario in 1965, 1966 and 1967 (Peschken 1971; Peschken and Beecher 1973) and at Indian Head, Saskatchewan in 1973 (Williamson 1974). A colony became established at one of four sites in Ontario, and in a 400 m² area the number of thistle shoots decreased to 4% of original density between 1968 and 1972 (Peschken and Beecher 1973). Increased incidence of rust (*Puccinia punctiformis*) may have contributed to the decrease.

Urophora cardui L. (Diptera) seems to be a promising control agent but has not yet been released. The female lays eggs in the terminal buds and a gall develops, from which the adult insects emerge in the following spring (Peschken 1971).

(b) Microorganisms and viruses —
FUNGI
Several species of fungi attack Canada thistle in Canada and the United States but do not seriously harm it and have not been considered for biological control. The fungi are the following: *Albugo tragoponis* Pers. ex S.F. Gray (USDA 1960; Conners 1967); *Erysiphe cichoraceum* DC. (USDA 1960); *Fusarium* sp. (USDA 1960); *Ophiobolus porphyrogonus* (Tode) Sacc., on dead stems (Conners 1967); *Phialea cyathoidea* Bull. ex Gill. (Conners 1967); *Phyllosticta cirsii* Desm. (USDA 1960); *Puccinia punctiformis* (Strauss) Rohling (*P. obtegens* Tul.) (USDA 1960; Conners 1967); *Puccinia cirsii* Lasch (USDA 1960); *Pyrenochaeta erysiphoides* Sacc. (Conners 1967); *Sclerotinia sclerotiorum* (Lib.) de Barry (USDA 1960; Conners 1967); *Sclerotium rolfsii* Sacc. (USDA 1960); *Septoria cirsii* Niessl (USDA 1960; Conners 1967).

Aster yellow virus has been reported from New Brunswick (Conners 1967).

(c) Higher plant parasites — Dodder (*Cuscuta* spp.) has been reported on *Cirsium arvense* in New York state (USDA 1960).

ACKNOWLEDGMENTS

Dr. P. Harris and Dr. M. G. Maw of Canada Agriculture Research Station, Regina, Saskatchewan, have kindly contributed information regarding the insects associated with *Cirsium arvense* and Dr. Maw has provided the author with a copy of "An annotated list of insects found associated with Canada thistle (*Cirsium arvense* (L.) Scop.) in Canada" (in press in The Canadian Entomologist). Dr. Maw has permitted quotations from this list. Figure 2 is reproduced from "The thistles of Canada" (Canada Agriculture Research Branch Monograph no. 10) by courtesy of Canada Department of Agriculture. For the sake of uniformity, non-metric units used in some of the papers reviewed have been converted to metric units.

ALEX, J. F. 1966. Survey of weeds of cultivated land in the prairie provinces. Experimental Farm, Res. Branch, Canada Agric., Regina, Sask. 68 pp.

AMOR, R. L. and HARRIS, R. V. 1974. Distribution and seed production of *Cirsium arvense* (L.) Scop. in Victoria, Australia. Weed Res. **14**: 317–323.

ANONYMOUS. 1959–60. The climate of Canada. Reprinted from The Canada year book 1959 and 1960. Dominion Bureau of Statistics, Ottawa, Ont.

BAKKER, D. 1960. A comparative life history study of *Cirsium arvense* (L.) Scop. and *Tussilago farfara* L., the most troublesome weeds in the newly reclaimed polders of the former Zuiderzee. *In* J. L. Harper, ed. The biology of weeds. Blackwell, Oxford.

BENDALL, G. M. 1975. The allelopathic activity of Californian thistle (*Cirsium arvense* (L.) scop.) in Tasmania. Weed Res. **15**: 77–81.

BRUNS, V. F. and RASMUSSEN, L. W. 1957. The effects of fresh water storage on the germination of certain weed seeds. II. White Top, Russian Knapweed, Canada thistle, Morning Glory and Poverty Weed. Weeds **5**: 20–24.

BURT, G. W. 1974. Translocation and metabolism of atrazine in Canada thistle. Weed Sci. **22**: 116–119.

159

CANADA WEED COMMITTEE. 1969. Common and botanical names of weeds in Canada. Canada Dep. Agric. Publ. 1397. 67 pp.

CHIPIL, W. S. 1946. Germination of weed seeds. Sci. Agric. **26**: 307–346.

CONNERS, I. L. 1967. An annotated list of plant diseases in Canada. Can. Dep. Agric. Publ. 1251.

DERSCHEID, L. A. and SCHULTZ, R. E. 1960. Achene development of Canada thistle and perennial sow thistle. Weeds **8**: 55–62.

DETMERS, F. 1927. Canada thistle, *Cirsium arvense* Tourn. Ohio Agric. Exp. Sta. Bull. 414. 45 pp.

DEWEY, H. L. 1901. Canada thistle. U.S. Dep. Agric. Bur. Bot. Circ. 27. 14 pp.

DOYON, D. 1968. La végétation des pâturages naturels de Saint-Ferréol et de Saint-Tite-des-Caps, Comté de Montmorency. Nat. Can. **95**: 367–397.

FERRON, M. et CAYOUETTE, R. 1971. Noms des mauvaises herbes du Québec. Min. Agric. Colonisation du Québec. Publ. 288. 133 pp.

FRIESEN, G. and SHEBESKI, L. H. 1960. Economic losses caused by weed competition in Manitoba grain fields. I. Can. J. Plant Sci. **40**: 457–467.

GROH, H. and FRANKTON, C. 1949. Canadian weed survey. Seventh report, 1948. Canada Dep. Agric. 144 pp.

HAMEL, A. et DANSEREAU, P. 1949. L'aspect écologique du problème des mauvaises herbes. Bull. Serv. Biogéogr. **5**: 1–47. (Agriculture **5**: 23–36; 369–379. 1949. **6**: 143–161. 1949).

HANSEN, A. A. 1918. Canada thistle and methods of eradication. U.S. Dep. Agric. Farmers Bull. 1002. 15 pp.

HARRIS, P. 1964. Host specificity of *Altica carduorum* Guern. (Coleoptera: Chrysomelidae). Can. J. Zool. **42**: 857–862.

HAY, W. D. 1937. Canada thistle seed production and its occurrence in Montana seeds. Seed World, March 26, pp. 6–7.

HAYDEN, A. 1934. Distribution and reproduction of Canada thistle in Iowa. Amer. J. Bot. **21**: 355–373.

HEGI, G. 1929. Illustrierte Flora von Mittel-Europa. Vol. 6(2). München.

HODGSON, J. M. 1964. Variations in ecotypes of Canada thistle. Weeds **12**: 167–171.

HODGSON, J. M. 1968a. The nature, ecology and control of Canada thistle. U.S. Dep. Agric. Tech. Bull. 1386. 32 pp.

HODGSON, J. M. 1968b. Canada thistle and its control. U.S. Dep. Agric. Leafl. No. 523. 8 pp.

HODGSON, J. M. 1970. The response of Canada thistle ecotypes to 2,4-D Amitrole and intensive cultivation. Weed Sci. **18**: 253–255.

HODGSON, J. M. and MOORE, H. D. 1972. Stomata variations in Canada thistle and response to herbicides (*Cirsium arvense*). Weed Sci. **20**: 68–70.

HOPE, A. 1927. The dissemination of weed seeds by irrigation water in Alberta. Sci. Agric. **7**: 268–276.

HUNTER, J. H. and SMITH, L. W. 1972. Environment and herbicide effects on Canada thistle ecotypes (*Cirsium arvense*). Weed Sci. **20**: 163–167.

KOLK, H. 1947. Studies on germination biology of weeds. (in Swedish) Publ. Inst. Plant Husbandry, R. Agric. Coll. of Sweden. No. 2 pp. 108–167.

KOLOKOLNIKOV, L. B. 1931. The weeds of the Vyatka region. (in Russian) Bull. Appl. Bot. Genet. Plant Breed. **25**: 257–279.

KORSMO, E. 1930. Unkräuter im Ackerbau der Neuzeit. Springer, Berlin.

LEAVITT, F. D. 1973. *In* Weeds and their control. Sask. Dep. Agric.

LINK, A. J. and KOMMEDAHL, T. 1958. Canada thistle — spotlight on a troublesome weed. Minn. Farm Home Sci. **15**: 21–22.

LUND, S. and ROSTRUP, E. 1901. Marktdisteln, *Cirsium arvense*. Bianco Lunos, Copenhagen.

MALVEZ, A. I. 1931. Weeds of the cotton plant (in Russian). Bull. Appl. Botany, Genetics Plant Breed. **26**: 288–330. Part 2.

MOORE, R. J. 1968. *In* IOPB chromosome number reports. XVIII. Taxon **17**: 419–422.

MOORE, R. J. and FRANKTON, C. 1965. Cytotaxonomy of *Cirsium hookerianum* and related species. Can. J. Bot. **43**: 597–613.

MOORE, R. J. and FRANKTON, C. 1974. The thistles of Canada. Res. Br., Canada Dep. Agric. Monograph No. 10. Ottawa, Ont.

PESCHKEN, D. P. 1971. *Cirsium arvense* (L.) Scop., Canada thistle (Compositae). Commonwealth Inst. Biol. Contr., Tech. Commun. **4**: 79–83.

PESCHKEN, D. P. and BEECHER, R. W. 1973. *Ceutorhynchus litera* (Coleoptera: Curculionidae): biology and first releases for biological control of the weed Canada thistle (*Cirsium arvense*) in Ontario, Canada. Can. Entomol. **105**: 1489–1494.

PESCHKEN, D., FRIESEN, H. A., TONKS, N. V. and BANHAM, F. L. 1970. Releases of *Altica carduorum* (Chrysomelidae: Coleoptera) against the weed Canada thistle (*Cirsium arvense*) in Canada. Can. Entomol. **102**; 264–271.

PRENTISS, A. N. 1889. On root propagation of Canada thistle. Cornell Univ. Agric. Exp. Sta. Bull. **15**: 190–192.

PROCTOR, M. and YEO, P. 1973. The pollination of flowers. Collins, London.

REED, C. F. and HUGHES, R. D. 1970. Selected weeds of the United States. U.S. Dep. Agric., Agric. Res. Ser., Agric. handb. 366. 463 pp. USDA–ARS Washington, D.C.

ROGERS, C. F. 1928. Canada thistle and Russian Knapweed and their control. Colo. Agric. Exp. Sta. Bull. 434. 44 pp.

ROGERS, C. F. 1929. Winter activity of the roots of perennial weeds. Sci. **69**: 299–300.

ROUSSEAU, C. 1968. Histoire, habitat et distribution de 220 plantes introduites au Québec. Nat. Can. **95**: 49–169.

SAGAR, G. R. and RAWSON, H. M. 1964. The biology of *Cirsium arvense* (L.) Scop. Proc. 7th Br. Weed Control Conf. 553–562.

SHARMA, M. P. and VANDEN BORN, W. H. 1973. Fate of picloram in Canada thistle, soybean and barley. Weed Sci. **21**: 350–353.

SCHREIBER, M. M. 1967. Effect of density and control of Canada thistle on production and utilization of alfalfa pasture. Weeds **15**: 138–140.

SEELY, C. I. 1952. Controlling perennial weeds with tillage. Idaho Agric. Exp. Sta. Bull. 288. 43 pp.

TOOLE, E. H. and BROWN, E. 1946. Final results of the Duval buried seed experiment. J. Agric. Res. **72**: 201–210.

U.S. DEPARTMENT OF AGRICULTURE. 1960. Index of plant diseases in the United States. Agric. handb. 165. USDA–ARS, Washington, D.C.

WELTON, F. A., MORRIS, V. H. and HARTZLER, A. J. 1929. Organic food reserves in relation to the eradication of Canada thistle. Ohio Agric. Exp. Sta. Bull. 441.

WILLIAMSON, G. D. 1971. Insect liberations in Canada. Parasites and predators 1970. Canada Dep. Agric. Ottawa, Ont.

WILLIAMSON, G. D. 1974. Insect liberations in Canada. Parasites and predators 1973. Canada Dep. Agric., Ottawa, Ont.

ZWÖLFER, H. 1965. Preliminary list of phytophagous insects attacking wild Cynareae (Compositae) in Europe. Commonw. Inst. Biol. Control. Tech. Bull. No. 6. pp. 81–154.

161

THE BIOLOGY OF CANADIAN WEEDS.
14. *Gypsophila paniculata* L.

A. L. DARWENT

Research Station, Agriculture Canada, Beaverlodge, Alberta T0H 0C0.
Contribution no. NRG 75-2, received 1 Apr. 1975, accepted 22 July 1975.

DARWENT, A. L. 1975. The biology of Canadian weeds. 14. *Gypsophila paniculata* L. Can. J. Plant Sci. **55**: 1049–1058.

This contribution on *Gypsophila paniculata* L., baby's breath (Caryophyllaceae), is part of a series that presents biological information on plants that are weedy in Canada. *G. paniculata*, an ornamental which has escaped from gardens, is a weed problem in sandy, submarginal farmlands, roadside drainage ditches and various ruderal habitats. It occurs across Canada and has been found at 60° N latitude. Largest infestations of the species occur in the southern portions of the three most western provinces.

Cette contribution à l'étude la gypsophile paniculée (Caryophyllacée), *Gypsophila paniculata* L., fait partie d'une série d'articles sur la biologie des mauvaises herbes du Canada. *G. paniculata* est une plante ornementale échappée de culture, qui infeste les terres agricoles sableuses sub-marginales, les fossés d'écoulement des routes et divers habitats rudéraux. On la trouve partout au Canada jusqu'à 60° de latitude nord. Les infestations les plus importantes de cette espèce ont été relevées dans la partie sud des trois provinces situées les plus à l'ouest.

1. Names

Gypsophila paniculata L.—**baby's breath** (Canada Weed Committee 1969), maiden's breath, tall gypsophyll; **brouillard,** oeillet d'amour, gypsophile paniculée (Perron 1971). Caryophyllaceae, pink family, Caryophyllacées.

2. Description and Account of Variation

A much-branched perennial herb up to 0.75 m in height (Fig. 1A); stems erect or ascending at the base, single to many in number, freely branching throughout, thickened at base to form caudex; leaves opposite, lanceolate to linear-lanceolate, gradually tapering to a point, usually one-nerved and covered on both sides with a dense "bloom" of glandular hairs; inflorescence a panicle-like compound dichasium of small white flowers; pedicels 5–12 mm long; calyx of 5 coalescent sepals, with 5 nerves alternating between broad hyaline intervals, widely bell-shaped, 1.5 to 2 mm long, united nearly to the tip; corolla of 5

wedge-shaped, white petals, 1.5 to 2 times as long as the calyx; stamens 10; styles 2; capsule spherical or egg-shaped, four-valved, slightly exceeding the calyx in length (Fig. 1B); seeds black in color, 1.5 to 2 mm long, prominently cross-corrugated, papillate in longitudinal, concentric rows and resemble the shape of a compressed snail.

Chromosome numbers have not been reported from Canadian populations, but Baksay (1956) and Reese (1961) report diploid chromosome numbers of 28 and 34, respectively, for material collected in central Europe.

G. elegans Bieb. is probably the species most resembling *G. paniculata* in Canada. It occurs as an ornamental or occasionally as a garden escape in waste areas, but it is an annual, grows to only 0.3 to 0.4 m in height and has flowers that are twice as large as those of *G. paniculata*. According to Bailey (1941) *G. paniculata* can also be confused with *Galium mollugo* L. The latter species occurs as a. weed in southern

Canada from Ontario to Newfoundland (United States Department of Agriculture 1970) and sparingly in British Columbia (Abrams and Ferris 1960). *G. mollugo* can be distinguished by its square stem and leaves which occur in whorls of 6–8.

G. paniculata, as an adventive species, appears morphologically quite uniform throughout its Canadian range. Darwent and Coupland (1966) did not observe any significant difference in the percent germination of mature seeds collected from three,

Fig. 1.   (A) Mature plant (.073X), (B) flowers and capsules (2X) and (C) seedling (4X) of *G. paniculata*.

163

widely-separated infestations in Saskatchewan. However, there were minor variations in the size, color and rate of germination of the seeds. Barkoudah (1962) has observed variations in the pubescence of stems, leaves, bracts and pedicels of *G. paniculata* populations in Hungary and has divided the species into two varieties based on this pubescence: *G. paniculata* var. *paniculata* Bark. has glabrous stems, leaves, bracts and pedicels whereas *G. paniculata* var. *adenopoda* Borbás ex Hallier-Koch has pubescence on the lower part of the stem, lower leaves and on the bracts and pedicels. Jankulov (1969) and Yankulov (1973) have found variation in the saponin content of selected lines of *G. paniculata* in Bulgaria. Bailey (1958) reports considerable variation within the species as a garden plant. *G. paniculata* var. *compacta* Hort. is a dwarf garden form while the cultivars Double, Ehrle and Bristol Fairy have flowers that are double the size of those on unselected plants of the species.

The main diagnostic features of a *G. paniculata* seedling are shown in Fig. 1C.

3. Economic Importance

(a) Detrimental — *G. paniculata* is a weed problem in submarginal, sandy farmlands that have been seeded to introduced perennial grasses or where the native grass cover has been otherwise disturbed. The species can also reach high densities in vacant lots and along fencelines. *G. paniculata* can reduce the crude protein content of hay produced in fields that it infests (Darwent et al. 1967). In the fall, when the plants become brittle and dry, they create an untidy appearance along roadsides and in urban areas. In addition, entanglement of detached shoots in fences, farm machinery and around buildings is a nuisance.

(b) Beneficial—The major economic use of *G. paniculata* has been largely as an ornamental in flower gardens. It is used extensively by the flower industry in the preparation of bouquets. Jankulov (1961) reports the use of the root for its saponin content in Europe. Livestock have been observed to graze on plants in the vegetative phase (Darwent et al. 1967).

(c) Legislation — *G. paniculata* is not listed in any Canadian, federal or provincial weed or seed act.

4. Geographical Distribution

G. paniculata occurs in east and central Europe, extending westward to central Austria, southward to Bulgaria, and northward to approximately 57° N in Russia (Barkoudah and Chater 1964). It occurs in Asiatic U.S.S.R., Mongolia and west China (Barkoudah 1962). The center of origin of the genus *Gypsophila* includes the Black Sea region, the Caucasus, north Iraq and north Iran (Barkoudah 1962). Barkoudah (1962) reports it as an adventive species in west Europe, while in North America taxonomists (Fernald 1950; Gleason and Cronquist 1963; Hitchcock et al. 1964; Moss 1969) have reported it as an adventive species between the latitudes of 40° and approximately 60°. In Canada, *G. paniculata* occurs as a garden escape or adventive species in most provinces (Fig. 2). Infestations have been observed as far north as Fort Smith, Northwest Territories (60°00′ N–111°53′ W). Largest infestations of the species occur in Saskatchewan, Alberta and British Columbia.

5. Habitat

(a) Climatic requirements — Although little specific information is available, it is apparent that *G. paniculata* can withstand considerable variation in both temperature and moisture. Within the area of Canada where *G. paniculata* occurs as an adventive species the mean annual number of degree days above 5.56 C range between 832 and 2,220 and the mean annual precipitation ranges between 25 and 112 cm (Canada Department of Mines and Technical Surveys 1957). In Eurasia, the genus *Gypsophila* is common to regions of low total precipitation with a winter–spring rainfall

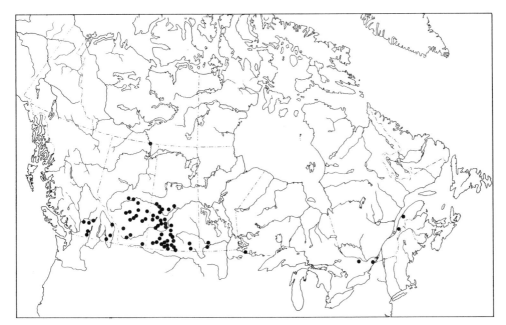

Fig. 2.　Canadian distribution of *Gypsophila paniculata* from specimens in the herbaria of Department of Agriculture Herbarium, Ottawa, Ontario and herbaria of the Department of Botany, University of British Columbia, Vancouver, British Columbia; and from reports by Agricultural Fieldmen of the Alberta Agricultural Service Boards and by personnel surveys.

pattern. Summers are hot and winters are cold. Day–night temperature contrasts are typical for a semidesert climate (Barkoudah 1962). *G. paniculata* is one of the few perennial ornamentals recommended for gardens located on permafrost (Harris 1970). In Yugoslavia, Tucakov (1958) has shown that the species is resistant to drought, wind and blown sand. In Canada, the species is most aggressive in areas of low rainfall. Darwent et al. (1967) observed at Beaver Creek, Saskatchewan (51°54′ N–106°43′ W) that the mean number of shoots and mean height of 40 mature plants were not significantly less in 1964 than in 1963 despite the fact that the April to August rainfall in 1964 was 34% below the long-term mean (14.5 cm), and in 1963, 35% above the long-term mean (30.2 cm). However, lack of rainfall during 1964 resulted in severe seedling mortality (Darwent and Coupland 1966).

(b) Substratum — *G. paniculata* has been found growing on fine-textured as well as coarse-textured soils, but it is most aggressive on the latter. In Saskatchewan, Darwent et al. (1967) reported seven out of the eight large infestations (1 ha or more in size) discovered in the province were located on sandy loam to loamy sand soils. In Alberta and British Columbia most infestations are also associated with coarse-textured soils. Barkoudah (1962) reports *G. paniculata* growing mainly on sandy and calcareous hills in eastern Europe and western Asia, while in other parts of Europe it grows in dry, sandy and stony places (Barkoudah and Chater 1964) and is characteristic of chalk outcrops (Core 1955). Fine-textured soils retard root development of *G. paniculata* (Tucakov 1958).

(c) Communities in which the species occurs — *G. paniculata* has been observed in a wide variety of habitats. In Saskatche-

wan, large infestations occurred in a lightly-grazed pasture located on stabilized sand dunes and containing native vegetation similar to that described by Hulett et al. (1966), in a roadside ditch, in hayfields and pastures dominated by *Bromus inermis* Leyes. or *Agropyron cristatum* (L.) Gaertn., in a shallowly cultivated field of *Secale cereale* L. and in an abandoned field dominated by annuals (Darwent et al. 1967). *G. paniculata* density in these habitats varied from 8 plants/are in a heavily-grazed pasture dominated by native species to 1,052 plants/are in a lightly-grazed *A. cristatum* pasture. Small infestations (< 1 ha in size) usually occurred in ruderal habitats such as roadside drainage ditches, cemetaries, vacant lots, etc. In one instance the species was observed growing in a grove of *Populus tremuloides* Michx., but the plants were spindly and seed production was delayed. In Eurasia, Barkoudah (1962) reports the species as growing in steppe communities and along the edges of pine forests.

6. History

G. paniculata was probably introduced into North America as a garden ornamental by early settlers. Macoun (1888) reports its first introduction into Manitoba in 1887. The first report of the weedy nature of the species in western Canada was noted in 1953 by members of the Saskatchewan Weed Survey (Darwent et al. 1967). They reported a large infestation in a *B. inermis* hayfield in western Saskatchewan. The species has now been reported as an adventive species, or garden escape, from numerous locations across Canada and northern United States north of 40°N latitude (Gleason and Cronquist 1963; Stevens 1963; Scoggan 1957; Moss 1959; Weber 1961; Hitchcock et al. 1964).

7. Growth and Development

(a) Morphology — The mature plant is characterized by a thick, deep-penetrating root system. At a site located on stabilized

sand dunes at Beaver Creek, Saskatchewan, the maximum depths reached by the roots of three well-developed plants ranged from 235 cm to more than 394 cm (Darwent and Coupland 1966). This deep rooting habit is probably the most important factor in allowing mature plants to withstand prolonged periods of drought.

(b) Perennation — *G. paniculata* survives by a persistent root system. These roots, with abundant food reserves, overwinter easily. New shoots arise from the caudex in the spring. Hill (1967) reports root formation in callus cultures of *G. paniculata*.

(c) Physiological data — De Groate (1957) obtained a marked increase in stem elongation from treatment of 2-wk-old plants sprayed with gibberellic acid. Jankulov and Mladenowa (1970) observed no reduction in viability when seeds of *G. paniculata* were soaked in a solution containing 10 mg/liter gibberellic acid or in a solution of 10 mg/liter thiamine. However, plants grown from treated seeds had less chlorophyll *a* and *b* and carotene in their leaves, greater weight of aerial parts and lower root weight than those grown from untreated seeds. Canham and Grafiedelli (1969) grew *G. paniculata* in an air-supported greenhouse in England, applied a 3-h period of light from incandescent lamps during the night and obtained a positive response in the amount of flowering.

(d) Phenology — The progress of shoot and flower development of 40 mature *G. paniculata* plants was followed at Beaver Creek, Saskatchewan during 1964 (Darwent and Coupland 1966). In late April the first shoots began to appear above the ground. They had a succulent appearance, being dark green in color and covered by dense glandular hairs. The mean number of shoots produced by each plant was 18. The shoots elongated very rapidly (approximately 8 cm/wk) during the first 2 mo after emergence. The pith of the shoots was filled with thin-walled cells for the first 2 mo after emergence, but then it became

166

hollow. Lateral branches developed on the shoots during early May. At this stage of development the plants had a leafy appearance. In early June, flower buds began to form. The buds were located in clusters with a covering of light green, hyaline bracts. Expansion of these clusters began approximately 2 wk after initial formation and continued until late June and early July when the flower buds began to open. The buds continued to open throughout July and into August. Fruits began to form in mid-July and matured and began to split open by late July. Dehiscence of the fruits continued from late July until the end of the growing season.

Darwent and Coupland (1966) observed seedling development at Beaver Creek, Saskatchewan in 1964, a year of lower than average rainfall. The few seedlings that emerged did so in early May. The first pair of secondary leaves appeared within 2 wk after emergence and by mid-June six pairs had developed. The seedlings attained an average height of 6 cm after 6 wk of growth. The cotyledons dried up and dropped off during the latter part of June. Only one shoot (with no lateral branches) developed on each plant during the first year of growth. The shoots remained green until killed by frost in the fall.

Root elongation is rapid during the first 2 yr of growth. At Beaver Creek, the average length of the tap roots of 10 plants approximately 1 yr after emergence was 62.0 cm, while the average height of the shoots was only 11.5 cm (Darwent and Coupland 1966).

In Saskatchewan, inflorescences of adventive plants do not appear to be produced during the first or second year of growth. However, in Florida Raulston et al. (1972) have reported the production of flowers 4–6 mo after the seed has been planted.

(e) Mycorrhiza — No data available.

8. Reproduction

(a) Floral biology — The mode of *G. paniculata* pollination is unknown. The structure of the flower suggests the possibility of cross-pollination (Darwent and Coupland 1966). The styles develop into long, spreading structures and tend to diverge outwards, while the filaments diverge in such a manner that the anthers are turned outwards. When in bloom the flowers have a pleasant, sweet odor. Milliron (1971) has observed floral visitations by bumble-bees (*Bombus terricola occidentalis* Grne.). At Beaverlodge, Alberta (55°13′ N–119°26′ W) honey bees (*Apis mellifera* L.) have been observed to visit *G. paniculata* growing in a garden (personal observation). However, since mature plants often have a multitude of flowers at various stages of development, it is likely that pollination can occur within the same plant.

(b) Seed production and dispersal — In North Dakota, Stevens (1957) reported that a single plant produced 13,700 seeds with a weight of 86 mg/100 seeds. The average weight of five samples of 100 seeds collected in Saskatchewan was 67 mg (Darwent and Coupland 1966). In Saskatchewan, wind was the most important agent of seed dispersal in the field (Darwent and Coupland 1966). During the latter part of the period of fruit development, the shoots became brittle and dry. Breakage occurred at the base and the plants were blown across the field. Most of the seeds in the capsules were loosely held and the majority dropped on the ground near the position of the parent plant. However, some capsules did not open completely, and seeds therein were carried for distances of nearly 1 km.

(c) Viability of seeds and germination — The seeds exhibit little or no dormancy (Darwent and Coupland 1966; Ichihara 1954). In germinators, maximum total germination of seeds collected in Saskatchewan occurred between 10 and 28 C. Germination at these temperatures ranged between 91 and 97%. Significant percentage germination reductions occurred at temperatures higher than 28 C and lower than 10 C (Darwent and Coupland 1966). Thompson (1973) observed a slightly wider range (10

167

to 38 C) of maximum germination from seeds collected in Hungary. Presence or absence of light did not have an effect on total germination (Darwent and Coupland 1966). Darwent and Coupland (1966) observed that under greenhouse conditions, 91–94% of the seeds planted at a depth of 0.25 cm or less produced seedlings. When placed at 1.0 cm, 84% of the seeds produced seedlings whereas only 51, 21 and 0.4% of the seeds placed at 2.0, 3.0 and 5.0 cm, respectively, produced seedlings. Soil texture also influenced seedling emergence. Total emergence of seedlings from a 0.25-cm depth was 95% in a sandy loam soil and only 79% in a clay soil.

(d) Vegetative reproduction — The only type of vegetative reproduction observed under natural conditions in Saskatchewan was an increase in the number of shoots per plant associated with an increase in the diameter of the caudex. Occasionally breaking of the caudex into two or more segments resulted in a greater, but still inconsequential, horizontal increase in area occupied by one plant. When segments of the root and caudex from various depths were planted in flats, only segments from the uppermost soil layers, and containing the caudex, produced shoots and none of the segments produced roots (Darwent and Coupland 1966).

9. Hybrids

There have been no reports of hybrids involving *G. paniculata* when it occurs as a garden escape or adventive species. However, under garden conditions a hybrid (*G. Bodgeri*) has been produced from a cross between a horticultural race of *G. paniculata* and *G. repens* L. var. *rosea* Hort. (Bailey 1958).

10. Population Dynamics

G. paniculata has exhibited an ability to invade and compete with other plant species in a number of habitats. In Saskatchewan, changes in the percentage area infested with *G. paniculata* in six belt transects distributed on three different habitats were studied by Darwent et al. (1967) between 1956 and 1965. The percentage area occupied by *G. paniculata* increased over a 9-yr-period in two of the three belt transects located on a *B. inermis* hayfield. The percentage area occupied by *G. paniculata* also increased over a 6-yr period in the belt transect located on a roadside drainage ditch and over a 4-yr period in the two belt transects located on a lightly grazed native pasture. The increases were not continuous. In years when rainfall was considerably below normal, the percentage area occupied by *G. paniculata* declined, presumably due to the death of immature plants. However, recovery was rapid wherever this occurred. The density of plants within the infested portions of the transects did not increase during the study period, except in the lightly grazed native pasture.

The life span of *G. paniculata* plants is unknown. In Saskatchewan there were no deaths among 50 mature plants over a 2-yr period. While it is possible that these plants were the same age, it probably indicates that the life span of *G. paniculata* plants, once established, is quite long. However, mortality was high in immature plants. Of 621 seedlings counted at Beaver Creek, Saskatchewan, in July 1963, only 8 remained alive 1 yr later. Unfavorable moisture conditions in 1964 caused the death of most plants (Darwent and Coupland 1966).

Topography and the presence of brush influenced the distribution of *G. paniculata* plants within infested areas in Saskatchewan (Darwent et al. 1967). On level grassland the species usually occurred as widely-spaced, single plants whereas on protected slopes and in small ravines where the supply of soil moisture and opportunity for trapping mature tumbling, seed-bearing plants were greater than on level land, the species frequently occurred in dense stands. The species also showed a tendency to have a greater density along fencelines (Darwent et al. 1967).

11. Response to Herbicides and Other Chemicals

Limited research suggests that *G. paniculata* is susceptible to dicamba (3,6-dichloro-o-anisic acid) at 2.24 kg/ha or more and picloram (4-amino-3,5,6-trichloropicolinic acid) at 1.12 kg/ha or more (Vanden Born and Schraa 1972). Fenoprop (2-(2,4,5-trichlorophenoxy) propionic acid) at 1.57 kg/ha and mecoprop [2-((4-chloro-1-tolyl)oxy) propionic acid] at 7.73 kg/ha provided good control in Saskatchewan (Skoglund and Darwent 1964a); 2,4-D [(2,4-dichlorophenoxy)acetic acid] at 1.12 to 2.24 kg/ha provided only partial *G. paniculata* control (Skoglund and Darwent 1964b).

12. Response to Other Human Manipulations

In Saskatchewan, heavy, continuous grazing suppressed the growth of mature plants and prevented the establishment of seedlings. However, light or infrequent grazing had little effect on the species. The vigor of *G. paniculata* was not measurably reduced by mowing or clipping. Disturbance of the soil by cultivation followed by abandonment increased the density as well as the standing crop biomass. Annual cultivation at a depth which severed the caudex from the root was very effective in destroying *G. paniculata* plants (Darwent et al. 1967).

13. Response to Parasites

(a) Insects and other non-domestic animals—

INSECTA

HOMOPTERA: *Macrosteles fascifrons* (Stal) — North America (Pirone et al. 1960) and *Myzuz persicae* (Sulzer) — Florida (Raulston et al. 1972).

THYSANOPTERA: *Frankliniella* spp. — Florida (Raulston et al. 1972).

LEPIDOPTERA: *Trichoplusia ni* (Hübner), *Pseudoplusia includens* Walk, *Spodoptera exigua* (Hübner), *S. eridania* (Cramer), and *Feltia subterranea* (Fab.) — Florida (Raulston et al. 1972).

DIPTERA: *Liriomyza* spp. — Florida (Raulston et al. 1972).

ARTHROPODA

Tetranychus spp.; the red spider mite are known to feed on *G. paniculata* in Florida (Raulston et al. 1972).

NEMATODA

Heterodera marioni (Cornu) Goodey causes nematode root knot in *G. paniculata* growing in North America (Westcott 1950).

(b) Microorganisms and viruses—

FUNGI

In North America *G. paniculata* is attacked by *Fusarium* spp. causing root rot disease (Conners 1967), by *Botrytis cinerea* Pers. causing blight, and by *Pythium debaryanum* Hesse, *Pellicularia filamentosa* (Pat.) Rogers and *Rhizoctonia solani* Kühn causing damping-off (Pirone et al. 1960; Westcott 1950).

VIRUSES

G. paniculata is reported to be susceptible to two virus diseases in North America; aster-yellows caused by callistephus virus 1 (Conners 1967); Pirone et al. 1960; United States Department of Agriculture 1960; Westcott 1950) and beet curly top (United States Department of Agriculture 1960).

BACTERIA

In North America, *Agrobacterium gypsophilae* Brown causes crown-gall and *Corynebacterium fascians* (Tilf.) Dowson causes faciation (Pirone et al. 1960; Westcott 1950).

ACKNOWLEDGMENTS

The author is grateful for the cooperation and assistance of G. A. Mulligan, Dr. P. Harris, J. Pinder-Moss and members of the Alberta Agricultural Service Board. The assistance of Dr. R. T. Coupland is also acknowledged. G. McLean of the Beaverlodge Research Station prepared the photographs.

ABRAMS, L. R. and FERRIS, R. S. 1960. Illustrated flora of the Pacific states Washington, Oregon and California. IV. Bignoniaceae to Compositae. Stanford Univ. Press, Stanford, California. 732 pp.

BAILEY, L. H. 1958. Manual of cultivated plants. The MacMillan Company, New York. 1116 pp.

BAKSAY, L. 1956. Cytotaxonomical studies in the flora of Hungary. Ann. Hist.—Nat. Mus. Natl. Hungary S.N. **7**: 321–334.

BARKOUDAH, Y. I. 1962. A revision of *Gypsophila, Bolanthus, Ankyropetalum,* and *Phryna.* Wentia **9**: 1–203.

BARKOUDAH, Y. I. and CHATER, A. O. 1964. *Gypsophila* L. *In* T. G. Tutin, V. H. Heywood, N. A. Burges, D. H. Valentine, S. M. Walters and D. A. Webb. Flora Europaea. Univ. Press., Cambridge, England. pp. 181–184.

CANADA DEPARTMENT OF MINES AND TECHNICAL SURVEYS. 1957. Atlas of Canada. Queen's Printer, Ottawa, Ontario. 110 pp.

CANADA WEED COMMITTEE. 1969. Common and botanical names of weeds in Canada. Canada Dep. Agr. Publ. 1397: 167 pp.

CANHAM, A. E. and GRAFIEDELLI, Z. 1969. Night-break lighting for cut flowers grown in an air-supported plastics greenhouse. Shinfield Progress **14**: 33–35.

CONNERS, I. L. 1967. An annotated index of plant diseases in Canada and fungi recorded on plants in Alaska, Canada and Greenland. Canada Dep. Agr. Res. Br. Publ. 1251: 381 pp.

CORE, E. L. 1955. Plant taxonomy. Prentice-Hall, Inc., Englewood Cliffs, New Jersey. 459 pp.

DARWENT, A. L. and COUPLAND, R. T. 1966. Life history of *Gypsophila paniculata.* Weeds **14**: 313–318.

DARWENT, A. L., COUPLAND, R. T. and SKOGLUND, N. A. 1967. The potential of *Gypsophila paniculata* as a weed in Saskatchewan. Can. J. Plant Sci. **47**: 125–134.

DE GROOTE, R. 1957. Résultats d'un essai d'orientation de la pulvérisation d'une solution du sel potassique de l'acide gibberellique sur quelques plantes ornementales. Bull. hort. Liege **12**: 279–280.

FERNALD, M. L. 1950. Gray's manual of botany. Eighth ed. American Book Co., New York. 1632 pp.

GLEASON, H. A. and CRONQUIST, A. 1963. Manual of vascular plants of northeastern United States and Canada. D. Van Nostrand Co., Inc., Princeton, New Jersey. 810 pp.

HARRIS, R. E. 1970. Gardening on permafrost. Canada Dep. Agr. Publ. 1408. 16 pp.

HILL, G. P. 1967. Root formation in callus cultures of *Gypsophila paniculata* L. Naturwissenschaften **54**: 522.

HITCHCOCK, C. L., CRONQUIST, A., OWNBEY, M. and THOMPSON, J. W. 1964. Vascular plants of the Pacific Northwest. Part 2. Salicaeae to Saxifragaceae. Univ. Washington Press, Seattle, Washington. 597 pp.

HULETT, G. K., COUPLAND, R. T. and DIX, R. L. 1966. The vegetation of dune sand areas within the grassland region of Saskatchewan. Can. J. Bot. **44**: 1307–1331.

ICHIHARA, J. 1954. Dormancy of the seeds of herbaceous flowers. (Abstr.) Hort. Abstr. **25**: 1895.

JANKULOV, J. K. 1961. Positive geotropism in the roots of *Gypsophila paniculata* L. and ways of overcoming it. (Abstr.) Hort. Abstr. **32**: 3538.

JANKULOV, J. K. 1969. Results of selection work with gypsophila (Abstr.) Hort. Abstr. **40**: 6997.

JANKULOV, J. and MLADENOWA, J. 1970. The effect of some growth substances on the root yield of *Gypsophila paniculata* L. and on the roots' foam-forming ability. (Abstr.) Hort. Abstr. **41**: 7369.

MACOUN, J. 1888. Catalogue of Canadian plants: IV Endogens. Dawson Bros., Montreal, Quebec. 428 pp.

MILLIRON, H. E. 1971. A monograph of the western hemisphere bumblebees (Hymenoptera: Apidae:Bombinae). I. The genera *Bombus* and *Megabombus* subgenus *Bombias* Mem. of Entomol. Soc. Canada. No. 82. 80 pp.

MOSS, E. H. 1959. Flora of Alberta. Univ. Toronto Press, Toronto, Ontario. 546 pp.

PERRON, W. H. 1971. Encyclopédie du jardinier horticulteur. Les Editions de L'Homme, Montreal, Quebec. 415 pp.

PIRONE, P. P., DODGE, B. P. and RICKETT, H. W. 1960. Diseases and pests of ornamental plants. Ronald Press Co., New York. 776 pp.

RAULSTON, J. C., POE, S. L. and MARONSKY, F. J. 1972. Cultural concepts of *Gypsophila paniculata* L. production in Florida. Proc. Florida State Hort. Soc. **85**: 423–428.

REESE, G. 1961. Unpublished data, p. 153. *In* A. Löve and D. Löve. Chromosome numbers of central and northwest European plant species. Opera Bot. **5**: 1–581.

SCOGGAN, H. J. 1957. Flora of Manitoba. Nat. Mus. of Canada Bull. No. 140. 619 pp.

SKOGLUND, N. A. and DARWENT, L. 1964a. The effect of herbicides on *Gypsophila paniculata* L. (baby's breath). Res. Rep., Canada Weed Comm., Western Section. pp. 209.

SKOGLUND, N. A. and DARWENT, L. 1964b. The effect of 2,4-D on baby's breath (*Gypsophila paniculata* L.). Res. Rep., Canada Weed Comm., Western Section. pp. 208–209.

STEVENS, O. A. 1957. Weights of seeds and numbers per plant. Weeds **5**: 46–55.

STEVENS, O. A. 1963. Handbook of North Dakota plants. North Dakota Inst. Regional Stud., Fargo, North Dakota. 324 pp.

THOMPSON, P. A. 1973. Geographical adaptations of seeds. *In* W. Heydecker, ed., Seed ecology. Pennsylvania State Univ. Press, University Park, Pennsylvania. pp. 31–58.

TUCAKOV, J. 1958. Plantes médicinales et aromatiques de sables dé Danube (Déliblato) en Yougoslavie. Importance économique. Possibilité de culture. Qual. Plant. Maveq. **5**: 108–120.

UNITED STATES DEPARTMENT OF AGRICULTURE. 1960. Index of plant diseases in the United States. Agr. Res. Service, United States Dep. Agr. Agr. Handbook No. 165. 531 pp.

UNITED STATES DEPARTMENT OF AGRICULTURE. 1970. Selected weeds of the United States. Agr. Res. Service, United States Dep. Agr. Agr. Handbook No. 366. 463 pp.

VANDEN BORN, W. H. and SCHRAA, R. J. 1972. Control of baby's breath with dicamba and picloram. Res. Rep., Canada Weed Comm., Western Section. pp. 358–359.

WEBER, W. A. 1961. Handbook of plants of the Colorado Front Range. Univ. Washington Press, Boulder, Colorado. 232 pp.

WESTCOTT, C. 1950. Plant disease handbook. D. Van Nostrand Co., Inc., Toronto, Ontario. 746 pp.

YANKULOV, Y. 1973. Changes in foam-production in *Gypsophila* roots during the vegetation period. (Abstr.) Hort. Abstr. **44**: 7019.

171

THE BIOLOGY OF CANADIAN WEEDS.
15. *Pteridium aquilinum* (L.) Kuhn

WILLIAM J. CODY and CLIFFORD W. CROMPTON

*Biosystematics Research Institute, Agriculture Canada, Ottawa, Ontario K1A 0C6.
Received 4 June 1975, accepted 29 July 1975.*

CODY, WILLIAM J. AND CROMPTON, CLIFFORD W. 1975. The biology of Canadian weeds. 15. *Pteridium aquilinum* (L.) Kuhn. Can. J. Plant Sci. **55**: 1059-1072.

A summary is provided of information on the biology of *Pteridium aquilinum* (L.) Kuhn, bracken, a fern species, cosmopolitan in its distribution and comprising several subspecies and varieties. Two varieties occur in Canada where they are particularly weedy in pastures and rough terrain. Bracken has been shown to be carcinogenic in rats, to be responsible for enzootic bovine haematuria in cattle, and to cause vitamin B_1 avitaminosis in horses and other nonruminants.

Les auteurs présentent un résumé des données sur la biologie de la ptéridie d'aigle (*Pteridium aquilinum* (L.) Duhn), espèce de fougère à distribution cosmopolite et comprenant plusieurs sous-espèces et variétés. Deux variétés sont répandues au Canada où elles infestent particulièrement les pâturages et les terrains accidentés. La ptéridie d'aigle s'est révélée cancérigène chez le rat, responsable de l'hématurie enzootique bovine, et de l'avitaminose B_1 chez le cheval et d'autres non ruminants.

1. Name

I. *Pteridium aquilinum* (L.) Kuhn var. *latiusculum* (Desv.) Underw. — **eastern bracken** (Canada Weed Committee 1969), brake; **grande fougère**, fougère d'aigle, pteride aigle, pteride aigle-imperiale, fougère imperiale, fougère-paille, polypode à feuilles recourbées, ptéridie, ptéris, ptéridium aquilin, ptéridium des aigles, ptéridium large (Ferron et Cayouette 1971).

II. *Pteridium aquilinum* (L.) Kuhn var. *pubescens* Underw. — **western bracken** (Canada Weed Committee 1969), brake, eagle fern; **grande fougère.** Polypodiaceae, fern family, Polypodiacées.

2. Description and Account of Variation

The genus *Pteridium* is monotypic. The single species, *P. aquilinum*, comprises several subspecies and varieties (Tryon 1941). In Canada, two varieties occur: var. *latiusculum* which is eastern in range, and var. *pubescens* which is found in British Columbia and the foothills of the Rocky Mountains in southern Alberta. In addition, Boivin (1952) has described a variety *champlainense* from Quebec to eastern Manitoba, which is doubtfully distinct.

In this species, the fronds arise singly from alternate sides of an extensively creeping and forking subterranean hairy rhizome. The frond consists of a stiff upright stipe and a bipinnate or often tripinnate blade which becomes coarse later in the year. The pinnae are subopposite, the pinnules alternate, with the ultimate divisions very numerous, oblong to linear, with revolute margins. Sporangia are borne in marginal sori on the under surface of the pinnules and are covered by a mostly continuous false outer indusium formed by the revolute margin, and a minute, often nearly obsolete, hyaline inner indusium.

I. *Pteridium aquilinum* var. *latiusculum* — Fronds 3-7 dm or more tall, the blade usually broadly triangular, the stipe longer or shorter than the blade; plants growing in the shade tend to have ternate fronds with the rachis bent so that the blade is presented

Can. J. Plant Sci. 55: 1059-1072 (Oct. 1975)

Fig. 1. *Pteridium aquilinum* var. *latiusculum* growing in the open. Constance Bay, Carleton Co., Ont. on 15 Sept. 1974.

to the available light, while plants growing in the open tend to be upright and stiff, with shorter ascending pinnae which are twisted at right angles to the rachis (Fig. 1); pinnules more or less at an oblique angle to the rachis; margins of the pinnules ciliate; the mid-nerve on the underside of the pinnules usually more or less short-pubescent and occasionally the underside of the pinnules more or less pubescent; indusium eciliate or occasionally ciliate (Fig. 2A).

II. *Pteridium aquilinum* var. *pubescens* — Fronds usually taller than var. *latiusculum*, up to 15 or more dm tall, the blade broadly triangular, but rarely ternate; the pinnules nearly at right angles to the rachis; the lower surface of the pinnules more or less densely villous or villous-puberulent and the inner indusium ciliate and sometimes also pubescent (Fig. 2B).

A chromosome number of $n = 52$ has been obtained from material of *Pteridium aquilinum* var. *latiusculum* from Virginia, U.S.A. (Wagner and Wagner 1966) and Ontario (Britton 1953; Mulligan and Cody unpublished). No counts have been reported on material of *P. aquilinum* var. *pubescens*.

3. Economic Importance

(a) Detrimental — Tryon (1941) considered bracken to be a serious agricultural pest in Europe, North America, Australia and New Zealand. Recently, bracken poisoning has been shown to be synonymous with chronic and acute enzootic haematuria in cattle (Rosenberger 1971). Groh (1941) discussed the possible relationship of bracken to this disease and related it to the distribution of bracken in British Columbia. Bankier (1943) reported that "redwater disease", enzootic bovine haematuria, had been known to occur in the Fraser Valley area of British Columbia for many years, as well as in Oregon, Washington, Australia, India, the British Isles, France and Germany.

Rosenberger (1971) also discussed vitamin B_1 avitaminosis which is caused by feeding on bracken, which occurs in horses and other nonruminants. Braid (1959), in a review of the bracken literature, stated that bracken had serious poisoning properties and had been responsible for many livestock deaths, mainly of cattle and horses, but to a much lesser extent of sheep and swine. Bracken poisoning is difficult to detect and diagnose (Hall 1964). This is due to a delayed toxicity (Evans and Mason 1965; Rosenberger 1971). The plants have been shown to be equally toxic in green forage or in a dry condition by Lodge et al. (1968). Recently, bracken has been the subject of research and discussion as a possible carcinogen or mutagen in man as well as in animals. Tests with rats fed on bracken (Evans and Mason 1965) proved that tumors and lesions could be caused throughout the small intestine of experi-

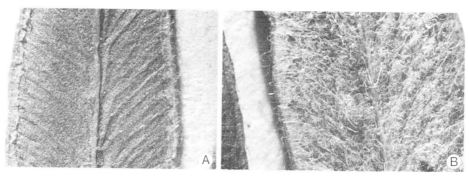

Fig. 2.   Undersurface of pinnule. A. *Pteridium aquilinum* var. *latiusculum*. B. *Pteridium aquilinum* var. *pubescens*.

mental animals. Pamukcu and Price (1969) suggested that the high degree of stomach cancer in the people of Japan might be attributed to the large quantities of bracken croziers eaten. Hirono et al. (1972) in comparing bracken croziers prepared by boiling in water with wood ash or sodium bicarbonate, or sometimes boiled fresh, or stored in salt and immersed in boiling water before use, suggested that the carcinogenic content was less on processed than on unprocessed bracken. The carcinogenic factor was, however, still evident. They further implied that the degree of carcinogenic activity of bracken varied geographically. Dobereiner et al. (1966) presented a world map of the reported cases of enzootic bovine hematuria as known to them. No cases of the disease have been reported from many areas such as eastern North America where bracken is quite plentiful. This would seem to indicate that bracken may be less toxic in some geographic regions than in others.

Recently, Hirono et al. (1973), in tests with rats, compared the toxicity of various parts of the plant viz: croziers, fronds, stalks and rhizomes. They discovered that croziers were more carcinogenic than young stalks and that rhizomes of adult plants were more carcinogenic than the fronds.

Tests for the active toxin in milk from cattle fed on bracken have been conducted in England (Evans et al. 1972). These tests gave positive results, proving evidence of the toxin being passed into the milk.

Numerous authors of works on edible plants (Fernald and Kinsey 1958) have recommended bracken croziers as a food, but in view of current investigations it was suggested by Hodge (1973) that bracken should be removed by botanists from their publications on edible plants.

In New Brunswick, dense growth of bracken fern has proved to be detrimental to the germination and early survival of spruce (*Picea* spp.) and balsam fir (*Abies balsamea* (L.) Mill.) seedlings (Place

1953). Bracken was considered by Eaton (1943) to be a troublesome weed of blueberries (*Vaccinium* spp.) in New England.

(b) Beneficial — Bracken has been used for composts, pig feeding, litter and manure, thatching and as a source of potash (Braid 1959). No present-day utilization for food appears possible for this plant, due to its carcinogenic, mutagenic and weedy properties. The use for thatching and as a source for potash is no longer feasible for economic reasons. McCulloch (1942) reported that in plots of Douglas fir seedlings in northwest Oregon, more seedlings survived when permitted to grow under bracken cover than where bracken had been cleared.

(c) Legislation — *Pteridium aquilinum* is not listed in any Canadian federal or provincial weed or seeds act.

4. Geographical Distribution

Pteridium aquilinum is worldwide in distribution. Tryon (1941) proposed two subspecies and 12 varieties and gave their distributions as known to him. The distribution map presented here (Fig. 3) is based on specimens from three herbaria (DAO, CAN and TRT (standard abbreviations for herbaria as in Holmgren and Keuken (1974)) and also includes data from Taylor (1970) and Rousseau (1974).

I. Var. *latiusculum* is native in Canada and is widespread from Newfoundland to eastern Manitoba. It is rare in eastern British Columbia and the foothills of the Rocky Mountains in Alberta, and is absent from the dry grassland regions of the Prairie Provinces.

II. Var. *pubescens* is native in Canada and is found only in the provinces of British Columbia and Alberta. In British Columbia the plant is either coastal or occurs adjacent to the tributaries of the Fraser, Columbia and Kootenay rivers. In Alberta it is rare in the foothills of the Rocky Mountains.

175

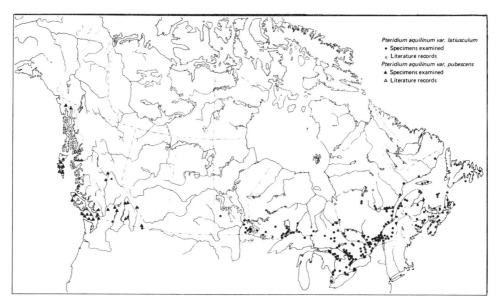

Pteridium aquilinum var. latiusculum
• Specimens examined
○ Literature records
Pteridium aquilinum var. pubescens
▲ Specimens examined
△ Literature records

Fig. 3. Canadian distribution of *Pteridium aquilinum* var. *latiusculum* and *P. aquilinum* var. *pubescens*.

5. Habitat

(a) Climatic requirements — Pteridium in Canada occurs from the border of the United States, north to 60° latitude in the west, and north to 45° latitude in the east. It is absent in the prairies. Where bracken occurs, temperatures vary from −15 C (5 F) mean in winter to 21 C (70 F) mean in summer. Rainfall varies from 61 cm (24 inches) to 165 cm (65 inches) per year. The amount of snowfall is also quite variable, from 10 cm (4 inches) to 51 cm (20 inches) per year (Anonymous 1957–58).

(b) Substratum — Both eastern and western bracken in Canada are mainly associated with Podzol and Brunisol soil types. In Michigan, Hellum (1964) stated that differences in bracken frond size can be directly attributed to Podzol soil profile development. As podzolization proceeds, the size of the plant increases.

(c) Communities in which the species occurs — Pteridium taxa in Canada are associated with abandoned fields, pastures, burnt-over areas, subacid soils, mixed, deciduous or coniferous forests, grassy slopes along roadsides, swamps, waste places, beaches, peat bogs and thickets. In Quebec, eastern bracken is associated with plant communities contained in nine bioclimatic zones as defined by Rousseau (1974). He listed *Pteridium* as being found in bioclimatic zones from the subarctic to the Great Lakes–St. Lawrence forest. There appears to be no apparent difference in the habitat requirements for either eastern or western bracken.

6. History

The two varieties of *Pteridium aquilinum* occurring in Canada are both considered by botanists to be of native origin (Tryon 1941; Fernald 1950; Cody 1956; Gleason 1963). The species is indigenous throughout much or all of its present distribution.

Cushing (1963) assumed that the majority of the trilete spores found in his Cedar Bog Lake borings from Minnesota (radiocarbon-dated from 10,000 yr) were *P. aquilinum*. In his *Pinus–Pteridium* zone assemblage he found *Pteridium* spores to be as characteristic of the zone as *Pinus* pollen.

176

7. Growth and Development

(a) Morphology — Although *Pteridium aquilinum* produces a myriad of spores each growing season, there is no record of the germination of these spores under natural conditions in Canada. The plant can survive burning and cutting because new fronds will arise from the deeply buried underground stem. From experiments carried out in Scotland, Conway (1952) found that a small fragment of stem buried in April and dug up 5½ mo later, grew 31.75 cm and produced seven side branches. In the place of 1 original frond bud, there were two expanded fronds and 25 frond buds. These buds do not all develop at the same time, but the younger ones form a reserve which soon take the place of the first set of fronds if these are destroyed by late spring frosts or mechanical damage. In a second experiment by Conway, a young plant growing in an experimental trough produced 45 fronds in its second growing season, 136 in the third and 297 in the fourth season; and again the underground stem had formed many branches, each bearing a number of fronds.

In eastern Canada, at least in years of good forage production, the mature fronds are apparently not palatable to cattle, and are left undisturbed by them in the pastures (personal observation). However, Wells (1949) observed that in 1948 in the west Midlands of England, cattle that had been feeding on lush and rank grass developed a craving for fibrous material which they would satisfy with bracken, if nothing else was available. Based on extensive excavation of root systems in England, Watt (1940) showed that the terminal bud of a rhizome might remain dormant for at least a year, or might produce two internodes in 1 yr, although the production of two internodes was not common. From his studies he estimated the average growth of a main rhizome in one area at a little over 5 cm per annum; a rhizome which measured about 250 cm was established to be about 50 yr old. In another area the average yearly growth over three seasons was 74.2 cm; main dead rhizomes were found 26 m from the advancing front; the bracken plant was estimated to be 35 yr old at the dying end, but the plant was actually about 72 yr old. No similar studies have been undertaken in Canada, but Hellum (1964) observed that the rhizome system and age of plants of var. *latiusculum* in Michigan was similar to that observed by Watt (1940, 1945) in England on var. *aquilinum*.

(b) Perennation — In Canada and elsewhere, bracken survives and spreads primarily by means of the extremely persistent underground stem. This stem, with abundant food reserves, overwinters and produces new fronds in the spring. The rhizome structure of bracken has been well demonstrated by Long and Fenton (1938), Watt (1940) and Hellum (1964). There are usually two systems of rhizomes, a deeper one, 1.25–2.50 cm in diameter, which is chiefly for food storage and for growth, and a second layer of smaller rhizomes nearer the surface, from which arise most of the fronds. The deeper system has lateral branches but usually only a few fronds, while the rhizomes near the surface bear numerous petioles and a dense covering of fine roots. Watt (1950) on the basis of observations in England over the period 1934–1949 concluded that the killing or crippling of fronds by frost stimulated new fronds to differentiate and grow, or removed the inhibition to do so. Watt (1950), in addition, reported that serious winter frosts kill a high proportion of frond initiates and rhizome apices located near the ground surface, and that winter frost conditions affect the number of emergent fronds and the length of the petiole and of the lamina. Hellum (1964) obtained comparable results for var. *latiusculum* in Michigan. No similar studies have been conducted in Canada.

(c) Physiological data —Ferguson and Armitage (1944) examined the chemical composition of bracken using material gathered

approximately every 14 days, from two sites in Berkshire, England.

Greshoff (1908) and Moon and Raafat (1951a) reported the presence of HCN in bracken.

Evans and Evans (1949) suggested that bracken-poisoning of farm animals was primarily an avitaminosis B_1 produced by the action of an unknown inactivating principle in bracken which destroyed the vitamin in the fodder, and also that part contributed by the microflora of the alimentary tract. Later, Evans et al. (1950) and Evans et al. (1951) reported the presence of a thiaminase in *P. aquilinum* [*Pteris aquilina*], which by virtue of its property of splitting aneurin into its components denies this essential intact vitamin to the animal. Moon and Raafat (1951b) found that postmortem tissue analyses of experimentally "bracken-poisoned" sheep showed relatively low concentrations of vitamin C in liver, kidney, heart and adrenal glands. Moon and McKeand (1953) reported that in the terminal stages of bracken "poisoning" in ruminants, there may be an increased destruction of vitamin C, but there is no evidence of a simple deficiency of this vitamin resulting from bracken feeding. They confirmed the occurrence of leucopenia in sheep suffering from bracken "poisoning", an occurrence previously reported for cattle, and suggested that the differences in the blood picture between bracken-fed cattle and sheep might be due to the ability of sheep to tolerate bracken feeding for much longer periods. Smith and Agiza (1951) in comparing the amino aicds of several species of grass, clover and bracken, based on material gathered in Scotland, found that the ranges of values for the amino acids for bracken were narrow, being much less than in the cases of all other species examined. Various writers (Conway 1952; Watt 1955) who have studied the ecology of bracken have suggested that this weedy plant brings pressure to bear on other plants associated with it, through competition for water, light and nutrients. Gliessman and Muller (1972), from studies in California, have found that phytotoxina released from bracken fronds may often be the limiting factor rather than direct competition for nutrients. These toxins are readily dissolved from the fronds and transmitted to the soil by precipitation. Phenolic acids were suspected and cinnamic acid was tentatively identified by these authors.

Workers in Japan (Hikino et al. 1970, 1971, 1972) have isolated several glycosides, pterosides A, B, C, D and Z, from Japanese material of *Pteridium aquilinum* var. *latiusculum*. These were described and stereostructures presented.

Evans and Osman (1974), in tests on mice that were injected with shikimic acid extracted from bracken, determined that chemical as being responsible for glandular stomach cancer, lymphocytic leukaemia, and reticulum cell leukaemia in their test animals. They further believed that a second carcinogenic substance is responsible for acute bovine bracken poisoning (Evans, Jones, Jones and Evans, unpublished).

(d) Phenology — Conway (1952), from studies of rhizome development in western Scotland in specially prepared trenches, found that the rhizome grows particularly strongly in the autumn, when large numbers of frond buds are initiated. In the spring the emergent frond first completes the extension of the petiole before the lamina appreciably unfolds. Watt (1945) presented a table and graph showing extension of growth of petiole and lamina of two fronds growing in England during the period 15–28 May 1943. Watt (1950) observed that new fronds would develop after the initial mid-May burst of growth up to as late as mid-July, if the first fronds were crippled or killed. In eastern North America the span of emergence appears to be shorter because of weather conditions. Hellum (1964) measured the rates of emergence of bracken at several site locations in Lower Michigan in 1962 and 1963. The rates of emergence were slower in 1963 than in 1962: 43 days

178

as compared to 28 days. The rates at which the leaves matured after emergence from the soil did not, however, change from 1962 to 1963, but did have a measurable influence on the blade size. Hellum concluded that bracken emergence times are so closely adjusted to temperature regimes that any abnormal or unusually high temperature variation during the early days of May caused early bracken emergence and could result in subsequent setbacks by frost. Figure 4 demonstrates the unfolding of the lamina of emergent fronds of *Pteridium aquilinum* var. *latiusculum* near Ottawa, Ontario. An examination of herbarium material at DAO, CAN and TRT revealed that sporulating specimens of var. *latiusculum* had been gathered as early as 23 August in Newfoundland, 1 August in Prince Edward Island, 16 July in Nova Scotia, 29 July in New Brunswick, 29 June in Quebec, 24 June in Ontario and 5 August in Manitoba; and specimens of var. *pubescens* as early as 22 July in British Columbia. It should be noted, however, that the sporangia of *Pteridium* on any one frond do not mature simultaneously. The fronds of *Pteridium* in Ontario and Quebec yellow before the first killing frost (Cody and Crompton unpublished). It is not known whether the yellowing is caused by maturity, soil moisture, changes in light values, or some critical temperature point inherent to the plant. Germination of spores is discussed in section 8(c).

(e) Mycorrhiza — In two areas of western Scotland, Conway and Arbuthnott (1949) discovered endotrophic mycorrhiza occurring irregularly in the middle cortical cells of the *Pteridium* root. The soil from these locations was peaty, contained much humus and possessed a pH of 4.4.

8. Reproduction

(a) Sporophyll biology — The reproductive mechanism in ferns has been described in numerous text books (McLean and Ivimey-Cook 1951; Foster and Gifford 1959). Briefly, reproduction of *Pteridium aquilinum* is by means of spores that are produced in sporangia which are found under the marginal indusium on the under side of the pinnules. A spore germinates to

Fig. 4.A,B,C. unfolding stages of the lamina of three separate fronds of *Pteridium aquilinum* var. *latiusculum* at Crown Pt., Ont. on 25 May 1974.

179

form a small green prothallus which may bear only antheridia or both antheridia and archegonia. Motile spermatozoids from the antheridia fertilize the oosphere or egg. The resultant zygote then germinates and produces the familiar fern plant. Only one zygote matures on any one prothallus.

(b) Spore production and dispersal — Many thousands of spores may be produced by a single well developed frond. Conway (1952) estimated 300,000,000. However, not all fronds of *Pteridium* produce sporangia, even though the marginal indusium is nearly always present. The light spores are readily distributed by the wind.

(c) Viability of spores and germination — According to Conway (1952), the spores may germinate without any period of dormancy; in experimental conditions, sporeling plants may be found within 6–7 wk after the spores have been shed. However, Smith (1938) stated that it is very probable that under natural conditions the spores of *Pteridium aquilinum* do not germinate until the spring after they are shed. Spores of some fern genera have been germinated as much as 48 yr after production (Smith 1938; Hill and Wagner 1974; Britton, *in litt.*). There are no figures available on the percentage germination of *Pteridium* spores, although it is obvious that only a very small number of spores will find a suitable moist niche on the soil and subsequently germinate. Since the spermatozoids are motile and thus require a moist situation through which to move to the archegonia, a dry season will restrict fertilization, or even kill the prothallus which is only one cell in thickness, and thus readily subject to desiccation. Gametophytes (prothalli) growing under unfavorable conditions may become branched or strap-like, and produce antheridia only (Smith 1938).

(d) Vegetative reproduction — Numerous fronds may arise along the forking underground stem. These, on the surface, will appear to be separate plants. New plants may be formed by the fragmentation of the underground stem either by rotting or by mechanical damage (Conway 1952). In Canada it is suspected that reproduction in bracken is mainly by vegetative means. Whittier (1966) has shown that what had been considered by earlier authors as natural apospory was actually a "prothalloid" growth or gall caused by two species of mites, *Eriophyes* spp. (*see* section 13 (a)).

9. Hybrids

Tryon (1941) reported the presence of intermediates between var. *pubescens* and var. *latiusculum* along the eastern border of the range of var. *pubescens:* Arizona, New Mexico, Colorado, Utah, Wyoming, Michigan, and Wisconsin. In 1949, Tryon also annotated specimens from Ontario in the Herbarium of the University of Toronto (TRT) as being intermediate between these two varieties. It was from specimens of this nature that Boivin (1952) described his var. *champlainense*. Intermediates between var. *aquilinum* and var. *latiusculum* in Europe were also reported by Tryon (1941). There is, however, no conclusive evidence that the plants reported as intermediates were of hybrid origin.

10. Population Dynamics

Of the many millions of spores which are released each year, only a limited number will find a moist protected niche which is a suitable site for germination. Conway (1949, 1957) demonstrated that germination of spores takes place most readily on sterilized soils which have a pH of between 5.5 and 7.7. Spores will germinate readily under laboratory conditions (Hofmeister 1857), but are not readily observed in the field. Indeed no published observations of prothalli or sporelings in Canada have been found. Long and Fenton (1938) reported that in eastern Britain the prothallial stage was rare or unknown, but that in western Britain where there is more precipitation, young plants were not uncommon. Lousley (1943–44) and Weatherby (1946) reported that sporelings of bracken had invaded sites in England which had been sterilized by bombing during the war. Oinonen (1967) reported that regeneration of bracken by spores in the northern part of the distribution of the species in Finland was clearly less frequent than in the southern parts of the country. Braid and Conway (1943) found that a juvenile plant could produce rhizomes which extended through a 1.8-m earth-filled tank by the autumn of the year planted. Oinonen (1967) found that on average sites in Finland, bracken spreads about 36 cm annually or about 18 cm annually in the frontal direction. Watt (1943) described the bracken plant as having a main axis whose direction of growth and predominance are determined by the freedom from competition in front and the increasing competition from neighboring plants farther back. An independent plant derived by the detachment of a branch shows a bush form with no predominant main axis, but a number of laterals of more or less equal size. No similar studies have been carried out in Canada. Watt (1943, 1945, 1947, 1954, 1956, 1969, 1970, 1971) compared the size and concentration of fronds of bracken from the advancing front, near hinterland, and remote hinterland and related these factors to those of frost, moisture, litter cover, depth of rhizome and senescence. Pioneer fronds and fronds from the remote hinterland were shorter in overall height as well as in length of petiole and lamina than fronds from the near hinterland. See also, under section 7 (c), the report of work on phytotoxins in California by Gleissman and Muller (1972).

11. Response to Herbicides and Other Chemicals

There is scant evidence of control work on *Pteridium* in Canada. 2,4D amine coupled with sodium chlorate was reported as giving good control in Nova Scotia (Leefe 1952).

In Europe, Japan, Australia and New Zealand many chemicals and selective herbicides have been tried for the control of bracken. Of these, MCPA, 4-CPA, dicamba, picloram and aminotriazole were prom-

ising, but proved quite variable in their effectiveness. Asulam is presently the most effective herbicide when applied at full frond emergence between July and September (McKelvie and Scragg 1973). They reported that asulam gave 90–100% control with little resulting harm to other vegetation. Borate compounds and dichlobenil consistently give good control for three seasons or more, but the total kill of the underlying sward and resulting soil sterility precludes this treatment on agricultural land (Erskine 1966). Hodgson (1963) stated that the difficulty in the control of bracken is the enormous number of underground frond buds (up to 40–60 tons of rhizome per acre bearing up to 500,000 frond buds, four fifths of the buds remaining dormant).

In the western United States (Stewart 1972) reported *Pteridium aquilinum* as being susceptible to dicamba at ca. 5.0 kg/ha (4 lbs/acre) when applied in June or ca. 9.80 kg/ha (8 lbs/acre) when applied in August, but that the plant was resistant to picloram, dichlobenil and bromacil.

12. Response to Other Human Manipulations

Pteridium is resistant to various types of cutting, slashing and bruising. These methods are sometimes used to reduce bracken infestations on unploughable grazing land, particularly in the British Isles, Europe, Australia, and New Zealand. Bruising the fronds by specially designed machines was, according to Wardrop (1951), the most effective means of mechanical eradication. Braid (1948), however, compared several bruising, slashing and cutting machines on their effectiveness in controlling bracken in test plots. He found that after several years all the cut plots contained less bracken. *Pteridium* responds to mechanical cutting and bruising by the rapid development of fresh fronds, which in turn must be removed when quite young to prevent foodstores being added to the rhizome. This constant removal of frond growth eventually exhausts the food reserves of the plant and the plant dies (Anonymous 1952).

In Washington and Oregon, experiments have been conducted in seeding down greater birdsfoot trefoil (*Lotus major* Sm.) with alta fescue (*Festuca arundinacea* Schreb.) and creeping red fescue (*F. rubra* L.) amongst western bracken infestations. Apparently, western bracken cannot compete with this particular legume–grass mixture and is effectively crowded out after 4 or 5 yr (Angell 1950).

Grazing bracken with beef cattle in New Zealand effectively reduced the size and vitality of selected stands (Inch 1964). In view of recent findings on the carcinogenic and mutagenic properties of *Pteridium*, this practice is, however, highly questionable.

Whilst the size of *Pteridium* infestations can be reduced by the aforementioned practices, the plant is difficult to eradicate totally.

13. Responses to Parasites

(a) Insects and other nondomestic stock — Thirty-three species of insects are listed by Simmonds (1967) as being found attacking *Pteridium*. Of the insects he listed, the following taxa are present and their larvae have been found feeding on *Pteridium* in Canada (J. E. H. Martin, personal communication). HYMENOPTERA: *Tenthredo livida* L.; *Selandria* sp.; *Strongyloaster (Thrinax)* sp., *Embria* sp.; *Aneugmenus (Strombocerus)* sp. DIPTERA: *Chirosa* sp.; *Pycnoglossa* sp.; *Anthomyia* sp.; *Dasyneura* sp.; LEPIDOPTERA: *Callopistria* sp.; *Euplexia* sp.

Forbes (1948) stated that the larvae of *Homochlodes fritillaria* Guenèe Geometridae: LEPIDOPTERA occur and feed on *Pteridium* from Quebec to Nova Scotia. Forbes (1954) further reported that the larvae of *Papiapema pterisii* Bird, a moth occurring in Canada, eats bracken rhizomes.

Whittier (1966) discussed the problem on natural apospory in *Pteridium* and pictured what had been described by earlier authors as prothalloid outgrowths. Whittier con-

cluded that the abnormality was a gall, caused by two species of mites of the genus *Eriophyes*. The condition was reported from New Hampshire, Wisconsin and Massachusetts. Canadian specimens showing this "prothalloid" condition were found from the following localities: in Ontario — Dunk's Bay, Bruce Co., Moore Lake, Bruce Co., Sibbalds Pt., York Co., Port Carling, Muskoka Dist., Queenston, Lincoln Co., Papineau Lake, Hastings Co.; in Quebec — Oka, Co. Deux Montagnes.

(b) Microorganisms and viruses — Conners (1967) listed the following fungal species as being found on Canadian *Pteridium*: *Ceratobasidium anceps* (Bres. and Sacc.) Jackson (stat. sclerot. *Sclerotinum deciduum* Davis); *Cryptomycina pteridis* (Reb. ex Fr.) Hohn; *Dothidella osmundae* (Pk. & Clint.) Sacc.; *Mycosphaerella indistincta* (Pk.) Lindau.; *Uredinopus haskiokai* Hirats and *U. pteridis* Diet. & Holw.

In addition, there are specimens of *Cladosporium grumosum* Pers. ex Lk., *Uredinopsis macrosperma* (Ckc.) Magn. and *Mycosphaerella pteridicola* Dearn. & House on *Pteridium* in the Mycological Herbarium of the Canada Department of Agriculture at Ottawa.

Puccinia spp. are also found on *Pteridium* occurring in Canada. The alternate hosts of these rusts are *Abies* spp. (D. B. O. Savile, personal communication).

No Canadian field surveys have been conducted to assess the result of fungal infestations or the damage caused by them on *Pteridium*.

The parasitic fungi *Corticium anceps* (Bres. and Syd.) Gregor and *Fusarium* sp. were reported by Gregor (1938) as having been used in experiments on the biological control of bracken, but without positive results.

(c) Higher plant parasites — Tryon (1941) reported that two species of Orobanchaceae, *Orobanche trichocalyx* (Webb and Berth.) G. Beck and *O. Schultzii* Mut. are parasitic on *Pteridium* in the Canary Islands.

ANGELL, G. 1950. Bracken fern control is another use for *Lotus major*. Wash. Farmer **75**: 289, 296–297.

ANONYMOUS. 1952. The control of bracken. G. B. Min. Agric. Fish. Adv. Leafl. 28.

ANONYMOUS. 1957-1958. Atlas of Canada. Geographical Branch, Canada Dep. of Mines and Technical Surveys, Ottawa, Ont.

BANKIER, J. C. 1943. Enzootic bovine haematuria (redwater of cattle) in British Columbia. Can. J. Compar. Med. **7**: 101–107, 146–151, 178–181.

BOIVIN, B. 1952. Two variations of *Pteridium aquilinum*. Amer. Fern J. **42**: 131–133.

BRAID, K. W. and CONWAY, E. 1943. Rate of growth of bracken. Nature **152**: 750–751.

BRAID, K. W. 1948. Bracken control— artificial and natural. J. Br. Grassl. Soc. **3**: 181–189.

BRAID, K. W. 1959. Bracken, a review of the literature. Commonwealth Bureau of Pastures and Field crops, England. Publ. 3. 69 pp. mimeo.

BRITTON, D. M. 1953. Chromosome studies on ferns. Amer. J. Bot. **40**: 575–583.

CANADA WEED COMMITTEE. 1969. Common and botanical names of weeds in Canada. Publ. 1397. Can. Dep. Agric. Ottawa, Ont. 67 pp.

CODY, W. J. 1956. Ferns of the Ottawa district. Can. Dep. Agric. Publ. 974. 94 pp.

CONNERS, I. L. 1967. An annotated index of plant diseases in Canada and fungi recorded on plants in Alaska, Canada, and Greenland. Canada Agric. Res. Br. Publ. 1251. 381 pp.

CONWAY, E. 1949. The autoecology of bracken (*Pteridium aquilinum* Kuhn). The germination of the spore, the development of the prothallus and the young sporphyte. Proc. R. Soc. Edinb. **163**: 325–343.

CONWAY, E. 1952. Bracken — the problem plant, a review of recent conclusions about its spread and dominance. Scot. Agric. **31**: 181–184.

CONWAY. E. 1957. Spore production in bracken. J. Ecol. **45**: 273–284.

CONWAY, E. and ARBUTHNOTT, M. 1949. Occurrence of endotrophic mycorrhiza in the roots of (bracken) *Pteridium aquilinum*. Nature **163**: 609–610.

CUSHING, E. J. 1963. Late Wisconsin pollen stratigraphy in east-Central Minnesota. University Microfilms, Ann Arbor, Michigan. 165 pp.

DOBEREINER, J., OLSON, C., BROWN, R. R., PRICE, J. M. and YESS, N. 1966. Metabolites in urine of cattle with experimental bladder lesions and fed bracken fern. Pesq. Agropec. Bras. **1**: 189–199.

EATON, E. L. 1943. The blueberry. Dom. Canada Publ. Farm Bull. 754. 120 pp.

ERSKINE, D. S. C. 1966. Chemical control of bracken. Edinburgh School of Agriculture. Experimental Work, 114 pp.

EVANS, E. T., EVANS, W. C. and ROBERTS, H. E. 1951. Studies on bracken poisoning in the horse. Part II. Br. Vet. J. **107**: 399–411.

EVANS, I. A., JONES, R. S. and MAINWARING-BURTON, R. 1972. Passage of bracken fern toxicity into milk. Nature **237**: 107–108.

EVANS, I. A. and MASON, J. 1965. Carcinogenic activity of bracken. Nature **208**: 913–914.

EVANS, I. A. and OSMAN, M. A. 1974. Carcinogenicity of bracken and shikimic acid. Nature **250**: 348–349.

EVANS, W. C. and EVANS, E. T. R. 1949. Studies on the biochemistry of pasture plants. No. 3. The effects of the inclusion of bracken (*Pteris aquilina*) in the diet of rats, and the problem of bracken poisoning in farm animals. Br. Vet. J. **105**: 175–186.

EVANS, W. C., JONES, N. R. and EVANS, R. A. 1950. The mechanism of the anti-aneurin activity of bracken (*Pteris aquilina*). Proc. Biochem. Soc. XXXVIII–XXXIX.

FERGUSON, W. S. and ARMITAGE, E. R. 1944. The chemical composition of bracken (*Pteridium aquilinum*). J. Agric. Sci. [England] **34**: 165–171.

FERNALD, M. L. 1950. Gray's manual of botany. 8th ed. American Book Co., New York, N.Y. 1632 pp.

FERNALD, M. L. and KINSEY, A. C. 1958. Edible wild plants of Eastern North America. Harper Brothers, New York, N.Y. 452 pp.

FERRON, M. and CAYOUETTE, R. 1971. Nom des mauvaises herbes du Québec. Min. de l'Agric. et de la Colonisation du Québec Publ. 288–71. 2ème ed. 113 pp.

FORBES, W. T. M. 1948. Lepidoptera of New York and neighbouring states. Part II. Cornell Univ. Agric. Exp. Sta. Mem. 274.

FORBES, W. T. M. 1954. Lepidoptera of New York and neighbouring states. Part III. Cornell Univ. Agric. Exp. Sta. Mem. 433.

FOSTER, A. S. and GIFFORD, E. M. 1959. Comparative morphology of vascular plants. W.

H. Freeman and Co. San Francisco and London. 555 pp.

GLEASON, H. A. 1963. The new Britton and Brown illustrated flora. Vol. I. Hafner Publishing Co., New York, N.Y. 482 pp.

GLIESSMAN, S. R. and MULLER, C. H. 1972. The phytotoxic potential of bracken, *Pteridium aquilinum* (L.) Kuhn. Madrōno 21: 299–304.

GREGOR, M. T. F. 1938. Associations with fungi and other lower plants. *In* Fr. Verdoorn, Manual of pteridology. Martinus Nijhoff. The Hague, Netherlands. 640 pp.

GRESHOFF, M. 1908. "Bracken poisoning". Pharm. Weekbl. 45: 770.

GROH, H. 1941. The distribution of bracken in its possible relation to bovine haematuria in British Columbia. Sci. Agric. 21: 703–710.

HALL, W. T. K. 1964. Plant toxicoses of tropical Australia. Aust. Vet. J. 40: 176–182.

HELLUM, A. 1964. Factors influencing frond size of bracken on sandy soils in northern lower Michigan. University Microfilms Inc. Ann Arbor, Mich. 106 pp.

HIKINO, H., TAKAHASHI, T., ARIHARA, S. and TAKEMOTO, T. 1970. Structure of pteroside B., glycoside of *Pteridium aquilinum* var. *latiusculum*. Chem. Pharm. Bull. 18: 1488–1489.

HIKINO, H., TAKAHASHI, T. and TAKEMOTO, T. 1971. Structure of pteroside Z and D, glycosides of *Pteridium aquilinum* var. *latiusculum*. Chem. Pharm. Bull. 19: 2424–2425.

HIKINO, H., TAKAHASHI, T. and TAKEMOTO, T. 1972. Structure of pteroside A. and C., glycosides of *Pteridium aquilinum* var. *latiusculum*. Chem. Pharm. Bull. 2: 210–212.

HILL, R. H. and WAGNER, W. H. Jr. 1974. Seasonality and spore type of the Pteridophytes of Michigan. Mich. Bot. 13: 40–44.

HIRONO, I., FUSHIMI, K., MORI, H., MIWA, T. and HAGA, M. 1973. Comparative study of carcinogenic activity in each part of bracken. J. Nat. Cancer Inst. 50: 1367–1371.

HIRONO, I., SHIBUYA, C., SHIMIZU, M. and FUSHIMI, K. 1972. Carcinogenic activity of processed bracken used as human food. J. Nat. Cancer Inst. 48: 1245–1250.

HODGE, W. H. 1973. Fern foods of Japan and the problem of toxicity. Amer. Fern J. 63: 77–80.

HODGSON, G. L. 1963. Possibilities of chemical control of bracken, *Pteridium aquilinum*. Quart. Rev. Nat. Agric. Advis. Serv. 14: 100–105.

HOFMEISTER, W. 1857. Beitrage zur Kenntniss des Gefasskryptogamen. Abh. Sach. Ges. (Acad.) Wiss. 3: 603–682.

HOLMGREN, P. K. and KEUKEN, W. 1974. Part 1, The herbaria of the world. *In* F. A. Stafleu, ed. Index herbariorum. Regnum Veg. 92: 1–397.

INCH, R. 1964. Fern control at a profit. N.Z. J. Agric. 108: 426–428.

LEEFE, J. S. 1952. Renovation of rough pastures by the use of commercial fertilizers and herbicides. Proc. 5th Meet. E. Sect. Nat. Weed Conf. (Canada). pp. 113–115.

LODGE, R. W., McLEAN, A. and JOHNSTON, A. 1968. Stock poisoning plants of western Canada. Agric. Can. Publ. 1361, Ottawa, Ont.

LONG, H. C. and FENTON, E. W. 1938. The story of the bracken fern. J. R. Agric. Soc. 99: 15–36.

LOUSLEY, J. E. 1943–44. The flora of the bombed sites in the city of London in 1944. Bot. Soc. Exch. Club Rep. 12: 882.

McCULLOCH, W. F. 1942. The role of bracken fern in Douglas-fir regeneration. Ecology 23: 484–485.

McKELVIE, A. D. and SCRAGGE, E. B. 1973. Control of bracken by asulam. Scot. Agric. 51: 474–480.

McLEAN, R. C. and IVIMEY-COOK, W. R. 1951. Textbook of theoretical botany. Vol. I. Longmans, Green and Co. London, England. 1069 pp.

MOON, F. E. and McKEAND, J. M. 1953. Observations on the vitamin C status and haematology of bracken fed ruminants. Br. Vet. J. 109: 321–326.

MOON, F. E. and RAAFAT, M. A. 1951a. Some biochemical aspects of bracken poisoning in the ruminant animal. I. Vitamin factors. J. Sci. Food Agric. 2: 327–336.

MOON, F. E. and RAAFAT, M. A. 1951b. The experimental production of bracken poisoning in sheep. J. Comp. Path. Ther. 61: 88–100.

OINONEN, E. 1967. Sporal regeneration of bracken *Pteridium aquilinum* (L.) Kuhn in Finland in the light of the dimensions and age of its clones. Acta Forest. Fenn. 83(1): 1–96.

PAMUKCU, A. M. and PRICE, J. M. 1969. Induction of intestinal and urinary bladder cancer in rats by feeding bracken fern. J. Nat. Cancer Inst. 43: 275–281.

184

PLACE, I. M. M. 1953. The influence of bracken fern [*Pteridium latiusculum*] on establishment of spruce and fir seedlings. Pulp Paper Mag. Can. **54**: 169–170, 172.

ROSENBURGER, G. 1971. Nature, manifestations, cause and control of chronic enzootic haemeturia in cattle. Vet. Med. Rev. **2/3**: 189–206.

ROUSSEAU, C. 1974. Geographie floristique du Québec-Labrador. Les Presses de l'Université Laval, Québec. 799 pp.

SIMMONDS, F. J. 1967. Possibilities of biological control of bracken, *Pteridium aquilinum*. PANS (Pest Articles News Sum.) Sect. C. Weed. Contr. **13**: 200–203.

SMITH, A. M. and AGIZA, A. H. 1951. The amino acids of several grassland species, cereals and bracken. J. Sci. Food Agric. **2**: 503–520.

SMITH, G. M. 1938. Cryptogamic botany, Vol. II. Bryophytes and pteridophytes. McGraw-Hill Book Company Inc. New York and London. 380 pp.

STEWART, R. E. 1972. Field screening of foliage applied herbicides on western swordfern and western bracken. Research Progress report, Western Society of Weed Science, 20. U.S. Dep. Agric. Roseburg, Oregon.

TAYLOR, T. M. C. 1970. Pacific northwest ferns and their allies. University of Toronto Press, Toronto, Ont. 247 pp.

TRYON, R. M. JR. 1941. Revision of the genus *Pteridium*. Rhodora **43**: 1–31, 37–67.

WAGNER, W. H. JR. and WAGNER, F. S. 1966. Pteridophytes of the Mountain Lake area, Giles Co., Virginia: Biosystematic studies, 1964–65. Castanea **31**: 121–140.

WARDROP, G. 1951. Bracken eaten on the braes. Farmer and Stock Breeder **65**: 94–95.

WATT, A. S. 1940. Contributions to the ecology of bracken I. The rhizome. New Phytol. **39**: 401–422.

WATT, A. S. 1943. Contributions to the ecology of bracken II. The frond and the plant. New Phytol. **42**: 103–126.

WATT, A. S. 1945. Contributions to the ecology of bracken III. Frond types and the make-up of the population. New Phytol. **44**: 156–178.

WATT, A. S. 1947. Contributions to the ecology of bracken IV. The structure of the community. New Phytol. **46**: 97–121.

WATT, A. S. 1950. Contributions to the ecology of bracken V. Bracken and frost. New Phytol. **49**: 308–327.

WATT, A. S. 1954. Contributions to the ecology of bracken VI. Frost and the advance and retreat of bracken. New Phytol. **53**: 117–130.

WATT, A. S. 1955. Bracken versus heather, a study in plant sociology. J. Ecol. **43**: 490–506.

WATT, A. S. 1956. Contributions to the ecology of bracken VII. Bracken and litter. 1. The origin of rings. New Phytol. **55**: 369–381.

WATT, A. S. 1969. Contributions to the ecology of bracken. VII. Bracken and litter. 2. Crown form. New Phytol. **68**: 841–859.

WATT, A. S. 1970. Contributions to the ecology of bracken VII. Bracken and litter. 3. The cycle of change. New Phytol. **69**: 431–449.

WATT, A. S. 1971. Contributions to the ecology of bracken VIII. The marginal and the hinterland plant: a study in senescence. New Phytol. **70**: 967–986.

WEATHERBY, C. A. 1946. Bracken in the bombed areas of London. Amer. Fern J. **36**: 122–123.

WELLS, H. E. 1949. Bracken poisoning. J. G. B. Min. Agric. **56**: 204–205.

WHITTIER, D. P. 1966. Natural aspory in *Pteridium?* Amer. Fern J. **56**: 61–64.

185

THE BIOLOGY OF CANADIAN WEEDS
16. *Comptonia peregrina* (L.) Coult.

IVAN V. HALL[1], LEWIS E. AALDERS[1], and C. FRED EVERETT[2]

[1]*Research Station, Agriculture Canada, Kentville, Nova Scotia, and* [2]*Research Station, Agriculture Canada, Fredericton, New Brunswick. Contribution no. 1561, Research Station, Agriculture Canada, Kentville, N.S., received 8 Sept. 1975, accepted 25 Sept. 1975.*

HALL, IVAN V., AALDERS, LEWIS E. AND EVERETT, C. FRED. 1976. The biology of Canadian Weeds 16. *Comptonia peregrina* (L.) Coult. Can. J. Plant Sci. **56**: 147–156.

Comptonia peregrina (L.) Coult., sweet-fern (Myricaceae), is a weed of pastures, Jack-pine *(Pinus banksiana* Lamb.) stands, and lowbush blueberry *(Vaccinium angustifolium* Ait. and *V. myrtilloides* Michx.) fields of Eastern Canada. It is particularly prevalent on light sandy gleysolic and luvisolic soils from Nova Scotia in the east to the Ontario–Manitoba border in the central portion of Canada. The pruning of shoots by cutting or burning merely stimulates growth of dormant buds on the rhizome. Reproduction is also by seeds that are produced on bur-like inflorescences. Fortunately, this species is quite susceptible to several herbicides such as 2,4–D, dicamba and picloram.

Comptonia peregrina (L.) Coult., la comptonie voyageuse (Myricacées), est une mauvaise herbe que l'on rencontre dans les pâturages, les peuplements de cyprès *(Pinus banksiana* Lamb.) et dans les champs de bleuets sauvages *(Vaccinium angustifolium* Ait. et *V. myrtilloides* Michx.) de l'est du Canada. On la trouve surtout dans les gleysols et luvisols sablonneux de la Nouvelle-Ecosse à la frontière occidentale de l'Ontario et du Manitoba au centre du Canada. Le brûlage ou émondage des pousses ne font que stimuler la croissance des bourgeons en dormance du rhizome. La comptonie se reproduit par des semences produites sur des inflorescences ressemblant à des boutons. Heureusement, l'espèce est assez sensible à plusieurs herbicides dont le 2, 4–D, le dicamba et le piclorame.

1. Name

Comptonia peregrina (L.) Coult. *(Myrica asplenifolia* L.) **sweetfern** (Canada Weed Committee 1969); **comptonie,** bois-chaud, bois de savane, comptonie à feuilles d'asplénie, comptonie voyageuse, fougère odorante, myrice, myrice à feuille d'asplénie (Ferron and Cayouette 1971). Myricaceae, wax-myrtle family, Myricacées.

2. Description and Account of Variation

A woody shrub (Fig. 1A) up to 1 m in height; new shoots arising from buds on the rhizome; stems and leaves densely pilose to slightly pubescent; leaves alternate, stipulate, simple and pinnately lobed, the margin slightly reflexed, the entire leaf producing a fern-like odor; plants generally monoecious; staminate catkins (Fig. 1B) olive green in color, up to 3.5 cm in length at anthesis, borne directly on the tip of the previous year's wood; female catkins dark red in color at the beginning of anthesis, borne below the staminate catkins (Fig. 1B), up to 0.7 cm in length; fruit with 8 linear bracts surrounding the ovary (Fig. 1C); this latter organ develops into a nut (Fig. 1D) at maturity.

Chromosome numbers have not been reported from Canadian populations, but Stokes (1937) reports $n = 16$ for *C. peregrina* from Thornton, Illinois. An examination of cells from actively growing shoot meristems of this species collected

Can. J. Plant Sci. 56: 147-156 (Jan. 1976)

near Kentville, Nova Scotia revealed $2n = 32$.

The Myricaceae are believed to have originated from the Hamamelidaceae or their relatives, and the genus *Comptonia* is considered the most advanced of the family (Lawrence 1951). Gleason (1952) retained this species within the genus *Myrica* under the binomial *Myrica asplenifolia* L. According to Macdonald (1974) the basis for

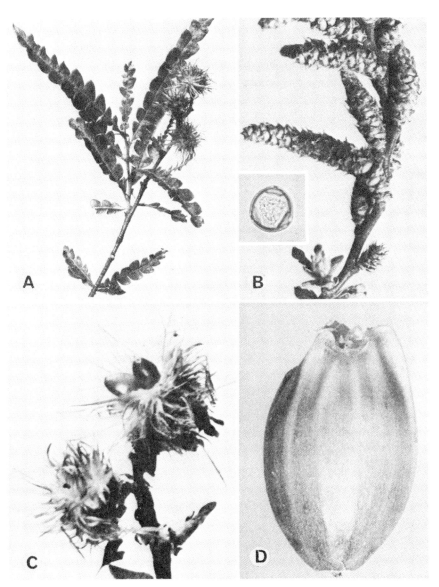

Fig. 1. (A) A shoot with young inflorescence (1.25×); (B) flowering, the staminate catkins terminal and one pistilate catkin below the others (1.5×) pollen grains as inset (1,000×); (C) bracts surrounding developing fruits (2.5×); (D) fruit 16×. All parts of sweet-fern, *Comptonia peregrina*.

187

separating *Comptonia* as a separate genus from *Myrica* is the presence of lanceolate-shaped structures on either side of the fruit and the presence of stipulate leaves in *C. peregrina*. He also stated that the axillary scale-like bracts were third-order bracts.

Within populations, marked differences have been reported in leaf shape and degree of hairiness. On the basis of leaf shape, Fernald (1950) recognized var. *asplenifolia* (L.) Fern., but this taxon occurs only from Long Island, New York to Virginia.

The stage at which *C. peregrina* is the most difficult to recognize is the seedling stage (Fig. 2A). The closely related *Myrica pensylvanica* Loisel. is shown by comparison in Fig. 2B.

3. Economic Importance

(a) Detrimental — *Comptonia peregrina* is an abundant species of eastern North America, especially from North Carolina northward. Muenscher (1952) considered it

a particular problem in hillside pastures, old fields and open woods. In lowbush blueberry *(Vaccinium angustifolium* Ait. and *V. myrtilloides* Michx.) stands, it not only competes for space, but the heavier stems of this species jam in the rakes and consequently most pickers will avoid areas where even scattered stems are present. It is one of the most serious weed problems in the commercial lowbush blueberry fields of New Brunswick. It generally occurs in areas which have been cleared from forest, but occasionally it can be found in run out fields abandoned from agriculture. It is more prevalent along the east coast of the province where it constitutes about 10% of the total weed population. In southern New Brunswick its status as a problem weed is limited to some of the barrens or marginal blueberry land. A herbicide cost of $20.00–$60.00 per hectare is estimated in 1975 for chemical control of this weed.

Wodehouse (1971) states that all members of the Myricaceae are wind-pollinated

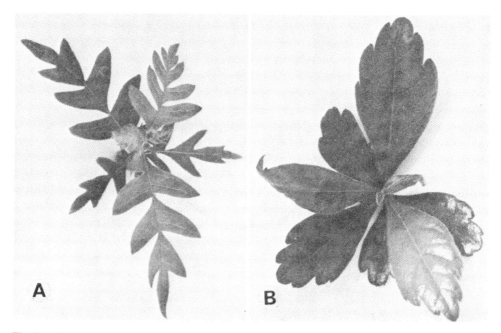

Fig. 2.   Seedlings of (A) sweet-fern, *Comptonia peregrina* and (B) bayberry, *Myrica pensylvanica* at 12-leaf stage (2×).

188

and shed fairly large amounts of pollen, and are therefore considered hay fever plants.

Fraser (1969) found that water extracts of foliage and roots of *C. peregrina* adversely affected survival, but not germination or growth, of *Pinus resinosa* Ait. seedlings.

(b) Beneficial — Martin et al. (1951) state that *C. peregrina* has limited value as a source of food for wildlife. The U.S.D.A. Forest Service (1948) reports that the extensive colonies of *C. peregrina* are useful for soil protection and as a source of wildlife cover. Marie-Victorin (1964) states that this species has great aesthetic value, for it is the chief vegetation in many burned areas and the clonal nature of growth breaks much of the dullness of northern landscapes.

(c) Legislation — *Comptonia peregrina* is not listed in any Canadian federal or provincial weed or seeds act.

4. Geographical Distribution

In Canada, this species is commonly found in all three Maritime Provinces, Ontario, and certain parts of Quebec (Fig. 3). The distribution map shows a hiatus from the middle of New Brunswick across to the Richelieu River in southern Quebec. It has been suggested that it is found on light sandy soils in the Canadian Shield and on sandy outwashes left by the glaciers. Marie-Victorin (1964) reported it as being common north of Quebec City, the Ottawa Valley, and in the region of Lac Saint-Pierre. Elsewhere it was rare. Scoggan (1950) did not report it from Bic and the Gaspé Peninsula, and Rouleau (1956) did not list it in his check-list of vascular plants of Newfoundland, Labrador, and St. Pierre and Miquelon. Fernald (1950) gives its North American distribution as Cape Breton Island to Manitoba and south to Virginia and in the upland to northern

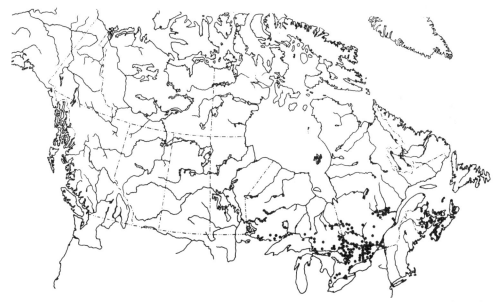

Fig. 3. Canadian distribution of sweet-fern, *Comptonia peregrina,* based on specimens from the herbaria of Department of Agriculture Herbarium, Ottawa, Ontario; National Museum of Canada, Ottawa, Ontario; Acadia University, Wolfville, Nova Scotia; University of Manitoba, Winnipeg, Manitoba; Herbier Louis-Marie, Université Laval, Québec; University of Toronto, Toronto, Ontario.

189

Georgia. With regard to its presence in Manitoba Scoggan (1957) states, "No specimens have been seen, however, and it must be excluded from our flora for the present."

5. Habitat

(a) Climatic requirements — Since *C. peregrina* grows much further south in North America than the 49th parallel, the extremes of the northern climate become of considerable interest to us because they limit the northern distribution. All locations found on the distribution map (Fig. 3) have 1,500 or more degree days above 5.6 C (42 F) (Department of Energy, Mines and Resources 1971). Start of the growing season is generally by 5 May and the end of the growing season would be approximately 11 Oct. The frost-free period is about 100 days. The mean daily minimum temperature is −24.9 C for January, based on the period 1931–1960. However, this is ameliorated to some extent by the fact that the depth of snow in the northern limits of the range during the same period is 76 cm.

(b) Substratum — On the gleysolic soils surrounding Lac St. Jean, *C. peregrina* probably grows in greatest abundance. The soils on the south side of Lac St. Jean are mainly gleysol, whereas on the north side they are humic gleysol. In Nova Scotia and New Brunswick *C. peregrina* occurs in the dominantly luvisolic soils, especially the gray luvisol. Most of these and other locations have very sandy or gravelly soils on which most species except *C. peregrina* and *Pinus banksiana* survive with difficulty.

(c) Communities in which the species occurs — The frequency of occurrence of *C. peregrina* and other associated species in three lowbush blueberry fields of the Lac St. Jean (Lake St. John) area is given in Table 1. For a more detailed analysis of the frequency and abundance of *C. peregrina* in the Comptonio–Vaccinietum association and sub-associations of the Lac. St. Jean area see Lavoie (1968). Data on relative foliage cover produced by various species in weedy lowbush blueberry stand are given in Table 2.

6. History

Since the entire area where *C. peregrina* now exists in Canada was heavily glaciated

Table 1.   Composition of lowbush blueberry fields at three locations in the Lac St. Jean area. Points 1 m apart on 100-m transect

Species	Ste. Jeanne d'Arc	St. Eugene	L'Ascension
Bare ground	28	17	29†
Pteridium aquilinum var.			
latiusculum (Desv.) Underw.	0	6	0
Populus tremuloides Michx.	0	9	4
Comptonia peregrina (L.) Coult.	9	18	30
Prunus pensylvanica L. f.	0	6	1
Aralia hispida Vent.	0	0	1
Cornus canadensis L.	0	0	1
Kalmia angustifolia L.	9	8	3
Vaccinium myrtilloides Michx.	1	0	0
Vaccinium angustifolium Ait.			
forma *angustifolium*	50	33	21
Vaccinium angustifolium			
forma *nigrum* (Wood) Boivin	3	2	8
Viburnum cassinoides L.	0	0	2
Solidago puberula Nutt.	0	1	0
	100	100	100

†Data collected 25 and 26 Aug., 1964.

Table 2. Average percentage of foliage cover produced by seven species from three 1×10-m quadrants from a field at Onslow, Col. Co, Nova Scotia. Data taken 4 June 1958

Species	Foliage cover (%)
Bare ground	17.0
Comptonia peregrina (L.) Coult.	11.0
Amelanchier laevis Wieg.	0.5
Rhododendron canadensis (L.) Torr.	6.0
Kalmia angustifolia L.	26.0
Gaultheria procumbens L.	3.0
Vaccinium angustifolium Ait.	30.5
Viburnum cassinoides L.	6.0

in recent times, it obviously has moved into the area following the retreat of the last glaciers. The prevalence of this species has fluctuated tremendously with the occurrence of local forest fires. Few species are favored by burning, but *C. peregrina* is definitely favored.

Hall (1949) was not able to distinguish pollen of this species in analysis of peat samples taken from a bog in Cape Breton Island. The pollen grains of the Myricaceae are quite similar in sculpturing, shape and size (polar view 32 μ) (Fig. 1B inset) to several species of *Betula* (Erdtman 1943).

7. Growth and Development

(a) Morphology — The rhizome with its adventitious buds is of prime importance in the colonization of newly burned areas. Especially in early spring or late fall, fires do not normally generate enough heat to kill this organ. Following the burn-prune, new shoots develop in full sunlight and the plant is able to grow rapidly by absorbing the necessary minerals and water through a well established root system. Marie-Victorin (1964) states that the protective coating of the seed allows germination in a xerophytic habitat and the resinous secretion protects the plant from the intense heat of summer. Detailed descriptions of the comparative morphology of seedlings, roots, stems, root tubercles, leaves, inflorescences, and fruits of *C. peregrina* and several other members of the Myricaceae

are contained in the work of Youngken (1919).

(b) Perennation — *Comptonia peregrina* passes the winter as a chamaephyte. Leaves remain on the plant until mid-winter and no evidence of winterkilling was noted on any of the specimens examined from the locations shown in Fig. 3.

(c) Physiological data — This species was one of several non-bog deciduous species examined as to photosynthetic rates by Small (1972). He found that bog deciduous species manufacture about 60% more photosynthate per acquired unit of nitrogen than do nonbog deciduous species. Recently, using an acetylene reduction technique, Morris et al. (1974) have shown that the closely related *Myrica pensylvanica* Loisel. is capable of fixing nitrogen and thus plays an important role in coastal communities or associations. Future work may show a similar role for this species on sandy outwash plains. The major constituents of the oil extracted from the foliage were 1–8 cineole, γ-terpinene, β-myrcene, β-caryophyllene, linalool and α-pinene (Halim and Collins 1970). Minshall (1957) found that *C. peregrina* contained one of the highest amounts of rubber and resin of many Canadian plants, 23.7% of dry weight after extraction with acetone.

(d) Phenology — Rhizomes began to grow in the Kentville, Nova Scotia, area in 1974 about 4 June. Pollen production had ceased

191

on 10 June. Data collected from herbarium specimens on times of development of catkins, leaves, fruit and flower buds are given in Table 3. Leaves were still present on the stems on 25 Oct. 1974 at the Kentville Research Station.

(e) Mycorrhiza — Short hypertrophic roots that resemble mycorrhizae (Zak 1971) were found on *C. peregrina* plants collected on 4 June 1974 near Kentville; Youngken (1919) presents a detailed description of similar tubercles found on three species of *Myrica* and *C. asplenifolia* Ait. (*C. peregrina* of present-day authors) growing in New Jersey and Pennsylvania. Youngken stated that the abnormal roots resulted from more compact and increased layers of cortex, 15–24 in the hypertrophic tissue as compared with 5–12 in the normal. He found that the parasite was a species of *Actinomyces*.

8. Reproduction

(a) Floral biology — Flowers are wind-pollinated with the staminate catkins at the end of the previous year's growth and the pistilate catkin is immediately below the male catkins. The mean number of staminate catkins per shoot based on 42 shoots was 6.43 ± 0.48 (SE) and for the pistilate catkins was 0.60 ± 0.01 (SE).

(b) Seed production and dispersal — Based on 15 samples taken on 15 July 1974, each 100 g of shoot produced 15.07 g of fruit and 29.96 burs. Another sample of 25 burs taken on the same date showed that the average weight in grams of the bur was 0.3614 ± 0.0271 (SE). The average number of seeds per bur was 5.52 ± 0.43 (SE) and the average weight of seeds per bur was 9.07 ± 0.87 mg (SE).

(c) Viability of seeds and germination — A number of germination tests of seed collected locally and in Ontario and subjected to various treatments of cold, light and scarification have been carried out at Kentville in the glasshouse. Freshly harvested seed seldom, if ever, germinates. The U.S. Department of Agriculture Forest Service (1948) also reports difficulty in germinating seeds: "Seed which had been stored dry in sealed bottles at 41°F for almost 2 years and then stratified in moist sand for 60 days at 41° gave no germination in 60 days, although 4 percent of the seed was found sound at the close of this period." A period of after-ripening as found in *Myrica pensylvanica* (Hall 1975) is probably necessary.

(d) Vegetative reproduction — In *C. peregrina*, lateral growth of the plant is by rhizome (Laycock 1967). Earlier, Hall and Mack (1959) had stated that it was by a root, and a section of the root was illustrated. It is difficult to see the transition point of rhizome to adventitious root in this species and the root section probably came from an adventitious root associated with the rhizome.

On highway 101 near Falmouth, Hants Co., Nova Scotia, *C. peregrina* has grown down the embankment 7.5 m in 6 yr.

9. Hybrids

None known.

10. Population Dynamics

In 1951 a small patch not more than 5 m in diameter of *C. peregrina* was noted in a large blueberry field at Tower Hill, Charlotte Co., New Brunswick. At that time the owners of the field were urged to clean up the infestation, but no action was taken. By 1973 more than 5 ha of the same field were populated with this weed (personal communication R. B. Scott).

11. Response to Herbicides and Other Chemicals

Comptonia peregrina is quite susceptible to a number of herbicides. The members of the Ontario Herbicide Committee (Guide to chemical weed control 1973) consider this species to be intermediate in susceptibility to 2,4-D (2, 4–dichlorophenoxyacetic acid) and in the susceptible to intermediate class for 2,4,5-T (2,4,5–trichlorophenoxyacetic acid); 2,4-D and 2,4,5-T; and ammonium sulfamate. Trevett (1952) recommended, in

192

Table 3. Phenological development of *Comptonia peregrina* in Eastern Canada

	Catkins fully expanded	Vegetative condition expressed in leaf length† (cm)				Green bur with immature seeds	Brown bur with mature seeds	Flower buds
		0–2	2–4	4–6	6–10			
Quebec								
Lac St. Jean,	9 June	9 June	11 June	8 July–9 Aug.	15 July–22 Sept.	8–27 July	15 July–21 Aug.	14 Aug.–22 Sept.
Gatineau–Pontiac southern portion	26 May–13 June	–	6 June	6–8 June	8 July–30 Aug.	16 June–3 July	8 July–14 Aug.	14 Aug.–30 Aug.
Deux Montagnes	15 May–25 May	15 May	21 May–15 June	30 June	17 Aug.	30 June	9 July	–
Ontario								
Algonquin Park	29 May	–	11 June–13 June	18 June	9 Aug.	20 June–2 July	6 July–9 Aug.	16 Aug.–9 Sept.
Nova Scotia								
Kentville Kings County	24 May	17 May–24 May	24 May–30 May	30 May–6 June	6 June–† 15 Sept.	24 June–3 July	18 July–30 Sept.	5 Aug. on

†Leaf size varies greatly, one largely vegetative clone had leaves on 21 July up to 16 cm.

193

Table 4. Reduction of the stand of *Comptonia peregrina* and *Kalmia angustifolia* in lowbush blueberries by selected herbicides and the effects on yield

Herbicides	Rates	Effects on stand†				Yield of blueberries 1972
		C. peregrina		K. angustifolia		
		1971	1972	1971	1972	
	kg a.i./ha					tonnes/ha
2,4–D ester	2.25	2	4	7	7	2.52
2,4–D ester	3.4	2	3	6	8	2.42
2,4–D ester+dicamba	3.4+1.12	6	6	10	9	2.27
Dicamba	3.4	8	10	8	9	3.43
Dicamba	6.8	10	10	10	10	2.72
Check (no herbicide)		1	3‡	2	3	–§

†Rating based on scale 0–10 where 0 = no effects and 10 = stand reduced 100%.

‡*C. peregrina* covered 19% of the ground area in the check areas (average of 48 observations).

§Not possible to rake the check areas for yield. Herbicides sprayed in 188 liters of water per hectare on 29 Sept. 1970 in Gloucester County, New Brunswick. The plots were burnt in May 1971. Cooperative experiment with Eagle Fisheries Ltd. and Armand Lavoie, District Agriculturist, New Brunswick Department of Agriculture.

lowbush blueberry fields, spraying *C. peregrina* with a 2,000 ppm water solution of 2,4–D from the amine formulation. In Maine and the Maritime Provinces the more common practice in moderate stands of this weed at the present time is to wipe or roll the bushes with 2,4–D (G. D. Palfrey and J. Sibley personal communication). Dicamba (3,6–dichloro-o-anisic acid) is also effective in controlling *C. peregrina* at 3.4 kg a.i./ha (Table 4). Jackson (1974) reports that picloram (4–amino-3,5,6–trichloropicolinic acid) at 0.5 kg/ha eliminated *C. peregrina* from grassland.

12. Response to Other Human Manipulations

Muenscher (1952) reported that close mowing two or three seasons in succession would control *C. peregrina*. We would agree that removing most of the shoot growth weakens the growth of this weed, but we believe it is impracticable for most growers at the present time.

13. Response to Parasites

Connors (1967) reports that the rust *Cronartium comptoniae* Arth. has been found growing on *C. peregrina* from both Quebec and Ontario. This fungus grows as thin, thread-like horns on the undersurface of the leaves and according to Pironne et al. (1960) is of no importance to its host.

ACKNOWLEDGMENTS

We wish to thank A. Brydon, G. Brown and A. Lightfoot for technical assistance. W. J. Cody and K. W. Spicer of the Biosystematics Research Institute, Agriculture Canada in Ottawa kindly sent seed samples. The loan of specimens from the herbaria listed in Fig. 3 is gratefully acknowledged. We also thank W. J. Cody of the Biosystematics Research Institute, Agriculture Canada, Ottawa, Ontario for helpful suggestions in the preparation of this manuscript.

CANADA WEED COMMITTEE. 1969. Common and botanical names of weeds in Canada. Can. Dep. Agric. Publ. 1397. 67 pp.

CONNORS, I. L. 1967. An annotated index of plant diseases in Canada and fungi recorded on plants in Alaska, Canada and Greenland. Can. Dep. Agric. Res. Br. Publ. 1251. 381 pp.

DEPARTMENT OF ENERGY, MINES AND RESOURCES. 1971. The national atlas of Canada. Folios A. & B. Queen's Printer, Ottawa, Ont.

ERDTMAN, G. 1943. An introduction to pollen analysis. Chronica Botanica Company, Waltham, Mass. p. 108.

FERNALD, M. L. 1950. Gray's manual of botany. 8th ed. American Book Co., New York, N.Y. 1632 pp.

FERRON, M. and CAYOUETTE, R. 1971. Nom des mauvaises herbes du Québec. Minist. Agric. et Colonisation Québec. Publ. 288. 133 pp.

FRASER, J. W. 1969. Influences of sweet-fern on germination, survival, and early growth of red pine. Can. J. Bot. 47: 1681-1683.

GLEASON, H. A. 1952. The new Britton and Brown. Illustrated flora of the northeastern United States and adjacent Canada. Vol. 2. The choripetalous Dicotyledoneae. Lancaster Press Inc., Lancaster, Pa. 655 pp.

HALIM, A. F. and COLLINS, R. P. 1970. Volatile oil composition of foliage from sweet fern. Lloydia 33: 7-10.

HALL, I. V. 1949. A paleoecological study of forest successions in northeastern Cape Breton Island as determined by pollen analysis. M.Sc. Thesis. Acadia University, Wolfville, N.S. 49 pp.

HALL, I. V. 1975. The biology of Canadian weeds. 7. *Myrica pensylvanica* Loisel. Can. J. Plant Sci. 55: 163-169.

HALL, I. V. and MACK, G. J. A. 1959. Weeds. Pages 16-19 *in* Blueberry substation Tower Hill, New Brunswick progress report 1954-1959. Can. Dep. Agric., Ottawa, Ont.

JACKSON, L. P. 1974. Perennial weeds in lowbush blueberry. Page 312 *in* Research report Canada Weed Committee Eastern Section, Halifax, N.S.

LAVOIE, V. 1968. La phytosociologie et l'aménagement des bleuetières. Natur. Can. 95: 397-412.

LAWRENCE, G. H. M. 1951. Taxonomy of vascular plants. The Macmillan Company, New York, N.Y. 823 pp.

LAYCOCK, W. A. 1967. Distribution of roots and rhizomes in different soil types in the pine barrens of New Jersey. U.S. Dep. Inter. Geol. Surv. Profes. Pap. 563-C. p. 10.

MACDONALD, A. D. 1974. Floral development of *Comptonia peregrina* (Myricaceae). Can. J. Bot. 52: 2165-2169.

MARIE-VICTORIN, Frère. 1964. Flore laurentienne. Deuxième ed. Les Presses de L'Université de Montréal. Montréal 3, Que. 925 pp.

MARTIN, A. C., ZIM, H. S. and NELSON, A. L. 1951. American wildlife and plants. McGraw-Hill Book Company, Inc., New York, N.Y. 500 pp.

MINSHALL, W. H. 1957. Rubber and resin content of native and introduced plants of Canada. Can. Dep. Agric. Mimeo. 53 pp.

MORRIS, M., EVELEIGH, D. E., RIGGS, S. C. and TIFFNEY, W. N. Jr. 1974. Nitrogen fixation in the bayberry *(Myrica pensylvanica)* and its role in coastal succession. Amer. J. Bot. 61: 867-870.

MUENSCHER, W. C. 1952. Weeds. The Macmillan Company, New York, N.Y. 579 pp.

ONTARIO HERBICIDE COMMITTEE. 1971. Guide to chemical weed control. Ont. Dep. Agric. Publ. 75. 78 pp.

PIRONE, P. P., DODGE, B. O. and RICKETT, H. W. 1960. Diseases and pests of ornamental plants. The Ronald Press Company, New York, N.Y. 494 pp.

ROULEAU, E. 1956. Studies on the vascular flora of the Province of Newfoundland (Canada). III. A check-list of the vascular plants of the Province of Newfoundland. Contrib. de l'Institut Botanique de l'Université de Montréal – No. 69. pp. 41-106.

SCOGGAN, H. J. 1950. The flora of Bic and the Gaspe Peninsula, Quebec. Can. Dep. Res. and Develop. National Museum of Canada Bull. 115: 399 pp.

SCOGGAN, H. J. 1957. Flora of Manitoba. Can. Dep. Northern Aff. Nat. Res. National Museum of Canada Bull. 140. p. 239.

SMALL, E. 1972. Photosynthetic rates in relation to nitrogen recycling as an adaptation to nutrient deficiency in peat bog plants. Can. J. Bot. 50: 2227-2233.

STOKES, J. 1937. Cytological studies in the Myricaceae. Botanical Gaz. 99: 387-399.

TREVETT, M. F. 1952. Control of woody weeds in lowbush blueberry fields. Maine Agric. Exp. Sta. Bull. 499. 23 pp.

U.S. DEPARTMENT OF AGRICULTURE FOREST SERVICE. 1948. Woody-plant seed manual. U.S. Gov. Printing Office, Washington, D.C. Misc. Publ. 654. 244 pp.

WODEHOUSE, R. P. 1971. Hay-fever plants. Their appearance, distribution, time of flowering, and their role in hay fever. Hafner Publishing Company, New York, N.Y. 280 pp.

YOUNGKEN, H. W. 1919. The comparative morphology, taxonomy, and distribution of the Myricaceae of the eastern United States. Contrib. Bot. Lab. Univ. Pennsylvania 4: 339-400.

ZAK, B. 1971. Characterization and identification of Douglas-fir mycorrhizae. Pages 38-53 *in* Mycorrhizae Proc. of the first North American conference on mycorrhizae, April 1969. Misc. Publ. 1189 U.S. Dep. Agric. Forest Serv.

THE BIOLOGY OF CANADIAN WEEDS. 17. *Cyperus esculentus* L.

GERALD A. MULLIGAN and BONNY E. JUNKINS

Biosystematics Research Institute, Research Branch, Agriculture Canada, Ottawa, Ontario K1A 0C6. Received 30 Dec. 1975, accepted 22 Jan. 1976.

MULLIGAN, GERALD A. AND JUNKINS, BONNY E. 1976. The biology of Canadian weeds. 17. *Cyperus esculentus* L. Can. J. Plant Sci. **56**: 339–350.

This account of *Cyperus esculentus* L. (yellow nut sedge) summarizes biological information on this species as part of a series of contributions on plants that are weedy in Canada. Yellow nut sedge is weedy in cultivated fields of Nova Scotia, New Brunswick, southern Quebec and southern Ontario and has only become a prominent weed in Canada during the last two decades.

Dans le cadre de la série d'articles sur les mauvaises herbes au Canada, le présent document résume les renseignements que nous possédons sur la biologie de *Cyperus esculentus* L. (souchet comestible). Le souchet comestible est considéré comme une mauvaise herbe des cultures de la Nouvelle-Écosse, du Nouveau-Brunswick, du sud du Québec et du sud de l'Ontario, mais n'est devenu important au Canada qu'au cours des deux dernières décennies.

1. Name

Cyperus esculentus L. — **yellow nut sedge** (Canada Weed Committee 1969), northern nutgrass (Hauser 1968); **souchet comestible**, amande de terre, souchet rampant, souchet-sultan, souchet traçant, trasi (Ferron et Cayouette 1971). Cyperaceae, sedge family, Cypéracées.

2. Description and Account of Variation

Perennial with rhizomes terminating in tubers or leafy plants; stems triangular, 25–65 cm tall, unbranched, glabrous, with grass-like leaves towards base or just below inflorescence; inflorescence golden-brown, umbelliform; spikelets strongly flattened; rachilla of spikelets not disarticulating at maturity; scales ovate to obtuse, 2–3 mm long, golden-brown, keeled, nerved; stigma 3-parted; stamens 3; 1-seeded; seeds 3-angled, ellipsoid, whitish to yellowish brown, 1.2–1.8 mm long.

Yellow nut sedge plants from native and weedy habitats in Ontario and Quebec had n = ca. 48 chromosomes. Hicks (1929) previously reported $2n$ = ca. 108 for plants collected at Boston, Massachusetts.

Can. J. Plant Sci. 56: 339-350 (Apr. 1976)

Cyperus esculentus is sometimes confused with a number of other species of *Cyperus*: *C. rotundus* L. (purple nut sedge), a perennial that occurs in the United States but not in Canada; *C. strigosus* L., a perennial occurring from southern Quebec to Saskatchewan; *C. schweinitzii* Torrey, a perennial occurring from southern Ontario to Saskatchewan; *C. erythrorhizos* Muhl., *C. engelmannii* Steudel and *C. ferruginescens* Boeckl., annuals that are found in southern Ontario. The last-named species also occurs in Quebec. *Cyperus esculentus* can be distinguished from all of the above species by the conspicuous scales on its rhizomes and by its terminal tubers. Both of these characteristics are entirely absent in the other species.

Two clones of yellow nut sedge from Delaware and Georgia, space-planted at Tifton, Georgia, exhibited different gross morphological characteristics (Hauser 1968). Georgia plants were taller, flowered later, produced plants located further from the parent tuber, and produced larger tubers than did plants from Delaware. Plants from Kemptville, Ontario grown in a greenhouse at Ottawa with plants from Thorndale,

Ontario flowered earlier and had more flowers than Thorndale plants. Hauser (1968) found that plants from different geographical areas have different responses to herbicides, 2,4-D proving ineffective in New York and Rhode Island but partially effective in Georgia. There is strong evidence that there are significant genetic differences between populations of *C. esculentus* and that some of these differences are relevant to the control of yellow nut sedge. However, there is no doubt that

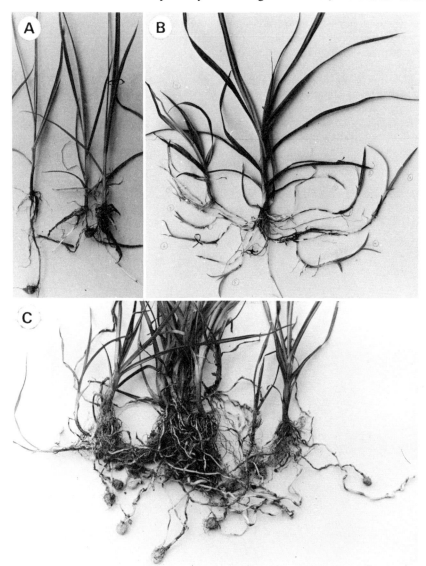

Fig. 1. Vegetative growth of *C. esculentus*. A. In spring, overwintered tubers with determinate rhizomes and primary leafy shoots. B. In summer, large primary leafy shoot with indeterminate rhizomes and secondary leafy shoots. C. In autumn, new tubers forming at apices of indeterminate rhizomes.

197

the North American weed is a single species.

Cultivated chufa, often considered to be the same species as weedy yellow nut sedge, differs from yellow nut sedge in many characteristics. Although chufa sometimes is planted in Canada it does not become weedy under our conditions. Chufa never produces seed, rarely produces flowers, and the whole plant, including the tubers, is killed by winter conditions.

Figure 1 shows the vegetative growth of *C. esculentus*; overwintering tubers, determinate and indeterminate rhizomes, primary and secondary leafy shoots, and new tubers. Flowering plants in both native and weedy habitats are shown in Fig. 2.

3. Economic Importance

(a) Detrimental — In Canada, yellow nut sedge is a persistent weed in many fields of vegetables, corn (*Zea mays* L.) and oats (*Avena sativa* L.). It causes yield reductions and cannot be eradicated by using present control methods. In the eastern United States it is a serious weed in about 10–15% of land devoted to corn, alfalfa (*Medicago sativa* L.), potatoes (*Solanum tuberosum* L.), vegetables, ornamentals, small fruits and tree fruits (Bayer, Libby, Meade and Sweet *in* Sweet 1974). In Delaware, yellow nut sedge not only competes with potatoes and lima beans (*Phaseolus limensis* Macf.) but it also spoils their quality (Bundy 1960). Yellow nut sedge tubers grow into potato

Fig. 2.   Flowering plants of *C. esculentus*. A. Small patch. B. Infestation in cornfield.

tubers, causing them to be graded as culls, and pass through with shelled lima beans, making costly hand-sorting necessary. Nut sedge, competing with cotton (*Gossypium hirsutum* L.) for a complete growing season, reduced cotton yields by 34% (Keeley and Thullen 1975). Yellow nut sedge reduces yields and increases production costs due to increased cultivation and handweeding, lowers crop quality and increases harvesting and production costs (Bell et al. 1962).

Cyperus esculentus and *C. rotundus* L. are between them considered the most serious weeds of Africa (Little 1965). These two species, grouped as a single entity, were placed on a list of the 10 worst weeds of field crops in the United States by the editors of *Crops & Soils Magazine* (Lewis and Worsham 1970).

Recent control of many weeds in fruit orchards has resulted in reduced competition for yellow nut sedge and more vigorous nut sedge plants (Meade *in* Sweet 1974). Sweet (1974) states that as quack grass (*Agropyron repens* (L.) Beauv.) becomes less prevalent in cornfields due to weed control, yellow nut sedge becomes more abundant.

Yellow nut sedge is the host for two nematode species that are serious pathogens to cotton in Georgia (Bird and Hogger 1973).

It has been suggested by Tamés et al. (1973) and Taylorson (1963) that growth in some cultivated crops is inhibited by an exudate from *C. esculentus*.

(b) Beneficial — Chufa and yellow nut sedge are closely related, but differ in many characteristics (Lorougnon 1969); they are considered separate species by some workers and the same species by others. The larger tubers and lack of tuber winter hardiness in chufa are probably the differences of greatest economic importance.

Chufa tubers are used throughout the world for a variety of purposes: to produce the summer beverage "horchata de chufa," roasted tubers for use as "earth almonds"; tubers and vegetation for use as a forage crop; ground tubers as a substitute for coffee; tubers for the production of a vegetable oil, and cellulose (Bruno 1945; Power and Chesnut 1923; Dolev and Mokady 1970; Lafuente et al. 1965; Driga 1959; Killinger and Stokes 1946; Putnina 1953). Chufa is not grown commercially in Canada because of serious harvesting problems and because it cannot at the present time compete with other crops economically. A prototype mechanical harvester for chufa was designed by Reid et al. (1972).

(c) Legislation — Yellow nut sedge is not mentioned in any Canadian Federal or Provincial Weed or Seeds Acts.

4. Geographical Distribution

In Canada, yellow nut sedge occurs in Nova Scotia, New Brunswick, southen Quebec and southern Ontario (Fig. 3). It occurs both in native habitats and cultivated fields throughout this area. The most westerly location in Canada is at the foot of Long Sault Rapids, Birchdale Landing, Roseberry Township, Rainy River District, Ontario. At this site it occurs in alluvial soil in depressions among boulders on a small rocky islet. In the United States, *C. esculentus* occurs in all States except North Dakota according to Reed and Hughes (1970). However, we have seen a specimen from North Dakota.

Cyperus esculentus occurs from southern Canada, in North America, to northern Argentina, in South America, in southern Europe, and in Africa including Madagascar (Kükenthal 1936; Cour 1960).

5. Habitat

(a) Climatic requirements — Yellow nut sedge tubers survive freezing temperatures during winters, whereas tubers of cultivated chufa and purple nut sedge do not survive. Tubers are the only vegetative part of a yellow nut sedge plant that overwinters. All other plant parts are killed by frost.

199

Stoller (1973) found that yellow nut sedge tubers survive in areas of low air and soil temperatures, partly because of the tuber's ability to harden to the cold and withstand low temperatures for long periods and partly because the extreme coldness of the air on the soil surface is not usually transmitted down to soil layers where some tubers reside. He found that 50% of yellow nut sedge tubers were killed at −6.5 C. This tuber mortality due to cold winter temperatures may account for the limited range of *C. esculentus* in Canada (*see* Fig. 3).

Bell et al. (1962) reported on the winter mortality of tubers in Delaware. In October of 1958 only 15% of tubers were soft and presumed dead whereas by April of 1959, 75% were in this condition. Of the tubers overwintering in New York at latitude 42°N, 90% or more sprouted when buried 5–10 cm deep whereas only 40% of the tubers at the soil surface sprouted and all those above the surface failed to sprout (Doty 1973).

(b) Substratum — Yellow nut sedge occurs in a wide range of soil types: sand, sandy-loam, sandy-gravel, loam, muck, clay-loam and clay. In native habitats the soil is always flooded in the spring whereas in cultivated fields it often grows in drier soils. Bell et al. (1962) found that tuber sprouting was greatly reduced when soil was compacted and that plants grown at 100% moisture produced significantly more tubers and vegetative material than those grown at 50% moisture.

The type of substrate influences tuber production. Tumbleson and Kommedahl (1961) found that shoots from tubers planted in sand emerged sooner than those in sandy silt-loam, but tubers in sandy silt-loam produced more plants at the end of 6 wk. Tubers planted in peat produced the most shoots per tuber initially and finally.

(c) Communities in which the species occurs — Yellow nut sedge is usually confined to habitats that have recently been disturbed. It occurs as a native along the margins of rivers, streams and lakes, and in bogs and marshes. These native habitats are usually flooded in the spring and there is little competition from other plants early in the growing season. It also grows as a weed in cornfields, oats, gardens, soybeans (*Glycine max* Merr.) and vegetable crops. In cultivated fields, nut sedge is associated

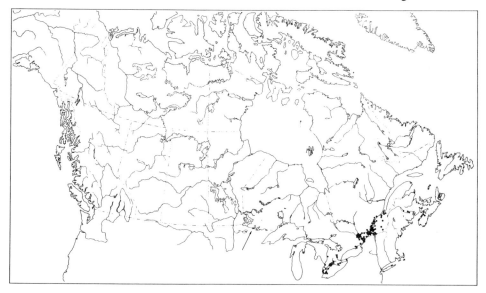

Fig. 3.   Distribution of *C. esculentus* from herbarium specimens.

200

with a wide variety of colonizing weeds. Yellow nut sedge appears to compete poorly with other weeds. Since yellow nut sedge is resistant to most herbicides, there is often a rapid increase in the abundance of nut sedge when other weeds in a field are controlled by herbicides.

6. History

Yellow nut sedge occurs in both native and weedy habitats throughout its Canadian range. Label data on herbarium specimens indicate that this nut sedge was found mostly in native habitats previous to 1950 and that it has only recently become troublesome in many cultivated fields. Although a few weedy fields of yellow nut sedge date back to the 1930's, most weed workers agree that yellow nut sedge has become more abundant as a weed only during the last two decades. It is probably not coincidental that the increased weediness of yellow nut sedge corresponds with the increased use of selective herbicides. The spread of yellow nut sedge from native to cultivated fields seems to be largely due to tubers being carried by implements of cultivation. Recently, several weed workers have observed yellow nut sedge tubers attached to the bases of young tomato transplants.

7. Growth and Development

(a) Morphology — Under certain conditions a tuber is formed at the apical end of an indeterminate rhizome. When first formed the tuber is white but it gradually turns brown and finally at maturity, nearly black. Overwintering tubers are hard, oblong, slightly flattened and are from 0.2 to 1.5 cm long. According to Bendixen (1973), tubers have a hard, tough lignified epidermal layer, well developed buds, a vascular system and roots. Starch-filled cells occupy the bulk of the tuber. He found that buds develop in the axils of closely appressed scale leaves that form a cone at the tip of the tuber. Buds have never been observed along rhizomes.

Tubers are dormant after they are formed in summer and autumn, and usually sprout the following spring (Bell et al. 1962; Stoller and Wax 1973; Taylorson 1967; Tumbleson and Kommedahl 1961, 1962). Most tubers are in the top 15 cm of the soil, although some have been reported as deep as 30 cm. Stoller and Wax (1973) reported that in Illinois, maximum emergence and viability of tubers occurred at a depth of 10.2 cm. Tubers usually produce from one to three sprouts (determinate rhizomes). These determinate rhizomes grow directly towards the soil surface and form a primary basal bulb just below the surface. At a point 1–2 cm below the soil surface, the scale leaves, at the tip of the determinate rhizome, elongate to about three times the normal size and the adjacent portion of the rhizome suddenly enlarges to form the primary basal bulb (Jansen *in* Sweet 1974). Each primary basal bulb produces a primary vegetative plant above the soil surface. The underground primary basal bulb enlarges considerably as the plant grows larger. A determinate rhizome and the original tuber may remain alive and attached to a primary basal bulb for as long as 12 wk (Stoller et al. 1972). The basal bulb produced by the original tuber also gives rise to many fibrous roots and indeterminate rhizomes. These indeterminate rhizomes develop secondary basal bulbs and tubers.

According to Jansen (1971), each indeterminate rhizome has a series of internodes, nodal scale leaves 0.5–1.0 cm in length, and a terminal pointed bud. He found one plant with indeterminate rhizomes, ranging in size from 2 to 60 cm long, with from 4 to 33 internodes.

The formation of secondary basal bulbs by indeterminate rhizomes is identical to the formation of primary basal bulbs by determinate rhizomes (tuber sprouts). Secondary basal bulbs behave like primary basal bulbs. Each secondary basal bulb produces a leafy plant, many fibrous roots and indeterminate rhizomes.

The formation of a tuber at the tip of an

indeterminate rhizome is characterized by a number of changes at the rhizome tip, a progressive shortening of internodes, an increase in the rhizome diameter, starch accumulation in the cells and the production of numerous scale leaves by the meristem (Bendixen 1973; Jansen 1971). The entire shoot apex swells rapidly to form the young white tuber encased in scale leaves.

(b) Perennation — Tubers are the only portion of yellow nut sedge plants that overwinter; all above-ground parts, basal bulbs, fibrous roots and rhizomes are destroyed by winter conditions (*see* Sections 5a and 7a). Unsprouted tubers are reported to be viable in the soil for as long as $3^1/_2$ yr after they are produced (Doty 1973). However, relatively few tubers survive over two winters. The importance of tubers in the establishment and spread of yellow nut sedge is obvious when it is realized that this species rarely, if ever, reproduces by seed.

(c) Physiological data — There appears to be one or more substances in or on the tuber epidermis that inhibits the sprouting of buds on tubers (Tumbleson 1960; Tumbleson and Kommedahl 1961, 1962). They found that washing yellow nut sedge tubers resulted in a great increase in the sprouting of fall harvested tubers and that the sprouting of washed tubers was inhibited when tubers were submerged in the wash-water. Tumbleson and Kommedahl (1962) reported that the basal portion of a tuber inhibits the sprouting of buds at the apical end. When the basal half of a bulb was detached from the apical half, the buds in the apical end broke dormancy and sprouted. Basal bulbs are formed at the tips of rhizomes, just below the soil surface, in response to the stimulus of daylight (Stoller et al. 1972). According the Jansen (1971) the rate of differentiation of the tips of rhizomes into basal bulbs is maximum at 16 h daylight and into tubers at 8–12 h daylight. However, tubers can be formed at any photoperiod.

Under artificial conditions, alternating temperatures of 20 C to 35 C promoted maximum seed germination (Bell and Larssen 1960; Durfee 1960; Bell et al. 1962; Larssen 1960). Temperatures lower than 10 C were detrimental to seed germination. Germination was inhibited by complete darkness at temperatures other than those optimal for germination (Durfee 1960). Seed treatment with potassium nitrate, potassium nitrite, sulphuric acid, ethylene chlorohydrin, ammonium nitrate and gibberellic acid stimulated germination (Durfee 1960; Larssen 1960).

(d) Phenology — Tubers are dormant until they have overwintered. The following spring, March or April in Georgia (Taylorson 1967) and mid-May or early June in Canada, the first tubers sprout. According to Jansen (1971), this is probably in response to warm temperatures that do not occur until the photoperiod is longer than 14 h. Increasingly longer daylight periods and higher temperatures promote the formation of many basal bulbs, indeterminate rhizomes and leafy plants. In Canada, the development of basal bulbs and leafy plants is at its maximum from late June to mid-August. When the diminishing photoperiod reaches 14 h, vegetative growth ceases, plants reportedly initiate flowering, and the formation of tubers at the end of indeterminate rhizomes accelerates (Jansen 1971). Flowering in Canada commences early in July and continues until September. This seems to be in response to high temperatures rather than to the photoperiod. Plants from Kemptville and Thorndale, Ontario flowered in a greenhouse in Ottawa without supplementary lighting on 21 June 1975, the longest day of the year. This is in agreement with Durfee (1960) who states that the length of photoperiod has a definite effect on the vegetative development of nut sedge but appears to have no effect on flower initiation.

Many stands of yellow nut sedge do not form mature seed. At the locations where seed is produced no seedlings were found in nature. A letter in the October 1975 issue of the *WSSA Newsletter* (Mulligan *in* Santelmann 1975) asked American weed workers if they had evidence that yellow nut sedge can become established in nature by seed. Seven U.S. weed workers answered the letter. Several had either grown plants from seed in the greenhouse or had successfully grown plants outside in flats using seed stored indoors over the winter. Two of the writers, Ellis W. Hauser of Georgia and Robert J. Thullen of California, had repeatedly looked for seedlings in the field without any success. There is, therefore, no concrete evidence that seed is a factor in the establishment or spread of yellow nut sedge. However, since germinating seedlings of yellow nut sedge are very minute, it is possible that we are missing some germination in nature.

(e) Mycorrhiza — None reported.

8. Reproduction

(a) Floral biology — Yellow nut sedge flowers are perfect, wind-pollinated and self-incompatible.

(b) Seed production and dispersal — Flowers of yellow nut sedge from Kemptville, Ontario and Thorndale, Ontario that were selfed in the greenhouse at Ottawa did not produce seed. However, when Kemptville flowers were crossed with Thorndale flowers all of the pollinated flowers formed viable seed.

Seed set of yellow nut sedge is very variable throughout its range; at many sites no seed is produced. These stands are undoubtedly the result of vegetative reproduction, the entire infestation being genetically the same plant. At other locations the amount of seed set varies from year to year; during one year seed set may be very high whereas during another year it may be extremely low. The amount of seed set is probably correlated with the distance between genetically different nut sedge plants and the weather conditions at the time of cross-pollination.

No seed was produced during 1975 at any of the 11 weedy and native stands of yellow nut sedge studied in the Ottawa and Brockville areas. Since weather conditions were favorable for cross-pollination at the times of flowering, we assume that each of these stands is genetically one plant that is spreading vegetatively.

Of 115 studied, only 13 herbarium specimens with mature inflorescences had well-formed seed. Specimens with seed had been collected in Nova Scotia, Quebec, Ontario, New York, Vermont, Florida, Montana and North Dakota. The amount of seed set ranged from very little on a specimen from Senneville, Quebec to nearly 100% on a specimen from Fargo, North Dakota. It appears that only about 1 infestation in 10 produces seed.

Justice and Whitehead (1946) found that 25 inflorescences of yellow nut sedge from a Maine population yielded 50,260 seeds with an average germination of 75.6%, the equivalent of 1,521 potential seedlings per inflorescence. Hill et al. (1963) stored *C. esculentus* seed indoors overwinter and planted it in the field the following spring. During one growing season they found that a single seedling developed into a stand of plants that produced a yield of 90,000 seeds with a germination of 51%.

(c) Viability of seed and germination — There is no evidence that yellow nut sedge seed produces plants in nature. However, there is ample evidence that plants produce abundant seed under some conditions and that this seed is viable. Larssen (1960) and Bell et al. (1962) report that seed of yellow nut sedge becomes viable as soon as 2–3 wk after the start of flowering. Bell and Larssen (1960) reported the following germination from a number of locations: 84 and 89% from New York; 61 and 76% from Rhode Island; 58% from Delaware and 28% from Maine. New York seed planted 0.6 cm deep germinated 31% whereas seed planted at 4.8 cm did not germinate. Seed produced by crossing Kemptville and Thorndale plants germinated immediately in the greenhouse in Ottawa. At maturity some yellow nut sedge seeds are dormant whereas other seeds are semidormant to non-dormant

(Durfee 1960; Justice and Whitehead 1946). Although there is no record of seeds producing yellow nut sedge plants in nature, during 1975 we obtained a healthy plant from 20 seeds taken from a herbarium specimen collected at Glenmount, Albany Co., New York on 5 September 1919. In addition, nine plants were obtained from 27 seeds taken from a herbarium specimen collected at Île à Cavale, Berthier Co., Que. in 1968. Bellue (1946) reported that seed stored 20 yr germinated 17%. Seed obviously would be a factor in the spread of yellow nut sedge if they could overwinter under dry and warm conditions. The only suggestion of this is a report by Bellue (1946) that yellow nut sedge is found in commercial grass seed and Ladino clover (*Trifolium repens* L.).

(d) Vegetative reproduction — The vegetative system of yellow nut sedge is an interconnected complex system of many tubers, rhizomes, basal bulbs and above-ground leafy plants (*see* Section 7a). During one growing season at Rosemount, Minnesota, 1 tuber produced 1,900 plants and 6,900 tubers to a depth of 23 cm in a patch 21 dm in diameter (Tumbleson and Kommedahl 1961).

9. Hybrids
There are no known hybrids between *C. esculentus* and any other *Cyperus* species.

10. Population Dynamics
Populations of yellow nut sedge were studied at 13 stations in eastern Ontario and adjacent Quebec during 1975. No seedlings were seen at any of these sites nor did any of the plants examined produce seed.

At Kemptville, overwintering tubers sprouted in mid-May, and by 1 June primary leafy shoots were 14 cm tall. By 17 June rhizomes were well developed, secondary leafy shoots were 2 or 3 cm tall, and a few small white tubers had been produced. On 8 July 10% of the plants were in flower and by 17 July about 50% were flowering. Some indeterminate rhizomes were 40 cm

long but there were very few new tubers. At this location, tuber production did not increase until after mid-August when the formation of secondary leafy plants virtually ceased. On 26 August about 90% of the leafy shoots had flowers or flower buds and some mature new tubers appeared.

Plants of yellow nut sedge often behave very differently at various locations. On 26 June plants in a Brockville field had many tubers whereas plants in a Kemptville field had none. On 9 July there were no flowering plants in a native stand along the flood shoreline at Eardley, Quebec whereas 40–50% of the plants were in flower 30 miles away at Kemptville.

11. Response to Herbicides and Other Chemicals
Yellow nut sedge has emerged as a critical problem since 1958 in the Coastal Plain region of the United States (Hauser 1968). He attributes its increased importance as a weed to changes in agricultural practices, particularly the widespread use of herbicides. Bird and Hogger (1973) reported that yellow nut sedge has greatly increased as a weed in cotton-producing areas of the United States due to the annual use of herbicides in this crop. In eastern Canada, yellow nut sedge has become a serious weed in many cultivated fields only within the last two decades, a period when selective herbicides came into prominence.

It was suggested by Stoller et al. (1972) that the opportune time for chemical control in the life cycle of yellow nut sedge may be between the time when overwintering tubers sprout and the time when new tubers are produced. They claim that it is nearly impossible to kill tubers buried in the soil.

Single applications of bentazon (3-isopropyl-1H-2, 1, 3-benzothiadizin-(4)3H one 2, 2-dioxide), with or without surfactants, at 0.85–1.14 kg/ha, applied on 28 June 1974 at Ridgetown, Ontario did not give adequate yellow nut sedge control (Pitblado et al. 1974). However, second applications at the same rates, 10 days later controlled yellow nut sedge for the immediate season. The surfactants themselves had no or very little effect on yellow nut sedge.

Riley and Smith (1974) obtained adequate control of yellow nut sedge at Macdonald College, Quebec with EPTC (S-ethyl dipropylthiocarbamate) on 17 July 1974 at 4.5 kg/ha. EPTC at 4.5 kg/ha and alachlor (2-chloro-2, 6-diethyl-N-(methoxymethyl) acetanilide) at 2.3 kg/ha gave good control of yellow nut sedge (souchet comestible) in corn and alfalfa (Ferron 1974). Ferron found that atrazine (2-chloro-4-(ethylamino)-6-(isopropylamino)-s-triazine) at 5.6 kg/ha plus 6.8 liters of oil gave better control of yellow nut sedge but reduced the yield of corn.

12. Response to Other Human Manipulations

In New York, land badly infested with yellow nut sedge was kept fallow for 4 consecutive yr. At the end of 4 yr, 11 tubers per 9 dm^2 were found in the top 15 cm of soil compared to 539 in the control (Bell et al. 1962). Two years of mechanical fallow were necessary to obtain a 90% reduction of viable tubers in the soil. Similar results were obtained in Minnesota by Tumbleson and Kommedahl (1962).

According to Sweet (1974) the majority of viable tubers in the plow layer were formed the previous season; perhaps 25% were formed 2 yr previously and less than 10% two seasons ago. He states that if no new tubers are allowed to form, and if deep plowing is avoided, severe infestations can be reduced to manageable levels in two seasons. Tubers beneath the plow depth will remain viable, but dormant, for four or five seasons. After this length of time they will die and decay.

Cultivation of infested fields in the fall when most tubers are dormant has little effect. Cultivation should commence as soon as tubers start sprouting in the spring and should continue throughout the growing season as long as tubers continue to sprout.

This will ensure that no new tubers are formed. Hauser (1968) obtained good control of yellow nut sedge by rotating crops along with the rotation of herbicides.

Potato growers have observed that there is much less yellow nut sedge the year after the planting of the cultivar Kennebec as compared to the year after either Irish Cobbler or Katahdin cultivars (Bundy et al. 1960; Libby in Sweet 1974). This is probably due to the shading effect of the more vigorous top growth of Kennebec.

13. Response to Parasites

(a) Insects and other nondomestic animals —
INSECTA
COCCIDAE: *Chorizococcus rostellum* (Hoke) on leaves and roots, southern California (Poinar 1964).
LEPIDOPTERA: *Bactra verutana* Lella; this insect may be greatly parasitized in some areas thus limiting its value in the biological control of yellow nut sedge, California (Poinar 1964; Keeley et al. 1969, 1970).
NEMATODA
Heterodera cyperi Golden (Schindler and Golden 1965); *Heterodera mothi* Khan & Husain (Minton et al. 1973); *Meloidogyne incognita* (Kofoid & White) Chitwood and *Hoploliaimus columbus* Sher.; yellow nut sedge is a host to these two nematodes that are severe parasites of cotton in Georgia (Bird and Hogger 1973).

(b) Microorganisms and viruses —
FUNGI
Ascochyta sp., on leaves, Georgia; *Phyllachora cyperi* Rehm, *Puccinia canaliculata* (Schw.) Legh. (U.S. Department of Agriculture 1960). Specimens of the rust *P. canaliculata* on yellow nut sedge from Ontario and Quebec are in the National Mycological Herbarium at Ottawa.

ACKNOWLEDGMENT

We thank Patricia Ferguson for her valuable assistance during the summer of 1975.

BELL, R. S., LACHMAN, W. H., RAHN, E. M. and SWEET, R. D. 1962. Life history studies as related to weed control in the northeast. 1. Nutgrass. Rhode Island Agric. Exp.Sta. Bull. 364. 33 pp.

BELL, R. S. and LARSSEN, E. 1960. Experiments with the germination of northern nutsedge (C. esculentus) seed. Northeast. Weed Contr. Conf. Proc. 14: 45–48.

BELLUE, M. K. 1946. Weed seed handbook — Series V. Bull Dep. Agric. Calif. 35: 87–94.

BENDIXEN, L. E. 1973. Anatomy and sprouting of yellow nutsedge tubers. Weed Sci. 21: 501–503.

BIRD, G. W. and HOGGER, C. 1973. Nutsedges as hosts of plant parasitic nematodes in Georgia cotton fields. Plant Dis. Rep. 57: 402.

BRUNO, F. 1945. Investigations of some raw materials for cellulose production. Lavori R. Inst. Bot. R. Giard. Colon. Palermo 12: 230–251.

BUNDY, O. M. 1960. Growth and development of northern nutgrass as affected by certain environmental conditions. Masters thesis, University of Delaware, Newark. 62 pp.

BUNDY, O.M., DONNALLY, W. F. and RAHN, E. M. 1960. Growth and development of northern nutgrass as affected by certain environmental conditions. Proc. Northeast. Weed Contr. Conf. 14: 44.

CANADA WEED COMMITTEE. 1969. Common and botanical names of weeds in Canada. Can. Dep. Agric. Publ. 1397. Ottawa, Ont. 67 pp.

COUR, P. 1960. Cyperus esculentus L., C. rotundus L., et C. rotundus var. brevibracteatus Legr. Bull. Cent. Etud. Rech. Sci. Biarritz 3: 181–192.

DOLEV, A. and MOKADY, S. 1970. Nutritional evaluation, possible uses and enrichment of "Horchata de Chufa". Nutr. Rept. Int. 2: 297–303.

DOTY, C. H. 1973. Effects of some environmental factors and postemergence herbicide applications on germination and growth of yellow nutsedge tubers. Masters thesis, Cornell University, Ithaca, N.Y. 133 pp.

DRIGA, I. E. 1959. Experiment on the cultivation of sweet potatoes and nutsedge plant in the Kiev climate, Trudy Bot. Inst. Akad. Nauk SSSR (Ser. 6) 7: 135–137.

DURFEE, J. W. 1960. Life history and the control of northern nutgrass Cyperus esculentus L. Masters thesis, University of Massachusetts, Amherst. 68 pp.

FERRON, M. 1974. Comportement de quelques herbicides sur le souchet en présence de luzerne ou de maïs. Res. Rep. Canada Weed Comm. (East. Sect.), Halifax, N.S. p. 336.

FERRON, M. and CAYOUETTE, R. 1971. Noms des mauvaise herbes du Québec. Min. Agric. Colonisation, Québec, Qué. 113 pp.

HAUSER, E. W. 1968. Yellow nutsedge — problems, research, trends and outlook. Proc. Northeast. Weed Contr. Conf. 22: 37–48.

HICKS, G. C. 1929. Cytological studies in Cyperus, Eleocharis, Dulichium, and Eriophorum. Bot. Gaz. 88: 132–150.

HILL, E. R., LACHMAN, W. H. and MAYNARD, D. N. 1963. Reproductive potential of yellow nutsedge by seed. Weeds 11: 160–161.

JANSEN, L. L. 1971. Morphology and photoperiodic responses of yellow nutsedge (Cyperus esculentus). Weed Sci. 19: 210–219.

JUSTICE, O. L. and WHITEHEAD, M. D. 1946. Seed production, viability, dormancy in the nutgrasses. J. Agric. Res. 73: 303–318.

KEELEY, P. E. and THULLEN, R. J. 1975. Influences of yellow nutsedge competition on furrow-irrigated cotton. Weed Sci. 23: 171–175.

KEELEY, P. E., THULLEN, R. J. and MILLER, J. H. 1969. Biological control studies on yellow nutsedge. Proc. 21st Calif. Weed Conf. p. 121.

KEELEY, P. E., THULLEN, R. J. and MILLER, J. H. 1970. Biological control on yellow nutsedge by Bactra verutana Zeller. Weed Sci. 18: 393–395.

KILLINGER, G. B. and STOKES, W. E. 1946. Chufas in Florida. Univ. Florida Agric. Sta. Bull. 419. 16 pp.

KÜKENTHAL, G. 1936. Cyperaceae–Scirpoideae–Cyperaceae. Das Pflanzenreich, IV, 20: 107, 116.

LAFUENTE, B., ALONSO, I. and LÓPEZ, J. J. 1965. Pasterización de la horchata con radiaciones infrarrojas. Rev. Agro. Tecnol. Aliment 5: 92–98.

LARSSEN, E. R. 1960. Factors influencing the germination of northern nutgrass (Cyperus esculentus). Masters thesis, University of Rhode Island, Kingston. 44 pp.

LEWIS, W. M. and WORSHAM, A. D. 1970. Nutsedge. Crops & Soils Magazine 22: 14–16.

LITTLE, E. C. S. 1965. Notes from a liaison officer III. PANS, Sect. C. Weed Contr. 11: 113–118.

LOROUGNON, G. 1969. Étude morphologique et biologique de deux variétés de *Cyperus esculentus* Linn. (Cyperacées). Cah. ORSTOM, Sér. Biol. **10**: 35–63.

MINTON, N. A., TUCKER, E. T. and GOLDEN, A. M. 1973. Occurrence of *Heterodera mothi*, a cyst nematode, in the United States. Plant Dis. Rep. **57**: 946.

MULLIGAN, G. A. *in* P. Santelman, ed. 1975. Yellow nutsedge seedlings. WSSA Newsletter **3**(4): 1–8.

PITBLADO, R. E., BROWN, R. H. and DILLON, C. 1974. Nutsedge control with bentazon. Res. Rep. Canada Weed Comm. (East. Sect.), Halifax, N.S. p. 346.

POINAR, G. O. 1964. Studies of nutgrass insects in California and their effectiveness on biological control agents. J. Econ. Entomol. **57**: 379–383.

POWER, F. B. and CHESNUT, V. K. 1923. Chemical examination of Chufa, the tubers of *Cyperus esculentus* Linné. J. Agric. Res. **26**: 69–75.

PUTNINA, C. 1953. New oil crop — Chufa (*C. esculentus*). Latv. PSR Zinátnu Akad. Vest. **8**: 81–84.

REED, C. F. and HUGHES, R. O. 1970. Selected weeds of the United States. U.S. Dep. Agric. Handb. 366. 463 pp.

REID, W. S., HERGERT, G. B. and FAGAN, W. E. 1972. Development of a prototype mechanical harvester for Chufa (*Cyperus esculentus* L. var. *sativus* Beek). Can. Agric. Eng. **14**: 89–95.

RILEY, W. R. and SMITH, A. L. 1974. Nutsedge control with alfalfa and EPTC. Res. Rep. Canada Weed Comm. (East. Sect.), Halifax, N.S. p. 347.

SCHINDLER, A. F. and GOLDEN, A. M. 1965. Significance of males in reproduction of *Heterodera cyperi*, a cyst nematode parasite of nut-grass. Plant Dis. Rep. **49**: 5.

STOLLER, E. W. 1973. Effect of minimum soil temperature on differential distribution of *Cyperus rotundus* and *C. esculentus* in the U.S.A. Weed Res. **13**: 209–217.

STOLLER, E. W. and WAX, L. M. 1973. Yellow nutsedge shoot emergence and tuber longevity. Weed Sci. **21**: 76–81.

STOLLER, E. W., NEMA, D. P. and BHAN, V. M. 1972. Yellow nutsedge tuber germination and seedling development. Weed Sci. **20**: 93–97.

SWEET, R., ed. 1974. Yellow nutsedge workshop. Suppl. Proc. Northeast Weed Sci. Soc. **28**: 20–34.

TAMÉS, R. S., GESTO, M. D. V. and VIEITEZ, E. 1973. Growth substances isolated from tubers of *C. esculentus* var. *aureus*. Physiol. Plant. **28**: 195–200.

TAYLORSON, R. B. 1963. A preliminary investigation on competitive effects of sweet potatoes on growth of *C. esculentus*. Proc. 16th South. Weed Conf., Tifton, Ga. p. 389.

TAYLORSON, R. B. 1967. Seasonal variation in sprouting, and available carbohydrate in yellow nutsedge tubers. Weeds **15**: 22–24.

TUMBLESON, M. E. 1960. Germination inhibitor in tubers of *C. esculentus*. Res. Rep., N. Central Weed Contr. Conf. **17**: 106–107.

TUMBLESON, M. E. and KOMMEDAHL, T. 1961. Reproductive potential of yellow nutsedge. Weeds **9**: 646–653.

TUMBLESON, M. E. and KOMMEDAHL, T. 1962. Factors affecting dormancy in tubers of *C. esculentus*. Bot. Gaz. **123**: 186–190.

U. S. DEPARTMENT OF AGRICULTURE. 1960. Index of plant disease in the United States. Agric. Handb. 165. U.S. Gov. Print. Off., Washington, D.C. 531 pp.

THE BIOLOGY OF CANADIAN WEEDS. 18.
Potentilla recta L., *P. norvegica* L., and *P. argentea* L.

PATRICIA A. WERNER[1] and JUDITH D. SOULE[2]

[1]*W. K. Kellogg Biological Station and Department of Botany and Plant Pathology, Michigan State University, Hickory Corners, Michigan 49060, and* [2]*Department of Zoology, Michigan State University, E. Lansing. Contribution no. 288, W. K. Kellogg Biological Station. Received 20 Oct. 1975, accepted 13 Feb. 1976.*

WERNER, PATRICIA A. AND SOULE, JUDITH D. 1976. The biology of Canadian weeds. 18. *Potentilla recta* L., *P. norvegica* L. and *P. argentea* L. Can. J. Plant Sci. **56**: 591–603.

Original research and information from other studies are incorporated into a summary of the biology of weedy species of *Potentilla* found in Canada: *P. recta* L. (sulphur cinquefoil, an introduced perennial), *P. norvegica* L. (rough cinquefoil, an annual, biennial, or rarely perennial), and *P. argentea* L. (silvery cinquefoil, a perennial).

Les auteurs présentent, à partir de recherches originales et des résultats d'autres travaux, un résumé sur la biologie des espèces adventices de *Potentilla* qu'on trouve au Canada. Il s'agit de *P. recta* L., potentille dressée, vivace introduite, *P. norvegica* L., potentille de Norvège, annuelle, bisannuelle ou rarement pérenne, et *P. argentea* L., potentille argentée, pérenne.

1. Name

There are more than 50 species of *Potentilla* in North America. Of those that occur in Canada, the three described below are considered among the weedy.

I. *Potentilla recta* L., (synonym: *P. sulphurea Lam.*) — **sulphur cinquefoil** (Canada Weed Committee 1969), upright cinquefoil, (Fernald 1950); **potentille dressée**, potentille droite (Ferron et Cayouette 1970).

II. *Potentilla norvegica* L. (synonyms: *P. monspeliensis* L., *P. monspeliensis* L. var. *norvegica* (L.) Rydb.) — **rough cinquefoil** (Canada Weed Committee 1969), **potentille de Norvège**, potentille, potentille de Montpellier, potentille dressée, potentille jaune (Ferron et Cayouette 1971) (see also section 6: History).

III. *Potentilla argentea* L. — **silvery cinquefoil** (Canada Weed Committee 1969), **potentille argentée**, argentine, potentilles (Ferron et Cayouette 1970).

The common name "five-finger" is frequently used for the genus *Potentilla* in the literature. Rosaceae, rose family, Rosacées.

2. Description and Account of Variation

(a) I. *Potentilla recta* is a perennial, reproducing by seeds (actually fruits, achenes); a woody rootstock producing one to several erect stems, 30–70 cm high; stems are simple up to the inflorescence, very leafy, stout, hairy; leaves with 5–7 coarsely serrate oblong leaflets, longest leaflet 3–14 cm long, green and rough-hairy both above and below, veins depressed above, prominent below, basal leaves on long petioles, upper leaves smaller with shorter petioles and finally sessile; inflorescence a many-flowered, nearly leafless, open cyme standing above the principal foliage; flower 1.5–2.5 cm across, petals 5, pale to sulphur yellow, as long as or longer than calyx, stamens mostly 30, 5 green sepals and 5 additional bracts (a characteristic of the genus); fruits are achenes (again characteristic of the genus), numerous in each flower, ovate, about 1.2 mm long, dark brown with lighter, prominent, branched ridges, and narrow, winged margin (Frankton and Mulligan 1970; Fernald 1950; Phillips 1956; Clapham, et al. 1952; Kelley 1953). Chromosome counts from material from two sites in Ontario and two in British Columbia all gave $2n = 28$ (Mulligan 1959). Other counts from European specimens have given both $2n = 28$, and $2n = 42$ (Darlington and Wylie 1956). The basic chromosome number for the genus *Potentilla* is $n = 7$ (Robertson 1974; Goswami and Matfield 1975).

II. *P. norvegica*, an annual, biennial or (rarely) short-lived perennial, reproducing by achenes; root simple, vertical, often rather thick in biennial and perennial forms, may have one or several stems rising from single rootstock; stems 20–60 cm high, robust, hairy, branched; leaves alternate, hairy, green on both sides, the lower on long petioles, upper nearly or quite sessile, each leaf consisting of 3 oval, coarsely toothed leaflets; inflorescence a leafy cyme at the ends of the branches; flowers 0.7–1.0 cm across, the 5 separate petals yellow, not longer than the green sepals, stamens 15–20; achenes ovoid to nearly round, 0.8–1.3 mm long, pale brown with shallow longitudinal ridges. (Frankton and Mulligan 1970; Clapham et al. 1952; Darlington et al. 1940; Kelley 1953). A chromosome number of $2n = 70$ was found for Canadian plants and agrees with that for most European sources (Mulligan 1959; Darlington and Wylie 1956). An exception is Asker (1970a) who lists $2n = 56$ for *P. monspeliensis* (N. American *P. norvegica*; see section 4).

III. *P. argentea*, a perennial, reproducing by achenes; woody root from which arises one to several radially branched, tomentose, whitish depressed or ascending stems, 10–50 cm long, paniculately branched at summit; leaves divided into 5 (or 7) wedge-shaped pinnatifid or incised leaflets with long teeth, dark green above, silvery white and densely tomentose (woolly) below, lower leaves with longer petioles than upper; flowers similar in size (0.7–1.5

cm) and color to *P. norvegica*, but borne in open cyme rather than in tight clusters, achenes about 0.6 mm long, ovoid, brown, smooth to distinct longitudinal, branched ridges (Frankton and Mulligan 1970; Clapham et al. 1952; Kelley 1953; Darlington et al. 1940). The chromosome number varies simultaneously with morphological features in different populations (Frankton and Mulligan 1970; however, Mulligan earlier (1959) disagreed, stating that there were no characters that distinguish chromosome races). Counts of $2n = 14, 28, 35, 42, 56$ have been reported for strains from various localities in Europe (Darlington and Wylie 1956), and counts of $2n = 28$ and 42 from Canada (Mulligan 1959). The Canadian counts represent only three locations, so other genotypes may yet be found in North American populations.

(b) *Similar species and distinguishing characteristics* — Because of the five-parted leaves, *P. recta* has sometimes been confused with hemp, *Cannabis* sp. (Darlington et al. 1940). The best distinguishing characteristic in the vegetative state is the cinquefoil's hairiness, since the hemp is smooth; in the flowering state the inflorescences and the dioecious nature of *Cannabis* are strikingly different from *Potentilla*.

P. intermedia L. resembles *P. argentea*, but has deeply toothed five-parted leaves which are more grayish and hairy below than white and woolly as in the latter species. The cyme is leafier and more woolly than in *P. argentea* (Gray 1889). The European species, *P. collina* Wibel, found occasionally in North America, also resembles *P. argentea*, but the former is more prostrate in habit, with broader leaflets and larger calyx (Britton and Brown 1897).

The most abundant species in the genus in Canada, *P. norvegica*, is best distinguished from the many other species of cinquefoil by its small flowers and three-parted leaves that are green on both sides (Frankton and Mulligan 1970).

(c) *Intraspecific variation* — According to Robertson (1974) *P. recta* shows much more intra-specific variation in Europe than in North America. Perhaps this is partly explained by the fact that only one chromosome count has been found in North America ($2n = 28$), whereas there are two in Europe ($2n = 28, 42$).

Boivin (1952) reported three varieties of *P. recta* growing in eastern Canada. The most common, *P. recta* L. var. *sulphurea* (Lam. and DC.) Peyr., is distinguishable from the others by its 7-parted middle and lower leaves, rather than the 5-parted leaves of *P. recta* L. var. *obscura* (Nestler) Koch., and *P. recta* var. *pilosa* (W.) Led.

P. norvegica varies in its life history in different situations. A specimen of *P. norvegica* from the Kolyma River area in Siberia had a perennial rootstock (Hooker 1884), whereas this species is usually an annual in cultivated ground or a biennial in dry waste areas (Darlington et al. 1940). It may be generally true that this species is found in its perennial form in cold regions, and so there may be a latitudinal and altitudinal separation of the annual–biennial and perennial forms in Canada, but this remains to be demonstrated.

P. argentea occurs with several genotypes (*see* section 1 above), and in Europe there is a pattern to the distribution of some of these. In Sweden, *P. argentea* with $2n = 14$ are more common in the most northern region, while to the south, the more common genotype is $2n = 42$ (Asker 1970b). It is not known ,whether any north–south pattern of genotype distribution also occurs in Canadian *P. argentea*, since extensive samples have not been made.

(d) Figure 1 compares the growth form of the mature plants, Fig. 2 the leaves and flowers, and Fig. 3 the achenes of the three species.

3. Economic Importance

(a) *Detrimental* — *Potentilla recta* is often continuous over large areas of roadside, waste places, and unworked fields and is not controlled by occasional mowing. However, according to Darlington et al. (1940) it is not a serious agricultural weed, since it can be controlled by plowing and planting to a clean-cultivated crop. The same source notes that this plant "is often mistaken for hemp (marijuana) and laboriously exterminated by zealous officials," thus wasting time and money.

Numerous organisms are known to cause disease in *P. recta* (U.S. Department of Agriculture (USDA) 1960). However, only one has been identified as a pathogen for economically important plant species in N. America: *Sphaerotheca humuli* (DC) Burr., which causes mildew on several crop plants (e.g. species of *Fragaria, Rubus, Rosa, Phlox*) (U.S. Department of Agriculture 1926, 1930). In Germany, Nienhaus (1960, *fide* Moore et al. 1964) reported that *P. recta* is susceptible to *Phytopthora cactorum* (Leb. & Cohn) Schroet., a fungus which causes crown rot in apple trees (McIntosh 1972).

Potentilla argentea (common in dry meadows, pastures, lawns, and other areas where the ground is not plowed) is not an important weed in agricultural crops, since it may be eradicated in most cases by improving the fertility of the soil or planting a vigorous-growing crop (Darlington et al. 1940). None of the diseases that attack this species is known to infect economically important plants.

Potentilla norvegica is common in cultivated ground where it grows rapidly as an annual. In dry waste places it may be found as a biennial. The seeds of *P. norvegica* have been among the most common early contaminants in North American seed crops of clover, timothy and red top (Francois 1941; Hillman 1897; Pammell and King 1910). One of the species of parasitic fungus reported on *P. norvegica* in Texas, *Rhizoctonia solani* Kuehn, causes root rot and seedling blight of flax, peas, sweet clover and alfalfa in Canada (Canada Department of Agriculture 1967).

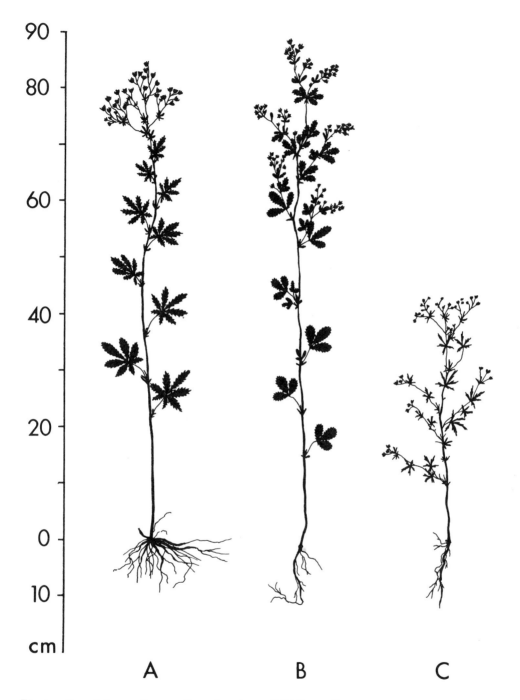

Fig. 1.   Growth forms of mature flowering plants of (A) *Potentilla recta*, (B) *P. norvegica*, and (C) *P. argentea*.

211

A

B

C

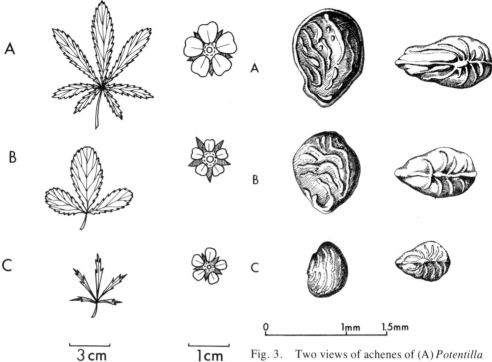

0   1mm   1.5mm

3cm   1cm

Fig. 2. Leaves and flowers of (A) *Potentilla recta*, (B) *P. norvegica*, and (C) *P. argentea*. Flowers emphasize the relative sizes of petals to sepals.

Fig. 3. Two views of achenes of (A) *Potentilla recta*, (B) *P. norvegica*, and (C) *P. argentea*.

No insects that infest other plants have been reported on *P. recta*, *P. norvegica* or *P. argentea*. None of the species is known to be allelopathic, allergenic, or poisonous to humans or farm animals. However, a fairly high tannin content (17–22% dry weight) has been reported in underground portions of *P. recta* (Herrmann 1957) which, if also present in above-ground parts, may make it poor forage for animals, due to the protein-binding action of tannins (cf. Whittaker and Feeny 1971).

(b) *Beneficial* — All three species are classified as horticultural plants by Darlington and Wylie (1956), who define the uses of such plants as "decoration, instruction, experiment, protection, curiosity or religious edification." In addition, all

species, but especially *P. argentea*, may aid in binding the soil on poor sites. Savile (1951) found that *P. argentea* and *Poa* spp. provided the main cover in an area where soil was almost lacking, several years after a severe spring flood had killed nearly all the vegetation on a grassland site in Ontario.

P. recta and *P. norvegica* have no reputed medicinal value, but *P. argentea* was recommended by Starostenko and Starostenko (1971) to be included among the active agents used for treating cirrhosis of the liver in humans. The reputation of *P. argentea* and other members of the genus as medicinal plants or astringents originally gave the genus its name, *Potentilla*, which is the diminutive of Latin *potens*, meaning powerful (USDA 1960; Robertson 1974; Stuhr 1933). Several species of the genus have been used for tanning hides (Stuhr 1933).

4. Geographical Distribution

In Canada, *P. recta* occurs mainly in Ontario, Quebec, and eastern provinces where the soils were formed from sedimentary rock; scattered populations also occur in Manitoba and southern British Columbia. *P. argentea* is found in every province but Alberta, mainly below 50°N. *P. norvegica* extends further north (to the MacKenzie River Delta) and is more widely dispersed throughout every province of Canada than the other two species. Figure 4 gives the distribution of *P. recta, P. norvegica,* and *P. argentea,* respectively, in Canada and bordering the U.S.A.

In North America, *P. recta* reaches south to Georgia and Texas, and is also found in Montana, Oregon and Washington. It occurs sparsely in England; in central and southern Europe from central France and Germany to central Spain, Sicily and the Middle East; in the mountains of North Africa; western and central Asia to approx. 100°E; south to Asia Minor; and northern Iran. *P. norvegica* is circumboreal. In the Western hemisphere it reaches south from Canada to South Carolina, Texas and California and extends in the Rocky Mountains into Mexico. It is found in southeast England; North and Central Europe from Scandinavia to Switzerland, Hungary and central Russia; from northern Asia to Kamchatka. (see also section 6). In the U.S.A., *P. argentea* extends south to Maryland, westward through Ohio to Kansas and north to North Dakota; also Oregon and Washington. In Europe: southern England and Scandinavia to central Spain, Italy and Greece; and in Asia: western and central parts to Asia Minor, Turkistan and Lake Baikal (Robertson 1974; Clapham et al. 1952; Kelley 1953; Rydberg 1898).

5. Habitat

a) *Climatic requirements* — In Canada, the distribution of *P. recta* corresponds to those areas with 750–1,250 mm (30–50 inches) mean annual precipitation (cf. Brooks and Connor 1936), or where less than 1% of the minimum daily temperatures fall below 0 C in May and less than 5% below 10 C in July (cf. Rayner 1961). *P. argentea* extends into slightly drier and colder areas. The northern limit of *P. norvegica* follows as isopleth where 70% of the minimum daily temperatures fall below 0 C in May but less than 1% fall below 0 C in July; mean annual precipitation is 500 mm (20 inches). All species extend southward into the United States. No more specific information is available.

b) *Substratum* — *P. recta* grows mainly in dry fields and waste areas; Fogg (1956) states that it flourishes best in limey or stony soils. Sandy soils are apparently optimum for *P. argentea* (Beal 1910). *P. norvegica* grows best on moist or wet land (Beal 1910), but may be found also on dry soils.

c) *Communities in which the species occur* — In abondoned fields *P. recta* is found from the earliest stages of succession until extensive woody cover is present. It is also seen along wood margins, but not under a forest canopy. Besides its common occurrence in abandoned fields, along roadsides and in openings in thickets, *P. norvegica* is also common in agricultural fields of clover, timothy, and red top. *P. argentea* thrives in open sandy areas of abandoned fields, meadows, pastures and lawns.

Populations of *Potentilla* species were examined in August 1975, in Kalamazoo Co., Mich., U.S.A. In a first-year fallow field, *P. norvegica* (17% ground cover, average of five plots, each 0.5 × 0.5 m) was growing in association with the following dominants (species > 10% cover): *Erigeron annuus* (L.) Pers. (24%), *Barbarea vulgaris* R. Br. (15%), *Aster pilosus* Willd. (12%), *Potentilla recta* L. (12%), *Achillea millefolium* L. (12%). In a 3rd-yr fallow field, *P. argentea* (4% cover) was found with the following dominants: *Bromus inermis* L. (14%), *Ambrosia artemisiifolia* L. (14%), *Poa compressa* L. (14%), *Potentilla recta* L. (14%), *Aster pilosus* Willd. (12%). In a 10th-yr fallow field, *P. recta* L. (24% cover) was found with the following dominants: *Aster pilosus* Willd. (39%), *Rhus typhina* L. (20%), *Achillea millefolium* L. (11%), *Daucus carota* L. (11%), *Poa compressa* L. (11%).

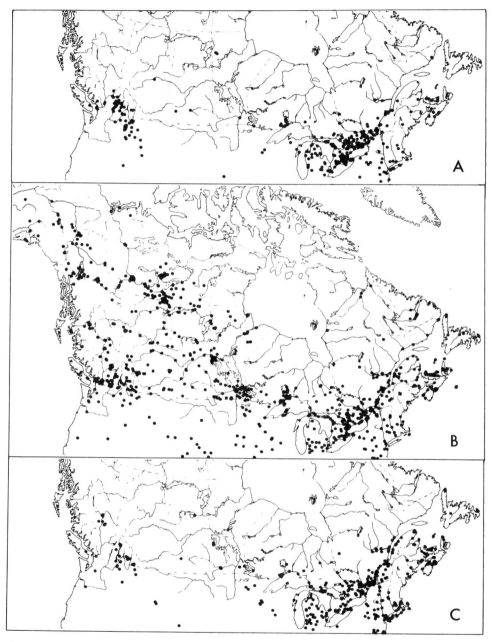

Fig. 4. Distribution of three species of *Potentilla* in Canada and adjacent United States: A. *P. recta*, B. *P. norvegica*, C. *P. argentea* from herbarium specimens (see acknowledgments).

6. History

The first introduction of *Potentilla recta* from Europe to North America occurred sometime before 1900, first referred to in the 1897 edition of Britton and Brown, where it was reported in Ontario. Fernald's 1950 revision of Gray's Manual of Botany gives its Canadian distribution as Newfoundland and Nova Scotia to Ontario, and notes that it was rapidly spreading. The exact time and place of the original introduction is not known.

P. norvegica is probably native to both Eurasia and North America. However, there has been some confusion as to whether what is called *P. norvegica* in North America is the same species as that in Europe. In Rydberg's monograph on *Potentilla* (1898) two subspecies of *P. monspeliensis* L. are recognized: var. *monspeliensis*, the North American variety, and var. *norvegica*, the European variety (the latter originally *P. norvegica* L.). Clapham et al. (1952) identified, but did not name, a North American variety of the European species *P. norvegica* L. Although most literature now refers to both forms simply as *P. norvegica* L., the classification has never been entirely resolved; as recently as 1970 Asker (1970a) referred to *P. norvegica* as only occasionally introduced in North America, and *P. monspeliensis*, the "substitute species," as indigenous to N. America. Probably the clearest statement of the problem is offered by Frankton and Mulligan (1970) who recognize that there exist undefined differences between native North American and the Old World forms and that probably both are present in Canada now, with eastern Canadian populations being largely introduced from Europe. *P. norvegica* is noted as one taxon or another in the earliest floras of North America and no significant changes in its distribution have occurred in the last 100 yr.

Even less is known of the history of *P. argentea* in Canada. It is probably native to both Eurasia and North America (cf. Macoun 1883; Rydberg 1898).

7. Growth and Development

(a) *Morphology* — The usual pattern of yearly regeneration of the perennial *P. recta* is by new shoots appearing near the edges of root "mass," while the old central core slowly rots away, probably taking 6 yr or more to disintegrate completely. The result is that long-lived plants are in the form of a circle of upright stems with only old stem and leaf tissue in the center. Grasses and seedlings of *Daucus carota* L. have been observed in this central area. The growth pattern is similar to that of *P. erecta* in the Soviet Union (Rabotnov, personal communication).

The ability of *P. recta* to develop a massive woody root is an aid to its survival along roadsides and other areas that are cut periodically. This root, acting as a storage organ, sends up new shoots quickly when others are cut off (see section 12).

Plasticity of growth form is an aid to the survival of *P. argentea* and *P. norvegica*. In Siberia, with cold winters, winds and night frosts in the spring, *P. argentea* develops a large rosette, with many leaves and the ability to produce up to 64 stems per plant in one growing season (Kott 1944). *P. norvegica* is a perennial in Siberia (Hooker 1884), a biennial in dry waste areas, and an annual in cultivated ground (Darlington et al. 1940).

(b) *Perennation* — Both *P. recta* and *P. argentea* are classified as semirosette hemicryptophyte only, while *P. norvegica* may also be a therophyte in its annual form (Clapham et al. 1952).

(c) *Physiological data* — None are available.

(d) *Phenology* — In Michigan in 1975 (a dry summer), *Potentilla* species began flowering about 1 June, with the peak (majority of buds in anthesis) about 21 June for *P. recta*, 15 June for *P. argentea*, and 27 June for *P. norvegica*. On any individual plant, flowers are produced for many weeks, the earliest forming mature seed heads at the same time the later buds are coming into flower. Flowering in *P. recta* and *P. argentea* continued until approximately 7 August. At that time 59.8% of the seed heads had produced mature seeds in *P. recta* and 54.9% in *P. argentea*. At that time, *P. norvegica* had only begun to produce mature seed heads (2.7%); flowering continued through early September.

(e) *Mycorrhiza* — None known.

8. Reproduction

(a) *Floral biology* — While polypoloidy is common, aneuploidy and odd-level polyploids are rare (Robertson 1974) and triploids are unknown (Asker 1970b) in the genus *Potentilla*. *P. recta* is polyploid and sexually reproducing, often with extensive ecotype formation (Robertson 1974). *P. norvegica* (European specimens) are thought to be obligate apomictic (Asker and Frost 1972). *P. argentea* is predominately apomictic, but some genotypes (e.g., $2n = 14$) have been reported to be sexual in reproduction (Asker 1970a).

In the summer of 1975, a field experiment was conducted in Michigan to determine whether plants of *P. recta* are out-crossers. In early June, prior to flower development, the inflorescence of each of six plants was covered with a nylon airflow pollination bag that allowed passage of moisture and air, but not pollen or insects. Each was secured tightly under the head close to the stem. The nearest *P. recta* plant to each bagged plant was designated a control. In August, after flowering was finished, the bagged and control heads were removed to the laboratory where 10 seeds from each plant were randomly selected and weighed using a Cahn electrobalance. No mold or visible differences between heads was observed.

When cross-pollination was prevented, fewer seeds developed to maturity: 7.6 ± 1.8 (SE) per flower compared to 57.8 ± 4.5 (SE) for the controls. However, the few seeds that did develop when cross-pollination was prevented were heavier than the seeds from the control plants: 0.40 ± 0.02 (SE) mg, compared to 0.25 ± 0.01 (SE) mg for controls (Table 1). Paired t tests produced a t value of -10.440 (df = 5) with a probability of < 0.01 that the two groups of flowers had the same number of seeds and a t value of 6.108 (df = 5) with a probability of < 0.01 that the two groups of seeds were the same weight. The above results indicate that allogamy is the most common means of fertilization in *P. recta*, but that a few seeds are produced by some type of selfing. When a reduced number of seeds are developed to maturity, they are heavier in weight than when all seeds develop. Further research into the effects of pollination and fertilization in development of the achenes is called for. Bees of the subfamily Andreninae with large amounts of pollen on their last pair of legs have been observed visiting *P. recta*, although their effectiveness as pollinators is unknown.

Table 1. Effects of preventing cross pollination on numbers and weight of developed seeds (achenes)

Plant no.	Mean number of seeds per flower		Mean weight of all seeds (mg)	
	Cross pollination prevented	Control	Cross pollination prevented	Control
1	1.8	54.6	0.48	0.26
2	7.1	45.0	0.42	0.26
3	10.1	49.0	0.41	0.26
4	13.6	67.0	0.40	0.23
5	3.7	57.0	0.30	0.26
6	9.2	74.0	0.39	0.23
$\bar{x}$ ($\pm$ SE)	7.6 ($\pm$ 1.8)	57.8 ($\pm$ 4.5)	0.40 ($\pm$ 0.02)	0.25 ($\pm$ 0.01)

(b) *Seed production and dispersal* — Populations of *Potentilla* described in section 5c were examined for seed (achene) production. *P. recta* (10th-yr field only) averaged 61.5 ± 28.0 (SD; $n = 15$) seeds per flower, 25.0 ± 10.7 (SD; $n = 20$) flowers per stem, and 1.1 ± 0.4 (SD; $n = 15$) stems per plant; hence a single plant might be expected to produce approximately 1,650 seeds. *P. norvegica* averaged 98.7 ± 45.1 (SD; $n = 15$) seeds per flower, 102.5 ± 45.1 (SD; $n = 10$) flowers per stem, and 1.3 ± 0.5 (SD; $n = 10$) stems per plant; therefore a single plant might be expected to produce approximately 13,150 seeds. *P. argentea* averaged 30.9 ± 23.9 (SD; $n = 15$) seeds per flower, 16.3 ± 14.6 (SD; $n = 20$) flowers per stem, and 1.7 ± 1.6 (SD; $n = 10$) stems per plant; hence a single plant might be expected to produce approximately 860 seeds. When mature, the seeds fall passively from the parent plant.

(c) *Viability of seeds and germination* — Kelley (1953) tested germinability of seeds of these three species of cinquefoil. Maximum germination, 17.5% ($\bar{x}$, two replications) for *P. recta* occurred with seeds stored under moist conditions, after 1 mo of storage in sand or 2 mo in peat. Germination was very low in seeds stored in dry conditions. For *P. argentea*, maximum germination also occurred with seed from wet storage, with a high of 60% ($\bar{x}$, two reps) after 3 mo storage in peat. *P. norvegica* displayed a maximum of only 4.5% ($\bar{x}$, two reps) germination and no noticeable trends in duration or type of storage.

Taylorson (1969) found that germination in *P. norvegica* is under photocontrol. Exposure to light after 3 days' imbibition caused full promotion of germination. Twenty-four hours of continuous unfiltered fluorescent light was enough to give 96% germination. When a temperature shift to 40 C for 2 h was added at the conclusion of the normal imbibition period (at 25 C), the time required in continuous light to give maximum germination decreased. When the seeds were imbibed in 0.2% KNO_3 and given the temperature shift, germination was 100% with 24 h of light exposure, and 50% with only one second exposure to red light. Photocontrol of germination for *P. recta* or *P. argentea* has not been tested.

Natural environmental conditions that allow seedling survival are undefined.

(d) *Vegetative reproduction* — None of these species possesses vegetative reproduction in the usual sense, such as by stolons, elongated rhizomes, rooting canes, etc. However, individual plants of *P. recta* may eventually become several independent, closely spaced plants (see section 7a).

9. Hybrids

Hybridization does not occur readily between *Potentilla* species; incompatibility barriers vary in type with species. (Goswami and Matfield 1975).

It is thought that *P. intermedia* is of hybrid origin, being the result of crosses between *P. argentea* and *P. norvegica*; however, such crosses have been unsuccessful when attempted artificially in the lab (Asker 1970a). It is thought that *P. collina* derived from a cross where one of the parents was *P. argentea* and that *P. canescens* resulted from the natural cross of *P. argentea* and *P. recta*. Hence, all three weedy *Potentilla* species are implicated in natural hybrid crosses, but none of these has been supported through experiment and no data are available on such crosses actually occurring in nature.

At least some of the $2n = 14$ races of *P. argentea* are sexual, making hybridization possible. Plants with morphologies intermediate between *P. argentea* and *P. canescens* have frequently been reported (cf. Asker 1970c), but are only very rarely found in herbaria specimens. Since *P. norvegica* is probably never sexual (Asker and Frost 1972), it is an unlikely hybrid parent.

Artificial crosses of several *Potentilla* species (including *P. argentea*) and *Fragaria* spp. (cultivated strawberry) have been attempted in the hope of gaining another economically important plant, but have not been successful to date (Asker 1971).

10. Population Dynamics

A cinquefoil population may extend over several hectares, or along several kilometers of a roadway. Densities of the *Potentilla* populations in the fields described in section 5c are as follows: *P. recta* (10th-yr field only), 2.67 flowering stems per m^2; *P. norvegica*, 0.04 flowering stems/m^2; and *P. argentea*, 1.67 flowering stems/m^2 in vegetation dominated by *Bromus inermis* L., 3.67/m^2 where *Ambrosia artemisiifolia* L. is dominant. In areas other than those described above, *P. recta* has been recorded with densities as high as 39.0 flowering plants/m^2 (Soule and Werner, in prep).

Aging of *Potentilla* plants by counting rings ("frost signatures") in the root crown is not possible after approximately the 6th yr, since the central core disintegrates (see section 7a); estimates based on total diameter of the plants indicate that 20-yr-old plants are not unusual (Soule and Werner, in prep).

A prediction of growth potential of a population can be made from the number of seeds produced, germination rate, and seedling survival rate. On an areal basis, the populations described in section 5c produced the following mean number of seeds: *P. recta* (10th-yr field only), 4,400/m^2; *P. norvegica*, 530/m^2; and *P. argentea*, 1,440–3,160/m^2. Rates of germination and seedling survival are unknown at the present time.

11. Response to Herbicides and Other Chemicals

Repeated applications of 2,4-D, 2, 3, 4-T or Silvex (or a single application > 16 oz/acre) in the spring or fall (the rosette stage) provides control of *Potentilla recta*. *P. norvegica* may be controlled by the same methods with 2,4-D or Silvex (Ontario Herbicide Committee 1968). No herbicide control is specified in the literature, but *P. argentea* can be eradicated by planting to a vigorous-growing crop or enriching the soil (Darlington et al. 1940).

12. Response to Other Human Manipulations

P. recta subjected to monthly mowing may develop bulky, horizontally spreading roots. In Kalamazoo Co., Mich., the mean dry weight of roots was significantly greater in plants growing in a mown strip (4.2 g per plant) than from plants in the adjacent undisturbed field (2.0 g per plant) (Soule and Werner, in prep).

Casual observations of *P. norvegica* and *P. recta* in a manured field in Michigan revealed vigorous plants with a large number of stems per plant which were thicker and taller than those described in the preceding paragraph and in section 5 c.

In a May-plowed field in Michigan, seedlings of *P. recta* and *P. argentea* were numerous by mid-June, as well as plants of *P. recta* emerging from old rootstock. The latter are distinguishable from seedlings in that their leaves, although no larger than the cotyledons of the seedlings, are of mature form, with 5-parted leaves and characteristic narrow, oblanceolate leaflets. Seedling leaves are rounded and are only 1- to 3-parted.

13. Response to Parasites

Insects — the only report of insects on these *Potentilla* spp. was from Poland — eriophid galls on *P. argentea* (Szulczewski 1932).

The USDA Index of Plant Diseases (1960) lists the following microorganism species on *P. recta* — *Septoria rectae* Greene; on *P. norvegica* — *Fabraea dehnii* (Rab.) Nannf., *Marssonina potentillae* (Desm.) Magn., *Mycosphaerella* sp. (*Sphaerella potentillae* Oud.), *Peronospora potentillae* d By., *Phoma potentillica* Allesch., *Phragmidium ivesiae* Syd., *P. potentillae* (Pers.) Karst., *Pucciniastrum potentillae* Kom., *Ramularia arvensis* Sacc., *Rhizoctonia solani* Kuehn, *Septoria purpurascens* Ell. and B. Martin, *Sphaerotheca humuli* (DC.) Burr., *Synchytrium aureum* Schroet., *Taphrina potentillae* (Farl.) Johans., yellow-virus (*Chlorogenus callistephi* Holmes, Calistephus virus 1 K.M. Sm.); and on *P. argentea* — Fabraea dehnii (Rab.) Nannf., *Marssonina potentillae* (Desm.) Magn., and *Peronospora potentillae* d By. Other sources also mention: on *P. recta* — *Phytophthora cactorum* (Leb. & Cohn) Schroet. (Moore et al. 1964), *Septoria potentillae* (Hollós 1926); on *P. norvegica* — *Fusarium acuminatum* Ell. and Ev., *Leptosphaeria doliolum* (Fr.) de Nat., *Leptotrochila repanda* (Fr.) Karst. (*Mollisia dehnii* (Fabh.) Karst.), *Ramularia punctiformis* Sacc. (Conners 1967) and on *P. argentea* — *Phragmidium potentillae* (Nicolas and Aggery 1947).

No higher plant parasites are recorded.

ACKNOWLEDGMENTS

Thanks are expressed to K. A. Erdman, C. E. Johnson, C. I. Weaver, T. L. Dangler, R. Soule, and G. Guth for their various roles in the field research, data analysis, and preparation of figures. The assistance of herbarium personnel at the following institutions is gratefully acknowledged: Department of Agriculture, Ottawa; University of British Columbia; University of Manitoba; Dalhousie University; New York Botanical Garden; University of Idaho; Washington State University; and Michigan State University. The research was supported in part by the National Science Foundation Grants GB-40425 and BMS 74-1602.

ASKER, S. 1970a. Apomictic biotypes in *Potentilla intermedia* and *P. norvegica*. Hereditas **66**: 101–108.

ASKER, S. 1970b. Apomixis and sexuality in the *Potentilla argentea* complex. II. Crosses within the complex. Hereditas **66**: 189–204.

ASKER, S. 1970c. Apomixis and sexuality in the *Potentilla argentea* complex. I. Crosses with other species. Hereditas **66**: 127–144.

ASKER, S. 1971. Some viewpoints on *Fragaria* × *Potentilla* intergeneric hybridization. Hereditas **67**: 181–190.

ASKER, S. and FROST, S. 1970. The "*Potentilla collina* problem" — a chemotaxonomic approach. Hereditas **66**: 49–70.

ASKER, S. and FROST, S. 1972. Plant age and chromatographic pattern in *Potentilla*. Hereditas **72**: 149–152.

BEAL, W. J. 1910. Seeds of Michigan weeds. Mich. State Agric. Coll. Exp. Sta. Div. of Bot. Bull. 260.

BOIVIN, B. 1952. Pugillus potentillarum. Phytologia **4**: 89–93.

BRITTON, N. L. and BROWN, H. A. 1897. An illustrated flora of the northern USA and Canada, Vol. II. Scribner, New York, 643 pp.

BROOKS, C. F. and CONNOR, A. J. 1936. Climatic maps of North America. Harvard Univ. Press, Cambridge, Mass.

CANADIAN DEP. AGRIC. 1967. Diseases of field crops in the prairie provinces. Can. Dep. Agric. Publ. 1008 (revised 1967), Ottawa, Ont.

CANADA WEED COMMITTEE. 1969. Common and botanical names of weeds in Canada. Can. Dep. Agric. Publ. 1397. Ottawa, Ont. 67 pp.

CLAPHAM, A. R., TUTIN, T. G. and WARBURG, E. F. 1952. Flora of the British Isles. Cambridge Univ. Press. 1591 pp.

CONNORS, I. L. 1967. An annotated index of plant diseases in Canada and fungi recorded on plants in Alaska, Canada and Greenland. Can. Dep. Agric. Publ. 1251, Ottawa, Ont.

DARLINGTON, H. T., BESSEY, E. A. and MEGEE, C. R. 1940. Some important Michigan weeds. Mich. State Coll. Agric. Exp. Sta. Spec. Bull. 304.

DARLINGTON, C. D. and WYLIE, A. P. 1956. Chromosome atlas of flowering plants. Macmillan, New York, 519 pp.

FERNALD, M. L. 1950. Gray's manual of botany (8th ed.). American Book Co., New York. 1632 pp.

FERRON, M. et CAYOUETTE, R. 1970. Noms de mauvaises herbes du Québec. Min. Agric. Colonisation, Québec, Qué. 113 pp.

FOGG, J. M. JR. 1956. Weeds of lawn and garden: a handbook for eastern temperate North America. Univ. of Pennsylvania Press, Philadelphia, Pa. 215 pp.

FRANCOIS, L. 1941. Les sémences des plantes commensales des légumineuses fourragères et des graminées des prairies [The seed of plants commensal with the forage legumes and grains of the prairies.] Ann. Epiphyt. Phytogénet. **7**: (spec. no.) 33–90.

FRANKTON, C. and MULLIGAN, G. A. 1970. Weeds of Canada. Queen's Printer, Ottawa, Ont. 217 pp.

GOSWAMI, D. A. and MATFIELD, B. 1975. Cytogenetic studies in the genus *Potentilla* L. New Phytol. **75**: 135–146.

GRAY, A. 1889. Manual of the botany of the northern United States. 6th ed. American Book Co., New York.

HERRMANN, K. 1957. The tannins of *Rhizoma tormentillae*. Arch. Pharm. U. Ber. deutsch pharm. Ges. **290**(62): 276–280.

HILLMAN, F. H. 1897. Nevada and other weed seeds. Nev. Agric. Exp. Sta. Bull. 38.

HOLLÓS, L. 1926. Új gombák Szekszárd vidékérviöl. Math. és Term.-Tud. Közlemen yekböl [Budapest] **35**: 1–64.

HOOKER, J. D. 1884. The student's flora of the British Isles. Macmillian Co., London. 563 pp.

KELLEY, W. R. 1953. Study of seed identification and seed germination of *Potentilla* spp. and *Veronica* spp. Cornell Univ. Agric. Exp. Sta. Mem. 317.

KOTT, S. O. 1944. Onekotorykh osobennostiakh razvitia sornykh rasteniy Sibiri. [Certain peculiarities of weed development in Siberia] Sovetskaia Bot. (Leningrad) (**4/5**): 81–84.

MACOUN, J. 1883. Catalogue of Canadian plants. Geological survey of Canada. Vol. 1. Dawson Bros., Montreal, Que.

McINTOSH, D. L. 1972. Effects of soil water suction, soil temperature, carbon and nitrogen amendments, and host rootlets on survival in soil of zoospores of *Phytophthora cactorum*. Can. J. Bot. **50**(2): 269–272.

MOORE, J. N., SCOTT, D. H. and CONVERSE, R. H. 1964. Pathogenicity of *Phytophthora fragariae* to certain *Potentilla* species. Phytopathology **54**(2): 173–176.

MULLIGAN, G. A. 1959. Chromosome numbers of Canadian weeds. II. Can. J. Bot. **37**: 81–92.

NICOLAS, G. and AGGERY, W. 1947. Notes phytopathologiques (5). Bull. Soc. Hist. Nat. Toulouse **82** (1/2): 123–130.

NIENHAUS, F. 1960. Das Wirtsspektrum von *Phytophthora cactorum* (Leb. & Cohn) Schroet. Phytopathol. Z. **38**: 33–68.

ONTARIO HERBICIDE COMMITTEE. 1968. Guide to chemical weed control. Ontario Dep. Agric. and Food, Toronto, Ont. 87 pp.

PAMMEL, L. H. and KING, C. M. 1910. Results of seed investigations for 1908-1909. Iowa Agric. Exp. Sta. Bull. 115.

PHILLIPS, C. E. 1956. Weeds of the northeast: aids to their identification by basal-leaf characteristics. Univ. of Delaware Agric. Exp. Sta. Field Manu. 1.

RAYNER, J. N., ed. 1961. Atlas of surface temperature frequencies for North America and Greenland. Arctic Meteorol. Res. Group Publ. 33., Montreal, Que.

ROBERTSON, K. R. 1974. The genera of Rosaceae in the southeastern United States. J. Arnold Arbor. **55**: 344–401.

RYDBERG, P. A. 1898. A monograph of the North American Potentilleae. Mem. Dep. Bot. Columbia Univ. **2**: 1–221.

SAVILE, D. B. 1951. Changes in grassland near Ottawa, Ontario, following prolonged flooding. Can. Field Nat. **65**(1): 42–45.

STAROSTENKO, N. T. and STAROSTENKO, V. N. 1971. Lechebnol deistvie serebristoi lapchatki pri tsirrozakh pecheni v otechno-astsiti cheskoi stadii [Therapeutic effect of the silver-leaved cinquefoil in cirrhosis of the liver in the edema-ascitic stage.] Zdravookhranenie (Kishinev) **14**(6): 15–19.

STUHR, E. T. 1933. A manual of Pacific Coast drug plants. Science Press, Lancaster, Pa. 189 pp.

SZULCZEWSKI, J. W. 1932. Ergänzung zum zooecidienverzeichnis gross polens. Bull. Soc. Amis. Sci. Poznan. Ser. B. **5**: 51–57.

TAYLORSON, R. B. 1969. Photocontrol of rough cinquefoil seed germination and its enchancement by temperature manipulation and KNO_3. Weed Sci. **17**(2): 144–148.

UNITED STATES DEPARTMENT OF AGRICULTURE. 1926. Check list of diseases of economic plants in the U.S.A. USDA Bull. 1336.

UNITED STATES DEPARTMENT OF AGRICULTURE. 1930. Strawberry diseases. USDA Farmer's Bull. no. 1458.

UNITED STATES DEPARTMENT OF AGRICULTURE. 1960. Index of plant diseases. U.S.A. Agric. Handb. 165. U.S. Gov. Print. Office, Washington, D.C. 531 pp.

WHITTAKER, R. H. and FEENY, P. P. 1971. Allelochemics: chemical interactions between species. Science **171**: 757–770.

220

THE BIOLOGY OF CANADIAN WEEDS
19. *Asclepias syriaca* L.

PRASANTA C. BHOWMIK and JOHN D. BANDEEN

Department of Crop Science, University of Guelph, Guelph, Ontario.
Received 8 Aug. 1975, accepted 9 Apr. 1976.

BHOWMIK, PRASANTA C. AND BANDEEN, JOHN D. 1976. The biology of Canadian weeds. 19. *Asclepias syriaca* L. Can. J. Plant Sci. **56**: 579–589.

This summary of biological data is for common milkweed (*Asclepias syriaca* L.), as a weed in Canada, particularly in eastern Canada. Weedy populations of this perennial occur in great abundance in southern Ontario and Quebec. It belongs to association of plants of roadsides, waste lands and river basins. Recently, this weed has spread into cultivated lands, especially cereals, row crops and forage crops.

Les auteurs récapitulent la biologie de l'Asclépiade commune (*Asclepias syriaca* L.) laquelle pousse à l'état adventice au Canada, et surtout dans l'est du pays. Des colonies abondantes de cette plante peuvent s'observer dans le sud de l'Ontario et du Québec. On la retrouve en associations sur les talus de routes, les terrains incultes et les berges des rivières. Ces dernières années, elle a envahi les terres en culture, surtout les céréales, les cultures sarclées et les cultures herbagères.

1. Name

Asclepias syricaca L. — **common milkweed** (Canada Weed Committee 1969), silkweed, cotton weed, wild cotton; **asclepiade de Syrie** (Ferron et Cayouette 1971). Asclepiadaceae, milkweed family, Asclepiadacées.

2. Description and Account of Variation

(a) Perennial with creeping underground rootstocks; reproducing by seeds and by adventitious root buds; simple stems up to 60–120 cm high, usually several together. All parts of the plant contain a milky juice. Leaves opposite, oblong and entire 5–15 cm broad and 7–20 cm long; short stalked, prominently veined, smooth margined, green on the upper surface but light colored and hairy on the lower surface. Flowers in umbels at the top of the stem or in the axils of the upper leaves; individual flowers on long, rather weak pedicels and about 0.95 cm in diameter; purplish or rarely white, fragrant; corolla lobes 6–9 mm long; hoods 3–4 mm high, ovate, obtuse; ovaries 2, the terminal portion of their styles united into a

fleshy disk, on the undersurface of which there are 5 stigmatic areas each of which is enclosed in a chamber formed by the margins of two adjacent stamen filaments; pollen contained in sacs (pollinia) which are set in pockets of the flattened filaments; 2 pollinia per stamen; pollinia attached in pairs (one from each of adjacent stamens) by a thin band (retinaculum); seed pods (follicles) grey; slenderly ovoid, hairy and covered with soft projections; 7–10 cm long and about 2.5 cm broad, splits open along one side exposing many seeds. Seeds 0.77–0.79 cm long, brown, flat and oval with a tuft of silky hairs.

Moore (1946b) and Mulligan (1961) have reported chromosome counts of $2n=22$ for Canadian material of *Asclepias syriaca*.

A. speciosa Torr. is very similar to common milkweed. It differs in having broad, oval and rounded or somewhat heart-shaped leaves, densely woolly flower stalks and fewer and longer flowers. Flowers have long and lanceolate hood (3 times as long as stamens) on corolla (Budd and Best 1964). The dogbanes (*Apocynum* spp.) also have milky juice and seeds with a tuft of hairs, but are unlike the milkweeds in their small bell-shaped flowers, very narrow fruits and small slender seeds (Frankton and Mulligan 1970).

Common milkweed plant parts at various stages of growth are shown in Fig. 1.

3. Economic Importance

(a) Detrimental — According to Evetts (1970), infestation of common milkweed caused an average yield loss of 720 kg/ha in sorghum (*Sorghum bicolor* (L.) Moench) and the yield loss became greater as the population of this weed increased in subsequent years.

(b) Beneficial — The Chippewa Indians used the flowers of *A. syriaca* in a stewed form and Iroquois ate young sprouts and buds (Berkman 1949). Kirkwood (1867) considered milkweed fiber as a textile material and also as a raw material in the paper industry. The literature referring to many uses of common milkweed has been summarized by Whiting in 1943. The possibilities of common milkweed have been studied particularly in France, Germany, the U.S.S.R., the United States and Canada (Senn 1944). These included the use of bast fiber of the stem as commercial fiber for textile, the floss as a substitute for kapok, the latex as a commercial rubber, the stems as raw material in the paper industry and the seeds as a source of oil and meal. The use of floss as an emergency material during the World War II established the plant's potential value (Berkman 1949).

Common milkweed flowers provide a source of honey for butterflies, bees and other insects. The leaves are the food for the larvae of an entire group of tropical insects, the Danainae (Brower 1969), including the familiar monarch and queen butterflies (Hutchings 1923).

(c) Legislation — Common milkweed is classified as a noxious weed in the Noxious Weeds Act of Ontario (Anonymous 1971), Manitoba (Anonymous 1968a) and Quebec

(Anonymous 1964). In the regulations to the Weed Control Act for Nova Scotia (Anonymous 1968b) common milkweed is considered 'class number one' noxious. This weed is not listed in Seeds Act and Regulations administered by Agriculture Canada (1967).

4. Geographical Distribution

The geographical boundary of this weed in North America is 35° and 50° north latitude and 60° and 103° west longitude (Woodson 1954; Doyon 1958). According to the Canadian Weed Survey (Groh 1943), common milkweed was found to be growing in all provinces from Saskatchewan eastward with the exception of Prince Edward Island. The recent study of herbarium specimens of *A. syriaca* by the authors reveals that this weed is found in all provinces from Manitoba eastwards with the exception of Newfoundland. The greatest concentration of this weed is found in the southern parts of Ontario and Quebec (Fig. 2).

5. Habitat

(a) Climatic requirements — According to Groh and Dore (1945), Woodson (1954) and Doyon (1958), the habital distribution is limited by 18 and 32 C mean July temperatures in the north and south, respectively, and growth is limited by a minimum of 50 cm rainfall in the three summer months. Excessive moisture, however, appears to be definitely harmful. Warm, dry soil resulting from good exposure and drainage is advantageous. Fully grown plants withstand drought well, but seedlings and young plants may easily be damaged by prolonged dry weather. Milkweed grows best in 30% to full sunlight (Berkman 1949).

(b) Substratum — Excellent stands of common milkweed are found in soils of all textural groups, especially when they tend to be of a loamy character and are well drained. Groh (1943) reported an alkaline preference of this species in eastern Canada. However, earlier studies indicated

Fig. 1. Common milkweed, *Asclepias syriaca*. Mature plants with (a) single stems as a clump and (b) inflorescence; plants (c) 9 mo old and (d) 2 mo old, grown from 5-cm-long rootstock, showing root establishment and root bud sprouting; seedlings (e) 14 days old and (f) $2^1/_2$ mo old, with root system.

223

that common milkweed was abundant in northern Michigan acid soils (Timmons 1946) and in soils with a *p*H range of 4–5 (Spurway 1941). The absence of boron from the soil prevents the occurrence of milkweed in some areas of the United States (Berkman 1949).

(c) Communities in which the species occurs — Common milkweed is abundant on roadsides, fencerows, railroads, waste lands and river basins. Recently, it has become more common in cereals, field crops and forage crops. Groh and Dore (1945) reported the presence of this weed in wooded areas (20%) and in cleared, grass- or marshland (80%) in Ontario. Common milkweed was found in succession in areas of Quebec, dominated by *Poa pratensis* L. and *Agrostis alba* L. (Doyon 1960).

6. History

Common milkweed is native in eastern North America (Fernald 1950) and is one of 13 species of *Asclepias* found in Canada (Boivin 1966). This weed was an early introduction from eastern North America to southern Europe.

7. Growth and Development

(a) Morphology — Common milkweed propagates by seeds and by underground rootstocks bearing adventitious buds which are capable of sprouting in a favorable environment. The sprouting usually occurs late in the season during the 1st yr of seedling growth, but can occur at any time during the growing season if the plant or rootstock is disturbed either by grazing or by agricultural practices.

(b) Perennation — The perennating activity is renewed annually from adventitious root buds. The buds are located either on the stem-base near the soil surface or on lateral roots (Bhowmik and Bandeen 1970a). The parent root survives for two or more growing seasons depending on soil conditions and frequency of tillage practices. Most buds remain viable throughout the severe winter months and sprout with the advent of spring weather.

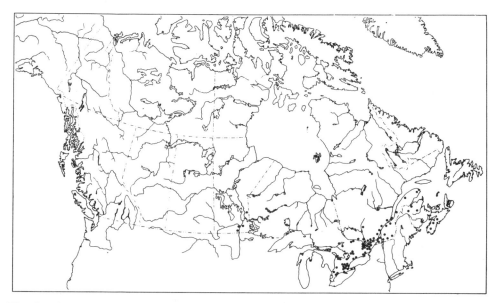

Fig. 2. Canadian distribution of *Asclepias syriaca* from specimens in Biosystematics Research Institute, Agriculture Canada, Ottawa; Royal Botanical Garden, Hamilton; Department of Botany, University of Toronto, Toronto; and Department of Botany, University of Guelph, Guelph.

(c) Physiological data — Limited physiological data are available at the present time. Our own results indicate that this species grows normally at a temperature of 27 C under 16-h photoperiod. Sixty-day-old seedlings produced as many as 52 buds on the root system at 27 C temperature and 16-h photoperiod (Bhowmik and Bandeen 1973a). The rate of seedling growth decreased, producing small plants with narrow leaves, as temperature decreased to 15 C. Interaction effects between temperature and photoperiod were significant on root and shoot growth as was evident by greater accumulation of dry matter with each increment of either temperature or photoperiod (Bhowmik and Bandeen 1968a,b).

(d) Phenology — The aerial shoots emerge in spring (April–May) from underground root buds. Active aerial growth commences as the weather becomes warmer. When there is ample foliage, surface root development becomes active. Root extension starts later in the year (July-August), but new shoots do not reach the surface until the following spring (Groh and Dore 1945). Root growth terminates during mid-August to mid-September when the majority of shoots become senescent. Seedlings do not flower during the 1st yr of growth (Kirkwood 1867; Bhowmik and Bandeen 1970a). However, newly developed shoots from the same root system flower normally during the next growing season. Flowering occurs in late June–July or early August depending on initial growth, weather and location. Doyon (1958) indicated that flowering in common milkweed does not occur before mid-June in Quebec.

(e) Mycorrhiza — None is known.

8. Reproduction

(a) Floral biology — *Asclepias syriaca* is allogamous (Mulligan and Kevan 1973) and this species is highly self-sterile (Moore 1947). Retinacula of the pollinia become entangled on legs of insects and the pollen sacs are inserted into the stigmatic chambers of the flower. The duration of flowering varies from plant to plant, umbel to umbel (Moore 1947) and clone to clone (Stolbin 1937). From the lowest umbel, flowering progresses rapidly upwards. Moore (1947) found that all flowers of an umbel usually opened within a period of 2–3 days. About 7 days elapsed between dates of full flowering of the lowest and the uppermost umbel of a stem of 4–6 inflorescences.

In our field study at the Elora Research Station, Guelph, Ontario, 3–7 inflorescences on each stalk and 8–128 flowers per inflorescence were found. A high percentage of flowers fell 10–12 days after opening. However, only 2–4% of the flowers produced matured pods.

The Hymenoptera, primarily wasps and bees, are largely responsible for pollination (Stevens 1951; Doyon 1960). Doyon (1960) did not think that the monarch butterfly (Danainae) played any role in insect pollination in contrast to Huchings (1923) who reported that the monarch butterfly was a pollinator.

(b) Seed production and dispersal — Enlargement of one or both of the ovaries of a flower follows successful pollination (Moore 1947). Young seeds increase in size, particularly at the micropylar end, and in a plane that is approximately at right angles to the placental ridge to which the seed is attached (Pearson 1948). Moore (1946a; 1947) found that about 50–75% of the enlarged ovaries of an umbel aborted. In our studies, an average of 4–6 pods per stalk, each with 150–425 seeds was found. The weight per 100 seeds ranged from 42.0 mg (Stevens 1932) and 43.4 to 73.1 mg (Bhowmik and Bandeen 1973a).

The seed pods mature and split open early in the fall (September–October) and the seeds are dispersed by wind, carried by the tufts of floss. Mature pods are found attached to dead stalks until late fall (November–December) and even in the following spring. According to our estimation, a hectare of common milkweed, consisting of 59,893 stalks, each with an average of five pods and each pod with an average of 290 seeds, could produce as many as 86,844,850 seeds.

(c) Viability of seeds and germination — At maturity or a few days after collection, seeds germinate poorly (Groh 1943; Bhowmik 1970; P. B. Cavers, personal communication). The initial viability of this weed was reported to be 97% based on a tetrazolium (0.1% solution of 2,3,5-triphenyl tetrazolium) test (Evetts and Burnside 1972a). Common milkweed seeds remained viable (32% germination) even after 9 yr of storage in glass jars (Groh 1943), but viability of the seeds declined sharply to about 8% after 7 yr when they were stored in an envelope. Crocker (1938) reported that Shull (1914) found that seeds of *A. syriaca* when kept in an inundated soil at the freezing point germinated after $4^1/4$ yr. On the other hand, normal viable seeds (54% germination) were destroyed when heated at 95 C for 15 min (Hopkins 1936).

Common milkweed seeds require a 1-yr period of after-ripening before they can germinate moderately well (Groh 1943; Bhowmik 1970). Storage at different temperatures (-12, 5, 21 C) did not improve germination for the first 3–4 mo of storage. However, germination was about 76% after 11 mo of storage at room temperature (21 C).

Seed treatments with gibberellic acid (10–400 ppm W), kinetin (25–400 ppm W) (Evetts and Burnside 1972a); thiourea (50 mM), potassium nitrate (25 mM), kinetin (0.1 mM), gibberellic acid (0.3 mM) (Oegema and Fletcher 1972); concentrated sulphuric acid (3-6 min) (Gerhardt 1929) all seemed to promote seed germination. Gerhardt (1929) found that germination of common milkweed seeds increased from 24 to 46% when they were incubated in pure oxygen. Stratifying seeds in water at low temperature caused a significant increase in germination (Poptsov and Kichyenova 1950; Jeffery and Robinson 1971; Evetts

and Burnside 1972a) and the optimum time was found to be 7–28 days at 5 C (Evetts and Burnside 1972a).

The maximum and minimum germinating temperatures were reported to be 35 C or 35–40 C and 15 C or 15–20 C, respectively (Evetts and Burnside 1972a). Our own experiments revealed that maximum seedling emergence occurred at 27 C air temperature compared to 21 or 10 C (Bhowmik 1970).

(d) Vegetative reproduction — Seedlings produce buds on the main root close to the ground surface within a period of 18–21 days after emergence (Bhowmik and Bandeen 1970a). Evetts and Burnside (1972a) found that 28% of the seedlings sprouted when the top growth of 21-day-old common milkweed seedlings was removed.

The sprouting activity increased and the number of days until sprouting decreased as days from planting to clipping increased (Evetts and Burnside 1972a; Bhowmik and Bandeen 1973b). The survival and regrowth of seedlings increased as seedlings developed additional leaf pairs. The number of sprouted buds ranged from 5 to 100% when the seedlings were clipped at the heights of 2–3 cm and 7.5–12.0 cm, respectively (Jeffery and Robinson 1971), and from 6 to 100% when the seedlings were clipped 16 and 48 days after emergence, respectively (Bhowmik and Bandeen 1973b). These observations show that sprouting does not occur in seedlings until they are clipped, indicating that apical dominance does play a role. Our studies indicated that one seedling, after 4 yr of natural (undisturbed) establishment, produced as many as 56 stalks vegetatively and 94 seedlings in an area of 9 m^2.

Common milkweed roots usually develop to a depth of 100–120 cm (Bhowmik and Bandeen 1970a). Numerous adventitious buds appear throughout the rootstocks, the majority remaining dormant (Gerhardt 1929; Groh and Dore 1945; Bhowmik and Bandeen 1969a) until conditions promote their activity. The lowest root bud dormancy was found in May (Bhowmik and Bandeen 1969a). An average of 13.2% of the rootstocks with a visible bud remained dormant in May compared to 52.2% in September. This dormancy of root buds was broken by high temperature. Thus, the rootstocks collected in May–August and September, sprouted to 80–95 and 67% respectively, when they were incubated at 27 C. On the other hand, rootstocks collected in May–July, sprouted to 25–72% at 15 C. However, there was no sprouting activity in August and September at 15 C. Smaller rootstocks required a longer time for sprouting. Similar observations were made by Groh (1943) who found 90–100% sprouting of rootstocks 30–45 cm in length as compared with a very insignificant sprouting of rootstocks of smaller length.

It has been reported in an earlier study related to the biology of common milkweed (Bhowmik 1970) that an increased root bud dormancy was evident as the total sugar level in rootstocks increased in the fall. The total sugar level in rootstocks reached a plateau (25%) in October after its sharp decline to about 10% in July (Bhowmik and Bandeen 1969b).

9. Hybrids

Moore (1946b) found some plants which appeared to be natural hybrids between *A. syriaca* and *A. speciosa* in experimental plots in which both species were growing.

10. Population Dynamics

According to Groh and Dore (1945), the density of common milkweed on Ontario roadsides ranges for 100 stalks/km in Lincoln County to about 1,863 stalks/km in Essex County. The field stand varied tremendously from 75 stalks/km in Lennox County to 10,954 stalks/km in Renfrew County. Our own observation in field sampling (southern Ontario) showed a variation of 11,819–88,226 stalks/ha.

Recently, a population shift has been observed from roadsides and waste places into fertile cultivated lands. The subsequent spreading into cultivated lands may be related to the removal of annual weeds by the increased use of herbicides that do not control common milkweed. Thus, seedlings become established in patches in cultivated land and spreading occurs into adjacent areas. The plants appear in abundance during June–July. With the advent of winter, the plants die leaving dormant root buds.

Common milkweed is not a good competitor in a cultivated area. Experiments at the Iowa Agricultural Experiment Station and the U.S. Department of Agriculture, at Beltsville, Maryland have established that it is difficult for milkweed to compete with bluegrass the first 2 yr after planting milkweed (Berkman 1949). According to Evetts and Burnside (1975), common milkweed height was significantly reduced by light, soil and full competition with green foxtail (*Setaria viridis* (L.) Beauv.), redroot pigweed (*Amaranthus retroflexus* L.) and sorghum (*Sorghum bicolor* (L.) Moench 'RS-626'), where only green foxtail caused a significant reduction in height due to light competition.

11. Response to Herbicides and Other Chemicals

Growth room studies (Bhowmik and Bandeen 1970b) indicated that the application of 2,4-D ((2,4-dichlorophenoxy) acetic acid) at the rate of 0.28–0.56 kg a.i./ha on 10- or 25-day-old seedlings activated top growth and bud production on the root. However, higher rates of 2,4-D (0.84–1.12 kg a.i./ha) produced restricted and abnormal shoot growth with fewer root buds.

Herbicides such as 2,4-D, Kil-mor (a commercial formulation of 2,4-D, mecoprop (2- ((4-chlor-o-tolyl) oxy) propionic acid) and dicamba (3, 6-dichloro-o-anisic acid)), MCPA (((4-chloro-o-tolyl) oxy) acetic acid) and dicamba destroyed the top growth without any appreciable effect on the root system. This led to vigorous growth of adventitious root buds. The application of amitrole-T (a commercial formulation of amitrole (3-amino-s-triazine) and ammonium thiocyanate) at the rate of 1.12–2.24 kg/ha proved to be effective during the 1st yr, although about 5–10% regrowth occurred in the next growing season (Bandeen 1971). Evetts and Burnside (1972b) found no regrowth of common milkweed in the following two growing seasons when plants were treated with amitrole-T at the rate of 4.48 kg/ha. Recently, the application of glyphosate (N-(phosphonomethyl) glycine), at the rate of 2.24–3.36 kg/ha in August or September 1971, killed the entire top growth in 1971 and allowed only 5–10% (Bandeen 1972) and 8–9% regrowth (Evetts and Burnside 1972b) in the 1972 season. Regrowth also occurred in 1972 season from plots treated in September 1971 with 2,4-D, 2,4,5-T ((2,4,5-trichlorophenoxy) acetic acid) and dicamba (Bandeen 1972). The early application (25 June) of either glyphosate at the rate of 2.24 or 3.36 kg/ha or amitrole-T at the rate of 1.12 or 2.24 kg/ha provided 100% control of common milkweed the following year as compared to late applications (30 July or 30 August) (Bandeen and Bhowmik 1973). Excellent control was obtained during the 1974 season (regrowth counts) from the application of glyphosate in 1973 (Bandeen and Bhowmik 1974). A decrease in control was apparent from late applications (Bandeen and Bhowmik 1973, 1974). At the present time, glyphosate seems to be effective for common milkweed control, although further field testing is needed.

12. Response to Other Human Manipulations

According to Timmons (1946), alfalfa was an effective competitive crop as a cultural practice for the eradication or control of common milkweed in northern Michigan. The density of common milkweed as compared with that on an adjacent unmowed 'old sod,' was 7.1% for alfalfa 3 or more yr old, 54.2% for alfalfa 1 or 2 yr old, 62.9% for wild grass meadow and 87.7% for red or alsike clover. The density of common milkweed in a row crop was 141.4% of that on an adjacent unmowed 'old sod.'

The practice of cultivation can induce a major problem, since underground rootstocks are most likely to be chopped into small fragments and each small fragment can produce a new plant. It is also noted that removal of stalks either by clipping or by other methods induces sprouting of underground root buds. Therefore, human manipulations such as clipping or cultivation can lead to the creation of a large colony of plants.

13. Responses to Parasites

Insects and disease organisms attack common milkweed but can hardly be credited with any great reduction in either density or incidence. Virus diseases result in a dense clumping of stems, together with yellowing or mottling and, finally, deforming of leaves, stems and flowers.

(a) Insects and other nondomestic animals — Doyon (1960) conducted a detailed study on insects found on common milkweed as follows.

HYMENOPTERA: *Tiphia clypeata* Robertson. (wasp), visitor to flower; *Microbembex monodonta* Say. (wasp), visitor to flower; *Formica fusca* L. (ant), lives on aphids; *Apis mellifica* L. (bee), visitor to flower. LEPIDOPTERA: *Phyciodes tharos* Dru., visitor to flower. COLEOPTERA: *Tetraopes teraophtalmus* Forst. (long-horned beetle of milkweed), lives in the stalks and roots; *Coccinella transversoguttata* Fald., lives on aphids; *Brachyacantha ursina* Fab., lives on aphids; *Labidomera clivicollis* kby. (milk butterfly), lives on leaves; *Adalia bipunctata* L., lives on aphids; *Macrodactylus subspinosus* Fab., ordinarily on rose bushes; *Ortholestes cingulatus* Gravenhorst., visitor to flower, lives on dead insects; *Chrysochus aurâtus* Fab., ordinarily on dogbane; *Lucidota corrusca* L., cosmopolitan. HEMIPTERA: *Lygaeus kalmii* Stal. (milkweed stink bug), lives on pith; *Phymata erosa* L., sucks the insects it captures; *Apateticus bracteatus* Fitch., insect predator; *Lygus pratensis* var. *oblineatus* Say. (dull stink bug), lives on grass; *Euschistus tristigmus* Say. (3-spotted stink bug), insect predator; *Sinea diadema* Fab., insect predator. HOMOPTERA: *Ceresa basalis* Wlk., lives on pith; *Ceresa diceros* Say., perhaps sucks from pith. ORTHOPTERA: *Amblycorypha oblongifolia* DeG., lives on grass.

(b) Microorganisms and viruses — The presence of flagella bacteria was recognized by Groh and Dore (1945) in the latex of common milkweed. The virus causing cucumber mosiac disease may winter in milkweed (Koch 1942). Connors (1967) found aster yellow virus (*Cellistephus virus* 1.) in Ontario.

According to Seymour (1929) and Shaw (1958) the following fungi are parasites of common milkweed, BASIDIOMYCETES: *Uromyces asclepiadis* Cke. and *Puccinia bartholomaei* Diet. ASCOMYCETES: *Phyllactinia guttata* Lev., *Erysiphe cichoracearum* DC. and *Glomerella fusarioides* Edgert. FUNGI IMPERFECTI: *Botrytis hypophylla* Ell. & Kell., *Septoria asclepiadis* Sacc., *Ascophyta asclepiadis* Ell. & Ev., *Fusarium roseum* Lk., *Cercospora asclepiadis* Ell. and *Cercospora clavata* (Ger) Cke.

The most frequent disease of common milkweed in Quebec is caused by *Cercospora clavata* (Ger) Cke. (Doyon 1960). Recently, Connors (1967) found this fungus to be widespread in Ontario. He also listed *Uromyces asclepiadis* Cke. (only states II and III are known) as a fungal disease of common milkweed. However, *Uromyces asclepiadis* Cke. appears not to overwinter in Canada and reinfection takes place each year by wind-borne spores from the United States. *Mollisia asclepiadis* Ell. & Ev. (found on dead stems of *Asclepias* spp. in Ontario), *Phyllosticta cornutti* Ell. & Kell, and *Fusarium acuminatum* Ell. & Ev. are other fungi found on common milkweed in Canada (Connors 1967).

ACKNOWLEDGMENTS

The authors acknowledge the cooperation of the herbarium personnel, Biosystematics Research Institute, Canada Department of Agriculture, Ottawa; Royal Botanical Garden, Hamilton; Department of Botany, University of Toronto; and Department of Botany, University of Guelph. The senior author wishes to thank Romain Rioux for English translation of the French papers by Doyon (1958, 1960).

AGRICULTURE CANADA. 1967. Seeds Act and Regulations. Queen's Printers, Ottawa, Ont.

ANONYMOUS. 1964. Réglement concernant les mauvaises herbes. Ministère de l'Agric. Québec. pp. 639–641.

ANONYMOUS. 1968a. The Noxious Weeds Act. Queen's Printer, Winnipeg, Man. 298 pp.

ANONYMOUS. 1968b. Regulations to the Weed Control Act. Queen's Printer, Halifax, N.S. 4 pp.

ANONYMOUS. 1971. The Weed Control Act. Ministry of Agric. and Food, Toronto, Ont. 4 pp.

BANDEEN, J. D. 1971. Milkweed control. Res. Rep. Can. Weed Comm. East. Sect. pp. 234–235.

BANDEEN, J. D. 1972. Milkweed control. Res. Rep. Can. Weed Comm. East. Sect. 258 pp.

BANDEEN, J. D. and BHOWMIK, P. C. 1973. Common milkweed control. Res. Rep. Can. Weed Comm. East. Sect. 292 pp.

BANDEEN, J. D. and BHOWMIK, P. C. 1974. Common milkweed control. Res. Rep. Can. Weed Comm. East. Sect. 329 pp.

BERKMAN, B. 1949. Milkweed — A war strategic material and a potential industrial crop for sub-marginal lands in the United States. Econ. Bot. **3**: 223–239.

BHOWMIK, P. C. 1970. The biology of common milkweed (*Asclepias syriaca* L.) M.Sc. Thesis, Univ. of Guelph, Guelph, Ont.

BHOWMIK, P. C. and BANDEEN, J. D. 1968a. Development of milkweed under different temperatures. Res. Rep. Nat. Weed Comm. East. Sect. 225 pp.

BHOWMIK, P. C. and BANDEEN, J. D. 1968b. Development of milkweed under different photoperiods. Res. Rep. Nat. Weed Comm. East. Sect. 225 pp.

BHOWMIK, P. C. and BANDEEN, J. D. 1969a. Root bud dormancy in milkweed. Res. Rep. Can. Weed Comm. East. Sect. 247 pp.

BHOWMIK, P. C. and BANDEEN, J. D. 1969b. Seasonal patterns of carbohydrate reserves in milkweed. Res. Rep. Can. Weed Comm. East. Sect. 248 pp.

BHOWMIK, P. C. and BANDEEN, J. D. 1970a. Life history of common milkweed. Weed Sci. Soc. Amer. Abstr. No. 12.

BHOWMIK, P. C. and BANDEEN, J. D. 1970b. Effect of 2,4-D on growth and development of milkweed seedlings. Weed Sci. Soc. Amer. Abstr. No. 73.

BHOWMIK, P. C. and BANDEEN, J. D. 1973a. Reproductive nature of common milkweed (*Asclepias syriaca* L.) Can. Bot. Assoc. 8th Annu. Meeting, 30 pp.

BHOWMIK, P. C. and BANDEEN, J. D. 1973b. Regrowth potential of common milkweed seedlings in growth room conditions. Res. Rep. Can. Weed Comm. East. Sect. 277 pp.

BOIVIN, B. 1966. Enumeration des plantes du Canada. Natur. Can. **93**: 424–425.

BROWER, L. P. 1969. Ecological chemistry. Sci. American. **220**: 22–29.

BUDD, A. C. and BEST, K. F. 1964. Wild plants of the Canadian Prairies. Res. Br. Can. Dep. Agric. Publ. 983. pp. 352–353.

CANADA WEED COMMITTEE. 1969. Common and botanical names of weeds in Canada. Can. Dep. Agric. Publ. 1397. 6 pp.

CONNERS, I. L. 1967. An annoted index of plant diseases in Canada and fungi recorded on plants in Alaska, Canada and Greenland. Can. Dep. Agric. Publ. 1251. pp. 44–45.

CROCKER, W. 1938. Life span of seeds. Bot. Rev. **4**: 235–274.

DOYON, D. 1958. Etude de la distribution géographique de l'asclépiade commune (*Asclepias syriaca* L.) en Amérique du Nord. Rapp. Soc. Québec Protect. Plantes **40**: 91–113.

DOYON, D. 1960. Etude bio-écologique d'*Asclepias syriaca* L. Quarante-deuxième Rapp. Soc. Québec Protect. Plantes. pp. 25–30.

EVETTS, L. L. 1970. Ecological studies with common milkweed. M.Sc. Thesis, Univ. of Nebraska, Lincoln, Neb. 70 pp.

EVETTS, L. L. and BURNSIDE, O. C. 1972a. Germination and seedlings development of common milkweed and other species. Weed Sci. **20**: 371–378.

EVETTS, L. L. and BURNSIDE, O. C. 1972b. Control of common milkweed. Res. Rep. Northcentral Weed Control Conf. pp. 36–38.

EVETTS, L. L. and BURNSIDE, O. C. 1975. Effect of early competitions on growth of common milkweed. Weed Sci. **23**: 1–3.

FERNALD, M. L. 1950. Gray's manual of botany, 8th ed. American Book Company, New York.

FERRON, M. and CAYOUETTE, R. 1971. Noms des mauvaises herbes du Québec, Division de la Recherche, Ministère de l'Agriculture et de la Colonisation du Québec. Publ. No. 288. 21 pp.

FRANKTON, C. and MULLIGAN, G. A. 1970. Weeds of Canada. Can. Dep. Agric. Publ. **948**: 217 pp.

GERHARDT, F. 1929. Propagation and food translocation in the common milkweed. J. Agric. Res. **39**: 837–851.

GROH, H. 1943. Notes on common milkweed. Sci. Agric. **23**: 625–632.

GROH, H. and DORE, W. G. 1945. A milkweed survey in Ontario and adjacent Quebec. Sci. Agric. **25**: 463–481.

HOPKINS, C. Y. 1936. Thermal death point of certain weed seeds. Can. J. Bot. **14**: 178–183.

HUTCHINGS, C. B. 1923. A note of the monarch or milkweed butterfly with special reference to its migratory habits. Can. Field Natur. **37**: 150 pp.

JEFFERY, L. R. and ROBINSON, L. R. 1971. Growth characteristics of common milkweed. Weed Sci. **19**: 193–196.

KIRKWOOD, A. 1867. A short treatise on the milkweed or silkweed and the Canadian nettle, viewed as industrial resources. Printed and Published by Hunter, Rose and Co. Ottawa, Ont. (cited by Senn 1944).

KOCH, L. W. 1942. Diseases of greenhouse cucumbers. Can. Dep. Agric. Publ. 741. (Farmer's Bull. 112).

MOORE, R. J. 1946a. Investigations on rubber-bearing plants. III. Development of normal and aborting seeds in *Asclepias syriaca* L. Can. J. Res. **24**: 56–65.

MOORE, R. J. 1946b. Investigations on rubber-bearing plants. IV. Cytogenic studies in *Asclepias* (Tourn.) L. Can. J. Res. **24**: 66–73.

MOORE, R. J. 1947. Investigations on rubber-bearing plants. V. Notes on the flower biology and pod yield of *Asclepias syriaca* L. Can. Field Natur. **61**: 40–66.

MULLIGAN, G. A. 1961. Chromosome numbers of Canadian weeds. III. Can. J. Bot. **39**: 1057–1065.

MULLIGAN, G. A. and KEVAN, P. G. 1973. Colour, brightness, and other floral characteristics attracting insects to the blossoms of some Canadian weeds. Can. J. Bot. **51**: 1939–1952.

OEGEMA, T. and FLETCHER, R. A. 1972. Factors that influence dormancy in milkweed seeds. Can. J. Bot. **50**: 713–718.

PEARSON, N. L. 1948. Observations on seed and seed hair growth in *Asclepias syriaca* L. Amer. J. Bot. **35**: 27–36.

POPTSOV, A. V. and KICHYENOVA, K. V. 1950. Biological growth of milkweed seeds (in Russian). Bull. Main Bot. Gard. **7**: 53–56 (cited by L. L. Evetts and O. C. Burnside 1972a).

SENN, H. A. 1944. Early studies of milkweed utilization in Canada. Can. Field Natur. **58**: 177–180.

SEYMOUR, A. B. 1929. Host index of the fungi of North America. XIII. Harvard Univ. Press. Cambridge, Mass. 732 pp.

SHAW, C. G. 1958. Host fungus for the Pacific Northwest, Wash. Agric. Exp. Sta., State College. Washington Circ. 335: 127 pp.

SHULL, G. H. 1914. The longevity of submerged seeds. Plant World. **17**: 329–337.

SPURWAY, C. H. 1941. Soil reaction (pH) preferences of plants. Mich. Agric. Exp. Sta. Special Bull. 906. 34 pp.

STEVENS, O. A. 1932. The number and weight of seeds produced by weeds. J. Bot. **19**: 784–794.

STEVENS, O. A. 1951. Further report on milkweed (*Asclepias*) culture. Bimon. Bull. N. Dak. Agric. Exp. Sta. **13**: 249–252.

STOLBINN P. A. 1937. Milkweed (*Asclepias syriaca*) as a subject of selection. Selektsiia Kauchukonosnykh rastenii. A collection of papers. No. **1**: 63–101. Abstract by G. Krotkov (cited by Moore 1947).

TIMMONS, F. L. 1946. Studies of the distribution and floss yield of common milkweed (*Asclepias syriaca* L.) in Northern Michigan. Ecology **27**: 212–225.

WHITING, G. A. 1943. A summary of the literature on milkweeds (*Asclepias* spp.) and their utilization. U.S. Dep. Agric. Bibl. Bull. No. 2: 41 pp.

WOODSON, R. E. JR. 1954. The North American species of *Asclepias* L. Ann. Mo. Bot. Gard. **41**: 211 pp.

231

THE BIOLOGY OF CANADIAN WEEDS
20. *Cornus canadensis* L.

IVAN V. HALL[1] and JACK D. SIBLEY[2]

*[1]Research Station, Agriculture Canada, Kentville, Nova Scotia B4N 1J5 and
[2]Nova Scotia Department of Agriculture and Marketing, Truro, N.S.*

Received 29 Mar. 1976, accepted 31 May 1976.

HALL, IVAN V. AND SIBLEY, JACK D. 1976. The biology of Canadian weeds. 20. *Cornus canadensis* L. Can. J. Plant Sci. **56**: 885–892.

Cornus canadensis L., bunchberry (Cornaceae), is a widespread, native herbaceous species generally growing in the litter under forest species or in the open where the climate is generally moist and cool. It occurs as a weed in lowbush blueberry fields recently developed from woodland. *Cornus canadensis* has been confused with *Cornus suecica* L. which it resembles. The two species grow side by side in Greenland, along the northern seacoasts of Eastern and Western Canada, and Alaska. The flesh of the fruit of *C. canadensis* is edible when cooked, but the berries with their stone-like seeds are unacceptable in the pack of frozen lowbush blueberry fruit. As *C. canadensis* is somewhat resistant to 2,4-D (2,4-dichlorophenoxyacetic acid), no chemical control is available at present for this species.

Le cornouiller du Canada (*Cornus canadensis* L.) est une plante herbacée indigène, très répandue dans les sous-bois des essences forestières ou en découvert, où le climat est généralement frais et humide. Il constitue une mauvaise herbe dans les champs de bleuets nains aménagés peu après coupe. On le confond parfois avec *Cornus suetica* L., auquel il ressemble. Les deux variétés se côtoient dans le Groenland, le long des côtes nord de l'Est et de l'Ouest du Canada et en Alaska. Les fruits de *C. canadensis* sont comestibles après cuisson, mais à cause de leurs graines dures, ils n'ont pas leur place dans un paquet de bleuets nains congelés. *C. canadensis* affichant une certaine résistance au 2,4-D (acide dichloro-2,4-phenoxyacétique), aucune répression chimique de cette mauvaise herbe n'est possible pour le moment.

1. Name

Cornus canadensis L. (=*Chamaepericlymenum canadense* B. & B., Rydb.) — **bunchberry** (Canada Weed Committee 1969), dwarf cornel, crackerberry, puddingberry; **cornouiller du Canada.** Cornaceae, dogwood family, Cornacées.

2. Description and Account of Variation

A low herb up to 23 cm in height (Fig. 1F), growing laterally by underground rhizomes and reproducing by seeds; shoots arising from buds on the rhizomes; leaves really alternate but growing as if in two whorls, the uppermost larger and with as many as or more leaves than the lower, entire, up to 8.5 cm in length and up to 5 cm in width, pinnately netted, lateral veins nearly parallel with the margin, lanceolate–ovate, apex acute, base acute; inflorescence subtended by four large, white bracts, flowers small in dense heads, sepals 4 and toothed, petals 4 and reflexed, stamens 4, and a stigma somewhat flattened; fruit a bright red drupe with a small stone usually containing a single seed.

One chromosome count $2n = 44$ on Canadian material has been recorded by Roy L. Taylor on specimen #118446 of DAO. During the preparation of this paper S. P. Vander Kloet of Acadia University informed the senior author that plants of *C.*

canadensis from Scatari Island, Nova Scotia had recently been examined and the chromosome number was $n = 22$. Dermen (1932) also reports $n = 22$ for *C. canadensis* collected from Pepperell, Massachusetts.

With the exception of Rydberg (1971), most North American taxonomists have retained the herbaceous *C. canadensis* within the genus *Cornus* (Rickett 1942). In addition to the herbaceous character, Rydberg used the two relatively minor characters, presence or absence of a bristle on the sepals and globose versus ellipsoid shape of the drupe, for separation at the generic level. These differences are more characteristic of separation at the specific level (Clausen 1944). Hara (1948) gives a detailed explanation why the generic name, *Cynoxylon*, is not appropriate.

Cornus canadensis is closely related to the boreal species, *Cornus suecica* L. (Fig. 1B). The two can be separated by the fact that the upper whorl of leaves of *C. canadensis* is larger than the lower one, whereas in *C. suecica* the leaves are similar in size and there are generally 5 or more pairs. In *C. suecica* the veins of the leaf all originate at or near the base of the blade, whereas in *C. canadensis* the uppermost pair originate partly up the midvein. The petals of *C. canadensis* are normally white, while those of *C. suecica* are purple. The fruit of *C. canadensis* is insipid while that of *C. suecica* is slightly acid.

A great many forms and varieties of *C. canadensis* have been described, especially by Lepage (1946, 1950, 1951, 1955) and by Lakela (1948). Some of these appear to have resulted from injury to growing point resulting in extra whorls of leaves, extension of the growing point, and/or dichotomous branching (Fig. 1E). Variation in color of the floral bracts was reported by Fernald (1941) and in the pubescence of the shoots by Lepage (1946) and Boivin (1960).

There are several habitats where the presence of abnormal types must be considered with caution. Such habitats are roadsides, powerline right-of-ways, approaches to airports, railway yards, etc. where weed spraying has often been carried out.

A mature shoot with fruit is shown in Fig. 1A.

3. Economic Importance

(a) Detrimental — The fruit of *C. canadensis* is often harvested along with lowbush blueberries during the harvest of that crop. Although the fruits of *C. canadensis* are edible (Hedrick 1919) they must be removed before freezing of the lowbush blueberry pack. Chief objection to *C. canadensis* is the presence of a large stone in each fruit. A survey conducted by one of us (J.D.S.) revealed that nearly 300 ha of lowbush blueberries in Nova Scotia were infested with this species and some fields had at least 20% coverage by this species.

(b) Beneficial — *Cornus canadensis* is one of the most attractive species of the understory of woodlands of Eastern Canada. In the late spring or early summer this wild flower with its whitish bracts is most attractive and in late summer or early fall the clusters of orange–red fruits are spectacular. *C. canadensis* grows exceedingly well in parks and campgrounds where the conifers have had the lower limbs removed allowing enough light to enter the canopy of the forest floor to provide ideal conditions for fruiting.

Martin et al. (1951) report that upland gamebirds, particularly grouse, feed on the

Fig. 1. (A) Fruiting stage of *C. canadensis* (0.5×). (B) Flowering stage of *C. suecica* (0.9×). (C) Cross section of rhizome of *C. canadensis* (100×). (D) *C. canadensis* from Peace River District of Alberta, altitude above 1,500 m (0.4×). (E) Specimen identified as *C. canadensis* forma *ramosa* Lepage (0.5×). (F) Habitat of *C. canadensis*.

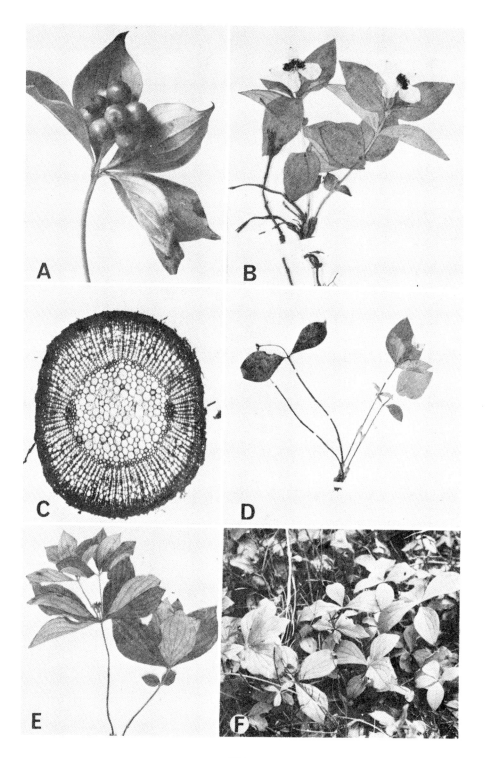

fruit and buds, and songbirds such as the Ipswich sparrow, veery thrush and vireos feed on the fruit.

(c) Legislation — *Cornus canadensis* is not listed in any Canadain federal or provincial, weed or seeds act.

4. Geographical Distribution

The Canadian distribution of *C. canadensis* is given in Fig. 2. Fernald (1950) states that *C. canadensis* occurs from southern Greenland to Alaska southward through Newfoundland and Nova Scotia to West Virginia across the United States in Illinois, Minnesota, South Dakota, New Mexico and California. Olsen (1921) states that it is native to the northern islands of Japan. *C. suecica* occurs in Greenland, Labrador, Alaska, Newfoundland, St. Pierre and Miquelon, Nova Scotia and the St. Lawrence of Quebec as well as Scandinavia.

5. Habit

(a) Climatic requirements — In the Canadian Arctic *C. canadensis* comes into bloom and fruits in no more than 6–7 wk. Also in the mountains of Alberta and British Columbia, as well as areas to the south, the plants of *C. canadensis* are generally depauperate (Fig. 1D) at elevations above 1,524 m (5,000 ft). Wherry (1934) studied soil conditions as to temperature, nitrogen content, and acidity of isolated areas where *C. canadensis* occurred along the Appalachian Mountains. He concluded that this species could not tolerate summer temperatures in excess of 18.3 C and this factor was limiting its southward migration.

(b) Substratum — The roots and rhizomes of *C. canadensis* are characteristically found in the litter of forest soils. Lutz and Chandler (1946) state that tree leaves are by far the largest source of plant material contributing to the organic matter. They further state that nutrient composition of the leaves varies according to the species of tree, age of leaves, and soil composition.

(c) Communities in which the species occurs — *Cornus canadensis* has been reported from notes on herbarium sheets as growing in the shade of the following trees: *Pinus strobus* L., *Pinus monticola* Dougl.,

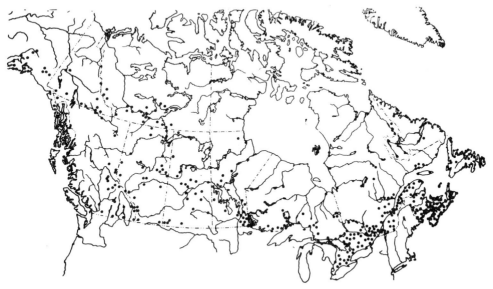

Fig. 2. Canadian distribution along with that from Alaska and Greenland of *Cornus canadensis* from specimens in the herbaria of Department of Agriculture Herbarium, Ottawa, Ontario and Acadia University, Wolfville, Nova Scotia.

Pinus banksiana Lamb, *Pinus contorta* Dougl., *Larix laricina* (Du Roi) K. Koch, *Picea glauca* (Moench) Voss, *Picea rubens* Sarg., *Picea mariana* (Mill.) B.S.P., *Tsuga canadensis* (L.) Carr., *Pseudotsuga menziesii* (Mirb.) Franco, *Abies balsamea* (L.) Mill., *Abies lasiocarpa* (Hook.) Nutt., *Thuja occidentalis* L., *Populus tremuloides* Michx., *Populus balsamifera* L., *Betula papyrifera* Marsh., *Betula populifolia* Marsh.

Based on five samples, the mean number of shoots of *C. canadensis* in an *Abies balsamea* and *Picea glauca* forest at the provincial park, Blomidon, Kings County, N.S. was $16.2 \pm SE\ 1.85$ per 20 cm². In the Maritime Provinces, the plants found growing in association with *C. canadensis* and their frequency of distribution are listed in the following field studies: Hall (1955), Hall (1959), Hall and Aalders (1968) and Hall (1972). In Quebec, Marie-Victorin (1964) states that this species forms one of the most important ecological associations found on the coniferous forest floor and to the north of the spruce forest.

6. History

Since Macoun (1883) stated that *C. canadensis* was common in woods all across the country, it must be considered part of the native vegetation.

7. Growth and Development

(a) Morphology — The rhizome (Fig. 1C) grows up to 30 cm per year in the soft, moist litter provided by the needles of several conifers, especially *Picea glauca*, and the leaves of several deciduous species.

The typical leaf of *C. canadensis* has a single layer of palisade parenchyma, several layers of spongy parenchyma and stomata present only on the under surface of the leaf. Olsen (1921) found marked differences in the leaf anatomy between Arctic populations in Greenland and those from Canada and Minnesota. Leaves from Greenland were thicker due to larger cells in the spongy parenchyma. The number of stoma was greater in the Arctic population, 160 per mm² from the Greenland population compared with 140 from Canadian material. The epidermal cells of both surfaces from the more southern populations were more undulating than their Arctic counterpart. The stem of *C. canadensis* was shown by Olsen to be more H-shaped in cross section than the closely related *C. suecica*, while the rhizome and root of the two species were nearly identical.

A study of the evolution of the inflorescence in the Cornaceae was carried out by Hutchinson (1942) who stated that only those species with a "loose corymbose cyme" should be retained in the genus *Cornus*. Wilkinson (1944) in an anatomical description of the floral anatomy of some 16 species of *Cornus* showed that the petal trace in *C. canadensis* was independent of the calyx trace, the latter being derived from the stamen bundles.

(b) Perennation — *Cornus canadensis* may pass the winter as a seed with the embryonic bud protected by a seed coat in which case it would be classified as a therophyte (Daubenmire 1947), but more generally it is a perennial with the buds of the rhizome below the surface of the soil, in which case, it is a cryptophyte.

(c) Physiological data — Work by Jensen et al. (1975) has shown that two distinct taxa or groups exist in the genus *Cornus* based on the presence of non-flavonoid glucosides. One group contains a hydroxycyclohexadienone glucoside along with salidrose, its reduced counterpart, while the other is characterized by various iridoid glucosides. *C. canadensis* is devoid of or very low in iridoid glucoside and presumably belongs to the first group.

A 200-g sample of fruit of *C. canadensis*, analyzed by the Food Processing Section of the Kentville Research Station, had 8% soluble solids and the titratable acidity was 0.07% expressed as citric.

(d) Phenology — Since *C. canadensis* has a wide distribution in Canada, blooming

dates range from late May to late July (Table 1). The orange–red fruit are generally developed before the end of August.

(e) Mycorrhiza — Olsen (1921) reports the presence of mycorrhiza in both *C. canadensis* and *C. suecica*.

8. Reproduction

(a) Floral biology — Flowers of *C. canadensis* are insect-pollinated by *Bombus terricola* Kirby and *B. ternarius* Soy. When inflorescences of *C. canadensis* were self-pollinated in the greenhouse no fruit developed, suggesting that the plants are self-incompatible.

(b) Seed production and dispersal — The number of fruit per inflorescence based on 25 shoots from a population sampled on 24 July 1975 at Cambridge, Kings County, N.S. was 11.8 ± SE 0.77. Twenty-five fruit taken from this sample on the same date had a mean individual weight of .077 g ± SE .002. Later in the season a sample taken from the provincial park at Blomidon, Kings County, N.S. on 11 September 1975 had 9.20 ± SE 0.96 fruits and the individual weight was .149 g ± .004. Sixty seeds from this sample weighed 1 g.

(c) Viability of seeds and germination — The Forest Service of the U.S. Department of Agriculture (1948) reported on the seed germination of some eight species of *Cornus* including *C. canadensis*. This species required 30–60 days at 25 C followed by 120–150 days at 0.5 C for germination. Although several habitats have been examined during 1974 and 1975, the later was exceedingly dry in Nova Scotia during the summer; no seedlings were found.

(d) Vegetative reproduction — *Cornus canadensis* grows laterally in the organic matter layer of forest soils by rhizomes that have several dormant buds (Hall and Mack 1959). Burning or pruning releases these buds from dominance by the apical bud and results in an increased number of shoots.

9. Hybrids

Hybrids between *C. canadensis* and *C. suecica* have been reported for considerable time, and are recognized by Fernald (1950) as X *C. unalaschkensis* Ledeb. Descriptions of three hybrid types and diagrams of the leaf, calyx and flower from *C. canadensis, C. suecica* and the hybrid *C. canadensis* × *C. suecica* are given by Lepage (1946). However, it should be noted that these were not produced under experimental conditions. Smith and Schofield (1952) found the two species growing in abundance at N.W. Cove, Scatari Island, but none of the X *C. unalaschkensis* Ledeb. was found.

Table 1. Phenological development of *Cornus canadensis* in Canada

Location or area	Degrees expressed in latitude and longitude if applicable	Avg date of	
		Bloom at anthesis	Orange–red fruit
Goose Bay, Nfld.	53°18′N 60°25′W	1 July	9 Aug.
Kentville, N.S.	45°04′N 64°30′W	6 June	16 Aug.
Fredericton, N.B.	45°57′N 66°40′W	8 June	8 Aug.
Lower St. Lawrence River, Que.	– –	6–7 June	10 Aug.
Saint Ambroise, Que.	48°33′N 71°20′W	21 June	–
Fort Chimo, Que.	58°10′N 68°15′W	23 July	–
Ottawa, Ont.	45°25′N 75°43′W	6 June	3 Aug.
Deep River, Ont.	46°04′N 77°29′W	16–21 July	11 Aug.
Thunder Bay, Ont.	48°27′N 89°12′W	2–6 July	16 Aug.
Northern Alta, B.C. and Yukon	– –	23 June–7 July	3–15 Aug.
Southern B.C.	– –	28 May–8 June	12–15 Aug.

10. Population Dynamics

Cornus canadensis is able to exist or grow slowly on the forest floor in the shade of many deciduous and coniferous species. Once the forest canopy has been removed, this species becomes the dominant vegetation. Unless the rhizomes are dug out of the soil, *C. canadensis* exists indefinitely until a new coniferous forest develops with complete foliage cover.

11. Response to Herbicides and other Chemicals

Trevett (1950) reported that bunchberry (*C. canadensis*) was resistant to 2,4-D (2,4-dichlorophenoxyacetic acid). Ragab and Jackson (1971) reported that *C. canadensis* could be killed by aminotriazole (3-amino-1,2,4-triazole). Plants that were sprayed on 24 October 1968 had no residues of this chemical in fruit harvested on 18 August 1969. In spite of this finding, aminotriazole is not recommended for even spot treatments in non-producing fields and consequently a chemical to control this weed is non-existant at this time.

12. Response to Other Human Manipulations

Since *C. canadensis* is a woodland species which seldom occurs on lowbush blueberry land that has been developed from former agricultural land (Hall 1959), the effects of most human manipulations are unknown. Intensive cultivation that included plowing to a depth of 30–40 cm followed by harrowing nearly eradicated *C. canadensis* in a lowbush blueberry field at West Brook, Cumb. Co., Nova Scotia (Hall 1963).

Removing part of the forest canopy had a marked effect on plants of *C. canadensis* in the understory. Under heavy shade of a spruce–fir canopy with 1% of full sunlight, plants were just able to survive. Moderate vegetative growth occurred in 20% of full sunlight and flowering and fruiting occurred in openings of the forest canopy giving 50% of full sunlight (Hall 1955).

13. Responses to Parasites

The principal insects which attack *Cornus* spp. are borers (*Chrysobothris femorata* Oliv. and *Thamnosphecia scitual* (Harr.), club-gall (*Mycodiplosis alternata* Felt.) and leaf-miner (*Chalepus dorsalis* Thunb.) and several scales (Pirone et al. 1960). Britton (1916) reported that larvae of *Macremphytus varianus* (Norton) feed on *Cornus* in Connecticut.

Several fungi have been reported as occurring on *C. canadensis* including *Glomerularia corni* Pk., *Phyllosticta corni-canadensis* Dearn and Bisby, *Pseudomassaria foliicola* Barr., *Puccinia porphyrogenita* Curt., *Septoria canadensis* Pk., *Valsa fallax* Nits., and *Venturia clintonii* Pk. (Conners 1967). On 11 September 1975 a sample of fruiting plants was collected in the provincial park at Blomidon, Kings Co., Nova Scotia and lesions were noted on the leaves and fruit (Fig. 1A). The organism responsible was *Septoria canadensis* Pk. (C. O. Gourley, personal communication).

All of the above organisms have little or no effect in changing population levels in stands that have been visited by the senior author.

ACKNOWLEDGMENTS

It is a pleasure to thank A. T. Lightfoot and A. C. Brydon for technical assistance. We wish to thank Dr. S. P. Vander Kloet who kindly read this manuscript and offered several helpful suggestions during its preparation.

BOIVIN, B. 1960. Centurie de plantes canadiennes. III. Natur. Can. **87**: 25–49.

BRITTON, W. E. 1916. Guide to insects of Connecticut. Part III. The Hymenoptera, or wasp-like insects of Connecticut. Hartford State geological and natural history survey. Bull. 22. p. 61.

CANADA WEED COMMITTEE. 1969. Common and botanical names of weeds in Canada. Can. Dep. Agric. Publ. 1397. p. 12.

CLAUSEN, R. T. 1944. A botanical study of the yam beans (Pachyrrhizus). Cornell Univ. Agric. Exp. Sta. Mem. 264 pp. 1–38.

CONNORS, I. L. 1967. An annotated index of plant diseases in Canada and fungi recorded on plants in Alaska, Canada and Greenland. Can. Dep. Agric. Res. Br. Publ. 1251. pp. 88–89.

DAUBENMIRE, R. F. 1947. Plants and environment. A textbook of plant autecology. John Wiley & Sons, Inc. New York, N.Y. p. 206.

DERMEN, H. 1932. Cytological studies of *Cornus*. J. Arnold Arboretum **13**: 410–417.

FERNALD, M. L. 1941. *Cornus canadensis* L. forma *rosea* f. nov. Rhodora **43**: 156.

FERNALD, M. L. 1950. Gray's manual of botany. 8th ed. American Book Co., New York, N.Y. p. 1106.

HALL, I. V. 1955. Floristic changes following the cutting and burning of a woodlot for blueberry production. Can. J. Agric. Sci. **35**: 143–152.

HALL, I. V. 1959. Plant populations in blueberry stands developed from abandoned hayfields and woodlots. Ecology **40**: 742–743.

HALL, I. V. 1963. Note on the effect of a single intensive cultivation on the composition of an old blueberry stand. Can. J. Plant Sci. **43**: 417–419.

HALL, I. V. 1972. Plants present in field being developed for lowbush blueberries at Coldbrook, Kings County, Nova Scotia. Pages 55-56 *in* Annual report of Research Station, Agriculture Canada, Kentville, N.S.

HALL, I. V. and AALDERS, L. E. 1968. The botanical composition of two barrens in Nova Scotia. Natur. Can. **95**: 393–396.

HALL, I. V. and MACK, G. J. A. 1959. Weeds. Pages 15-19 *in* Blueberry Substation Tower Hill, New Brunswick progress report 1954-1959. Can. Dep. Agric., Ottawa, Ont.

HARA, H. 1948. The nomenclature of the flowering dogwood and its allies. J. Arnold Arboretum **29**: 111–115.

HEDRICK, U. P. 1919. Sturtevant's notes on edible plants. Albany, J. B. Lyon Company, State Printers. p. 192.

HUTCHINSON, J. 1942. Neglected generic characters in the family Cornaceae. Ann. Bot. N.S. **6**: 83–93.

JENSEN, S. R., KJAER, A. and NIELSEN, B. J. 1975. The genus *Cornus*: non-flavonoid glucosides as taxonomic markers. Biochem. System. Ecol. **3**: 75–78.

LAKELA, O. 1948. Forms of *Cornus canadensis* in Minnesota. Rhodora **50**: 304–306.

LEPAGE, E. 1946. Variations taxonomiques de trois espèces laurentiennes. Natur. Can. **73**: 5–16.

LEPAGE, E. 1950. Variations mineures de quelques plantes du nord-est du Canada et de l'Alaska. Natur. Can. **77**: 228–231.

LEPAGE, E. 1951. Entités nouvelles dans la flore du Québec. Natur. Can. **78**: 341–352.

LEPAGE, E. 1955. Nouvelles formes du *Cornus canadensis* L. et du *Pontederia cordata* L. Natur. Can. **82**: 99–102.

LUTZ, H. J. and CHANDLER, R. F. 1946. Forest soils. New York, N.Y. John Wiley and Sons, Inc. pp. 140–153.

MACOUN, J. 1883. Catalogue of Canadian plants. Part 1. — Polypetalae. Dawson Brothers, Montreal, Que. p.190.

MARIE-VICTORIN, FRERE. 1964. Flore Laurentienne, 2nd ed. Les Presses de L'Université de Montréal. Montreal, Que. pp. 407–408.

MARTIN, A. C., ZIM, H. S. and NELSON, A. L. 1951. American wildlife and plants. McGraw-Hill Book Company, Inc., New York, N.Y. p. 352.

OLSEN, C. 1921. Cornaceae. Meddelelser om Gronland XXXVII: pp. 130–150.

PIRONE, P. P., DODGE, B. O. and RICKETT, H. W. 1960. Diseases and pests of ornamental plants. The Ronald Press, Company, New York, N.Y. pp. 285–287.

RAGAB, M. T. H. and JACKSON, L. P. 1971. Aminotriazole residues in lowbush blueberry fruit. Can. J. Plant Sci. **51**: 331–332.

RICKETT, H. W. 1942. The names of *Cornus*. Torreya **42**: 11–14.

RYDBERG, P. A. 1971. Flora of the prairies and plains of central North America. Vol. 2. Dover Publications, Inc., New York, N.Y. pp. 606–607.

SMITH, E. C. and SCHOFIELD, W. B. 1952. Contributions to the flora of Nova Scotia. Rhodora **54**: 220–228.

TREVETT, M. F. 1950. Weed control. Pages 32-35 *in* Producing blueberries in Maine. Agric. Exp. Sta. Bull. 479.

U.S. DEPARTMENT OF AGRICULTURE FOREST SERVICE. 1948. Woody-plant seed manual. Misc. Publ. 654. U.S. Gov. Printing Office, Washington, D.C. pp. 146–150.

WHERRY, E. T. 1934. Temperature relations of the bunchberry, *Cornus canadensis* L. Ecology **15**: 440–443.

WILKINSON, A. M. 1944. Floral anatomy of some species of *Cornus* Bull. Torrery Bot. Club **71**: 276–301.

THE BIOLOGY OF CANADIAN WEEDS.
21. *Urtica dioica* L.

I. J. BASSETT[1], C. W. CROMPTON[1], and D. W. WOODLAND[2]

[1]*Biosystematics Research Institute, Agriculture Canada, Ottawa, Ontario K1A 0C6; and*
[2]*Department of Plant Sciences, Macdonald Campus of McGill University, Ste. Anne de Bellevue, Quebec H0A 1C0. Received 15 Sept. 1976, accepted 13 Oct. 1976.*

BASSETT, I. J., CROMPTON, C. W. AND WOODLAND, D. W. 1977. The biology of Canadian weeds. 21. *Urtica dioica* L. Can. J. Plant Sci. **57**: 491–498.

A summary of biological information on *Urtica dioica* L. ssp. *gracilis* (Ait.) Selander (American stinging nettle) and ssp. *dioica* (European stinging nettle) is presented. American stinging nettle is widespread throughout Canada, while European stinging nettle is confined to a few disturbed habitats in Eastern Canada. American stinging nettle is often weedy in nutrient-rich soils such as are normally associated with cultivated row crops, old pastures, farmyards, irrigation canals, drainage ditches, orchards, and open woodlands. Airborne pollen of *Urtica dioica*, shed in large amounts, in known to cause hay fever. The stinging emergences (needles) of both subspecies produce a painful sting to the human flesh.

L'auteur présente des données biologiques sur *Urtica dioica* L. ssp. *gracilis* (Ait.) Selander (ortie dioïque d'Amérique) et ssp. *dioica* (ortie dioïque d'Europe). La première est répandue au Canada alors que la seconde se limite à quelques habitats dérangés de l'est du Canada. L'ortie d'Amérique est souvent une mauvaise herbe des sols fertiles, tels ceux qui sont normalement associés aux cultures sarclées, vieux pâturages, cours de ferme, canaux d'irrigation, fossés de drainage, vergers et boisés clairs. On sait que de grandes quantités de pollen en suspension dans l'air causent la fièvre des foins. Les poils urticants des deux sous-espèces causent des piqûres douloureuses à l'homme.

1. Names

Urtica dioica L. — **stinging nettle** (Canada Weed Committee 1969); **ortie dioïque**, ortie, ortie piquante (Ferron et Cayouette 1971). Two subspecies occur in Canada: 1. the common and widespread native taxon, *U. dioica* ssp. *gracilis* (Ait.) Selander — **American stinging nettle, ortie dioïque d'Amérique** 2. the rare introduced taxon, *U. dioica* L. ssp. *dioica* — **European stinging nettle, ortie dioïque du Europe.** Urticaceae, nettle family, Urticacées.

2. Description and Account of Variation

Urtica dioica ssp. *gracilis*. Erect or partially ascending perennials with extensive rhizome system; stems (0.5) 1–2 (2.5) m tall, slender, simple or with axillary branches, glabrous, except for stinging emergences, to slightly pilose, hispid or strigose; stipules 5–12 mm long, free, oblong to linear–lanceolate, acute to attenuate; leaves opposite, broadly ovate to lanceolate, rounded to cordate at base, acute to acuminate at tip; petioles slender (1/8) 1/4–2/3 the length of the blade, longer on lower stem leaves, shorter on upper leaves; blades glabrous on both surfaces to sparingly pilose or strigose beneath, coarsely serrate to dentate; cystoliths rounded; teeth directed forward, 1–5 mm deep, those of lower blades larger, upper blades smaller; plants predominantly monoecious, rarely dioecious; staminate flower clusters generally equal to or longer than the petioles, greenish yellow with four equal sepals and four stamens; pistillate flower clusters generally shorter than the petioles; inner sepals ovate, slightly to

Can. J. Plant Sci. 57: 491-498 (Apr. 1977)

moderately hispid, (0.5) 1.0–1.5 (2.0) mm long; outer sepal lobes on mature flowers generally 1/4–1/2 (2/3) longer than the inner lobes; achenes 1.0–1.5 mm long, ovate, tan to brown, smooth to tuberculate; wind-pollinated, flowering from late May to October.

The common American stinging nettle (ssp. *gracilis*) can be distinguished from the infrequent European stinging nettle (ssp. *dioica* by the features detailed in the following key:

Plants predominantly monoecious (pistillate plants occasional, staminate ones rare); stems rigid, the plants upright in habit; leaf blades and stems glabrous with stinging hairs usually on lower leaf surface only . . . . .*U. dioica* ssp. *gracilis*

Plants predominantly dioecious; stems weak, the plants with a sprawling, branching habit; leaf blades and stems usually strongly hispid with stinging hairs on both leaf surfaces . . . .*U. dioica* ssp. *dioica*

Chromosome numbers of $2n = 26$ and $2n = 52$ have been reported for ssp. *gracilis* and $2n = 52$ for ssp. *dioica* by Bassett et al. (1974).

Stinging nettle is sometimes confused with *Boehmeria cylindrica* (L.) Sm. (bog hemp), *Galeopsis tetrahit* L. (hemp nettle) and *Verbena urticifolia* L. (white vervain). However, these plants lack the stinging hairs that are present on stinging nettle from the two-leaf stage onwards.

Seedlings and flowering shoots of *Urtica dioica* ssp. *gracilis* are illustrated in Figs. 1 and 2. The seedlings of ssp. *dioica* are similar to those of ssp. *gracilis*.

Fig. 1.   Seedlings.   Fig. 2.   Flowering shoot.

3. Economic Importance

(a) Detrimental — Major infestations of American stinging nettle have been observed in orchards, market gardens, farm yards, nurseries, old pastures, along roadsides, drainage ditches, irrigation canals and stream banks in the southern portion of its Canadian range. The stinging emergences on the stem, leaves and flowers of stinging nettle plants produce a painful sting to the human flesh, followed by an immediate small reddish swelling and prolonged itching and numbness of the sensitized area. Initial reactions last a few minutes on first being exposed. After being stung repeatedly, the pain often intensifies and can last for several days.

The pollen of American stinging nettle, shed in large amounts, is an important contributor to summer hay fever. Solomon and Cathey (1970) tested 84 atopic patients epidermally with extracts of American stinging nettle pollen. Of the patients tested, 20% developed allergenic reactions exceeding their response to extracts of common ragweed (*Ambrosia artemisiifolia* L.). A 32-yr analysis of atmospheric pollen in Minnesota ranked *Urtica* spp. 10th in abundance among 50 plant genera (Hansen and Dahl 1965).

(b) Beneficial — Fernald and Kinsey (1958), and Woodland (1973) report that young American stinging nettle leaves make an excellent potherb, and can be boiled and substituted for spinach. They tell of the use of the European stinging nettle in Scotland in earlier times as a rennet to curdle milk for cheese. In Germany, during World War II, the European stinging nettle was gathered as food for human consumption because of its high nutritive value (Stern 1943). In Russia, nettle hay was tested agronomically and found very high in protein and low in fibre, and produced high yield on the second and third cuttings (Totev 1964). Cappa (1965), in Italy, compared the nutritive values of nettle meal versus alfalfa meal on pullets and hens. The birds fed on nettle meal reached sexual maturity earlier and produced more eggs per bird than birds fed on alfalfa meal.

European stinging nettle is sometimes used by foresters as an indicator of soils suitable for reforestation, since nettles grow mainly in areas with high soil fertility (Pigott 1964).

(c) Legislation — American stinging nettle (*U. dioica* ssp. *gracilis*), under the name tall nettle, is included in the list of noxious weeds for Manitoba (Anonymous 1970), and under the name *Urtica dioica* (*sensu lat.*) is designated a noxious weed by the Province of Alberta (Anonymous 1973).

4. Geographical Distribution

American stinging nettle occurs in all provinces as well as the Yukon Territory, and Mackenzie District, N.W.T. (Fig. 3). Although wide ranging, this plant is abundant mainly in lowland situations and is often associated with human habitation. Infestations are found in rich soils suited for market gardens, nurseries, and orchards. The distribution of American stinging nettle extends south to Virginia, Missouri, Louisiana, northern Texas, New Mexico, eastern Utah, Arizona, and California. European stinging nettle (Fig. 3) is cosmopolitan in temperate regions (Woodland 1975).

5. Habitat

(a) Climatic requirements — Within Canada, American stinging nettle occurs from the United States border north to 62° latitude in the west, and north to 53° latitude in the east. As indicated by this extensive distribution and the collecting sites shown in Fig. 3, various amounts of rainfall and snow cover are tolerated by this taxon. American stinging nettle will grow (based on 42°F) from under 600–800 degree-days in the forest tundra to 3,250 degree-days in the Great Lakes–St. Lawrence forest regions (Rousseau 1974).

(b) Substratum — Woodland (1975) sampled soil from 38 American stinging nettle

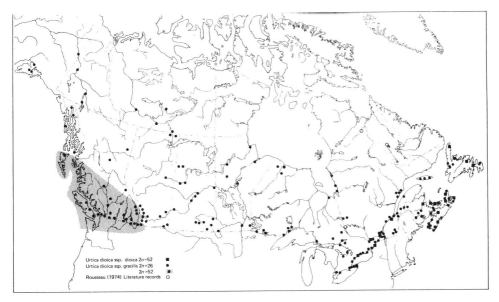

Fig. 3. Distribution of American stinging nettle (*Urtica dioica* ssp. *gracilis*), and European stinging nettle (*U. dioica* ssp. *dioica*) in Canada.

populations in the United States. The *p*H of these samples ranged from 5.6 to 7.6 on sites west of the Rocky Mountains and from 6.2 to 7.5 on more eastern sites.

In Canada, American stinging nettle grows in Podzol, Brunisol, Humic Gleysolic, Gleysolic, and Cyric Gleysol soils. It grows more commonly on Podzol and Brunisol soil types where leaching tends to cause rapid breakdown on any accumulating organic matter.

(c) Communities in which the species occurs — American stinging nettle grows in eight of the nine bioclimatic zones in Quebec defined by Rousseau (1974). These zones range from forest–tundra associations to Great Lakes–St. Lawrence Forest associations. American stinging nettle is rarely observed as a single plant with one or a few stems. It usually forms in large closed clones. The largest infestations seen on recent cross-Canada field surveys for stinging nettle were along the St. John River, N.B., in market garden areas south of Montreal and along drainage ditches and in orchards of the eastern townships, Quebec

and southern Ontario. A large population of American stinging nettle extends for 15 km along the highway embankment between Kenora, Ontario and Winnipeg, Manitoba. It is also common in coulees and along stream banks on the prairies, and on the periphery of orchard irrigation run-off in the Okanagan Valley, B.C.

6. History

American stinging nettle is undoubtedly native to North America. An Upper Cretaceous fossil resembling American stinging nettle was found in Alaska (Hollick and Martin 1930). It is considered by McAndrews et al. (1973) to form a portion of the Quaternary flora of the Great Lakes Region. After the Wisconsin glaciation, it evidently migrated northward into Canada during the Holocene. Cushing (1963) found fossil *Urtica*-type pollen in Minnesota borings, radiocarbon-dated from 7,800 B.P. until recent times. We have identified *Urtica* pollen in Holocene sediment samples 7,600–8,100 B.P. and 8.600–9,100 B.P. from southern Ontario (radiocarbon dates provided by the Geological Survey of Canada). The earliest botanical collection of this taxon was made in 1789 at Hudson Bay (Bassett et al. 1974).

The oldest collection of the introduced European stinging nettle is from Stone Mills, Bay of Quinte, Ontario, where it was first found in 1877 by J. Macoun. It has since been collected in scattered locations in Eastern Canada. It is usually found near ports, ballast heaps, and railway yards.

7. Growth and Development

(a) Morphology — The weediness of American stinging nettle can be attributed to the vigorous spread of the plant by means of rhizomes. The rhizomes can establish new colonies from which other species are virtually excluded, when scattered through the soil by disturbances such as mechanical cultivation. Stinging emergences also cause man to avoid hand-weeding smaller infestations.

(b) Perennation — American stinging nettle is killed back to ground level by frost each year. It survives in the soil through its perennating rhizomes.

(c) Physiological data — Because of nettle's injurious sting, the physiology and chemistry of its emergences have been studied extensively. Willis (1969), using gas-phase chromatography, thin-layer chromatography, and elemental analysis was unable to determine the chemical constitution of the toxin. He disproved the results of many previous authors who had tentatively identified the toxins as acids, alkaloids, enzymes, histamines, salts and proteins. The causative agent of the nettles' sting still remains unknown.

American stinging nettle will not persist in areas which are saline, or in habitats of low soil fertility. Rorison (1967) discovered that calcium reduced the permeability of *Urtica* root cells to phosphorus. Low phosphate levels resulted in slow growth rates; high phosphate levels resulted in fast growth rates. Nassery (1970) determined

that lacking an abundant supply of phosphate, *Urtica* will show deficiency symptoms and grow poorly.

Totev (1964) analyzed the chemical composition of *Urtica* hay. This hay contained 21–23% crude protein, 3 to 5% crude fats, 35–39% non-nitrogen extract substances, 9–21% crude fibre and 19–29% ash. Cappa (1965) found that the amino acids contained in dehydrated meal of *Urtica dioica* were nutritionally superior to the amino acid concentrations of dehydrated alfalfa meal.

(d) Phenology — Due to its wide geographical range, the phenology of American stinging nettle is somewhat variable. Maximum root development occurs in the late spring and early summer, prior to flowering and subsequent seed setting. American stinging nettle flowers from late May to early October. On the prairies and in the northern areas, flowering is condensed into the period from mid-June to late August. No seedlings have been observed in the field.

8. Reproduction

(a) Floral biology — American stinging nettle is anemophilous. As the staminate flowers mature, the anthers dehisce forcing the perianth parts to open. Meanwhile, the filaments which are bent spring-like, release, and the pollen grains are catapulted from the open anthers into the air. We have seen the pollen grains thrown up to 2 cm from the flower.

American stinging nettle is monoecious, bearing staminate and pistillate flowers on each shoot. Some panicles are entirely male, some entirely female, and some are mixed (occasionally hermaphroditic flowers are produced). Male flowers are produced in greater abundance during June and July and female flowers mostly later in the growing season. This has led to the mistaken view that the plants are dioecious.

American stinging nettle is self-compatible; pistillate flowers bagged together with staminate flowers of the same plant in greenhouse experiments produce viable seed.

(b) Seed production and dispersal — American stinging nettle produces one achene per flower. The flowers are arranged in four branching panicles at the nodes, between the petiole and shoot. Each cluster of four panicles produces approximately 1,000 seeds. Plants growing in the shade have loose, drooping, panicles with 500–5,000 seeds per shoot, whereas open grown plants have compact stiff panicles that are much more productive, with 10,000–20,000 seeds per shoot. Some American stinging nettle clones undoubtedly produce billions of seeds. The achenes normally remain on the plant until frost, when they fall to the ground. Some remain on the plant until they are removed by snowfall and ice.

(c) Viability of seeds and germination — American stinging nettle seeds require no vernalization. Seed collected directly from a plant will germinate in 5–10 days. Seeds will germinate in the greenhouse after 10 yr storage.

(d) Vegetative reproduction — American stinging nettle survives through vegetative reproduction by rhizomes. Plants established from seed in test situations initiate vegetative spread in the first growing season. A rhizome planted in the later summer can spread to 2.5 m in diameter by the following year.

9. Hybrids

The only other *Urtica* sp. in Canada is *U.urens* L. There is no evidence that *U. dioica* hybridizes with it.

10. Population Dynamics

In Canada, American stinging nettle is a minor constituent of woodland clearings, stream alluviums, coulees and open range. Upon opening land for agricultural development, the plant establishes itself in areas of high soil fertility and becomes weedy. In tests with European stinging nettle in Britain, Ivins (1952) proved that the plant could establish itself from seed when planted into herbage and forage test plots. Nettle became the dominant weed in legume mixtures, was less dominant in legume–grass mixtures, and was considerably reduced in pure grass plots. Field observations of American stinging nettle in Canada indicate that competition from grass species limits the spread of nettle clones.

The factors preventing American stinging nettle from becoming more widespread and abundant are: poor soil conditions, competition from soil binding plants, shade from forest trees, and the high mortality of seedlings. Several collecting sites of 25 yr ago were revisited to find the infestation still prevalent. A conservative estimate of the age of some nettle clones would be at least 50 yr.

11. Response to Herbicides and other Chemicals

As there is no specifically recommended chemical control for American stinging nettle in Canada, general control recommendations for perennial weeds in non-crop land will probably eradicate this plant (Anonymous 1975).

12. Response to Other Human Manipulations

Three small closed clones of American stinging nettle were cut close to the ground on 5 July 1974, near Ottawa, Ontario. The plant responded to this cutting by sending up numerous bushy shoots. Totev (1964) found that a higher percentage yield of European stinging nettle was obtained on third cutting for hay.

American stinging nettle will not survive repeated ploughing and mechanical cultivation. Several years of such practices will effectively reduce infestation by destroying its extensive rhizome system (Muenscher 1955).

13. Responses to Parasites

(a) Insects and other nondomestic stock — Sen and Jensen (1969) report that *Urtica*

245

spp. are the predominate hosts for the hop cyst nematode, *Heterodera humuli* Filipjev. Vegetables, forage crops, fruits, and cereals in Canada are infected by this nematode.

Beirne (1972) discussed the occurrence of two-spotted spider mite, *Tetranychus urticae* Koch, and of the bug, *Calocaris norvegicus* Gmel. on *Urtica dioica*. The former is resistant to insecticides and moves from the host to infest vegetables, clover (*Trifolium* spp.), and greenhouse plants. The latter has been found on strawberries (*Fragaria* spp.) and potatoes (*Solanum tuberosum* L.) in Newfoundland. Davis (1971) lists 28 species of insects confined to European stinging nettle and a further 18 species for which it is an important host. He describes the parts of the plant which are attacked by the various stages of the insects. More recently, Davis (1973) has reported on the Hemiptera and Coleoptera found on the European stinging nettle in England.

Other insects found associated with American stinging nettle in Canada are as follows (J. E. H. Martin, personal communication): *Vanessa atalanta* L., *Bolaria* sp., *Polygonia interrogationis* Fabricus, *P. coma* Harris, *P. satyrus* Edwards, *Nymphalis milberti* Latrielle (Lepidoptera: Nymphalidae); *Melagromyza martini* Spencer, *Phytomyza flavicornis* Fall., *Agromyza pseudorystans* Now., *A. reptans* Fall. (Diptera: Agromyzidae, from Spencer (1969)).

(b) Micro-organisms and viruses — Conners (1967) refers to the following fungi being found on American stinging nettle: *Dendryphium vinosum* (Berk. and Curt.) Hughes (*Helminthosporium utricae* Pk.), *Didymella eupyrina* Sacc., *Leptosphaeria acuta* (Moug.) Karst, *L. doliolum* (Pers.) de Not., *Pistillaria micans* Pers. ex Fr., *Puccini caricina* DC. (*P. caris* (Schum.) Schroet. var *urticata* (Kern) Arth.), *Ramularia urticae* Ces., *Sclerotinia sclerotiarum* (Lib.) de Bary, *Septoria urticae* Desm.

In addition D. B. O. Savile (personal communication) reports that powdery mil-

dew (*Erysiphe cichoraccarum* DC. ex Mérat), downy mildew (*Peronospora urticae* (Lib.) de Bary), and a rust alternating to *Carex* spp. (*Puccinia urticata* Kern OI) have been found on American stinging nettle. These fungi seldom cause severe damage to the plant.

(c) Higher plant parasites — Doder (*Cuscuta* spp.) occasionally parasitizes American stinging nettle in Ontario.

ACKNOWLEDGMENTS

We wish to thank J. McNeill and G. A. Mulligan of our Institute for helpful criticisms of the manuscript and R. J. Mott, Geological Survey of Canada, for providing us with Holocene pollen sediments.

ANONYMOUS. 1970. The Noxious Weeds Act. Queen's Printer, Winnipeg, Manitoba pp. 1-20.

ANONYMOUS. 1973. Regulations designating plants as noxious weeds. Alberta Regulation 147/73. Queen's Printer, Edmonton, Alberta, unpaginated.

ANONYMOUS. 1975. Guide to chemical weed control. Publ. 75, prepared by: Members of the Ontario Herbicide Committee, and Ministers of Agriculture, Newfoundland — New Brunswick, Nova Scotia — Prince Edward Island. 91 pp.

BASSETT, I. J., CROMPTON, C. W. and WOODLAND, D. W. 1974. The family Urticaceae in Canada. Can. J. Bot. **52**: 503–516.

BEIRNE, B. P. 1972. Pest insects of annual crop plants in Canada. IV. Hemiptera, V. Orthoptera, VI. Other groups. Mem. Entomol. Soc. Can. No. 85. 73 pp.

CANADA WEED COMMITTEE. 1969. Common and botanical names of weeds in Canada. Can. Dep. Agric. Publ. 1397. 67 pp.

CAPPA, V. 1965. On the nutritive value of *Urtica dioica*. Atti Soc. Ital. Sci. Vet. **19**: 261–264.

CONNERS, I. L. 1967. An annotated index of plant diseases in Canada and fungi recorded on plants in Alaska, Canada, and Greenland. Can. Agric. Res. Br. Publ. 1251. 381 pp.

CUSHING, E. J. 1963. Late Wisconsin pollen stratigraphy in East-Central Minnesota. Univ. Microfilms, Inc. Ann Arbor, Mich. 166 pp.

DAVIS, B. N. K. 1971. The insect fauna of stinging nettle (*Urtica dioica*). Monks Wood Exp. Sta. Annu. Rep. 1969-1971. pp. 33-35.

DAVIS, B. N. K. 1973. The Hemiptera and Coleoptera of stinging nettle (*Urtica dioica* L.) in East Anglia. J. Appl. Ecol. **10**: 213–237.

FERNALD, M. L. and KINSEY, A. C. 1958. Edible wild plants of Eastern North America. Harper Brothers, New York, N.Y. 452 pp.

FERRON, M. et CAYOUETTE, R. 1971. Nom des mauvaises herbes du Québec, ed. 2. Min. Agric. Colonisation du Québec. Publ. 288. 113 pp.

HANSEN, A. and DAHL, A. O. 1965. Long-term analysis of atmospheric pollen. Proc. Atmospher. Biol. Conf. pp. 145–150.

HOLLICK, A. and MARTIN, G. C. 1930. The upper Cretaceous floras of Alaska. U.S. Geol. Surv. Prof. Pap. 159. United States Government Printing Office, Washington, D.C.

IVINS, J. D. 1952. Concerning the ecology of *Urtica dioica* L. J. Ecol. **40**: 380–382.

McANDREWS, J. H., BERTI, A. A. and NORRIS, G. 1973. Key to the Quaternary pollen and spores of the Great Lakes Region. Life Sci. Misc. Publ., R. Ont. Mus. 61 pp.

MUENSCHER, W. C. 1955. Weeds. Macmillan Company, New York, N.Y. 560 pp.

NASSERY, H. 1970. Phosphate absorption by plants from habitats of different phosphate status. II. Absorption and incorporation of phosphate by intact plants. New Phytol. **69**: 197–203.

PIGOTT, C. D. 1964. Nettles as indicators of soil conditions. New Sci. **25**: 230–232.

RORISON, I. H. 1967. A seedling bioassay on some soils in the Sheffield area. J. Ecol. **55**: 725–741.

ROUSSEAU, C. 1974. Géographie floristique du Québec–Labrador. Les Presses de l'Université Laval, Québec. 799 pp.

SEN, A. K. and JENSEN, H. J. 1969. Host-parasite relationships of various plants and the hop cyst nematode, *Heterodera humuli*. Plant Dis. Rep. **53**: 37–40.

SOLOMON, W. R. and CATHEY, J. 1970. Pollen of nettles: a potential determinant of interactability in ragweed pollinosis. J. Allergy **45**: 99–100.

SPENCER, K. A. 1969. The Agromyzidae of Canada and Alaska. Mem. Entomol. Soc. Can. No. 64. 311 pp.

STERN, L. J. 1943. Identification of *Urtica*. Post Institute, New York, N.Y. 16 pp.

TOTEV, T. 1964. Research into growing common nettle for fodder. Rasteviev'd. Nauko **1**: 95–104.

WILLIS, C. L. 1969. Toxic constituents of the stinging nettle. M.S. Dissertation, Iowa State University, Ames, Iowa. Mineo. 42 pp.

WOODLAND, D. W. 1973. Stinging nettles, taste good! Macdonald J. **34**: 5–6.

WOODLAND, D. W. 1975. Biosystematics of the perennial North American species of *Urtica*. Univ. Microfilms Inc. Ann Arbor, Mich. 174 pp.

THE BIOLOGY OF CANADIAN WEEDS.
22. *Descurainia sophia* (L.) Webb

K. F. BEST

Research Station, Research Branch, Agriculture Canada, 5000 Wascana Parkway, Regina, Saskatchewan. Received 13 Jan. 1976, accepted 28 Oct. 1976.

BEST, K. F. 1977. The biology of Canadian weeds. 22. *Descurainia sophia* (L.) Webb. Can. J. Plant Sci. **57**: 499-507.

An account is given of the biology of *Descurainia sophia* (L.) Webb. This species, commonly known as flixweed, is found throughout Canada, but is particularly prevalent as a weed in the cultivated fields of the Prairie Provinces. The paper is one of a series of the biology of Canadian weeds and is concerned primarily with those characteristics of the species which appear to present the main obstacles to its effective control.

La présente étude porte sur la biologie de *Descurainia sophia* (L.) Webb. Cette espèce, communément appelée sagesse-des-chirurgiens, se retrouve partout au Canada mais se révèle particulièrement nuisible comme adventice dans les cultures des Prairies. Cette recherche s'insère dans une série d'études sur la biologie des mauvaises herbes canadiennes et s'intéresse surtout aux caractéristiques de l'espèce qui semblent constituer les principaux obstacles aux programmes de désherbage.

1. Name

Descurainia sophia (L.) Webb. — **flixweed** (Canada Weed Committee 1969), tansy mustard (Frankton and Mulligan 1970), **sagesse-des-chirurgiens**, asperge (Ferron and Cayouette 1971). Cruciferae, mustard family, Crucifères.

2. Description and Account of Variation

Annual or winter annual, the whole plant grayish-green due to minutely branched hairs; stems 2–10 dm high, branched above; leaves alternate, all divided two to three times into very narrow segments and strongly scented; flowers clustered at top of stem, petals yellow, 2–2.5 mm long and not longer than the sepals; siliques narrowly linear, 15–30 mm long, 0.5–1.0 mm wide ascending at right angles to the stem on short stalks 7–12 mm long; seeds 10–20 in one row in each half of the silique, oblong–ellipsoid, bright orange, about 0.8 mm long (Frankton and Mulligan 1970; Fernald 1950). Seedlings and mature plant are shown in Fig. 1.

Can. J. Plant Sci. 57: 499-507 (Apr. 1977)

The following description of flixweed seedlings is from Kummer (1951). Hypocotyl pubescent with a few stalked, star-shaped hairs, soon curved and not apparent above ground; seed leaves 0.75 × 4 to 1.5 × 6.5 mm; stalk pubescent with hairs similar to those of the hypocotyl, a definite stub remaining when the blade is shed; leaves alternate except for the first cotyledon leaves, which appear to be paired, pale green, rather thick, and a little rough, hoary with stalked, star-shaped hairs, each with six rays or less; leaves folded inward longitudinally in bud, the lobes lying side by side directed towards the leaf tip; tasteless, ordorless basal leaves in a rosette; stem not apparent.

Chromosome number $2n = 28$ has been obtained on North American and European material by Mulligan (1961) and other workers.

Flixweed can be distinguished from two close relatives and also from *Sisymbrium* species by the following characteristics (Frankton and Mulligan 1970). Green or short-fruited tansy mustard (*Descurainia*

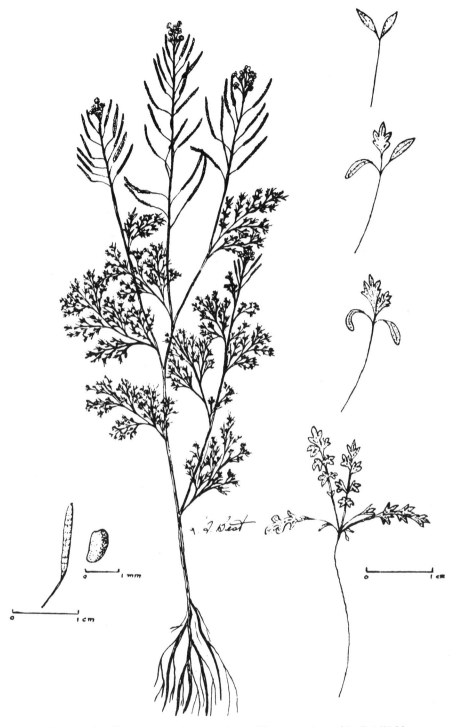

Fig. 1.   Seedling stages and mature plant of *Descurainia sophia* (L.) Webb.

pinnata (Walt.) Britt. var. *brachycarpa* (Richards.) Fern.) is a greenish plant with leaves divided into fine segments. It differs from flixweed in having glandular hairs, seeds in two rows in each half of the silique and siliques about 1.2 cm long on stalks of nearly the same length. Gray tansy mustard (*Descurainia richardsonii* (Sweet) E. Schulz) is a grayish plant with leaves less divided than those of flixweed. It is rather readily distinguished from flixweed and green tansy mustard as its siliques and stalks are erect and close to the main flowering stem. The siliques of gray tansy mustard are about 6 mm long and are on stalks 3 mm long. Both tansy mustards are native to North America and are widely distributed, although practically absent from the Atlantic Provinces. Like flixweed, they are more abundant in the Prairie Provinces. The *Sisymbrium* species, including tumble mustard (*Sisymbrium altissimum* L.), are similar to flixweed and the tansy mustards. However, the *Sisymbrium* species do not have branched hairs and the flowers are larger (2.5–8.0 mm) than those of the *Descurainia* species.

3. Economic Importance

(*a*) *Detrimental* — Anderson (1971) lists flixweed as one of the main weeds encountered during a 5-yr study in the semi-arid region of southwest Saskatchewan. Although Chepil (1946) noted that flixweed does not have the same competitiveness with grain crops as does wild mustard (*Sinapis arvensis* L.), an extra cultivation in the spring is often required to control rank growth from heavy infestations of overwintering plants that can crowd out grain and reduce crop yields (Slife et al. 1960).

(*b*) *Beneficial* — Overwintering stands of flixweed can afford protection from erosion on fields lacking good cover, of crop residues.

(*c*) *Legislative* — Flixweed is included in the category of "other weeds" under the Seeds Act and Regulations administered by Agriculture Canada (1967) and is listed as noxious in Alberta (1955) and in Manitoba (1970).

4. Distribution

Flixweed was introduced from Eurasia and now occurs in all provinces (Fig. 2). It is one of the most abundant weeds in the Prairie Provinces including the Peace River area (Groh 1930, 1937, 1949; Groh and Frankton 1947; Frankton and Mulligan 1970). In his survey of the weeds on cultivated land in the Prairie Provinces, Alex (1966) recorded flixweed from 76% of the districts in Alberta, from 96% of the districts in Saskatchewan and from 54% of the districts in Manitoba. It is very common throughout British Columbia to latitude 54° and is the annual weed most consistently found throughout the Cariboo and central portions of the province (Eastman 1944, 1947). It has also been found on disturbed soil in the Mackenzie River area of the North West Territories (Thieret 1963; Cody 1956). Montgomery et al. (1962) stated that the weed was less common in Eastern Canada than on the prairies. Flixweed plants have been found on railways and waste places in the Clay Belt of Northern Ontario and Quebec (Baldwin 1958). In Quebec, Rousseau (1968) reported the species at Sept-Iles and from Matane to Gaspé on the south bank of the St. Lawrence River.

According to Muenscher (1955) the species is widely established in the United States from Quebec to Washington, south to Delaware, Missouri and California, being more common in Eastern Oregon, Washington and the Great Basin region.

Apparently native throughout temperate Europe to 65°, it is found in North Africa, in Asia from Kashmir to Kumaon and extending to Buluchistan and to China and Japan (Clapham et al. 1962; Chopra et al. 1960). It has been introduced into South America (Anonymous 1971) and into New Zealand (Clapham et al. 1962).

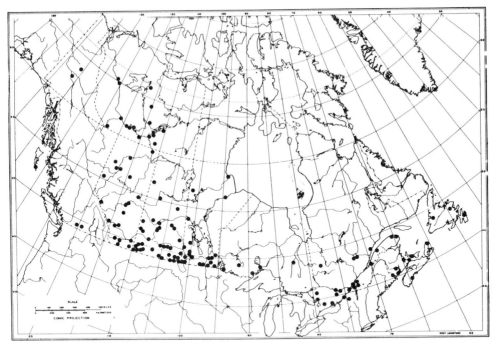

Fig. 2. The distribution in Canada of *Descurainia sophia* (L.) Webb based on specimens from various Canadian herbaria.

5. Habitat

(a) *Climatic requirements* — Plants germinating in the fall establish rosettes and survive the freezing conditions. Flixweed is better adapted to the climate of the Canadian Prairies than to the more humid eastern provinces (Rousseau 1968). It occurs in Canada from subalpine (Best, unpublished data) to sea level (Calder and Taylor 1968). In greenhouse studies at Swift Current, flixweed flowered earlier when root temperatures were maintained at a constant 5 C rather than at 12, 20 or 27 C (Best and Nielsen 1964).

(b) *Substratum* — Primarily found on open, warm, nutrient-rich sandy or stony soils in Europe, flixweed is often an indicator of sand (Hanf 1973). Pfeiffer (1957) noted that the species was often found in the rubble of bombed cities where ecological properties were uniform, being warm, excessively drained, rich in $CaCO_3$ and poor in humus. In Canada, it infests grainfields, gardens, roadsides, fencelines, drift soil and anywhere that land has been disturbed (Frankton and Mulligan 1970), and is not restricted to sandy soils on the prairies.

(c) *Communities in which the species occurs* — On the Canadian Prairies, flixweed is generally associated with *Thlaspi arvense* L., especially in fields that are not cultivated in the fall (Best and McIntyre, unpublished data). Both species germinate throughout the growing season and late into the fall, and overwinter as rosettes. According to Best (unpublished data) and the Canada Weed Committee (1973, 1974), other species associated with flixweed in Western Canada in the 2nd yr include: *Agropyron repens* (L.) Beauv., *Amaranthus albus* L., *A. blitoides* S. Wats., *A. retroflexus* L., *Avena fatua* L., *Bromus tectorum* L., *Capsella bursa-pastoris* (L.) Medic.,

251

Cerastium spp., *Chenopodium album* L., *C. fremontii* S. Wats., *Cirsium arvense* (L.) Scop., *Convolvulus arvensis* L., *Crepis tectorum* L., *Epilobium angustifolium* L., *Equisetum* spp., *Euphorbia esula* L., *E. serpyllifolia* Pers., *Hordeum jubatum* L., *Iva axillaris* Pursh, *Kochia scoparia* (L.) Schrad., *Malva pusilla* Sm., *Matricaria maritima* L. var. *agrestis* (Knaf) Wilmott, *Monolepis nuttalliana* (R. + S.) Greene, *Lactuca* spp., *Lappula echinata* Gilib., *Lygodesmia juncea* (Pursh) D. Don, *Salsola pestifer* A. Nels., *Saponaria vaccaria* L., *Senecio* spp., *Setaria viridis* L., *Sinapis arvense* L., *Sisymbrium altissimum* L., *Sonchus arvensis* L., *Taraxacum officinale* Weber, *Thlaspi arvense* L., *Tragopogon dubius* Scop. and *Veronica* spp.

In eastern Canada, flixweed has been found growing with *Camelina microcarpa* Andrz., *Amaranthus retroflexus* L., *Brassica juncea* (L.) Czern., *Ambrosia* spp., *Polygonum aviculare* L., *Sisymbrium altissimum* L., *Lactuca scariola* L., *Arenaria* spp. and *Viola arvensis* Murr. (Canada Weed Committee 1975).

6. History

When Torrey and Gray (1840) found *D. sophia* near Quebec, Montreal and in other parts of Lower Canada, they considered it to be native to Canada. In reality it moved across Europe with human migration and reached Canada with the French settlers (Marie-Victorin 1947). Holmes found the species near Montreal in 1821; Macoun, in 1882, recorded the species along Rivière Madeleine and Cté. de Gaspé-Nord (Rousseau 1968). The earliest specimens in the DAO herbarium at Ottawa are from Manitoba and Saskatchewan, dated 1901 (Groh 1944). Scoggan (1957) cited the earliest collection in Manitoba as being by Fletcher in 1901 at Plum Coulee. Specimens from Beaverlodge and Halcourt appear to be the first records for Alberta (Groh 1930).

Flixweed was collected at Yreka in California in 1908 by Jepson (Robbins 1940). It was introduced into North Dakota

about 1910 (Stevens 1950). Howell collected it in 1933 on the sandy open Mojave Desert, 11 mi south of Mojave, Kern County; this seems to be the first record of the plant in Southern California (Robbins 1940). Anderson (1946) classified flixweed as a weed introduced into Alaska from Europe.

7. Growth and Development

(a) *Morphology* — The low, rosette habit of the vegetative phase protects overwintering plants from low temperatures and drying winds, enabling them to gain maximum advantage from the insulating effect of snow cover. The plants rapidly develop numerous leaves and lateral branches in the spring. A rosette of a single plant of flixweed may produce as many as 15 lateral branches (Kott 1944). The racemose inflorescence and the capacity of the plant to produce numerous additional inflorescences from lateral branches, in response to favorable growing conditions, largely accounts for the prolific seed production characteristics of this species.

(b) *Perennation* — Flixweed may overwinter as seeds in the soil or as compact rosettes. These rosettes may vary in size and number of leaves depending on their stage of development at freeze-up

Physiological data — Flixweed was rather inefficient in usage of moisture in greenhouse studies at Swift Current, requiring 711 kg of water to produce 1 kg of dry matter (Anderson and Best 1965). In the same study, stinkweed (*Thlaspi arvense* L.), barley (*Hordeum vulgare* L.), Russian thistle (*Salsola pestifer* A. Nels.) and green foxtail (*Setaria viridis* (L.) Beauv.) required 894, 570, 550 and 470 kg of water, respectively, to produce 1 kg of dry matter.

(d) *Phenology* — In the recording of the flowering sequence of local flora at Swift Current by Budd and Campbell (1959) and its continuation by Best (unpublished data), it was found that over a 13-yr period, the average day of first flowering for flixweed was 29 May. The average date of emergence of flixweed seeded in late fall was 27 April, with the first flowering by 29 May (Best, unpublished data). Stevens (1956) recorded the average date of first flowering in North Dakota as 28 May. Flowering continues throughout the summer (Frankton and Mulligan 1970). The date of maturity at Swift Current was 22 July (Chepil 1946), while Thieret (1963) claimed that fruit matured as early as 13 July at Enterprise, N.W.T.

Best and McIntyre (unpublished data) investigated the importance of vernalization on the acceleration of flowering at Regina. Seeds stored for 8 mo at room temperature without natural vernalization and sown outdoors in early May required 95 days to flower, whereas spring-emerging plants from seed overwintered in the soil flowered within 45 days. Overwintering rosettes flowered 2 wk before spring-emerging flixweed.

Moistened seeds were vernalized at 2 C, germinated, and the seedlings grown in vermiculite under 16-h day, 20 C, 30,000 lx, and watered with a modified Hoagland's solution (Best and McIntyre 1972) containing 52.5 ppm N. Controls with no cold treatment did not flower within 119 days. Plants from seed held for 2 wk at 2 C flowered within 57 days. Seed vernalized for 4 and 6 wk flowered within 71 and 41 days, respectively.

Seedlings grown in soil for 1 mo (6-7 leaves) were vernalized at 2 C, grown under the above conditions and watered with tapwater. Plants held for 2 wk at 2 C flowered within 97 days, while those kept at 2 C for 4 and 6 wk flowered within 80 days.

Seedlings were grown in vermiculite under 16-h day, 20 C and were watered with a modified Hoagland's solution containing 52.5 ppm N. After 1 mo (6-7 leaves), gibberellic acid (GA) was applied to the stem apices with a micropipette on alternate days. Untreated plants flowered within 96 days; plants receiving 10 μg/liter of GA flowered within 71 days, while those

treated with 50 μg/liter of GA flowered within 63 days. The latter plants were 10 cm taller than those receiving the 10 μg/liter treatment and were five times taller than the controls.

(e) *Mycorrhiza* — No information available.

8. Reproduction

(a) *Floral biology* — The flowers are densely crowded in terminal racemes which elongate considerably after flowering (Anonymous 1971). Flixweed is autogamous and rarely visited by insects (Mulligan 1972). The flowers have been rated in their photometric brightness at 20.5% for the yellow portion of the insect visual spectrum (Mulligan and Kevan 1973).

(b) *Seed production and dispersal* — Stevens (1954) estimated the average number of seeds from a single plant as 75,650 and 0.12 g as the weight of 1,000 seeds. Chepil (1946) noted that the seeds of *D. sophia* shattered four times as readily as those of Thatcher wheat (*Triticum aestivum* L.). At harvest, many flixweed seeds are scattered in the vicinity of the parent plants, while others are included as impurities in cereal and forage seed.

The seeds of flixweed are spread by wind, animals and man (Anonymous 1971). Flixweed was 1 of the 21 species of Cruciferae found by Young and Evans (1973) to possess a mucilaginous substance. Salisbury (1961) suggested that mucilaginous seeds become attached to the feathers of birds feeding in ruderal communities and are removed into new areas by preening.

(c) *Viability of seeds and germination* — Flixweed germinated most readily in the autumn at Swift Current and its dormancy in cultivated soil exceeded 3 yr (Chepil 1946). When flixweed was seeded in the fall there was 43% germination over a 3-yr period, with yearly rates of 24, 8 and 11%. During the 1st yr, one third of the germination occurred by the end of May with another flush of over 50% in the fall. In the 2nd yr, the same general pattern was evident, with peak germinations in the spring and in the fall. The majority of the germination in the 3rd yr occurred in the fall.

Rogers and Stearns (1955) found that seeds germinated better soon after harvest than after 1 yr of storage. In the laboratory, optimum germination with both new and 1-yr-old seed was obtained by alternating diurnal temperatures of 16 h at 10 C and 8 h at 30 C with light of 1,000 lx fluorescent (Best, unpublished data).

9. Hybrids
Interspecific hybrids involving *Descurainia sophia* are unknown in Canada.

10. Population Dynamics
Flixweed infests gardens, roadsides, grain-fields, townsites and land that has been cultivated, or where the native vegetation has been destroyed by other means (Neatby and Greaney 1941). In the fall, on summer fallow land, stands of flixweed seedlings have been observed that were too dense to allow plants to grow to any great size (Groh 1944). On 25 September 1969, Molberg (1969) found 12.1 flixweed rosettes/m^2 on heavy clay summer fallow at Regina. This dropped to 7.1/m^2 by 5 May of the following year, a survival of 59%. He also reported a spring emergence of flixweed seedlings on the same sampling area of 7.25/m^2. Stevens (1957) recorded a maximum seed population of 704,582/m^2 in a North Dakota soil.

11. Response to Herbicides and Other Chemicals
Molberg and Hay (1968) reported excellent control of flixweed on summer fallow at Regina with paraquat at 1 kg/ha in 225 liters of water with 1% Agrol 90 (a cationic wetting agent). Late autumn applications of ester and amine formulations of 2,4-D at 0.42 kg/ha controlled winter annual forms of flixweed in Saskatchewan (Anderson 1969; Molberg 1969). Late autumn applications of 2,4-D at 0.42 kg/ha controlled

flixweed in winter wheat (Anonymous 1971). Sodium or amine formulations of 2,4-D at 0.8 to 1.0 kg/ha applied in winter wheat at shooting stage in the Ukraine, when *D. sophia* was in the rosette stage, reduced the population of flixweed by 95.6% and increased grain yields by 0.3 t/ha (Vorob'ev and Lebedev 1970). In Canada, flixweed is more difficult to kill with 2,4-D in the spring than in the fall (Hay 1975).

12. Response to Other Human Manipulations
Flixweed that germinates in the fall can be controlled by fall or early spring cultivation (Hay 1975). Overwintering rosettes that are not controlled by spraying, cultivation or during the seeding operation offer strong competition for the crop because of their rapid growth in the spring. In wet periods, cultivation may not kill the plants. In many areas, fall tillage is not a desirable practice, since standing stubble and other crop residues trap snow and offer protection against erosion by wind.

13. Response to Parasites
(*a*) *Insects and other nondomestic animals* — Larvae of *Colaphellus sophia transylvanicus* Schall (Coleoptera: Chrysomelidae) were collected from *Descurainia sophia* in Bulgaria (Gruev 1968). Two beetles were reported by Maw and Molloy (1975) from Saskatchewan collections: a leaf feeder, the red turnip beetle, *Entomoscelis americana* Brown (Coleoptera: Chrysomelidae) and an insect predator, the striped collops, *Collops vittatus* Say (Coleoptera: Melyridae).

(*b*) *Micro-organisms and viruses* — Conners (1967) cites references of *Albugo cruciferarum* S. F. Gray; *Peronospora parisitica* (Pers. ex Fr.) Fr.: *Puccinia aristidae* Tracy and *Sclerotinia sclerotiorum* (Lib.) de Bary as found on species of *Descurainia* in Canada.

(*c*) *Higher plant parasites* — No information available.

254

ACKNOWLEDGMENTS

I wish to thank Dr. G. I. McIntyre for his cooperation and Dr. J. R. Hay for his critical appraisal of the manuscript.

AGRICULTURE CANADA. 1967. Seeds Act and Regulations. Queen's Printer, Ottawa, Ontario. 50 pp.

ALBERTA. 1955. Noxious Weeds Act, Chap. 262, p. 4035.

ALEX, J. F. 1966. Survey of weeds of cultivated land in the prairie provinces. Exp. Farm, Res. Br., Agric. Can., Regina, Saskatchewan. 68 pp.

ANDERSON, C. H. and BEST, K. F. 1965. Water use efficiency of barley and weeds grown in the greenhouse. Soil Horizons 6(1): 15–16.

ANDERSON, C. H. 1969. Control of winter annual forms of stinkweed and flixweed. Can. J. Plant Sci. 49: 87–89.

ANDERSON, C. H. 1971. Comparison of tillage and chemical summerfallow in a semiarid region. Can. J. Soil Sci. 51: 397–403.

ANDERSON, J. P. 1946. Flora of Alaska and adjacent parts of Canada. Part V. Iowa State Coll. J. Sci. 20(3): 297–347.

ANONYMOUS 1971 CIBA-GEIGY Weed Tables. Ciba-Geigy Ltd., Basle, Switzerland.

BALDWIN, W. K. W. 1958. Plants of the clay belt of northern Ontario and Quebec. Nat. Mus. Can. Bull. 156: 165. 324 pp.

BEST, K. F. and NIELSEN, K. F. 1964. Soil Horizons 5(2): 14.

BEST, K. F. and McINTYRE, G. I. 1972. Studies on the flowering of Thlapis arvense L. I. The influence of some environmental and genetic factors. Bot. Gaz. 133: 454–459.

BUDD, A. C. and CAMPBELL, J. B. 1959. Flowering sequence of a local flora. J. Range Manage. 12(3): 127–132.

CALDER, J. A. and TAYLOR, R. L. 1968. Flora of the Queen Charlotte Islands. Part I. Systematics of the vascular plants. CDA Monog. No. 4(1): 366. 659 pp.

CANADA WEED COMMITTEE. 1969. Common and botanical names of weeds in Canada. CDA Publ. 1397. 67 pp.

CANADA WEED COMMITTEE. (West Sect.). 1973. Res. Rep. 438 pp.

CANADA WEED COMMITTEE. (West Sect.). 1974. Res. Rep. 496 pp.

CANADA WEED COMMITTEE. (East Sect.). 1975. Res. Rep. 330 pp.

CHEPIL, W. S. 1946. Germination of weed seeds. I. Longevity, periodicity of germination, and vitality of seeds in cultivated soil. Sci. Agric. 26(7): 307–346.

CHOPRA, I. C., ABROL, B. K. and HANDA, K. L. 1960. Arid zone research. XIII. Medicinal plants of the arid zones. UNESCO 1960: 31–32. Place de Fontenoy, Paris. 96 pp.

CLAPHAM, A. R., TUTIN, T. G. and WARBERG, E. F. 1962. Flora of the British Isles. Cambridge Univ. Press. 1962: 185. 1296 pp.

CODY, W. J. 1956. New plant records for northern Alberta and southern Mackenzie district. Can. Field-Natur. 70(3): 101–130.

CONNERS, I. L. 1967. An annotated index of plant diseases in Canada. Can. Dep. Agric. Publ. 1251. 381 pp.

EASTHAM, J. W. 1944. Stock-poisoning plants and weeds. B.C. Dep. Agric. Rep. 58: 63.

EASTHAM, J. W. 1947. Supplement to flora of Southern British Columbia, B.C. Provincial Museum, Dep. Educ. Spec. Publ. I. Victoria, B.C. 119 pp.

FERNALD, M. L. 1950. Gray's manual of botany. American Book Co., New York, N.Y. 1632 pp.

FERRON, M. and CAYOUETTE, R. 1971. Nom des mauvaises herbes du Québec. Min. de l'Agric. et de la Colonization du Québec. Publ. 288. 113 pp.

FRANKTON, C. and MULLIGAN, G. A. 1970. Weeds of Canada. Can. Dep. Agric. Publ. 948. 217 pp.

GROH, H. 1930. Grande Prairie weeds. Dom. Can., Dep. Agric. Pam. 117: 8. 12 pp.

GROH, H. 1937. Peace–Athabaska weeds. Dom. Can., Dep. Agric. Publ. 556: 27. 42 pp.

GROH, H. 1944. Canadian weed survey. 3rd Annu. Rep. 70 pp.

GROH, H. 1949. Plants of clearing and trail between Peace River and Fort Vermilion, Alberta. Field-Natur. 63(4): 119–134.

GROH, H. and FRANKTON, C. 1947. Canadian weed survey. 6th Annu. Rep. 25 pp.

GRUEV, B. 1968. A new dipteran parasite Macquartia flavipes (Meigen, 1924) in the larva of Colaphellus sophiae Schall (Coleoptera, Chrysomelidae). Mitt. Deut. Entomol. Ges. 27(3): 33.

HANF, M. 1973. Weeds and their seedlings. W. S. Cowell, Ltd., Ipswich, Great Britain. 348 pp.

KOTT, S. 1944. Certain peculiarities of weed development in Siberia. Soversk. Bot. (Leningrad) 1944(4/5).

KUMMER, A. P. 1951. Weed seedlings. Univ. of Chicago Press. 435 pp.

MANITOBA. 1970. Noxious Weeds Act. Chap. N110:1–20.

MARIE-VICTORIN, F. 1947. Flore laurentienne. Les Frères des Écoles Chrétiennes, Montréal, Qué. 916 pp.

MOLBERG, E. S. and HAY, J. R. 1968. Chemical weed control on summerfallow. Can. J. Soil Sci. 48: 255–263.

MOLBERG, E. S. 1969. Fall applications of 2,4-D for flixweed and stinkweed control. Canada Weed Committee (Western Section). Res. Rep. 315 pp.

MONTGOMERY, F. H., SWITZER, C. M. and KINGSBURY, C. H. 1962. Ontario weeds. Ont. Dep. Agric. Publ. 505: 42. 115 pp.

MUENSCHER, W. C. 1955. Weeds. The Macmillan Co., New York, N.Y. 560 pp.

MULLIGAN, G. A. 1961. Chromosome numbers of Canadian weeds. III. Can. J. Bot. 39: 1057–1066.

MULLIGAN, G. A. 1972. Autogamy, allogamy and pollination in some Canadian weeds. Can. J. Bot. 50(8): 1767–1771.

MULLIGAN, G. A. and KEVAN, P. G. 1973. Color, brightness, and other floral characteristics attracting insects to the blossoms of some Canadian weeds. Can. J. Bot. 51: 1939–1952.

NEATBY, K. W. and GREANEY, F. J. 1941. An illustrated guide to prairie weeds. Line Elevators Farm Serv. Bull. 2. Winnipeg, Man. 80 pp.

PFEIFFER, H. 1957. Development of plant communities on the rubble of bombed cities. Vegetatio 7(5/6): 301–320.

ROBBINS, W. W. 1940. Alien plants growing without cultivation in California. Univ. of Calif., Agric. Exp. Sta., Berkley, Calif. Bull. 637. 128 pp.

ROGERS, B. J. and STEARNS, F. W. 1955. Preliminary studies on the germination of weed seeds. NCWCC. Proc. 12: 7.

ROUSSEAU, C. 1968. Histoire, habitat et distribution de 220 plantes introduites au Québec. Natur. Can. 95(1): 49–171.

SALISBURY, E. J. 1961. Weeds and aliens. Macmillan Co., New York, N.Y. 330 pp.

SCOGGAN, H. J. 1957. Flora of Manitoba. Nat. Mus. Can. Bull. 140: 319. 619 pp.

SLIFE, F. W., BUCHHOLTZ, K. P. and KOMMEDAHL, T. 1960. Weeds of the North Central States. Univ. of Ill., Agric. Exp. Sta. Circ. 718: 82. 262 pp.

STEVENS, O. A. 1950 Handbook of North Dakota plants. N. Dak. Agric. Coll. 1950: 156. Knight Printing Co., Fargo, N. Dak. 324 pp.

STEVENS, O. A. 1954. Weed seed facts. N. Dak. Agric. Coll. Circ. A-218.

STEVENS, O. A. 1956. Flowering dates of weeds in North Dakota. N. Dak. Agric. Exp. Sta. Bimo. Bull. 18(6): 209–213.

STEVENS, O. A. 1957. Weights of seeds and numbers per plant. Weeds 5(1): 46–55.

THIERET, J. W. 1963. Botanical survey along the Yellowknife Highway, Northwest Territories, Canada. I. Catalogue of the flora. Sida 1(3): 117–170.

TORREY, J. and GRAY, E. 1840. A flora of North Dakota. 2 Vols., New York.

VOROB'EV, N. E. and LEBEDEV, E. M. 1970. *Descurainia sophia* in winter wheat in southern steppes of the Ukrainian SSR and its control. Osnovnye Rezul'taty Raboty Ismail'skoi Opytnoi Stantsii Dnepropretrovsk, Ukrainian SSR 1970: 61–64.

YOUNG. J. A. and EVANS, R. A. 1973. Mucilaginous and seed coats. Weed Sci. 21(1): 52–54.

THE BIOLOGY OF CANADIAN WEEDS
23. *Rhus radicans* L.

GERALD A. MULLIGAN and BONNY E. JUNKINS

Biosystematics Research Institute, Research Branch, Agriculture Canada, Ottawa, Ontario K1A 0C6. Received 8 Nov. 1976, accepted 17 Dec. 1976.

MULLIGAN, GERALD A. AND JUNKINS, BONNY E. 1977. The biology of Canadian weeds. 23. *Rhus radicans* L. Can. J. Plant Sci. **57**: 515–523.

Poison ivy (*Rhus radicans* L.) occurs in repeatedly disturbed habitats in every province except Newfoundland. Three varieties are recognized in Canada: var. *radicans*, var. *rydbergii* (Small *ex* Rydberg) Rehder, and var. *negundo* (Greene) G. A. Mulligan. Variety *rydbergii* is the most common and widespread. The biology of poison ivy and the dermatitis it causes in humans is discussed.

L'herbe à la puce (*Rhus radicans* L.) est répandue dans les habitats constamment dérangés de chaque province, sauf à Terre-Neuve. On trouve trois variétés au Canada, soit *radicans*, *rydbergii* (Small *ex* Rydberg) Rehder et *negundo* (Greene) G. A. Mulligan. La variété *rydbergii* est la plus commune. L'auteur étudie la biologie de l'herbe à la puce et la dermatite qu'elle cause chez l'homme.

1. Name

Rhus radicans L. — **poison ivy** (Canada Weed Committee 1969); **herbe à la puce** (Ferron and Cayouette 1971). Anacardiaceae, cashew family, Anacardiacées.

2. Description and Account of Variation

Woody perennial, spreading by seeds and woody rhizomes; a trailing vine, a subshrub to shrub from 0.5 to 12 dm high, or a vine climbing rough surfaces to 150 dm high; leaves alternate, 6.5–40 cm long, consisting of 3 leaflets, middle leaflets with stalks 8–55 mm long, lateral leaflets with shorter stalks 0.5–6.0 mm long, leaflet margins entire, toothed to rarely deeply lobed; leaves green during summer and colored various shades of yellow, orange, red or bronze in autumn; flowers clustered, small, whitish-green; male and female flowers normally on separate plants; fruits clustered, globose, green to yellow, waxy, 3–7 mm in diameter, 1-seeded.

Three recognizable varieties of *Rhus radicans* occur in Canada: var. *rydbergii* (Small *ex* Rydb.) Rehder is most common, var. *negundo* (Greene) G. A. Mulligan

Can. J. Plant Sci. 57: 515-523 (Apr. 1977)

(*Rhus radicans* var. **negundo** (Greene) G. A. Mulligan, comb. et stat. nov., *Toxicodendron negundo* Greene, Leafl. Bot. Observ. Crit. 1: 117. 1905) is next common, var. *radicans* is least common. Photographs of the three varieties are shown in Fig. 1. Although the morphology of the three varieties intergrades slightly where their ranges overlap, they can usually be distinguished by the following characteristics.

Var. *rydbergii* — a trailing vine, or a subshrub to shrub lacking aerial roots; pedicels glabrous or with short, appressed, ascending puberulence; hairs along midrib on undersurface of leaflets not tufted; hairs along sideveins on undersurface of leaflets spreading; usually fewer than 5 leaves on stems; leaflets toothed or mostly toothed.

Var. *negundo* — shrub to vine with aerial roots climbing rough surfaces; pedicels with long spreading pubescence (some plants with short, appressed, ascending puberulence in southwestern Quebec); hairs along midrib on undersurface of leaflets not tufted; hairs along sideveins on undersurface of leaflets spreading; usually 5 or more leaves on vertical stems; leaflets toothed or mostly toothed.

257

Fig. 1. *Rhus radicans*. A. var. *negundo* climbing tree. B. var. *radicans* in fruit. C. var. *rydergii* in flower. D. patch of var. *rydbergii* in fruit.

Var. *radicans* shrub to vine with aerial roots climbing rough surfaces; pedicels with short, appressed, ascending puberulence; undersurface of leaflets with tufts of hairs towards bases of midribs (especially in angle formed with main lateral veins); hairs ascending along lateral veins on undersurface of leaflets; usually 5 or more leaves on vertical stems; leaflets entire or mostly entire.

In addition to the variability of growth habit in poison ivy, there is great variability in leaf size and leaf shape (Fig. 2). Leaves vary in size from 6.5 to 40 cm long, and leaflets from entire and variously toothed to occasionally deeply lobed. Entire leaflets are most common in var. *radicans* and deeply lobed leaflets most prevalent in var. *negundo*. Although leaves of poison ivy normally have 3 leaflets, leaves with 5 leaflets sometimes occur. Leaves of poison ivy with 5 leaflets are probably rarer than a "four-leaved clover."

The chromosome number $n = 15$ was obtained on material of var. *rydbergii* from 3 locations in Ottawa District, Ont., and 1 location in Ottawa District, Que., and on plants of var. *negundo* from 2 locations in Ottawa District, Ont. Meiosis was regular at all stages and the chromosomes formed 15 pairs at diakinesis and metaphase I. Previous counts of $2n = 30$ were obtained on plants of *Rhus radicans* from southwestern Ontario (R. J. Moore unpublished), Manitoba (Löve and Löve 1973) and Michigan (Gillis 1971).

Poison ivy is often confused with three other plants that also occur in Canada: hog peanut (*Amphicarpa bracteata* (L.) Fern.), Manitoba maple (*Acer negundo* L.), and Virginia creeper (*Parthenocissus quinquefolia* (L.) Planch.) (Frankton and Mulligan 1970). Poison ivy has 3 leaflets, is woody with woolly winter buds, has cream to yellow-green flowers 0.2–0.5 cm broad, has alternate leaves and has clusters of globose, waxy, green to yellow fruits 3–7 mm in diam; hog peanut has 3 leaflets but is not woody and has larger lilac to white

flowers about 1 cm in diam; young seedlings of Manitoba maple have 3 leaflets but have opposite leaves, and mature plants

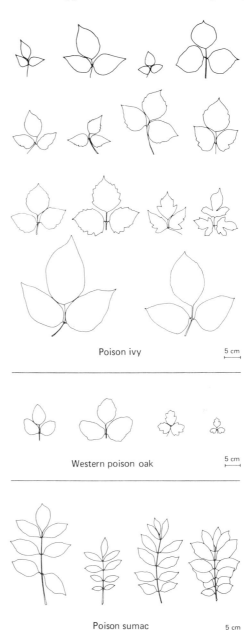

Poison ivy   5 cm

Western poison oak   5 cm

Poison sumac   5 cm

Fig. 2. Variation in size and shape of leaves in poisonous *Rhus* species.

259

have winged fruits; Virginia creeper has 5 leaflets and bluish, globose fruits 5–7 mm in diam.

A poisonous sap that causes a characteristic dermatitis on the skin of humans is present in *R. radicans* and two other species of *Rhus* that grow in Canada. The other two species are western poison oak (*R. diversiloba* Torr. & Gray) and poison sumac (*R. vernix* L.). The latter two species are rarely encountered in Canada and thus are not usually important causative agents of *Rhus* dermatitis. Western poison oak, a shrub with rounded apices on its three leaflets (Fig. 2), is confined, in Canada, to remote areas on the east coast of Vancouver Island and on some small adjacent islands (Fig. 3). Poison sumac occurs in some woody swamps of southern Ontario and southern Quebec (Fig. 3). It is a tall shrub or small tree with 6–12 leaflets arranged in pairs with an additional single leaflet at the end of the midrib (Fig. 2). Poison oak (*R. toxicodendron* L.) does not occur in Canada.

3. Economic Importance

(a) Detrimental — Poison ivy causes a dermatitis in humans. The poisonous principle is contained in the sap and is present in all parts of the plant except the anthers, pollen, xylem and epidermis. The surfaces of roots, stems, leaves and fruit must be ruptured to release the poisonous sap. Since the poisonous principle must penetrate the skin before poisoning results, the most severe dermatitis symptoms are in areas with thin skin and poisoning is less severe or does not occur in areas with thick skin or heavy hair. The first symptom of poisoning is a severe itching of the skin. Later, a red inflammation and a blistering of the skin occurs. In severe cases, oozing sores develop. The rash spreads only by contact with the poisonous principle, not as the result of exudates from sores.

There are four antigenic compounds in the poisonous sap of poison ivy. They are all 1, 2 dihydroxybenzenes (catechols) with a 15-carbon-atom side chain in the 3 position (Symes and Dawson 1954; Loev

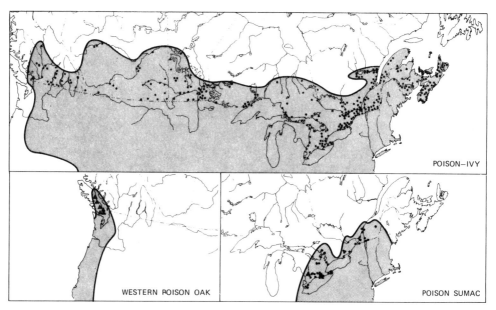

Fig. 3. Distribution of poisonous *Rhus* species in Canada and the northern United States. Dots and triangles represent sites of herbarium collections.

and Dawson 1956). The components differ only in the degree of unsaturation of the side-chain. The carbon skeleton of the active principle was first established by Hill et al. (1934).

The leaves, roots and stems do not vary in dermatitogenic capacity throughout the year and plants collected from many different habitats and geographic locations cannot be distinguished as to their dermatitogenic power when tested at the same time on the same person (Klingman 1958). It is, however, probably easiest to contact poison ivy dermatitis in the spring when leaves are tender and will bruise most easily. The interval between contact with the poisonous sap and appearance of the dermatitis is quite variable, rarely less than 6 h, but can be delayed as long as 12 days (Klingman 1958). In general, poison ivy dermatitis develops within 24 to 48 h after contact. Klingman (1958) states that the healing time may vary from a few days to several weeks and that healed sites will often remain supersensitive to any further contact with the sap for several months. The poisonous sap may be deposited at the site of the dermatitis by direct contact with the plant or by contact with contaminated objects, such as shoes, clothing, tools and domestic animals. Although the poisonous principle is not volatile, severe cases of poisoning have occurred as the result of contact with droplets of sap on plant particles contained in the smoke of burning poison ivy.

Under hot, humid conditions the poisonous samp becomes inert in about 1 wk. However, under dry conditions the poisonous principle can remain active for a long period of time. Contaminated gloves stored at room temperature for 16 mo still can cause poison ivy dermatitis (Shelmire 1941). Sap-contaminated clothing can be rendered harmless by washing in a laundering machine using soap flakes or a commercial detergent. Washing of the infected skin can never be done soon enough to prevent some dermatitis in sensitive individuals but it is useful in that it prevents the spread of the sap to uninfected parts of the body.

According to Klingman (1958), there is a great amount of variability in sensitivity, not only from person to person but even during different periods of the same person's life. Humans are not born sensitive to the sap of poisonous *Rhus* species. However, most people can be sensitized by a single contact with poison ivy. Most Americans residing in areas where poison ivy is common become sensitized by casual contact with the plant.

Although there is no racial immunity to poison ivy, clinical evidence shows that the white race is more sensitive than are the darkly pigmented races (Klingman 1958). In general, children are more sensitive than adults, with sensitivity to dermatitis generally decreasing with an increase in age (Dawson 1956; Klingman 1958). Cattle, horses, sheep, hogs, goats, birds and many other animals are apparently completely immune to poison ivy (Martin et al. 1951; Muenscher and Kingsbury 1964; Crooks et al. 1963).

(b) Beneficial — Poison ivy is of considerable wildlife value. Fruits are eaten by many birds, and fruits, stems and leaves are eaten by bears, muskrats, rabbits, small rodents and deer (Martin et al. 1951). Poison ivy berries completely filled the crop of a partridge killed near Ottawa. Where ground cover of poison ivy is dense it contributes to the protection of small animals. Bees make a non-poisonous honey from the nectar of poison ivy (Rostenburg 1955). Some North American Indians utilized the juice of poison ivy for a variety of purposes (Gillis 1971, 1975).

(c) Legislation — Poison ivy is classified as a noxious weed in the Revised Statutes of Nova Scotia 1964, Ontario 1973, Manitoba 1970, Alberta 1973 and British Columbia 1973.

4. Geographical distribution

Poison ivy occurs in all provinces of Canada except Newfoundland (Fig. 3). It

261

reaches its greatest abundance in southern Ontario and southern Quebec but is locally common throughout its Canadian range. Three varieties of poison ivy are found in Canada; var. *radicans* is in Prince Edward Island, southern Nova Scotia and southern New Brunswick, var. *negundo* is in southern Quebec and southern Ontario and var. *rydbergii* is in all provinces except Newfoundland and Prince Edward Island.

5. Habitat

(a) Climatic requirements — Very little is known about the climatic requirements of poison ivy. However, its distribution from the Atlantic to the Pacific Oceans and from $29°30'$ latitude in the south (Gillis 1971) to $53°30'$ in the north (Fig. 3) suggests that it is adapted to a wide range of climatic conditions. In Canada, sections of horizontal rootstalks and vertical stems are often winter-killed.

(b) Substratum — Poison ivy generally occurs on soils that have been repeatedly disturbed but not on soils that have recently been cultivated. It is found on sandy, stony or rocky shores of streams, rivers and lakes. It occurs on talus slopes and talus debris, on limestone cliffs and shores, and in various sandy habitats. Variety *rydbergii* generally occurs on sandier, more alkaline soils than the other two varieties. Variety *negundo* appears to grow best in soils of high nutrient value and good, but not excessive, drainage and in more acid soils than var. *rydbergii* and var. *radicans* (Gillis 1971).

Calcium is the most important element in the soil for the growth of poison ivy (Gillis 1971). Gillis states that maximum root development is in the A horizon of the soil and that poison ivy is virtually absent from soils that are highly leached by minerals, especially Ca and Mg.

(c) Communities in which the species occurs — Poison ivy occurs in many native and introduced plant communities. It is most common in thickets, along the borders of woods, and in wood openings. It is often associated with the fringes of dry trembling aspen groves in the west and wet woodlands in the east. Poison ivy frequently grows with pines (*Pinus* spp.), cedars (*Thuja* spp.), white elm (*Ulmus americana* L.), balsam fir (*Abies balsamea* (L.) Mill), trembling aspen (*Populus tremuloides* Michx.), maples (*Acer* spp.), ashes (*Fraxinus* spp.), and birches (*Betula* spp.).

6. History

The present Canadian range of poison ivy is probably very similar to that of the species at the time of first European settlement. However, there is no doubt that the felling of the native forest and the subsequent regular disturbance of the land has substantially increased the density of poison ivy within its native range.

7. Growth and Development

(a) Morphology — Colonization of new sites is mainly by seed that is dispersed by animals.

(b) Perennation — Although most horizontal rootstocks and vertical stems overwinter under our conditions, some of the rootstocks and vertical stems are winter-killed. Flower buds, formed on new growth in late summer and early autumn, overwinter and flower the following year.

(c) Physiological data — No information is available.

(d) Phenology — As soon as the soil warms up in the spring, leaves appear on the vertical stems that have overwintered. Flower buds, formed the previous year, open in late May or early June in Canada. First anthesis does not occur until initial leaves are fully expanded. Maximum flowering occurs in June, although some additional flowering occurs sporadically until early autumn. Male and female flowers, although on separate plants, open about the same time. Fruits mature in August and September but do not readily fall to the ground. Some clusters of fruits remain until the following spring. Many fruits are eaten

by birds and other animals during the autumn, winter and early spring, and the hard seeds pass through the digestive tracts of animals in a viable condition.

Each germinating seed produces a primary vertical stem and basal roots. In the first or second growing season, horizontal rootstocks are produced from the base of the primary vertical shoot. These rootstocks, which are really stem tissue with a root-like appearance, grow horizontally on or beneath the surface of the ground. Rootstocks have buds which produce secondary vertical stems similar to the primary vertical stem and usually also produce adventitious roots just below each bud. The secondary vertical stems produce further horizontal rootstocks, resulting in a large interconnected clone with many vertical stems and above or beneath the ground horizontal rootstocks. In var. *rydbergii*, the vertical stems are from 0.5 to 8 dm tall. In var. *negundo* and var. *radicans* the vertical stems can form shrubs from 1 to 12 dm high and vines climbing rough surfaces to 150 dm high. In these latter two varieties, a single clone may have some vertical shoots forming shrubs and other shoots producing vines.

In Canada, overwintering vertical stems of poison ivy start growing late in May or in early June. Horizontal rootstocks and new vertical shoots from the rootstocks are produced first in late June and reach their maximum development during July and August.

(e) Mycorrhiza — No information is available.

8. Reproduction

(a) Floral biology — Poison ivy is dioecious, with male and female flowers on separate plants. The flowers are creamy-white in appearance and are in compact clusters. Although flower clusters are often partly hidden in the axils of leaves, both male and female flowers are frequently visited by insects, and female flowers produce a high percentage of mature fruit. Five species of Hymenoptera were seen pollinating flowers of poison ivy at Ottawa, *Augochlora paura* (Say), *Agapostemon virescens* (Fab.), *Lasioglossum* sp., and two species of *Andrena*. Several ants were collecting pollen from male flowers. Gillis (1971) states that one of the chief pollinators of poison ivy is the honey bee (*Apis mellifera* L.). The frequent visits to poison ivy flowers is probably facilitated by the strong ultraviolet reflectance of flowers observed at Ottawa. Ultraviolet reflectance from the large compact flower clusters would provide a very visible target for pollinating insects (Mulligan and Kevan 1973).

(b) Seed production and dispersal — Most flowers on female plants are effectively insect-pollinated, producing numerous clusters of one-seeded fruits. Birds and other animals eat fruits in autumn, winter and early spring and are largely responsible for the dissemination of seeds (Gillis 1971). The passage of fruits through the digestive tracts may facilitate the germination of hard seeds of poison ivy (Martin et al. 1951; Gillis 1961, 1971).

(c) Viability of seed and germination — In a series of test, Gillis (1971) found that only two samples of our three varieties, out of samples from 18 sources, germinated without an after-ripening chill of 6 wk moist storage at 1 C. The two samples were from Florida and Bermuda. Germination was 0–3% for seed of var. *rydbergii* from 5 locations in the United States, was 11–62% for seed of var. *negundo* from 3 locations in U.S.A., and 4–82% for seed of var. *radicans* from 10 locations in U.S.A. Seeds of poison ivy remain viable for at least 6 yr (Gillis 1971). The low germination of var. *rydbergii* suggests that the hard seed coat needs special treatment to promote germination. Occasional seedlings of var. *rydbergii* have germinated in nature during June and early July at Ottawa.

(d) Vegetative reproduction — A plant of poison ivy is an interconnected system of underground and above-ground horizontal

rootstalks with numerous vertical stems arising from alternate buds along the rootstalks. A seedling that germinated on 25 April 1932 had its first horizontal rootstocks by August 1932 and two well developed rootstocks and two secondary vertical stems by September 1933 (Muenscher and Kingsbury 1964). Our experience is that the horizontal spread of poison ivy is slow, rarely more than 10 cm/yr and frequently less than this.

9. Hybrids

There are no natural interspecific hybrids in *Rhus* known to occur in Canada.

10. Population Dynamics

Poison ivy becomes established from seed and forms large patches by the slow vegetative spread of horizontal rootstocks. Although male and female flowers are on separate plants, very few female flowers fail to produce seed. This is not unexpected, since male and female plants often grow together or very near each other. Poison ivy rarely becomes established from plant fragments (Gillis 1971).

11. Response to Herbicides and Other Chemicals

Chemicals are recommended for the control of poison ivy in habitats that do not permit cultivation and where damage to other vegetation can be tolerated. Best results are obtained when plants are growing most actively. Chemicals recommended are fenoprop (silvex), ammonium sulphamate, sodium chlorate products, concentrated borate products, sodium borate — sodium chlorate mixtures, 2, 4-D + mecoprop + dicamba, and dicamba + 2,4-D (Canada Weed Committee 1975). Dead plants of poison ivy can still cause a dermatitis and must be handled with care.

12. Response to Other Human Manipulations

Since poison ivy does not usually become established from plant fragments it can easily be eradicated by repeated cultivation.

13. Response to Parasites

(a) Insects and other domestic animals — A large number of arthropods in the following orders feed on poison ivy: Lepidoptera, Hymenoptera, Diptera, Coleoptera, Homoptera (Aphididae) and Acarina (Harrison 1904; Tissot 1928, 1933; Steyskal 1951; Gillis 1971; Richards 1972). Criddle (1927) considered the larvae of *Epipaschia zelleri* Grote (Lepidoptera) the most destructive of all insects to poison ivy.

(b) Microorganisms and viruses — FUNGI: Conners (1967) lists the following fungi as infesting poison ivy in Canada: *Cercospora rhoina* Cke. & Ell.-Man., *Cylindrosporium irregulare* (Pk.) Dearn. — Ont., *Cylindrosporium toxicodendri* (Ell. & Mart.) Ell. & Ev. — Sask. and Man., *Phyllosticta rhoicola* Ell. & Ev. — Man., *Sphaeropsis sumachi* (Schw.) Cke. & Ell. — N.S., and *Pileolaria brevipes* Berk. & Rav. — Man., Ont., Que. & N.S. Parmelee and Elliott (1974) also list *Pileolaria brevipes* from British Columbia and Arthur (1934) states that this rust infects poison ivy throughout its range.

ACKNOWLEDGMENTS

We thank the herbarium Curators of the following institutions for lending us specimens of poisonous *Rhus* species; ACAD, UNB, QFA, MTJB, MT, SFS, DAO, CAN, QK, TRT, WIN, SASK, ALTA, UAC, UBC, and V.

ARTHUR, J. C. 1934. Manual of the rusts in the United States and Canada. Purdue Research Foundation, Lafayette, Ind. 438 pp.
CANADA WEED COMMITTEE. 1969. Common and botanical names of weeds in Canada. Can. Dep. Agric. Publ. 1397. Ottawa, Ont. 67 pp.
CANADA WEED COMMITTEE. 1975. Report of the Research Appraisal and Research Planning Committee, Eastern Section, Toronto, Ont. 117 pp.
CONNERS, I. L. 1967. An annotated index of plant diseases in Canada. Can. Dep. Agric. Publ. 1251. 381 pp.
CRIDDLE, N. 1927. Lepidoptera reared in Manitoba from poison ivy. Can. Entomol. 59: 99–101.

CROOKS, D. M., KEPHART, L. W. and KLINGMAN, D. L. 1963. Poison ivy and poison oak. Farmers Bull. 1972, U.S. Dep. Agric., Washington, D.C. pp. 1–27.

DAWSON, C. R. 1956. The toxic principle of poison ivy. J. Chem. Educ. **33**: 94–96.

FERRON, M. and CAYOUETTE, R. 1971. Noms des mauvaises herbes du Québec. Min. Agric. Colonisation, Québec, Qué. 113 pp.

FRANKTON, C. and MULLIGAN, G. A. 1970. Weeds of Canada. Can. Dep. Agric. Publ. 948. 217 pp.

GILLIS, W. T. 1961. Poison ivy and the poison oaks. Cranbrook Inst. Sci. News Letter **30**: 98–107.

GILLIS, W. T. 1971. The systematics and ecology of poison-ivy and the poison-oaks (*Toxicodendron, Anacardiaceae*). Rhodora **73**: 72–159, 161–237, 370–443, 465–540.

GILLIS, W. T. 1975. Poison ivy and its kin. Arnoldia **35**: 93–123.

HARRISON, G. D. 1904. Poison ivy caterpillars. J. New York Entomol. Soc. **12**: 249–250.

HILL, G. A., MATTACOTTI, V. and GRAHAM, W. D. 1934. The toxic principle of poison ivy. J. Amer. Chem. Soc. **56**: 2736–2738.

KLINGMAN, A. M. 1958. Poison ivy (*Rhus*) dermatitis. A.M.A. Arch. Derm. **77**: 149–180.

LOEV, B. and DAWSON, 1956. On the geometrical configuration of the olefinic components of poison ivy urushiol. The synthesis of a model compound. J. Amer. Chem. Soc. **78**: 1180–1183.

LÖVE, A. and LÖVE, D. 1973. IOPB chromosome number reports. 30. Taxon **22**: 285–291.

MARTIN, A. C., ZIM, H. S. and NELSON, A. L. 1951. American wildlife and plants. A guide to wildlife food habits. Dover Publ., New York, N.Y. 500 pp.

MUENSCHER, W. C. and KINGSBURY, J. M. 1964. Poison ivy and poison sumac. Cornell Ext. Bull. 191, Ithaca, N.Y. pp. 1–11.

MULLIGAN, G. A. and KEVAN, P. G. 1973. Color, brightness, and other floral characteristics attracting insects to the blossoms of some Canadian weeds. Can. J. Bot. **51**: 1939–1952.

PARMELEE, J. A. and ELLIOTT, M. E. 1974. *Pileolaria brevipes*. Fungi Canadensis 50, Agric. Canada, Ottawa, Ont. 2 pp.

RICHARDS, W. R. 1972. *Aulacorthum rhusifoliae* (Homoptera; Aphididae). A new poison ivy inhabiting aphid from Ontario. Can. Entomol. **105**: 173–174.

ROSTENBURG, A. 1955. Anecdotal biographical history of poison ivy. A.M.A. Arch. Derm. **72**: 438–445.

SHELMIRE, B. 1941. The poison ivy plant and its oleoresin. J. Invest. Derm. **4**: 337–348.

STEYSKAL, G. 1951. Insects feeding on plants of *Toxicodendron* section of the genus *Rhus*. Coleopterist's Bull. **5**: 75–77.

SYMES, W. F. and DAWSON, C. R. 1954. Poison ivy "urushiol." Amer. Chem. Soc. J. **76**: 2959–2965.

TISSOT, A. N. 1928. A new aphid on poison ivy (*Rhus radicans* L.). Fla. Entomol. **12**: 1–2.

TISSOT, A. N. 1933. Additions to the aphid fauna of Florida. Fla. Entomol. **17**: 37–45.

THE BIOLOGY OF CANADIAN WEEDS. 24.
AGROPYRON REPENS (L.) BEAUV.

PATRICIA A. WERNER[1] and R. RIOUX[2]

[1]*W. K. Kellogg Biological Station and Departments of Botany and Zoology, Michigan State University, Hickory Corners, Michigan 49060 and* [2]*Ferme Expérimentale, Agriculture Canada, C.P. 400, La Pocatière, Québec. Contribution nos.* [1]*315 and* [2]*88, received 22 Dec. 1976, accepted 5 Apr. 1977.*

WERNER, PATRICIA A. AND RIOUX, R. 1977. The biology of Canadian weeds. 24. *Agropyron repens* (L.) Beauv. Can. J. Plant Sci. **57**: 905–919.

Agropyron repens (L.) Beauv., quack grass, is an introduced perennial grass found in all provinces of Canada and the Northwest Territories. In most agricultural areas it is a serious weed of cultivated crops; alternately it can be used as pasture or hay. A summary of the biology of quack grass is presented as part of a series of the biology of Canadian weeds.

Le chiendent, *Agropyron repens* (L.) Beauv., est une graminée vivace introduite qu'on retrouve dans toutes les provinces du Canada et dans les Territoires du Nord-Ouest. C'est une mauvaise herbe importante des cultures de la plupart des régions agricoles; cependant elle peut aussi être utilisée comme plante à pâturage ou à foin. Dans le cadre de la série d'articles sur la biologie des mauvaises herbes du Canada, cette contribution résume les données de la biologie du chiendent.

[Traduit par les auteurs]

1. Name

Agropyron repens (L.) Beauv. — **quack grass, couch grass** (Canada Weed Committee 1969); **chiendent** (Ferron et Cayouette 1975). Poaceae (Gramineae), grass family, Graminées. The species has also been listed as *Elytrigia repens* (L.) Nevski or *Triticum repens* L. in some floras and scientific papers, especially European.

2. Description and Account of Variation

Perennial, spreading by seeds and rhizomes; rhizomes long (up to 1 m), slender (1.5 mm), smooth, whitish, and scaly; leaves, 9–10 mm wide, 6–20 cm long, finely pointed, flat, green, sometimes glaucous, scrabrous at the margin and on the upper surface, lower surface smooth; leaf sheaths round, split, short, with overlapping hyaline margins; ligules membranous, obtuse, 0.5–1 mm long, and sometimes ciliated; stem 30–120 cm long, hollow, round, slender to somewhat stout with three to five nodes; spikes erect, straight, 5–30 cm long, with rough margins; spikes green or sometimes bluish-green, loose or compact but with the axis hard; spikelets compressed, 10–20 mm long, 3–8 flowered, sessile; spikelets one-third to half their length apart, alternate in two rows on opposite sides of the axis with the broader size appressed to it; glumes herbaceous, lanceolate to oblong, blunt or pointed, 7–12 mm long, hard and 3–7 nerved; lemma overlapping, lanceolate oblong, keeled upward, 8–12 mm long, hard and 5-nerved; palea nearly as long as the lemma with 2 rough keels; anthers 4–8 mm long; fruit a caryopsis, lance-shaped in outline, straw to dirty-gray-colored, 8.0–9.0 mm long, 1.3–1.8 mm wide; sinus U-shaped, rachilla well exposed, about one-sixth to one-fifth the length of the caryopsis. The species is hexaploid (Palmer and Sagar 1963). Chromosome counts of $2n = 42$ have been obtained for Canadian material (Bowden 1965). In European plants $2n = 42$ is the standard chromosome count; however, counts of 28, 34, and 35 have also been recorded (Palmer and Sagar 1963).

The combination of matted, whitish rhizomes, auricles, hairy lower sheaths, and heads resembling a slender head of wheat distinguish quack grass from most other grasses. *Agropyron repens* resembles western wheat grass, *A. smithii* Rydb. but the latter has bluish rigid leaves that tend to roll in at the edges under dry conditions, while those of quack grass are lax, rarely bluish, and always remain flat (Frankton and Mulligan 1971). *A. trachycaulum* (Link) Malte has no rhizomes and much smaller anthers. The rye grasses, *Lolium* spp., also possess slender spikes but the spikelets occur with their edges tangential to the main stem, while in quack grass the spikelets are arranged with the broader surface appressed to the stem (Frankton and Mulligan 1971).

In a study of hybridization with the genus *Agropyron*, Bowden (1965) recognized two forms of *A. repens* in Canada: f. *repens*, which is awnless or very short-awned, and f. *aristatum* (Schum.) Holmb. Skand., where the lemmas have awns that are 2–9 mm long. The floristic composition within each province consists of 66–70% f. *repens*, as determined by an examination of herbarium specimens in the Department of Agriculture Herbarium, Ottawa.

Figure 1 shows the main diagnostic features of the seed and mature plant.

3. Economic Importance

(a) *Detrimental* — Quack grass competes strongly with a number of cultivated crops (see Muzik 1970) in almost all agricultural areas of Canada except the drier regions of Saskatchewan, Alberta and Manitoba (compare Friesen and Shebeski 1960). Reduced yields in Canadian crops attributed to the presence of quack grass have been reported for corn and oats (up to 85% and 30–70% reduction respectively; see references in Rioux 1973), and for barley and soybeans (Rioux 1973). Further, in corn, the presence of quack grass increases ear moisture at harvest and delays tasseling and silking (Bandeen and Buchholtz 1967).

Quack grass is a luxury consumer of key nutrients. By mid-July a stand of quack grass can tie up approximately 55, 45, and 68% of the total N, P, and K, respectively, that it removes from the soil for the entire season; in a stand of the size 2,000 kg shoot dry weight per hectare, this is equivalent to 118 kg/ha of N, 17 kg/ha of P, and 67 kg/ha of K (Bandeen and Buchholtz 1967). The value of grass seed crops may be greatly reduced if contaminated with quack grass seed. Quack grass serves as an alternate food plant for several pests of grain crops, such as the cereal leaf beetle, *Oulema melanopa* (L.) (Dr. Dean Haynes, personal communication).

(b) *Beneficial effects* — Quack grass may be used for pasture or hay and can be found on lists of preferred plants for rangeland. Total crude protein (dry) content of quack grass is comparable with timothy at the same stage of growth. Quack grass roots and rhizomes are efficient soil binders on slopes, embankments and sandy soils. It provides cover for wildlife, including small mammals, some song birds and game.

In current experimental studies underway in Michigan, *Agropyron repens* is one of the most effective oldfield plants for reclaiming nutrients from municipal sewage effluent sprayed on vegetation in abandoned fields. If left uncut, quack grass is active mainly in the spring, but efficient uptake can be maintained throughout the growing season by a schedule of repeated mowing and harvesting. The harvested quack grass has a level of nitrogen high enough to be appropriate for cattle feed, but low enough to avoid toxicity (Drs. F. P. Reed and S. N. Stephenson, personal communication).

A methanol extract prepared from *A. repens* has been effective against mosquito larvae (*Aedes aegypti* L.) even in low concentrations; only 2 of 36 plant species tested were as effective (Supavarn et al. 1974). Under the synonym *Triticum repens*, quack grass is recorded in most herbals with many useful properties (Palmer and Sagar 1963). The rhizomes, when dried and ground, can serve as a source of flour (Fernald and Kinsey 1958).

Fig. 1. *Agropyron repens* (L.) Beauv.: diagnostic features. (a) junction between leaf and sheath showing auricles; (b) spikelet; (c) caryopsis; (bottom) growth habit.

(c) *Legislation* — The species is listed in the category "Primary Noxious Weed Seeds" in the Seeds Act and Regulations administered by Agriculture Canada (1967).

4. Geographical Distribution

Although originally an Old-world species only (see section 6), the current distribution of quack grass is circumpolar (Hulten 1962). Its distribution extends throughout Europe, Australia, New Zealand and the temperate zones of Asia and North and South America.

In North America, *A. repens* is found in every state in the U.S.A. but is rarely troublesome as a crop weed south of Washington, D.C. and St. Louis, Mo. (Johnson 1958). In Canada, it is found from Newfoundland to British Columbia (Boivin 1967) and occurs as far north as Natasquan in Quebec (Rousseau 1968), Goose Bay in Labrador (Hustich 1971), Fort Smith, N.W.T. (Cody 1956) and Greenland and

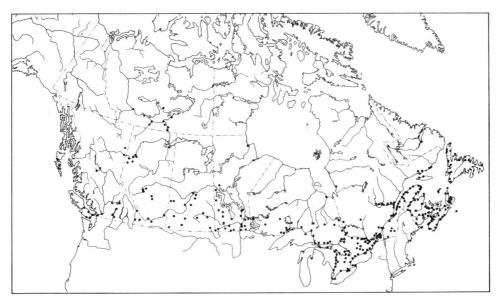

Fig. 2. The distribution of *Agropyron repens* (L.) Beauv. in Canada is based on specimens in the herbaria of the Canada Department of Agriculture and the National Museum of Canada, both in Ottawa, Ontario. The distribution of quack grass in the United States is common throughout the Northern States shown here except Alaska.

Alaska (Boivin 1967). It is especially common in Southeastern Canada (Bowden 1965) (see Fig. 2).

5. Habitat

(a) *Climatic requirements* — Specific information is unavailable. It is commonly designated as a "cool-season" grass. In Canada it is common in areas of moderate rainfall and is rare in areas of low rainfall.

(b) *Substratum* — Quack grass has been reported growing on a wide variety of soils, from dry sand to wet alluvium, and in pH ranges from 4.5 to 8.0 (see Doyon 1965, 1968; Rousseau 1968). In general, however, quack grass is most vigorous in neutral to alkaline soils (pH 6.5–8.0; King 1966; Dale et al. 1965). It has a high salt tolerance of 70–95 mg/100 g of soil (Tesu et al. 1972) and may be found on saline soils. In the British Isles, it is associated with arable clay soils (Palmer and Sagar 1963). In Canadian pastures, quack grass shows no drainage preference but does best on fine-structured soils (Dale et al. 1965). Rhizome growth is reduced in compacted soil (Wolcott and Carlson 1947).

(c) *Communities in which the species occurs* — Quack grass is a plant of open areas, mainly occurring where the native vegetation is disturbed. It is common in agricultural fields as well as in road margins, waste places, and abandoned fields and lots (Frankton and Mulligan 1971), and is especially vigorous in fallow land and in the first years after tillage ceases (Barralis 1961). Quack grass may make up > 90% of the biomass in an abandoned field for several years, and exclude colonization by herbaceous dicotyledonous species (see Werner 1975). When shrubs enter a field, quack grass is gradually reduced in biomass and finally dies out within a few years (Dr. John Cantlon, unpublished data). The species is not found under a continuous cover of shrubs and trees (Palmer and Sagar 1963). Permanent pasture tends to have very little of this grass, perhaps due to selective feeding by the grazers.

269

Quack grass is often found as a riparian plant on river banks (Rousseau 1968), freshwater beaches, salt beaches, and sand dunes. In maritime zones it is found on dunes and on alluvial soils, in salt and fresh water marshes, and on tidal flats.

6. History

Quack grass is a native of Europe and was introduced to New England during colonization. Josselyn (1672) who visited New England in 1639 and 1663, placed quack grass among ''such plants as have sprung up since the English planted and kept cattle here.'' Probably it was introduced to Quebec during the same period (Rousseau 1968). Similarly, it was introduced westward during the early years of European settlement. The rapid spread of quack grass in western Manitoba and eastern Saskatchewan is likely the result of sowing infested bromegrass (Carder 1961) and/or by transportation of infested hay and straw.

7. Growth and Development

(a) *Morphology* — The aerial shoots and rhizomes constitute a sympodial system. Rhizome growth is renewed annually from axillary buds at the base of the aerial shoots. Axillary buds along the rhizomes are mainly dormant due to strong apical dominance exerted by the terminal bud (see section 7c). Aerial shoots are formed mainly at the end of the growing season when a rhizome tip becomes erect; they are also formed from both terminal and axillary buds any time that a rhizome becomes detached from the parent plant (see also section 10). Adventitious roots form at nodes of the rhizome; roots are short in length relative to other grasses. See Palmer and Sager (1963) for detailed description of the morphology of quack grass, Håkansson (1967–1970, 1971) for experimental studies on morphological development under various conditions of burial depth, defoliation, rhizome breakage, etc., and Rogan and Smith (1975a,b) for detailed description of the developmental anatomy and morphology of the rhizomes, shoots and leaves.

(b) *Perennation* — Quack grass is an herbaceous perennial, classified as a geophyte.

(c) *Physiological data* — Axillary buds on rhizomes of quack grass are released from inhibition when the rhizome apex is removed or when the rhizome is severed from the parent plant. Isolated rhizome segments exhibit a polarity such that buds toward the apical end develop into aerial shoots, those toward the base develop into rhizomes or remain dormant (Rogan and Smith 1976). McIntyre (1965) showed that apical dominance in rhizomes could be controlled by changing level of nitrogen. He suggested (McIntyre 1969) that apical dominance (in high-N rhizomes which were isolated from the parent plant, i.e. from the source of carbohydrate), was due primarily to intra-plant competition for a limited carbohydrate supply, although the ability of the apex to compete successfully may depend on its ability to synthesize mobilizing hormones.

It has been suggested that indole-3-acetic acid (IAA) is produced in the apical region and transported into the lateral buds in sufficiently high levels to inhibit growth of the latter (Akhavein 1971). Rogan and Smith (1976) suggested that a continuous supply of gibberellin from the parent plant may be essential to maintain apical dominance. Leakey et al. (1975) found that various hormones can play a part in apical dominance in rhizome buds and that there are interactions between apical and basal factors; i.e., no single-factor explanation suffices. They suggested that auxin is the apical factor (see also Chancellor 1974) and that cytokinins (probably originating from the roots which occur both on the parent plant and at each node along the rhizome) are a major constituent of the parental factor.

Under longer photoperiods, heavier rhizomes (Williams 1971) and more numerous and thicker rhizomes are produced (Palmer 1958). The level of aboveground illumination affects the rhizomes more than it does the aerial shoots (Williams 1970a;

Palmer 1958) A reduction in level of light produces an increase in the percentage of rhizome buds developing as shoots and an increase in number of shoots produced at older (dormant) nodes along the rhizome. The formation of new rhizomes from buds is entirely suppressed at 2,690 lux (McIntyre 1970).

In a large field study (Bandeen and Buchholtz 1967), the application of nitrogen increased shoot dry weight and decreased rhizome dry weight, but the application of potassium or phosphorus had either no effect on shoots or rhizomes (K_2O) or increased shoot growth only (P_2O_5). Rogan and (Smith 1975a) found that at low levels of nitrogen (15 ppm), there was an increase in the tendency for the buds in the axils of leaves 1 and 2 to produce rhizomes or rhizome-tillers instead of tillers. Both low temperature (10 C) and low nitrogen (15 ppm) led to the production of relatively fewer secondary rhizomes and tillers. The number of leaf primordia increased with decreasing temperature and increasing nitrogen level (up to 960 ppm) (Rogan and Smith 1975b). Rhizome buds require oxygen for development to occur (Johnson and Buckholtz 1962).

Arny (1932) found a seasonal trend of sugar accumulation in rhizomes of *A. repens*. Total soluble sugars increased, reached an early season high (8%) in late May, then decreased to 3% from June until early October, followed by an increase to about 8% in November. In contrast, in a study of the carbohydrate level in quack grass rhizomes, Schirman and Buckholtz (1966) found a fairly constant level (46%) throughout the year, although the total available carbohydrate content was slightly higher during the major accumulation period, i.e. from August to November. By the following April, the total available carbohydrate was approximately 39% of the dry weight, but the dry weight of rhizomes had dropped from 7,000 to 5,500 kg/ha.

The pattern of translocation of carbohydrates varies with seasonal time, which may be significant for control with phloem-translocated herbicides. Fiveland et al. (1972) demonstrated that more ^{14}C-labelled carbohydrates were retained in the parent rhizomes at the 3- to 4-leaf stage than at the 2-leaf stage; shoots were photosynthetically independent at the 5-leaf stage. Rogan and Smith (1974) showed that with the growth of axillary shoots, assimilates were exported from the primary shoot to the daughter tillers and rhizomes; reciprocal translocation did not occur between tillers and the primary shoot although it did between the rhizome tillers and the primary shoot (see also Forde 1966). In mature plants the primary shoot and tillers were completely independent, but rhizome-tillers continued to receive small quantities of assimilate from the main shoot system. Shading a whole plant had no effect on tracer movement, but shading of all but one tiller caused a transfer of assimilates to the rest of the plant which was not observed in intact plants (Rogan and Smith 1974).

(d) *Phenology* — Seeds germinate in the early spring. The seedlings begin to produce tillers in the 4- to 6-leaf stage and rhizomes in the 6- to 8-leaf stage (Palmer and Sagar 1963). In Canada, the latter stage is usually reached 2–3 mo after seedling emergence. In contrast, new rhizomes start to develop at the 3- to 4-leaf stage in plants that have been developed from rhizome buds (Fiveland et al. 1972); this stage is reached around 15 May at Guelph, Ont. (Rioux 1973) and around 1 June at La Pocatière in eastern Quebec.

New rhizomes develop underground in greatest numbers during June, July and August (Evans and Ely 1935). The tip of each rhizome grows in a horizontal direction below the soil surface during the spring and summer before becoming erect in the autumn to form a primary aerial shoot (see section 7a). This shoot develops into a mature plant during the following year (in Britain; see Palmer 1958) but in a cold climate most of these newly formed shoots die in winter (Akhavein 1971). Flowering occurs in late June to July in Canada (Frankton and Mulligan 1971). Seeds ripen in early August to early September and drop from the parent plants by late September.

In general, the plants are most active in sexual reproduction and rhizome formation in the middle of the summer, and in tillering and photosynthesis in spring and autumn. The natural seasonal cycle may be altered by cultural practices. For examples, tillering and rhizome production will follow soil disturbance at any period of the year except mid-winter, and the growth cycle may be initiated in August after a cereal crop has been removed (Palmer and Sagar 1963).

(e) *Mycorrhiza* — None known.

8. Reproduction

(a) *Floral biology* — Quack grass is wind-pollinated and virtually self-sterile. However, seeds set by enclosed spikes have been reported (see Palmer and Sagar 1963). Much genetic variation is found when quack grass reproduces by seeds (Raleigh et al. 1962, Williams 1973a).

(b) *Seed production and dispersal* — The amount of seed produced is highly variable. Reports range from 15 to 400 seeds per plant stem, with 25–40 most common. In arable crops, the number of seeds depends on the crop in which the quack grass was growing, the proximity of different genotypes, humidity, and the length of time between anthesis and crop harvest (Williams and Attwood 1970, 1971). Further, it has been suggested that since plants tend to be self-sterile and large stands may be a single clone as the result of vegetative reproduction, then seed formation should be much higher at the margin of a clone where inflorescences are cross-pollinated than in the center of a large stand (see Palmer and Sagar 1963).

(c) *Viability of seeds and germination* — Little information is available on viability levels of quack grass seeds, except indirectly via germination studies. Alternating temperatures are a requirement for germination (Chepil 1946; Andersen 1968; Palmer

and Sagar 1963). Freshly harvested seed will not germinate at constant temperatures between 5 and 30 C in either light or darkness, but up to 90% germination is achieved if the temperature fluctuates diurnally between 15 and 25 C (Sagar 1961). There is no after-ripening period (Sagar 1961).

If buried, seeds may lie dormant for 2–3 yr (Carder 1961) and retain their viability for a maximum of about 4 yr (Brackney and Seely 1966). After passing through the digestive tracts of horses, cows and sheep, but not swine, seeds of quack grass retain their viability (Muenscher 1952). In the laboratory, germination is promoted by gibberellic acid and inhibited by abscissic acid but is not affected by sonication, liquid nitrogen and infrared light (Holm and Miller 1972).

The seeds possess no special morphological adaptation for dispersal, but fall passively from the parent plant. Means of long distance dispersal have not been identified to date.

(d) *Vegetative reproduction* — Given the relatively low number of seeds produced, and the generally higher probability of survival of vegetatively-produced plants relative to seedlings, vegetative cloning is much more important than sexual reproduction in maintaining a population on a site (see also section 10). Raleigh et al. (1962) reported that the diameter of spread of the 14 rhizomes of one parent plant was 3.04 m. The total length of rhizomes was 154 m, with 206 shoots having arisen from them.

Johnson and Buckholtz (1962) reported a seasonal activity of rhizome buds; there was a steady decrease in activity from mid-April to June, dormancy during June, and increased activity from July onward. Within broad limits, rhizome initiation and growth are not correlated with flowering of plants, e.g., flowering shoots produce the same amount of rhizome material as do vegetative shoots (at light levels above the minimum required for rhizome growth) (Palmer 1958).

Conceivably, every mature rhizome bud is capable of establishing a new plant. However, most buds along an intact rhizome are dormant and do not initiate any growth. See section 7c for a discussion of apical dominance in quack grass.

9. Hybrids
Palmer and Sagar (1963) reported hybrids between quack grass and *A. junceiforme* (A. & D. Löve) and between quack grass and *A. pungens* (Pers.) Roem and Schukt. Dewey (1965) formed synthetic but sterile hybrids between quack grass and *A. riparium* Scribn. & Smith. In Canada, hybrids have been reported with *Elymus arenarius* L. and *Elymus canadensis* L. (Lepage 1953). None of these hybrids is of known economic importance.

10. Population Dynamics
In open habitats an individual plant forms a clump during the first growing season due to extensive subtillering of primary tillers. Also, as many as 150 rhizomes or rhizome branches may be produced. In the second season the clump may develop into a patch as other clumps develop from the erected tips of the first season's rhizomes (see section 7a,d). Later, adjacent patches may coalesce to form a continuous stand or alternatively they may be contained by the presence of other species (Palmer and Sagar 1963). In a closed community an individual plant consists of a primary shoot, two or three primary tillers, and from two to four rhizomes, and clump formation does not occur (Palmer 1958 and Palmer and Sagar 1963).

Tripathi and Harper (1973) conducted a study which compared the reproductive strategies of two species of *Agropyron, A. repens* and *A. caninum,* growing them for 20 wk in the greenhouse in various mixtures and from initial starts of either seeds or tillers. In both species, plants established from tillers were more vigorous and aggressive than their counterparts produced from seeds. In *A. repens,* plants started from seed did not produce aboveground foliage for 10–12 days and lagged behind plants begun from tillers in biomass accumulation for the 1st 8 wk of the study. In pure stands, quack grass had 44–55% of its total biomass in underground structures at the 20-wk harvest date (in mixed stands the percentage was somewhat less). At the same time, the percentage of total biomass accumulated in seeds was 0.1–0.9% (slightly higher values in plants produced from tillers). The average number of seeds per plant was 30; average number of rhizome buds per plant was 215.

Williams (1973b) collected seeds from several clones of quack grass in several areas in Britain, germinated them in an unheated glasshouse, and examined the developing seedlings and clones. Comparisons of both seedlings and clones showed differences among genotypes: clones with the least weight of rhizome tended to have the most weight of spikes. Also, large variations occurred between clones established from seedlings from a given area, especially in the pattern of dry weight allocation between primary and secondary shoots and in the time the spikes emerged.

A long-term field study of quack grass is underway in an abandoned field in Kalamazoo County, Michigan. Two years previous to the initiation of the study, the field had been scraped clear of all vegetation by large earth-moving equipment during construction of a research facility. By the autumn of year 0, a uniform 2-yr old stand of quack grass was present; a portion of this area was plowed to a depth of 25 cm and then disked with a standard drag disk at two levels — 1 pass (low cultivation) and 20 passes on a single day (high cultivation). In years 1, 2, and 3, quack grass was sampled by harvest techniques (dried > 48 h at 100 C, forced-air oven) from the two areas; in years 2 and 3, samples were also taken from the continuous surrounding quack grass stands which were then 4 and 5 yr of age, respectively. On a per meter basis, the total biomass of plants increased with time, as did all plant organs except seeds-and-reproductive stems, which decreased after year 2. There was little difference in absolute biomass between quack grass growing in high levels compared to low levels of cultivation. Litter accumulated so that it was almost 600 g/m² by the 5th yr. The number of seeds per flower stem ranged from 12 to 30, with little pattern evident over time or treatment (Table 1). Although absolute biomass of plants steadily increased from year 1 to year

5, sexual reproduction reached highest values by several criteria in the intermediate years and then decreased dramatically (Table 1 and Werner, in preparation).

Quack grass reportedly is an allelopathic plant which inhibits the growth and germination of seeds of other plants through the release of toxic substances. However, living quack grass material has failed to produce inhibitory effects in numerous experiments (see discussion in Palmer and

Table 1. Growth and reproductive characteristics of *Agropyron repens* left undisturbed for 5 yr after initial major soil disturbance in a field in Kalamazoo County, Michigan

		Year				
		1	2	3	4	5
Biomass (g)/m²						
Seeds + flower stems	(C)†	–	–	–	95	99
	(L)	27	124	98	–	–
	(H)	20	113	86	–	–
Leaves	(C)	–	–	–	95	144
	(L)	22	75	98	–	–
	(H)	22	84	97	–	–
Roots‡	(C)	–	–	–	146	91
	(L)	16	114	49	–	–
	(H)	14	80	56	–	–
Rhizomes	(C)	–	–	–	291	426
	(L)	54	184	205	–	–
	(H)	23	197	274	–	–
Total	(C)	–	–	–	633	760
	(L)	121	497	446	–	–
	(H)	80	469	508	–	–
Litter	(C)	–	–	–	286	562
	(L)	Nil	82	164	–	–
	(H)	Nil	107	237	–	–
Sexual reproductive effort						
Biomass of seeds +	(C)	–	–	–	47%	41%
flower stems as a	(L)	60%	63%	50%	–	–
percentage of	(H)	47%	59%	52%	–	–
aboveground biomass						
No. flower stems/m²	(C)	–	–	–	69	18
	(L)	8	47	54	–	–
	(H)	4	35	36	–	–
No. seeds/m²	(C)	–	–	–	817	270
	(L)	128	786	886	–	–
	(H)	116	624	634	–	–
No. seeds/g	(C)	–	–	–	54.5	14.2
leaf biomass	(L)	5.8	52.4	40.3	–	–
	(H)	5.3	34.7	33.4	–	–

†C = area not plowed in year 0 (see text); L = area of low cultivation in year 0 (1 disk pass); H = area of high cultivation in year 0 (20 disk passes). All values are means of 8 samples.
‡Low values in years 3 and 5 may reflect difficulty of accurate root sampling and/or the fact that there was uncommonly low rainfall (year of sampling: 1976).

Sugar 1963), and it may be that only dead materials produce an inhibitory effect. In the field and greenhouse, a litter layer of dead stems and leaves of quack grass greatly inhibits the germination of teasel (*Dipsacus sylvestris*) seeds. The action is probably through chemical means, although it is not clear whether the inhibitor is leached from quack grass itself or is a product of microbial activity (Werner 1975).

The ability of quack grass to maintain high growth rates through very cool periods of the year, coupled with vegetative reproduction (section 8d), luxury uptake of minerals (section 3a) and possibly allelochemic toxins, make it a potentially strong competitor of crops (cf. Raleigh et al. 1962). Williams (1970a,b, 1975) demonstrated that quack grass grows faster than wheat and has a larger leaf area ratio, but has a competitive advantage only if it germinates before the wheat. The earlier that wheat was sown in pots infested with quack grass, the less it suffered from competition. So, early growth of cereal crops may have a suppressive effect on quack grass until anthesis; however, the advantage is lost when the crop begins to ripen and quack grass is freed from competition for light. In fact, the potential problem for the following year may be even greater, since quack grass plants that had early shading produced more shoots and seeds after mid-July than those that were not shaded earlier (Williams 1970a).

11. Response to Herbicides and Other Chemicals

Quack grass is thought to be encouraged by auxin herbicides, substituted phenols and modern crop husbandry techniques (Aberg 1964; Bachthaler 1969; Brimhall 1970; Hammerton 1968). Many herbicides are available but crop management methods that use herbicides to control quack grass require careful selection of herbicides and consideration of cropping sequences.

Lately, two new herbicides for the control of quack grass have been tested: pronamide and glyphosate. Pronamide is most phytotoxic to quack grass when placed in the rhizome zone (Carlson et al. 1975). Its continuous use on two soil types at La Pocatière gave an effective control of quack grass with promotion of alfalfa growth. Nevertheless, complementary control may be necessary to avoid a shift in weed problems (Table 2). Glyphosate has been shown to provide a high degree of quack grass control in fall and spring applications without residual effects on crops (Baird et al. 1971; Baird and Begeman 1972). Complete control has been achieved over an

Table 2. Species composition (relative proportions × 100) in an alfalfa (*Medicago sativa*) stand, in La Pocatière, Quebec, by level of pronamide treatments applied the previous year

Species	Pronamide (kg/ha)			
	0.0	0.84	1.68	3.36
Medicago sativa L.	2.5	14.5	14.5	28.3
Agropyron repens (L.) Beauv.	91.5	77.0	56.5	15.6
Taraxacum officinale Web.	0.0	1.0	7.8	15.0
Plantago major L.	0.0	2.5	2.5	8.0
Achillea millefolium L.	0.0	0.5	2.5	1.5
Chenopodium album L.	1.5	0.5	1.5	3.0
Capsella bursa-pastoris (L.) Medic.	3.0	3.0	13.5	22.0
Galeopsis tetrahit L.	0.0	0.0	1.0	4.0
Trifolium spp.	1.0	0.5	0.5	2.0
Vicia cracca L.	0.0	0.5	0.0	0.0
Sonchus arvensis L.	0.0	0.0	0.5	0.0
Equisetum arvense L.	0.5	0.0	0.0	0.0

advanced stage of development (see also Rioux et al. 1974). In quack grass, glyphosate is rapidly absorbed after surface-spraying, with a large portion transmitted to the rhizomes and untreated shoots; total photosynthesis is reduced more in quack grass than in wheat (Sprankle et al. 1975a). Mobility of the herbicide in the soil is very limited (Sprankle et al. 1975b).

12. Response to Other Human Manipulations

Careful and repeated tillage from the beginning of August until the ground becomes frozen often gives excellent control of quack grass (Godbout 1960). Moderate disking in a single soil operation may actually enhance quack grass growth by releasing dormant buds from apical suppression (Werner, unpublished data). The pattern of cultivation should be designed to break up the rhizomes and kill the resulting fragments by exhausting their food reserves (Muzik 1970; Cussans and Wilson 1970); deep burial will assist in the latter (Håkansson 1968). Programs involving rotation (or heavy cultivation) and herbicides have been particularly successful (Cussans and Wilson 1970; Evans 1968).

13. Responses to Parasites

(a) *Insects and other non-domestic organisms* — Insecta — Coleoptera: *Brachyrhinus ligustici* L. (Palm 1935); *Melanotus* spp. and *Phyllophaga* spp. (Metcalf et al. 1962). Diptera: *Rhytophage destructor* (Say) (Fenton 1952). Homoptera: *Macrosiphum granarium* (Kirby) and *Toxoptera graminum* (Rondani) (Metcalf et al. 1962). Hymenoptera: *Cephus cinctus* Norton (CDA 1944). Orthoptera: *Melanoplus* spp. (Herman and Eslick 1939). Palmer and Sagar (1963) list five species of Nematoda and 24 species of Insecta found on *A. repens* in Great Britain. Of the flies (Diptera), two, *Mayetiola destructor* (Say) and *Chlorops pumilionis* (Bjerk.) are thought to be specific to quack grass; several other flies use quack grass as their chief food plant. These may prove of value in control of the grass.

(b) *Microorganisms and viruses* — Conners (1967) lists 30 microorganism species on quack grass, and the Canadian provinces where each is found. These include five species of *Puccinia* and three species of *Ustilago*. Palmer and Sagar (1963) list 22 species of fungi on *A. repens* in Great Britain. Hudson and Webster (1958) give the succession of fungi on decaying shoots of quack grass. (Caution should be practiced in assuming that a species of fungus found on both quack grass and cereal crops are the same strain; Novakova and Zacha (1975) studied in detail *Tilletia contraversa* Kuhn on quack grass and wheat in Czechoslovakia and were unable to transmit the pathogen from quack grass to any wheat variety and finally concluded that the wild grass was not a source of infection for wheat in their area.)

Agropyron mosaic virus (also known as couch grass streak mosaic virus) is found on quack grass. This yellow-green streak mosaic, mainly seen on younger leaves, has little effect on the vigor of the plant. There is not much information on the virus from Canadian sources. The first report of its occurrence in Great Britain (Catherall and Chamberlain 1975) describes a virus that is serologically related to a Canadian isolate. It was experimentally transmitted by the mite *Abacarus hystrix* to wheat and by sap inoculation to 17 other species of festacoid grasses.

(c) *Higher plant parasites* — None recorded.

ACKNOWLEDGMENTS

The authors express thanks to G. M. Barnett, J. D. Bandeen, P. B. Cavers, and K. A. Erdman for their various roles in preparation of the manuscript; also to J. M. Gillett and W. J. Cody for assistance in the preparation of the distribution map. A portion of the research results reported here (e.g. Table 1) were supported by National Science Foundation grant BMS 74-01602 as part of a study on plants in successional environments.

ABERG, E. 1964. Susceptibility: Factors in the plant modifying the response of a given species of treatment. Pages 401–464 in L. J. Audus, ed. The physiology and biochemistry of herbicides. Academic Press, New York, N.Y.

AGRICULTURE Canada. 1967. Seeds Act and Regulations. Queen's Printer. Ottawa, Ont. 50 pp.

AKHAVEIN, A. A. 1971. Effects of 2-chloroethylphosphonic acid (ethrel) and selected environmental factors on growth of quack grass (Agropyron repens L. (Beauv.)) and field bindweed (Convolvulus arvensis L.). Ph.D. Thesis. Oregon State University.

ANDERSEN, R. N. 1968. Germination and establishment of weeds for experimental purposes. Weed Science Society of America, Urbana, Ill. 236 pp.

ARNY, A. C. 1932. Variations in the organic reserves in underground parts of five perennial weeds from late April to November. Minn. Agric. Exp. Sta. Tech. Bull. 84: 1–28.

BACHTHALER, G. 1969. Development of the weed flora in Germany in relation to changes in methods of cultivation. Angew Bot. 43: 59–60. (Weed Abstr. 19: 1677).

BAIRD, D. D. and BEGEMAN, G. F. 1972. Post emergence characterization of a new quack grass herbicide. Proc. North East. Weed Sci. Soc. 26: 100–106.

BAIRD, D. D., UPCHURCH, R. P., HOMESLEY, W. B. and FRANZ, J. E. 1971. Introduction of a new broadspectrum post emergence herbicide class with utility for herbaceous perennial weed control. Proc. North Cent. Weed Control Conf. 26: 64–68. Kansas City, Mo.

BANDEEN, J. D. and BUCHHOLTZ, K. P. 1967. Competitive effects of quack grass upon corn as modified by fertilization. Weeds 15: 220–224.

BARRALIS, G. 1961. Distribution et état d'infestation des graminées adventices en France. Pages 263-269. in Comptes rendus du symposium sur les herbicides et de la lère conférence du COLUMA. Paris.

BOIVIN, B. 1967. Enumération des plantes du Canada. VI. Monopsides (suite). Natur. Can. 94: 471–528.

BOWDEN, W. M. 1965. Cytotaxonomy of the species and interspecific hybrids of the genus Agropyron in Canada and neighboring areas. Can. J. Bot. 43: 1421–1448.

BRACKNEY, C. T. and SEELY, C. I. 1966. Quack grass control in Idaho. Agric. Exp. Sta. Bull. 455.

BRIMHALL, P. B. 1970. Modifications in the weed flora due to weed control techniques. Proc. 2nd Int. Mett. Selective Weed Control Beet Crops. Rotterdam. 249 pp.

CANADA DEPARTMENT of AGRICULTURE. 1944. Control of couch grass in Manitoba. Can. Dep. Agric. Publ. 765.

CANADA WEED COMMITTEE. 1969. Common and botanical names of weeds in Canada. Can. Dep. Agric. Publ. 1397. 67 pp.

CARDER, A. C. 1961. Couchgrass control in Alberta. Alta. Dep. Agric. Publ. 149.

CARLSON, W. C., LIGNOWSKI, E. M. and HOPEN, H. J. 1975. Uptake, translocation and adsorption of pronamide. Weed Sci. 23: 148–154.

CATHERALL, P. L. and CHAMBERLAIN, J. A. 1975. Occurrence of agropyron mosaic virus in Britain. Plant. Pathol. 24: 155–157.

CHANCELLOR, R. J. 1974. The development of dominance amongst shoots arising from fragments of Agropyron repens rhizomes. Weed Res. 14: 29–38.

CHEPIL, W. S. 1946. Germination of weed seeds. 1. Longevity, periodicity of germination and vitality of seeds in cultivated soil. Sci. Agric. 26: 307–346.

CODY, W. J. 1956. New plant records for northern and southern MacKenzie District. Can. Field Natur. 70(3): 101–130.

CONNERS, I. L. 1967. An annotated index of plant diseases in Canada and fungi recorded on plants in Alaska, Canada and Greenland. Can. Dep. Agric. Publ. 1251. Ottawa, Ont. 381 pp.

CUSSANS, G. W. and WILSON, B. J. 1970. Cultural and chemical treatments for the control of Agropyron repens and Agrostis gigantea in barley. Proc. 10th Br. Weed Control Conf. pp. 344–351.

DALE, H. M., HARRISON, P. J. and THOMSON, G. W. 1965. Weeds as indicators of physical site characteristics in abandoned pastures. Can. J. Bot. 43: 1319–1327.

DEWEY, D. R. 1965. Synthetic hybrids of new world and old world agropyrons. 11. Agropyron repens × Agropyron riparium. Amer. J. Bot. 52: 1039–1045.

DOYON, D. 1965. Les paturages semi-naturels à Festuca rubra sur certains sols dérivés de matériaux calcaires. Natur. Can. **92**: 109–120.

DOYON, D. 1968. La végétation des paturages naturels de St-Ferreol et de St-Tite-des-Caps, Comté de Montmorency. Natur. Can. **95**: 367–391.

EVANS, D. 1968. A system for controlling perennial grass weeds on a large cereal farm situated on a chalk soil. Proc. 9th Br. Weed Control Conf. pp. 197–199.

EVANS, N. W. and ELY, J. E. 1935. The rhizomes of certain species of grasses. Amer. Soc. Agron. J. **27**: 791–797.

FENTON, F. A. 1952. Field crop insects. 1st ed. Macmillan Co., New York, N.Y. 340 pp.

FERNALD, M. L. and KINSEY, A. C. 1958. Edible wild plants of eastern North America. Rev. by R. C. Rollins. Harper, New York, N.Y.

FERRON, M. and CAYOUETTE, R. 1975. Nom des mauvaises herbes du Québec. Agric. Québec. 3e ed. QA 38 R4-4. 113 pp.

FIVELAND, T. J., ERICKSON, L. C. and SEELY, C. I. 1972. Translocation of ^{14}C-assimilates and 3-amino-1, 2-, 4-trizole and its metabolites in *Agropyron repens*. Weed. Res. **12**: 155–163.

FORDE, B. J. 1966. Translocation in grasses. 11. Perennial ryegrass and couch grass. N. Z. J. Bot. **4**: 496–514.

FRANKTON, C. and MULLIGAN, G. A. 1971. Weeds of Canada. Can. Dep. Agric. Publ. 948. 217 pp.

FRIESEN, G. and SHEBESKI, L. H. 1960. Economic losses caused by weed competition in Manitoba grain fields. 1. Weed species, their relative abundance and their effect on crop yield. Can. J. Plant Sci. **40**: 457–467.

GODBOUT, E. 1960. Expériences sur les façons culturales. Agriculture **17**: 70–71.

HÅKANSSON, S. 1967–1970. Experiments with *Agropyron repens* (L.) Beauv. I–IX. Ann. Agric. Coll., Sweden [Uppsala, Lantbrukshogskolans Annals] **33**: 823–873; **34**: 3–29, 31–51; **35**: 61–78, 79–97, 869–894, 953–987; **36**: 135–151, 351–359. (in English).

HÅKANSSON, S. 1971. Experiments with *Agropyron repens* (L.) Beauv. X. Swed. J. Agric. Res. **1**: 239–246.

HAMMERTON, J. L. 1968. Past and future changes in weed species and weed floras. Proc. 9th Br. Weed Control Conf. pp. 1136–1145.

HERMANN, W. and ESLICK, R. 1939. Susceptibility of seedling grasses to damage by grasshoppers. Amer. Soc. Agron. J. **31**: 333–337.

HOLM, R. E. and MILLER, M. R. 1972. Weed seed germination. Responses to chemical and physical treatments. Weed Sci. **20**: 150–152.

HUDSON, H. J. and WEBSTER, J. 1958. Succession of fungi on decaying stems of *Agropyron repens*. Trans. Br. Mycol. Soc. **41**: 165–177.

HULTEN, E. 1962. The circumpolar plants. 1. Vascular cryptogams, conifers, monocotyledons. Kgl Svenska Vatenskasakad Handl. 4th Ser. **8**(5): 1–275. Almqoist and Wiksells, Stockholm.

HUSTICH, I. 1971. The introduced flora element in central Quebec–Labrador peninsula. Natur. Can. **98**: 425–441.

JOHNSON, B. G. 1958. Natural and induced dormancy of the vegetative buds on the rhizomes of quack grass (*Agropyron repens* (L.) Beauv.). Ph.D. Thesis Univ. of Wisconsin 154 pp. Madison, Wis.

JOHNSON, B. G. and BUCKHOLTZ, K. P. 1962. The natural dormancy of vegetative buds on the rhizomes of quack grass. Weeds **19**(1): 53–57.

JOSSELYN, J. 1672. New England rarities discovered in birds, beasts, fishes, serpents and plants of that country. London (facsimile edition, W. Junk. Berlin 1926). Cited by Rousseau 1968.

KING, L. 1966. Weeds of the world. Biology and control. Inter-Science, New York, N.Y. 526 pp.

LEAKEY, R. R. B., CHANCELLOR, R. J. and VINCE-PRUE, D. 1975. Parental factors in dominance of lateral buds on rhizomes of *Agropyron repens* (L.) Beauv. Planta **123**: 267–274.

LEPAGE, E. 1953. Nouvelles notes sur les hybrides de graminées. Natur. Can. **80**: 189–199.

McINTYRE, G. I. 1965. Some effects of the nitrogen supply on the growth and development of *Agropyron repens* (L.) Beauv. Weed. Res. **5**: 1–12.

McINTYRE, G. I. 1969. Apical dominance in the rhizome of *Agropyron repens*. Evidence of competition for carbohydrate as a factor in the mechanism of inhibition. Can. J. Bot. **47**: 1189–1197.

McINTYRE, G. I. 1970. Studies on bud development in the rhizome of *Agropyron repens*. 1. The influence of temperature, light intensity and bud position on the pattern of development. Can. J. Bot. **48**: 1903–1909.

METCALF, C. L., FLINT, W. P. and MET-CALF, R. L. 1962. Destructive and useful insects. Their habits and control. 4th ed. McGraw-Hill Book Co., New York, N.Y.

MUENSCHER, W. C. 1952. Weeds. MacMillan Co., New York, N.Y. 579 pp.

MUZIK, T. J. 1970. Weed biology and control. McGraw-Hill, Toronto, Ont. 273 pp.

NOVAKOVA, J. and ZACHA, V. 1975. [Contribution to the knowledge of *Tilletia contraversa* Kuhn on *Agropyron repens* (L.) P.B.] Ceska Mykol. 29: 83–89. [In Czech.].

PALM, C. E. 1935. The alfalfa snout beetle, *Brackyrlinus ligustici* L. Cornell Uni. Agric. Exp. Sta. Bull. 629: 47 pp.

PALMER, J. H. 1958. Studies in the behaviour of the rhizomes of *Agropyron repens* (L.) Beauv. 1. The seasonal development and growth of the parent plant and rhizome. New Phytol. 57: 145–159.

PALMER, J. H. and SAGAR, G. R. 1963. *Agropyron repens* (L.) Beauv. Biological flora of the British Isles. J. Ecol. 51: 783–794.

RALEIGH, S. M., FLANAGAN, T. R. and VEATCH, C. 1962. Life history studies as related to weed control in the northeast. 4. Quack grass. Rhode Island. Agric. Exp. Sta. Bull. 365.

RIOUX, R. 1973. Factors influencing glyphosate activity on quack grass. M.S. Thesis. Univ. Guelph, Ont. 73 pp.

RIOUX, R., BANDEEN, J. D. and ANDERSON, G. W. 1974. Effects of growth stage on translocation of glyphosate in quack grass. Can. J. Plant Sci. 54: 397–401.

ROGAN, P. G. and SMITH, D. L. 1974. Patterns of translocation of ^{14}C-labelled assimilates during vegetative growth of *Agropyron repens* (L.) Beauv. Z. Pflanzenphysiol. 73(5): 405–414.

ROGAN, P. G. and SMITH, D. L. 1975a. The effect of temperature and nitrogen level on the morphology of *Agropyron repens* (L.) Beauv. Weed Res. 15: 93–99.

ROGAN, P. G. and SMITH, D. L. 1975b. Rates of leaf initiation and leaf growth in *Agropyron repens* (L.) Beauv. J. Exp. Bot. 26: 70–78.

ROGAN, P. G. and SMITH, D. L. 1976. Experimental control of bud inhibition in rhizomes of *Agropyron repens* (L.) Beauv. Z. Pflanzenphysiol. 78(2): 113–121.

ROUSSEAU, C. 1968. Histoire, habitat et distribution de 220 plantes introduites au Quebéc. Natur. Can. 95: 49–169.

SAGAR, G. R. 1961. *Agropyron repens* — an introduction. Proc. 5th Br. Weed Contr. Conf. pp. 259–263.

SCHIRMAN, R. and BUCKHOLTZ, K. P. 1966. Influence of atrazine on control and rhizome carbohydrate reserves of quack grass. Weeds 14: 233–236.

SPRANKLE, P., MEGGITT, W. F. and PENNER, D. 1975a. Absorption, action, and translocation of glyphosate. Weed Sci. 23: 235–240.

SPRANKLE, P., MEGGITT, W. E. and PENNER, D. 1975b. Adsorption, mobility, and microbial degradation of glyphosate in the soil. Weed Sci. 23: 229–234.

SUPAVARN, P., KNAPP, F. W. and SIGNAFUS, R. 1974. Biologically active plant extracts for control of mosquito larvae. Mosquito News 34: 398–402.

TESU, C., PALADE, L., CARUNTO, V., NERLESCU, E. and AVARVARIS, I. 1972. (Contribution to the study of soil salinity in the flood plain of the river Bahlim in river landscape management.) Lucrasi Sti-Institut agronomic of Clonescu de la Brad; (Agron. Hortic. (1972) 312-323). (Herbage Abstr. 1974 (44:3886)).

TRIPATHI, R. S. and HARPER, J. L. 1973. The comparative biology of *Agropyron repens* (L.) Beauv. and *A. caninum* (L.) Beauv. I. The growth of mixed populations established from tillers and from seeds. J. Ecol. 61: 353–368.

WERNER, P. A. 1975. The effects of plant litter on germination in teasel. Amer. Midl. Natur. 94: 470–476.

WILLIAMS, E. D. 1970a. Effects of decreasing the light intensity on the growth of *Agropyron repens* (L.) Beauv. in the field. Weed Res. 10: 360–366.

WILLIAMS, E. D. 1970b. Studies on the growth of seedlings of *Agropyron repens* (L.) Beauv. and *Agrostis gigantea* Roth. Weed Res. 10: 321–330.

WILLIAMS, E. D. 1971. Effects of light intensity, photoperiod and nitrogen on the growth of seedlings of *Agropyron repens* (L.) Beauv. and *Agrostis gigantea* Roth. Weed Res. 11: 159–170.

WILLIAMS, E. D. 1973a. A comparison of the growth and competition behaviour of seedlings and plants from rhizomes of *Agropyron repens* (L.) Beauv. and *Agrostis gigantea* Roth. Weed Res. 13: 422–429.

WILLIAMS, E. D. 1973b. Variation in growth

of seedlings and clones of *Agropyron repens* (L.) Beauv. Weed Res. **13**: 24–41.

WILLIAMS, E. D. 1975. Growth of seedlings of *Agropyron repens* (L.) Beauv. and *Agrostis gigantea* Roth in cereal crops. Weed Res. **15**: 299–306.

WILLIAMS, E. D. and ATTWOOD, P. J. 1970. Seed production by couch grass (*Agropyron repens*). N.A.A.S.Q. Rev. **89**: 42–46.

WILLIAMS, E. D. and ATTWOOD, P. J. 1971. Seed production of *Agropyron repens* (L.) Beauv. in arable crops in England and Wales in 1969. Weed Res. **11**: 22–30.

WOLCOTT, A. R. and CARLSON, R. F. 1947. Preliminary report on field application of IPC in the control of quack grass in an established sod. Mich. Agric. Exp. Sta. Quart. Bull. **30**: 218–229.

THE BIOLOGY OF CANADIAN WEEDS.
25. *Silene alba* (Miller) E. H. L. Krause

J. McNEILL

Biosystematics Research Institute, Agriculture Canada, Ottawa, Ontario K1A 0C6.

Received 17 Mar. 1977, accepted 25 May 1977.

McNEILL, J. 1977. The biology of Canadian weeds. 25. *Silene alba* (Miller) E. H. L. Krause. Can. J. Plant Sci. **57**: 1103–1114.

A review is provided of information on the biology of *Silene alba* (*Lychnis alba, Melandrium album*), a weed species introduced from Eurasia, which occurs across the agricultural areas of Canada. A serious weed, especially of leguminous forage crops, white cockle is resistant to common herbicides such as 2,4-D and 2,4,5-T.

L'auteur fournit une documentation biologique sur la Lychnide blanche (*Silene alba, Lychnis alba, Melandrium album*), espèce de mauvaise herbe introduite d'Eurasie et répandu dans les régions agricoles du Canada. Particulièrement nuisible dans les cultures fourragères de légumineuses, elle résiste aux herbicides courants comme le 2,4-D et le 2,4,5-T.

1. Name

Silene alba (Miller) E. H. L. Krause (*Lychnis alba* Miller; *Melandrium album* (Miller) Garcke) (see McNeill 1976, p. 407) — **white cockle** (Canada Weed Committee 1969), white campion (Gleason and Cronquist 1963); **compagnon-blanc** (Coste 1900; Fournier 1946), lychnide blanche (Ferron and Cayouette 1971). Caryophyllaceae, pink family, Caryophyllacées.

2. Description and Account of Variation

Dioecious biennial or short-lived perennial (sometimes behaving as an annual) with a thick almost woody stock, bearing few short non-flowering shoots and usually several erect flowering shoots, 30–100 cm tall; stems and leaves covered with rather short, spreading hairs, those in the upper part of the flowering stems glandular. Leaves opposite, ovate to lanceolate, the lower narrowed into long stalks, the upper sessile. Bracts lanceolate to narrowly triangular, acute. Flowers large, ca. 25–30 mm diam., in a lax compound dichasium. Calyx fused, with 5 narrowly triangular teeth, greenish to purplish with rather long glandular hairs throughout; calyx tube of staminate flowers cylindrical, 15–22 mm long, 10-veined, with teeth 4–5.5 mm long; that of pistillate flowers narrowly ovoid, 20–30 mm long, 20-veined, becoming more or less inflated and accrescent in fruit, with teeth extending to 6.5 mm long. Petals 5, white, each with a long, slightly exserted claw, 2 coronal ligules and a spreading bifid limb. Stamens 10 (staminate flowers only). Styles usually 5 (pistillate flowers). Capsule ± ovoid, narrowing at the top, opening by suberect to spreading teeth, twice the number of the styles. Seeds 1.3–1.5 mm diam, grey, bluntly tubercled.

The chromosome number $n = 12$ has been reported for plants of white cockle growing as a weed in Ottawa (Mulligan 1957); this is the same number as that reported from West Liberty, Iowa (Crang and Dean 1971) and extensively from Eurasia.

Silene alba is frequently confused with *S. noctiflora* L. (night-flowering catchfly) and there has also been some confusion with *S. dioica* (L.) Clairv. (red cockle). *Silene noctiflora*, which is to be found throughout the country, although uncommon in Atlan-

Fig. 1.   Twelve-week-old plant of *S. alba* (× 2/9).   Fig. 2–3. Male (Fig. 2) and female (Fig. 3.) flowers of *S. alba*, also showing some of the variation in corolla lobing in the species (× 1½). Fig. 4. Seeds of *S. alba*, collected in Pontiac County, Quebec (× 8).   Fig. 5. Seeds of *S. alba* found as an impurity in imported red clover seeds; the grey bloom has been removed from some of the seeds in the cleaning of the clover seed (× 8).   Fig. 6. Seeds of *S. dioica* collected in Stanley Park, Vancouver (× 8).

tic Canada, differs in its consistently annual habit, in being densely viscid–hairy in the upper part so that living plants are sticky to the touch, in its more or less linear, attenuate bracts, in the calyx being whitish and glabrous between the 10 prominent green viscid hairy nerves which usually have prominent cross-connections, in the narrow attenuate calyx-teeth, 7–10 mm long, in the flowers always being closed during the day and having petals yellowish below and pinkish above, in the bisexual flowers with 3 styles, and in the capsule opening by 6 recurved teeth. Red cockle, *Silene dioica* (=*Lychnis dioica*), is extremely uncommon in Canada; it is not weedy and is only known to be naturalized in coastal British Columbia, a few places in Atlantic Canada and one wooded area in Manitoba (McNeill in prep.). In addition to its red or bright pink petals, red cockle can be distinguished by its more numerous non-flowering shoots arising in the axils of the lowest stem leaves, its eglandular stems, shorter pedicels, smaller flowers (calyx tube 10–15 mm long), broadly triangular calyx teeth less than 4 mm long, ± globose capsules dehiscing with recurved teeth, and smaller, reddish-black seeds with acute tubercles.

A young plant of *S. alba* is illustrated in Fig. 1 and male and female flowers in Figs.

2, 3, 7 and 8. Figures 4 6 show normal seeds of *S. alba* and of *S. dioica*, along with seeds of the former species which have undergone a seed-cleaning process such that some have lost their characteristic grey bloom. Seeds similar to these, found as an impurity in alfalfa and clover seed, have been mistaken for those of *S. dioica* (which is not classed as a noxious weed).

3. Economic importance

(a) *Detrimental* — In most agricultural areas of Canada, white cockle is an important weed of field crops such as alfalfa (*Medicago sativa* L.), clover (*Trifolium* spp.) and small grains. It is an increasingly troublesome weed in western Canada, especially in areas with a grain–forage rotation. Doersch (1964) indicated that in Wisconsin about 50% of the alfalfa acreage was infested with white cockle, while for the northeastern United States, Fertig (1968) calculated that 30% of the acreage of established legumes was infested, and that there had been a very significant increase in the abundance of the weed in the previous 5 yr. A United States Department of Agriculture survey in 1965 (USDA–ARS 1968) reported that white cockle was one of the five worst weeds in pastures and hay crops in six states from New Hampshire and

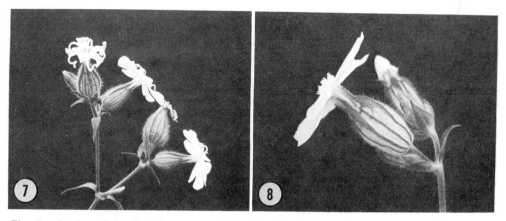

Fig. 7. Portion of female inflorescence of *S. alba*, showing 20-veined calcyes (× 1/2). Fig. 8. Male flowers and flower buds of *S. alba*, showing 10-veined calyces (× 1^1/3).

Connecticut to Minnesota, and that infestations were still increasing.

Faan and Johnson (1951) report that in Wisconsin, cucumber mosaic virus can overwinter in plants of *S. alba*; the virus was detected in 13 of 138 plants tested. Cucumber mosaic virus was not, however, found by Bruckart and Lorbeer (1976) in tests on *S. alba* plants in Orange and Oswego Counties, New York.

(b) *Beneficial* — In a survey of more than 325 plant species for possible sources of new insecticides (Patterson et al. 1975), it was found that extracts from the leaves and roots of white cockle were highly toxic to larvae of the mosquito, *Aedes aegypti*. As a relatively large-flowered dioecious species, *Silene alba* has long been noted as providing valuable experimental material for research in plant genetics and in particular on sex determination and fertilization (see e.g. Westergaard 1958; Zenkteler et al. 1975).

(c) *Legislation* — White cockle is listed as a noxious weed under the terms of the Noxious Weed Acts of Manitoba and Saskatchewan and of the Weed Control Act of Nova Scotia. It is also listed in the schedule to the Weed Control Act of Alberta and in the regulations under the Agricultural Abuses Act of Quebec. The species was deleted from the schedule of noxious weeds under the Ontario Weed Control Act in 1973. White cockle is a "primary noxious weed" under the Weed Seeds Order (1960) of the Seeds Act of Canada.

4. Geographical Distribution

Silene alba, introduced from Eurasia, now occurs across the southern portion of Canada (Fig. 7) and is found in every province, although it is very rare in Newfoundland and parts of the Maritime provinces; it is particularly abundant in British Columbia, Ontario, and Quebec. The species is not known from the Northwest or Yukon Territories, and Dearborn (1959) lists it as a weed "not now in Alaska" although specimens from the state are known (Fig. 9). Pedersen (1972) reports that it was once found in a vegetative state in southern Greenland. Reed (in Reed and Hughes 1970) records its occurrence throughout the northern half of the contiguous United States with greater economic importance east of the Dakotas and Nebraska. The species is widespread as a native weed throughout Europe (Chater and Walters 1964) and ranges eastward to Mongolia and S. E. Siberia (Shishkin 1936). *Silene alba* also occurs as an introduction in parts of Australia and New Zealand (Willis 1972) and has been found in India (Nair 1969).

5. Habitat

(a) *Climatic requirements* — White cockle appears to be limited climatically in its distribution northward primarily by its inability to ripen seed within the available growing season. Behrens (quoted in Pearson 1969) found that a temperature of 32 C was detrimental to seedling emergence, suggesting that high spring and summer temperatures are a factor in restricting its distribution in the southern United States.

Silene alba has long been recognized as a "sun-lover" (Baker 1947a). Willmot and Moore (1973) have shown that plants of *S. alba* can reach a much higher light-saturated rate of apparent photosynthesis than plants of the shade-tolerant *S. dioica*, and perform less well at very low light intensities, to the extent that they may show a net photosynthetic loss at light intensities below about 2,150 lx. Where *S. alba* occurs outside of cultivated fields it is a plant of open communities and appears able to tolerate low humidity and exposure to wind (Baker 1947a).

(b) *Substratum*— White cockle typically grows on dry, well aerated soils and is not found where the soil is waterlogged during the summer. Baker (1947a) reports that seedlings readily "damp off" in a humid atmosphere and he found unwilted plants in Britain in soil with a moisture content of only 3.4% of dry weight.

284

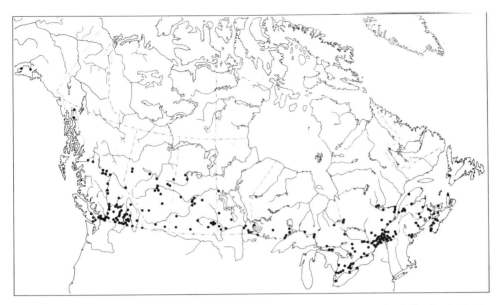

Fig. 9.   Distribution of *S. alba* in Canada and Alaska from specimens in the following herbaria: ACAD, ALTA, CAN, DAO, GH, ISC, MT, MTJB, NFLD, SCS, UBC, and V. (Herbarium abbreviations as in Holmgren and Keuken 1974).

(c) *Communities in which the species occurs* — White cockle occurs in waste places, along roadsides and at the edges of fields as well as being found as a weed of leguminous forage crops and small grains, often in association with yellow rocket (*Barbarea vulgaris* R. Br.) (Doersch 1964; Fertig 1968). It is particularly characteristic of new legume seedings and does not generally persist in closed communities. Baker (1947a) lists species associated with *S. alba* in various habitats in southern England.

6. History

Introduced into North America from Europe, *S. alba* first became established in the eastern United States probably in the early part of the 19th century, although the exact period is uncertain because of confusion with *S. dioica* and with *S. noctiflora*, an earlier introduction. *Silene alba* appears first (as *Lychnis vespertina*) in the fifth edition of Gray's *Manual* (1867); it is described there as "scarce," a term still used in the sixth edition (Gray 1890). According to Groh (1946), the first Canadian record was that by Gibson and Macoun (1875) from eastern Lake Huron. The species is included in Macoun's (1883) *Catalogue of Canadian Plants* where it is reported (under *Lychnis vespertina*) to be "a weed in a few gardens and waste places"; single collections from Nova Scotia, New Brunswick and two localities in Ontario are cited. The species is not included in Fletcher's (1897) *Weeds* but is illustrated in Clark and Fletcher (1906) where it is described as "by no means a common weed in Canada . . . but introduced occasionally with crop seeds . . . from Europe." It was said to be "abundant and troublesome" in the vicinity of Guelph and also to occur in a few other places in Western Ontario. Although the dumping on ballast heaps of rubbish from grain ships was probably another method of introduction (Baker 1948), that described by Clark and Fletcher seems to have been the main one. The subsequent spread of the species

285

across North America appears also to have been due to its dissemination with crop seed.

7. Growth and Development

(a) *Morphology* — Initial soil penetration is by a tap root which extends from 5 to about 40 cm, depending on the depth and porosity of the soil (Baker 1947a). Lateral roots then take over the main assimilative function and Mörchen (1972) illustrates the extent of such root growth in garden soil, where a depth of more than 1.2 m may be reached, much greater than that attainable by the less drought-resistant *S. dioica*. Near the soil surface the tap root may reach a diameter of more than 3 cm, and the root crown may bear numerous adventitious buds. In a field experiment in Wisconsin, such buds were found on all plants sampled from 7 September onwards, even those seeded only 1 mo earlier (Hastings and Kust 1970a). Pearson (1969) has found that crown-root segments with as little as 1 cm of root attached can produce new plants and all those buried at a depth of 13 cm showed regrowth within 2 mo. At a depth of 38 cm, 25% showed regrowth after 3 mo. Crown-root segments are, however, susceptible to air-drying; in a field experiment in Michigan, Pearson found that only one of five segments survived 2 days' exposure on the soil surface without rainfall, and none more than 2 days.

Ormrod and Renney (1968), in a survey of weed leaf stomata and trichomes, recognize *S. alba* as one of only a few species with sufficient pubescence to influence penetration of sprays. Baker (1946) found that hair density varied inversely with leaf size and moreover that plants growing in exposed situations were hairier than those in more mesic habitats. The types of glandular and eglandular hairs found in *S. alba* are illustrated by Tkachenko and Zykova (1975).

(a) *Perennation* — *Silene alba* may behave as an annual (under conditions of annual cultivation) or a biennial or it may persist for a few years. In most parts of Canada, flowering and fruiting can occur in the first season, but plants arising from later germinating seed overwinter as leaf rosettes on a substantial root that stores carbohydrate food reserves. Hastings and Kust (1970a) report that in Wisconsin, reserve carbohydrate storage was most rapid during September and early October and in all plants maximum storage levels were reached by the beginning of November. No winter injury was observed and minimum levels of reserve carbohydrate during spring growth were reached in mid-June. Plants that overwinter after flowering often lack any prominent leaf rosettes.

Pearson (1969) found that under field conditions of ploughing and seedbed preparation, few white cockle plants survived and subsequent infestation was almost entirely (98%) from seed.

(c) *Physiological data* — Willmot and Moore (1973) provide details of a wide range of photosynthetic parameters for ramets of *S. alba* previously grown under two different levels of light intensity (low — 4,300 lx and high — 21,500 lx).

(d) *Phenology* — In observations in Minnesota, Anderson (1967) found that rapid spring growth of semi-erect rosette leaves typically occurred in white cockle and that erect stems had emerged from the rosettes by early summer, at which time the basal rosette leaves had withered. Plants flower in most parts of Canada from June to October, the earlier flowering being usually those plants that have overwintered. Mathon (1961), Listowski (1966) and Pearson (1969) all report only slow and sporadic flowering under a short-day regime, whereas long or continuous days promote consistent rapid flowering. In Pearson's experiments the mean number of days to flowering was about 20 for continuous light and about 40 for a 16-h day. Ripe capsules are produced 4 to 5 wk after flowering, but Pearson and Meggitt (1969) report that immature seeds are viable 2–3 wk after pollination.

(c) *Mycorrhiza* — No mycorrhizal associations have been reported with *S. alba*.

8. Reproduction

(a) *Floral biology* — The flowers of *S. alba* are generally moth-pollinated. Richards and Baker in Baker (1947a) quote British reports of visits by members of the Noctuidae and Sphingidae. They also report on several Thysanoptera that have been found in the flowers, some with such regularity as to be probably involved in pollination. Brantjes (1976a) described the behavior of *Hadena bicruris* Hufn., which pollinates flowers of *S. alba* while visiting them to feed on nectar and oviposit.

Allogamy is obligate because of the separation of the sexes on different plants. The sex determination mechanism is a Y chromosome one, with the Y chromosome larger than the X. The system has probably been more extensively studied than that of any other dioecious plant species (van Nigtevecht 1966; Westergaard 1958).

(b) *Seed production and dispersal* — In Connecticut, Peters and Currey (1969) found that plants of white cockle produced an average of 500 seeds per capsule whereas Pearson (1969) found that 11-mo-old plants sampled in Michigan in mid-July had an average of 367 seeds per capsule and an average of 66 capsules per plant, giving an average seed potential of around 24,000 seeds per plant. Although these figures are higher than those observed in many Canadian samples (and much higher than Baker's (1947a) observations in Britain), white cockle is prolific in seed production. With flowering taking place from June to October seeds are produced and seedlings established over a long period. White cockle is spread chiefly as an impurity in crop seed.

(c) *Viability of seeds and germination* — Most germination tests indicate a high level of viability in white cockle seeds; those conducted under the most favorable conditions show over 90% germination within 8–15 days and generally over 80% at

constant temperatures in the range 20–30 C (Houser 1971; Pearson 1969; Thompson 1970c). Using his "germination curve" procedure (Thompson 1970a), Thompson (1970b) has found that seeds of *S. alba* from various parts of Europe had minimum optimal germination temperatures between 11 and 15 C and maximum optimal values ranging from 28 to 31 C.

None of the experiments cited above or the reports by Maguire and Overland (1959), and Rogers and Stearns (1955), working in North America, give any evidence of seed dormancy or of significant within-populational variation in this regard. Baker (1947a), however, found low germination (11% in 1 mo at 25 C) in seeds freshly gathered in Britain and suggested that a short period of dormancy existed in some seeds immediately after shedding. This is supported by observations on seed collected near Ottawa (Mulligan, pers. comm.) and the report by Steinbauer et al. (1955) from Michigan of 37–48% germination in seed sown within 1 mo of harvest compared with 82–93% for those tested after 10 mo of dry storage. In the latter experiment, the incorporation of 0.2% aequeous solution of potassium nitrate resulted in 87–94% germination in both freshly harvested and stored seed. There are also reports of dormancy in older seed; for example, a dormancy level of 58% in the previous year's seed was found by Lewis (1958); moreover the dormancy in such seed was as high as 87% when storage had been at a depth of 0.38 m in mineral soil. These reports suggest that substantial proportions of dormant seeds are produced in some populations, but that in others dormancy does not occur or is at a very much lower level.

Seeds of white cockle require light for germination but photoperiod and light intensities varying fom 540 to 21,500 lux were found in general to have no significant effects on germination (Pearson 1969). In a field experiment in Czechoslovakia, Kollár (1968) has found that whereas 17% of *S.*

alba seeds on the soil surface germinated within 75 days, none did so when buried at depths ranging from 25 to 150 mm; when recovered from these depths, 97% of the seeds were found to be intact and viable, as were most of the seeds (73%) that had not germinated on the surface. In greenhouse experiments in Michigan, Pearson (1969) found that emergence of seedlings was not adversely affected by planting depths up to 25 mm; at 50 mm emergence was only 10% in sandy loam and no seedlings at all emerged in silt or clay loams. At depths up to 25 mm, emergence was highest in sandy loam (43%) and lowest in clay loam (6%).

(d) *Vegetative reproduction* — No special structures adapted to vegetative reproduction exist in *S. alba*. Attempts to induce rooting of the stems in greenhouse soil were unsuccessful (Pearson 1969), nor do the developed leaf rosettes become independently rooted (Baker 1947a). Only the buds on the root-crown (see 7(a) above) permit vegetative regeneration, and so spread by vegetative means is restricted to the mechanical movement of entire roots and root-crown segments.

9. Hybrids

Hybrids between *S. alba* and *S. dioica* have long been known in Europe. The status of the two species and their hybrids has been the subject of study by several workers, notably Löve (1944) and Baker (1948, 1950a,b). Hybrids show various intermediate conditions in the characteristics which distinguish the species (see 2, above); the presence of a pale pink corolla is the most evident of these intermediate states. In Europe the species are generally distinguishable, but hybridize whenever they occur in close proximity (Chater and Walters 1964).

The status of the two species and their hybrids in North America has been more controversial. Although generally distinguished in floras and manuals, it has been suggested by Baker (1948) and Boivin (1967, 1968) that all the orginal introduc-

tions were of hybrid origin. Recent studies (McNeill in prep.) show that the material recognized as white cockle in North America is indistinguishable from European *S. alba*. Hybrids are found only in or near areas in which *S. dioica* occurs (see 2, above); they were common in the eastern coastal United States in the nineteenth century but seem less so today. No field weed populations showing hybrid origin have been found in Canada.

No other natural interspecific hybrids involving *S. alba* are known, but artificial F_1 hybrids have been obtained in crosses with a number of other species of *Silene* (Baker 1958; Kruckeberg 1962; Crang and Dean 1971; McNeill in prep.).

10. Population Dynamics

Following an August and a May seeding of alfalfa on land in Michigan heavily infested with white cockle, Pearson (1969) found that the number of new white cockle plants averaged between 120 and 180/m^2. After both seedings, 98% of all white cockle plants originated from seed. Very few white cockle seedlings appeared later than 4 wk after seeding, but the emergence of the weed was much slower than that of the alfalfa. After cutting, the competitive effects of the white cockle were much less severe.

In natural populations there is usually a predominance of female plants. For example, Mulcahy (1967) working in Georgia, U.S.A., found that the male/female sex ratio of plants in three populations ranged from 0.32 to 0.68. Various hypotheses have been developed to explain the female preponderance (Mulcahy 1967; Lloyd 1974). Pearson (1969) did not find significant differences in dry weight between male and female plants of white cockle grown in field and greenhouse experiments in Michigan.

11. Response to Herbicides and Other Chemicals

White cockle is resistant to foliar applications of 2,4-D, 2,4,5-T and MCPA and somewhat resistant to those of 2,4-DB and MCPB (Doersch 1964; Peters and O'Leary 1967; Ontario Herbicide Committee 1975; Canada Weed Committee 1976). Severe stunting or other reduction in vigor has been achieved with bromacil (0.6 kg/ha), simazine (2.25 kg/ha) and terbacil (0.6 kg/ha) (Peters and O'Leary 1967; Ilnicki and Hist 1969), and Hastings and Kust (1970b) report that simazine applied in the fall at 2.2 kg/ha was effective in controlling white cockle in established alfalfa. Control was achieved, however, without any increase in alfalfa yield over the untreated plot. Similar results were obtained by Anderson (1967) who found that of seven herbicides tested on white cockle in alfalfa (including dicamba, linuron and simazine) none increased forage yields. Pyrazon (Jaggard 1971) and chloroxurun (Putnam et al. 1969), used as pre-emergence herbicides, have provided effective control of white cockle in sugar beet and strawberries, respectively, but in the former case without significant effect on sugar or root yield.

In laboratory tests, Roberts (1965) found that primary root elongation in *S. alba* was reduced by 50% with chloropropham at a concentration of 0.04 ppm, whereas alfalfa was similarly inhibited only at a concentration of 4 ppm. In similar experiments with pronamide, Roberts and Ricketts (1973) found that *S. alba* was inhibited at 0.1 ppm and most members of the Leguminosae at 1–3 ppm.

12. Response to Other Human Manipulations

Mechanical injury during seedbed preparation together with deep burial or drying conditions near the surface of the soil cause a very low regeneration rate from root-crown segments (Pearson 1969); the species appears able to survive regular cultivation only by seed.

13. Responses to Parasites

(a) *Insects and nondomestic animals* — Richards and Baker in Baker (1947a) list 11 insect species that feed on *S. alba*. In addition, *Brachycaudus divaricata* Shaposhnikov and *Silenobium schusteri* Börner are reported by Richards (1976), and *Hadena bicruris* Hufn. by Brantjes (1976b).

(b) *Microorganisms and viruses* — Conners (1967) reports the following fungi as occurring on *S. alba* in Canada: *Phyllosticta lychnidis* A. Bondarzew, and *Uromyces verruculosus* Schroet. *Ustilago violacea* (Pers.) Rouss., the smut that induces an androecial development in female plants of *S. alba* and *S. dioica* (Baker 1947b, 1957), occurs widely on *S. alba* in Europe, and has been found on this host in Nova Scotia. Thirty-seven other species of fungi are reported as occurring on *S. alba* (and the closely related *S. dioica*) in Europe in Oudemans (1921, pp. 43-46).

Lychnis ringspot virus was first discovered by Bennett (1959) on plants of *S. alba* subsp. *divaricata* in greenhouse culture in California. The virus is capable of infecting crop plants such as sugar beet (*Beta vulgaris* L.) and spinach (*Spinacia oleracea* L.). Chessin et al. (1967) isolated a new strain of tobacco mosaic virus (TMV) from plants of *S. alba* growing in widely scattered locations in Montana; Sosnová and Polák (1974) also discovered TMV in plants of *S. alba* growing in Czechoslovakia.

(c) *Higher plant parasites* — No higher plant parasites are known on *S. alba*.

ACKNOWLEDGMENTS

It is with pleasure that I acknowledge the extensive technical and bibliographic assistance provided by Marion McCauley, the help given by Gail Bebee, and also the work of Patricia L. Ferguson in critically examining some of the herbarium material. I am also grateful to Professor W. F. Meggitt, Department of Crop Science, Michigan State University, East Lansing, for his kindness in lending me a copy of the thesis by J. O. Pearson, and to colleagues in the entomological sections of this Institute for information on insect visitors and parasites.

ANDERSON, R. H. 1967. An evaluation of several herbicides for the selective control of white cockle in alfalfa. M.S. Thesis. Univ. of Minnesota, St. Paul, Minn. 60 pp.

BAKER, H. G. 1946. The reaction of plants of the genus *Melandrium* to exposure. Proc. Leeds Phil. Lit. Soc. **4**: 359-366.

BAKER, H. G. 1947a. Biological flora of the British Isles: *Melandrium* (Roehling em.) Fries (*Lychnis* L. (1753) partim.). J. Ecol. **35**: 271-292.

BAKER, H. G. 1947b. Infection of species of *Melandrium* by *Ustilago violacea* (Pers.) Fuckel and the transmission of the resultant disease. Ann. Bot. Ser. 2, **11**: 333-348.

BAKER, H. G. 1948. Stages in invasion and replacement demonstrated by species of *Melandrium*. J. Ecol. **36**: 96-119.

BAKER, H. G. 1950a. Dioecious *Melandrium* in western North America. Madroño **10**: 218-221.

BAKER, H. G. 1950b. The inheritance of certain characters in crosses between *Melandrium dioicum* and *M. album*. Genetica **25**: 126-156.

BAKER, H. G. 1957. Expression of sex in flowering plants. Nature **180**: 614-615.

BAKER, H. G. 1958. Hybridization between dioecious and hermaphrodite species in the Caryophyllaceae. Evolution **12**: 423-427.

BENNETT, C. W. 1959. Lychnis ringspot. Phytopathology **49**: 706-713.

BOIVIN, B. 1967. Enumération des plantes du Canada. III — Herbidées, 1° partie: Digitatae: Dimerae, Liberae. Nat. Can. **93**: 583-646.

BOIVIN, B. 1968. Flora of the Prairie Provinces, part II — Digitatae, Dimerae, Liberae. Phytologia **16**: 219-339.

BRANTJES, N. B. M. 1976a. Riddles around the pollination of *Melandrium album* (Mill.) Garcke (Caryophyllaceae) during the oviposition by *Hadena bicruris* Hufn. (Noctuidae, Lepidoptera). I. Proc. K. Nederl. Akad. Wetensch. Ser. C, Biol. Med. Sci. **79**: 1-12.

BRANTJES, N. B. M. 1976b. Prevention of super parasitization of *Melandrium* flowers by *Hadena* (Lepidoptera). Oecologia **24**: 1-6.

BRUCKART, W. L. and LORBEER, J. W. 1976. Cucumber mosaic virus in weed hosts near commercial fields of lettuce and celery. Phytopathology **66**: 253-259.

CANADA WEED COMMITTEE. 1969. Common and botanical names of weeds in Canada. Publ. 1397. Canada Department of Agriculture, Ottawa, Ont. 67 pp.

CANADA WEED COMMITTEE. 1976. Report of the Research Appraisal and Research Planning Committee, Western Section, Vancouver, B.C., December 2-4, 1975. Canada Weed Committee, Agriculture Canada, Regina, Sask. 104 pp.

CLARK, G. H. and FLETCHER, J. 1906. Farm weeds of Canada. Canada Department of Agriculture, Ottawa, Ont. 56 pp., 103 pl.

CHATER, A. O. and WALTERS, S. M. 1964. *Silene* L. Pages 158-181 *in* T. G. Tutin et al., eds. Flora Europaea, Vol. 1. Univ. Press, Cambridge.

CHESSIN, M., ZAITLIN, M. and SOLBERG, R. A. 1967. A new strain of tobacco mosaic virus from *Lychnis alba*. Phytopathology **57**: 452-453.

CONNERS, I. L. 1967. An annotated index of plant diseases in Canada and fungi recorded on plants in Alaska, Canada and Greenland. Publ. 1251. Research Branch, Canada Department of Agriculture, Ottawa, Ont. 381 pp.

COSTE, H. 1900. Flore descriptive et illustrée de la France. vol. 1 (pp. 1-240). Paul Klincksieck, Paris.

CRANG, R. E. and DEAN, H. L. 1971. An intergeneric hybrid in the Sileneae (Caryophyllaceae). Bull. Torrey Bot. Club **98**: 214-217.

DEARBORN, C. H. 1959. Weeds in Alaska and some aspects of their control. Weeds **7**: 265-270.

DOERSCH, R. E. 1964. White cockle and yellow rocket. Proc. North Cent. Weed Control Conf. **20**: 58.

FAAN, HWEI CHUNG and JOHNSON, J. 1951. The overwintering of the cucumber mosaic virus. Phytopathology **41**: 1001-1010.

FERRON, M. and CAYOUETTE, R. 1971. Nom des mauvaises herbes du Québec. ed. 2. Publ. 288-71. Ministère de l'Agriculture et de la Colonisation du Quebec. 113 pp.

FERTIG, S. N. 1968. Broadleaf weed problems of the Northeast Weed Control Conference. Proc. Northeast. Weed Control Conf. **22**: 19-26.

FLETCHER, J. 1897. Weeds. Bull. 28, Canada Department of Agriculture, Ottawa, Ont. [47 pp.].

FOURNIER, P. 1946. Les quatre flores de la France. ed. 2. Paul Lechevalier, Paris. 1,093 pp.

GIBSON, J. and MACOUN, J. 1875. The plants of the eastern coast of Lake Huron, and their distribution throughout the northern and western portions of British North America. Can. J. **14**: 635-657.

GLEASON, H. A. and CRONQUIST, A. 1963. Manual of vascular plants of northeastern United States and adjacent Canada. van Nostrand, Princeton, N.J. 810 pp.

GRAY, A. 1867. Manual of botany of the northern United States. ed. 5. Ivison, Blakeman, Taylor, New York & Chicago.

GRAY, A. 1890. Manual of botany of the northern United States. ed. 6, revised by S. Watson and J. M. Coulter. American Book Co., New York, N.Y.

GROH, H. 1946. Canadian weed survey. Third annual report 1944. Canada Department of Agriculture, Ottawa, Ont. 70 pp.

HASTINGS, R. E. and KUST, C. A. 1970a. Reserve carbohydrate storage and utilization by yellow rocket, white cockle, and hoary alyssum. Weed Sci. 18: 140–148.

HASTINGS, R. E. and KUST, C. A. 1970b. Control of yellow rocket and white cockle in established alfalfa. Weed Sci. 18: 329–333.

HOLMGREN, P. K. and KEUKEN, W. 1974. Index herbariorum. Part I. The herbaria of the world. ed. 6. (Regnum Veg. 92) Oosthoek, Schetema & Holkema, Utrecht. 397 pp.

HOUSER, A. C. 1971. Laboratory germination of mature and immature white cockle (*Lychnis alba*) seeds. Proc. Assoc. Off. Seed Anal. 60: 118–122.

ILNICKI, R. D. and HIST, L. F. 1969. Weed control in dormant alfalfa. Proc. Northeast. Weed Control Conf. 23: 222–226.

JAGGARD, K. W. 1971. Herbicides and weed control: stubble cultivations. Rep. Rothamsted Exp. Sta. 1970(1): 268–269.

KOLLÁR, B. 1968. Sledovanie klíčivosti semien a vzchádzavosti niektorých druhov burín dozretých. v. oximnej pšenici z rozličnej hĺbky pôdy. Acta Fytotechn. 17: 103–110.

KRUCKEBERG, A. R. 1962. Intergeneric hybrids in the Lychnideae (Caryophyllaceae). Brittonia 14: 311–321.

LEWIS, J. 1958. Longevity of crop and weed seeds. 1. First interim report. Proc. Int. Seed Test. Assoc. 23: 340–354.

LISTOWSKI, A. 1966. Further observations on the development of hibernating annual plants (Observations on plant development. XIII). Acta Soc. Bot. Polon. 35: 455–460.

LLOYD, D. G. 1974. Female-predominant sex ratios in angiosperms. Heredity 32: 35–44.

LÖVE, D. 1944. Cytogenetic studies on dioecious *Melandrium*. Bot. Not. 1944 [97]: 125–213.

McNEILL, J. 1976. The taxonomy and evolution of weeds. Weed Res. 16: 399–413.

MACOUN, J. 1883. Catalogue of Canadian plants. Part I. — Polypetalae. Dawson, Montreal, Que. 192 pp.

MAGUIRE, J. D. and OVERLAND, A. 1959. Laboratory germination of seeds of weedy and native plants. Wash. Agric. Exp. Sta. Circ. 349: 1–15.

MATHON, C. C. 1961. Contribution à l'étude des exigences thermiques préalables et du photopériodisme chez différentes espèces de Phanérogames. Bull. Mus. Natl. Hist. Nat. Ser. 2, 33: 228–235; 348–356.

MÖRCHEN, G. 1972. Über den unterschiedlichen Wuchs zweier einheimischer Lichtnelken. Hercynia Ser. 2, 9: 271–274.

MULCAHY, D. L. 1967. Optimal sex ratio in *Silene alba*. Heredity 22: 411–423.

MULLIGAN, G. A. 1957. Chromosome numbers of Canadian weeds. I. Can. J. Bot. 35: 779–789.

NAIR, V. J. 1969. *Silene alba* (Mill.) Krause — a new record for India. Bull. Bot. Surv. Ind. 11: 201.

NIGTEVECHT, G. VAN 1966. Genetic studies in dioecious *Melandrium*. II. Sex determination in *Melandrium album* and *Melandrium dioicum*. Genetica 37: 307–344.

ORMROD, D. J. and RENNY, A. J. 1968. A survey of weed leaf stomata and trichomes. Can. J. Plant Sci. 48: 197–209.

ONTARIO HERBICIDE COMMITTEE. 1975. Guide to chemical weed control. Ontario Ministry of Agriculture and Food, Toronto, Ont. 91 pp.

OUDEMANS, C. A. J.A. 1921. Enumeratio systematica fungorum. Vol. 3. Nijhoff, The Hague. 1,313 pp.

PATTERSON, B. D., KHALIL, S. K. WAHBA, SCHERMEISTER, L. J. and QURAISHI, M. S. 1975. Plant–insect interactions. I. Biological and phytochemical evaluation of selected plants. Lloydia 38: 391–403.

PEARSON, J. O. 1969. A life history study of white cockle (*Lychnis alba* Mill.) and some competitive effects in alfalfa (*Medicago sativa* L.). Ph.D. Thesis. Department of Crop Science, Michigan State University, East Lansing, Mich. 78 pp.

PEARSON, J. O. and MEGGITT, W. F. 1969. Life history of white cockle and some competitive effects with alfalfa. Abstr. Meet. Weed Sci. Soc. Amer. 1969: 150-A. (Weed Abstr. 21: 150).

PEDERSEN, A. 1972. Adventitious plants and cultivated plants in Greenland. Medd. Gronl. 178(7): 1–99.

PETERS, R. A. and CURREY, W. L. 1969. Growth habits of white cockle as related to weed control. Proc. Northeast. Weed Control Conf. **23**: 414.

PETERS, R. A. and O'LEARY, R. M. 1967. Herbicidal response of white cockle (*Lychnis alba*) and other winter weeds associated with alfalfa. Proc. Northeast. Weed Control. Conf. **21**: 299–302.

PUTNAM, A. R., KESNER, C. D. and HESS, F. D. 1969. Herbicides and herbicide combinations for newly planted strawberries. Proc. North Centr. Weed Control Conf. **24**: 53.

REED, C. F. and HUGHES, R. O. 1970. Selected weeds of the United States. Agric. Handb. 366, Agricultural Research Service, United States Department of Agriculture, Washington, D.C. 463 pp.

RICHARDS, W. R. 1976. A host index for species of Aphidoidea described during 1935 to 1969. Can. Entomol. **108**: 499–550.

ROBERTS, H. A. 1965. Comparative tolerance of some dicotyledons to chlorpropham. Weed Res. **5**: 61–67.

ROBERTS, H. A. and RICKETTS, M. E. 1973. Comparative tolerance of some dicotyledons to pronamide and chlorpropham. Pestic. Sci. **4**: 83–87.

ROGERS, B. J. and STEARNS, F. W. 1955. Preliminary studies on the germination of weed seeds. Proc. North Centr. Weed. Control Conf. **12**: 7.

SHISHKIN, B. K. 1936. Sem. LX. Gvozdichnye — Caryophyllaceae Juss. *In* V. L. Komarov, Flora SSSR **6**: 386–870. Alademii Nauk, Moskva & Leningrad.

SOSNOVÁ, V. and POLÁK, Z. 1974. Further natural host plants of a necrotic TMV-strain . Biol. Plant. (Praha) **16**: 395–396.

STEINBAUER, G. P., GRIGSBY, B., CORREA, L. and FRANK, P. 1955. A study of methods for obtaining laboratory germination of certain weed seeds. Proc. Assoc. Off. Seed Anal. **45**: 48–52.

THOMPSON, P. A. 1970a. Characterization of the germination response to temperature of species and ecotypes. Nature **225**: 827–831.

THOMPSON, P. A. 1970b. Germination of species of Caryophyllaceae in relation to their geographical distribution in Europe. Ann. Bot. **34**: 427–449.

THOMPSON, P. A. 1970c. A comparison of the germination character of species of Caryophyllaceae collected in central Germany. J. Ecol. **58**: 699–711.

TKACHENKO, N. M. and ZŶKOVA, N. YA. 1975. Mikroskopichne doslidzhennya travỹ melandriyu biloho. Farm. Zh. **30**: 72–76.

UNITED STATES DEPARTMENT OF AGRICULTURE–AGRICULTURAL RESEARCH SERVICE. 1968. Extent and cost of weed control with herbicides and an evaluation of important weeds, 1965. Rep. ARS. 34–102. United States Department of Agriculture, Washington, D.C.

WESTERGAARD, M. 1958. The mechanism of sex determination in dioecious flowering plants. Adv. Genet. **9**: 217–281.

WILLIS, J. H. 1972. A handbook to plants in Victoria. Vol. II. Dicotyledons. Melbourne Univ. Press. 832 pp.

WILLMOT, A. and MOORE, P. D. 1973. Adaptation to light intensity in *Silene alba* and *S. dioica*. Oikos **24**: 458–464.

ZENKTELER, M., MISIURA, E. and GUZOWSKA, I. 1975. Studies in obtaining hybrid embryos in test tubes. Pages 180-187 *in* H. Y. Mohan Ram, J. J. Shah and C. K. Shah, eds. Form, structure and function in plants. Sarita Prakashan, Nauchandi, India.

THE BIOLOGY OF CANADIAN WEEDS.
26. *Dennstaedtia punctilobula* (Michx.) Moore

WILLIAM J. CODY[1], IVAN V. HALL[2], and CLIFFORD W. CROMPTON[1]

[1]*Biosystematics Research Institute, Agriculture Canada, Ottawa, Ontario K1A 0C6, and*
[2]*Research Station, Agriculture Canada, Kentville, Nova Scotia B4N 1J5.*

Received 2 Mar. 1977, accepted 13 July 1977.

CODY, WILLIAM J., HALL, IVAN V. AND CROMPTON, CLIFFORD W. 1977. The biology of Canadian weeds. 26. *Dennstaedtia punctilobula* (Michx.) Moore. Can. J. Plant Sci. **57**: 1159–1168.

A summary of biological information on *Dennstaedtia punctilobula* (Michx.) Moore, hay-scented fern, is presented. It has a native perennial herbaceous species of North America which has its center of distribution in the Appalachian region. In Canada it is found from the East Coast to Ontario. It is a weed in native lowbush blueberry fields, upland pastures and roadsides, particularly in the eastern parts of its range, where it forms dense colonies.

Les auteurs présentent un résumé de l'information biologique sur la fougère odorante, *Dennstaedtia punctilobula* (Michx.) Moore. C'est une plante vivace herbacée et indigène de l'Amérique du Nord, qui a le centre de distribution dans la région appalachienne. Au Canada, cette fourgère est trouvée du côté de l'est jusqu'en Ontario. C'est une mauvaise herbe répandue dans les champs de bleuets nains, dans les pâturages hauts et aussi au bord des routes, particulièrement dans l'est, où on trouve des colonies très denses.

1. Name

Dennstaedtia punctilobula (Michx.) Moore (=*Dicksonia pilosiuscula* Willd.; *Dicksonia punctilobula* (Michx.) A. Gray) — **hay-scented fern** (Canada Weed Committee 1969); **dennstaedtie punctilobulée**, (Ferron et Cayouette 1971). Pteridaceae (Copeland 1947), Polypodiaceae of many authors (Fernald 1950), fern family, Pteridacées.

2. Description and Account of Variation

Colonial perennial, the 30- to 74-cm tall fronds (Fig. 1) arising from the slender, naked, freely creeping and forking rhizome; stipe pale brown, lustrous, naked; rachis and under surface of the fronds minutely glandular–pubescent; blade lanceolate, bipinnate, the pinnae lanceolate, the pinnules pinnatifid with toothed lobes; sporangia borne in minute round sori situated on the upper margin of the under side of the lobes and covered by cup-shaped indusia. There is little variation within the species except in the length of the fronds, but the following forms which occur throughout the range of the species have been described: f. *schizophylla* (Clute) Rugg, with the ultimate segments deeply and sharply incised; f. *cristata* (Maxon) Clute, with the tips of many pinnae forked; f. *nana* (Gilbert) Weath., with the pinnules of the pinnae of the usually small fronds crowded, overlapping and rounded toward tips of the pinnae, and very small and scattered towards the base of the pinnae; f. *poyseri* Clute, with the blade bipinnate to bipinnatifid, with ovate pinnules and deeply lobed segments.

In sterile condition, *Dennstaedtia punctilobula* might possibly be confused with such other ferns as *Dryopteris spinulosa* (O. F. Muell.) Watt (spinulose wood fern), *Athyrium filix-femina* (L.) Roth (lady fern), *Cystopteris bulbifera* (L.) Bernh. (bulblet fern) and *Cystopteris fragilis* (L.) Bernh. (fragile fern). However,

Fig. 1. Fronds and rhizome of *Dennstaedtia punctilobula*. Reprinted from *Ferns of the Ottawa District* (Cody 1956).

it can be readily distinguished from these and all other species in its range, by the conspicuous hairs located both on the main rachis and the other axes. These multicellular hairs are of two kinds, one tipped by an acute colorless cell (acicular type) and the other by a rounded, colored cell (glandular type) (Morton and Neidorf 1954).

A chromosome number of $n = 33$ or 34 has been obtained on material from southern Ontario by Britton (1964) and $n = ca.$ 33 on material from eastern Ontario by Mulligan and Cody (unpublished).

3. Economic Importance

(a) *Detrimental* — *Dennstaedtia punctilobula* is a troublesome weed in lowbush blueberry fields especially in recently deforested areas in Nova Scotia and New Brunswick. The fern competes with blueberry shrubs for space, light, moisture and nutrients, thereby reducing fruit yield. Moreover, it creates difficulties in picking of berries (Jackson and Hall 1967). *D. punctilobula* has also been recorded as a weed of rough pastures and old fields in Nova Scotia, New Brunswick, Prince Edward Island and Quebec (Dore 1948; Erskine 1960; Muenscher 1955; Roland and Smith 1969). In such habitats it competes with grasses and forbs for space, and sometimes forms almost pure stands. It is not palatable to grazing animals (Roland 1941; Wherry 1961). Though a beautiful fern, this species spreads too rapidly for safe introduction into a small garden (Wherry 1961). Chrysler and Edwards (1947) state that this species shares with bracken the ability to take possession of a rocky or sterile field. *D. punctilobula* is one of only three ferns that are not protected by law in the State of New York, the other two being *Pteridium aquilinum* and *Onoclea sensibilis* (New York 1974).

(b) *Beneficial* — Following fires, *D. punctilobula* will quickly form a dense ground cover in areas where previously only a few fronds were present under a woodland canopy. This prevents soil crosion and leads to an accumulation of organic matter. The finely cut fronds of this species are pleasing to the eye.

4. Geographical Distribution

The main range of *D. punctilobula* is centered in the Appalachian region and extends into adjacent parts of eastern Canada and eastern United States. In Canada, *D. punctilobula* is rare in southern Newfoundland, and is common in Nova Scotia, New Brunswick and the eastern townships of Quebec. In Ontario it does not occur north of the southern townships of Nipissing and Parry Sound districts, or west of eastern Perth and Kent Counties (Fig. 2). Roberts (1935) is incorrect in depicting the range of *D. punctilobula* as extending north of Lake Superior in the districts of Sudbury, Algoma, Thunder Bay and west to Rainy River District. In the United States, *D. punctilobula* occurs as far west as Minnesota and south to Georgia and Alabama, but it is quite rare in the western part of its range (Mohlenbrock 1967; Billington 1952; Tryon et al. 1940).

5. Habitat

(a) *Climatic requirements* — *Dennstaedtia punctilobula* in eastern Canada occurs from the border of the United States north to latitude 48°30′N in western Newfoundland, to 47°45′N in Charlevoix Co., Quebec, and 45°10′N in Nipissing District, Ontario. Its western limit is close to Parry Sound in western Parry Sound District but does not extend west of 81°51′W in eastern Kent Co. These limits of range do not have an obvious correlation with isotherms, annual precipitation, length of growing season or average number of frost-free days (Anonymous 1974a). The rainfall varies from 89 to 127 cm; low temperature is about -29 C; high temperature is about 38 C; the mean annual frost-free period ranges from 120 to 180 days; and the mean annual length of growing season ranges from 160 to 220 days.

(b) *Substratum — D. punctilobula* is usually found on gently sloping well drained light sandy soils and about rock piles, but may also occur in swamps and limestone ledges. Wherry (1921) considered this species to be typically indifferent to soil acidity requirements. However, Hou (1950) reported soil pH of 4.8, 4.2 and 3.4 for stands of *D. punctilobula* that he studied in central Pennsylvania.

(c) *Communities in which the species occurs — Dennstaedtia punctilobula* fronds may be found widely spaced in mixed woodland, where the canopy is more or less

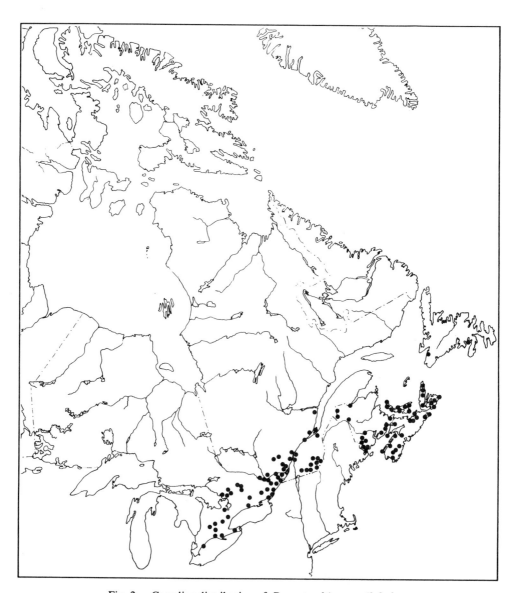

Fig. 2. Canadian distribution of *Dennstaedtia punctilobula*.

296

closed, but following burning or clearing will within a few years often form dense colonies to the exclusion of all other plant species. It is frequent in blueberry fields, upland pastures and along roadsides in the eastern part of its range.

6. History

Dennstaedtia punctilobula is of native origin throughout its present range. It undoubtedly moved in to Canada from the south following the retreat of the last glacial ice. Prior to the clearing of the land by the first white settlers, this species probably was found as scattered fronds in more or less closed canopy woodlands and formed dense colonies in natural forest clearings, in lighter soils and rough rocky situations, following wildfires and blowdowns.

7. Growth and Development

(a) *Morphology* — *Dennstaedtia punctilobula* produces large numbers of spores each growing season, but there is no record of the germination of these spores under natural conditions in Canada. The plant can survive burning and cutting because new fronds arise from the rhizome (Hall 1955).

Conard (1908) has presented an extremely detailed account of the structure and development of both the sporophyte and gametophyte generations of *D. punctilobula*. Two to five fronds is the common annual growth from each branch of the rhizome. Sterile and fertile fronds are similar in form, and both kinds are produced throughout the season, though the greatest development occurs in May and June. The stipe stands erect and the blade curves backwards facing the chief source of light.

(b) *Perennation* — In Canada and the eastern United States, *D. punctilobula* survives and spreads primarily by means of the persistent underground stem or rhizome. This rhizome, with abundant food reserves, overwinters and produces new fronds in the spring and throughout the growing season. The rhizome, which is long and branching, is found at from 5 to 15 cm below the surface of the ground. Branches may occur as direct forking of the rhizome or occasionally by stem-buds produced on the lower parts of the frond petioles (Conard 1908). Both branches of a forked rhizome tend to grow equally. Conard (1908) observed that about 20% of fronds produce shoots on the side of the petiole 3–8 mm from the rhizome. These shoots may remain dormant and papilla-like for 2 or 3 yr or their growth may be extremely slow. They may grow rapidly and nearly equal in size the fronds from which they spring. If the frond fails to develop, this shoot may. continue to grow alone. Ultimately all of these shoots produce normal rhizomes. At Ottawa, a clone measuring approximately 20 cm in diameter was planted in a light sandy loam in a lath house in August 1966. This clone had increased in size to a patch 242 × 182 cm by September 1976, the narrow measurement having been curtailed by trampling and cultivation. This would indicate an outward growth from the center of about 11 cm a year, but the actual growth of a single rhizome would average greater than 11 cm because of the repeated forking and thus changing of the direction of growth.

(c) *Physiological data* — *D. punctilobula* forms extensive colonies which will often exclude all other vascular plant species due to competition for light, nutrition and moisture, or the plant may be producing some inhibiting phytotoxins such as that released by *Pteridium aquilinum* fronds (Gliessman and Muller 1972). Phenolic acids were suspected and cinnamic acid was tentatively identified by these authors in *P. aquilinum*. Bohm and Tryon (1967) identified several cinnamic acid and benzoic acid derivatives from fronds of *D. punctilobula* and noted that among the 46 fern species representing 28 genera and eight families, this species was unique in possessing coumarin.

Hou (1950) analyzed the chemical composition of 10 ferns and fern allies gathered from acid soil localities in central Pennsylvania. He found that *D. punctilobula* is characterized by relatively large amounts of manganese, which varied markedly with the *p*H of the soil: as the *p*H of the soil decreased, the availability of manganese in the soil increased.

In a study of photoperiod of certain ferns (Benedict 1963), it was found that the copious fronds of *D. punctilobula* grown under long photoperiod (15–16 h) were sterile.

The fronds after being killed by frost turn a characteristic, chocolate-brown color which can readily be recognized in the fields and along roadsides.

(d) *Phenology* — New fronds arise all summer from May through September, or until the first sharp frost kills the fronds. The minute spores may be gathered in July and August; in culture they will start to develop in about 16 days. The young sporophyte will be visible in $3^1/2$ mo or less, the forked rhizome will develop in 1 yr, and the plants are mature in 3 yr (Roberts 1935). A more detailed account of germination of spores is described in section 8(c).

During the months of May, June and July 1975, detailed observations were made on two plots of *D. punctilobula*, the first on a steep, hilly, semiwooded slope in Gatineau Co., Quebec, and the second in a lath house at the Central Experimental Farm, Ottawa. Fronds grew quickly after they appeared above the ground. The growing frond remains in a fiddlehead conformation until the stipe has reached about half its final length, then the fiddlehead expands rapidly. Tiny green sori were first observed on 1 June. These increased in size and turned brown after 14 July. By 23 July many of the fronds had sori that were nearly black and were shedding spores.

Conard (1908) reported that in eastern Pennsylvania and Maryland in 1905, the young fronds appeared above the ground in the latter half of April and by 4 June 1905, spores were nearly mature at Loch Raven, Maryland.

(e) *Mycorrhiza* — Conrad (1908) reported the presence of fungal hyphae running through root cells of *D. punctilobula*. The fungus was not isolated.

8. Reproduction

(a) *Sporophyll biology* — The reproductive mechanism in ferns has been described in numerous textbooks (McLean and Ivimey-Cook 1951; Foster and Gifford 1974), and for *D. punctilobula*, in great detail by Conard (1908). The reproduction of *D. punctilobula* occurs by means of spores that are produced in sporangia clustered under the cup-shaped indusium of the small round sorus situated on the upper margin of the under sides of the lobes of the pinnules. A spore germinates to form a small green prothallus. The male prothallus is always only one cell thick. Antheridia may arise at any point on the shaded side and the prothallus may continue to grow for 5 mo or more and produce great numbers of antheridia. The female prothallus is always cordate in shape and about three cells in thickness. The archegonia are borne on the under side of a central thickening or swelling. Only rarely are prothalli hermaphroditic. A motile spermatozoid from the antheridium (one from each of the 32 sperm mother cells) fertilizes the egg or oosphere. The resultant zygote then germinates and produces a sporeling (Fig. 3) which grows into the familiar fern plant. Archegonia will continue to be produced on a prothallus until one is fertilized, but only one sporeling per prothallus will grow to maturity.

(b) *Spore production and dispersal* — Several millions of tetrahedral spores may be produced by a single well developed fertile frond, but it should be noted that not all fronds are fertile. Sterile and fertile fronds are similar in form but the reasons for the production of sori on some fronds is not known. One frond which bore about 11,000 sori was estimated to have produced over 7,000,000 spores. Thus a single clone growing in an open situation with several

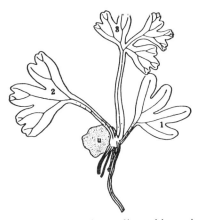

Fig. 3. Three-leaved sporeling with portion of prothallus (u) still attached. First, second and third leaves are indicated 1, 2, 3. Reprinted with permission from Carnegie Institute of Washington, Publication 94(1908).

hundreds of fronds would produce many millions of spores. These light spores are readily distributed by the wind as they are hurled from a sporangium. Sporangia in individual sori, and on the frond as a whole, do not mature evenly, so spore production is staggered.

(c) *Viability of spores and germination* — According to Roberts (1935), spores of *D. punctilobula* will germinate in about 16 days. Conard (1908) stated that spores sown on moist micaceous earth in October 1905 had mostly germinated and formed protonemata in 23 days. No published information has been found regarding the germination of spores and the production of gametophytes in natural situations in Canada, but such occurrences have been reported by Conard (1908) near Baltimore, Maryland, presumably from spores shed the year that they were found. There are no data available on the longevity of spores of this species. Spores of some fern genera have, however, been germinated as much as 48 yr after production: e.g. *Pellaea* (34 yr), *Dicksonia* (22 yr) and *Asplenium* (48 yr) (Smith 1938; Hill and Wagner 1974; Britton *in litt.*). There are no figures available on

the percentage of germination of *D. punctilobula* spores, although it is obvious that only a very small number of spores will find a suitable moist niche on the soil and subsequently germinate and produce a prothallus sufficiently close to one of the other sex, for a motile spermatozoid to fertilize an egg. Since the spermatozoids require a moist situation through which to move to the archegonia, a dry season restricts fertilization, and may result in the death of the prothallus which is readily subject to desiccation.

(d) *Vegetative reproduction* — Numerous fronds arise along the forking rhizome. On the surface, these appear to be separate plants. New plants may be formed by the fragmentation of the rhizome, either by rotting or mechanical damage. New plants formed however, still remain adjacent to sister plants.

9. Hybrids

No hybrids involving *D. punctilobula* are known.

10. Population Dynamics

In the fall of 1949, Hall (1955) cleared a second-growth stand of trees (about 25 yr old) in which *D. punctilobula* fronds occurred as small, spaced fronds. The area was then burned in April 1951 and again in 1952. Fronds of *D. punctilobula* were counted in a belt transect 39 m long and 0.9 m wide with the following results: 144(1949); 326(1950); 2,326(1951); 6,359(1952); and the percentage of foliage cover increased from 1.6% in 1949 to 3.2% in 1950, 23.0% in 1951 and 35.6% in 1952. Hall also reported that 1% full sunlight allowed for minimal growth (i.e. just survival) in a spruce-fir canopy; 10% full sunlight allowed moderate vegetative growth (but not spore production) in a wire birch canopy; and that 50% full sunlight in openings in the forest canopy allowed fruiting (the production of fertile fronds).

11. Response to Herbicides and Other Chemicals

Egler (1950) reported that in northwestern Connecticut all ferns tested were resistant to 2,4,5-T and 2,4-D — 2,4,5-T mixtures, and that *Dennstaedtia punctilobula, Onoclea sensibilis* and *Pteridium aquilinum* required constant attention because they tended to reproduce rapidly. Palfrey (*in litt.*) advised that the major herbicide, Brushkill (2,4-D + 2,4,5-T) used by the Nova Scotia Department of Highways, applied at recommended rates (Anonymous 1973) had not proven effective in controlling hay-scented fern along roadsides.

Jackson and Hall (1967) stated that *D. punctilobula* was difficult to control in lowbush blueberry fields and ought to be eradicated before production started. At that time a concentration of 5.5 kg/ha of amitrole (3-amino-5-triazole) active ingredient in 560 liters of water was recommended (5 lb a.i. in 50 gal of water/acre). They cautioned against harvesting any nearby berries because the crop must not contain any residue of this chemical.

In 1974 May and Baker Ltd. published a report entitled ''Asulox for the control of bracken'' (Anonymous 1974b). The rate recommended was 4.48 kg Asulox/ha, and it was stated that *Athyrium filix-femina, Blechnum spicant, Dryopteris borreii, D. dilatata, Thelypteris limbosperma* and *T. phegopteris* were also susceptible. Since this chemical was effective in the control of bracken and other ferns in England, it was tested by L. Jackson, Canada Agriculture, Experimental Station, Nappan, Nova Scotia in 1975 with considerable success. Because of the good results with bracken, Jackson laid out and treated plots of hay-scented fern with Asulox at Nappan in 1976. Results of this study will not be available until the summer of 1977.

12. Responses to Other Human Manipulations

Farmers in North Carolina have practiced cutting by hand with some success in pastures. This must be done before the spores mature, usually in June, and then again before the second crop produces spores. Such cutting will not, however, totally eliminate the fern (Cox 1936). This fern will not persist in cultivated land or in situations where the fronds are continually broken off by trampling. Muenscher (1955) suggested that the fronds should be mowed close to the ground before the spores matured and that small patches could be grubbed out by hand, but this is usually not practical in the situations where this species occurs.

It has been suggested that salt could be sprinkled among ferns where they occur in pastures, because in their eagerness for the salt, cattle and other domestic stock would practically destroy the leaf growth of the ferns by trampling (Cox 1936).

13. Responses to Parasites

(a) *Insects and other non-domestic stock* — No records of insects feeding or laying eggs on *D. punctilobula* were found nor were any records found of its use for food or bedding by any non-domestic animal.

(b) *Micro-organisms and viruses* — Fungi do not play an important role in the control of *D. punctilobula*, however, the following have been reported as occurring on this fern species: *Ceratobasidium anceps* (Bres. & Syd.) Jackson, in Quebec (Conners 1967); *Helotrum scutula* (Pers.) Karst., in Virginia (Anonymous 1960); and *Pezizella pteridina* (Nyl.) Rehm in Pennsylvania. No records of viruses were found for this species.

(c) *Higher plant parasites* — None recorded.

ACKNOWLEDGMENTS

It is with pleasure that we acknowledge the technical help provided in the field by Derek Munro. We are also grateful to Professor D. Britton for information provided on the Ontario distribution of *D. punctilobula*.

ANONYMOUS. 1960. Index of plant diseases in the United States. U.S. Agric. Handb. No. 165. 531 pp.

300

ANONYMOUS. 1973. Guide to chemical weed control. Publ. 75. Prepared by: Members of the Ontario Herbicide Committee, Minister of Agric. Newfoundland–New Brunswick–Nova Scotia, Prince Edward Island. 87 pp.

ANONYMOUS. 1974a. The national atlas of Canada. 4th ed. (rev.) Macmillan Co. of Canada, Toronto, and Dep. Energy Mines and Resources, Ottawa, Ont. 266 pp.

ANONYMOUS. 1974b. Asulox for the control of bracken. May and Baker Ltd., Dagenham, Essex, England. 16 pp.

BENEDICT, R. C. 1963. The effect of photoperiod on certain ferns. Amer. Fern J. **53**: 126–128.

BILLINGTON, C. 1952. Ferns of Michigan. Cranbrook Inst. Sci. 240 pp.

BOHM, B. A. and TRYON, R. M. 1967. Phenolic compounds in ferns. I. A survey of some ferns for cinnamic acid and benzoic acid derivatives. Can. J. Bot. **45**: 585–593.

BRITTON, D. M. 1964. Chromosome numbers of ferns in Ontario. Can. J. Bot. **42**: 1349–1354.

CANADA WEED COMMITTEE. 1969. Common and botanical names of weeds in Canada. Can. Dep. Agric. Publ. 1397. 67 pp.

CHRYSLER, M. A. and EDWARDS, J. L. 1947. The ferns of New Jersey. Rutgers University Press, New Brunswick, N.J. 201 pp.

CODY, W. J. 1956. Ferns of the Ottawa District. Canada Agric. Publ. 974. 94 pp.

CONARD, H. S. 1908. The structure and life-history of the hay-scented fern. Carnegie Inst. Wash. Publ. **94**: 1–106.

CONNERS, I. L. 1967. An annotated index of plant diseases in Canada and fungi recorded on plants in Alaska, Canada and Greenland. Canada Agric. Res. Br. Publ. 1251. 381 pp.

COPELAND, E. B. 1947. Genera *Filicum*. Chronica Botanica Co., Waltham. 270 pp.

COX, H. R. 1936. Eradication of ferns from pasture lands in the eastern United States. U.S. Dep. Agric. Farmers' Bull. 687. 8 pp.

DORE, W. G. 1948. Pasture associations of Eastern Canada. Ph.D. Thesis. The Ohio State University, Columbus, Ohio. 144 pp.

EGLER, F. E. 1950. Herbicide effects in Connecticut vegetation, 1949. Bot. Gaz. **112**: 76–85.

ERSKINE, D. S. 1960. The plants of Prince Edward Island. Can. Dep. Agric. Publ. 1088. 270 pp.

FERNALD, M. L. 1950. Gray's manual of botany. 8th ed. American Book Co., New York, N.Y. 1632 pp.

FERRON, M. and CAYOUETTE, R. 1971. Nom des mauvaises herbes du Québec. Minist. Agric. et Colonisation, Québec. Publ. 288. 113 pp.

FOSTER, A. S. and GIFFORD, E. M. JR. 1959. Comparative morphology of vascular plants. W. H. Freeman & Co., San Francisco and London. 555 pp.

GLIESSMAN, S. R. and MULLER, C. H. 1972. The phytotoxic potential of bracken, *Pteridium aquilinum* (L.) Kuhn. Madroño **21**: 299–304.

HALL, I. V. 1955. Floristic changes following the cutting and burning of a woodlot for blueberry production. J. Agric. Sci. **35**: 143–152.

HILL, R. H. and WAGNER, W. H., JR. 1974. Seasonality and spore type of the Pteridophytes of Michigan. Mich. Bot. **13**: 40–44.

HOU, H-Y. 1950. The chemical composition of certain ferns and fern allies of central Pennsylvania. Amer. Fern J. **40**: 233–240.

JACKSON, L. P. and HALL, I. V. 1967. Weeds and their control. Pages 15-20 *in* I. V. Hall, L. E. Aalders, L. P. Jackson, G. W. Wood, and C. L. Lockhart. Lowbush blueberry production in Canada. Can. Dep. Agric. Publ. 1278. 39 pp.

McLEAN, R. C. and IVIMEY-COOK, W. R. 1951. Textbook of theoretical botany. Vol. I. Longmans, Green and Co., London, England. 1069 pp.

MOHLENBROCK, R. H. 1967. The illustrated flora of Illinois: Ferns. Southern Illinois University Press, Carbondale and Edwardsville. 191 pp.

MORTON, C. V. and NEIDORF, C. 1954. The hay-scented fern, *Dennstaedtia punctilobula*. Amer. Fern J. **44**: 65–68.

MUENSCHER, W. C. 1955. Weeds 2nd ed. Macmillan Co., New York, N.Y. 560 pp.

NEW YORK. 1974. Environmental Conservation Law 9-1503 Regulation NYCRR 193.3.

ROBERTS, E. A. 1935. American ferns, how to grow and use them. Nat. Hortic. Mag. **14**: 105–131.

ROLAND, A. E. 1941. The ferns of Nova Scotia. Proc. N.S. Inst. Sci. **20**(3): 64–120.

ROLAND, A. E. and SMITH, E. C. 1969. The flora of Nova Scotia, Part I. Proc. N.S. Inst. Sci. **26**(1): 1–238.

SMITH, G. M. 1938. Cryptogamic botany, Vol. II. Bryophytes and Pteridophytes. McGraw-Hill Book Co., Inc. New York and London. 380 pp.

TRYON, R. M., FASSETT, N. C., DUNLOP, D. W. and DIEMER, M. E. 1940. The ferns and fern allies of Wisconsin. University of Wisconsin, Madison, Wis. 158 pp.

WHERRY, E. T. 1921. The soil reactions of the ferns of woods and swamps. Amer. Fern. J. **11**: 5–16.

WHERRY, E. T. 1961. The fern guide, northeastern and midland United States and adjacent Canada. Doubleday and Co. Inc. Garden City, N.Y. 318 pp.

THE BIOLOGY OF CANADIAN WEEDS.
27. AVENA FATUA L.

M. P. SHARMA and W. H. VANDEN BORN

Department of Plant Science, University of Alberta, Edmonton, Alta. T6G 2E3.
Received 27 Jan. 1977, accepted 15 Aug. 1977.

SHARMA, M. P. AND VANDEN BORN, W. H. 1978. The biology of Canadian weeds. 27. *Avena fatua* L. Can. J. Plant Sci. **58**: 141-157.

This contribution on *Avena fatua* L., wild oats, is part of a series which presents biological information on plants that are weedy in Canada. Wild oats rate as by far the most serious annual weed of cultivated fields in the prairie provinces of Canada. The weed occurs in a wide variety of habitats: spring cereal and oilseed crop fields, fallow fields, roadsides, waste places, gardens and other habitats disturbed by man. Seed dormancy and irregular germination throughout the growing season are the most important features contributing to the persistence of wild oats. The weed is susceptible to a number of soil-and foliage-applied herbicides.

Cette monographie sur la folle avoine, *Avena fatua* L., fait partie d'une série de documents sur la biologie des plantes vivant à l'état adventice au Canada. La folle avoine est de loin la mauvaise herbe annuelle la plus sérieuse pour les cultures dans les provinces des prairies canadiennes. On la trouve dans toutes sortes d'habitats: champs de céréales de printemps et d'oléagineux, jachères, talus de routes, terrains vagues, jardins et autres milieux remués par l'homme. La dormance et l'aptitude à germer en tout temps de la saison de végétation sont les principaux caractères expliquant la persistance de cette espèce. On peut toutefois la combattre dans une certaine mesure au moyen de plusieurs herbicides appliqués au sol ou au feuillage.

1. Name

Avena fatua L. — **Wild oats** (Canada Weed Committee 1969), oatgrass, poor oats and wheatgrass (Britton and Brown 1913); **avoine sauvage**, folle avoine (Ferron and Cayouette 1964). Gramineae, grass family, Graminées.

2. Description and Account of Variation

(a) Annual; plants 60–150 cm high, often much tufted, with terete, smooth and erect stems; leaves linear-lanceolate, leaf blades long, flat and broad about 20–30 cm long and 1 cm wide; leaf sheaths and bases of leaf blades usually variable in hairiness — individual plants vary from none to very hairy; ligule about 5 mm long, greyish white, lacerate at the top; spikelets in a loose open panicle, drooping; each spikelet with 2 glumes within which are 2 or 3 florets, glumes longer than the florets;

glumes membranous with convex dorsal side, with several veins, the lower glume 2–2.5 cm long, the upper one somewhat shorter; lemma hairy or glabrous, with several veins, black, brown, gray, yellow or white, with a bent twisted bristle (awn) 3–4 cm long; seeds consisting of 2 flowering scales (lemma and palea) enclosing the caryopsis; all seeds with a slanting, circular, depressed scar (also called sucker mouth) at the base, scar often with a circle of hairs.

Wild oats are hexaploid with a chromosome number $2n = 42$ (Thurston 1957).

(b) Wild oats resemble cultivated oats (*Avena sativa* L.) but there are some features that can be used to distinguish the two species. In the field, even at long range, wild oat plants usually can be readily distinguished from cultivated oats by their greater height and vigor as well as by their whitish straw and chaff at maturity. The panicles are usually loose, large and drooping. The spikelets separate from their pedicels by disarticulation, thus leaving distinct basal scars, or sucker mouths. The callus at the base of the first floret of the spikelet usually is covered with a dense growth of hairs. The florets separate from each other by disarticulation of their respective floret rachilla segments. Each floret usually carries a rather long, twisted and geniculate awn (bristle), whereas in cultivated oats bristles are absent or confined to the lowest floret and then are usually straight. Because of variability in color of lemma, the seeds of wild oats may be yellowish white, gray, brown or black in color, whereas in cultivated oats the seeds are usually yellowish white. Wild oat seeds exhibit a characteristic dormancy (delayed germination), but the seeds of cultivated oats usually can germinate soon after maturity.

Baum (1968) described characters in the micromorphology of the lodicules and epiblasts of *A. sativa* and *A. fatua* that can be used in combination with the traditionally used differences in gross morphology of the spikelets to separate the two species. The lodicule of *A. sativa* is more or less cylindrical at the base. The upper part of the lodicule is open, forms a trough and is attenuate towards the apex. The main feature of the lodicule of *A. sativa* is its side lobe which is obliquely attached to the cylindrical base. The lodicule of *A. fatua* is also three-dimensional as in *A. sativa*, but differs by the absence of a side lobe. Instead, there is a delicate and thin, mostly wavy, short wing or flag-like appendage. The margin of the apex of the epiblast in *A. sativa* is almost entire although usually depressed or with a small notch at the middle. In *A. fatua* the apical margin is irregularly crenate, eroded, or sinuate.

The close relationship between *A. fatua* and *A. sativa* has been emphasized by Malzew (1930) by classifying the latter as subspecies of *A. fatua*. Thus, the botanical studies of cultivated oats contain much information that is applicable to wild oats. The reviews by Rajhathy and Thomas (1974) and Stanton (1961), for example, aid in the understanding of the weed species.

(c) Iman and Allard (1965) found genetic differences in wild oats from different geographic regions and these were related to habitat differences. They used material from seven localities representing three regions of California, an arable area at 15–30 m elevation in the Sacramento valley, a region of infested grazing-lands in the inner Coast Range, and another in the foothills of the Sierra Nevada mountains where wild oats were distributed through a wide range of habitats. Families from the same site, and also single plants progenies, contained many different genotypes, and the genetic flexibility was considered to contribute to the success of *A. fatua* in establishing in a wide range of habitats. Differences in seed dormancy, germination, emergence and growth of wild oat populations collected from natural infestations in various localities have been demonstrated by a number of investigators (Marshall and Jain 1970; Naylor and Jana 1976; Sexsmith 1967). Naylor and Jana (1967) suggest that these differences result in part from genetic adaptation to agronomic practices. Intraspecific variations in response of wild oats to herbicides have been reported by Jacobsohn and Anderson (1972).

(d) Figures 1–3 show morphological features of wild oat plants.

3. Economic Importance

(a) *Detrimental* — Wild oats is the most serious annual grassy weed of cultivated land in the prairie provinces of Canada. The weed is responsible for reductions in crop yields, dockage losses, cleaning costs, lowering of grade and quality, and costly chemical and cultural control measures. Wild oats markedly reduce the yield of wheat (*Triticum aestivum* L.) (Bell and Nalewaja 1968b; Bowden and Friesen 1967), barley (*Hordeum vulgare* L.) (Bell

304

and Nalewaja 1968b; McBeath et al 1970), flax (*Linum usitatissimum* L.) (Bowden and Friesen 1967) and rapeseed (*Brassica napus* L.) (Dew and Keys 1976). Crop losses due to competition may also affect crop quality. Protein content of wheat and barley seed may be decreased (Friesen et al. 1960) or unaffected (Bell and Nalewaja 1968b). Bell and Nalewaja (1968a) noted a reduction in the oil content of flax seed due to wild oat competiton.

Estimates of total annual losses due to wild oats in the prairie provinces vary from $120 million up to $500 million (Friesen 1973).

Wild oats produce allelopathic effects on other plant species (Tinnin and Muller 1972). Water leachates from wild oat straw contained a group of phenolic compounds that were inhibitory to germination and seedling growth of other plant species.

Fig. 1. *Avena fatua* L. plant at the 2-leaf stage.

(b) *Beneficial* — Wild oats are used extensively for hay and as a range grass in the interior and coastal valleys of California, where it is estimated that approximately 16,000 ha are harvested annually for that purpose (Stanton 1961). Wild oat screenings are used as cattle feed. Ground wild oats may be sold under somewhat disguised names, for instance, 'mill oats' in the U.S.A. Wild oat grain has about 90% of the feeding value of cultivated oat (Christensen and Hopper 1938). Samples studied had 15.5% crude fibre, 61.6% total digestible nutrients and 9.6% digestible proteins compared with figures for cultivated oats of 10.3, 69.2 and 9.6, respectively.

The discovery of new genes in *A. fatua* and other wild species exhibiting resistance to cold (Suneson and Marshall 1967) and to several destructive plant pathogens, such as the organisms causing powdery mildew, crown and stem rust, cereal root nematode and barley yellow dwarf virus (Zillinsky and Murphy 1967), has an immediate practical value in the improvement of cultivated oat varieties. Another example of the usefulness of wild oats in a breeding program is the development of dormoats (Burrows 1970) (see Section 9. Hybrids).

(c) *Legislation* — Wild oats are classified as 'noxious weeds' in the Provincial Weed Acts of Alberta, Saskatchewan and Manitoba (Anonymous 1965, 1970, 1972). The Federal Seeds Act and Regulations, administered by Agriculture Canada (1967) and enforced in all provinces and territories, lists wild oats under "Secondary Noxious Weed Seeds."

4. Geographical Distribution

Figure 4 gives the geographical distribution of wild oats in Canada. The weed is most abundant in cultivated fields of the three prairie provinces, Alberta, Saskatchewan and Manitoba (Alex 1966; Wood 1953). It also occurs to a minor extent in northeast British Columbia and southern Ontario. Wild oats rate as by far the most troublesome weed of almost the entire cultivated

Fig. 2. A mature *Avena fatua* plant with inflorescence.

portion of the Northern Plains of the Great Plains Region of North America (Wood 1953). This includes the prairie provinces of Canada, the northern half of South Dakota, the northwest fringe of Minnesota, North Dakota and Montana. The total area infested with wild oats in Canada and the United States is estimated at over 25 million ha (Nalewaja 1970; Wood 1953).

Wild oats are a major weed problem in arable lands, especially in cereals, in several European countries, e.g., United Kingdom, Belgium, Denmark, France, Germany, Netherlands, Spain, Greece and Italy, and in North Africa, the U.S.S.R., Australia and New Zealand (Bowler 1973; Dadd 1957; Malzew 1930; Quail and Carter 1968; Thurston 1954).

5. Habitat

(a) *Climatic requirements* — While occurring over a wide range of soil, climatic and other conditions, wild oats are inclined to be choosy as to environment. They prefer temperate and cool climates and moist soil conditions. This is observed in two ways. First, wild oats are seldom a serious weed in the more arid and hot sections of the Northern Plains, except where moisture becomes available through irrigation. Second, wild oats are usually more abundant on the lower, moister parts of a field, especially on water runs, than they are on the knolls or southern exposures.

(b) *Substratum* — In general, wild oats seem to prefer the heavy clay and clay loam soils and those of parkland areas rather than more arid sections.

(c) *Communities in which species occur* — Wild oats occur in a wide variety of habitats in Canada: spring cereal and oilseed crop fields, fallow fields, roadsides, waste places, gardens and other habitats disturbed by man. The weed is most common in cultivated fields and may form almost solid

Fig. 3.   Left: A spikelet containing seeds (× 5). Right: A seed showing awn and basal scar (× 5).

stands in fields of spring-sown cereals and oilseed crops if left uncontrolled. Species with which it is frequently associated in the cereal and oilseed crops include *Amaranthus retroflexus* L., *Chenopodium album* L., *Equisetum arvense* L., *Fagopyrum tatricum* (L.) Gaertn., *Polygonum convolvulus* L., *Polygonum persicaria* L., *Polygonum scabrum* Moench, *Saponaria vaccaria* L., *Setaria viridis* (L.) Beauv., *Sinapis alba* L. and *Thlaspi arvense* L.

6. History

Wild oats were introduced into North America by early European settlers as impurities in seeds and feed. Published records on wild oats indicate the occurrence of this species in Canada for more than three centuries (Baum 1968). Mason (1853) stated that oats were cultivated in Newfoundland in 1622, according to Coffman (1961), and wild oats occurred as an impurity in the grain. Provancher (1862) stated that *Avena sativa* (cultivated oats) began to be extensively cultivated from the 1840's and that *A. fatua* was already

infesting cultivated fields. Since then, the cultivation of *A sativa* has been extended throughout the range of agricultural lands of Canada and wild oats has spread along with it and the other cereals.

7. Growth and Development

(a) *Morphology* — Wild oats exceed wheat, barley and rye in their ability to emerge from soil layers well below the surface. This is because the first internode or mesocotyl of the wild oats has a great ability to elongate and can push the stem apex and surrounding leaf tissue up through the soil for a considerable distance. This usually allows the first leaf to emerge with the protection of the coleoptile.

The early shedding of wild oat seeds on the ground, usually before or at the time of crop harvest, allows the reinfestation of fields. The strong twisted awn on the lemma of wild oat seeds responds to changes in humidity by bending. The hygroscopic action takes place with considerable force and often may push the shed seed under clods or into cracks in the soil.

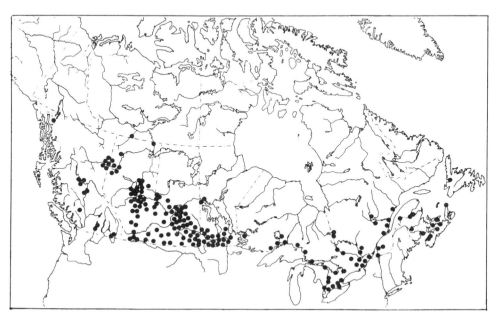

Fig. 4.   Geographical distribution of *Avena fatua* in Canada.

(b) *Perennation* — Wild oats is an annual weed with one generation per year under Canadian conditions. Wild oat plants that started growth in late summer or fall did not survive the winter in the prairie provinces (Aamodt and Platt 1934). The weed can perennate in coastal areas of California where mowing and irrigation allows summer survival.

(c) *Physiological data* — In a growth cabinet study (Sharma et al. 1977a) it was found that low light intensity and short photoperiod severely restricted growth and delayed the heading and maturity of wild oats (Table 1). Plants grew much taller under low light intensity (10.5 klx) but weighed only one-third or less as compared to plants grown under high light intensity (34.0 klx). The average numbers of leaves and tillers per plant were 5.3 and 1.7 under low light intensity and 7.1 and 8.6 under high light intensity, respectively. Root growth also was severely inhibited under low light intensity. Wild oats grew better at day–night temperatures of 20–12 C than at 12–12 C and 28–20 C. However, the initial rate of growth was enhanced and periods to heading and maturity were shortened at the high temperature regime (28–20 C).

Thurston (1959) reported that wild oat seedlings were smaller than those of cultivated cereals of the same age in total dry weight, nitrogen content, leaf area and number of leaves. However, very young wild oat plants had higher net assimilation rates than the cultivated cereals and they soon caught up and passed the crop plants in dry weight, height, etc. Nitrogen deficiency symptoms in wild oats were the same as in crops grown in pots (Thurston 1959).

Transpiration of wild oat plants was markedly reduced after foliar treatment with five post-emergence wild oat herbicides (Sharma et al. 1977c). Suppression of transpiration increased with increasing rates of herbicides.

(d) *Phenology* — The main flush of germination of wild oats is in the spring and early fall, but some germination may occur throughout the growing season (Banting 1962, 1974). Cool, moist conditions promote maximum emergence and thus the crops seeded early are usually the most heavily infested. Seedlings can emerge from depths up to 20 cm, if conditions are right, and produce vigorous plants (Sharma et al. 1976; Thurston 1961).

Shoot and root growth of wild oats is slow initially (up to 2 wk after emergence) but increases rapidly thereafter (Pavlychenko 1937; Sharma et al. 1977a). Tillering occurs mainly during the period 2–4 wk after emergence (Sharma et al. 1977a). Pavlychenko and Harrington (1934) reported that 5 days after emergence, wild oats had a root system 87 cm in length, and 21 days after emergence the length was 24 m. Eighty days after emergence the total length of the root system was 256 m. This root system, at 80 days, was more extensive than that of cereal crops: barley, wheat, spring rye and oats.

Table 1. Effects of light intensity and photoperiod on wild oats

Treatment	DW shoot† (g/pot)	Tillers/plant†	Wk to heading	Wk to maturity
Light intensity				
Low (10.5 klx)	2.7	1.7	9	14
High (34.0 klx)	6.8	8.6	7	10
Photoperiod				
8 h	3.0	3.7	16	22
16 h	7.4	5.6	8	12
24 h	22.4	5.1	6	9

†Data taken 6 wk after emergence. From Sharma et al. (1977a).

The root system of wild oats was less than one-ninth as long (24 m) under competition with Hanchen barley as when competing with Marquis wheat (225 m).

The rapid development, early maturity and ready shattering ability of wild oats are well known. Less widely known is the uneven ripening of seed in the panicle from top to bottom and also in the individual stalk. Wild oat plants produce panicles in succession over a longer period than cultivated oats (Thurston 1959). Flowering may take place for as long as 6 wk in any one crop. Under western Canadian conditions, plants usually start heading (flowering) in early July and shed their seeds by about the middle of August. Seeds at the tip of the main axis of the panicle may ripen and fall to the ground before the seeds at the base are filled.

(e) *Mycorrhiza* — None known.

8. Reproduction

(a) *Floral biology* — Wild oats are normally self-pollinated, so isolated plants set viable seeds (Dadd 1953). Nevertheless, there is a large body of evidence that suggests that natural crossing does, in fact, occur (Aamodt et al. 1934; Imam and Allard 1965). On the basis of observed monogenic characters in naturalized populations of *A. fatua* in California, Imam and Allard (1965) estimated the outcrossing in these populations to range from 1 to 12%. Natural crossing between *A. fatua* and *A. sativa* is extremely low. Derrick (1933) planted *A. sativa* cv. Alaska around a 0.91 m² block of *A. fatua* and reported approximately 0.1% natural crossing.

(b) *Seed production and dispersal* — Wild oats usually have two to three seeds per spikelet. The number of seeds per inflorescence and per plant depends on the growing conditions and may reach as high as 500 seeds per plant (Dadd 1953), but 100–150 seeds per plant is a common occurrence. Chancellor and Peters (1972) reported that wild oats competing in a heavy crop of

spring barley may produce only 1–2 panicles with 20–30 seeds per plant, whereas under less intense competition in field beans it produces up to 140 seeds per plant. Wild oat seeds usually fall to the ground in the immediate vicinity of the parent plants as soon as they ripen. Seeds that do not fall remain as an impurity in the crop seed.

(c) *Viability of seeds and germination* — Freshly shattered mature seeds of wild oats are usually completely dormant (Banting 1974). Seeds lose their dormancy most readily following "afterripening" under warm, dry storage conditions. Banting (1966b) at Regina found that of seeds stored at 18 C or at alternating 18 and 40 C, 49 and 67%, respectively, lost their dormancy during the 1st yr. At these temperatures 1% of the seeds were still dormant after 5 yr. Seeds stored at 40 C probably would have afterripened or lost their dormancy in the shortest period of time, but the supply of seeds was depleted after 1 yr. Cool, moist conditions, on the other hand, delayed the process of afterripening, and at 2 C more than 50% of the seeds remained dormant after 5 yr. Seeds will persist for 3–6 yr in cultivated soil (Banting 1962; Tingey 1961). Seeds in undisturbed soil or under sod survive longer than in soil cultivated annually (Banting 1974). Survival of wild oat seeds under leys on clay soils was investigated by Thurston (1966) in England. She found that during the 1st yr under ley the number of seeds decreased by 41 and 86%, respectively, at two locations. Subsequent decreases were less, and after 5 yr under ley there were still enough of the original seeds left to produce an infestation of a cereal crop. Investigations in Canada (Banting 1966a), U.S.A. (Tingey 1961), England (Thurston 1961) and Australia (Quail and Carter 1968) have shown that deep burial of seeds (below 5 cm) extended the period of persistence and, therefore, should be avoided.

The viability of wild oat seeds is completely destroyed after heating at 105 C for 15 min (Hopkins 1936). Molberg and

Banting (1973) were able to destroy a large number of wild oat seeds in straw windrows by burning immediately after harvest. Seeds that fell into cracks or worked their way into the soil were not included in the test. Wilson and Cussans (1975) reported a 50% reduction in total viable seeds as a result of straw burning.

Investigations of the causes of wild oat seed dormancy and methods of breaking it have received considerable attention. Unripe seeds of wild oats are viable but non-dormant (Thurston 1962b). Conditions during ripening affect the speed of onset of viability and initial development of dormancy, referred to as primary dormancy. Sexsmith (1969) found that both high temperature and low soil moisture decreased dormancy; temperature had a greater effect than soil moisture. Position of seeds on the panicle also affects the dormancy in wild oats. Johnson (1935) observed that there was a progressive increase in the germinability of primary grains in passing from the lower to upper, earlier maturing whorls.

The mechanism of dormancy in wild oats has been studied by a number of workers. Opinions differ on the role of the husk or hull, consisting of lemma and palea, in dormancy of wild oats. Atwood (1914) suggested that delay in germination is brought about by a restriction in the supply of oxygen, probably by the seed coat. Hay (1962) and Thurston (1962b) observed that removing the hulls completely or pricking the caryopses through the enveloping hulls increased the germination of wild oats. In contrast, Black (1959) found that loosening the hull or removing the palea and edges of the lemma did not break dormancy; he concluded that gaseous exchange to the caryopsis was not the cause of dormancy of seeds enclosed in wet hulls.

Several workers have extracted germination inhibitors from intact or ground hulls of wild oat seeds (Black 1959; Kommedahl et al. 1958). Hay (1962) extracted the same kind and amount of inhibitor from dormant and non-dormant seeds, so the inhibitor may or may not be a cause of dormancy. Work by Simpson (1965) and Simpson and Naylor (1962) has shown that primary dormancy in wild oats involves a restriction in (a) sugar production in the endosperm of the seed (due to a block in the release or synthesis of the enzyme maltase) and (b) sugar utilization in the embryo axis or the scutellum (the adjacent tissue) or both. These restrictions can be overcome in the laboratory by treatment with gibberellic acid. In further work, Simpson (1966) suggested that loss of dormancy in wild oats may be regulated by the loss of a naturally occurring growth retardant that prevents the synthesis of a gibberellin in the embryo. These observations suggest that dormancy in wild oats may be controlled by a gibberellin-inhibitor antagonism. The onset of seed dormancy can be prevented by treating the developing seeds with gibberellic acid (Black and Naylor 1959).

Non-dormant wild oat seeds may undergo a ''secondary'' dormancy if the conditions for their germination are not favorable. Hay and Cumming (1959) were able to induce such dormancy when seeds were immersed in water for 4 days. Kommedahl et al. (1958) observed a similar situation with alternate wetting and drying.

A number of chemicals have been shown to break, at least partially, the wild oat seed dormancy. These include plant growth regulators, gibberellic acid and cytokinins (Black and Naylor 1959; Corns 1960; Hay and Cumming 1959; Sharma et al. 1976), nitrate salts, especially potassium nitrate (Hay and Cumming 1959), thiourea (Sharma et al. 1976) and gases such as ethylene at high pressure (Hoffman 1961). Under field conditions, fall or early spring application of nitrogen fertilizers has been shown to stimulate the germination of wild oats (Sexsmith and Pitman 1963; Sharma et al. 1977b).

Some confusion exists regarding the optimum temperature for wild oat germination. Mather (1946) reported that wild oats germinate best at temperatures between 0 and 10 C. Friesen and Shebeski (1961) later reported the optimum temperature for wild oat germination to be between 15 and 21 C. These workers observed that emergence was slow at 15 C and no germination occurred at 4.4 C. Banting (1974) and Sharma et al. (1976) found that seeds germinated well at temperatures between 15 and 26.5 C. Germination was slow at lower temperatures. Several workers have reported that light inhibits the germination of wild oats. White, blue and far-red light are most inhibitory (Hsiao and Simpson 1971). Shallow tillage in the fall to lightly cover seeds on the soil surface has been shown to stimulate the germination of wild oats (Bibbey 1935; Sharma et al. 1977b).

(d) *Vegetative reproduction* — There is no vegetative reproduction as such in wild oats, although there is some evidence (Kirk and Pavlychenko 1932) that cut wild oat stems under certain conditions can propagate vegetatively.

9. Hybrids

A. Interspecific hybrids with species of identical chromosome numbers. B. Interspecific hybrids with species of different chromosome numbers. Hybrids in the first category involve those with other hexaploid species, *A. sativa, A. byzantina* and *A. sterilis*. Natural and artificial hybrids between *A. fatua* and *A. sativa* have been reported by numerous investigators, for example, Aamodt et al. 1934, Baum 1968, 1969a and Derrick 1933. Hybridity was assumed because many intermediate forms between *A fatua* and *A. sativa* had been recorded and described. Artificial crosses have been made to check the hypothesis that "fatuoids" originate from natural crossing between *A. fatua* and *A. sativa*.

Sterile hybrids between *A. fatua* and other *Avena* species with different chromosome numbers have been reported. These include hybrids of *A. fatua* × *A. strigosa*, *A. fatua* × *A. barbata*, *A. fatua* × *A. magna* and *A. fatua* × *A. murphyi* (Rajhathy and Thomas 1974).

The hybrids between *A. fatua* and *A. sativa* generally can be recognized on the basis of spikelet and floret characters such as spikelet separation, floret disjunction, rachilla length, awns, pubescence, lemma color, hullessness, multiflorous spikelet, and size and shape of kernel. The heavier protruding awns make them readily distinguishable at maturity. There may also be color differences. In the threshed grain the awn, scar (sucker mouth) and rachilla are similar to those of wild oats but the general size and the surface of the grain are similar to those of cultivated oats. The hairs on the scar are very much shorter than those of the wild oats. There is, however, some overlap in external morphology of spikelets and florets between wild oats, cultivated oats, the fatuoids, and the hybrids between these. Baum (1969a,b) used the micromorphological features of the lodicules as markers in recognizing the *Avena* hybrids and fatuoids. It was demonstrated in his studies that the *sativa*-type lodicule is diagnostic of *A. sativa* and fatuoids and that the *fatua*-type lodicule is indicative of *A. fatua* or of F_1 hybrids between these two taxa.

Natural hybrids between wild oats and cultivated oats, fatuoids and other off-types deteriorate the purity of oat seeds. Recently a new class of oats (dormoats) has been developed at Ottawa by Burrows (1970) from crosses between *A. fatua* and *A. sativa*. They possess the dormancy of wild oats coupled with the kernel characteristics of the cultivated oats and have the potential to be economically exploited as a winter crop (Burrows 1970).

10. Population Dynamics

Wild oats require 2–3 mo to produce mature plants from seed and they never overwinter under Canadian conditions. The weed is most common in spring-planted annual crops, particularly cereals, and is virtually absent from land that has not been disturbed recently. When pastures, hayfields, roadsides, etc. are cultivated, wild oat plants often appear in abundance because of the germination of seeds present in the soil.

Marshall and Jain (1967) reported census data on the relative abundance of *A. fatua* over several sites in the central California grasslands. The total density of seeds in the soil during early summer was found to vary from 28 to 92/m², of which 20-80% failed to produce a seedling in the following generation. Of those which germinated, varying proportions of seedlings (5-80%) failed to survive to maturity. As a result, the density of adult *Avena* plants in these populations was seldom greater than 20 plants/m², and usually less than 15 plants/m². Marshall and Jain (1970) further reported that estimates of seed loss due to animal predation in *Avena fatua* over a number of sites in the California annual-type grasslands varied from 0 to 65% of the total seed load. Wild oats showed complex patterns of variation in germination both between and within populations. Both of these factors played a significant role in regulation of wild oat populations.

Imam and Allard (1965), in population studies on wild oats from three regions of central California, observed that three sources of genetic variability could be distinguished and measured for the quantitative characters that included percentage emergence, days to flowering, number of tillers per plant, height and seed number per panicle. The sources of variability were: differences between regions, differences between sites within regions, and plant-to-plant differences within sites. The measurements indicated that wild oats are differentiated geographically, and the differentiations observed were those one would expect to permit each population to meet the requirements imposed by its habitat. For example, earliness in flowering in populations from a vacant city lot site may be related to the practice of controlling weeds by late spring cultivation, which would presumably favor early maturity.

Thurston (1962a) in England studied the effects of winter wheat, winter rye, winter barley, spring barley and fallow cultivated as for a winter cereal on germination and growth of wild oats on a naturally-infested field. Data were collected on plant number, dry weight and seed production. Wild oats were controlled by a dense crop of autumn-sown cereal. Type of crop was unimportant provided it grew well on the site; its effectiveness depended on its density when the wild oats germinated in spring. Even in a light crop of barley, wild oats grew much less vigorously than on the fallow plots. Chancellor and Peters (1972) reported that the earliest germinating wild oat plants in spring barley had a greater chance of survival, tended to have more tillers and produced a greater number of panicles than the later germinating ones. Bate (1970) studied the effect of barley population on the growth of wild oats and found that barley competition affected some attributes of wild oat growth more than others. Plant numbers and height were altered little but tiller, panicle and seed numbers were altered significantly. More tillering occurred at the low barley population than at the high one. Wilson and Cussans (1975) in England studied population changes on plots subjected to a range of cultivation treatments with or without straw burning. Where seed was allowed to shed, the average increase factor was 3.4 on plots where straw was removed, and 2.5 on burnt plots. In each case, early stubble cultivation greatly increased the rate of population increase so that the overall range for the increase factors was from 1.6 to 4.4.

The competitive success of wild oats depends greatly on the plants with which they are competing. Pavlychenko and Harrington (1934) studied the competing abilities of certain weeds, including wild oats, and crops. Based on the development of the root system, development of assimilation surface and stomatal number, the authors concluded that wild oats were the most vigorous competitors among weeds studied. Recently, Dew (1972) and Dew and Keys (1976) reported the relative competitive ability of various crops (Table 2) as expressed by yield losses due to wild

313

oat competition. Flax is a very poor competitor, while barley is a strong competitor. Rapeseed falls somewhere between barley and wheat. A number of factors such as the relative date of emergence of wild oats and crop, relative rate of growth of crop and the density of wild oats and crop influence the competition. If the weed emerges before the crop, yield loss is greater than if the weed emerges later. Serious competition starts before the 2- to 3-leaf stage of wild oats (Chancellor and Peters 1976; Sharma and Hunter 1975).

11. Response to Herbicides and Other Chemicals

Wild oats are susceptible to a number of soil- and foliage-applied herbicides and several of these are used for their selective control in cereal and oilseed crops. Emerging seedlings of wild oats are killed by soil-applied diallate (S-(2,3-dichloroallyl) diisopropylthiocarbamate) and triallate (S-(2,3,3-trichloroallyl) diisopropylthiocarbamate) at rates of 1.12–1.40 kg/ha (Molberg et al. 1964; Parker 1963). Differential placement of these heribicides in relation to the seed of wild oats and crop has been used to selectively control this weed. The presence of a mesocotyl in wild oats, immediately below the coleoptile, that can elongate to move the coleoptilar node up into the herbicide-treated soil layer, is the basis for selective action of these her-

bicides. Banting (1970) found that the shoot tissue of wild oats was damaged more readily than the root tissue by diallate and triallate. Herbicides caused mitotic abnormalities that included short, thick chromosomes, dumbbell-shaped nuclei, clumps of chromosome material and doubling of the chromosome number, bridges and micronuclei.

Friesen and Bowren (1973) reported that wild oats are susceptible to soil-applied trifuluralin (α,α,α-trifluoro-2,6-dinitro-N,N-dipropyl-p-toluidine). It can be used to control wild oats in rapeseed, wheat and barley at rates of 0.84–1.12 kg/ha.

Wild oats are susceptible to several herbicides applied to the foliage in cereal and oilseed crops. They include barban (4-chloro-2-butynyl-m chlorocarbanilate) (Friesen 1961), asulam (methyl sulfanilyl-carbamate) (Sharma et al. 1977b), dichlorfop methyl (methyl 2-[4-dichloro-phenoxy) phenoxy] propionate) (Friesen et al. 1976, difenzoquat (1,2-dimethyl-3,5-diphenyl-1 H pyrazolium) (Friesen and Litwin 1975), benzoylprop ethyl [ethyl ($\pm$)2-N-benzoyl-3,4-dichloroanilino) propionate] and its analogue flamprop methyl (methyl N-benzoyl-N-(3-chloro-4-fluoro-phenyl)-2-aminopropionate) (Kirkland and Ashford 1976). Table 3 gives the recommended rates, the leaf stages of wild oats and the crops in which they are used, for various post-emergence herbicides. Mix-

Table 2. Effect of wild oat populations on yield of various crops

Wild oat plants/m²	Percentage loss due to wild oats			
	Wheat	Barley	Rapeseed	Flax
0	0	0	0	0
5	8	5	7	13
10	11	7	9	19
20	15	10	13	27
30	19	13	16	33
50	24	16	21	42
70	28	19	25	50
100	34	23	30	60
150	41	28	37	74

Adapted from Dew (1972) and Dew and Keys (1976).

tures of some post-emergence herbicides such as barban plus benzoylprop ethyl or flamprop methyl have been shown to have a synergistic effect on wild oats (O'Sullivan and Vanden Born 1975).

12. Response to Other Human Manipulations

Kirk and Pavlychenko (1932) found that small sections of wild oat seedlings, about 2.5 cm in length and containing the coleoptile node, became rooted under favorable conditions and produced fully developed plants. With young seedlings at the time of emergence, regrowth occurred mostly from a small area located between ground level and about 2.5 cm below the surface. Under practical conditions, however, wild oats do not reproduce from vegetative parts and the plants can be killed easily by cultivating the soil after seeds have germinated. Various cultural practices such as delayed seeding, summer-fallowing, fall and spring tillage, and post-seeding cultivation are based on this principle. In a study carried out at different locations in the prairie provinces (Banting 1974), delayed seeding of wheat and barley caused a 12–95% reduction in wild oat populations at harvest. Fall-seeded crops such as fall rye and winter wheat can reduce wild oat infestations due to winter-killing of plants that grow after crop seeding and the smothering effect of crops that have an early start in the spring. The use of forage crops such as grasses and legumes may provide control of wild oats if they are used in a crop rotation (Banting 1974).

The effect of fertilizers containing nitrogen and/or phosphorus on wild oat infestations has been studied by a number of investigators, for example, Bell and Nalewaja 1968b, Bowden and Friesen 1967, McBeath et al. 1975. Although added fertilizers enhance the growth of both wild oats and crop they effectively reduce crop yield losses, especially in crops that are strong competitors. Sexsmith and Russell (1963) found that nitrogen fertilizer increased the number of seed-bearing stems, plant height, straw weight, and seed yield of wild oats in spring wheat. Phosphorus fertilizer, on the other hand, had no apparent effect on any aspect of wild oats but increased the wheat yield as did the nitrogen fertilizer. McBeath et al. (1975) showed that differential placement of phosphorus fertilizer had a pronounced effect on the competitive ability of wild oats in barley. When phosphorus was available to barley, the enchanced growth of barley helped to smother the wild oats and to reduce wild oat seed production. On the other hand, when phosphorus was available to wild oats, the weed offered strong competition to barley and reduced the crop yield.

13. Response to Parasites

Wild oats are generally susceptible to the same range of parasites as cultivated oats. The occurrence on wild oats of a parasite of

Table 3.   Post-emergence herbicides for wild oat control in various crops

Herbicide	kg/ha	Leaf stage of wild oats	Crops
Barban	0.28–0.42	1½–2	Wheat, barley Flax, rapeseed
Asulam	1.12	3	Flax
Dichlorfop methyl	0.70	2–5	Wheat, rapeseed, Flax
Difenzoquat	0.84	3–5	Barley
Benzoylprop ethyl	1.40	3–5	Wheat, rapeseed
Flamprop methyl	0.56	3–5	Wheat

315

cultivated oats does not necessarily indicate that the weed is an important host in the biology of that parasite.

(a) INSECTS. The weed is a host of *Oscinella frit* Linn. and *Toxoptera graminum* (Rond.) (Cunliffe 1929).

(b) NEMATODES. Wild oats are host to the eel worms *Heterodera major* Schmit (Thomas et al. 1946) and *Ditylenchus dipsaci* Kuehn (Steiner and Buhrer 1932).

(c) FUNGI. The weed is susceptible to *Puccinia graminis* Pers., *Erisyphe graminis* DC., *Ustilago avenae* Pers. Rosta and *Puccinia coronata* Corda (Dadd 1957).

(d) VIRUS. Natural infection of wild oats with barley stripe mosaic virus (BSMV) was detected in Manitoba (Chiko 1975).

ACKNOWLEDGMENT

The financial support from the Alberta Hail and Crop Insurance Corporation and the Alberta Agricultural Research Trust is gratefully acknowledged. The assistance of weed control specialists of various provincial agriculture departments in plotting the geographical distribution of wild oats is much appreciated. R. J. Schraa assisted in the preparation of photographs.

AAMODT, O. S. and PLATT, A. W. 1934. Resistance of wild oats and some common cereal varieties to freezing temperatures. Sci. Agric. 14: 645–650.

AAMODT, O. S., JOHNSON, L. P. V. and MANSON, J. M. 1934. Natural and artificial hybridization of *Avena sativa* with *A. fatua* and its relation to the fatuoids. Can. J. Bot. 11: 701–727.

AGRICULTURE CANADA. 1967. Seeds Act and Regulations. Queen's Printer, Ottawa, Ont. 50 pp.

ALEX, J. F. 1966. Survey of weeds of cultivated land in the prairie provinces. Research Branch, Agriculture Canada, Regina, Sask. 68 pp.

ANONYMOUS. 1965. An Act Respecting Noxious Weeds. Queen's Printer, Regina, Sask. pp. 3937–3953.

ANONYMOUS. 1970. The Noxious Weed Act. Queen's Printer, Winnipeg, Man. pp. 1–20.

ANONYMOUS. 1972. The Weed Control Act. Queen's Printer, Edmonton, Alta. 13 pp.

ATWOOD, W. M. 1914. A physiological study of the germination of *Avena fatua*. Bot Gaz. 57: 386–414.

BANTING, J. D. 1962. The dormancy behavior of *Avena fatua* L. in cultivated soil. Can. J. Plant Sci. 42: 22–39.

BANTING, J. D. 1966a. Studies on the persistence of *Avena fatua*. Can. J. Plant Sci. 46: 129–140.

BANTING, J. D. 1966b. Factors affecting the persistence of *Avena fatua*. Can. J. Plant Sci. 46: 469–478.

BANTING, J. D. 1970. Effect of diallate and triallate on wild oat and wheat cells. Weed Sci. 18: 80–84.

BANTING, J. D. 1974. Growth habit and control of wild oats. Agric. Can. Publ. 1531. 34 pp.

BATE, P. G. 1970. The effect of barley population and row width on the growth of *Avena fatua*, wild oat. Proc. 10th Br. Weed Contr. Conf. pp. 826–830.

BAUM, B. R. 1968. On some relationships between *Avena sativa* and *A. fatua* (Gramineae) as studied from Canadian material. Can. J. Bot. 46: 1013–1024.

BAUM, B. R. 1969a. The role of the lodicule and epiblast in determining natural hybrids of *Avena sativa* × *fatua* in cultivated oats. Can. J. Bot. 47: 85–91.

BAUM, B. R. 1969b. The use of lodicule type in assessing the origin of *Avena fatuoids*. Can. J. Bot. 47: 931–944.

BELL, A. R. and NALEWAJA, J. D. 1968a. Competitive effects of wild oat in flax. Weed Sci. 16: 501–504.

BELL, A. R. and NALEWAJA, J. D. 1968b. Competition of wild oat in wheat and barley. Weed Sci. 16: 505–509.

BIBBEY, R. O. 1935. The influence of environment upon the germination of weed seeds. Sci. Agric. 16: 141–150.

BLACK, M. 1959. Dormancy studies in seed of *Avena fatua*. 1. The possible role of germination inhibitors. Can. J. Bot. 37: 399–402.

BLACK, M. and NAYLOR, J. M. 1959. Prevention of the onset of seed dormancy by gibberellic acid. Nature 184: 468–469.

BOWDEN, B. A. and FRIESEN, G. 1967. Competition of wild oats (*Avena fatua* L.) in wheat and flax. Weed Res. 7: 349–359.

BOWLER, D. J. 1973. Economic benefits from controlling wild oat. Span 16(2): 79–81.

BRITTON, N. L. and BROWN, A. 1913. An

illustrated flora of the Northern United States, Canada and the British possessions. Vol. I. Charles Scribner's Sons, N.Y. 680 pp.

BURROWS, V. D. 1970. Yield and disease-escape potential of fall-sown oats possessing seed dormancy. Can. J. Plant Sci. **50**: 371–377.

CANADA WEED COMMITTEE. 1969. Common and botanical names of weeds in Canada. Can. Dep. Agric. Publ. 1397. Ottawa, Ont.

CHANCELLOR, R. J. and PETERS, N. C. B. 1972. Germination periodicity, plant survival and seed production in populations of *Avena fatua* L. growing in spring barley. Proc. 10th Br. Weed Control Conf. pp. 218–225.

CHANCELLOR, R. J. and PETERS, N. C. B. 1976. Competition between wild oats and crops. Pages 99-112 in D. P. Jones, ed. Wild oats in world agriculture. Agric. Res. Counc., London.

CHIKO, A. W. 1975. Natural occurrence of barley stripe mosaic virus in wild oats (*Avena fatua*). Can. J. Bot. **53**: 417–420.

CHRISTENSEN, F. W. and HOPPER, T. H. 1938. Digestible nutrients and metabolizable energy in certain silages, hays and mixed rations. J. Agric. Res. **57**: 477–491.

COFFMAN, F. A. 1961. Origin and history. Pages 15-39 in F. A. Coffman, ed. Oats and oat improvement. Amer. Soc. Agron., Madison, Wis.

CORNS, W. G. 1960. Effects of gibberellin treatments on germination of various species of weed seeds. Can. J. Plant Sci. **40**: 47–51.

CUNLIFFE, N. 1929. Studies on *Oscinella frit* Linn. Ann. Appl. Biol. **16**: 135.

DADD, C. V. 1953. Wild oats. Natl. Agric. Advis. Serv. Q. Rev. **21**: 1–7.

DADD, C. V. 1957. Wild oats. Field Crop Abstr. **10**: 1–10.

DERRICK, R. A. 1933. Natural crossing with wild oats, *Avena fatua*. Sci. Agric. **13**: 459.

DEW, D. A. 1972. An index of competition for estimating crop loss due to weeds. Can. J. Plant Sci. **52**: 921–927.

DEW, D. A. and KEYS, C. H. 1976. An index of competition for estimating loss of rape due to wild oats. Can. J. Plant Sci. **56**: 1,005–1,006.

FERRON, M. and CAYOUETTE, R. 1964. Noms des mauvaises herbes du Québec. Min. Agric. Colonisation, Québec, Qué. 68 pp.

FRIESEN, G. and SHEBESKI, L. H. 1961. The influence of temperature on the germination of wild oat seeds. Weeds **9**: 634–638.

FRIESEN, G., SHEBESKI, L. H. and ROBINSON, A. D. 1960. Economic losses caused by weed competition in Manitoba grain fields. II. Effect of competition on the protein content of cereal crops. Can. J. Plant Sci. **40**: 652–658.

FRIESEN, H. A. 1961. Some factors affecting the control of wild oats with barban. Weeds **9**: 185–194.

FRIESEN, H. A. 1973. Identifying wild oats yield losses and assessing cultural control methods. Pages 20-25 in Let's clean up wild oats. Agric. Can. and U.G.G. Ltd., Saskatoon, Sask.

FRIESEN, H. A. and BOWREN, K. E. 1973. Factors affecting the control of wild oats in rapeseed with trifluralin. Can. J. Plant Sci. **53**: 199–205.

FRIESEN, H. A. and LITWIN, O. B. 1975. Selective control of wild oats in barley with AC 84777. Can. J. Plant Sci. **55**: 927–934.

FRIESEN, H. A., O'SULLIVAN, P. A. and VANDEN BORN, W. H. 1976. HOE 23408, a new selective herbicide for wild oat and green foxtail in wheat and barley. Can. J. Plant Sci. **56**: 567–578.

HAY, J. R. 1962. Experiments on the mechanism of induced dormancy in wild oats (*Avena fatua* L.). Can. J. Bot. **40**: 191–202.

HAY, J. R. and CUMMING, B. G. 1959. A method for inducing dormancy in wild oats (*Avena fatua* L.). Weeds **7**: 34–40.

HOFFMAN, O. L. 1961. Breaking wild oat dormancy with gases at high pressure. Weeds **9**: 493.

HOPKINS, C. Y. 1936. Thermal death point of certain weed seeds. Can. J. Res. C-D **14**: 178–183.

HSIAO, A. I. and SIMPSON, G. M. 1971. Dormancy studies in seed of *Avena fatua*. 7. The effects of light and variation in water regime on germination. Can. J. Bot. **49**: 1347–1357.

IMAM, A. G. and ALLARD, R. W. 1965. Population studies in predominantly self-pollinated species. VI. Genetic variability between and within natural populations of wild oats from differing habitats in California. Genetics **51**: 49–62.

JACOBSOHN, R. and ANDERSON, R. N. 1972. Intraspecific differential response of wild oat and barley to barban. Weed Sci. **20**: 74–80.

JOHNSON, L. P. V. 1935. General preliminary studies on the physiology of delayed germination in *Avena fatua*. Can. J. Res. C. **13**: 283–300.

KIRK, L. E. and PAVLYCHENKO, T. K. 1932. Vegetative propagation of wild oats,

Avena fatua, and other economically important species of *Avenae* and *Hordeae*. Can. J. Res. **7**: 204–220.

KIRKLAND, K. J. and ASHFORD, R. 1976. Benzoylprop ethyl and its analogue for the control of wild oat in wheat. Weed Sci. **24**: 316–318.

KOMMEDAHL, T., DEVAY, J. E. and CHRISTENSEN, C. M. 1958. Factors affecting dormancy and seedling development in wild oats. Weeds **6**: 12–13.

MALZEW, A. I. 1930. Wild and cultivated oats (Sectio Euavena Griseb). Bull. Appl. Bot. Gener. Plant Breed. Suppl. 38. Leningrad.

MARSHALL, D. R. and JAIN, S. K. 1967. Cohabitation and relative abundance of two species of wild oats. Ecology **48**: 656–659.

MARSHALL, D. R. and JAIN, S. K. 1970. Seed predation and dormancy in the population dynamics of *Avena fatua* and *Avena barbata*. Ecology **51**: 886–891.

MASON, C. 1853. Report of the Commissioner of Patents for the year 1853. Agric. Rep. Oats, 158–159.

MATHER, H. J. 1946. The control of wild oats in Alberta. Alta. Dep. Agric. Circ. No. 71.

McBEATH, D. K., DEW, D. A. and FRIESEN, H. A. 1970. Competition between barley and wild oats as affected by nitrogen, barban and time of seeding. Can. J. Plant Sci. **50**: 541–550.

McBEATH, D. K., SHARMA, M. P. and VANDEN BORN, W. H. 1975. Effect of P fertilizer placement on yield of barley and wild oat seed. Res. Rep. Can. Weed Comm. (West. Sect.). pp. 631-632.

MOLBERG, E. S. and BANTING, J. D. 1973. Effect of burning wheat stubble on the viability of wild oat seeds. Res. Rep. Can. Weed Comm. (West. Sect.) pp. 352–353.

MOLBERG, E. S., FRIESEN, H. A., McCURDY, E. V. and DRYDEN, R. D. 1964. Placement of diallate and triallate for control of wild oats in wheat. Can. J. Plant Sci. **44**: 351–358.

NALEWAJA, J. D. 1970. Wild oat: A persistent and competitive weed. Weeds Today 1(2): 10–13.

NAYLOR, J. M. and JANA, S. 1976. Genetic adaptation for seed dormancy in *Avena fatua*. Can. J. Bot. **54**: 306–312.

O'SULLIVAN, P. A. and VANDEN BORN, W. H. 1975. Wild oat herbicide combinations. Res. Rep., Dep. Plant Sci., University of Alberta. 97 pp.

PARKER, C. 1963. Factors affecting the selectivity of 2,3-dichloroallyl diisopropylthio-carbamate (diallate) against *Avena* spp. in wheat and barley. Weed Res. **3**: 259–276.

PAVLYCHENKO, T. K. 1937. Quantitative study of the entire root systems of weed and crop plants under field conditions. Ecology **18**: 62–79.

PAVLYCHENKO, T. K. and HARRINGTON, J. B. 1934. Competitive efficiency of weeds and cereal crops. Can. J. Res. **10**: 77–94.

PROVANCHER, L. 1862. Flore canadienne ou description de toutes les plantes des forêts, champs, jardins et eaux du Canada. Vol. 2., Québec. pp. 689-691.

QUAIL, P. H. and CARTER, O. G. 1968. Survival and seasonal germination of seeds of *Avena fatua* and *A. ludoviciana*. Aust. J. Agric. Res. **19**: 721–729.

RAJHATHY, T. and THOMAS, H. 1974. Cytogenetics of oats (*Avena* L.). The Genetics Society of Canada, Ottawa, Ont. 90 pp.

SEXSMITH, J. J. 1967. Varietal differences in seed dormancy of wild oats. Weeds **15**: 252–255.

SEXSMITH, J. J. 1969. Dormancy of wild oat seed produced under various temperature and moisture conditions. Weed Sci. **17**: 405–407.

SEXSMITH, J. J. and PITMAN, U. J. 1963. Effect of nitrogen fertilizers on germination and stand of wild oats. Weeds **11**: 99–101.

SEXSMITH, J. J. and RUSSELL, G. C. 1963. Effect of nitrogen and phosphorus fertilization on wild oats in spring wheat grown on stubble. Can. J. Plant Sci. **43**: 64–69.

SHARMA, H. C. and HUNTER, J. H. 1975. Effect of time of removal of wild oats on competition in wheat. Res. Rep. Can. Weed Comm. (West. Sect.) 13. pp.

SHARMA, M. P., McBEATH, D. K. and VANDEN BORN, W. H. 1976. Studies on the biology of wild oats. I. Dormancy, germination and emergence. Can J. Plant Sci. **56**: 611–618.

SHARMA, M. P., McBEATH, D. K. and VANDEN BORN, W. H. 1977a. Studies on the biology of wild oats. II. Growth. Can. J. Plant Sci. **57**: 811–817.

SHARMA, M. P., McBEATH, D. K. and VANDEN BORN, W. H. 1977b. Wild oats: Herbicide–fertilizer interactions. Res. Rep., Dep. Plant Sci., Univ. of Alberta, Edmonton, Alta. and Agric. Can. Res. Sta., Lacombe, Alta. 80 pp.

SHARMA, M. P., VANDEN BORN, W. H. and McBEATH, D. K. 1977c. The effect of postemergence wild oat herbicides on the transpiration of wild oats. Can. J. Plant Sci. **57**: 127-132.

SIMPSON, G. M. 1965. Dormancy studies in seed of *Avena fatua*. 4. The role of gibberellin in embryo dormancy. Can. J. Bot. **43**: 793-816.

SIMPSON, G. M. 1966. The suppression by (2-chlorethyl) trimethylammoniumchloride of synthesis of gibberellin-like substance by embryos of *Avena fatua*. Can. J. Bot. **44**: 115-116.

SIMPSON, G. M. and NAYLOR, J. M. 1962. Dormancy studies in seed of *Avena fatua*. 3. A relationship between maltase, amylases, and gibberellin. Can. J. Bot. **40**: 1659-1673.

STANTON, T. R. 1961. Classification of *Avena*. Pages 75-95 *in* F. A. Coffman, ed. Oats and oat improvement. Amer. Soc. Agron., Madison, Wis.

STEINER, G. and BUHRER, E. M. 1932. A list of plants attacked by *Ditylenchus dipsaci*. Plant Dis. Rep. **16**(8): 76-85.

SUNESON, C. A. and MARSHALL, H. G. 1967. Cold resistance in wild oats. Crop Sci. **7**: 667-668.

THOMAS, I., BROWN, K. B. and WILLIS, R. J. 1946. The cereal root eel worm (*Heterodera major*) in Wales. Ann. Appl. Biol. **33**: 63-65.

THURSTON, J. M. 1954. A survey of wild oats (*Avena fatua* and *A. ludoviciana*) in England and Wales in 1951. Ann. Appl. Biol. **41**: 619-636.

THURSTON, J. M. 1957. Morphological and physiological variation in wild oats (*Avena fatua* L. and *A. ludoviciana* Dur.) and in hybrids between wild and cultivated oats. J. Agric. Sci. **49**: 259-274.

THURSTON, J. M. 1959. A comparative study of the growth of wild oats (*Avena fatua* L. and *A. ludoviciana* Dur.) and of cultivated cereals with varied nitrogen supply. Ann. Appl. Biol. **47**: 716-739.

THURSTON, J. M. 1961. The effect of depth of burying and frequency of cultivation on survival and germination of seeds of wild oats (*Avena fatua* L. and *Avena ludoviciana* Dur.). Weed Res. **1**: 19-31.

THURSTON, J. M. 1962a. The effect of competition from cereal crops on the germination and growth of *Avena fatua* L. in a naturally-infested field. Weed Res. **2**: 192-207.

THURSTON, J. M. 1962b. Biology and control of wild oats. Rothamstead Exp. Sta. Rep. pp. 236-253.

THURSTON, J. M. 1966. Survival of seeds of wild oats (*Avena fatua* L. and *Avena ludoviciana* Dur.) and charlock (*Sinapsis arvensis* L.) in soil under leys. Weed Res. **6**: 67-80.

TINGEY, D. C. 1961. Longevity of seeds of wild oats, winter rye, and wheat in cultivated soil. Weeds **9**: 607-611.

TINNIN, R. O. and MULLER, C. H. 1972. The allelopathic influence of *Avena fatua*: The allelopathic mechanism. Bull. Torrey Bot. Club **99**: 287-292.

WILSON, B. J. and CUSSANS, G. W. 1975. A study of the population dynamics of *Avena fatua* L. as influenced by straw burning, seed shedding and cultivations. Weed Res. **15**: 249-258.

WOOD, H. E. 1953. The occurrence and the problem of wild oats in the great plains region of North America. Weeds **2**: 292-294.

ZILLINSKY, F. J. and MURPHY, H. C. 1967. Wild oat species as sources of disease resistance for the improvement of cultivated oats. Plant Dis. Rep. **51**: 391-395.

THE BIOLOGY OF CANADIAN WEEDS. 28.
Verbascum Thapsus L. and *V. Blattaria* L.

KATHERINE L. GROSS[1] and PATRICIA A. WERNER[1,2]

[1]*W. K. Kellogg Biological Station and Department of Zoology, and* [2]*Department of Botany and Plant Pathology, Michigan State University, Hickory Corners, Michigan 49060. Contribution no. 336, received 21 July 1977, accepted 14 Nov. 1977.*

GROSS, KATHERINE L. AND WERNER, PATRICIA A. 1978. The biology of Canadian weeds. 28. *Verbascum thapsus* L. and *V. blattaria* L. Can. J. Plant Sci. **58**: 401–413.

Verbascum thapsus L., common mullein, and *V. blattaria* L., moth mullein, are introduced weeds of pasture, abandoned fields, and roadsides occurring in widely-spaced, but dense patches in Southern Ontario, Quebec, the Maritime Provinces, British Columbia and throughout the U.S.A. Original research and information from other studies are incorporated into a summary of the biology of these two fugitive plant species.

Verbascum thapsus L., la molène vulgaire, et *M. blattaria* L., molène blattaire, sont deux mauvaises herbes importées qu'on trouve dans les pâturages, les champs abandonnés et les talus de route, en plaques isolées mais néanmoins denses, dans le sud de l'Ontario, le Québec, les provinces Maritimes, la Colombie-Britannique et un peu partout à travers les Etats-Unis. Le tableau biologique de ces deux espèces incorpore les recherches originales des auteurs aux renseignements tirés d'autres travaux.

1. Name

Eight of the 250 European species of *Verbascum* have been introduced into North America. By far the most prevalent are the two weedy species described below.

I. *Verbascum thapsus* L. — **common mullein** (Canada Weed Committee 1975), high taper, cow's lungwort, flannel plant, mullein dock, Aaron's rod, Adam's flannel, torches (among 40 common English names) (Millspaugh 1974; Britton and Brown 1913); **grande molène**, bouillon-blanc, tabac du diable, molène médicinale (Ferron et Cayouette 1970).

II. *Verbascum blattaria* L. — **moth mullein** (Canada Weed Committee 1975), **molène blattaire** (Marie-Victorin 1964). Scrophulariaceae, figwort family, Scrophulariacées.

2. Description and Account of Variation

(a) I. *Verbascum thapsus* is a biennial or, rarely, annual; producing a low vegetative

rosette up to 60 cm in diameter which overwinters and is followed in a succeeding growing season by a stout flowering stem 0.3–2.0 m tall; deep tap root; flower stem longitudinally ridged by the bases of decurrent leaves, densely woolly with branched hairs; leaves alternate; lower leaves oblong or oblanceolate, 10–30 cm long, decurrent on the internode below; inflorescence a spike-like raceme 20–50 cm × 3 cm, very dense, rarely with axillary racemes from the upper leaves; flowers sessile, slightly irregular, corolla rotate, yellow or, rarely, white; petals five; stamens irregular attached to corolla, three upper filaments shorter, densely white-villous, lower two longer, glabrous, anthers larger and colored; ovary superior, 2-celled; capsule 3–6 mm long, ovoid, longer than calyx, splitting into two valves at maturity; seeds numerous, columnar, light to dark brown, 0.5–1.0 mm long, lateral surface angular and six-sided (Beal 1910; Darlington et al. 1940; Gleason and Cronquist

Can. J. Plant Sci. 58: 401-413 (Apr. 1978)

1963; Clapham et al. 1952). Chromosome counts from plants collected in Ottawa and British Columbia gave $2n. = 36$ (Packer 1964; Mulligan 1961). Other counts from European material have given $2n = 34$ and $2n = 36$ (Darlington and Wylie 1955). Basic chromosome numbers for the genus *Verbascum* are $n = 8, 15, 18$ (Darlington and Wylie 1955; Löve and Löve 1961) and $n = 9, 11, 17$ (Löve and Löve 1961).

II. *Verbascum blattaria* is also a biennial reproducing by seed, the flowering stem 0.6–1.2 m tall arising from an overwintered rosette, glandular pubescent with single hairs; leaves glabrous, variable; stem leaves alternate, 2–6 cm long, oblong, ovate, or lanceolate, sessile, but not decurrent, margins dentate, lacinate, or pinnatified; basal leaves longer, oblanceolate, pinnatified, sessile or slightly petioled, may not persist at the time of flowering; racemes 10–60 cm long, loose; flower pedicels spreading, 5–15 mm long, bracts at the base; corolla yellow or white, 1.0–2.5 cm wide, petals five; stamens five, attached to petals, all filaments villose with violet hairs, anthers of upper three stamens small, anthers of lower two obliquely inserted and adnate to the filament; ovary superior, 2-celled; capsule depressed–globose, 5–8 mm long, equalling, or longer than, the calyx; stigma persistent; seeds 6-sided, not distinct from *V. thapsus* (Beal 1910; Darlington et al. 1940; Gleason and Cronquist 1963). Chromosome counts for plants collected in Canada are not available; material collected from Europe and Northern Asia gave $2n = 30$ and $2n = 32$ (Darlington and Wylie 1955).

(b) *Similar species and distinguishing characteristics* — *Verbascum thapsus* may be distinguished from *V. lychnitus* L. by its dense terminal raceme (the inflorescence is a panicle in the latter) and from *V. phlomoides* L. by its strongly decurrent leaves (Britton and Brown 1913). Two *Verbascum* species resemble *V. blattaria* in North America: *V. virgatum* Stokes, on the Pacific coast, which has a fruiting pedicel shorter than the calyx (Britton and Brown 1913), and *V. phoenicium* L. which has a purple corolla and leaves that are only sparsely hairy (Gleason and Cronquist 1963). (c) *Intraspecific variation* — In Europe, both *V. thapsus* and *V. blattaria* exhibit much phenotypic variation. Two distinct subspecies of *V. thapsus* and three separate varieties of *V. blattaria* have been described (Murbeck 1933). In North America, variation appears to be much reduced (or perhaps not examined closely) and mainly concerns pigmentation of the corolla. *Verbascum thapsus* f. *candicans* House, a white form, occurs only rarely (Fernald 1950). *Verbascum blattaria* f. *albiflora*, with white corolla and purplish base, sometimes occurs as a pure population or in mixed stands with the yellow form. Genetically, the two characters are non-blending (Pennell 1935).

(d) Figure 1 shows the growth form of both species and details of the leaves, seeds, and flowers.

3. Economic Importance

(a) *Detrimental* — Although extracts from *V. thapsus* can inhibit growth of wheat seedlings (Johnson 1961), neither *Verbascum* species is a serious agricultural weed, since they can be controlled by cultivation of the soil. In overgrazed or poor pastures, the presence of *V. thapsus* represents a further degradation of the pasture because grazing animals avoid eating mullein (Dr. D. Isely, personal communication). Of the numerous organisms that cause disease in *V. thapsus*, two are destructive to economically important plants: *Erysiphe cichoracearum* D.C. (powdery mildew) which affects a large variety of vegetables and garden plants, especially species of *Cucumis, Helianthus,* and *Dahlia* (United States Department of Agriculture (USDA) 1926, 1960; Westcott 1960) and *Phymatotrichum omnivorum* (Shear) Dug. (root rot) which is a pathogen of cotton. *Phymatotrichum omnivorum* is also found on *V. blattaria* (USDA 1960). Recently, the cucumber mosaic virus (CMV) has been reported on *V. thapsus* (Bruckart and Lorbeer 1976). It is important to point out that a pathogen strain on a wild plant is not necessarily the same strain as that on a crop plant and may not be transferable (e.g. with *Agropyron repens* (L.) Beauv., Werner and Rioux 1977); appropriate studies have not been conducted with mullein species and crops. Neither species is known to be alleopathic, allergenic, or poisonous to humans.

(b) *Beneficial* — Both species of *Verbascum* are classified as medicinal herbs, although *V. thapsus* is the more widely known. Since ancient times *V. thapsus* has been used as an anodyne-pectoral and remedy for coughs and diarrhea, and is believed to be the "phlemos" described by Hippocrates (Millspaugh 1974). The leaves may provide some stimulatory effects when smoked (Wilhelm 1974). Mullein was recorded as a fish poison in Aristotle's *Historia Animalium* (Wilhelm 1974). An insect associated with mullein species, the mirid bug (*Campylomma verbasci*), may prove to be of beneficial economic importance in some cases. Although the bug has been listed as a pest on apples (e.g. Madsen et al. 1975), a study in pear orchards showed that it causes little economic damage and may be beneficial. It is only partially phytophagous, cannot complete its life cycle without insect prey, and feeds on several species of mites and insects that attack the fruit crop, including the European red mite *Paronychus ulmi* (Mulligan and Jong 1970).

Verbascum blattaria is often grown as an ornamental (USDA 1960). A methanol extract derived from the species has been effective against mosquito larvae (*Aedes aegypti* L.) even in low concentrations; only 5 of the 36 plant species tested were as effective (Supavarn et al. 1974).

4. Geographical Distribution

In Canada, *V. thapsus* occurs mainly in southern Ontario, Quebec, the eastern provinces and British Columbia; scattered populations occur throughout the cental plains region. *Verbascum blattaria* occurs mainly in southern Ontario and Quebec with a few populations in southern British Columbia (see Fig. 2). In North America, *V. thapsus* extends throughout the Midwest and Eastern coast as far south as Florida and Texas, and then westward through the Rocky Mountains to Washington and California. Populations are scattered but locally abundant. *Verbascum thapsus* occurs throughout the British Isles (rare in northern Scotland) and Europe (except for Iceland and Crete) to 64°N. in Norway, east into the U.S.S.R., and south to the Caucasus Mountains and Western Himalayas; Murbeck (1933) reported its occurrence in Asia Minor and China. *Verbascum blattaria* is rare in the British Isles, but occurs commonly throughout Europe from the Netherlands to Central Spain, eastward to Afganistan and Central Asia, and south to North Africa (Murbeck 1933; Clapham et al. 1952; Britton and Brown 1913). The center of distribution of *Verbascum* congeners is Western and Central Asia.

5. Habitat

(a) *Climatic requirements* — Both species occur mainly in continental areas characterized by cool summers (mean temperature of the warmest month less than 22°C, but with at least 4 mo over 10°C). *Verbascum thapsus* occurs in areas where the mean annual precipitation is 500–1,500 mm (20–60 inches) and the growing season at least 140 days (cf. Atlas of Canada 1957). The northern limit of distribution follows isopleths where less than 1% of the minimum daily temperatures fall below 0°C in May and less than 5% fall below 10°C in July (cf. Rayner 1961). *Verbascum blattaria* is more restricted in its distribution in Canada, occurring mainly in warmer, wetter areas, with minimum annual precipitation of 700–1,500 mm (30–60 inches) and a 180-day growing season (cf. Atlas of Canada 1957). Both species extend southward into the United States.

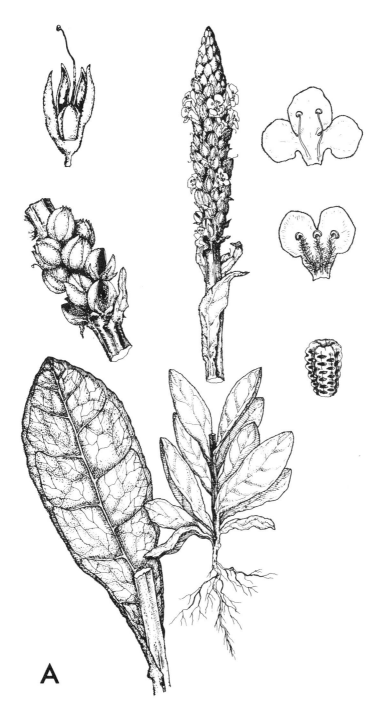

A

Fig. 1.   A (left) *Verbascum thapsus* and B (right) *V. blattaria*, each showing flowering habit, details of leaf, developing capsules on the stem, ovary within the calyx, dissected corolla with attached stamens, and a mature seed. For size dimensions, see text.

GUTH · 1977

B

(b) *Substratum* — *Verbascum thapsus* is found mainly on dry, sandy soils. In England, it is common in chalk and limestone districts (Furneaux 1909; Good 1948) with highly calcareous soils. In Canada, it grows abundantly in, but is not restricted to, pastures with well-drained soil, and a pH range of 6.5–7.8 (Dale et al.

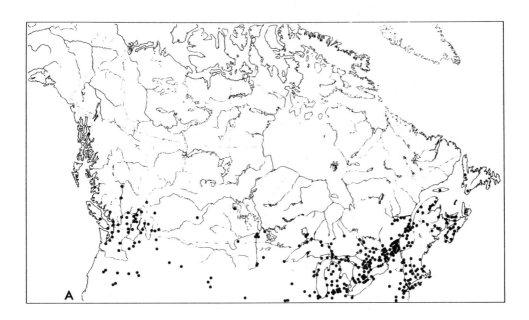

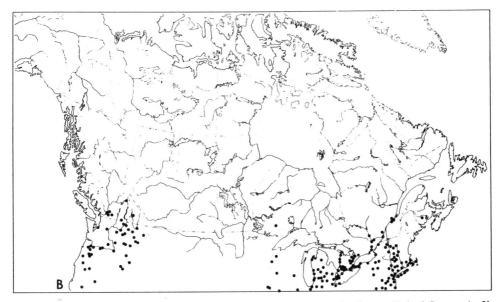

Fig. 2. Distribution of two species of *Verbascum* in Canada and adjacent United States: A. *V. thapsus*, B. *V. blattaria*, from herbarium specimens (see acknowledgments.)

1965). *Verbascum blattaria* is found mainly in waste places, but grows best in rich soils (Hanes and Hanes 1947).

(*c*) *Communities in which the species occur* — In abandoned agricultural fields, *V. thapsus* is an early colonizer, the tall flowering stalks usually appearing the 2nd yr after abandonment. In such areas, its success may be attributed to its reported herbicide resistance (Burton 1964) (see section 7 on Growth and Development). *Verbascum blattaria* may be found along the margins of cultivated fields, roadsides, and meadows; populations may cover entire fields where the ground has been left unbroken for 1–2 yr (Darlington et al. 1940).

In Kalamazoo Co., Michigan, in a field in its 3rd yr after abandonment from a barley crop, *V. thapsus* was a dominant part of the vegetation, growing in association with *Potentilla recta* L., *Lychnis alba* Mill., *Rumex crispus* L., *Aster* spp., *Solidago canadensis* L., *Poa* spp. and *Medicago sativa* L. each with > 10% cover. In a nearby 12-yr-old field, *V. thapsus* was sparse, although the density of dead flowering stalks from previous years indicated an earlier dominance; the perennials *Solidago canadensis, Agropyron repens* (L.) Beauv., and *Poa canadensis* L. made up the major portion of the vegetation.

6. History

Verbascum thapsus was probably introduced into North America several times as a medicinal herb and accidentally. Its introduction as a piscicide in the mid-1700's was apparently limited to a few families in the Blue Ridge Mts. of Virginia (Wilhelm 1974). The species apparently naturalized and spread very rapidly, since by 1818 Eaton (erroneously) described it as a native species. The introduction of *V. blattaria* into North America is less well known. It too was recorded by Eaton (1818), who described it as being common along the East Coast and into Pennsylvania. Both species

were present as far west as Michigan in 1839 (Darlington et al. 1940).

7. Growth and Development

(*a*) *Morphology* — Both species possess a tap root and overwintering rosette, from which the flowering stalk emerges in the spring. The dense cover of trichomes on the leaves of *V. thapsus* makes them unpalatable to cattle (Fogg 1945), and some phytophagous insects (Dr. P. Harris, personal communication). Muzik (1970) reports that these epidermal hairs protect the species from aqueous solutions of 2, 4-D because the droplets are held away from the leaf surface. Ice crystals are held away in the same manner.

(*b*) *Perennation* — Both *V. thapsus* and *V. blattaria* are classified as semi-rosette hemicryptophytes (Clapham et al. 1952).

(*c*) *Physiological data* — Williams and Kemp (1976) have shown that seedlings of *V. thapsus* collected from a range of cold to warm temperature habitats (based on altitude and latitude) exhibit similar rates of photosynthesis within a temperature range of 20–35°C. Only at the highest temperature tested, 40°C, did seedlings from the warmest habitat (low altitude and latitude) exhibit a higher photosynthetic rate than those from the coolest habitat. They concluded that the ability of an individual plant to photosynthesize over a broad range of temperature has contributed to mullein's success across a diversity of habitats.

Williams et al. (1975) reported a CO_2 compensation point of 58 vpm CO_2 for *V. thapsus* and on this basis concluded that the species had a C_3 photosynthetic pathway (although Parkhurst (1976) has hypothesized it may be a C_4 on the basis of leaf anatomy). Wuenscher (1970) shaved the dense trichomes off the leaves of *V. thapsus* and found that the transpiration rate was lower in the unshaved portion of the leaves. Parkhurst (1976), evaluating the work of Wuenscher (1970), showed by calculation that the main effect of the trichomes was to increase stomatal resistance, with only a slight increase in boundary layer resistance. Electron micrographs of these trichomes have revealed an abundance of highly active organelles (Miroslavov 1970).

Glier and Caruso (1973) demonstrated that low temperatures induce the degradation of starch in roots of *V. thapsus*, which may provide cryoprotection for the overwintering rosette.

(*d*) *Phenology* — Seeds of *V. thapsus* germinate in the early spring, forming a rosette that continues to grow into late autumn and overwinter. After a vernalization period (Glier and Caruso 1973), the plant produces a tall flower stalk. Flowering begins in late June, and peaks in early August. Flowers mature on the stalk from the bottom to the top in successive spirals so that at any one point in time, they appear in a loose spiral pattern up the raceme. As the season progresses, each successive spiral begins slightly higher on the stem, but overlaps for most of its length with the former spirals. Growth of the flower stalk is indeterminate. The length of the flowering period appears to be a function of stalk height, taller stalks continuing to flower into late September and early October.

Verbascum blatteria also flowers from late June into early September. Flowering proceeds from the bottom of the raceme upwards. In midseason, capsules are maturing on the bottom while buds are just opening at the top (Darlington et al. 1940).

(*e*) *Mycorrhiza* — None reported.

8. Reproduction

(*a*) *Floral biology* — Individual flowers of *V. thapsus* are ephemeral, opening before dawn and closing before midafternoon of the same day (C. A. Thompson, personal communication). They are protogynous, the style maturing first and then bending downward once the anthers appear (Kerner von Marilann 1895). The two anterior stamens are naked, and provide most of the fertilizing pollen. The hairs of the posterior three probably provide a foothold for visitors, for example hover-flies, which gather nectar and pollen from the posterior anthers while their abdomens are dusted with pollen from the anterior pair (McLean and Ivimey-Cook 1956). Although visited by a wide variety of insects, only short- and long-tongued bees are effective vectors of cross-pollination (Pennell 1935). Flowers are also autogamous, self-pollination occurring at the end of the day if cross-pollination has not occurred. The style returns to its original position, and the corolla closes, pushing the still receptive stigma against the anthers (Kerner von Marilann 1895).

Verbascum blattaria is homogamous, the anthers and style of individual flowers maturing simultaneously (Clapham et al. 1952). The style protrudes from the corolla, encouraging outcrossing since an insect visitor lands there before entering the corolla. Self-pollination may occur as the flower closes. The anthers adhere together under the stigma such that when the corolla abscises the attached anthers are suspended on the stigma and dump pollen on it (Kerner von Marilann 1895).

(*b*) *Seed production and dispersal* — Seeds of *V. thapsus* are contained in a capsule with two cells. Salisbury (1942) reports the mean number of capsules per plant as 226 ± 42 (SD; $n = 37$), with an average of 596 ± 30 (SD; $n = 16$) seeds per capsule. This gives an approximate average of 136,000 seeds per plant. The number of seeds for a population from a 3-yr-old Michigan field (see 5c) in August of 1976 ranged from 0 to 749 per capsule, with a mean of 208 ± 200 (SD; $n = 18$), for a total of 175,000 per plant. The lower mean number and higher variation in the latter estimate of seed set is attributed to heterogeneous predation by weevil larvae (*Gymnaetron tetrum* Fab.). Of the 18 capsules examined, 11 had no seeds and showed evidence of weevil activity: in eight of these a larva was present and in one, an adult weevil; in two, an emergence hole and frass indicated earlier presence of a weevil.

The seeds possess no specialized morphological adaptations for dispersal by wind or animals. The capsule splits open along its longitudinal axis when mature, and movement of the stalk by wind or a large animal is required to release the seeds from the parent (McLean and Ivimey-Cook 1956). Seeds are dispersed as far as 11 m, although 93% of them fall within 5 m and 75% of them fall within 1 m of the parent plant (Fig. 3).

There is little information on seed production in *V. blattaria*. It is reported to have produced over 1,100 capsules per plant in Kalamazoo Co., Michigan (Hanes and Hanes 1947).

(c) Viability and germination — Seeds of both species remain viable, although dormant, for extended periods of time; up to 35 yr in *V. thapsus* (Darlington and Steinbauer 1961) and at least 90 yr in *V. blattaria* (Kivilaan and Bandurski 1973). In Denmark, viable seeds of *V. thapsus* were

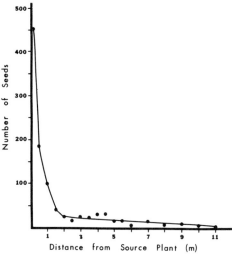

Fig. 3. Pattern of seed deposition in *Verbascum thapsus*. The number of seeds deposited (*y*) as a function of distance from the parent plant (*x*) exhibits a power function such that $\log y = 1.84 - 1.06 (\log x)$ and the correlation coefficient, *r*, is -0.908. This pattern is in contrast to the log-normal distribution reported by Salisbury (1942). The pattern was determined in field trials using seed traps as described by Werner (1975).

collected from soil samples archeologically dated from 1300 A.D. (Ødum 1965).

The seeds apparently do not have an after-ripening period (Gardner 1921; S. D. Getz, unpublished data). Gardner (1921) obtained 53–94% germination of *V. thapsus* seeds on filter paper in the light, and none in the dark. There apparently is an effect of substrate, since, by using sand or soil as a substrate, Gardner was able to increase germination in the dark to 20 and 34%, respectively.

Seeds collected from a Michigan population of *V. thapsus* (see 5c) were separated by sieves into three size classes and put to germinate in petri dishes (Whatman no. 3 filter paper) in a glasshouse (11 h of sunlight, temperature 19–23°C) in October 1976, immediately after harvest from the parent plant. The largest seeds (>500 μm) gave 30% germination, the intermediate (250–500 μm) 42%, and the smallest seeds (<250 μm) 0% germination; germination was complete in 8 days. Of the two larger size categories, the non-germinated seeds generally had fully developed embryos, but a tetrazolium test did not demonstrate that they were alive; seeds in the smallest size category did not have fully developed embryos. (The proportion of seeds produced by an individual plant averaged 6% large seeds, 85% intermediate seeds, and 9% small seeds.)

This same lot of seeds (not separated by size) gave 5–10% field germination across experimentally sown densities of 50–10,000 per 0.25 m² the following spring (1977); this was done in the same field where the seeds had been collected, but where a portion had been plowed the previous autumn (K. L. Gross, unpublished data).

(d) Vegetative reproduction — Not reported or observed by these authors.

9. Hybrids

Though not common, natural hybrids of *V. thapsus* occur with *V. lychnitis* and *V. nigrum* (Clapham et al. 1952). Darwin

(1889) worked with a natural population of *V. thapsus* × *lychnitus* and found the hybrid to be intermediate in character between the two parents, and uniformly sterile. Two specimens of this hybrid from the Eastern U.S.A. are in the herbarium of the Field Museum of Natural History, Chicago, Illinois. No natural hybrids of *V. blattaria* have been reported in North America. Several are reported in Europe, however, including a *V. thapsus* × *blattaria* cross (Murbeck 1933).

The first artificial hybrids within the genus *Verbascum* were done by Koelreuter in 1762 (see Murbeck 1933). Species hybrids within the genus can be produced artificially relatively easily, although they are almost universally sterile (Arts-Damler 1960). Application of a colchicine treatment has produced fertile hybrids in crosses with *V. phoeniceum, V. nigratum, V. phlomoides, V. lychnitus,* and *V. gnaphlodes* (Arts-Damler 1960). Occasionally spontaneous chromosome doubling occurs.

10. Population Dynamics

A population of *V. thapsus* may extend over several hectares or along several kilometers of roadway. Salisbury (1942) reports that densities of 5.2 flowering plants/m² have been observed in coppiced woodlands in England, 2 yr after they were cut.

In the 3-yr-old field (in 1976, see 5c), flowering plants were randomly distributed (by a test of distance to nearest neighbor) at an average density of 1.0/m²; and with a mean height of 119 ± 36 cm (SD; $n = 51$). Plants within the 12-yr-old field were found at a lower density (0.17/m²) and were significantly shorter (Student's t-test; $t = 11.83, P < .001$), 48.8 ± 15 cm (SD; $n = 23$). Populations are quite ephemeral in such oldfields if the area is left undisturbed. In the younger field above, the density of the vegetative rosettes was only 0.021/m² in 1976; furthermore, there were almost no seedlings the following spring in spite of the estimated 175,000 seeds/m² produced the previous year (see also section 8c). Prelimi-

nary results of current studies on the population dynamics of *V. thapsus* indicate that the typical pattern of the species is one of ephemeral adult populations and long-lived seed pools.

Flowering plants of *V. thapsus* were sampled from the 3-yr-old field described in 5c in August 1976 to determine biomass allocation within individual plants; plants were removed to the laboratory, separated by component parts, dried for 24 h at 100°C in a forced-air drying oven, and weighed to the nearest 0.1 g. The total mean weight of a flowering plant was 145.1 g ($\pm$ 42.5 SE; $n = 15$). The mean percentage biomass allocated to the flowers and underlying flower stalk was 19.0% ($\pm$ 1.2 SE); to supporting stem, 23.6% ($\pm$ 1.3 SE); to leaves still alive, 15.7% ($\pm$ 1.1 SE); to leaves now dead, 30.3% ($\pm$ 2.5 SE); to roots, 11.5% ($\pm$ 0.7 SE).

11. Response to Herbicides and other Chemicals

A single application of a 2, 4-D/2, 4, 5-T mixture at 16 oz/acre in June or early September (the rosette stage) provides control of *V. thapsus* and is not harmful to livestock (Ontario Herbicide Committee 1968). Good, long-term control of this species can be achieved with an initial application of Tebuthiuron at 4-6 lb/acre. Repeated applications at half the initial rate will suppress regrowth (Lade et al. 1974). No herbicide control is specified in the literature for *V. blattaria.*

12. Response to Human Manipulations

Cutting the rosette below the crown will prevent either species from flowering (Darlington et al. 1940; Fogg 1945). Repeated mowing of *V. thapsus* prevents the flowering stalk from bolting, but the basal rosette will increase in size. If mowing is discontinued, the plant will then bolt, and produce flowers. Damage to the terminal raceme (e.g. clipping) will cause increased growth of the axillary branches.

13. Response to Parasites

A curculionid weevil (*Gymnaetron tetrum* Fab.), specific to *V. thapsus*, was introduced to North America from Europe (Burcham 1937). The larvae mature in the capsules (Sleeper 1954) and destroy up to 50% of the seeds (see Section 8b). Eight other species of Coleoptera which are injurious to *V. thapsus* in Poland (Popov 1972) have not been reported in North America.

The USDA (1960) lists the following micro-organisms on both species: *Cercospora verbasciola* Ell. and Ev., *Phymotrichium omnivorum* (Shear.) Dug., *Phoma thapsi* (Ell. and Ev.), *Phyllosticta verbasciola* Ell. and Kell.; on *V. thapsus* only: *Erisphye cichoracearum* D.C., *Heterodera maroni* (Cornu) Goody, *Meloidogyne* sp., *Mycosphaerella verbasciola* (Schw.) Fairm., *Ramularia variabilis* (Fckl.); and on *V. blattaria* only: *Septoria verbasciola* (Berk. and Curt.), *Phoma verbasciola* Fairm., *Oidium* sp. Westcott (1960) also reports *Septoria verbasciola* and *Oidium pyrinum* on *V. thapsus*. Six species of leaf-inhabiting parasitic fungi are reported on *V. thapsus*, and three on *V. blattaria* (USDA 1953).

ACKNOWLEDGMENTS

Thanks is expressed to J. D. Soule, G. G. Mittelbach, K. A. Erdman, G. Guth, H. Caswell, and G. A. Mulligan for their various roles in the field research, preparation of figures, and manuscript reviews. D. K. Young verified the identification of *Gymnaetron tetrum*. Special thanks is expressed to S. D. Getz for permission to use unpublished data on seed germination in *V. thapsus*. The assistance of herbarium personnel at the following institutions is gratefully acknowledged: Department of Agriculture, Ottawa; University of British Columbia; University of Manitoba; University of Toronto; New York Botanical Garden; The Field Museum of Natural History, Chicago; Missouri Botanical Garden, St. Louis; The Gray Herbarium, Harvard University; and Michigan State University. The research was supported in part by National Science Foundation Grants BMS-74-1602 and DEB-77-14811; publication costs were paid in part by a grant to K.L.G. from the Department of Zoology, Michigan State University.

ARTS-DAMLER, T. 1960. Cytogenetical studies on six *Verbascum* species and their hybrids. Genetica 31: 241–328.

ATLAS OF CANADA. 1957. Department of Mines and Technical Surveys, Geographical Branch, Ottawa, Ont. (110 maps).

BEAL, W. J. 1910. Seeds of Michigan weeds. Mich. State Agric. Coll. Exp. Sta., Div. of Bot. Bull. 260.

BRITTON, N. L. and BROWN, H. C. 1913. An illustrated flora of the Northern United States, Canada, and the British possessions. Scribner, New York. 637 pp.

BRUCKART, W. L. and LORBEER, J. W. 1976. Cucumber mosaic virus in weed hosts near commercial fields of lettuce and celery. Phytopathology **66**: 253–259.

BURCHAM, E. L. 1937. Notes on Curculionidae (Coleoptera). J. Wash. Acad. Sci. 27: 312–316.

BURTON, J. E. 1964. Methods and problems of weed control along highways. Proc. 20th N. Cent. Weed Cont. Conf. **43**: 6.

CANADA WEED COMMITTEE. 1975. Common and botanical names of weeds in Canada. Canada Dep. Agric. Publ. 1397. Ottawa, Ont. 67 pp.

CLAPHAM, A. R., TUTIN, T. G. and WARBURG, E. F. 1952. Flora of the British Isles. University Press, Cambridge. 1591 pp.

DALE, H. M., HARRISON, P. J. and THOMSON, G. W. 1965. Weeds as indicators of physical site characteristics in abandoned pastures. Can. J. Bot. **43**: 1319–1327.

DARLINGTON, C. D. and WYLIE, A. P. 1955. Chromosome atlas of flowering plants. 2nd ed. Allen and Unwin Ltd., London. 519 pp.

DARLINGTON, H. T., BESSEY, E. A. and MEGEE, C. R. 1940. Some important Michigan weeds. Mich. State Coll. Agric. Exp. Sta. Spec. Bull. 304.

DARLINGTON, H. T. and STEINBAUER, G. P. 1961. The eighty-year period for Dr. Beal's seed viability experiment. Amer. J. Bot. **48**: 321–325.

DARWIN, C. R. 1889. The different forms of flowers on plants of the same species. D. Appleton and Co., New York. 352 pp.

EATON, A. 1818. Manual of botany for the northern and middle states. Webster's and Skinners, Albany. 524 pp.

FERNALD, M. L. 1950. Gray's manual of botany. American Book Co., New York. 1632 pp.

FERRON, M. and CAYOUETTE, R. 1970. Noms des mauvaises herbes du Québec. Min. Agric. Colonisation Québec, Qué. 113 pp.

FOGG, J. M. 1945. Weeds of lawn and garden. University of Pennsylvania Press, Philadelphia. 215 pp.

FURNEAUX, W. S.. 1909. Field and woodland plants. Longmans, Green and Co., London. 383 pp.

GARDNER, W. A. 1921. Effect of light on germination of light sensitive seeds. Bot. Gaz. **71**: 249–288.

GLEASON, H. A. and CRONQUIST, A. 1963. Manual of vascular plants of Northeastern United States and adjacent Canada. D. van Nostrand, Princeton, N.J. 810 pp.

GLIER, J. H. and CARUSO, J. L. 1973. Low temperature induction of starch degradation in roots of a biennial weed. Cryobiology **10**: 328–330.

GOOD, R. D. 1948. A geographical handbook of the Dorset flora. Dorset Nat. Hist. Arch. Soc., Dorchester. 255 pp.

HANES, C. R. and HANES, F. N. 1947. Flora of Kalamazoo Co., Mich. vascular plants. Anthoensen Press, Portland, Mich. 295 pp.

JOHNSON, D. A. 1961. Growth inhibitors in native plants of Northern Arizona. Res. Notes Rocky Mt. For. Range Exp. Sta. **61**: 2.

KERNER VON MARILANN, A. J. 1895. The natural history of plants. Vol. II. Part 1. (Trans. from German) Holt and Co., New York. 496 pp.

KIVILAAN, A. and BANDURSKI, R. S. 1973. The ninety-year period for Dr. Beal's seed viability experiment. Amer. J. Bot. **60**: 140–145.

LADE, D. H., BARRENTINE, J. L., DOHNER, L. D. HOBBS, C. D., KEATON, J. A., PAFFORD, J. L., WALKER, J. C. and WATSON, J. H. 1974. Tebuthiuron, a new herbicide for total vegetation control. Pages 266–269 *in* Proc. 27th Annu. Meet. South. Weed Sci. Soc. Eli Lilly Co., Greenfield, Ind.

LÖVE, A. and LÖVE, D. 1961. Chromosome numbers of central and the Northwest European plant species. Opera Bot. **5**: 1–581.

MADSEN, H. F., PETERS, H. F. and VAKENTI, J .M. 1975. Pest management: experience in six British Columbia apple orchards. Can. Entomol. **107**: 873–877.

MARIE-VICTORIN, FR. 1964. Flore Laurentienne. Les Presses de L'Université Montréal. 925 pp.

McLEAN, R. C. and IVIMEY-COOK, W. R. 1956. Textbook of theoretical botany. Vol. II. Longmans, Greene, and Co., London. 1130 pp.

MILLSPAUGH, C. F. 1974. American medicinal plants. Dover Publ. Inc., New York. 806 pp.

MIROSLAVOV, E. A. 1970. Submikros Kopiche skaya morfologiya Kroyuschikh trikhome *Verbascum thapsus* L. [Submicroscopic morphology of the covering trichomes of *Verbascum thapsus* L.] [In Russian, English abstract.] Dokl. Akad. Nauk SSSR Ser. Biol. **195**: 467–468.

MULLIGAN, G. A. 1961. Chromosome numbers of Canadian weeds. Can. J. Bot. **37**: 1057–1066.

MULLIGAN, R. D. and JONG, C. 1970. The biology and influence of pesticides on *Campylomma verbasci* (Heteroptera: Miridae) Can. Entomol. **102**: 1390–1394.

MURBECK, S. S. 1933. Monographie der Guttang *Verbascum*. [In Swedish and Latin]. Lunds Univers. Arsskr., N. F., Avd. 2, **29**: 1–630.

MUZIK, T. J. 1970. Weed biology and control. McGraw-Hill, New York. 273 pp.

ØDUM, S. 1965. Germination of ancient seeds. Dan. Bot. Ark. **24**: 70.

ONTARIO HERBICIDE COMMITTEE. 1968. Guide to chemical weed control. Ont. Dep. Agric. Food. Toronto, Ont. 87 pp.

PACKER, J. G. 1964. Chromosome numbers and taxonomic notes on Western Canadian and Arctic plants. Can. J. Bot. **42**: 473–494.

PARKHURST, D. F. 1976. Effects of *Verbascum thapsus* L. leaf hairs on heat and mass transfer: A reassessment. New Phytol. **76**: 453–457.

PENNELL, F. W. 1935. The Scrophulariaceae of Eastern Temperate North America. Acad. Nat. Sci. Mono. (No. 1). 650 pp.

POPOV, P. 1972. Insect pests of medicinal crops in Bulgaria. III. Coleoptera. [In Russian; English summary]. Rasteniev 'd. Nauki. **9**: 167–175.

RAYNER, J. N., ed. 1961. Atlas of surface temperature frequencies for North America and Greenland. Arct. Meteorol. Res. Group. Publ. 33. Montreal, Que.

SALISBURY, E. J. 1942. The reproductive capacity of plants. G. Bell and Sons, Ltd., London. 244 pp.

SLEEPER, E. L. 1954. A European weevil in North America. Entomol. News **65**: 129–130.

SUPAVARN, P., KNAPP, F. W. and SIGAFUS, R. 1974. Biologically active plant extracts for control of mosquito larvae. Mosq. News **34**: 398–402.

UNITED STATES DEPARTMENT OF AGRICULTURE. 1926. Checklist of diseases of economic plants in the USA. U.S. Dep. Agric. Bull. 1366.

UNITED STATES DEPARTMENT OF AGRICULTURE. 1953. Plant diseases. Yearbook of agriculture. Washington, D.C. 940 pp.

UNITED STATES DEPARTMENT OF AGRICULTURE. 1960. Index of plant diseases. USA. Agric. Handb. 165. U.S. Govt. Print. Office, Washington, D.C. 531 pp.

WERNER, P. A. 1975. A seed trap for determining patterns of seed deposition in terrestrial plants. Can. J. Bot. **53**: 810–813.

WERNER, P. A. and RIOUX, R. 1977. The biology of Canadian weeds. 24. *Agropyron repens* (L.) Beauv. Can. J. Plant Sci. **57**: 905–919.

WESTCOTT, C. L. 1960. Plant disease handbook. P. van Nostrand Co., Inc. Princeton, N.J. 825 pp.

WILHELM, G., JR. 1974. The mullein: plant piscicide of the mountain folk culture. Geogr. Rev. **64**: 235–252.

WILLIAMS, G. J. III and KEMP, P. R. 1976. Temperature relation of photosynthetic response in populations of *Verbascum thapsus* L. Oecologia (Berl.) **25**: 47–54.

WILLIAMS, G. J. III, LAZOR, R. and YOUNGRAU, P. 1975. Temperature adaptations in the Hill reaction of altitudinally and latitudinally diverse populations of *Verbascum thapsus* L. Photosynthetica **9**: 35–39.

WUENSCHER, J. W. 1970. The effect of leaf hairs on *Verbascum thapsus* on leaf energy exchange. New Phytol. **69**: 65–73.

THE BIOLOGY OF CANADIAN WEEDS.
29. *Melilotus alba* Desr. and *M. officinalis* (L.) Lam.

ROY A. TURKINGTON[1], PAUL B. CAVERS, and ERIKA REMPEL

Department of Plant Sciences, University of Western Ontario, London, Ontario N6A 5B7.

Received 21 Sept. 1977, accepted 18 Nov. 1977.

TURKINGTON, ROY A., CAVERS, PAUL B. AND REMPEL, ERIKA. 1978. The biology of Canadian weeds. 29. *Melilotus alba* Desr. and *M. officinalis* (L.) Lam. Can. J. Plant Sci. **58**: 523–537.

This summary of biological data is for white sweet-clover (*Melilotus alba* Desr.) and yellow sweet-clover (*M. officinalis* (L.) Lam.) which occur as weeds of roadsides and waste places across the southern half of Canada. *M. alba* extends into the Canadian Shield region and is found in a greater variety of habitats.

Cette étude monographique porte sur le mélilot blanc (*Melilotus alba* Desr.) et le mélilot jaune (*M. officinalis* (L.) Lam.) qu'on rencontre comme adventices le long des routes et dans les terrains vagues dans toute la partie sud du Canada. *M. alba* étend son habitat jusque dans la région du Bouclier canadien et fait preuve d'une grande adaptabilité écologique.

1. Names

Melilotus alba Desr. — **white sweet-clover** (Canada Weed Committee 1969); **mélilot blanc** (Ferron and Cayouette 1971).
Melilotus officinalis (L.) Lam. — **yellow sweet-clover** (Canada Weed Committee 1969); **mélilot jaune** (Ferron and Cayouette 1971), Leguminosae, bean (pulse) family, Légumineuses.

2. Description and Account of Variation

(a) Both species are annual or biennial herbs; the presence of a single gene pair distinguishing between annual and biennial forms (Clarke 1935). Each species has a strong tap root, a crown which produces from 1 to 10 upright stems, trifoliate leaves with the terminal leaflet stalked and numerous small leaves (Fig. 2). The following description has been taken chiefly from Stevenson (1969).

I. *Melilotus alba* — Stem 0.3 - 2.6 m high, upright, coarse or fine, grooved or channelled, usually pubescent or pilose near the tip. Leaflets of the lower trifoliate leaves broadly ovate, obovate, or rhomboidal, rounded or truncate at the tip, irregularly dentate, 1.5–5 cm long: those of the upper leaves oblong–lanceolate, usually rounded or truncate near the tip, dentate or almost entire. Stipules 7–10 mm long, entire, narrowly cuneate, those of the lower leaves with one or two teeth near the broadened base. Each raceme 40–80, rarely 120 flowered, elongated at maturity, 8–15 cm long or occasionally up to 28 cm in some annual varieties. Pedicels 1.5–2 mm long. Flowers white, 4–6 mm long, single, 10 stamens, 2 ovules in ovary, style and stigma all hidden inside a pair of keel petals which are more or less fused along the outer margin to form the keel. Calyx 2–2.5 mm long, teeth as long as the tube, rarely shorter, triangular–lanceolate. Wings and standard more or less equal and longer than keel. Pod 3–4 mm long, 2–2.5 mm broad, 1.5–2 mm thick, obliquely ovate, reticulately nerved, black, dark grey or tawny, tip obtuse, base of style persisting (Fig. 1c,d). Pods usually have 1 seed, rarely 2 or 3. Seeds oval (Fig. 1a,b) 2–2.5 mm long, 1.5 mm broad, yellow or rarely greenish-yellow; endosperm present, two-layered and completely encloses the embryo.

[1]Present address (R.A.T.): Department of Botany, University of British Columbia, Vancouver, B.C. V6T 1W5.

II. *Melilotus officinalis* — This species is almost indistinguishable from *M. alba* by most characteristics except its yellow flower. *M. officinalis* is somewhat smaller than *M. alba,* flowers earlier and is more xeric (Heitlinger 1975). Dahlberg (cited in Kirk and Stevenson 1931a) and Stevens and Long (1926) state that seeds marked with purple specks can be definitely assigned to *M. officinalis*. Schulz (1901) says that *M. alba* has two ovules per ovary and *M. officinalis* usually has six, whereas Coe and Martin (1920) state 2-5 and 3-6, respectively. The pods of *M. officinalis* have a few simple or forked ridges, chiefly transverse. On the pods of *M. alba* the ridges are more irregular and tend to form reticulations (Fig. 1c). The mature pods of *M. alba* are usually dark brown to black and those of *M. officinalis* are pale brown. The seeds of *M. officinalis* are oblong in shape with a shallow lateral notch at one end. They are a little more rounded than those of *M. alba* (Fig. 1a,b).

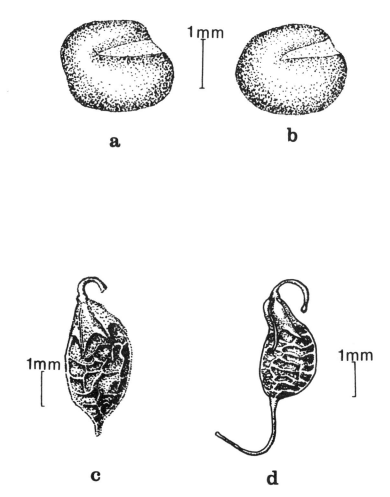

Fig. 1. Drawings of the seeds and pods of *Melilotus alba* (a and c) and *Melilotus officinalis* (b and d). Scale as shown. Diagrams of seeds re-drawn from Stevens and Long (1926); diagrams of pods re-drawn from Stevenson (1969).

Chromosome numbers have been reported for 17 of the 20 *Melilotus* spp. and all have $n = 8$ (Darlington and Wylie 1955). Chromosome counts of $2n = 16$ have been reported for Canadian specimens of *M. alba* (Mulligan 1957) and *M. officinalis* (Fryer 1930). No natural polyploids are known although tetraploids have been produced artificially (Atwood 1936).

(b) *Melilotus alba* is distinguished from all other sweet-clovers by its white flowers.

Yellow-flowered *M. altissima* and *M. indica* are similar in appearance to *M. officinalis* but differ in distribution and plant height. *M. altissima* is a very tall (1.6 m) biennial or perennial and is found from British Columbia to Nova Scotia (Roland and Smith 1969). It can be distinguished from *M. officinalis* by its pubescent ovaries and pods (Stevenson 1969). *M. indica* is an annual having a low growth form (0.5 m) and is abundant in the south and Pacific states (Gleason 1963). Its flowers are smaller (2–3 mm long) and much more densely arranged in the raceme than those of *M. officinalis* (Stevens and Long 1926). Seed pods in *M. indica* are papery, the seeds are yellowish-green and minutely tuberculate (Stevenson 1969). *M. indica* has been introduced on occasion throughout Canada and scattered individuals may be found across the country.

(c) I. *M. alba* is a polymorphic species which Suvorov (cited in Stevenson 1969) divided into three subspecies and a large number of ecotypes and forms. European material is much more variable than North American. Characters that show great variation are height, thickness of stem, bushiness, date of maturity (Stevens and Long 1926), amount and color of foliage (Clarke 1935), shape and size of leaves (Kirk and Armstrong 1934), amount of bloom and size of flowers (Stevenson 1969), and color of seeds (Fowlds 1939). Swenson (1942) describes four seed colors: normal yellow, pale yellow, pale green and green. Even the relative size of keel, wing and standard vary (Stevenson 1969). The

occurrence of dwarf-branching types of *M. alba* has been described by Kirk (1924). The typical erect and ascending form of white blossom sweet-clover is dominant to the dwarf-branching type (Stevenson 1937). Goplen (1962) reported a mutant with extremely large wrinkled leaves.

A comprehensive list of the different cultivated varieties is given by Smith and Gorz (1965).

II. *M. officinalis* is a variable species comprising, according to Suvorov's interpretation, three subspecies and about 16 ecotypes or forms. The cultivated varieties include Erector, Madrid and Aura (Stevenson 1969; Smith and Gorz 1965).

(d) Figure 1 shows the main diagnostic features of seeds and seed pods of each species. Since seedlings and adult plants of the two species are so similar morphologically, only those of *M. alba* have been shown in Fig. 2.

3. Economic Importance

(a) Detrimental — Sweet-clover possesses typical weedy attributes, i.e. reproduces in large numbers, is persistent and grows singly or in small clumps along roadside edges, railway rights-of-way, pastures and disturbed areas. Its tall and vigorous growth often masks guide rails and sign posts, creating a hazard for motorists. It is only a minor problem in Southern Ontario but a much greater nuisance in Northern Ontario where the plants grow much taller (R. M. Dell, pers. comm.). The flowers of sweet-clover also attract many bees and insects which could be a detriment along highways. Sweet-clover has been considered a noxious weed in Iowa, New England and the central U.S.A. because it sometimes occurs as "an adulteration in other crops" (cited in York and Pammel 1919). Both sweet-clover species have been classed as noxious weeds in various publications (e.g. Pammel 1912, cited in York and Pammel 1919; Mulligan 1976).

A condition known as sweet-clover disease (Greenshields 1957) or 'bleeding disease' (Smith and Gorz 1965) in cattle frequently results from the feeding of spoiled sweet-clover hay or ensilage. It is generally believed that cattle are more susceptible to the disease than sheep (Linton et al. 1963). *M. alba* is a weed of wheat crops (Pirzada and Rajput 1969). Melilot taint of wheat, also referred to as sweet-clover taint, is caused by sweet-clover in wheat fields being harvested with the wheat. If the sweet-clover is still green or if the harvesting is done in wet conditions, the wheat absorbs the characteristic odor of sweet-clover (Greenshields 1957). Yellow sweet-clover has appeared as a weed in barley fields in Saskatchewan (A. G. Thomas, personal communication). McArthur and Miltimore (1969) claimed

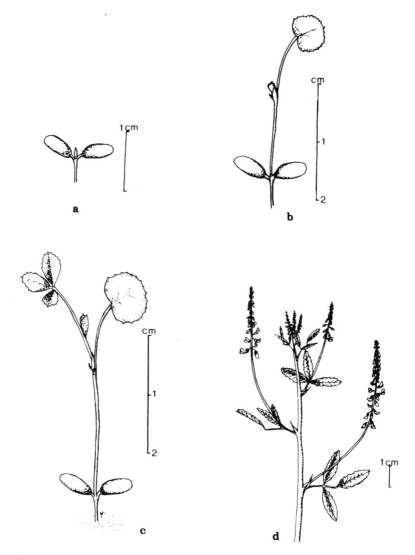

Fig. 2. Four stages in the growth of *Melilotus alba* (a) 6 days, (b) 17 days and (c) 24 days from emergence. A portion of an adult is shown in (d) (re-drawn from Robinson 1949). Scale as shown.

336

that the Arctic variety of *M. alba* causes bloat. The use of sweet-clover agriculturally has been restricted due to the coarseness of its stems, which detracts from its value as a hay crop, and the impermeability of the seed coat, which necessitates scarification of the seed before it is sown (Stevenson 1937).

(b) Beneficial — Sweet-clovers have a variety of uses in agriculture. As pasture plants they are amongst the most productive available if properly managed (Greenshields 1957); they can provide good quality hay rich in protein and minerals (Smith and Gorz 1965); they are satisfactory for making good quality silage (Smith and Gorz 1965) and when harvested for seed, the straw will provide a roughage of considerable value (Greenshields 1957).

The soil-improving qualities of sweet-clover are well known and both species are used extensively in the more humid regions of western Canada to improve soil fertility and soil structure (Greenshields 1957). The species are often used for commercial seed production (Smith and Gorz 1965).

Both species have long been recognized as most valuable plants for honey (Bohart 1960, cited in Smith and Gorz 1965). *M. alba* has a higher pollen content than *M. officinalis* (Packer 1971). Plants of *M. officinalis* provide less honey than those of *M. alba* (Marie-Victorin 1964).

The ring-necked pheasant *(Phasianus colchicus torquatus)* will nest in stands of *M. alba* growing along roadsides although it prefers a mixture of alfalfa and crested wheatgrass (Hoffman 1973).

Since they are invading species, they quickly colonize freshly disturbed soils on well-drained river banks, construction sites etc. and reduce soil erosion.

(c) Legislation — In Iowa seed law, sweet-clover has been included in the list of noxious weeds (York and Pammel 1919).

Although neither *M. alba* nor *M. officinalis* is listed as a noxious weed in Canada, the Canada Seeds Act and Regulations (Agriculture Canada 1967) specifies a maximum number of sweet-clover seeds that are permissible per ounce for registered and certified seed of many grasses and legumes.

4. Geographical Distribution

I. *Melilotus alba* — Native to Europe and Western Asia. Naturalized in Britain, throughout Europe and Asia eastward to Tibet (Clapham et al. 1962). It has been introduced and is naturalized in Australia (Burbidge and Gray 1970), South Africa (Adamson and Salter 1950) and Argentina (Lavado and Nella 1972). It has been observed in western Greenland (Polunin 1959). It has been planted as a crop in Russia (Pel'men'ov 1972), Germany, Poland, Argentina and throughout the U.S.A. and Southern Canada. In Canada *M. alba* has been collected from every province and territory (Fig. 3). Data for Figs. 3 and 4 have been obtained from herbarium specimens (special thanks to Mr. W. J. Cody) and from Rousseau (1968), Calder and Taylor (1968), Marie-Victorin and Rolland-Germain (1969), Erskine (1960) and Baldwin (1958).

II. *Melilotus officinalis* — Native to Eurasia (Smith and Gorz 1965). Naturalized from Ireland throughout Europe and Asia to western China (Clapham et al. 1962). It has been introduced to several continents but is less widely distributed than *M. alba*, probably because it has been used less often as a crop. In Eastern Canada it does not extend as far north as *M. alba* (Baldwin 1958; Scoggan 1957) and is less common than *M. alba* along roads in the Canadian Shield region. It occurs across the south of the country (Fig. 4).

5. Habitat

(a) Climatic requirements — Both species are adapted to a wide range of climatic conditions. They are drought-tolerant (Butovssii 1971), only requiring enough moisture for establishment after which they will develop under extremely dry conditions. Kirk (1931b, cited in Dunham 1933)

grew both sweet-clover species in Saskatchewan with precipitation ranging from 18 to 26 cm. Both species are winter-hardy and have extended their ranges into high latitudes including the Yukon and the North West Territories (Figs. 3 and 4).

Neither species can withstand prolonged flooding. *M. alba* is slightly more tolerant and it is occasionally found on gravelly open banks beside rivers in Southern Ontario where flooding continues for several weeks during the winter and spring. In an experiment in London, Ontario, less than 10% of plants of either species survived a 5-day immersion in Thames River water at 20°C. A major cause of death was fungal attack which continued after the plants dried out (Weekes and Cavers, unpublished).

Plant heights are always greater under longer day lengths (9–17 h). Increased day length restricts crown bud formation (Smith 1942). Low temperatures (<13.3°C) retard flowering (Smith 1942).

(b) Substratum — *M. alba* is found growing on a wide range of soil types and textures, from Fargo clay (Stoa 1933) and loam to dune sand and river gravel. It is found most commonly on calcareous soils (Dunham 1933), and is reported to be unsuited to acid soils (Smith and Gorz 1965), although Ramakrishnan (1968a,b, 1970) has identified calcicole and calcifuge populations in Southern Ontario. Greenshields (1957) has reported that best growth occurs on rich loams and clay loams. *M. alba* has also been observed to invade and grow on coal ash dumps with no pathological alteration in morphology (Seraya and Komov 1971). *M. officinalis* is a pioneer species on asbestos tips (Banásová 1970) and occurs on gypsum tips (Roland and Smith 1969). Salt tolerance has been shown by Lavado and Nella (1972) for *M. officinalis* in Argentina and by Shestakov and Vladimirov (1973) for *M. alba* in Moldavia. Ashford and Bolton (1961) have shown that a sulphur deficiency restricts growth and that nitrogen application depresses fixation and nodulation. Sweet-clover is quite tolerant of high boron concentrations (Holliday et al. 1958).

Sweet-clovers have strong and deep tap roots and can make good growth on soils of moderately low fertility (Smith and Gorz 1965).

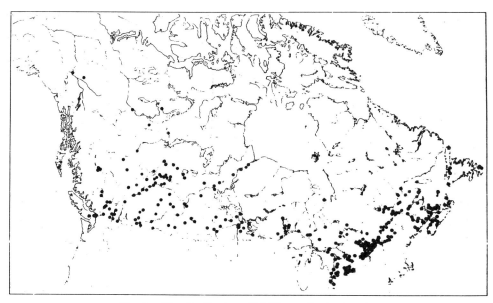

Fig. 3.   The distribution of *Melilotus alba* in Canada.

(c) Communities in which the species occurs — Sweet-clover grows in a variety of communities ranging from agricultural land (Smith and Gorz 1965) to roadside verges (Haney et al. 1974; Roland and Smith 1969) railway embankments, river banks and waste areas. Consequently, the species with which it associates also vary. In a prairie grassland in Minnesota, Heitlinger (1975) reported the presence of a number of herbs and grasses growing with *M. alba*. Sweet-clovers are weeds of wheat (Pirzada and Rajput 1969) and barley (Thomas, personal communication) yet they are also used as companion crops for *Avena sativa* (Haskins and Gorz 1975). In Minnesota, Robinson (1968) found that experimental plots of sweet-clover were infested by a range of weedy species.

In a calcareous, well drained abandoned field near Exerter, Ontario, *M. officinalis* was restricted to the upper half of a long gradual slope, while *M. alba* was restricted to the lower third of the slope. Common species associated with both sweet-clovers were *Agropyron repens* (L.) Beauv., *Daucus carota* L., *Medicago lupulina* L., *Plantago lanceolata* L., *Solidago* spp., *Taraxacum officinale* Weber. Species primarily found with *Melilotus officinalis* were *Asclepias syriaca* L., *Phleum pratense* L., *Trifolium pratense* L. and *Trifolium repens* L. Species found primarily with *M. alba* were *Convolvulus arvensis* L., *Dipasacus sylvestris* Huds., *Erigeron strigosus* Muhl., *Oenothera biennis* L., *Oxalis* sp., and *Sonchus* sp. (Cavers and Parks, unpublished).

Neither species persists in shaded sites. Isolated plants growing in partial shade are less vigorous than those in the open and produce very few seeds.

6. History

The genus *Melilotus* originated in Eurasia. The subgenus *Eumelilotus* Schultz, which includes *M. alba* and *M. officinalis* is native to the Mediterranean area through central Europe to Tibet (Smith and Gorz 1965). Smith and Gorz also noted that sweet-clover plants were used by the ancient Greeks for medicinal purposes.

The earliest report of *Melilotus* in North America was in 1664 by Boucher but the species was not identified (Stevenson

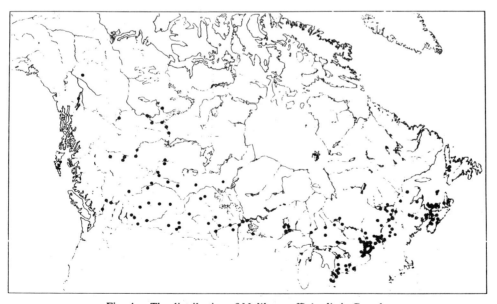

Fig. 4. The distribution of *Melilotus officinalis* in Canada.

1969). *M. alba* was included by Gronovius in his *Flora Virginica* of 1739 (Stevenson 1969). Gilmore (1931) stated that M. alba was first established as a despised weed.

In North America sweet-clovers have been the subject of a love–hate relationship with humans. Erskine (1960) reported that *M. officinalis* was cultivated as a fodder crop in Prince Edward Island before 1850, and *M. alba* before 1888. In Canada the usefulness of sweet-clovers was gradually deemed less important. By 1906, Clark and Fletcher wrote in *Farm Weeds of Canada* that both species were "common wayside weeds — often complained of by farmers." In the early years of this century sweet-clovers regained favor as agents of soil reclamation on eroded slopes and for renovation of worn-out fields (Smith and Gorz 1965). In recent years the overall use of sweet-clover in North America has declined.

Without doubt, the recurring popularity of both white and yellow sweet-clover has been a major factor in their dispersal throughout the U.S.A. and Canada. Their dispersion has probably been hastened by bee-keepers (Heitlinger 1975).

7. Growth and Development

(a) Morphology — The flowering shoots of the second year arise from the overwintering portion of the crown and roots. Contractile roots pull the crown 5 cm or more below the soil surface in the fall, protecting it from severe winter conditions. The mature strong, deep tap root exceeds 120 cm in depth. It enables the species to withstand droughts and is also the food storage organ which aids winter survival and promotes rapid growth of flowering shoots in the spring (Martin 1934). Adventitious roots enlarge the root diameter to 30 or 40 cm and help keep the tall heavy plant upright in windy habitats.

W. Abrahamson (personal communication) compared the two species in terms of the percentage total biomass assigned to each part of the plant at the peak of flowering. In *Melilotus alba,* 10.5% was belowground structures, 57% stem, 10.5% leaves and 22% flowers, seeds and associated structures. In *M. officinalis,* 11% was belowground structures, 52% stem, 7% leaves and 30% flowers, seeds and associated structures.

(b) Perennation — Annual individuals overwinter as seeds and are therophytes. The biennials are hemicryptophytes and overwinter alternately as seeds and as thick tap roots with a crown and winter buds. Although fall seedlings have been observed (personal observation, unpublished data), very few survived the winter. Natural vegetative reproduction was not observed. *M. alba* is typically self-fertile but does not set seed unless the flowers are manipulated (Coe and Martin 1920). A few plants that have been clipped rigorously during the growing season have survived into a third growing season in London, Ontario, but plants always die after flowering (Cavers unpublished).

(c) Physiological data — Both species possess root nodules and have symbiotic relationships with *Rhizobium* bacteria. The highest nitrogen content is in vegetative plants in the late fall (Dunham 1933). Coumarin is characteristic of *Melilotus* plants and is concentrated in flower buds and fresh leaves from the tips of branches (2.5%, Linton et al. 1963). Roots, stems and mature leaves have very low levels.

Flower induction in biennial sweet-clovers is influenced by day length. When grown at 25.5°C day and 20°C night temperatures in a greenhouse, *M. alba* required at least a 17-h photoperiod for flowering (Wiggans 1953). Annual plants of *M. alba* flowered during photoperiods of 12–20 h. Kasperbauer et al. (1962) found that vernalization reduced the photoperiodic requirement. Smith (1942) reported that the height of *M. alba* and *M. officinalis* increased under longer days, and that low temperatures retarded flowering.

(d) Phenology — In Southern Ontario, seedlings can appear in any month of the year although there are pronounced peaks

of emergence in March–April and September–October. During the winter, seedlings of both species emerge whenever there is a thaw of 3 days or more. Winter seedlings appearing on gravel bars of the Thames River in February or March usually flowered the same year, whereas seedlings appearing in April or later remained vegetative and usually died over the following winter.

Smith and Graber (1948) described in detail the development of the biennial sweet-clover during the seedling year. After a few weeks, the primary stem becomes much branched and a prominent primary root develops. As the season progresses the crown develops. Top growth reaches a maximum in late summer when a rapid increase in the size of the roots begins and continues into the fall. As root size increases, crown buds develop, and there is a marked increase in the percentage of available carbohydrate. In the spring of the second year, the crown buds give rise to rapidly growing stems. Growth in the second year consists almost entirely of tops (Smith and Gorz 1965). Both *M. alba* and *M. officinalis* flower in June/July (Stevens and Long 1926) but the latter generally flowers a few weeks earlier than the former (Heitlinger 1975). In Southern Ontario, *M. officinalis* is usually in flower by the first week of June, *M. alba* by the last week of June. The first flowering date is more variable in the former species (late May to late June) and varies with the habitat (Rempel, unpublished). On later developing plants, flowers continue to appear until freezing weather in the fall. The progression of flowering in the racemes of *M. officinalis* is twice as rapid as in *M. alba*. Flowers remain in fresh condition for approximately 2 days (Stevens and Long 1926). In Ontario, seeds of *M. officinalis* are ripe by late July; the first ripe seeds of *M. alba* do not appear until early August (Rempel, unpublished). Seeds continue to ripen until the late autumn and many remain on the plant over the winter.

The annual and biennial forms are quite similar in growth habit in the early part of the seedling year. However, by midsummer the top growth of the biennial is much more decumbent than that of the annual and buds begin to appear on the crown. As the season progresses, growth is mainly in the tops in the annual and there is rapid development of the root and crown rhizomes in the biennial (Smith and Gorz 1965).

(e) Mycorrhiza — No mycorrhizal system has been found in either species.

8. Reproduction

(a) Floral biology — Kirk and Stevenson (1931b) pointed out that in *M. alba*, the close proximity of stigmas and anthers seems to facilitate self-pollination, but this does not always hold with *M. officinalis*. With *M. alba*, Clarke (1935) found that when pistil and stamens are of the same length, self-pollination readily takes place, but when the pistil is longer than the stamens, there is very little self-pollination. Brink (1934) has shown that self-incompatibility in *M. officinalis* is caused by a reduced rate of germination of a plant's own pollen on its stigma and the subsequent slow growth of the pollen tube. More recently, Barcikowska (1966) found that white sweet-clover, although cross-fertile, sometimes exhibits high self-fertility in both the annual and biennial forms, contrary to yellow sweet-clover which has little self-fertility. Gorz and Haskins (1971) recorded 67% cross-fertilization in annual *M. alba*.

Sweet-clover is highly attractive to honey bees. Although the honey bee is the most important pollinator, Bohart (cited in Smith and Gorz 1965) indicated that *M. officinalis* is attractive also to a number of bee species and halictids, and *M. alba* is attractive to a much wider array of insects, including many wasps and flies. Coe and Martin (1920) listed a wide variety of insects pollinating sweet-clover blossoms.

(b) Seed production and dispersal — Sweet-clover seed production is influenced

by many interacting factors, including weather and soil conditions, plant spacing, management practices, number of pollinating insects, variety of sweet-clover and the incidence of diseases and harmful insects (Smith and Gorz 1965). Both species usually produce one seed/fruit but sometimes two or three. Stevens (1932) quoted a weight of 2.0 g/1,000 seeds for *M. alba* and estimated 14,235 seeds/plant (with five stems). However, Coe (1917, in Heitlinger 1975) estimated 350,000 seeds/plant. In London, Ontario, plants of *M. alba* are generally 1/3 larger than those of *M. officinalis*. Large plants of *M. alba* growing in the open with little competition produced 200,000–350,000 seeds each. Large plants of *M. officinalis* seldom produced more than 100,000 seeds. Damaged plants, those in sterile ground, or those suffering intense competition may produce fewer than 100 seeds each (Rempel and Cavers, unpublished).

Sweet-clover seeds are readily dispersed with crop seeds as the Canadian Seed Regulations (Agriculture Canada 1967) attest. The large seeds can be blown over short distances (a few meters) by strong winds, but rain wash and stream flow are probably much more important for dispersal. In tests in 2 successive yr in London more than 2/3 of the seeds of *M. alba* remained floating after 15 min in violently agitated water. Propagules with the outer fruit layers attached will become attached to both wet and dry clothing (unpublished undergraduate experiments, University of Western Ontario).

(c) Viability of seeds and germination — A large proportion of well-ripened, mature seeds are "hard" i.e. temporarily impermeable to water at temperatures suitable for germination (Harrington 1916) and thus few freshly harvested seeds will germinate (Bashinov 1970). The impermeable layer is outermost on the seed coat (Smith and Gorz 1965). Fully developed seeds, collected before they are thoroughly dry, will be soft; as they lose moisture, they become hard and

may remain hard for many years. Helgeson (1932) concluded that impermeability in sweet-clover seeds is brought about by dehydration in the late stages of maturity. Immature seeds are practically all permeable and these may be induced to the impermeable state by storage in a dry place. In contrast, hardness may be prevented for at least 19 mo by storage in moist, cold conditions.

Stoa (1941, in Smith and Gorz 1965) noted that hard seeds of sweet-clover remained viable in the soil for more than 20 yr, and Munn (1954, in Smith and Gorz 1965) found that 17% of an original lot of hard seeds remained hard for almost 40 yr when stored in stoppered vials in a dry room, but 60% of them germinated when scarified. Stoa (1933) documented work in North Dakota where sweet-clover (species not mentioned) was allowed to mature in plots in 1918. In the following 14 years the plots were cultivated and cropped yearly. By 1932, the 11th distinct volunteer crop of sweet-clover appeared; all 11 crops were known to have come from the original 1918 seed. Stevens and Long (1926) estimated that scarification of seeds in both species resulted in an average loss of viability of 50%. Crocker (1938) cites several different records of seed longevity; *M. alba* 33% after 40 yr, 1.25% after 41 yr, 0.6% after 81 yr; *M. officinalis* 33% after 40 yr. Pel'men'ov (1972) recorded the lowest percentage germination and vigor in sweet-clover from freshly harvested seeds. Values increased with storage and were at a maximum after 9 yr.

Amongst the factors which affect the germination of sweet-clover are cold and alternating temperatures (McElgunn 1973; Dunn 1939; Busse 1930; Martin 1945; Knapp 1955), moisture (Smith 1975; Dunn 1939), coumarin (Stoker 1964), high hydrostatic pressure (Davies 1928) and seed color (Stevenson 1937; Svoboda 1969 (unpublished undergraduate thesis, Univ. of Western Ontario)).

(d) Vegetative reproduction — No vegetative reproduction has been observed to occur naturally but it may be induced artificially using a commercial rooting hormone (Rempel, unpublished data).

9. Hybrids

Natural interspecific hybrids in *Melilotus* are rare. Most reports of natural hybrids are subject to doubt (Stevenson 1969). Practically all sweet-clovers in cultivation are varieties and not hybrids.

Artificially produced interspecific hybrids have been reported by numerous authors (Greenshields 1954; Kirk 1929, 1931a; Smith 1954; Smith and Gorz 1965; Stevenson and Kirk 1935; Webster 1955).

10. Population Dynamics

Most of the following observations have been made in or near London, Ontario by P. B. Cavers.

Seedlings of both species can appear in any month of the year, but the major flush of germination occurs in March or early April with a second smaller flush possible in late September, October or November. The timing of seedling emergence is most important, since almost all seedlings appearing in late summer, autumn and early winter die before spring. Many seedlings appearing in late winter also perish but occasional groups survive and give rise to plants which flower during the same year. In contrast, seedlings appearing from late March to early May have the best chance of survival but invariably are biennial.

Seedlings in fertile loam or clay often arise in clumps. The majority die, presumably from lack of light, during the period of rapid growth of neighboring plants. In a greenhouse experiment utilizing constant densities of 600 plants/m², more than 75% of the plants started from seedlings became moribund or dead within a 5-mo period. Approximately 30 plants survived and grew in each square meter.

In gravelly, sandy or stony ground, flowering plants are often large and widely spaced; seldom more than 1 or 2/m².

Seedling mortality is always high, with less than 5% of emergent seedlings surviving for more than 4 mo. Late summer counts on sandy or gravelly locations revealed densities of 50–125 plants/m² of non-flowering plants. The vast majority of these plants died before the following spring.

In sites such as steep, eroded banks and frequently disturbed ground, few seedlings emerge and subsequent mortality is much lower. Widely spaced plants are often large with many flowering racemes.

Mowing of roadsides or waste areas usually favors populations of *M. alba* and *M. officinalis*. Individual non-flowering plants have a better chance of survival.

At the seedling or early vegetative stages, neither species is a good competitor with vigorous plants of other species. As a result, plants of sweet-clover are restricted to disturbed, ploughed or eroded ground. Second-year plants do grow rapidly in the spring and can compete effectively with newly arising weeds. Dunham (1933) found that weeds were a severe problem in pure stands of sweet-clover; a wheat companion crop tended to alleviate this problem.

In Southern Ontario in sites where both species are persistent, they often flower in alternate years.

11. Response to Herbicides and Other Chemicals

Sweet-clover is extremely susceptible to injury from the widely used phenoxy-type herbicides such as 2,4-D at 0.42 kg/ha (Greenshields and White 1954), MCPA, MCPB, 2,4-DB, 2,4-DP etc., and to dicamba (Banvel-D) (R. Brown, personal communication). If sweet-clover is allowed to persist until its 2nd yr, it is more difficult to kill with 2,4-D (Greenshields 1957). Aflon (linuron 50%) at 5 kg/ha controlled *M. alba* in wheat crops (Ahmad 1969). Residues from Tordon (picloram) at 5.6 ℓ/ha prevented establishment of sweet-clover (Alley 1967; Byrd and Nyman 1966) and *M. alba* was killed with neburon or dalapon (7.5-10 kg/ha) (Gimesi 1969). Ozone

(0.15 ppm) has been shown to damage *M. alba* (Brennan et al. 1969).

12. Response to Other Human Manipulations

Burning aids in the establishment of sweet-clover in grassland (Graber 1927). Heitlinger (1975) reported that (1) a fire in early May was followed by an increased number of 1st-yr sweet-clover plants but a decreased number of 2nd-yr plants, (2) a fire in early June decreased the number of both 1st and 2nd-year sweet-clover plants and (3) an early fall burn between the 1st and 2nd yr of sweet-clover growth increased winter mortality and decreased the vitality of 2nd-yr plants.

M. alba cut the same year as it was seeded had a reduced yield in its 2nd yr and was less competitive with weeds, although a greater yield was obtained from plants cut both 1st and 2nd yr. Second-year plants cut at the "pre-bud" stage made a more vigorous recovery than those cut later; also, plants cut at a height of 30 cm were damaged less than those cut at 15 cm (Garber et al. 1934).

The removal of tops just previous to or at the beginning of the special growth period of roots and crowns (late August or early September) inhibited subsequent growth and was followed by low winter resistance and by poor growth of surviving plants in the second season. On the other hand, the removal of tops after the special growth period was over (any time after September) had little or no detrimental effect (Martin 1934).

Both species can be eliminated from an area within 2 yr if the ground surface is covered by perennial species. Seedlings of sweet-clover cannot survive in a perennial sward. However, Stoa (1933) demonstrated that seeds can remain viable in the soil for at least 20 yr to perpetuate a population.

13. Parasites

A comprehensive treatment of this subject is presented by Smith and Gorz (1965) and Conners (1967).

The following insects are common on sweet-clover in London, Ontario: *Coccinella trifasciata* L., *Philaenus leucophthalamus* (Fall), *Tetrastichus* sp., *Adelphocris lineolatus* (Goeze), *Sphaerophoria* sp., *Ctenucha virginica* Charpentier, *Artylone (delaware) logan* Edwards and *Chauliognathus pennsylvanicus* (De Geer) (E. Rempel, unpublished).

On Griffith Island in Georgian Bay near Owen Sound, Ontario, white-tailed deer were observed to graze intensively on both *M. alba* and *M. officinalis*. Flowering specimens of each species were restricted to a large, deer-proof enclosure and the interior of pheasant pens (Cavers, unpublished).

ACKNOWLEDGMENTS

The authors are grateful for financial assistance from Agriculture Canada (Contract Grant arranged through G. A. Mulligan). We thank Anita Payne for drawing the figures and Muriel Heagy for preparing the maps. The assistance of scientists across Canada in supplying us with herbarium records is gratefully acknowledged. In particular, we appreciate the assistance of Madeleine Dumais from the University of Alberta. Insect identification by Murray Maw, Peter Harris and John George was most helpful.

ADAMSON, R. S. and SALTER, T. M. 1950. Flora of the Cape Peninsula. Juta, Cape Town. 889 pp.

AGRICULTURE CANADA. 1967. Seeds Act and Regulations. Queen's Printer, Ottawa, Ont. 50 pp.

AHMAD, M. 1969. Studies on the pre-emergence treatment of the weedicide Afalon on weeds in wheat. West Pak. J. Agric. Res. **7**: 8–12.

ALLEY, H. P. 1967. Crop tolerance to Tordon and Banvel-D tested. Crops Soils **20**: 24–25.

ASHFORD, R. and BOLTON, J. L. 1961. Effects of sulphur and nitrogen fertilization, and inoculation with *Rhizobium meliloti* on the growth of sweet clover (*Melilotus alba* Desr.). Can. J. Plant Sci. **41**: 81–90.

ATWOOD, S. 1936. Tetraploid and aneuploid *Melilotus alba* resulting from heat treatment. Amer. J. Bot. **23**: 674–677.

BALDWIN, W. K. W. 1958. Plants of the clay belt of Northern Ontario and Quebec. Natl. Mus. Can. Bull. 156. 324 pp.

BANÁSOVÁ, V. 1970. Vegetation of Dobšiná asbestos heaps. Biologia (Bratisl.) **25**: 699–708.

BARCIKOWSKA, B. 1966. Self fertility and inbreeding depressions in white and yellow sweet clover (*Melilotus albus* Desr. and *M. officinalis* (L.) Desr.). Genet. Pol. **7**: 1–11.

BASHINOV, M. N. 1970. Seed germination of sweet clover and lucerne. Tr. Buriat. S-KH. Opytn. Stn. **5**: 138–144.

BRENNAN, E., LEONE, I. A. and HALISKY, P. M. 1969. Response of forage legumes to ozone fumigations. Phytopathology **59**: 1458–1459.

BRINK, R. A. 1934. Self-incompatibility in yellow sweet-clover, *Melilotus officinalis*. J. Amer. Soc. Agron. **26**: 307–312.

BURBIDGE, N. T. and GRAY, M. 1970. Flora of the Australian Capital Territory. Australian National University Press, Canberra. 447 pp.

BUSSE, W. F. 1930. Effect of low temperatures on germination of impermeable seeds. Bot. Gaz. **89**: 169–179.

BUTOVSSII, B. G. 1971. Biological characteristics of *Lotus corniculatus* and *Melilotus alba* grown in the Sakhalin region. Tr. Sakhalinskii KompleksnoiNauchno-Issledovatel'skii Inst. **23**: 124–130.

BYRD, B. C. and NYMAN, F. A. 1966. Progress report on highway vegetation control experiments using Tordon 101 mixture and Norbak particulating agent. Down Earth **22**: 28–31.

CALDER, J. A. and TAYLOR, ROY L. 1968. Flora of the Queen Charlotte Islands. Part I. Systematics of the vascular plants. Queen's Printer, Ottawa, Ont. 659 pp.

CANADA WEED COMMITTEE. 1969. Common and botanical names of weeds in Canada. Can. Dep. Agric. Publ. 1397, Ottawa, Ont. 67 pp.

CLAPHAM, A. R., TUTIN, T. G. and WARBURG, E. F. 1962. Flora of the British Isles. Cambridge University Press. 1269 pp.

CLARK, G. H. and FLETCHER, J. 1906. Farm weeds of Canada. Canada Department of Agriculture, Ottawa, Ont. 103 pp.

CLARKE, A. E. 1935. Inheritance of annual habit and mode of pollination in an annual white sweet clover. J. Amer. Soc. Agron. **27**: 492–496.

COE, H. S. and MARTIN, J. N. 1920. Sweet-clover seed. U.S. Dep. of Agric. Bull. **844**. pt. 2.

CONNERS, I. L. 1967. An annotated index of plant diseases in Canada and fungi recorded on plants in Alaska, Canada and Greenland. Can. Dep. Agric. Publ. 1251. Ottawa, Ont. 381 pp.

CROCKER, W. 1938. Life-span of seeds. Bot. Rev. **4**: 235–274.

DARLINGTON, C. D. and WYLIE, A. P. 1955. Chromosome atlas of flowering plants. Allen and Unwin, London, England. 519 pp.

DAVIES, P. A. 1928. High pressure and seed germination. Amer. J. Bot. **15**: 149–156.

DUNHAM, R. S. 1933. Effect of method of sowing on the yield and root and top development of sweetclover in the Red River Valley. J. Agric. Res. **47**(12): 979–995.

DUNN, L. E. 1939. Influence of low temperature treatments on the germination of seeds of sweet clover and smooth vetch. J. Amer. Soc. Agron. **31**: 687–694.

ERSKINE, D. S. 1960. Plants of Prince Edward Island. Can. Dep. Agric. Publ. 1088. 270 pp.

FERRON, M. et CAYOUETTE, R. 1971. Noms des mauvaises herbes du Québec. 2e éd. Min. Agric. Colonisation, Québec, Que. 113 pp.

FOWLDS, M. 1939. Seed color studies in biennial white sweet clover, *Melilotus alba*. J. Amer. Soc. Agron. **31**: 678–686.

FRYER, J. R. 1930. Cytological studies in *Medicago, Melilotus* and *Trigonella*. Can. J. Res. **3**: 3–50.

GARBER, R. J., HOOVER, M. M. and BENNETT, L. S. 1934. The effect upon yield of cutting sweet clover (*Melilotus alba*) at different times and at different heights. J. Amer. Soc. Agron. **26**: 974–977.

GILMORE, M. R. 1931. Plant vagrants in America. Mich. Acad. Sci. Arts Letters **15**: 65–79.

GIMESI, A. 1969. New experience in the chemical weeding and defoliation of lucerne. Ochr. Rost. **5**: 31–38.

GLEASON, H. A. 1963. The new Britton and Brown illustrated flora of the Northeastern United States and adjacent Canada. Vol. 2. Hafner Publ. Co. Inc., New York, N.Y.

GOPLEN, B. P. 1962. A recessive gene with major pleiotropic effects in sweetclover, *Melilotus alba* L. Can. J. Genet. Cytol. **4**: 141–146.

GORZ, H. J. and HASKINS, F. A. 1971. Cross-fertilization in *Melitotus alba*. Crop Sci. **11**: 767–768.

345

GRABER, L. F. 1927. Improvement of permanent bluegrass pasture with sweet clover. J. Amer. Soc. Agron. **19**: 994–1006.

GREENSHIELDS, J. E. R. 1954. Embryology of interspecific crosses in *Melilotus*. Can. J. Bot. **32**: 447–465.

GREENSHIELDS, J. E. R. 1957. Sweet clover in Western Canada. Can Dep. of Agric. Publ. 998, Ottawa, Ont. 14 pp.

GREENSHIELDS, J. E. R. and WHITE, W. J. 1954. The effects of 2,4-D spray drift on sweet clover plants in the second year of growth. Can. J. Agric. Sci. **34**: 389–392.

HANEY, A., CARLSON, J. A. and ROLFE, G. L. 1974. Lead contamination of soils and plants along highway gradients in east central-Illinois. Tran. Ill. State Acad. Sci. **67**: 323–335.

HARRINGTON, G. T. 1916. Agricultural value of impermeable seeds. J. Agric. Res. **6**: 761–796.

HASKINS, F. A. and GORZ, H. J. 1975. Influence of seed size, planting depth, and companion crop on emergence and vigor of seedlings in sweetclover. Agron. J. **67**(5): 652–654.

HEITLINGER, M. E. 1975. Burning a protected tallgrass prairie to suppress sweetclover, *Melilotus alba* Desr. Pages 123–132 *in* M. K. Wali, ed. Prairie: a multiple view, Conference, Grand Forks, N.D.

HELGESON, E. A. 1932. Impermeability in mature and immature sweet clover seeds as affected by conditions of storage. Trans. Wisc. Acad. Sci. Arts Letters **27**: 193–206.

HOFFMAN, D. M. 1973. Pheasant nest site selection. Colo. Div. Wildl. Spec. Rep. **32**: 1–27.

HOLLIDAY, R., HODGSON, D. R., TOWNSEND, W. N. and WOOD, J. W. 1958. Plant growth on 'Fly Ash'. Nature **181**: 1079–1080.

KASPERBAUER, M. J., GARDNER, F. P. and LOOMIS, W. E. 1962. Interaction of photoperiod and vernalization in flowering of sweet clover (*Melilotus*). Plant Physiol. **37**: 165–170.

KIRK, L. E. 1924. Aberrant forms in Arctic sweet clover. Sci. Agric. **5**: 113–116.

KIRK, L. E. 1929. Natural crossing between white flowered and yellow flowered sweet clover. Sci. Agric. **9**: 313–315.

KIRK, L. E. 1931a. Inheritance of dwarf branching habit in a new variety of sweet clover and its potential economic value in breeding. Sci. Agric. **11**: 315–325.

KIRK, L. E. 1931b. Sweet clover and soil improvement. Univ. of Saskatchewan Agric. Leafl. (Mimeographed).

KIRK, L. E. and ARMSTRONG, J. M. 1934. A single factor mutation in *Melilotus alba* Desr. having multiple effects on homologous structures. Can. J. Res. **10**: 787–792.

KIRK, L. E. and STEVENSON, T. 1931a. Seed colour markings in white flowered sweet clover *Melilotus alba* Desr. Sci. Agric. **11**: 607–611.

KIRK, L. E. and STEVENSON, T. M. 1931b. Factors which influence spontaneous self-fertilization in sweet clover (*Melilotus*). Can. J. Res. **5**: 313–326.

KNAPP, R. 1955. Über den Verlauf der Keimung von einigen Gräsern, Leguminosen und *Iberia amara* bei unterschiedlichen Temperaturen. Angew. Bot. **29**: 125–138.

LAVADO, R. S. and NELLA, J. C. 1972. Modifications to a saline–alkaline soil after 2 years of cropping with forage species. Idia **291**: 77–80.

LINTON, J. H., GOPLEN, B. P. BELL, J. M. and JAQUES, L. B. 1963. Dicoumarol studies. II. The prothrombin time response of sheep to various levels of contamination in low coumarin sweetclover varieties. Can. J. Anim. Sci. **43**: 353–360.

MARIE-VICTORIN, F. 1964. Flore laurentienne, 2nd éd. revue par E. Rouleau. Les presses de l'Université de Montréal, Montréal, Qué. 924 pp.

MARIE-VICTORIN, F. and ROLLAND-GERMAIN, F. 1969. Flore de l'Anticosti-Minganie. Les Presses de l'Université de Montréal, Montréal, Qué. 527 pp.

MARTIN, J. N. 1934. The relative growth rates and interdependence of tops and roots of the biennial white sweet clover, *Melilotus alba* Desr. Amer. J. Bot. **21**: 140–159.

MARTIN, J. N. 1945. Germination studies of sweet clover seed. Iowa State Coll. J. Sci. **19**: 289–300.

MULLIGAN, G. A. 1957. Chromosome numbers of Canadian weeds. I. Can. J. Bot. **35**: 779–789.

MULLIGAN, G. A. 1976. Common weeds of Canada. McClelland and Stewart, Toronto, Ont. 140 pp.

McARTHUR, J. M. and MILTIMORE, J. E. 1969. Bloat investigations. Studies on soluble proteins and nucleic acids in bloating and non-bloating forages. Can. J. Anim. Sci. **49**: 69–75.

McELGUNN, J. D. 1973. Germination response

of forage legumes to constant and alternating temperatures. Can. J. Plant. Sci. **53**: 797–800.

PARKER, J. S. 1971. The flight and foraging behaviour of the alkali bee (*Nomia melanderi* (Ckll.)) and the alfalfa leaf cutter bee (*Megachile rotundata* (F.)). Ph.D. Thesis, University of Utah. (Disser. Abstr. Int. B. **32**: 3988–3989).

PEL'MEN'OV, E. K. 1972. Biology of seed germination in sweet clover. Bdzhil'nitsvo. Resp. Mizvid. Temat. Nauk. Zb. **8**: 44–48.

PIRZADA, M. H. and RAJPUT, M. J. 1969. Association of weed seeds with field crop seeds. I. Wheat. West Pak. Agric. Res. **7**: 1–7.

POLUNIN, N. 1959. Circumpolar arctic flora. Oxford Press. 514 pp.

RAMAKRISHNAN, P. S. 1968a. Nutritional requirements of the edaphic ecotypes in *Melilotus alba* Medic. I. pH, calcium and phosphorus. New Phytol. **67**: 145–157.

RAMAKRISHNAN, P. S. 1968b. Nutritional requirements of the edaphic ecotypes in *Melilotus alba* Medic. II. Aluminium and manganese. New Phytol. **67**: 301–308.

RAMAKRISHNAN, P. S. 1970. Nutritional requirements of the edaphic ecotypes in *Melilotus alba* Medic. III. Interference between the calcareous and acidic populations in the two soil types. New Phytol. **69**: 81–86.

ROBINSON, D. H. 1949. Leguminous forage plants. 2nd ed. Arnold and Co., London, England.

ROBINSON, R. G. 1968. Management of land diverted from crop production. I. Perennial forages. Agron. J. **60**: 619–622.

ROLAND, A. E. and SMITH, E. C. 1969. The flora of Nova Scotia. Proc. Nova Scotian Institute of Science **26**(2): 3–238 and **26**(4): 277–743.

ROUSSEAU, C. 1968. Histoire, habitat et distribution de 220 plantes introduites au Québec. Natur. Can. **95**: 49–171.

SCHULZ, O. E. 1901. Monographie der Gattung *Melilotus*. Bot. Jahrb. **29**: 660–753.

SCOGGAN, H. J. 1957. Flora of Manitoba. Nat. Museum of Canada Bull. 140, Biol. Ser. 47. 619 pp.

SERAYA, G. P. and KOMOV, S. V. 1971. Seed growth and shoot formation in flowering plants on coal ash. Ekologiya **2**: 91–93.

SHESTAKOV, I. L. and VLADIMIROV, P. M. 1973. Salt tolerance of cultivated plants and kinetics of uptake of ash elements during the reclamation of saline soils in Moldavia. Voprosy soleustoichivosti rastenii. Tashkent, Uzbek SSR, 'Fan'. pp. 279–284.

SMITH, D. 1975. Forage management in the North. Wm. C. Brown Book Co., Dubuque, Iowa.

SMITH, D. and GRABER, L. F. 1948. The influence of top growth removal on the root and vegetative development of biennial sweet clover. J. Amer. Soc. Agron. **40**: 818–831.

SMITH, T. J. 1942. Responses of biennial sweet clover to moisture, temperature, and length of day. J. Amer. Soc. Agron. **34**: 865–876.

SMITH, W. K. 1954. Viability of interspecific hybrids in *Melilotus*. Genetics **39**: 266–279.

SMITH, W. K. and GORZ, H. J. 1965. Sweetclover improvement. Adv. Agron. **17**: 163–231.

STEVENS, O. A. 1932. The number and weight of seeds produced by weeds. Amer. J. Bot. **19**: 784–794.

STEVENS, O. A. and LONG, H. D. 1926. Sweet clover seed studies. North Dakota Agric. Exp. Sta. Bull. 197. 20 pp.

STEVENSON, G. A. 1969. An agronomic and taxonomic review of the genus *Melilotus* Mill. Can. J. Plant Sci. **49**: 1–20.

STEVENSON, T. M. 1937. Sweet clover studies on habit of growth, seed pigmentation and permeability of the seed coat. Sci. Agric. **17**: 627–654.

STEVENSON, T. M. and KIRK, L. E. 1935. Studies in interspecific crossing with *Melilotus*, and intergeneric crossing with *Melilotus*, *Medicago* and *Trigonella*. Sci. Agric. **15**: 580–589.

STOA, T. E. 1933. Persistence of viability of sweet clover seed in a cultivated soil. J. Amer. Soc. Agron. **25**: 177–181.

STOKER, J. R. 1964. The germination of seeds of *Melilotus alba*. Can. J. Biochem. **42**: 851–857.

SWENSON, S. P. 1942. Inheritance of seed color in biennial white sweet clover, *Melilotus alba*. J. Amer. Soc. Agron. **34**: 452–459.

WEBSTER, G. T. 1955. Interspecific hybridization of *Melilotus alba* × *M. officinalis* using embryo culture. Agron. J. **47**: 138–142.

WIGGANS, S. C. 1953. The relationship of photoperiod to growth and flowering of *Melilotus* species. Proc. Iowa Acad. Sci. **60**: 278–284.

YORK, G. W. and L. H. PAMMEL. 1919. Sweet clover a weed. Amer. Bee J. **59**: 412–413.

THE BIOLOGY OF CANADIAN WEEDS
30. *Pyrus melanocarpa* (Michx.) Willd.

IVAN V. HALL[1], GEORGE W. WOOD[2], and LLOYD P. JACKSON[3]

[1]*Researc'. Station, Agriculture Canada, Kentville, Nova Scotia B4N 1J5,* [2]*Research Station, Agriculture Canada, Fredericton, New Brunswick E2B 4Z7,* and [3]*Experimental Farm, Agriculture Canada, Nappan, N.S. B0L 1C0. Received 30 Nov. 1977, accepted 18 Jan. 1978.*

HALL, IVAN V., WOOD, GEORGE W. AND JACKSON, LLOYD P. 1978. The biology of Canadian weeds. 30. *Pyrus melanocarpa* (Michx.) Willd. Can. J. Plant Sci. **58**: 499–504.

Pyrus melanocarpa (Michx.) Willd., black chokeberry (Rosaceae) is a native shrub occurring from Newfoundland to the head of Lake Superior in Ontario. It tolerates a wide variety of substrates but in all of its habitats there is a high incidence of sunlight. It is a major weed problem of lowbush blueberry (*Vaccinium angustifolium* Ait. and *V. myrtilloides* Michx.) fields, especially following the application of fertilizer.

Pyrus melanocarpa (Michx.) Willd., cerisier à grappes (Rosaceae), est un arbuste indigène qu'on rencontre de Terre-Neuve à la tête du lac Supérieur en Ontario. Il s'adapte à un vaste éventail de substrats pour autant qu'ils soient fortement éclairés. C'est un parasite sérieux des plantations de bleuets (*Vaccinium angustifolium* Ait. et *V. myrtilloides* Michx.), surtout après l'épandage d'engrais.

1. Name

Pyrus melanocarpa (Michx.) Willd. (*Aronia melanocarpa* (Michx.) Ell., *Aronia nigra* (Sarg.) Koehne and *Sorbus melanocarpa* (Michx.) Heynh.) — **black chokeberry** (Canada Weed Committee 1969), chokepear, barrenberry; **gueules noires.** Rosaceae, rose family, Rosacées.

2. Description and Account of Variation

A slender woody shrub up to 1 m in height; new shoots arising from the rhizome; new shoot-growth (Fig. 1A) pubescent with the pubescence diminishing on the older growth; leaves glabrous above, pubescent below, especially on the veins, alternate, simple, serrate–glandular, oblanceolate, acute at both apex and base, the upper surface pale green with a row of brownish-black glands (Fig. 1C) along the mid vein, the lower surface greyish-white in color; flowers (Fig. 1B) in cymes, sepals 5 green, petals 5 white, stamens numerous, pistil 1; fruit about 1 cm in diameter, black, containing several bony seeds (Fig. 1D).

Although Darlington and Wylie (1955) reported a chromosome number of $2n = 34$,

a check of the article cited by them (Moffett 1931) did not show a count for this species. In Canada a specimen collected on 5 Aug. 1953 from a boggy marsh near McGowan Lake, 3.2 km east of Maberly, Lanark Co., Ontario by W. G. Dore (Dore 14521 (DAO)) had a chromosome count of $2n = 34$ (det. R. Moore).

Pyrus melanocarpa resembles closely *P. arbutifolia* (L.) L. f. and *P. floribunda* Lindl. *P. arbutifolia* has red fruit whereas the other two species are dark-fruited. *P. melanocarpa* is less hairy on the leaves, pedicels and fruit than the other two species.

3. Economic Importance

(a) Detrimental — Prior to the use of commercial fertilizer on stands of lowbush blueberries (*Vaccinium angustifolium* Ait. and *V. myrtilloides* Michx.), the competition offered by scattered shoots of *P. melanocarpa* was of minor importance. The use of a fertilizer causes a marked increase in the vigor and number of shoots per unit area of this species.

Fernald and Kinsey (1943) stated that the fruit of *P. melanocarpa* with its deep color and high pectin content made an acceptable jam. However, taste panelists at the University of Maine (Murphy et al. 1974) preferred lowbush blueberry products without impurities of *P. melanocarpa* and *P. floribunda*. In raw berries 10% by number of black chokeberry impurity imparted a detectable undesirable flavor, in sauce 9%, and in muffins 17%.

(b) Beneficial — Martin et al. (1951) reported that the fruits of *P. melanocarpa* were of minor importance to wildlife: the chickadee and the cedar waxwing ate the fruit and the ruffed grouse ate both the fruit and buds.

E. Karmo (personal communication 14 June 1977) found that wild bees, *Andrena* and *Halictus* species, worked *Pyrus* spp. in lowbush blueberry fields for both pollen and nectar, whereas the honeybee, *Apis mellifera* L., gathered mostly pollen from the same species.

(c) Legislation — *Pyrus melanocarpa* is not listed in any Canadian federal or provincial weed or seeds act.

4. Geographical Distribution

The range of *P. melanocarpa* extends from Newfoundland in the east to Northern Ontario in the central part of Canada (Fig. 2). Fernald (1950) stated that it occurs as far south as South Carolina and Tennessee.

5. Habitat

(a) Climatic requirements — A study of the distribution of *P. melanocarpa* (Fig. 2) using maps of soil temperature (produced by the Department of Energy, Mines and Resources 1973) revealed that this species occurred in the "mild mesic", "moderately cool boreal", and the "cool boreal areas". With regard to soil moisture, the species is located in the "perhumid area" with no significant water deficit or within the "humid" which has a slight water deficit. Most of the area where *P. melanocarpa*

occurs receives 100 cm of rainfall annually. Average daily minimum temperatures for February do not exceed −20°C. Since *P. melanocarpa* frequently occurs at the edges of salt marshes in the Maritime Provinces, it must have considerable resistance to salt spray.

(b) Substratum — The two most common soil types on which *P. melanocarpa* occurs in Canada are the Humo-Ferric Podzol and the Grey Brown Luvisol (Clayton et al. 1977).

(c) Communities in which the species occurs — *Pyrus melanocarpa* grows in several habitats including the heads of salt marshes, meadows, bogs, edges of lakes, and barrens, all of which have a high incidence of sunlight during the growing season. The burning of woodland or abandoned hayfields for lowbush blueberry production gives rise to a habitat where black chokeberry also grows and fruits exceptionally well.

6. History

Macoun (1883) in discussing *Pirus arbutifolia* var. *melanocarpa* stated that var. *melanocarpa* was far less common in Nova Scotia than *P. arbutifolia*, whereas in New Brunswick and Ontario *melanocarpa* was the more common taxon.

Pyrus melanocarpa is an indigenous species that has persisted in certain habitats such as peat bogs and exposed headlands.

7. Growth and Development

(a) Morphology — The rhizome is an important organ in the survival of this species with new shoots arising from buds located on this organ.

(b) Perennation — *Pyrus melanocarpa* passes the winter as a dormant, woody shrub (Fig. 1A). The berry-like fruits persist until late fall or early winter. At Nappan, Cumberland Co., N.S., fruits were collected as late as 29 Nov. 1976.

Fig. 1A. Dormant shoot of *P. melanocarpa* showing flower buds at distal end. B. Flower showing five petals and several stamens. C. Glands on the midrib of the leaf (10×) and a typical leaf below. D. Seeds (10×).

350

(c) Physiological data — Small (1972a) reported nutrient element data for several plants growing in Mer Bleue Bog and adjacent fields near Ottawa, Ontario. The mean content of N, P and K on a leaf dry weight basis for this species was found to be 1.74, 0.139 and 1.06%, respectively. Bog species including *P. melanocarpa,* had relatively low concentrations of Al and Mn in the leaves in spite of the large concentrations available (Small 1972b). The leaf resistance and water potential of *P. melanocarpa* is as high as or greater than most species of bog or neighboring plants studied by this same author (1972c).

A 200-g sample of fruit of *P. melanocarpa* analyzed on 26 Aug. 1977 by the Food Processing Section of the Kentville Research Station had 15.5% soluble solids measured by refractometer and the titratable acidity was 0.70% expressed as citric acid.

(d) Phenology — *P. melanocarpa* flowered in the Maritime Provinces during the first 3 wk of June and the fruits matured during the latter 2 wk of August. In 1977, *P. melanocarpa* was in bloom at Nappan, Cumberland Co., Nova Scotia from 6 to 14 June. The fruit began to turn red on 4 Aug. and by 19 Aug., 50% of the fruit were red and 50% were black. Rhizome growth commenced about the same time as vegetative growth. A piece of rhizome excavated on 9 June 1977 at Aylesford, Kings Co., N.S. had 20 cm of new growth on that date.

(e) Mycorrhiza — Information on presence or absence of mycorrhiza is lacking.

8. Reproduction

(a) Floral biology — Flowers of *P. melanocarpa* are insect-pollinated. Small (1976) found that flowering of *P. melanocarpa* occurred from about 31 May to nearly 20 June at the Mer Bleue peat bog near Ottawa. Although a preponderance of bog species were in bloom during this period, *P. melanocarpa* received 8.3% of the total number of insects. Insects that visited *P. melanocarpa* were 1 species of Lepidoptera, 1 Coleoptera, 28 Diptera and 16 Hymenoptera. In Charlotte Co., New Brunswick, during 1977, *P. melanocarpa*

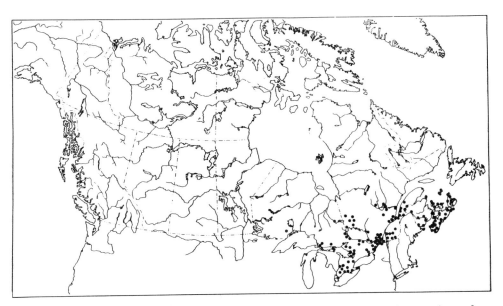

Fig. 2.   Canadian distribution of black chokeberry, *Pyrus melanocarpa,* based on specimens from the herbaria of Department of Agriculture Herbarium, Ottawa, Ontario; National Museum of Canada, Ottawa, Ontario; and Acadia University, Wolfville, Nova Scotia.

was more attractive to solitary bees than *V. angustifolium* when the bloom of the two species overlapped to some extent. The following list of Andrenidae and Halictidae were found pollinating *P. melanocarpa* on 1 June 1977 at Tower Hill, Charlotte Co., N.B.: *Andrena carlini carlini* Ck., *A. crataegi* Robt., *A. wheeleri* Groen., *A. miserabilis* Cr., *A. thaspii* Groen., *Andrena* sp. *Lasioglossum cressone* Robt., *Lasioglossum* spp.

In a greenhouse trial at Kentville, Kings Co., N.S. flowers of *P. melanocarpa* were found to be nearly self-sterile as evidenced by only 1 out of 31 self-pollinated flowers setting fruit, whereas 12 out of 15 cross-pollinated flowers were successful. Flowers were pollinated on 5 May and the fruit reached maturity on 20 July 1977.

(b) Seed production and dispersal — The mean fruit weight of *P. melanocarpa* based on 50 observations from a population sampled on 25 Aug. 1977 at Aylesford, Kings Co., N.S. was 0.269 g ± SE 0.010. The mean number of seeds from the above fruit was 7.96 ± SE 0.185. The correlation coefficient of 0.22 between fruit weight and seed number was not significant. A sample of 60 seeds weighed 0.15 g.

(c) Viability of seeds and germination — The Forest Service of the U.S. Department of Agriculture (1948) reported that commercial seed had a purity of 82% and a soundness of 95%. To promote germination of seed they recommended 90 or more days at 5°C in moist sand as a pretreatment. A potential germination of 45–58% was given. Seed germination tests conducted at Kentville are in agreement with the above findings. Seeds extracted from ripe berries on 27 Sept. and sown immediately on soil failed to germinate by 29 Dec. 1977. Seeds extracted from the same sample of fruit but held for 65 days in a refrigerator at 2°C before extraction and planting on 1 Dec. germinated 33% (18, 15, 17 germinated in three samples of 50 seeds) by 29 Dec. 1977. Environmental conditions for germination tests were 21°C during the 16-h light period and 18°C during the 8-h dark period of each 24-h period.

(d) Vegetative reproduction — For horticultural purposes, propagate *P. melanocarpa* by suckers, layers or cuttings of greenwood in the greenhouse (Hortus Third 1976).

9. Hybrids

According to Rehder (1956) X *Sorbaronia sorbifolia* (Poir.) Schneid. is the hybrid *Aronia melanocarpa* × *Sorbus americana.* X *Sorbaronia fallax* Schneid. similarly is *Aronia melanocarpa* × *Sorbus aucuparia,* and X *Sorbaronia dippelii* (Zab.) Schneid. is a combination of *Aronia melanocarpa* and *Sorbus aria.* All of these hybrids are cultivated but do not grow naturally in Canada.

10. Population Dynamics

Pyrus melanocarpa establishes itself from seed. The rapidity with which it spreads in open habitats depends to a large degree on the fertility of the soil. In several locations where we have noted *P. melanocarpa*, it appeared that the area of germination and seedling establishment had never been plowed. Once established in such places as the edges of rock piles or poorly drained areas it grew rapidly into adjoining areas.

11. Response to Herbicides and Other Chemicals

Trevett (1952) reported that *P. melanocarpa* was moderately resistant to 2,4-D.

Recently, the means of combatting *P. melanocarpa* in Maine has changed to promoting early abscission of the fruit rather than attempting to kill the plant. Trevett and Durgin (1972) found that an application of 2.2 kg/ha of 2-chloroethylphosphonic acid (ethephon) applied about 1 wk after 100% petal fall gave a 96% reduction in number of fruit. In a subsequent study, Ismail (1974) provided further data that ethephon at three different rates effectively reduced yields of *P. melanocarpa* without affecting the yield and quality of *V. angustifolium.*

12. Response to Other Human Manipulations

Typical shoot length, diameter at base of shoot, fresh weight, and dry weight of 100 stems 1 yr after burning are respectively. 30.4 cm ± SE 0.5; 0.3 mm ± SE 0.0; 317.5 g; 136.0 g (60 h at 80°C). Data were taken on 19 Aug. 1977 at Nappan, Cumberland Co., Nova Scotia.

13. Response to Parasites

Conners (1967) reports the following fungi on *Aronia melanocarpa* (*P. melanocarpa*): *Gymnosporangium clavipes* (Cke. & Pk.) Cke. & Pk., *Isariopsis* sp., and *Podosphaera clandestina* (Wallr. ex Fr.) Lev. He also states that this species was shown to be susceptible to fire blight, *Erwinia amylovora* (Burr.) Winsl. et al., by artificial inoculation.

Several lowbush blueberry fields in New Brunswick were surveyed during the summer of 1977 and no defoliating insects were found on *P. melanocarpa*. Berries of this species were also examined and no maggots or fruit worms were found.

ACKNOWLEDGMENTS

We wish to thank D. R. Blenkhorn, A. C. Brydon, L. C. Coldwell, S. J. Conrad and A. T. Lightfoot for technical assistance. The loan of specimens from the herbaria listed in Fig. 2 is gratefully acknowledged.

CANADA WEED COMMITTEE. 1969. Common and botanical names of weeds in Canada. Can. Dep. Agric. Publ. 1397. p. 5.

CLAYTON, J. S., EHRLICH, W. A., CANN, D. B., DAY, J. H. and MARSHALL, I. B. 1977. Soils of Canada. Vol. 1. Soil report. Research Branch, Can. Dep. Agric. Res. Br. pp. 114–120.

CONNERS, I. L. 1967. An annotated index of plant diseases in Canada and fungi recorded on plants in Alaska, Canada and Greenland. Can. Dep. Agric. Res. Br. Publ. 1251. p. 43.

DARLINGTON, C. D. and WYLIE, A. P. 1955. Chromosome atlas of flowering plants. London, George Allen & Unwin Ltd. p. 145.

DEPARTMENT OF ENERGY, MINES AND RESOURCES. 1973. The national atlas of Canada. 4th ed. Survey and Mapping Branch, Ottawa, Ont.

FERNALD, M. L. 1950. Gray's manual of botany. 8th ed. American Book Co., New York, N.Y. p. 760.

FERNALD, M. L. and KINSEY, A. C. 1943. Edible wild plants of Eastern North America. Idlewild Press. Cornwall-on-Hudson, N.Y. p. 229.

HORTUS THIRD. 1976. A concise dictionary of plants cultivated in the United States and Canada. MacMillan Publishing Co., Inc., New York. p. 110.

ISMAIL, A. A. 1974. Selective thinning of black barrenberry fruit in lowbush blueberry fields with ethephon. HortScience 9: 346–347.

MACOUN, J. 1883. Catalogue of Canadian plants. Part 1 — Polypetalae. Dawson Brothers, Montreal, Que. p. 146.

MARTIN, A. C., ZIM, H. S. and NELSON, A. L. 1951. American wildlife and plants. McGraw-Hill Book Company, Inc., New York, N.Y. p. 322.

MOFFETT, A. A. 1931. A preliminary account of chromosome behaviour in the Pomoideae. J. Pomol. Hortic. Sci. 9: 100–110.

MURPHY, E. F., TRUE, R. H., ISMAIL, A. A. and HOGAN, J. M. 1974. Effects of foreign edible berries on the flavor and texture of lowbush blueberry products. HortScience 9: 22–24.

REHDER, A. 1956. Manual of cultivated trees and shrubs. The MacMillan Company, New York, N.Y. pp. 382–383.

SMALL, E. 1972a. Photosynthetic rates in relation to nitrogen recycling as an adaptation to nutrient deficiency in peat bog plants. Can. J. Bot. 50: 2227–2233.

SMALL, E. 1972b. Ecological significance of four critical elements in plants of raised sphagnum peat bogs. Ecology 53: 498–503.

SMALL, E. 1972c. Water relations of plants in raised sphagnum peat bogs. Ecology 53: 726–728.

SMALL, E. 1976. Insect pollinators of the Mer Bleue peat bog of Ottawa. Can. Field Nat. 90: 22–28.

TREVETT, M. F. 1952. Control of woody weeds in lowbush blueberry fields. Maine Agric. Exp. Sta. Bull. 499. 23 pp.

TREVETT, M. F. and DURGIN, R. E. 1972. Progress report on the selective abortion of black barrenberry fruit in lowbush blueberry fields with ethephon, (2-chloroethyl) phosphonic acid. Res. Life Sci. Univ. Maine 20: 1–8.

U.S. DEPARTMENT OF AGRICULTURE FOREST SERVICE. 1948. Woody-plant seed manual. Misc. Publ. 654. U.S. Gov. Printing Office, Washington, D.C. pp. 90–91.

THE BIOLOGY OF CANADIAN WEEDS. 31.
Hordeum jubatum L.

K. F. BEST, J. D. BANTING, and G. G. BOWES

Research Station, Research Branch, Agriculture Canada, Regina, Saskatchewan S4P 3A2.
Received 22 Sept. 1977, accepted 13 Feb. 1978.

BEST, K. F., BANTING, J. D. AND BOWES, G. G. 1978. The biology of Canadian weeds. 31. *Hordeum jubatum* L. Can. J. Plant Sci. **58**: 699–708.

An account is given of biology of *Hordeum jubatum* L. It is found throughout Canada but is particularly prevalent as a weed of rangeland and pastures of the Prairie Provinces. The paper is one of a series on the biology of Canadian weeds and is concerned primarily with those characteristics of the species which appear to present the main obstacles to its effective control.

Les auteurs font état de la biologie de *Hordeum jubatum* L., espèce adventice qu'on retrouve partout au Canada, mais plus particulièrement dans les parcours et les pâturages des provinces des Prairies. Ce document s'inscrit dans une série de rapports traitant de la biologie des mauvaises herbes du Canada et portant surtout sur les caractéristiques qui en rendent la lutte particulièrement difficile.

1. Name

Hordeum jubatum L. — **foxtail barley** (Canada Weed Committee 1975). Other common names include wild barley, skunk grass, skunk-tail grass, squirrel-tail grass and tickle grass (Best 1965), **orge queue d'écureuil** (Ferron et Cayouette 1971). Gramineae (grass family) Graminées.

2. Description and Account of Variation

Frankton and Mulligan (1970) and Best et al. (1971) describe the species as follows: a tufted perennial with fibrous roots, spreading by seed. Stems 0.3–0.6 m high, smooth; blades to 6 mm wide, 5–15 cm long, flat or U-shaped, grayish green, often purplish, acuminate, twisted with long and short hairs on inner surface, short hairs on outer surface; sheaths round, split, distinctly veined, margins overlapping, lower sheaths sometimes hairy; ligules to 1 mm long, membranous, obtuse or truncate, lacerate, finely ciliate; collar medium broad, continuous, pale green, often purplish, sometimes oblique; auricles absent or rudimentary; heads 5–12 cm long, tassel-like at first but nearly as broad as long at maturity;

heads break up readily into seven-bristled clusters consisting of three spikelets at each joint; central spikelet of each cluster with a single floret and three bristles (awns), each outer spikelet represented by two bristles and lacking a floret; bristles to 8 cm long, green or reddish at early stages, becoming a shiny cream color at maturity. Delorit (1970) describes the fertile floret as elliptical, sessile, broadest at middle or slightly below, plano–convex; palea flat, almost completely exposed and having a prominent wrinkle, pointed at tip and rachilla about two-thirds to three-quarters length of palea, yellow, 5.0–7.5 mm long, 1.0–1.5 mm wide; sterile spikelets with flank fertile floret are borne on a stalk, have unexpanded lemmas and the glumes are reduced to long, flexible, awn-like structures. Foxtail barley may be distinguished from *Elymus canadensis*, *E. innovatus* and *E. condensatus* in that it lacks rhizomes, and from *E. virginicus* and *E. glaucus* by having leaf blades less than 10 mm in width. It may also be distinguished from *Sitanion hystrix* by having blades with soft pubescence and lacking claw-like auricles.

Can. J. Plant Sci. **58**: 699-708 (July 1978)

Pollen grains in *Hordeum* species are large, ranging from 47 to 62 microns in diameter (Wodehouse 1965). *H. jubatum* is tetraploid and has a chromosome count of $2n = 28$ (Mulligan 1960; Gross 1960). Bowden (1962) treats the *Hordeum jubatum* complex as three subspecies: ssp. *jubatum*; ssp. X *intermedium* (ssp. *breviaristatum* X ssp. *jubatum*); and ssp. *breviaristatum*. His key to the subspecies of *H. jubatum* is as follows:

a[1]. Glumes straight or almost straight, or arcuate usually from the bases or sometimes from the middle or near the apices, rarely bent near the apex, ascending, or often widely spreading obliquely or at right angles to the rachis axis rarely weakly recurved, sometimes spreading and strongly recurved especially when ripe; glumes (0.8)– 1.1–7.0–(8.0–9.0) cm long; awns of lemmas of central spikelets, (0.75)– 0.95–7.0–(8.0–9.0) cm long . . . . .b.

  b[1]. Glumes (3.3)–4.7–7.0–(8.0–9.0) cm long; awns of lemmas of central spikelets, (3.3)–4.1–7.0–(8.0– 9.0) cm long . . . . . 1di ssp. *jubatum*.

  b[2]. Glumes (8.0)–1.1–2.4–(3.0–3.6) cm long; awns of lemmas of central spikelets, (0.75)–0.95–2.5– (3.0–3.6) cm long . . . . 1dii ssp. X *intermedium*.

a[2]. Glumes usually straight or almost straight, rarely arcuate from the middle or near the apices or bent near the tips, ascending, sometimes slightly spreading obliquely; glumes (0.6–0.75)–0.8– 1.3–(1.4–1.8) cm long; awns of lemmas of central spikelets (0.4)–0.5–0.9– (1.0–1.35) cm long . . . . 1dlii ssp. *breviaristatum*.

Hordeum jubatum L. emend. ssp. *jubatum* occurs in all provinces of Canada, but is apparently absent from the Queen Charlotte Islands.

Hordeum jubatum L. emend. ssp. X *intermedium* Bowden. There is good evidence that this subspecies is of hybrid origin from the crossing of ssp. *jubatum* with ssp.

breviaristatum (Bowden 1962). It occurs where both parental subspecies grow in adjacent habitats. The hybrid swarms, however, have spread beyond the sites where both parental subspecies are found. In such areas only *H. jubatum* ssp. *jubatum* may be present while *H. jubatum* ssp. *breviaristatum* is absent. It has been recorded from Alaska, Yukon, district of Mackenzie, British Columbia, Alberta, Saskatchewan, Manitoba and Quebec.

Hordeum jubatum L. emend. ssp. *breviaristatum* Bowden occurs over a wide area of Canada, from the Queen Charlotte Islands, Yukon, through Alberta, southwestern Saskatchewan, southern Labrador and Newfoundland. It has not been reported from eastern Saskatchewan, Manitoba, Ontario, Quebec or the Maritime Provinces.

However, in all other papers reviewed, the species was not classified to the subspecies level. Therefore, in this paper, the authors stipulate that what is referred to as *H. jubatum* includes all of ssp. *jubatum* and parts of ssp. X *intermedium*.

3. Economic Importance

(a) *Detrimental* — Cattle and sheep do not graze *H. jubatum* plants once the heads have been formed (United States Department of Agriculture (USDA 1937). The bearded heads with their stiff awns readily break apart with sections of the rachis remaining as sharp points on the spikelets. When grazed or fed as hay, parts of the head become embedded in mouth tissues, nostrils and eyes of cattle, horses, sheep and game animals (Rush 1930, 1932; USDA 1937). Cattle are injured to a lesser extent than horses because the mucous membrane of their mouths is thicker and less easily penetrated. Infection following injury from *H. jubatum* has been reported to cause necrotic stomatitis or calf diphtheria, lumpy jaws and pus-forming abscesses (USDA 1937). Wool or pelts are also downgraded from the effects of this plant (Kingsbury 1964).

355

H. jubatum harbors wheat rust (Thornton and Durrell 1933; Jackson 1918), and the blackstem rust of grains (Stevens 1927).

(b) *Beneficial* — *H. jubatum* is palatable forage for cattle, horses and sheep until the barbed awns of the flowering spike develop (Whitman and Stevens 1941; USDA 1937). It has a high content of protein and phosphorus, a low crude fibre rating but is low yielding (Campbell et al. 1966; Clark and Tisdale 1945). *H. jubatum* is grazed by deer and elk (USDA 1937).

(c) *Legislation* — *H. jubatum* is listed under "other weeds" in the Seeds Act and Regulations administered by Agriculture Canada (1967). It is classified as noxious by the Government of Manitoba (1971).

4. Geographic Distribution

H. jubatum is found across Canada from Newfoundland to the Yukon (Figs. 1 and 2), and is well adapted to subarctic regions (Mitchell 1967). It is more common in western Canada than in eastern Canada (Clark and Fletcher 1909; Craigie et al. 1944). It occurs throughout all of the United States except for the southern Altantic and Gulf Coast States (Clark and Fletcher 1909; Gates 1936; Greaney 1947; Craigie et al. 1944; Reed 1970; USDA 1937). *H. jubatum* has been reported from South America, Asia, and Europe (Fernald 1950; Bailey 1966).

5. Habitat

(a) *Climatic requirements* — *H. jubatum* is adapted to a wide range of environmental conditions as evident from its very wide distribution. Although it grows commonly in saline soils at low elevations on the plains, it also exists at subalpine elevations in the spruce belt (USDA 1937).

(b) *Substratum* — A facultive halophyte, *H. jubatum* grows best on wet, fertile, non-alkaline soils (Wilson 1967). It often forms a vegetative border around small lakes (sloughs) and marshes where soils are alkaline and where spring flooding may occur (Batho 1939; Moss 1953; Love and Love 1954; Dodd et al. 1964; Dodd and Coupland 1966; Best et al. 1971). While many prairie species grow adjacent to but do not invade saline soils due to their inability to absorb water, *H. jubatum* is one of the dominant perennial grasses in saline vegetation, being mid-way in order of salt tolerance. It grows on soils with a high water table, 0.2–1.5% salinity, pH of 7.3–8.1, with conductivity ranging from 6 to 26 mmhos, and on all soils from sandy loam to clay, in fields, meadows, pastures and waste places under arid to marshy conditions (Thornton and Durrell 1933; Dodd et al. 1964; Dodd and Coupland 1966; Ungar 1967, 1970).

(c) *Communities in which the species occurs* — *H. jubatum* was found to be a dominant species of the halophyte vegetation in Saskatchewan and South Dakota (Dodd et al. 1964; Dodd and Coupland 1966; Ungar 1970). The four perennial grasses generally associated with *H. jubatum*, in decreasing order of salt tolerance, were *Puccinellia nuttallii* (Schultes) Hitchc., *Distichlis stricta* (Torr.) Rydb., *Muhlenbergia richardsonis* (Trin.) Rydb. and various species of *Agropyron*. Where periodic flooding occurred, *Triglochin maritima* L. occupied the coarse-textured soils while *Salicornia rubra* Nels. was the dominant species of fine-textured soil. *Sarcobatus vermiculatus* (Hook.) Torr. was found to be the principle shrub, but was limited to the very dry area of southwestern Saskatchewan, occurring as an overstory to *Agropyron smithii* Rydb.

Zonation was pronounced on saline soils in flat to depressed areas with poor drainage (Dodd and Coupland 1966). Central portions were generally bare of all vegetation, although some growth of *Scirpus paludosus* Nels. was found. Adjacent to the highly saline area, pure or mixed stands of *Salicornia rubra* Nels., *Suaeda depressa* (Pursh) Wats. and *Atriplex patula* L. var. *hastata* (L.) Gray were found. An outer zone generally supported a mixture of *H. jubatum, Triglochin maritima* L., *Distichlis stricta* (Torr.) Rydb., *Spartina gracilis* Trin., *Eleocharis palustris* (L.) R. + S., *Chenopodium rubrum* L. and *Glaux maritima* L.

Coupland (1952) observed concentric rings of vegetation around small lakes (sloughs) in the Canadian mixed prairie where drainage was poor. The inner circumference was generally occupied by *Eleocharis palustris* (L.) R. + S., *Bechmannia syzigachne* (Steud.) Fern. and species of *Carex* with *H. jubatum* in the

Fig. 1.   Mature plant of *Hordeum jubatum* L. with details of spikelet and leaf attachment.

next area. An outer zone was dominated by *Calamagrostis canadensis* (Michx.) Beauv. and *C. inexpansa* A. Gray. Other associated species included *Agrostis scabra* Willd., *Deschampsia caespitosa* (L.) Beauv., *Glyceria grandis* S. Wats., *Hierochloa odorata* (L.) Beauv., *Urtica procerus* Muhl., *Rumex mexicanus* Meisn., *Stellaria* spp., *Ranunculus* spp., *Geum aleppicum* Jacq., *Gaura glabra* Lehm., *Collomia linearis* Nutt. and *Stachys palustris* L. There was often a fringe of shrubs, chiefly *Symphorocarpos occidentalis* Hook. on the outer edge of the herbaceous species. *H. jubatum* was often observed in shallow coulee bottoms and was usually associated with *Deschampsia caespitosa* (L.) Beauv., *Poa canbyi* (Scribn.) Piper, *Agrostis scabra* Willd. and species of Carex.

6. History

H. jubatum is indigenous to western North America (Frankton and Mulligan 1970).

The oldest specimen in the Biosystematics Research Institute herbarium (DAO) was from Dufferin, Manitoba dated 1873 and Scoggan (1957) cited a listing on the Red River Valley by Dawson in 1875.

7. Growth and Development

(a) *Morphology* — Foxtail barley is an erect, densely tufted perennial with fibrous roots (Best et al. 1971). When mature, the stems break off and the heads are blown about, often in tangled masses, spreading seed over a wide area (Taylor et al. 1958; Stevens 1927). The rough awns stick to animals and seeds are also scattered in this manner (USDA 1937). The ability to germinate in the fall and overwinter gives the species a competitive advantage and an opportunity to colonize new areas.

(b) *Perennation* — *H. jubatum* is a hemicryptophyte (Gates 1940), a short-lived perennial regenerating from buds in the crown just below the surface of the

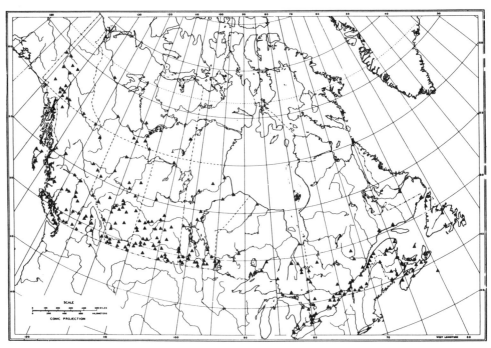

Fig. 2. The distribution in Canada of *Hordeum jubatum* L. based on specimens from various Canadian herbaria (DAO, CAN, OAC, SASK).

ground. It also overwinters as seed in the soil.

(c) *Physiological data* — Wilson (1967) grew *H. jubatum* with orchard grass (*Dactylis glomerata* L.) in pots of soil at controlled root temperatures of 7, 12, 20 and 27°C with ambient air temperature of about 24°C. He found that the foxtail barley responded more to increases in temperature than did the orchard grass, and consequently at higher temperatures there was proportionately more *H. jubatum* in the mixture. When grown alone in the greenhouse, the species developed best under low salinity and high moisture and fertility. Root extracts from foxtail barley had little or no effect on germination of wheat (*Triticum aestivum* L.), barley (*Hordeum vulgare* L.) and 12 other species in tests at Swift Current (Lawrence and Kilcher 1962).

(d) *Phenology* — Seeds of *H. jubatum* usually germinate in late August or September and the following year, under favorable conditions, the plants develop tufts 20–30 cm high and 5–10 cm in diameter with first flowering varying from mid-June to early July (Clark 1914; Stevens 1927, 1960). Thirty-five percent of seeds planted in late July in North Dakota emerged by the end of October and about two-thirds of these survived the following spring. Flowering in these plants occurred during the 1st wk in July and was general by mid-July. Individual plants had as many as 48 stalks, some of which were up to 35 cm in height. In the 2nd yr, the average diameter of the plants was 4.4 cm and there were 55 flowering spikes per plant. In the 3rd yr, the plants had an average diameter of 9.1 cm with 188 spikes per plant. Spikes began to appear in early July and spike production was heaviest for the first 2 wk, but continued well into September.

(3) Mycorrhiza—No information available.

8. Reproduction

(a) *Floral biology* — The central, long-awned spikelet is fertile, producing a single grain or seed, and on each side of it, attached to its base, are two sterile florets, each with three shorter awns (Clark and Fletcher 1909). Mulligan and Findlay (1970) determined that the species was self-compatible, producing viable seed when the flowering heads were isolated.

(b) *Seed production and dispersal* — The slender, sharp-pointed caryopsis with its long, barbed awn begins to mature in early July (Clark 1914; Whitman and Stevens 1941). The caryopsis is hairy at the apex, usually adherent to the palea at maturity (Gates 1936). The heads shatter readily and the seeds are scattered as they mature with the joints of the rachis and their three attached spikelets falling apart (Montgomery 1964; Muenscher 1960). At maturity, the stems break off and the heads are blown about, thus spreading seeds over a wide area (Taylor et al. 1958).

(c) *Viability of seeds and germination* — Chepil (1946) found that fewer than 2% of the seeds buried to a depth of 7.5 cm in a clay, loam, or sandy loam soil were alive after 1 yr. Banting (unpublished data) suggested that loss of viability depended on the seed population and the environmental conditions that applied during the period of burial. In one population, over 97% of the seeds were dead after 2 yr burial. In another, mortality was greater in the first 2–3 yr in buried than in surface seeds. However, the surface seeds did not remain viable as long and a few of the buried seeds were still alive after 7 yr in the soil. The amount of induced dormancy in the seeds on the surface was high in the spring following placement in the field the previous autumn. Small but significant increases in induction were also evident in buried seeds at this time.

Stevens (1960) and Ungar (1974) reported that germination was greater at alternating than at constant temperature. Banting (unpublished data) found that germination in darkness was increased more by alternating temperatures of 20° and 30°C for 18 and 6 h, respectively, as did Stevens

(1960), than by 10° and 15°C for 10 and 14 h, respectively, as did Ungar (1974). Germination was reduced by light, the effect being most pronounced when the light was continuous and at constant temperatures, conditions similar to those used by Cords (1960). The results indicated that the level of the alternating temperatures, the duration of the light period and the depth of dormancy in the seeds were factors determining the germination potential.

The effect of depth of planting on emergence of foxtail barley in various soils was also tested (Banting, unpublished data). Emergence was good in the top 2.5 cm of Regina heavy clay and was much less or absent in Weyburn loam and Asquith fine sandy loam except for the seeds on the surface. No emergence occurred in any of the soils from a depth of 7.5 cm or more.

Maw (unpublished data) at Regina noted little difference in the production of viable seed whether the heads matured on intact plants or on cut stems. Mowing should be done within 10 days of the inflorescence emerging from the sheath. Mowing after 10 days will not prevent production of viable seed although some decrease in germination may be obtained.

(d) *Vegetative reproduction* — The species reproduces vegetatively from buds that overwinter on the crown and produce new shoots the following spring.

9. Hybrids

A hybrid of *H. jubatum* and *Agropyron trachycaulum* is considered by some to be the so-called *Elymus macounii,* now known as *Agrohordeum macounii* (Fernald 1950). Boyle and Holmgren (1955) as well as Gross (1960) referred to hybrids between *H. jubatum* and *Agropyron trachycaulum* and reported that natural hybrids could occur with either species as maternal parents. Wagenaar (1960) cytologically examined two hybrids of *H. jubatum* ($2n = 28$) $\times$ *Secale cereale* ($2n = 14$) and one hybrid of *H. jubatum* $\times$ *H. bulbosum.* Davis and Heywood (1965) also noted that vigorous hybrids between *H. jubatum* and *Secale cereale* have been raised by embryo culture.

As mentioned previously (Bowden 1962), *H. jubatum* ssp. *jubatum X intermedium* results from a cross between *H. jubatum* ssp. *jubatum* and *H. jubatum* ssp. *breviaristatum.* Rajhathy (1966) indicated that both *H. jubatum* and *H. breviaristatum* are self-pollinated, so it is not surprising that they do not hybridize at some sites of contact. The natural hybrid swarms are more similar morphologically to *H. jubatum* than to *H. brachyantherum* because foxtail barley is usually the recurrent parent. Schooler et al. (1966) obtained a highly fertile amphiploid ($2n = 42$) between *H. jubatum* ($2n = 28$) and *H. compressum* ($2n = 14$). The F_1 plants were sterile, taller than either parent and had a chromosome count of $2n = 21$.

10 Population Dynamics

H. jubatum is adapted to a wide range of water table conditions and prevalence depends on competition from other plants (Cords 1960). In the presence of hydrophytes (*Eleocharis* spp.), *H. jubatum* is only a minor component of the vegetation. When the water table is low, *Festuca elatior* L. and *Agropyron elongatum* (Host.) Beauv. were reported to reduce the population of *H. jubatum*. Unless improved species are introduced, drainage of meadows and pastures generally results in an increase of *H. jubatum*. On wet, non-saline soils, the growth of *H. jubatum* was restricted by competition from *Dactylis glomerata* L. (Wilson 1967). On wet, saline soils where *D. glomerata* offered little competition, the foxtail barley grew well. On dry or infertile soils it grew sparsely.

The size of an *H. jubatum* population, which included seedlings and mature plants in a low to moderately saline area in Saskatchewan, was greater in the spring than the fall of the year (Maw and Bowes, unpublished data). Severe competition from invading *Poa* spp. reduced the population of *H. jubatum* by 75% over a 1-yr period. Based on a growing season of 28 wk, the mean half life of *H. jubatum* seedling cohorts was 4.7–5.0 yr for pure stands and only 0.6 yr when there was severe competition from *Poa* spp. The high rate of seedling mortality which occurred following emergence decreases as *H. jubatum* became established. The mortality was greater for seedlings emerging in the spring than fall.

11. Response to Herbicides and Other Chemicals

In Canada, there are no herbicides recommended for the selective control of *H. jubatum* although two herbicides, glyphosate and pronamide, are presently being tested (Canada Weed Committee 1976). Tolerance of *H. jubatum* seedlings to siduron was found to be genetically controlled by three complementary dominant factors (Schooler et al. 1972). This suggests that plants that are tolerant of siduron could evolve by natural selection. When chemicals are used in place of tillage during summer fallow, *H. jubatum* has been reported to persist (Bowren et al. 1976).

12. Response to Human Manipulation

Foxtail barley should be cut for hay before the seeds are formed. In wet seasons a second cutting may be necessary to prevent any seed ripening. However, successive mowing increases the competitive ability of the species. Seeding of cultivated pastures to a highly competitive grass effectively reduces the amount of *H. jubatum* (USDA 1937). Conservative grazing on uncultivated range enables the reestablishment of more palatable native perennial grasses and is probably the most feasible method of reducing the weed. Artificial reseeding of badly depleted areas to aggressive but palatable grasses may be necessary to hasten the improvement of the range. Muenscher (1955) noted that early spring grazing of infested pastures by sheep or cattle will give *H. jubatum* a severe setback. Deep plowing and an annual smother crop followed by plowing and

alfalfa (*Medicago sativa* L.) is an effective control. A clean cultivated crop for a year before reseeding to grass may also be used.

13. Response to Parasites

(a) *Insects and other nondomestic animals* — Maw and Molloy (personal communication 1977) at the Regina Research Station have collected the following insects on *H. jubatum*: Coleoptera: *Ceutorhynchus sulcipennis* LeC., *Crepidodera* spp., *Phylliodes punctulata* Melsh, *Phyllotreta cruciferae* Guez., Diptera: *Hylemya platura* Mg., Hemiptera: *Thyreocoris pulicaria* Germar., Homoptera: *Aceratagallia sanguinolenta* Prov., *Aphalara rumicis* Mlly., *Euscelidius schenki* (Kirsch.), *Macrosteles fascifrons* Stal, *Palus bilineatus* (Gill. & Bak.), *Rhopalosiphum maidis* Fitch.

Visitors or insect predators found on *H. jubatum* include Coleoptera: *Coccinella transversoguttata* Faldermann, *Hippodamia tridecimpunctata tribialis* (Say); Diptera: *Meromyza saltatrix* L.; and Hemiptera: *Nabis roseipennis* Reuter; *Orius insidiosus* (Say).

(b) *Micro-organisms and viruses* — Thornton and Durrell (1933) maintained that *H. jubatum* was a major host in harboring wheat rust. At almost any time of the summer, rust may be found on foxtail barley. Stevens (1927) also noted that *H. jubatum* was an important agent in the distribution of black stem rust of grains. When the spores are blown up from the south they may grow on the *H. jubatum* and produce a continuous crop of spores which infest cereals and other grasses. Sanford and Broadfoot (1933) found that stripe rust (*Puccinia glumarum*), commonly found on *H. jubatum* also affects wheat and the *Agropyron* species including *A. richardsonii*, *A. tenerum*, *A. dasystachyum*, *A. smithii* and *A. griffithii*. Of the native hosts in Alberta, *H. jubatum* is outstanding, both in susceptibility to *P. glumarum* and in prevalence. It is the grass on which the rust is first found when apparently absent from other susceptible species in the vicinity.

Seedlings and older plants growing in moist habitats appear to be the principle carriers of stripe rust during September.

Cherewick (1944) reported the occurrence of powdery mildew (*Erysiphe graminis* DC.) on *H. jubatum* from Nova Scotia to British Columbia and to within 100 km of the Arctic Circle.

(c) Higher plant parasites — No information available.

ACKNOWLEDGMENTS

The authors wish to thank Dr. J. R. Hay, Regina, for his appraisal of the manuscript, Dr. A. C. Hamill, Harrow and Dr. A. L. Darwent, Beaverlodge for their seed supply and Phil Mueller for his field research.

AGRICULTURE CANADA. 1967. Seeds Act and Regulations. Queen's Printer, Ottawa, Ontario. 50 pp.

BAILEY, L. H. 1966. Manual of cultivated plants. The Macmillan Co., New York, N.Y. 1116 pp.

BATHO, G. 1939. A B C of Manitoba weeds. Man. Dep. Agric. Immigr. Circ. **131**: 24 pp.

BEST, K. F. 1965. Common names of weeds of Canada. Agric. Can. Res. Br., Exp. Farm, Swift Current, Sask. S.C. 110. 27 pp.

BEST, K. F., LOOMAN, J. and CAMPBELL, J. B. 1971. Prairie grasses. Agric. Can. Publ. 1413. 239 pp.

BOWDEN, W. M. 1962. Cytotaxonomy of the native and adventive species of *Hordeum, Eremopyrum, Secale, Sitanion* and *Triticum* in Canada. Can. J. Bot. **40**: 1675–1711.

BOWREN, K. E., EDWARDS, W. S. and HENNING, R. E. 1976. Herbicides and tillage for summerfallow. Canada Weed Committee Research Report (Western Section). pp. 527–528.

BOYLE, W. S. and HOLMGREN, A. H. 1955. A cytogenetic study of natural and controlled hybrids between *Agropyron trachycaulum* and *Hordeum jubatum*. Genetics **40**: 539–545.

CAMPBELL, J. B., BEST, K. F. and BUDD, A. C. 1966. 99 range forage plants of the Canadian prairies. Agric. Can. Publ. 964. 102 pp.

CANADA WEED COMMITTEE. 1975. Common and botanical names of weeds in Canada. Agric. Can. Publ. 1375. 67 pp.

CANADA WEED COMMITTEE. 1976. Report, Research Appraisal and Research Planning Committee. p. 40.

CHEPIL, W. S. 1946. Germination of weed seeds. 1. Longevity, periodicity of germination, and vitality of seeds in cultivated soil. Sci. Agric. **26**(7): 307–346.

CHEREWICK, W. J. 1944. Studies on the biology of *Erysiphe graminis* DC. Can. J. Res. 22 Sec. C. **2**: 52–86.

CLARK, G. H. 1914. Weeds and weed seeds. Agric. Can. Seed Br. Bull. S-8. 67 pp.

CLARK, G. H. and FLETCHER, J. 1909. Farm weeds of Canada. Agric. Can. 192 pp.

CLARKE, S. E. and TISDALE, E. W. 1945. The chemical composition of native forage plants of southern Alberta and Saskatchewan in relation to grazing practices. Agric. Can. Publ. **769**: 21–22.

CORDS, H. P. 1960. Factors affecting the competitive ability of foxtail barley (*Hordeum jubatum* L.). Weeds **8**(4): 636–644.

COUPLAND, R. T. 1952. Grassland communities of the western Canadian prairies — Climax and subclimax. Proc. 6th Int. Grassl. Congr. **1952**: 625–631.

CRAIGIE, J. H., SWAINE, J. M. and GROH, H. 1944. Canadian weed survey — Third annual report. Agric. Can. Sci. Serv. **1944**: 9.

DAVIS, P. H. and HEYWOOD, V. H. 1965. Principles of angiosperm taxonomy. Oliver and Boyd, Edinburgh. 558 pp.

DELORIT, R. J. 1970. Illustrated taxonomy manual of weed seeds. Agronomy Publications, River Falls, Wis. 175 pp.

DODD, J. D., RENNIE, D. A. and COUPLAND, R. T. 1964. The nature and distribution of salts in uncultivated soils in Saskatchewan. Can. J. Soil Sci. **44**: 165–175.

DODD, J. D. and COUPLAND, R. T. 1966. Vegetation of saline areas in Saskatchewan. Ecology **47**(6): 958–963.

FERNALD, M. L. 1950. Gray's manual of botany. American Book Co., New York, N.Y. 1632 pp.

FERRON, M. and CAYOUETTE, R. 1971. Noms des mauvaises herbes du Québec. Ministère de l'Agriculture et de la Colonisation du Québec. Publ. 288, 113 pp.

FRANKTON, C. and MULLIGAN, G. A. 1970. Weeds of Canada. Agric. Can. Publ. 948, 217 pp.

GATES, F. C. 1936. Grasses of Kansas. Rep. Kansas State Board of Agric. **55**(220-A): 133.

GATES, F. C. 1940. Flora of Kansas. Agric. Exp. Sta., Kansas State Coll. Agric. and Appl. Sci., Topeka, Kans. 266 pp.

GREANEY, F. J. 1947. An illustrated guide to prairie weeds. Line Elevator Farm. Serv. Bull. No. 2. 80 pp.

GROSS, A. T. H. 1960. Distribution and cytology of *Elymus macounii* Vasey. Can. J. Bot. **38**: 63–67.

JACKSON, V. W. 1918. Lessons on weeds. Man. Dep. Agric. Immigr. Ext. Bull. 30. 50 pp.

KINGSBURY, J. M. 1964. Poisonous plants of the United States and Canada. Prentice Hall Inc., Englewood Cliffs, N.J. 626 pp.

LAWRENCE, T. and KILCHER, M. R. 1962. The effect of 14 root extracts upon germination and seedling length of 15 plant species. Can. J. Plant Sci. **42**(2): 308–313.

LOVE, A. and LOVE, D. 1954. Vegetation of a prairie marsh. Bull. Torrey Bot. Club. **81**(1): 23.

MANITOBA. 1971. The Noxious Weeds Act. Chap. N. **110**: 15.

MITCHELL, W. W. 1967. On the *Hordeum jubatum – H. brachyantherum* question. Madrono **13**(4): 108–110.

MONTGOMERY, F. H. 1964. Weeds of Canada and the northern United States. The Ryerson Press, Toronto, Ont. 226 pp.

MOSS, E. H. 1953. Marsh and bog vegetation in northwestern Alberta. Can. J. Bot. **31**: 448–470.

MUENSCHER, W. C. 1955. Weeds. The Macmillan Co., New York, N.Y. 560 pp.

MUENSCHER, W. C. 1960. Poisonous plants of the United States. The Macmillan Co., New York, N.Y. 277 pp.

MULLIGAN, G. A. 1960. Polyploidy in Canadian weeds. Can. J. Genet. Cytol. **2**: 150–161.

MULLIGAN, G. A. and FINDLAY, J. N. 1970. Reproductive systems and colonization in Canadian weeds. Can. J. Bot. **48**: 859–860.

RAJHATHY, T. 1966. Notes on the *Hordeum jubatum* complex. Madrono **18**: 243–244.

REED, C. F. 1970. Selected weeds of the United States. U.S. Dep. Agric. Handb. No. 336. 463 pp.

RUSH, W. M. 1930. Foxtail grass is killing elk. Mont. Wildl. **3**(7): 10–11.

RUSH, W. M. 1932. Northern Yellowstone elk study. Missoula, Mont. 131 pp.

SANFORD, G. B. and BROADFOOT, W. C. 1933. The relative susceptibility of cultivated and native hosts in Alberta to stripe rust. Sci. Agric. **13**(11): 714–721.

SCHOOLER, A. B., NELSON, J. and ARFSTEN, A. 1966. *Hordeum jubatum* L. crosses with *Hordeum compressum* Griseb. Crop Sci. **6**: 187–190.

SCHOOLER, A. B., BELL, A. R. and NALEWAJA, J. D. 1972. Inheritance of siduron tolerance in foxtail barley. Weed Sci. **20**: 167–169.

SCOGGAN, H. J. 1957. Flora of Manitoba. Natl. Mus. Can. Bull. **140**: 109. 619 pp.

STEVENS, O. A. 1927. North Dakota weeds. N.D. Agric. Exp. Sta. Bull. 162, 46 pp.

STEVENS, O. A. 1960. Weed development notes. N.D. Agric. Exp. Sta. Res. Rep. **1**: 6–7.

TAYLOR, R. L., WILTON, A. C. and KLEBESDEL, L. J. 1958. Weeds in Alaska. Univ. of Alaska Agric. Exp. Ser. Bull. 600. 32 pp.

THORNTON, B. J. and DURRELL, L. W. 1933. Colorado weeds. Colo. Agric. Exp. Sta. Bull. 403. 115 pp.

UNGAR, I. A. 1967. Vegetation–soil relationships on saline soils in northern Kansas. Amer. Midl. Nat. **78**(11): 98–120.

UNGAR, I. A. 1970. Species–soil relationships on sulfate dominated soils in South Dakota. Amer. Midl. Nat. **83**(2): 343–357.

UNGAR, I. A. 1974. The effect of salinity and temperature on seed germination and growth of *Hordeum jubatum*. Can. J. Bot. **52**(6): 1357–1362.

UNITED STATES DEPARTMENT OF AGRICULTURE. 1937. Range plant handbook. USDA, Washington, D.C. G74.

WAGENAAR, E. B. 1960. The cytology of three hybrids involving *Hordeum jubatum* L. Can. J. Bot. **38**: 69–85.

WHITMAN, W. and STEVENS, O. A. 1941. Grass. Agric. Exp. Sta., N. Dak. Agric. Coll. Bull. 300, 112 pp.

WILSON, D. B. 1967. Growth of *Hordeum jubatum* under various soil conditions and degrees of plant competition. Can. J. Plant Sci. **47**: 405–412.

WODEHOUSE, R. P. 1965. Pollen grains. McGraw-Hill Book Co. Inc., New York, N.Y. 574 pp.

363

THE BIOLOGY OF CANADIAN WEEDS. 32
Chenopodium album L.

I. J. BASSETT and C. W. CROMPTON

Biosystematics Research Institute, Agriculture Canada, Ottawa, Ontario K1A 0C6.
Received 29 May 1978, accepted 14 July 1978.

BASSETT, I. J. AND CROMPTON, C. W. 1978. The biology of Canadian weeds. 32. *Chenopodium album* L. Can. J. Plant Sci. **58**: 1061–1072.

In Canada, lamb's-quarters (*Chenopodium album* L.) occurs in disturbed habitats in every province, the Yukon and the Northwest Territories. A key is provided separating two other closely related weedy species, *C. berlandieri* Moq. ssp. *zschackei* (Murr.) Zobel and *C. strictum* Roth var. *glaucophyllum* (Aellen) Wahl from *C. album*. The biology of *C. album*, the most common weedy species in the genus, is discussed.

Au Canada, le chénopode blanc (*Chenopodium album* L.) se rencontre dans les habitats perturbés de toutes les provinces ainsi que du Yukon et des Territoires du Nord-Ouest. Les auteurs proposent une clé pour distinguer *C. album* de deux proches parents adventices, *C. berlandieri* Moq. spp. *zschackey* (Murr.) Zobel et *C. strictum* Roth var. *glaucophyllum* (Aellen) Wahl. L'article passe en revue la biologie de *C. album*, l'espèce adventice la plus répandue du genre.

1. Name

Chenopodium album L. — **lamb's-quarters** (Canada Weed Committee 1969), fat-hen, pigweed, white goosefoot; **chénopode blanc,** amarante commune, ansérine, chou gras, farineuse, herbes grasses, poulette grasse (Ferron et Cayouette 1971). Chenopodiaceae, goosefoot family, Chénopodiacées.

2. Description and Account of Variation

Annual, 10–250 cm high, stems angular, branched, brownish-yellow and ridged with green or reddish parallel stripes; leaves alternate, petioled, without stipules, mealy-farinose to nearly glabrous, deep green to light green, ovate–lanceolate to rhombic–lanceolate, sinu-dentate to entire, lamina 1–12 cm long, 0.5–8.0 cm wide, 1–5 times longer than wide; plants monoecious; flowers perfect, clustered in contiguous glomerules, 5-merous, farinose to glabrous, perianth basally united, clasping and nearly enclosing the mature fruit (utricle); stamens 5, rarely 3 or 4; pistil having a short style and 2 papillate stigmas; seeds mostly shiny black, horizontal, 1.2 mm wide by 1.3 mm long, circular in outline; testa with radiating faint rugulate ridges or smooth; pericarp easy or difficult to remove, mottled–farinose or smooth. Wind-pollinated, flowering from late May to October (Fig. 1).

In Canada, *Chenopodium album* has been found to have chromosome numbers of $2n = 54$ or $n = 27$ (Taylor and Mulligan 1968; Bassett and Crompton 1971; Crompton and Bassett 1976). Atrazine-tolerant biotypes of *C. album* from southern Ontario had chromosome numbers of $n = 27$, with completely regular meiosis in all cases (Crompton and Bassett, unpublished). The same counts have been reported for this species in America by Homsher (1967) and Guisti (1964).

Aellen (1929) recognized 34 subspecies, varieties, and forms of *C. album* in North America. Abrams (1944) concluded that all these taxa were minor variants of *C. album*. *C. album* is often confused with a number of other closely related weedy annual species of which the most common in

Canada are *C. berlandieri* Moq. ssp. *zschackei* (Murr.) Zobel, $2n = 36$ (Bassett and Crompton 1971), and *C. strictum* Roth var. *glaucophyllum* (Aellen) Wahl, $n = 18$ or $2n = 36$ (Bassett and Crompton 1971; Keener 1970). An error ($2n = 18$) was printed for the chromosome count of this species in Bassett and Crompton (1971).

Seedlings of *C. album* (Fig. 2A) and *C. berlandieri* ssp. *zschackei* are *very* similar and cannot be distinguished from each other. Seedlings of *C. strictum* var. *glaucophyllum* (Fig. 2B), with their shallow serrate leaves, can be separated from the seedlings of *C. album* (Fig. 2A). At reaching full maturity, *C. album* can best be distinguished from *C. berlandieri* ssp. *zschackei* and *C. strictum* var. *glaucophyllum* by the features detailed in the following key:

A. Seeds with adherent reticulate or honeycombed pericarp, showing a yellow area (stylopodium) around the base of the style, circular (Fig. 3, C and D.), radicle not prominent; calyx-lobes (perianth parts) very prominently keeled along the center, not covering the achenes ....*C. berlandieri* ssp. *zschackei*
A. Seeds with non-adherent or adherent non-reticulate pericarp without a yellow stylopodium, oval or circular (Fig. 3,A,B,E,F), with or without a prominent radicle; perianth parts normally not strongly keeled, covering the achenes
  B. Seeds circular, averaging 1.2 mm wide by 1.3 mm long (Fig. 3, A.); pericarp easy or difficult to remove, testa marked by faint reticulations or striations (20X), radicle not prominent and only shallowly notched (flowering late May to late August) .....
  ....*C. album*
  B. Seeds oval, averaging 1.0 mm wide by 1.3 mm long (Fig. 3, E.); pericarp difficult to remove, testa smooth (20X), radicle prominent and deeply notched (flowering late August to late October) ....*C. strictum* var. *glaucophyllum*

C. berlandieri ssp. *zschackei* is most abundant in the three Prairie Provinces and relatively infrequent in other parts of Canada (Fig. 4). *C. strictum* var. *glaucophyllum* is most common in southern Ontario, southwestern Quebec and the Okanagan region of British Columbia and infrequent in Manitoba and Saskatchewan (Fig. 4). *C. strictum* var. *glaucophyllum* is absent from Alberta, New Brunswick, Nova Scotia, and Newfoundland; in Prince Edward Island only one population has been observed. Further biological information is required for *C. berlandieri* ssp. *zschackei* and *C. strictum* var. *glaucophyllum*.

3. Economic Importance

(a) *Detrimental* — Lamb's-quarters ranks amongst the 10 most important weeds of cropland in Saskatchewan (Thomas 1977). Light to heavy concentrations of *Chenopodium album* were found by Alex (1966) throughout agricultural areas of the Prairie Provinces during surveys in 1963–64. Of the 103 weedy species surveyed in southern Ontario, Alex (1964) determined that lamb's-quarters ranked second in abundance in 50 tomato fields sampled in the counties of Essex, Kent and Prince Edward. On a world basis, according to Holm et al. (1977), lamb's-quarters is ranked as the most important weed in potatoes and sugar beets and seventh in abundance in corn crops. They also state that in England *Chenopodium* seeds constitute 1/3 of the weed seed impurities of carrot seed. It was found to be the dominant weed in kale plantings in England (Holmes and Pfieffer 1964). In the United States, Welker (1966) considers lamb's-quarters to be a primary weed in asparagus plantings and Wisk and Cole (1966) regard it to be the predominant weed in soybeans. The most common weed of sugar beet and potatoes in Sweden is considered to be lamb's-quarters (Aamisepp 1976).

C. album has been found to be poisonous to sheep and swine when they ingest large quantities over a sufficient period. In Iowa, Buck et al. (1966) attributed a seasonal disease of swine, perirenal edema, to the ingestion of *C. album* and *Amaranthus* *retroflexus* L. Herweijer and Den Houter (1970), in the Netherlands, determined that poisoning of sheep occurred after they were put in a re-sown pasture dominated by

Fig. 1.   Lamb's quarters, *Chenopodium album*. Adult plant [drawing from ''Weeds of Canada'' by Frankton and Mulligan (1970)].

366

lamb's-quarters. In both swine and sheep the causative agent was suspected to be oxalic acid.

The airborne pollen of lamb's-quarters causes summer hay fever (Wodehouse 1971).

(b) *Beneficial* — Lamb's-quarters seeds are an important source of food for many species of North American birds (Martin et al. 1951). Young leaves and shoots can be boiled and used as a pot herb (Fernald and Kinsey 1951; Knapp 1975), and the seeds can be milled into a dark palatable flour (Fernald and Kinsey 1951).

Ascaridole, an oil used as an anthelmintic to treat round worms and hook worms (Boche and Runquist 1968), can be extracted from *C. album* leaves.

(c) *Legislation* — Lamb's-quarters has been designated a noxious weed by the provinces of Quebec, Manitoba and Alberta (Anonymous 1964, 1970, 1973).

4. Geographical Distribution

Lamb's-quarters occurs in all provinces of Canada, the Yukon Territory, and the Mackenzie District, N.W.T. (Fig. 4). It is a cosmopolitan weed and occurs between latitudes 70°N and 50°S, except in areas having extreme desert conditions (Holm et al. 1977).

5. Habitat

(a) *Climatic requirements* — Where *C. album* occurs in Canada, the average annual precipitation varies from 30 to 325 cm and the snow cover from 0 to 76 cm; the growing season ranges from 160 to 200 days and the degree days above 42°F range from 1,500 to 3,500 (Anonymous 1974).

Fig. 2A.   Seedling of *Chenopodium album*. Seedling of *C. berlandieri* ssp. *zschackei* is very similar to *C. album*. B. Seedling of *Chenopodium strictum* var. *glaucophyllum*.

367

(b) *Substratum* — Lamb's-quarters has been found growing in soils which range from strongly acid to alkaline; it grows in chernozemic, podzol or gleysolic soil types in well-drained conditions, having gravel or stony phases. It prefers cultivated calcareous and occasionally non-calcareous soils (Williams 1963).

(c) *Communities in which the species occurs* — Lamb's-quarters is an anthropophilic plant, usually found growing in association with other weeds in disturbed open habitats. It is often found in construction sites and gravel pits. It does not usually grow in natural situations such as native woodland and prairie.

6. History

The monographer of the Chenopodiaceae family, Moquind-Tandon (1840, 1849), considered lamb's-quarters a weed of agriculture throughout temperate regions. Standley (1916) could not decide upon its origin. *C. album* is the most common species of this genus occurring in Canada. The earliest herbarium collections in CAN and DAO (Holmgren and Keuken 1974) were taken in 1858, 1887, 1891, 1895, 1896, and 1898.

7. Growth and Development

(a) Morphology — Cumming (1963), Williams and Harper (1965), Wentland (1965),

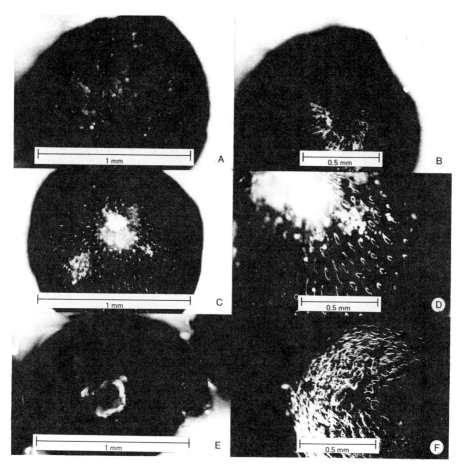

Fig. 3A,B. Testa of *Chenopodium album*.   C. and D. Pericarp attached to testa of *C. berlandieri* ssp. *zschackei*. E. and F. Testa of *C. strictum* var. *glaucophyllum*.

and Henson (1970) have shown experimentally that high percentages of (black) dormant seeds are produced under long day length. These seeds are smaller and have a thicker testa than the occasional brown-reticulate, non-dormant seeds that are produced under short days. Cumming (1963) also demonstrated that *C. album* can germinate over a wider range of conditions than the less weedy species of the genus. Dormancy factors contribute to the success of *C. album* as a weed.

(b) *Perennation* — Lamb's-quarters, an annual, maintains itself by its seeds which overwinter on or under the surface of the soil.

(c) *Physiological data* — Cumming (1963) found different germination responses by lamb's-quarters to the ratio of red, far-red light.

When plants were exposed to an abrupt shift in day length from long to shorter days, Gifford and Stewart (1965) found that floral apices were formed and flowering occurred in spite of the fact that the time was insufficient for a flowering hormone,

"florigen," to be translocated from the mature leaves.

Wentland (1965) discovered that seed dormancy was markedly influenced by a shift in photoperiod. He determined that the critical developmental stage in the production of dormant versus non-dormant seeds was the appearance of the terminal floret bud. He also found that germination inhibitors were produced in the perianth of fruits that had been initiated under long photoperiod (20 h). Barrett and Peters (1976) studied the effect of drought on germinating *C. album* seeds. Total germination was reduced 14% by conditions of drought. Karssen (1976) found that seeds of lamb's-quarters collected over consecutive years varied in the percentage of dormant seeds: 1971 seeds had low dormancy whereas the seeds of 1972 had high dormancy.

C. album has been shown by Pandy et al. (1971) to take up large amounts of phosphate at early and late stages of its growth cycle. Allebone et al. (1970) found that the leaf surface waxes of *C. album* contained 13

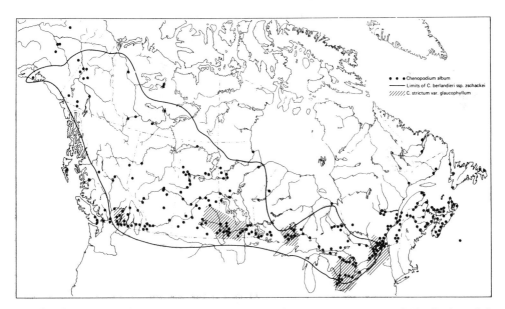

Fig. 4. Distribution of *Chenopodium album* in Canada, including the general distribution of *C. berlandieri* ssp. *zschackei* and *C. strictum* var. *glaucophyllum*.

aldehydes and acetates. The alkaloid trigonelline was discovered in lamb's-quarters by Drost (1970).

(d) *Phenology* — Plants of lamb's-quarters were examined during field surveys in southern portions of Canada and from herbarium specimens collected throughout Canada and Alaska. Plants flowered from May to October in all portions of the range. This is due partly to the plant's response to photoperiod and partly to the germination strategy of the seeds (see sections 7a & c). In the Ottawa region, seedlings were first observed 20 and 24 May, 1976 and 1977 respectively. They continued to emerge until early August. Our field observations are consistent with the results of Roberts (1964) on the emergence of *C. album* in England.

We have observed that plants emerging in July produce more foliage and remain in a vegetative condition longer than plants emerging in late May and early June. Roberts (1972) points out that species without seed dimorphism have germination peaks similar to that of *C. album*. He also states that the factors affecting the loss of dormancy may occur on more than one occasion each year. Taylorson and Borthwick (1969) showed that low red/far-red ratios of light (simulating a shaded canopy of leaves) inhibit germination of lamb's-quarters seed. Henson (1970) demonstrated that fluctuations of temperature increased the germination response to light. Further research into the factors affecting dormancy is still required.

(e) *Mycorrhiza* — None is reported occurring on *Chenopodium album*.

8. Reproduction

(a) *Floral biology* — The flowers of *Chenopodium album* are perfect, possess 5(4–3) anthers and are wind-pollinated. The stigmas (2) protrude and are receptive prior to the shedding of pollen in each flower. Mulligan (1972) did not observe insects visiting the flowers of *C. album*. Our studies and the findings of Mulligan and Findlay (1970) indicate that *C. album* is self-compatible and reproduces both by self- and cross-pollination. We bagged 10 immature inflorescences of *C. album* at Kars and at Eganville, Ont. and from these, viable seeds were obtained from seven inflorescences.

(b) *Seed production and dispersal* — Stevens (1932) found that *C. album* produced approximately 72,450 seeds on an average-sized plant, and that 1,000 seeds have a mean seed weight of 0.7 g. Herron (1953) presented data on the seed weight, germination percentage and seed morphology of 14 *Chenopodium* spp. (including *C. album*). He compared some of his results with those of Stevens (1932) and other workers.

Lamb's-quarters has no obvious mechanism for the dispersal of its seeds. It has been recorded arising from faeces of cattle, pigs, sheep, and sparrows. The germination percentage is augmented from 32 to 100% after passing through birds (Salisbury 1961). *C. album* has been dispersed by man's agricultural practices, road construction, moving of debris and ballast, and similar activities.

(c) *Viability of seeds and germination* — Wentland (1965) determined experimentally that seeds produced under short days (8 h) had 94 and 83% germination in the light and in the dark, respectively. He also showed that seeds produced under long days (17 h) had 20 and 2% germination in the light and in the dark. He determined, with seeds produced under 8-h and 17-h photoperiods, that pericarp inhibitors reduced germination from 58% (8 h) to 21% (17 h). The inhibiting substances in the pericarps produced under 8-h photoperiod were found to be different from those produced under 17-h photoperiod. Other factors involved in seed germination are given in section 7c. Toole and Brown (1946), in completing the results of the Durvel buried seed experiment, germinated seeds 39 yr old from soil depths of 45–55 cm and 90–105 cm, where conditions of moisture, temperature and oxygen were assumed to be nearly constant. Lewis (1973) found that 23% seed survival was obtained from C. album buried in soil for 20 yr.

(d) *Vegetative reproduction* — Lamb's-quarters does not reproduce vegetatively.

9. Hybrids

There is no evidence in the current botanical literature or from our own field work of natural interspecific hybrids in lamb's-quarters.

10. Population Dynamics

Ervio (1971) studied stem diameters, number of main branches, size and number of leaves, seed and dry-matter yield as related to intra-specific competition. In these experiments carried out over 3 yr, seed production/plant was highest the first year and decreased over subsequent years. Over the experiment's duration the population density did not affect seed weight. At a density of 16 plants/m² the plants produced a maximum average of 41,930 seeds per plant and at 567 plants/m² produced a minimum of 366 seeds/plant. Therefore, maximum production/m² was 671,000 seeds and the minimum production was 210,800 seeds/m².

Williams (1963) presented an analysis of the frequency of C. *album* in various habitats in Britain. Its highest frequency was on cultivated calcareous and occasionally non-calcareous soils. It rarely occurs as a single plant because its non-specialized mode of seed dispersal (see section 8b) results in concentrations of seed near parent plants. The plant's reaction to increased density, photoperiod and its germination peaks results in the production of individuals varying in height, inflorescence type, and degree of leafiness (Williams 1963, 1964; Ervio 1971). Extremes range from short (5 cm) depauperate plants with few seeds to tall (1–1.5 m) leafy plants with many thousands of seeds.

11. Response to Herbicides and Other Chemicals

Lamb's-quarters is susceptible to the commonly recommended herbicidal foliage sprays (Anonymous 1977). Holliday and Putwain (1974) found that plants of *Chenopodium album* were more resistant to simazine than plants of *Senecio vulgaris* L. Lamb's-quarters proved to be highly susceptible to MCPA regardless of the application time during the day (Weaver and Nylund 1965). Cylocate gave 90% control of C. *album* in tests on sugar beets (Lee et al. 1974). Handley and King (1974) found that control was variable using bentazon when the plants of C. *album* were "well developed." Bandeen and McLaren (1976) reported on biotypes of C. *album* resistant to the triazine group of herbicides. Jensen et al. (1977) determined that there was little difference in atrazine uptake between resistant and susceptible lamb's-quarters selections. Radosevich (1977) suggested the presence of a biochemical protective mechanism with chloroplasts of the resistant biotypes.

Souza Machado et al. (1978) determined that photochemical activity, in particular the Hill reaction, was inhibited in chloroplasts of atrazine-susceptible biotypes but not in chloroplasts from the resistant selection.

12. Response to Other Human Manipulations

Chenopodium album is unable to withstand clipping. Roberts (1963) showed that the number of emerging C. *album* plants/.0929 m² did not vary as a result of primary cultivation, ploughing and rototilling at depths of 15–46 cm. Other weeds, particularly *Poa annua* L., increased in density as a result of rototilling. Roberts (1963) states that if plants are cut or trampled during early stages of growth they will not survive.

During the summers of 1976 and 1977 at Kars, Ontario we cut off the upper stems of 50 plants at the three leaf stage, leaving the lowermost pair of leaves. In both years the plants did not survive.

371

13. Responses to Parasites

(a) *Insects and nondomestic animals* — Williams (1963) lists 33 insect taxa occurring on lamb's-quarters in the British Isles. The following parasitize is in Canada (J. E. H. Martin, personal communication): **Collembola:** *Bourletiella hartensis* Fetch (feeds on seedlings). **Thysanoptera:** *Aeolothrips fasciatus* L., *Taeniothrips vulgatissimus* (Hal.), *Thrips fuscipennis* (Hal.), *Thrips tabaci* Lindemann. **Miridae:** *Melanotrichus flavosparus* Sahlb., *Lygus lineolaris* P. de B., *Atomoscelis modestus* Van Duzee, *Melanotrichus coagulatus* Uhler. **Aphidae:** *Aphis fabae* Scop., *Hayhurstia atriplicis* L. **Lepidoptera:Noctuidae:** *Scotogramma trifolii* (Rottenburg) (feeds on young plants); **Geometridae:** *Eupithecia subnotata* Hb. (larva feed on flowers and seeds); **Glechiidae:** *Chrysoesthia hermonella* Fab., *Scrobipalpa absaletella* Fisch. v. Rossl. (mines leaves), *S. atriplicella* Fisch. v. Rossl., *S. nitentella* Fuchs (eats flowers and seeds); **Coleophoridae:** *Coleophora annulatella* Tengstr. (larva eats seeds of *Chenopodium* spp. and *Atriplex* spp.).

The following taxa in the Aphidae have been compiled as feeders on *C. album* by Patch (1938): *Aphis abbreviata* Patch, *A. fabae* Scopoli, *A. gossypi* Glover, *A. laburni* Kaltenbach, *A. maidi-radicis* Forbes, *A. medicaginis* Koch, *A. middletonii*, *A. papaveris* Fabricus, *A. rumicis* L., *A. spiraecola* Patch, *Hyalopterus atriplicis* L., *Macrosiphum gei* Koch, *M. solanifolii* Ashmead, *Myzus persicae* Sulzer, *M. pseudosolani* Theobald. Patch (1938) also lists *Phemhigus betae* Doane of the Eriosomatinae as a feeder on lamb's-quarters.

(b) *Microorganisms and viruses* — Conners (1967) list the following fungi as occurring on *C. album: Cercospora dubia* (Riess) Wint., *Diplodia ellisii* Sacc., various *Fusarium* spp., *Peronospora farinosa* (Fr.) Fr., *Phoma longissima* (Pers.) West, *Physoderma pulposum* Wallr., *Puccinia aristidae* Tracy, *Septoria* spp., *Stagonospora atriplicis* (West.) Lind, *Uromyces peckianus* Farl. Conners reports that clover yellow mosaic virus is found on *C. album* in British Columbia. *Peronospora farinosa* (Fr.) Fr. has developed a special form spp. *chenopodii* Byford (Byford 1967). He suggests that if downy mildews attacking *Chenopodium* spp. are distinct, they should be considered as strains of f. *chenopodii*.

In the United States (Anonymous 1960), the following fungi, nematodes and viruses are found on lamb's-quarters: **Fungi:** *Albugo bliti* (Biv.-Bern.) Kuntze, *Alternaria amaranthi* (Pk.) Van Hook, *Aphanomyces cochlioides* Drechs., *Cercospora beticola* Sacc., *C. dubia* (Riess) Wint., *Diplodia natalensis* P. Evans, *Diplodina ellisii* Sacc., *Dothidella longissima* (Pers. ex West.) Ell. & Ev., *Gloeosporium melleum* Dearn. & Overh., *Hadrotrichum chenopodinum* Pk., *Metasphaeria anthelmintica* (Cke.) Dearn. *Peronospora* spp., *Phymatotrichum omnivorum* (Shear) Dug., *Puccinia aristidae* Tracy, *Rhizoctonia solani* Kuehn., *Sclerotinia sclerotiorum* (Lib.) d By., *Stagonospora atriplicis* (West.) Lind, *Uromyces peckianus* Farl. **Nematodes:** *Ditylenchus dipsaci* (Kuehn) Filip., *Meloidogyne* sp. *Pratylenchus pratensis* (De Man) Filip. **Viruses:** Mosaic-virus, *Marmor betae* Holmes, Betavirus 2. *C. album* has been found to be a virus reservoir for tobacco etch virus which infects bell peppers (Weinbaum and Milbrath 1976). Williams (1963) lists the following viruses on *C. album:* beet mosaic, beet yellows, potato virus X, M, S, lettuce mosaic, carnation ring spot, lucerne (alfalfa) mosaic, vine mosaic and black ring spot.

ACKNOWLEDGMENTS

We thank the herbarium curators of the following institutions for lending us specimens of lamb's quarters and closely related species: ACAD, UNB, MT, MTMG, CAN, OAC, TRT, LKHD, WIN, SASK, SCS, ALTA, and UBC.

AAMISEPP, A. 1976. Weed control in potatoes and sugar beet. Swed. Weed Conf. (SWDCA) **17**: D-30, D-32.

ABRAMS, I. 1944. Illustrated flora of the Pacific States. Vol. II. Stanford Univ. Press. Stanford, Calif. 635 pp.

AELLEN, P. 1929. Beitrag zur systematik du *Chenopodium* – Arten Amerikas vorwiegend auf Grund der Sammlung des United States National Museums in Washington, D.C. 1 & 2. Rep. Spec. Nov. Regn. Veget. **26**(1): 31–64. **26**(2): 119–160.

ALEX, J. F. 1964. Weeds of tomato and corn fields in two regions of Ontario. Weed Res. **4**: 308–318.

ALEX, J. F. 1966. Survey of weeds of cultivated land in the prairie provinces. Exp. Farm, Res. Br., Agric. Can., Regina, Sask. mimeo. 68 pp.

ALLEBONE, J. E., HAMILTON, R. J., KNIGHTS, B. A., MIDDLEDITCH, B. S. and POWER, D. M. 1970. Cuticular leaf waxes. Part II. *Chenopodium album* L. and *Lolium perenne* L. Chem. Phys. Lipids **4**: 37–46.

ANONYMOUS. 1960. Index of plant diseases in the United States. U.S. Dep. Agric. Handb. No. 165. 531 pp.

ANONYMOUS. 1964. Agricultural Abuses Act. 1. Regulations concerning noxious weeds. Ministère de l'Agriculture, Que. pp. 639–641.

ANONYMOUS. 1970. The Noxious Weeds Act. Queen's Printer, Winnipeg, Man. pp. 1–20.

ANONYMOUS. 1973. The Weed Control Act. Regulations designating plants as noxious weeds. Ab. regulation 147/73.

ANONYMOUS, 1974. The national atlas of Canada (4th ed., revised) Macmillan Co. of Canada Ltd. Toronto, Ont. Department of Energy, Mines and Resources and Information Canada. 254 pp.

ANONYMOUS. 1977. Guide to chemical weed control. Ont. Ministry of Agric. and Food. Publ. 75. 104 pp.

BANDEEN, J. D. and McLAREN, R. D. 1976. Resistance of *Chenopodium album* to triazine herbicides. Can. J. Plant Sci. **56**: 411–412.

BARRETT, M. and PETERS, R. A. 1976. Germination of corn, lamb's quarters, and fall panicum under simulated drought. Proc. Northeast. Weed. Sci. Soc. **30**: 98–103.

BASSETT, I. J. and CROMPTON, C. W. 1971. *In* A. Love, ed. IOPB chromosome number reports. XXXIV. Taxon **20**: 785–797.

BOCHE, J. and RUNQUIST, O. 1968. Kinetics of the thermal rearrangement of ascaridole. J. Organ. Chem. **33**: 4285.

BUCK, W. M., PRESTON, K. S., ABEL, M. and MARSHALL, M. S. 1966. Perirenal edema in swine: a disease caused by common weeds. Amer. Vet. Med. Assoc. J. **148**: 1525–1531.

BYFORD, W. J. 1967. Host specialization of *Peronospora farinosa* on *Beta*, *Spinacia* and *Chenopodium*. Trans. Br. Mycol. Sci. **50**: 603–607.

CANADA WEED COMMITTEE. 1969. Common and botanical names of weeds in Canada. Can. Dep. Agric. Publ. 1397. 67 pp.

CONNERS, I. L. 1967. An annotated index of plant diseases in Canada. Can. Dep. Agric. Res. Br. Publ. 1251. 381 pp.

CUMMING, B. G. 1963. The dependence of germination on photoperiod, light quality and temperature in *Chenopodium* spp. Can. J. Bot. **41**: 1211–1233.

CROMPTON, C. W. and BASSETT, I. J. 1976. *In* A. Love, ed. IOPB chromosome number reports. LIV. Taxon **25**: 631–649.

DROST, K. 1970. Chromatographic studies on basic substances in some species of Chenopodiaceae. Acta Polon. Pharm. **27**: 161–166.

ERVIO, L. R. 1971. The effect of intra-specific competition on the development of *Chenopodium album* L. Weed Res. **11**: 124–134.

FERNALD, M. L. and KINSEY, A. C. 1951. Edible wild plants of Eastern North America. Harper Brothers, New York, N.Y. 452 pp.

FERRON, M. and CAYOUETTE, R. 1971. Nom des mauvaises herbes du Québec, ed. 2, Min. Agric. Colonisation du Québec. Publ. 288 113 pp.

FRANKTON, C. and MULLIGAN, G. A. 1970. Weeds of Canada. Can. Dep. Agric. Publ. 948. 217 pp.

GIFFORD, E. M. and STEWART, K. D. 1965. Ultrastructure of vegetative and reproductive apices of *Chenopodium album*. Science **149**: 75–77.

GUISTI, L. 1964. Notas citotaxonomicas sobre *Chenopodium album* L. en Argentina. Darwiniana **13**: 486–505.

HANDLEY, R. P. and KING, J. M. 1974. The evaluation of bentazone for weed control in processing legumes. Proc. 12th Br. Weed Control Conf. pp. 403–410.

HENSON, I. E. 1970. The effects of light, potassium nitrate and temperature on the germination of *Chenopodium album*. Weed Res. **10**: 27–39.

HERRON, J. W. 1953. Study of seed production, seed identification and seed germination of *Chenopodium* spp. Cornell Univ. Agric. Exp. Sta. Mem. **320**: 24 pp.

HERWEIJER, C. H. and DEN HOUTER, L. F. 1970. Poisoning in sheep caused by *Chenopodium album*. Tijdschr. Diergeneesk. **95**: 1134–1136.

HOLLIDAY, R. J. and PUTWAIN, P. D. 1974. Variation in susceptibility to simazine in three species of annual weeds. Proc. 12th. Br. Weed Control Conf. 649–654.

HOLM, L. G., PLUCKNETT, D. L., PANCHO, J. V. and HERBERGER, J. P. 1977. The world's worst weeds. East-West Center Book, Univ. Press of Hawaii, Honolulu, Hawaii. 609 pp.

HOLMES, H. M. and PFIEFFER, R. K. 1964. The control of *Chenopodium album* in kale with a methylmercapto triazine (desmetryne). Pest. Abstr. News Sum. Sect. C. **10**: 159–163.

HOLMGREN, P. K. and KEUKEN, W. 1974. Index herbariorum. Part 1. The herbaria of the world. ed. 6. Oosthock, Scheltama & Holkema, Utrecht. 397 pp.

HOMSHER, P. J. 1967. Cytological and taxonomic studies in *Chenopodium*. University Microfilms, Ann Arbor, Mich. 127 pp.

JENSEN, K. I. N., BANDEEN, J. D. and SOUZA MACHADO, V. 1977. Studies on the differential tolerance of two lamb's-quarters selections to triazine herbicides Can. J. Plant Sci. **57**: 1169–1177.

KARSSEN, C. M. 1976. Two sites of hormonal action during germination of *Chenopodium album* seeds. Physiol. Plant **36**: 264–270.

KEENER, C. S. 1970. Documented plant chromosome numbers 70: 1. Sida **3**(7): 533–536.

KNAPP, A. H. 1975. Wild harvest. Pagurian Press Ltd., Toronto, Ont. 190 pp.

LEE, G. A., ALLEY, H. P., GALE, A. F. and McNAMEE, M. A. 1974. Weed control in sugarbeets. Res. J. Agric. Res. Sta. Univ. of Wyoming. No. 83. pp. 1–22.

LEWIS, J. 1973. Longevity of crop and weed seeds: survival after 20 years in soil. Weed Res. **13**: 179–191.

MARTIN, A. C., ZIM, H. S. and NELSON, A. L. 1951. American wildlife and plants. McGraw-Hill Book Co. Inc. New York, N.Y. 500 pp.

MOQUIN-TANDON, A. 1840. Chenopodearum monographica enumeratio. P.-J. Loss, Paris. 182 pp.

MOQUIN-TANDON, A. 1849. Ordo CLVII. Salsolaceae. *In* De Candolle Alph. L.P.P., Prodromus systematis naturalis regni vegetabilis **13**(2): 41–219. Masson, Paris.

MULLIGAN, G. A. 1972. Autogamy, allogamy and pollination in some Canadian weeds. Can. J. Bot. **50**: 1767–1771.

MULLIGAN, G. A. and FINDLAY, J. N. 1970. Reproductive systems and colonization in Canadian weeds. Can. J. Bot. **48**: 859–860.

PANDY, H. N., MISRA, K. C., and MUKHERJEE, K. L. 1971. Phosphate uptake and its incorporation in some crop plants and their associated weeds. Ann. Bot. **35**: 367–372.

PATCH, E. M. 1938. Food plant catalogue of the aphids of the world including the Phyllosceridae. Bull. 393. Maine Agric. Exp. Sta., Orono. 431 pp.

RADOSEVICH, S. R. 1977. Mechanism of atrazine resistance in lamb's quarters and pigweed. Weed Sci. **35**: 316–318.

ROBERTS, H. A. 1963. Studies on the weeds of vegetable crops. III. Effect of different primary cultivations on the weed seeds in the soil. J. Ecol. **51**: 83–95.

ROBERTS, H. A. 1964. Emergence and longevity in cultivated soil of seeds of some annual weeds. Weed Res. **4**: 296–307.

ROBERTS, E. H. 1972. *In* E. H. ROBERTS, ed. Viability of seeds. Chapter 11. Dormancy: a factor affecting seed survival in the soil. Syracuse University Press, Syracuse, N.Y. 448 pp.

SALISBURY, E. Sir. 1961. Weeds and aliens. Collins Clear-Type Press, London and Glasgow. 384 pp.

SOUZA MACHADO, V., BANDEEN, J. D., STEPHENSON, G. R. and JENSEN, K. I. N. 1978. Differential atrazine interference with the Hill reaction of isolated chloroplasts from *Chenopodium album* L. biotypes. Weed Res. **17**: 407–413.

STANDLEY, P. C. 1916. North American flora. Chenopodiaceae **21**: 1–93. New York Botanical Garden, New York, N.Y.

STEVENS, O. A. 1932. The number and weight of seeds produced by weeds. Amer. J. Bot. **19**: 784–794.

TAYLOR, R. L. and MULLIGAN, G. A. 1968. Flora of the Queen Charlotte Islands. Res. Br., Can. Dep. Agric. Monogr. No. 4, Part 2. Queen's Printer, Ottawa, Ont.

TAYLORSON, R. B. and BORTHWICK, H. A. 1969. Light infiltration by foliar canopies;

significance for light controlled weed seed germination. Weed Sci. **17**: 144–147.

THOMAS, A. G. 1977. 1977 weed survey of cultivated land in Saskatchewan. Agric. Can. Res. Sta. Regina, Sask. Mimeo. 103 pp.

TOOLE, E. H. and BROWN, E. 1946. Final results of the Durvel buried seed experiment. J. Agric. Res. **72**: 201–210.

WEINBAUM, Z. and MILBRATH, G. M. 1976. The isolation of tobacco etch virus from bell peppers and weeds in southern Illinois. Plant Dis. Rep. **60**: 469–471.

WELKER, W. V. 1966. Weed control in asparagus. Northeast. Weed Conf. Proc. 20th Annu. Meeting. p. 35.

WEAVER, M. L. and NYLUND, R. E. 1965. The susceptibility of annual weeds and Canada thistle to MCPA applied at different times of day. Weeds **13**: 110–113.

WENTLAND, M. J. 1965. The effect of photoperiod on seed dormancy of *Chenopodium album*. University Microfilms, Ann Arbor, Mich. 117 pp.

WILLIAMS, J. T. 1963. Biological flora of the British Isles: *Chenopodium album* L. J. Ecol. **51**: 711–725.

WILLIAMS, J. T. 1964. A study of the competitive ability of *Chenopodium album* L. I. Interference between kale and *C. album* grown in pure stands and in mixtures. Weed Res. **4**: 283–295.

WILLIAMS, J. T. and HARPER, J. L. 1965. Seed polymorphism and germination. I. The influence of nitrates and low temperatures on the germination of *Chenopodium album*. Weed Res. **5**: 141–150.

WISK, E. L. and COLE, R. H. 1966. Effect of date of application of two pre-plant herbicides on weed control and crop injury in soybeans. Northeast. Weed. Conf. Proc. 21st Annu. Meeting pp. 366–367.

WODEHOUSE, R. P. 1971. Hay fever plants. Ed. 2. Hafner Publ. Co., New York, N.Y. 280 pp.

Index